WOLF AND STANLEY ON ENVIRONMENTAL LAW

Fourth Edition

Cavendish
Publishing
Limited

London • Sydney • Portland, Oregon

This book is supported by a Companion Website, created to keep *The English Legal System* up to date and to provide enhanced resources for both students and lecturers.

Key features include:

◆   termly updates
◆   links to useful websites
◆   links to 'ebooks' for introductory and further reading
◆   revision guidance
◆   'ask the author' – your questions answered

www.cavendishpublishing.com/envlaw

WOLF AND STANLEY ON ENVIRONMENTAL LAW

Fourth Edition

Susan Wolf, BA (Econ) (Hons), LLB (Hons)
Principal Lecturer in Law
University of Northumbria

Neil Stanley, LLB (Hons)
Lecturer in Law and Solicitor
University of Leeds

Cavendish
Publishing
Limited

London • Sydney • Portland, Oregon

Fourth edition first published in Great Britain 2003 by
Cavendish Publishing Limited, The Glass House,
Wharton Street, London WC1X 9PX, United Kingdom
Telephone: + 44 (0)20 7278 8000   Facsimile: + 44 (0)20 7278 8080
Email: info@cavendishpublishing.com
Website: www.cavendishpublishing.com

Published in the United States by Cavendish Publishing
c/o International Specialized Book Services,
5824 NE Hassalo Street, Portland,
Oregon 97213-3644, USA

Published in Australia by Cavendish Publishing (Australia) Pty Ltd
45 Beach Street, Coogee, NSW 2034, Australia
Telephone: + 61 (2)9664 0909   Facsimile: +61 (2)9664 5420
Email: info@cavendishpublishing.com.au
Website: www.cavendishpublishing.com.au

© Wolf, S and Stanley, N	2003
First edition	1995
Second edition	1997
Third edition	2001
Fourth edition	2003

This title was previously published in the Cavendish Principles series

British Library Cataloguing in Publication Data
Wolf, Susan, 1959 –
Wolf and Stanley on environmental law – 4th ed
1 Environmental law – Great Britain
I Title II Stanley, Neil
344.4'1046

Library of Congress Cataloguing in Publication Data
Data available

ISBN 1-85941-832-5

1 3 5 7 9 10 8 6 4 2

Printed and bound in Great Britain

PREFACE

The authors' objectives in writing this text are as follows:

- to provide the reader with a succinct and accessible account of the core features of *pollution control* law in England and Wales;

- to design and write a book with the needs of both *law* and *non-law* students, at both *undergraduate* and *postgraduate* levels, firmly in mind. The authors teach a variety of law modules to undergraduate students (on law, environmental science, environmental management and other degree programmes) to students who include employees of the regulators (the Environment Agency, local authorities and DEFRA) and the regulated (waste and water industries);

- to focus on the topics which feature most often and are therefore of *most relevance* to students on environmental law courses offered by Higher Education institutions in England and Wales;

- to set the law in its policy and practical context;

- to provide the reader with *research assistance* through *links* to key sources of further information; and

- to provide non-lawyers with basic advice on how to access case reports, journal articles, etc, either in the library or via online databases/websites.

We provide the reader with a simple framework to guide him or her through this text. We have arranged the material from the perspectives of the regulators (who 'police' compliance with the law), the regulated (those who are subject to the law), and those legal persons (individuals and companies) and groups who wish either to challenge decisions made by government or the regulators, or claim compensation for pollution-related damage. In Chapter 1, we introduce the reader to the legal framework which controls polluting emissions in England and Wales against the backcloth of EC environmental and international environmental law. We also examine the sources of environmental law, the ethical underpinning of the law, relevant legal principles and the emergence of alternative methods (to the basic 'Command and Control' regulatory system) to control polluting activity. In Chapter 2, we outline the administrative and enforcement roles of the regulators and the role of the courts. In Chapter 3, we consider the impact of the UK's membership of the EC on the rapid development of environmental law and policy. In Chapters 4–10, we describe and analyse the main pollution control regimes, largely from the perspective of the regulator: water pollution, waste management, Integrated Pollution Control and Integrated Pollution Prevention and Control, contaminated land, atmospheric pollution, statutory nuisance and noise. In Chapters 11 and 12, we discuss the use of environmental law by individuals and others to protect property interests, human health and the environment, and to oversee the activities of the regulators and to mount private prosecutions. Chapter 11 addresses the torts of nuisance, negligence, trespass and the rule in *Rylands v Fletcher*, whilst Chapter 12 covers access to environmental information, human rights, public concern, judicial review and private prosecutions. Neil was responsible for updating Chapters 1, 2, 4, 5, 8, 11 and 12 whilst Sue has updated Chapters 3, 6, 7, 9 and 10.

This textbook focuses on those laws in England and Wales which are concerned with the regulation of polluting substances emitted into the environment from industrial, commercial, agricultural and domestic premises. Whilst we concede that environmental law extends well beyond pollution control, we have been guided in the selection of content by the needs of our primary readership. We concentrate on an analysis of the main vehicle which is used by the government to control polluting emissions in the UK: the series of 'Command and Control' laws (that is, legislation is enacted by Parliament which 'commands' the UK subject to do, or refrain from doing, something – usually obtaining a licence to authorise an activity – and thereby the legislation 'controls' the UK subject's activities) which address specific environmental problems. Whilst we do discuss EC law and international law, we discuss developments at these levels in terms of how they impact upon national regulation, often by driving the development of our law forward.

Since this is a textbook, and reasons of space require us to be selective, we recognise that we run the risk of generalising at the expense of accuracy in some cases. Short of writing an encyclopaedia, this problem is inescapable. We would therefore recommend any reader with a specific environmental problem to resolve should seek professional advice.

We would like to thank our publishers for their help in writing this book. Special thanks go to our editor Jon Lloyd for keeping us on task. We have endeavoured to strike the right balance between broad structure and detailed analysis. If we have disappointed the reader in any way then we would urge him or her to contact us at lawnks@leeds.ac.uk. We are committed to continuous improvement of this text and value all constructive comments.

We hope that you find the suggested further reading lists at the end of chapter helpful in kickstarting your research. Please let us know if you locate any article, report, case, etc, which you found useful and which we have not yet included in our further reading references. We also hope that non-lawyers in particular will appreciate the advice we provide to help you access case reports, journal articles, etc.

Susan Wolf
Neil Stanley
August 2003

CONTENTS

Preface		*v*
Table of Cases		*xiii*
Table of Statutes		*xxv*
Table of Statutory Instruments		*xxxiii*

1 ELEMENTS OF ENVIRONMENTAL LAW   **1**

1.1   Introduction   1

1.2   What is environmental law?   1

1.3   Environmental law: an overview   1

1.4   Preliminary issues   2

1.5   The public regulation of private pollution   5

1.6   Private law: the role of the individual, companies and non-governmental organisations in the regulation of pollution   11

1.7   The sources of environmental law   12

1.8   Legal and policy principles   13

1.9   Alternatives to the Command and Control approach to pollution regulation   16

1.10   Further information   21

2 THE ADMINISTRATION AND ENFORCEMENT OF ENVIRONMENTAL LAW   **29**

2.1   Introduction   29

2.2   The system of pollution control prior to the Environment Act 1995   30

2.3   Reasons for change   35

2.4   The Environment Agency   37

2.5   The local authorities   54

2.6   Other bodies concerned with environmental protection   55

2.7   The role of the courts in the administration and enforcement of environmental law   59

2.8   Further information   67

3 EUROPEAN COMMUNITY ENVIRONMENTAL LAW AND POLICY   **69**

3.1   Introduction   69

3.2   The development of the European Union (EU)   69

3.3   The aims of the EC   71

3.4   EC competences   71

3.5   Sources of EC law   73

3.6   The institutional framework   76

3.7   The legislative procedure   81

3.8   Enforcement of EC law   83

3.9   Indirect enforcement through the national courts   87

3.10   The EC as a new legal order   88

3.11   Supremacy of EC law   89

3.12   Effect of EC law   90

3.13   The duty of interpretation approach   93

3.14   State liability   94

3.15   The development of a Community environmental policy   96

3.16   Further information   118

4	**WATER POLLUTION**	**121**
4.1	Introduction	121
4.2	Control over water pollution: an overview	121
4.3	Polluting substances and polluting activities	122
4.4	The historical development of the public regulation of water pollution	124
4.5	The water industry and the WIA 1991	125
4.6	Controlled waters	126
4.7	The regulator's statutory water pollution responsibilities	127
4.8	Discharge consent licences	129
4.9	Water pollution offences	137
4.10	Statutory and other defences	146
4.11	Proving water pollution	149
4.12	Enforcement	149
4.13	Preventive approaches to water pollution control	151
4.14	The prevention and remediation of polluted water	157
4.15	Access to information (s 83 of the WRA 1991)	159
4.16	The private regulation of water pollution	160
4.17	Disposal of wastes into sewers	162
4.18	Water abstraction	165
4.19	Controls relating to drinking water	168
4.20	The interface of the WRA 1991 and WIA 1991 with other statutory water pollution controls	171
4.21	Water pollution: the EC and the pace of regulatory change	173
4.22	Marine pollution	178
4.23	Further information	182
5	**WASTE MANAGEMENT**	**185**
5.1	Introduction	185
5.2	The problem of waste	185
5.3	The historical development of statutory waste controls	188
5.4	Part II of the the EPA 1990	190
5.5	What is waste?	190
5.6	The legal definition of waste	191
5.7	The system of waste regulation	202
5.8	The waste management licensing system	205
5.9	Licence conditions	213
5.10	Administration and enforcement powers	215
5.11	Surrender of licences (s 39)	218
5.12	Rights of appeal (s 43)	219
5.13	Public registers (s 64)	220
5.14	Supervision and monitoring (s 42)	220
5.15	Clean-up powers (s 59)	222
5.16	Waste offences	224
5.17	Special waste offences	230
5.18	Waste strategy for England and Wales	232

5.19	Waste planning	242
5.20	The interface between the waste management regime and other regulatory pollution controls	244
5.21	The duty of care	246
5.22	Further information	256
6	**INTEGRATED POLLUTION CONTROL AND INTEGRATED POLLUTION PREVENTION AND CONTROL**	**259**
6.1	Introduction	259
6.2	The development of an integrated approach to pollution control	260
6.3	IPC: achieving the best practical environmental option	261
6.4	Overview of IPC	262
6.5	Prescribed processes and substances	263
6.6	Licensing: the need for an authorisation	268
6.7	IPC applications	270
6.8	Conditions	273
6.9	The BATNEEC condition	275
6.10	BATNEEC and the best practical environmental option (BPEO)	277
6.11	Public registers	279
6.12	Transfer of an authorisation	280
6.13	Monitoring of an IPC authorisation	280
6.14	Powers of enforcement	281
6.15	Offences	286
6.16	Rights of appeal	288
6.17	The interface between IPC and other pollution controls	289
6.18	IPC and IPPC	290
6.19	IPPC permits	292
6.20	Enforcement powers	299
6.21	Appeals and public registers	301
6.22	Criminal law enforcement	301
6.23	The interface of IPPC with other regulatory controls	303
6.24	Further information	305
7	**CONTAMINATED LAND**	**307**
7.1	The contaminated land legacy	307
7.2	The contaminated land regime	310
7.3	The statutory framework of the contaminated land regime	313
7.4	The appropriate person	317
7.5	Allocating the cost of remediation	319
7.6	The Remediation Notice	321
7.7	Interface with other controls	323
7.8	Further information	326
8	**ATMOSPHERIC POLLUTION**	**327**
8.1	Introduction	327
8.2	Problems caused by air pollution	327
8.3	Historic controls	328

8.4	Government policy	328
8.5	The Environment Act 1995	330
8.6	Other legislative controls	332
8.7	Local Authority Air Pollution Control (LAAPC)	334
8.8	The Clean Air Act (CAA) 1993	335
8.9	Statutory nuisances relating to air quality	342
8.10	Pollution from motor vehicles	342
8.11	EC legislation	344
8.12	Acid rain, ozone, global warming and the international dimension	346
8.13	Further information	348
9	**STATUTORY NUISANCE**	**349**
9.1	Introduction	349
9.2	What are statutory nuisances?	350
9.3	Prejudicial to health or a nuisance	350
9.4	Exemptions	354
9.5	Responsibility of the local authorities	355
9.6	Abatement Notices	357
9.7	Appeals against an Abatement Notice	360
9.8	Non-compliance with an Abatement Notice	362
9.9	Defences against non-compliance with an Abatement Notice	363
9.10	Action by citizens	366
9.11	Advantages of the statutory nuisance provisions	367
9.12	Contaminated land and statutory nuisances	367
9.13	Further information	369
10	**NOISE POLLUTION**	**371**
10.1	The problem of noise pollution	371
10.2	The legal regulation of noise	372
10.3	Damage to health	374
10.4	Measuring noise	375
10.5	Neighbourhood noise	376
10.6	Common law	377
10.7	Contract and licensing	382
10.8	Statutory controls	382
10.9	Noise as a statutory nuisance	383
10.10	Noise Abatement Notices	387
10.11	Appeals against an Abatement Notice	391
10.12	Non-compliance with an Abatement Notice	392
10.13	An aggrieved citizen's action – s 82 of the EPA 1990	395
10.14	The Noise Act 1996	396
10.15	Bylaws	399
10.16	Specific noise controls	399
10.17	Preventing neighbourhood noise	404
10.18	The EC dimension	407

10.19 Alternative dispute resolution 408
10.20 Further information 409

11 THE PRIVATE REGULATION OF ENVIRONMENTAL POLLUTION: THE COMMON LAW **411**

11.1 Introduction 411
11.2 Common law actions 411
11.3 Remedies 413
11.4 General defences to intentional torts 415
11.5 Torts 416
11.6 Nuisance 417
11.7 Private nuisance 417
11.8 Public nuisance 428
11.9 Defences in public nuisance and private nuisance actions 430
11.10 Remedies in nuisance actions 431
11.11 Negligence 431
11.12 Trespass 439
11.13 The rule in *Rylands v Fletcher* 441
11.14 *Cambridge Water Co v Eastern Counties Leather plc* 445
11.15 An evaluation of the common law as a means of environmental protection 448
11.16 Civil actions under statute 451
11.17 Statutory provisions which alter rights under common law 453
11.18 The EC and civil liability 453
11.19 Further information 455

12 THE PRIVATE REGULATION OF ENVIRONMENTAL POLLUTION: THE PUBLIC CONCERN, PRIVATE PROSECUTION, JUDICIAL REVIEW, ACCESS TO INFORMATION AND HUMAN RIGHTS **457**

12.1 Introduction 457
12.2 Public concern 457
12.3 Private prosecutions 464
12.4 Judicial review in English law 466
12.5 Access to information 470
12.6 Recognition of the need for public participation 476
12.7 Environmental pressure groups 477
12.8 Human rights 480
12.9 Further information 491

APPENDIX: LEGAL RESOURCES: A BASIC GUIDE FOR NON-LAWYERS **493**

Index 497

TABLE OF CASES

AB v South West Water Services Ltd [1993] 1 All ER 609 428

AMEC Building Ltd v London Borough of Camden [1997] Env LR 330 364

ARCO Chemie Nederland Ltd v Minister van
Volkshuivesting and EPON [2000] ECR I-4475 194

ASA Abfall Services AG v Bundesminister fur Umwelt,
Jugend und Familie (Case C-6/00) [2002] ECR I-1961 197

Aher-Waggon GmbH v Germany (Case C-389/96) [1998] ECR I-4473 ....104, 106

Alconbury
See R (on the Application of Alconbury Developments Ltd)
v Secretary of State for the Environment, Transport and the Regions—

Allen v Gulf Oil Refining Ltd [1981] AC 1001;
[1981] 2 WLR 188; [1981] All ER 353 ....415, 419, 424, 438

Allison v Merton, Sutton and Wandsworth AHA [1975] CLY 2450 427

Alphacell Ltd v Woodward [1972] 2 WLR 1320; [1972] All ER 475 ....139, 140, 163

Amministrazione delle Finanze dello Stato v Simmenthal
(Case 106/77) [1978] ECR 629; [1978] 3 CMLR 263 90

Andreae v Selfridge & Co Ltd [1938] Ch 1; [1937] 3 All ER 259 ....378, 379

Armour v Skeen 1976 SLT 71 229

Attorney General (Gambia) v N'Jie [1961] 2 WLR 845 366

Attorney General v Gastonia Coaches Ltd [1977] RTR 219 427

Attorney General v PYA Quarries Ltd [1957] 2 WLR 770 ....381, 428

Attorney General's Reference (No 2 of 1988) [1990] QB 771 213

Attorney General's Reference (No 1 of 1994) [1995] 2 All ER 1007 140

AvestaPolarit Chrome Oy (Case C-114/01)
(2003) unreported, judgment of 11 September 194

Ballard v Tomlinson (1885) 29 Ch D 115 446

Barnes v Irwell Valley Water Board [1939] 1 KB 21 432

Barnett v Chelsea and Kensington Hospital Management
Committee [1969] 1 QB 428 433

Becker v Finanzamt Munster-Innenstadt (Case 8/81) [1982] ECR 53 90

Beju-Bop Ltd v Home Farm (Iwerne Minister) Ltd
[1990] Water Law 90 449

Bellew v Cement Ltd [1948] Ir R 61 414

Benthem v Netherlands (1985) 8 EHRR 1 487

Berridge Incinerators v Nottinghamshire County Council
(1987) unreported, 14 April 223

Betts v Penge Urban District Council [1942] 2 All ER 61 ....350, 383

Bishop of Rochester v Bridges (1831) 1 B & Ad 847 452

Blackburn v ARC Ltd [1998] Env LR 469 ....342, 412, 418, 422, 425, 427, 438

Blackland Park Exploration Ltd v Environment Agency
[2003] EWHC 691 237

Blair v Deakin (1887) 57 LT 522 426

Bliss v Hall (1838) 4 Bing NC 183 426

Blue Circle v Ministry of Defence [1998] 3 All ER 385; [1999] Env LR 22 ....308, 433, 434

Blythe v Birmingham Waterworks Co (1856) 11 Exch 781 431

Boddington v British Transport Police [1999] 2 AC 143 146
Bolam v Friern Hospital Management Committee [1957] 1 WLR 582 432
Bolton v Stone [1951] AC 850 421
Booker Aquaculture Ltd v Secretary of State for Scotland
  (1998) The Times, 24 September 486
Bouhelier (Case 53/76) [1997] ECR 197 106
Brasserie du Pêcheur SA v Germany (Cases C-46 and
  48/93) [1996] 2 WLR 506; [1996] All ER (EC) 301 ....95, 96
Brazil v Secretary of State for Transport, Local
  Government and the Regions [2001] 1 All ER 192 485
Bristol City Council v Huggins (1995) unreported 363, 393
British Celanese Ltd v AH Hunt (Capacitors) Ltd
  [1969] 1 WLR 959; [1969] 2 All ER 1252 ....421, 443
Bruton and National Rivers Authority v Clarke
  [1993] Water Law 145 157
Buckley v UK (1996) 23 EHRR 101 485
Budden and Albery v BP Oil Ltd and Shell Oil Ltd [1980] JPL 586 ....415, 438
Burton v Winters [1993] 1 WLR 1077 415
Busch v Klinikum Neustadt GmbH (Case C-320/01)
  [2003] ECR I-12041 93

CPC (UK) Ltd v National Rivers Authority [1995] Env LR 131 141
Cambridge Water Co v Eastern Counties Leather plc
  [1994] 2 AC 264; [1994] 2 WLR 53; [1994] 1 All ER 53 ....12, 20, 64, 308, 418,
                                                      422, 425, 433, 434, 442–45,
                                                                 448–50, 485
Caparo Industries v Dickman [1990] 2 AC 605 432
Carr v Hackney London BC [1995] Env LR 372 ....352, 354, 359
Catscratch Ltd and Lettuce Holdings Ltd
  v Glasgow Licensing Board [2001] SC 218 486
Chapman v Gosberton Farm Produce Co Ltd [1993] Env LR 191 ....365, 372, 394
Chapman v UK [2001] BHRC 48 485
Chasemore v Richards (1859) 7 HL Cas 349 160
Christie v Davey [1893] 1 Ch 316 380
CILFIT v Ministry of Health (Case 283/81) [1982] ECR 3415 PD 68 88
City of London Corp v Bovis Construction Ltd
  [1992] 3 All ER 697; [1989] JPL 263 400
Clarke v Secretary of State for Transport, Local Government
  and the Regions [2001] 1 All ER 120 485
Clayton v Sale Urban District Council [1926] 1 KB 415 ....359, 390
Comitato Di Coordinamento per la Difesa Della Cava
  v Regione Lombardia (Case C-236/92) [1994] ECR I-483 235
Commission v Belgium (Case C-42/89) [1990] ECR I-2821 116
Commission v Belgium (Walloon Waste) (Case 2/90)
  [1992] 1 ECR 4431 ....106, 107
Commission v Council (Titanium Dioxide Waste)
  (Case C-300/89) [1991] ECR I-2867; [1993] 3 CMLR 359 103

Commission v Council (Waste Disposal) (Case C-155/91)
[1993] ECR I-939 103

Commission v Denmark (Danish Bottles)
(Case 302/86) [1988] ECR 460; [1989] 1 CMLR 619 . . . . .20, 101, 102, 106

Commission v Germany (Re Beer Purity Laws)
(Case 178/84) [1987] ECR 1227 95

Commission v Germany (Case C-361/88)
[1991] ECR I-2567; [1993] 2 CMLR 821 116

Commission v Germany (Case C-131/93) [1994] ECR 3302 105

Commission v Germany (Case C-228/00) 197, 198

Commission v Greece [2000] ECR I-5047 85

Commission v Ireland (Souvenir Jewellery)
(Case 113/80) [1980] ECR 1625 106

Commission v Ireland (Case 151/84) [1981] ECR 3573 84

Commission v Luxembourg (Case C-458/00) 197

Commission v Portugal (Case C-214/97) OJ C 258, 15/8/1998 117

Commission v UK (Case 246/89) [1989] ECR 3125 83

Commission v UK (Case C-337/89)
(Re Drinking Water Directive)
[1993] Water Law 59; [1992] I-ECR 6103 . . . . .83, 92, 96, 116

Commission v UK (Bathing Water)
(Case 56/90) [1993] Water Law 168;
[1993] Env LR 472 . . . . .83, 115, 117, 175, 478

Commission v UK (Case C-340/96) [1999] ECR I-2023 83

Commission v UK (Case C-69/99) [2002] ECR I-10979 156

Confédération Nationale des Producteurs de Fruits et
Legumes v EEC Council (Cases 16 and 17/62)
[1962] ECR 471; [1963] CMLR 160 73

Cook v South West Water plc
[1992] 3(4) Water Law 103; (1992) ENDS 207 160

Costa v ENEL (Case 6/64) [1964] ECR 585;
[1964] CMLR 425 89

Coventry City Council v Cartwright [1975] 1 WLR 845;
[1975] 2 All ER 99 . . . . .351, 355

Criminal Proceedings against Ditlev Bluhme
(Case C-67/97) [1999] 1 CMLR 612 105

Crown River Cruises Ltd v Kimbolton Fireworks Ltd
[1996] 2 Lloyd's Rep 533 . . . . .418, 421

Cunningham v Birmingham City Council [1998] Env LR 1 351

Customs and Excise Commissioners v APS Samex
[1983] 1 All ER 1042 . . . . .87, 88

Customs and Excise Commissioners v Darfish Ltd
[2001] Env LR 3 17

Customs and Excise Commissioners v Parkwood
Landfill Ltd [2002] EWHC Ch 47; [2002] STC 417 17

De Keyser's Royal Hotel Ltd v Spicer Bros Ltd
(1914) 30 TLR 257 . . . . .379, 421

Dear v Thames Water Ltd (1992) WLAW 116 432

Dennis & Dennis v Ministry of Defence [2003] EWHC 793 . . . . .372, 375, 380, 423
Devonshire WRA v Roberts, Warren and Snow (1995) 7 ELM 105 222
Dillenkoffer and Others v Germany (Cases C-178–79/94)
    [1996] ECR I-4845 96
Donoghue v Stevenson [1932] AC 562 431
Douglas v Hello! Ltd [2001] 2 WLR 992 485
Drinking Water Inspectorate v Severn Trent Water
    (1995) 243 ENDS 45 169
Durham County Council v Peter Connors Industrial
    Services Ltd [1993] Env LR 197 228
Dusseldorp BV (Case C-203/96) [1998] ECR I-4075 106

East Devon District Council v Farr [2002] Env LR 31 365
East Northamptonshire District Council
    v Fossett [1994] Env LR 388 . . . . .378, 388
East Riding of Yorkshire County Council v Yorkshire
    Water Services Ltd [2000] Env LR 113 354
Empress Car Co (Abertillery) Ltd v National Rivers
    Authority [1998] 1 All ER 481; [1998] Env LR 396 . . . . .64, 139–43
Envirocor Waste Holdings Ltd v Secretary of State for the
    Environment (1995) EGCS 60 . . . . .334, 461
Environment Agency v British Steel plc (1999) 29 ENDS, December .142
Environment Agency v Brock plc [1998] Env LR 607 . . . . .141, 145
Environment Agency v Clarke, Re Rhondda Waste
    Disposal Ltd [2000] Env LR 600 219
Environment Agency v Melland [2002] EWHC 904 226
Environment Agency v Milford Haven Port Authority
    and Andrews [1999] 1 Lloyd's Rep 673 48
Environment Agency v Newcomb and Son Ltd and
    Another [2002] EWHC 2095 208
Esso Petroleum Co Ltd v Southport Corp [1956] AC 218 440
Express Dairies Distribution v Environment Agency [2003] EWHC 448 147

Fairchild and Others v Glenhaven Funeral Services Ltd
    [2002] 3 All ER 305 436
Firma Foto-Frost v Hauptzollamt Lübeck-Ost
    (Case 314/85) [1987] ECR 4199; [1988] 3 CMLR 57 88
Foster v British Gas (Case C-188/89) [1991] 2 AC 306;
    [1991] 2 WLR 1075; [1991] 2 All ER 705 93
France v Commission of the European Communities (PCP case)
    (Case C-41/93) [1994] Water Law 120 108
Francovich and Bonifaci v Italian State (Cases C-6 and 9/90)
    [1991] ECR I-5357; [1993] 2 CMLR 66 94–96
Fredin v Sweden (1991) 13 EHRR 784 486

Gateshead Metropolitan BC v Secretary
    of State for the Environment and Northumbrian
    Water Group [1995] Env LR 37; [1995] JPL 432 . . . . .187, 333

Gibbons and Others v South West Water Services
  [1992] 2 WLR 507; [1993] Env LR 244 . . . . .414, 453

Giles v Walker (1890) 24 QBD 656 443

Gillingham BC v Medway (Chatham)
  Dock [1993] QB 343; [1992] 3 WLR 449;
  [1992] 3 All ER 923; [1992] Env LR 98 . . . . .379, 419, 420

Gilli and Andres (Case 788/79) [1980] ECR 2071 106

Godfrey v Conwy County BC [2000] Env LR 674 384

Graham and Graham v Rechem International Ltd [1996] Env LR 158 . . . . .412, 437

Greenpeace v ICI (1994) 234 ENDS, July 161

Greenpeace Schweiz v Switzerland (1997) 23 EHRR CD 116 470

Gregory v Piper (1829) 9 B & C 591 440

Griffin v South West Water [1995] Water Law 5; [1995] IRLR 15 . . . . .93, 474

Grimaldi v Fonds des Maladies Professionnelles
  (Case C-322/88) [1989] ECR 4407; [1991] 2 CMLR 265 75

Groenveld (PB) BV (Case 15/79) [1979] ECR 3409 106

Guerra v Italy (1998) 26 EHRR 357 . . . . .481, 482, 490

Guthrie v SEPA [1998] Env LR 128 . . . . .214, 216

HMIP v Safety Kleen UK Ltd (1994) ENDS 236 264

HMIP v Southern Refining Services Ltd (1994) unreported,
  DoE news release 5/12/94 288

Halsey v Esso Petroleum Co Ltd [1961] 1 WLR 683;
  [1961] 2 All ER 145 . . . . .342, 376, 377, 427, 429

Hammersmith London BC v Magnum Automated
  Forecourts Ltd [1978] 1 WLR 50 363

Hanrahan v Merck Sharp and Dohme [1988] 1 LRM 629 449

Hatton v UK (2001) The Times, 8 October 483

Heaney and McGuinness v Ireland [2001] Crim LR 481 490

Heath v Brighton Corp (1908) 98 LT 718 . . . . .380, 421

Hertfordshire CC ex p Green Environmental Industries
  Ltd and John Moynihan [2000] 1 All ER 773; [1998] Env LR 153 488

Hollywood Silver Fox Farm Ltd v Emmett
  [1936] 2 KB 468; [1936] 1 All ER 825 . . . . .380, 421

Hope Butuyuyu v London Borough of Hammersmith
  and Fulham [1997] Env LR D 13 364

Hotson v East Berkshire AHA [1987] AC 750 436

Huckerby v Elliott [1970] 1 All ER 194 230

Hughes, Re [1943] 2 All ER 269 230

Hunter v Canary Wharf Ltd [1997] 2 WLR 684;
  (1995) 139 SJ LB 214 . . . . .381, 412, 418, 423, 428, 429,
                                                                                 434, 435, 449, 485

Imperial Chemical Industries v Shatwell [1965] AC 656 453

Impress (Worcester) Ltd v Rees [1971] 2 All ER 357 142

Inter-Environment Wallonie ASBL
  v Regione Wallonie [1998] Env LR 625 194

JB and M Motor Haulage Ltd v London Waste
    Regulation Authority [1993] Env LR 243 222
John Young & Co v Bankier Distillery Co [1893] AC 691; [1891] All ER 439 160
Jones v Llanrwst Urban District Council [1911] 1 Ch 393; [1908] All ER 922 . . . . .161, 440

Kampelmann v Landschafts verband Westfalen-Lippe
    (Cases C-243–58/96) [1997] ECR-I 6907 93
Katte Klitsche de la Grange v Italy (1994) 19 EHRR 368 487
Kennaway v Thompson [1980] 3 WLR 361; [1980] 3 All ER 329 422
Kent County Council v Beaney [1993] Env LR 225 225
Khatun and Others v UK (1998) 26 EHRR 212 484
Kiddle v City Business Properties Ltd [1942] 1 KB 269 430
Kirklees Metropolitan Council v Field and Others [1998] Env LR 337 358

LCB v UK (1998) 27 EHRR 212 481
Lake Lanoux Arbitration (1957) ILR 101 178
Lambert (A) Flat Management Ltd v Lomas
    [1981] 1 WLR 898; [1981] 2 All ER 280 394
Lambie v Thanet District Council [2001] Env LR 21 . . . . .388, 389
Leakey v National Trust [1980] 2 WLR 65; [1980] 1 All ER 17 424
Leeman v Montagu [1936] 2 All ER 1677 378
Leigh Land Reclamation Ltd v Walsall Metropolitan BC (1991) 3 JEL 281 225
Leonesio v Ministero dell'Agricoltura e delle Foreste
    (Case 93/71) [1972] ECR 287; [1973] CMLR 343 74
Levy v Environment Agency [2003] Env LR 11 276
Lewisham London BC v Hall [2003] Env LR 4 393
Liverpool City Council v Maudsley (1992) LMELR 51 362
Lloyd v Symonds and Others (1998) Lawtel, 20 March 363
Lloyds Bank v Guardian Assurance, Trollope and
    Colls Ltd (1987) 35 Build LR 34 415
Lochgelly Iron and Coal Co v McMullen [1934] AC 1 . . . .
Lockhart v NCB 1981 SLT 161 139
Lodge Holes Colliery Co Ltd v Wednesbury Corp [1908] AC 323 441
London Borough of Haringey v Jowett
    [1999] NPC 52; [2000] Env LR D6 . . . . .354, 385
London Borough of Lewisham v Fenner (1995) 44 ENDS 248 353
Lopez Ostra v Spain (1995) 20 EHRR 277 . . . . .483, 484

McColl v Strathclyde Regional Council [1984] JPL 351 168
McDonald v Associated Fuels Ltd (1954) DLR 775 439
McGhee v National Coal Board [1973] 1 WLR 1 . . . . .435, 436
McGinley and Egan v UK (1998) 27 EHRR 1 482
McKenna and Others v British Aluminium Ltd
    (2002) The Times, 25 April 485
McLeod v Buchanan [1940] 2 All ER 179 138

Maile v Wigan Metropolitan BC [2001] Env LR 11 314

Malton Board of Health v Malton Manure Co (1879) 4 ExD 302 355

Manley v New Forest District Council [1999] EWCH Admin 752 365

Marcic v Thames Water Utilities Ltd [2001] 3 All ER 698;
    [2002] 2 All ER 55 . . . . .160, 422, 485

Margate Pier v Town Council of Margate (1869) 33 JP 437 355

Marleasing SA v La Commercial Internacional de
    Alimentacion SA (Case 106/89) [1990] ECR I-4135; [1992] CMLR 305 94

Marjury v Sunbeam Corp Ltd (1974) 1 NSWLR 659 139

Marshall v Southampton AHA (Case 152/84)
    [1986] 2 WLR 780; [1986] ECR 723; [1986] 1 CMLR 688; 87, 92

Mayer Parry Recycling Ltd v Environment Agency [1999] Env LR 489 194

Merlin v British Nuclear Fules plc [1990] 2 QB 557 434

Middlesbrough County Council v Stevens
    (1993) The Times, 7 September 375

Miles v Forest Rock and Granite Co (Leicestershire) Ltd (1918) 34 TLR 500 443

Miller v Jackson [1977] 3 WLR 20; [1977] All ER 338 439

Miner v Gilmore (1859) 12 Moo PCC 131 165

Murphy v Brentwood District Council
    [1990] 3 WLR 414; [1990] 2 All ER 908 438

Myatt v Teignbridge District Council [1994] Env LR D 18 389

National Coal Board v Neath BC [1976] 2 All ER 478 . . . . .351, 384

National Coal Board v Thorne [1976] 1 WLR 543 . . . . .351, 384

National Rivers Authority and Anglers Co-operative
    Association v Clarke (1994) 232 ENDS 45 450

National Rivers Authority v Egger (UK) Ltd [1992] Env LR 130 144

National Rivers Authority v McAlpine Homes East Ltd [1994] 4 All ER 286 142

National Rivers Authority v Welsh Development Agency [1993] Env LR 407 140

National Rivers Authority v Wright Engineering Co Ltd [1994] 4 All ER 281 142

National Rivers Authority v Yorkshire Water Services Ltd
    [1995] 1 All ER 225; [1994] Env LR 177 . . . . .140, 148, 162, 163

Network Housing Association Ltd v Westminster City
    Council (1995) 27 HLR 189 . . . . .358, 390

Nicaragua v United States (Merits) (1986) ICJ 14 178

North West Leicestershire ex p Moses [2000] JPL 733 467

Northavon District Council v Secretary of State for the
    Environment (1980) 40 P & CR 332 243

Northwestern Utilities v London Guarantee and
    Accident Co Ltd [1936] AC 108 445

O'Toole v Knowsley Metropolitan BC [1999] Env LR D 29 351

Official Receiver v Environment Agency,
    Re Celtic Extraction Ltd [2000] Env LR 86 219

Orkem v Commission (Case 374/87) [1989] ECR 3283 489

Ortenberg v Austria (1994) EHRR 524 487

Osman v UK (1999) 5 BHRC 293 482
Overseas Tankship (UK) Ltd v Morts Dock &
 Engineering Co Ltd (The Wagon Mound)
 [1961] AC 388; [1961] 2 WLR 126 433

Palin Granit Oy v Vemassalon kansanterveystoyn
 kuntayhtyman hallitus (Case C-9/00) [2002] ECR I-3533 195
Penwith District Council v Secretary of State for the
 Environment [1977] JPL 371 406
Pine Valley Developments v Ireland (1991) 14 EHRR 319 486
Plaumann & Co v EEC Commission (Case 25/62)
 [1963] ECR 95; [1964] CMLR 29 . . . . .86, 479, 480
Polychronakis v Richards and Jerrom Ltd [1998] Env LR 346 364
Porter v South Buckinghamshire District Council [2001] 1 All ER 184 485
Powell and Rayner v UK (1990) 12 EHRR 355 . . . . .403, 482–84, 486
Practice Direction (Crime: Costs) [1991] 1 WLR 498 466
Price v Cromack [1975] 1 WLR 988; [1975] 2 All ER 113 . . . . .139, 143
Procureur de la République v ADBHU (Case 240/83) [1985] ECR 531 100
Procureur du Roi v Dassonville (Case 8/74)
 [1974] ECR 837; [1974] 2 CMLR 436 . . . . .101, 104
Publico Ministero v Tullio Ratti (Case 148/78)
 [1979] ECR 1629; [1980] 1 CMLR 96 . . . . .87, 91

R v Avon County Council ex p Terry Adams Ltd [1994] Env LR 442 .204
R v Birmingham City Justices ex p Guppy (1988) 152 JP 159 388
R v Boal [1992] QB 591; [1992] 2 WLR 890; [1992] 3 All ER 178 . . . . .211, 229
R v Bolton Metropolitan BC ex p Kirkman [1998] Env LR 719 .235, 278
R v Bristol City Council ex p Everett [1999] Env LR 587 351
R v Cardiff City Council ex p Gooding Investments Ltd (1995) 7 ELM 134 204
R v Carrick District Council ex p Shelley [1996] Env LR 273 . . . . .355, 356
R v Daventry District Council [2002] All ER 149 235
R v Derbyshire County Council ex p Murray [2001] Env LR 26 278
R v Director of Serious Fraud ex p Smith [1993] AC 1 466
R v Dovermoss Ltd [1995] Env LR 258; [1995] ELM 106 144
R v Environment Agency and Redland Aggregates Ltd
 ex p Gibson [1999] Env LR 73 . . . . .262, 270, 278
R v Ettrick Trout Co Ltd v Baxter [1994] Env LR 165 145
R v Exeter CC ex p JL Thomas and Co Ltd [1991] 1 QB 471 426
R v Falmouth and Truro Port Health Authority
 ex p South West Water Ltd [2000] NPC 36 . . . . .356, 358
R v Fenny Stratford JJ ex p Watney Mann [1976] 1 WLR 1101 .388, 389
R v Friskies Petcare UK Ltd [2000] 2 Cr App R (S) 401 . . . . .61, 62
R v Hertfordshire County Council ex p Green
 Environmental Industries Ltd [2000] 2 WLR 373; [2000] 1 All ER 773 . . . . .222, 466
R v HM Inspector of Pollution ex p Greenpeace (No 2)
 [1994] 4 All ER 329; [1994] Env LR 76 . . . . .65, 468

R v Howe (F) & Son (Engineers) Ltd [1999] 2 Cr App R(S) 37 . . . . .60, 62

R v Inland Revenue Commissioners ex p National
Federation of the Self-Employed and
Small Businesses Ltd (1982) [1982] AC 617 467

R v Johnson [1996] 2 Cr App R 434 429

R v Leicestershire County Council ex p Blackfordby
and Boothorpe Action Group Ltd [2001] Env LR 2 486

R v Leicestershire CC, Hepworth Building Products and
Onyx (UK) Ltd ex p Blackfordby and Boothcorpe
Action Group [2001] Env LR 35 235

R v Leighton and Town and Country Refuse
Collections Ltd [1997] Env LR 411 224

R v Metropolitan Stipendiary Magistrate
ex p London Waste Regulation Authority
[1993] 3 All ER 113 226

R v Metropolitan Stipendiary Magistrate
ex p Mahmed Ali [1997] Env LR D 15 360

R v North Somerset District Council ex p Garnett [1998] Env LR 91 467

R v Poole BC ex p Beebee and Others [1991] 2 PLR 27; [1991] JPL 643 469

R v Rotherham Metropolitan BC ex p Rankin [1990] JPL 503 193

R v Secretary of State for Foreign Affairs
ex p World Development Movement Ltd
[1995] 1 WLR 386; [1995] 1 All ER 611 469

R v Secretary of State for the Environment
ex p Friends of the Earth and Andrew Lees [1994] 2 CMLR 760 . . . . .83, 92, 469

R v Secretary of State for the Environment
ex p Greenpeace [1994] 2 CMLR 737 94

R v Secretary of State for the Environment
ex p Rose Theatre Trust [1990] 2 WLR 186; [1990] 1 All ER 754 467–69

R v Secretary of State for the Environment
ex p RSPB [1995] NPC 22; [1995] 7 JEL 245 88

R v Secretary of State for the Environment and MAFF
ex p Standley and Metson [1997] Env LR 589 156

R (on the Application of Alconbury Developments Ltd)
v Secretary of State for the Environment,
Transport and the Regions [2001] 2 All ER 929 488

R v Secretary of State for Trade and Industry
ex p Duddridge and Others (1995) The Times,
26 October; [1995] Env LR 151; [1995] JEL 224; [1996] Env LR 325 . . . . .16, 463, 470

R v Secretary of State for Trade and Industry
ex p Greenpeace Ltd [1998] Env LR 415 66

R v Secretary of State for Transport ex p Factortame Ltd
and Others (Cases C-46 and 48/93)
[1996] 2 WLR 506; [1996] All ER (EC) 301 . . . . .83, 95, 96

R v Somerset District Council ex p Dixon [1998] Env LR 111 467

R v South West Water Authority (1991) 3 LMELR 65 . . . . .161, 429

R v Stewart [1896] 1 QB 300 464

R v Swale BC and Medway Ports Authority ex p RSPB [1991] JPL 39 470

R v Tunbridge Wells Justices ex p Tunbridge Wells BC [1996] Env LR 88 388
R v Vale of Glamorgan BC and ABP
    ex p James [1996] 8 ELM 12; [1997] Env LR 195 219
R v Wicks [1998] 2 AC 92 146
R v Yorkshire Water Services Ltd (2001) The Times, 12 December 61, 169
Rainham Chemical Works v Belvedere Fish Guano
    [1921] 2 AC 465; [1921] All ER 48 444
Read v Lyons & Co Ltd [1947] AC 156; [1946] 2 All ER 471 ....417, 422, 425, 442–45
Rewe-Zentral AG Bundesmonopolver-wältung für
    Branntwein (Cassis de Dijon case) (Case 120/78)
    [1979] ECR 649; [1979] 3 CMLR 494 ....101, 104–06
Rickards v Lothian [1913] AC 263; [1911–13] All ER 71 ....442, 443
Roberts v Vale District Council (1997) 78 LGR 368 243
Robinson v Kilvert (1884) 41 Ch D 88 ....380, 421
Rookes v Barnard [1964] 2 WLR 269 413
Roskell v Whitworth (1871) 19 WR 804 379
Rugby Joint Water Board v Walters [1967] Ch 397 166
Rushmer v Polsue and Alfieri Ltd [1906] Ch 234; [1907] AC 121 ....379, 420
Rylands v Fletcher (1868) LR 3 HL 330 ....20, 64, 416, 431, 433,
                                                          441–47, 449, 451, 485

SITA EcoService Nederland BV v Minister van
    Volkshuisvesting, Ruimtelijke Ordening en
    Milieubeheer (Case C-116/01) (2003) unreported, judgment of 3 April 198
Saddleworth Urban Development Corporation
    v Aggregate and Sand (1970) 114 SJ 931 363
Sandwell Metropolitan BC v Bujok [1990] 1 WLR 1350 366
Saunders v UK (1997) 23 EHRR 313 489
Saunders-Clark v Grosvenor Mansions and
    D'Allesandri [1900] 2 Ch 373 419
Schulmans Inc v NRA [1993] Env LR D 1 143
Scott v Berkshire County Council [1984] JPL 94 205
Scott v London & St Katherine's Docks Co (1865) 3 H & C 596 435
Scott-Whitehead v National Coal Board
    [1987] 2 EGLR 227; (1987) 53 P & CR 263 ....161, 432
Secretary of State for Wales v Dwr Cymru (1995) 242 ENDS 169
Sedleigh-Denfield v O'Callaghan [1940] AC 880; [1940] 3 All ER 349 381
Sergius Oebel (Case 155/80) [1981] ECR 1993 106
Severn Trent Water Authority v Express Foods Group Ltd
    (1988) 153 JP 126 145
Shanks and McEwan (Teeside) Ltd
    v Environment Agency [1997] 2 All ER 332 ....225, 226
Sheffield City Council v ADH Demolition Ltd
    (1984) 82 LGR 177 336
Smith v Giddy [1904] 2 KB 448 415
Smith v Great Western Railway (1926) 135 LT 112 443

Southern Water Authority v Pegrum [1989] Crim LR 442 139

Southwark BC v Simpson [1999] 21 HLR 504; [1999] Env LR 553 351

Southwark London BC v Ince [1989] COD 549 ....354, 384

St Helens Smelting Co v Tipping
  (1865) 11 HL Cas 642; (1865) 11 ER 1483 ....342, 418

Star Fruit Co v Commission (Case 247/87)
  [1989] ECR 291; [1990] 1 CMLR 733 84

Sterling Homes v Birmingham City Council [1996] Env LR 121 358

Stevenage Borough Council v Wilson [1993] Env LR 214 354

Stichting Greenpeace Council and Others
  v EC Commission (Cases T-585/93 and C-321/95P)
  [1995] ECR II-2205 ....86, 479

Stokes v GKN [1968] 1 WLR 1776 438

Stott (Procurator Fiscal Dunfermline) v Brown
  [2001] 2 WLR 817; [2001] 2 All ER 97 489

Sturges v Bridgman (1879) 11 Ch D 852 ....352, 378, 420, 426, 430

Tandridge District Council v P & S Civil Engineering Ltd
  [1995] Env LR 67 268

Tate & Lyle Industries Ltd v GLC [1983] AC 509 ....424, 429

Tennent v Earl of Glasgow (1864) 2 Macph (Ct of Sess) (HL) 22 445

Tetley v Chitty [1986] 1 All ER 663 ....381, 424

Thames Waste Management Ltd v Surrey County Council
  [1997] Env LR 148 226

Thompson v Gibson (1841) 7 M & W 456 424

Thompson v Smiths Shiprepairers (North Shields) Ltd [1984] 1 All ER 881 433

Tombesi Litigation [1997] All ER 639; [1998] Env LR 59 ....193, 194

Tower Hamlets LBC v Manzoni and Walder [1984] JPL 436 ....384, 385

Trail Smelter Arbitration (1940) 3 RIAA 1905 178

Trevett v Secretary of State for Transport, Local
  Government and the Regions and Others [2002] EWHC 2696 Admin 464

Twyford Parish Council v Secretary of State for the
  Environment and Secretary of State for Transport
  [1991] COD 210; [1992] 1 CMLR 276; [1993] 3 Env LR 37 92

UK v Commission (Cases C-157/96 and C-180/99)
  [1998] ECR I-2265; [1998] ECR I-2211 16

United Kingdom Renderers Association Ltd,
  John Pointon and Sons Ltd v Secretary of State for
  the Environment, Transport and the Regions [2002] EWCA Civ 749 277

Van Duyn v Home Office (Case 41/74) [1974] ECR 1337; [1975] 1 CMLR 1 ....91, 92

Van Gend en Loos v Nederlandse Administratie
  der Belastingen (Case 26/62) [1963] ECR 1; [1963] CMLR 105 89–91

Vanderpant v Mayfair Hotel Co Ltd [1930] 1 Ch 138 378

Vessoso v Ministere Public of Italy and Zanetti
  v Same (Joined Cases C-206/88 and C-207/88) [1990] ECR I-1462 193

R (on the Application of Vetterlein)
v Hampshire County Council [2001] All ER (D) 146 487
Von Colson v Land Nordrhein-Westfalen (Case 14/83) [1984] ECR 1891 94

Walter v Selfe (1851) 4 De G & S 315 . . . . .378, 418
Waste Incineration Services Ltd
v Dudley Metropolitan BC [1993] Env LR 29 228
Webb v EMO Air Cargo (UK) Ltd [1993] 1 WLR 49;
[1992] 4 All ER 929; [1992] 2 All ER 43; [1992] 1 CMLR 793 (CA) 94
Wellingborough District Council v Gordon (No 1)
[1991] COD 154; [1991] JPL 874 361
Wellingborough District Council v Gordon (No 2) [1993] Env LR 218 364
Welsh Water Authority v Williams Motors (Cymdu) Ltd
(1988) The Times, 5 December 142
West v Bristol Tramway Co [1908] 2 KB 14; [1908–10] All ER 215 443
Wheeler and Another v JJ Saunders Ltd and Others
[1996] Ch 19; [1995] 3 WLR 466; [1995] 2 All ER 697 .379, 419, 420, 425
Wilsher v Essex AHA [1986] 3 All ER 801 436
Wivenhoe Port v Colchester BC [1985] JPL 175 . . . . .352, 365
Woodhouse v Walsall Metropolitan BC [1994] Env LR 30 . . . . .211, 229
Wrothwell (FJH) v Yorkshire Water Authority [1984] Crim LR 43 139
Wychavon District Council v NRA [1993] 2 All ER 440 140
Wychavon District Council v Secretary of State for the
Environment and Velcourt Ltd [1994] COD 205; [1994] JEL 351 94

TABLE OF STATUTES

Alkali Act 1863 ....260, 328, 335
Alkali Act 1874 328
Alkali Works Regulation
  Act 1906 ....31, 328
Ancient Monuments and
  Archaeological Areas
  Act 1979 468

Building Act 1984 407

Civil Aviation Act 1982 .....374, 382, 383, 402
  s 68(1), (3) 403
  ss 76, 77 403
  s 78 402
  s 79 403
Clean Air Act 1956 ....328, 335, 354, 460
Clean Air Act 1968 ....328, 335
Clean Air Act 1993 ....7, 54, 327, 328,
                    333, 335–37, 341–43,
                    354, 473
  Pts I–III 335
  s 1 ....336, 337
  s 1(1), (2) 336
  s 1(3) 338
  s 1(4) 338
  s 2 336–39
  s 2(3) 337
  s 2(4) 339
  s 3 337
  s 4 339
  s 5 339
  ss 6–8 340
  s 7 340
  s 14 340
  ss 18, 19 341
  s 20 337
  s 30 343
  s 33 336
  s 34 341
  s 34(2) 473
  s 36 341
  s 35 341
  s 35(1)(b) 341
  s 36 342
  s 36(6) 342
  s 37 341
  s 38 341
  s 39 342
  s 41 335
  s 43 336
  s 44 336
  s 51 339
  s 61(3) 341
  Sched 1 341

Company Directors
  Disqualification
  Act 1986 63
Comprehensive Environmental
  Response Compensation
  and Liability Act 1980 (USA) 310
Control of Pollution
  Act 1974 ....11, 124, 185, 188–90,
                    202, 206, 211–13,
                    218, 229, 349, 360, 373,
                    374, 382–84, 391
  Pt III 399
  s 6(3) 161
  s 17 198
  ss 31(1)(a), 32(1)(a) 450
  ss 57–59 384
  ss 58, 59 355
  s 59A 399
  ss 60–67 395
  s 60 ....380, 399–401, 404
  s 60(2) 399
  s 60(4) 400
  s 61 ....380, 399, 404
  s 61(3) 400
  s 62 401
  s 62(2) 401
  ss 63–67 404
  s 63 404
  s 64 405
  s 65 405
  s 68 403
  s 69 405
  s 71 ....364, 394, 400, 403
  s 72 400
  s 74 405
  s 75(1) 415, 438
  Sched 1 404
Control of Pollution
  (Amendment) Act 1989 ....39, 204, 211,
                    250, 251
  s 1(1) 205, 250
  s 1(3) 205
  s 2 250
  ss 5, 6 205
Countryside and Rights of Way
  Act 2000 58
Crime and Disorder Act 1998 371
  s 51 403
Criminal Justice Act 1991 63
Criminal Justice and Public Order
  Act 1994 404
  s 63 404

Deposits of Poisonous Wastes
  Act 1972 . . . . .188, 460
Diseases of Animals Act 1894 464
Disqualification of Directors
  Act 1986 . . . . .62, 229

Electricity Act 1989 .470
Environment Act 1995 . . . .9, 10, 29, 30, 38–41,
                    43, 44, 54, 121, 123,
                    125, 129–31, 133, 158,
                    185, 190, 202, 210, 232,
                    242, 282, 284, 313,
                    327, 328, 330, 331, 473
  Pt IV 39, 330, 333
  s 1 261
  s 1(1) 38
  s 2 . . . . .39, 128
  s 2(1)(a)(i) 127
  s 2(2) 39
  s 3 39
  s 4 . . . . .14, 40, 128, 166
  s 5 41
  s 6 . . . . .41, 128, 166
  s 6(1) 44
  s 7 .41, 42, 44, 128
  s 7(1)–(3) 43
  s 8 . . . . .41, 43, 44
  s 8(4) 43
  s 9 44
  ss 11–12 38
  s 13 39
  s 39 . . . . .41, 43, 44, 149
  s 39(2) 44
  s 41 . . . . .210, 271
  ss 51–52 159
  s 56(1) 40, 44
  s 57 . . . . .39, 54, 309, 349
  s 80 330
  s 80(4) 330
  s 81 330
  s 82 331
  s 83 331
  s 84 331
  s 85 . . . . .331, 332
  s 85(5), (7) 332
  s 86 331
  ss 87, 88 332
  s 92 190
  ss 93–95 190
  s 93 240
  s 99 242
  ss 108–10 221
  s 108 . . . . .32, 34, 44, 45, 136,
                    149, 284, 285, 314, 315
  s 111 137

s 114 . . . . .132, 289
s 120 146
Sched 2 324
Sched 2B 237
Sched 22 . . . . .39, 129, 146, 157,
                    159, 214, 237, 283, 344
Environmental
  Protection Act 1990 . . . .12, 31, 39, 123, 125,
                    172, 185, 188–91, 199,
                    205, 206, 211, 218, 219,
                    234, 244, 246, 255, 261,
                    264, 269, 278, 279, 281,
                    302, 303, 308, 309, 349,
                    352, 354–56, 363, 373,
                    374, 378, 381–86, 391,
                    393, 395, 398–400, 405,
                    411, 412, 425, 452,
                    464, 466, 471, 473
  Pt I 6, 10, 30, 31, 33, 35, 36,
                    39, 41, 44, 54, 127, 128, 146,
                    172, 261–63, 269, 270,
                    272, 284, 287, 289–91,
                    298, 327, 332, 334, 335
  Pt II 10, 34, 35, 39, 41, 44, 147, 172,
                    185, 187, 189–92, 198, 202,
                    206, 213, 227, 235, 245,
                    259, 272, 285, 289,
                    296, 303, 488
  Pt IIA 10, 54, 172, 290, 307,
                    309, 311, 313, 349, 367
  Pt III 10, 54, 289, 304, 313, 333, 349,
                    354, 365, 367, 374, 377
  Pt IV 464
  Pt VII 58
  s 1 263
  s 1(2) 3, 263
  s 1(3) 41, 264, 292
  s 1(4) 264
  s 2 264
  s 2(1) 268, 269
  s 2(5) 266
  s 3 . . . . .274, 275
  s 3(5) 18, 274
  s 4(9) 276
  s 5(1) 251
  s 6 . . . . .205, 222, 226, 262, 266,
                    268, 283
  s 7 . . . . .226, 273–76, 278, 282, 334
  s 7(2) 263, 274, 275
  s 7(4) 275, 298
  s 7(7) 276, 277
  s 8 271
  s 8(8) 272
  s 10 282
  s 10(3) 282
  s 10(7) 270

Environmental Protection
  Act 1990 (contd)—
  s 11 . . . . .270, 282, 288
  s 12 283
  s 12(1) 283
  s 12(3) 283
  s 13 . . . . .283, 284
  s 13(4) 284
  s 14 284
  s 14(2) 284
  s 15 288
  s 15(8) 283
  s 17 . . . . .32, 44, 284
  s 20 279
  s 21 279
  s 22 . . . . .279, 288
  s 22(11) 280
  s 23 . . . . .277, 284, 286, 287
  s 23(1) 279, 288
  s 23(1)(a) 262
  s 23(1)(b) 284
  s 24 284
  s 26 286
  s 27 . . . . .286, 290, 303, 324
  s 28 289
  s 28(1) 244
  s 29 212
  s 29(3) 41
  s 29(9) 207
  s 30 202
  s 30(5) 203
  s 30(7) 203
  s 32 203
  s 33 . . . . .16, 147, 209, 220, 223,
                             225, 226, 228, 247–49,
                                    252, 255, 489
  s 33(b) 226
  s 33(1) 223, 224, 226, 228, 452, 488
  s 33(1)(a) 206, 208, 224–28
  s 33(1)(b) 206, 208, 224, 225, 227, 228
  s 33(1)(c) 206, 208, 222, 224, 225, 228
  s 33(2) 208, 227
  s 33(3) 208, 250
  s 33(4) 208
  s 33(5) 226, 227, 251
  s 33(6) 226
  s 33(7) 228
  s 33(7)(a) 147, 228
  s 33(7)(c) 228
  s 33(9) 228, 229
  s 34 . . . . .203, 235, 246, 247, 249, 255
  s 34(1) 247, 248
  s 34(1)(b) 248
  s 34(2) 247
  s 34(3) 250
  s 34(4) 250, 252

  s 34(5) 247, 252
  s 34(6) 227, 247
  s 34(10) 254
  ss 35–42 235
  s 35 . . . . .185, 207, 224
  s 35(3) 213
  s 35(4) 214, 217
  s 35(5) 214
  s 35(6) 213, 215
  s 35(7) 213, 214
  s 35(8) 210, 214
  s 35A 214
  s 36 209
  s 36(1)(a) 209
  s 36(2) 209, 213, 242, 245
  s 36(3) 209, 212, 213
  s 36(4) 210
  s 36A 210, 214, 216, 217
  s 36A(3) 210
  s 36A(4) 214
  s 37 215
  s 37(1)(a) 216
  s 37(2) 215
  s 37A 216
  s 37A(9) 216
  s 38 220
  s 38(1)–(13) 218
  s 38(1), (2) 217
  s 38(3), (4) 216
  s 38(6) 217
  s 38(9) 217, 218
  s 38(9A) 214
  s 38(9C) 217
  s 39 . . . . .218, 298
  s 40 . . . . .216, 244
  s 41 209
  s 41(7) 217
  s 42 . . . . .217, 220
  s 42(3) 223
  s 42(6) 217
  s 43 219
  s 43(4) 220
  s 43(5) 220
  s 43(6) 220
  s 43(7) 217, 220
  s 44 . . . . .209, 227
  s 44A 190, 232, 242
  s 44B 232
  s 45 204
  s 46(2) 244
  s 48 204
  s 49 . . . . .204, 244
  s 50 . . . . .232, 242
  s 51 203
  s 52 244
  s 59 . . . . .16, 19, 222, 223, 245, 324

Environmental Protection
Act 1990 (contd)—
s 59(3) 222
s 59(4) 223
s 59(5) 223
s 59(6) 222
s 59(7) 223
s 59(8) 223
s 60 227
s 61 190
s 62 ....199, 202
s 63(2) 223, 227, 452
s 64 220
s 64(6) 220
s 65 220
s 65(5) 220
s 71 ....222, 226, 489
s 71(2) 488, 489
s 73(b) 223
s 73(6) 16, 223, 247, 255, 451, 452
s 74 ....211, 212
s 74(3) 211
s 74(4) 209, 211
s 74(7) 211
s 75(2) 192
s 75(3) 192
s 75(4)–(7) 191
s 75(4) 237
s 78 202
s 78(4) 311
s 78(7) 315
s 78(9) 313
ss 78A–78YC 309
s 78A 319
s 78A(2) 311, 324, 368
s 78A(4) 312
s 78B 315
s 78B(1) 314
s 78C 315
s 78E 317
s 78E(1) 317, 321
s 78E(4) 316, 317
s 78E(5) 316, 317
s 78F(2) 317, 318
s 78F(3) 318
s 78F(4) 318, 319
s 78F(6) 320
s 78H 316
s 78H(5)(a)–(c) 317
s 78H(6), (7) 316
s 78K 317
s 78L(1) 322
s 78M 322
s 78M(3), (4) 322
s 78N 317, 322
s 78N(3) 316

s 78P 322
s 78P(8) 322
s 78Q 315
s 78R 323
ss 78U, 78X(2) 313
s 78X(3) 319
s 78YB(1) 290, 324
s 78YB(2) 324
s 78YB(3) 245, 324
ss 79–82 ....188, 349, 417
s 79 ....289, 290, 350, 383–85, 394
s 79(1) 349, 355, 385
s 79(1)(a) 354, 365, 367
s 79(1A) 349
s 79(1)(b) 354, 365, 367
s 79(1)(c) 354, 365
s 79(1)(d) 246, 354, 365
s 79(1)(e) 245, 355, 365, 390
s 79(1)(f) 355, 365
s 79(1)(g) 355, 360, 361, 365, 383,
				384, 391, 392, 395, 398
s 79(1)(ga) 355, 360, 361, 365, 383,
				385, 392, 395
s 79(1)(h) 355, 365
s 79(2)–(6) 354
s 79(3) 354
s 79(6A) 385
s 79(7) 351, 354, 359, 383, 390
s 79(9) 364, 400
s 80 ....290, 356–60, 385, 387, 389, 391
s 80(a) 389
s 80(1) 353
s 80(1)(a), (b) 388
s 80(2) 360, 390, 391
s 80(2)(c) 359
s 80(3) 360, 391
s 80(4) 349, 362–64, 392, 393
s 80(5), (6) 363
s 80(7) 363, 364
s 80(8) 364
s 80(8)(aa) 394
s 80(9) 394
s 80A 356, 385
s 81(1) 360, 390
s 81(3) 362, 392, 398
s 81(4) 362, 392
s 81(5) 363, 393
s 81A 362, 392, 393
s 82 ....290, 304, 353, 366, 395,
				401, 452, 465
s 87A(7) 316
s 89(1)(ga) 361
s 118(10) 464
s 143 ....308, 309
s 152 334
s 157 ....36, 63, 146, 227, 229, 230, 287

Environmental Protection
  Act 1990 (contd)—
  s 158 287
  Sched 1 . . . . .270, 282
  Sched 2 . . . . .203, 232
  Sched 2A 232
  Sched 2B 192
  Sched 3 . . . . .356, 357, 386

European Communities
  Act 1972 . . . . .74, 89
  s 3(2) 75

Factories Act 1961 191

Finance Act 1996 .17, 241
  ss 43–46 17
  ss 43A–43C 17

Finance Act 2001 323

Fire Precautions Act 1971 229

Food and Environment
  Protection Act 1985 208
  Pt II 147, 181
  s 5 181

Freedom of Information
  Act 2000 471

Gulf Oil Refining Act 1965 415

Health and Safety at
  Work etc
  Act 1974 . . . . .31, 57, 334, 382, 383
  Pt I 39
  s 2(1) 60
  s 37 229

Highways Act 1980—
  s 100 148
  s 161 334
  s 161A 334

Human Rights Act 1998 . . . . .457, 480, 481,
                                        484, 488
  s 6 485
  s 7(3) 470

Insolvency Act 1986 219

Land Compensation
  Act 1973 . . . . .382, 383

Land Drainage Act 1991 39

Land Drainage Act 1994 125

Law Reform (Contributory
  Negligence) Act 1945 445
  s 1 416

Licensing Act 1964—
  s 4 382

Limitation Act 1980 450
  s 2 450
  s 11(4) 450
  s 14 435

Local Government (Access to
  Information) Act 1985 473

Local Government Act 1972 471
  s 201 343
  s 222 430
  s 235(1) 399

Local Government and
  Planning Act 1980 404

Local Government (Miscellaneous
  Provisions) Act 1976 374

Local Government (Miscellaneous
  Provisions) Act 1982 382

London Government Act 1963 382

Magistrates' Court Act 1980—
  s 101 . . . . .268, 394

Medicines Act 1968—
  s 58 201
  s 130 . . . . .198, 201

Merchant Shipping Act 1988 83

Merchant Shipping Act 1995—
  s 100A 180
  s 131 180
  s 136 180
  s 137 180
  s 138A 180
  s 141 180
  s 144 180

Mines and Quarries Act 1954 355

Mines and Quarries (Tips)
  Act 1969 243

Natural Heritage (Scotland)
  Act 1991—
  s 1 14

Noise Abatement Act 1960 399

Noise Act 1996 . . . . .373, 374, 383, 392,
                                    393, 396–99
  s 1 396
  s 4 397
  s 7 397
  s 7(6) 397
  s 10 397
  Sched 1 398

Noise and Statutory
   Nuisance Act 1993 . . . . . .349, 350, 361, 362,
                    374, 382, 383, 385, 389,
                    391, 392, 403, 417
   s 2 385
   s 7 401
   s 8 401
   s 9 402
   s 10 393
   Sched 2 401
Nuclear Installations Act 1965 434

Petroleum Act 1998—
   Pt IV 181
Planning (Hazardous)
   Substances Act 1990 . . . . .54, 246
   s 28 473
Police and Criminal Evidence
   Act 1984 489
   s 78 465
Pollution Prevention and
   Control Act 1999 . . . . .10, 11, 41, 54,
                    125, 147, 172, 236, 259,
                    269, 271, 291, 327, 332,
                    334, 335, 344, 467, 471, 473
Powers of Criminal
   Courts Act 1973—
   s 35 396
   s 43 392
Prevention of Oil Pollution
   Act 1971 180
Private Places of Entertainment
   (Licensing) Act 1967 382
Public Health Act 1848 188
Public Health Act 1875 . . . . .124, 328, 349
Public Health Act 1936 . . . . .188, 328, 349, 351,
                    352, 366, 384
   s 92(1)(c) 351
   s 99 . . . . .388, 452
Public Health (Smoke
   Abatement) Act 1926 . . . . .328, 335

Radioactive Substances
   Act 1993 . . . . .31, 39
   s 38 464
Rehabilitation of Offenders
   Act 1974 . . . . .212, 251
River Boards Act 1948 125
Rivers Pollution Prevention
   Act 1876 124

Rivers (Prevention of
   Pollution) Act 1951 124
   s 2 139
Rivers (Prevention of
   Pollution) Act 1961 124
Road Traffic Act 1972—
   s 172 489
Road Traffic Act 1988 . . . . .343, 374
   s 42 343
Road Traffic Regulation
   Act 1984 344
   s 1 344
   s 6 344
   s 122 344

Salmon and Freshwater
   Fisheries Act 1975 . . . . .34, 39, 125, 173
   s 4 . . . . .138, 173
   s 4(1) 143, 173, 450
Salmon Fisheries Act 1861 124
Supreme Court Act 1981 467
   s 31(3) 466, 467

Town and Country Planning
   Act 1947 188
Town and Country Planning
   Act 1990 . . . . .188, 383, 466
   s 38 243
   s 54A 243, 333, 484
   s 55 242
   s 55(1) 242
   s 55(3)(b) 242
   s 70(2) 333
   s 77 488
   Sched 1 242
Transport Act 2000 .329

Water Act 1945 166
Water Act 1973 125
Water Act 1989 . . . . . .30, 33, 124, 125, 127, 135
   Pt III 127
   s 107(1)(a) 140, 143
Water Industry Act 1991 . . . . . . .10, 31, 57, 121,
                    124, 125, 148, 162,
                    164, 168, 171, 172,
                    245, 304, 467, 471, 473
   Pts II–IV 34, 128
   s 2 42
   s 7(4) 161, 464
   s 18 169
   s 67 168

Water Industry Act 1991 (contd)—
  s 68 ....169, 171
  s 69 171
  s 70 169
  s 70(1) 61
  s 71 171
  s 72 171
  s 73 171
  s 74 171
  s 76 171
  s 77 171
  s 77(3) 171
  s 78 171
  s 80 172
  ss 81–85 172
  s 118 ....57, 162, 163, 290
  s 120(1) 165
  s 121 164
  ss 122, 129 164
  s 141 163
  s 165 147
  s 210 229
  s 211 ....161, 464

Water Industry Act 1999 ....10, 121, 124,
                                          125

Water Resources Act 1963 ....125, 166
  s 33 166

Water Resources
  Act 1991 ....6, 9, 10, 31, 33–35,
                          38, 39, 41, 44, 121,
                          123, 124, 126–31, 133,
                          134, 137, 146, 147, 151,
                          158, 162, 164, 166–68,
                          171–73, 208, 211, 245,
                          259, 263, 285, 411, 412,
                          446, 450, 466, 471, 473
  Pt II 127
  Pt III 127, 150
  Pt IV 127
  Pt V 127
  s 2 ....33, 127
  s 7 33
  s 15 ....34, 128
  s 16 ....34, 127
  s 17 43
  s 18(1) 128
  ss 19–20 166
  s 19 ....128, 165
  ss 20–23 128
  s 20 128
  s 21 166
  s 21(7) 166
  s 22 166
  s 23 166
  s 24 167

  s 27 167
  s 28 167
  s 29 167
  s 34 167
  s 37 167
  s 38 167
  s 39 452
  ss 41–42 ....130, 132, 167
  ss 43–45 168
  ss 46–47 167
  s 48 ....167, 170
  ss 49–50 167
  ss 51–53 168
  s 60 452
  s 61 168
  s 73(1) 168
  s 73(2) 168
  s 78 168
  s 79 168
  s 79A 168
  s 80 168
  ss 82–84 134–36
  s 82 ....135, 136, 315
  s 83 ....131, 135, 136, 159
  s 84 136
  s 85 ....16, 64, 129, 137–39, 144,
                  146–48, 161–63, 304
  s 85(1)–(5) 138
  s 85(1) 53, 138–43, 161
  s 85(3) 53, 138, 143
  s 85(6) 131, 138, 145, 150
  s 86 ....129, 134, 138, 148
  s 87 ....148, 162
  s 87(1) 148
  s 87(2) 132, 148, 163
  s 88 ....129–31, 146, 147
  s 89 ....147, 148
  s 89(1)(a), (c) 147
  s 89(2) 148
  s 89(4) 146, 148
  s 89(5) 148
  s 90 146
  s 90(1) 146
  s 90(2) 146
  s 90A 146
  s 90B 159
  s 90B(1) 146
  s 91 ....132, 159
  s 91(2F) 132
  s 91(2G) 132
  s 91(2H) 133
  ss 92–95 151
  s 92 153
  s 93 154
  s 94 155
  s 95 155

Water Resources Act 1991 (contd)—
  s 100(b) 124
  s 102 136
  s 104 . . . . .126, 144
  s 161 . . . . .16, 19, 122, 151, 157–59, 324
  s 161(1) 157
  s 161(1A), (3) 157
  s 161A–161D 158
  s 161A 157, 158
  s 161A(4) 158
  s 161B 158, 159
  s 161B(5) 159
  s 161C 159
  s 161D 159
  s 161D(4) 159
  s 163 147

  ss 169–73 34
  s 190 159
  ss 202–04 160
  s 206 129
  s 209 137
  s 217 . . . . .36, 63, 146, 229
  s 221 145
  Sched 5 . . . . .128, 166
  Sched 8 168
  Sched 9 168
  Sched 10 . . . . .129, 130, 133, 159
  Sched 11 154
  Sched 12 155
Wildlife and Countryside
  Act 1981 58

TABLE OF STATUTORY INSTRUMENTS

Action Programme for Nitrate Vulnerable Zones (England
and Wales) Regulations 1998 (SI 1998/1202) 156

Aeroplane Noise Regulations 1999 (SI 1999/1452) 402

Aggregates Levy (General) Regulations 2002 (SI 2002/761) 18

Aggregates Levy (Registration and Miscellaneous
Provisions) Regulations 2001 (SI 2001/4027) 18

Air Navigation (Noise Certification) Order 1990
(SI 1990/1514) 402

Air Quality (England) Regulations 2000 (SI 2000/928) 7, 330

Anti-Pollution Works Notices Regulations 1999
(SI 1999/1006) 154, 158

Bathing Waters (Classification) Regulations 1991
(SI 1991/1597) 7, 135

Civil Procedure Rules—
Pt 54 466

Clean Air (Arrestment Plant) (Exemptions) Regulations
1969 (SI 1969/1262) 340

Clean Air (Emissions of Dark Smoke) (Exemptions)
Regulations 1969 (SI 1969/1263) 338

Clean Air (Emissions of Grit and Dust from Furnaces)
Regulations 1971 (SI 1971/162) 339

Contaminated Land (England) Regulations 2000
(SI 2000/227) 313, 315
reg 2(1)(d) 290
reg 4 321
reg 7 323
Sched 3 323

Contaminated Land (Wales) Regulations 2001 (SI 2001/2197) 313

Control of Noise (Appeals) (Amendment)
Regulations 1990 (SI 1990/2276) 400

Control of Noise (Appeals) Regulations 1975
(SI 1975/2116) 400, 405

Control of Noise (Code of Practice for Construction
and Open Sites) Order 1984 (SI 1984/1992) 394, 403

Control of Noise (Code of Practice for Construction
and Open Sites) Order 1987 (SI 1987/1730) 394, 403

Control of Noise (Code of Practice on Noise from
Audible Intruder Alarms) 1981 (SI 1981/1829) 394, 403

Control of Noise (Code of Practice on Noise from
Ice-Cream Van Chimes etc) 1981 (SI 1981/1828) 394, 403

Control of Noise (Code of Practice on Noise from
Model Aircraft) 1981 (SI 1981/1830) 394, 403

Control of Noise (Measurement and Registers)
Regulations 1976 (SI 1976/37) 375, 405

Control of Pollution (Applications, Appeals and
Registers) Regulations 1996 (SI 1996/2971) 129, 130, 132, 159

Control of Pollution (Oil Storage) (England)
   Regulations 2001 (SI 2001/2954) 153
Control of Pollution (Silage, Slurry and Agricultural
   Fuel Oil) Regulations 1991 (SI 1991/324) 153
Control of Pollution (Special Waste)
   Regulations 1980 (SI 1980/1709) 198, 199, 253
   Sched 1 198
Controlled Waste (Registration of Carriers and Seizure
   of Vehicles) Regulations 1991 (SI 1991/1624) .185, 205, 250
   reg 1(2) 205
   reg 2 205
   reg 5(1) 205
   regs 20–25 . . . . .205, 222
   Sched 1 205
Controlled Waste (Registration of Carriers and Seizure
   of Vehicles) Regulations 1998 (SI 1998/605) 205, 250
Controlled Waste Regulations 1992 (SI 1992/588) 191
   Sched 2 204
Crop Residues (Burning) Regulations 1993 (SI 1993/1366) 334

Dark Smoke (Permitted Periods) Regulations 1958
   (SI 1958/498) 338
Drinking Water (Undertakings) (England and Wales)
   Regulations 2000 (SI 2000/1297) 169

Electricity at Work Regulations 1989—
   reg 4(2) 60
Environmental Information Regulations 1992
   (SI 1992/3240) 314, 471, 473
   reg 2(1) 474
Environmental Protection (Applications, Appeals
   and Registers) Regulations 1991 (SI 1991/507) 263, 270, 273, 288, 289
Environmental Protection (Control of Substances
   that Deplete the Ozone Layer) Regulations 1996
   (SI 1996/506) 345
Environmental Protection (Duty of Care)
   Regulations 1991 (SI 1991/2389) 247, 252, 255
   reg 2(3) 252
Environmental Protection (Non-Refillable Refrigerant
   Containers) Regulations 1994 (SI 1994/199) 345
Environmental Protection (Prescribed Processes and
   Substances) Regulations 1991 (SI 1991/472) 263, 264, 267, 334
   reg 4 . . . . .267, 268
   Sched 1 . . . . .264, 265
   Sched 2 266
   Sched 3 269
   Sched 4 . . . . .264, 266
   Sched 5 . . . . .264, 266, 268
   Sched 6 . . . . .264, 266, 267

Groundwater Regulations 1998 (SI 1998/2746) 154, 238, 245

Landfill (England and Wales) Regulations 2002
    (SI 2002/1559) 236–38
    reg 3 236
    reg 3(2) 238
    reg 5 236
    reg 6 236
    reg 7 236
    reg 9 237
    reg 16 236
    reg 17 236
    Sched 1 236
    Sched 4 237
Landfill Tax (Contaminated Land) Order 1996 (SI 1996/1529) 241
Landfill Tax (Qualifying Materials) Order 1996 (SI 1996/1528) 241
Landfill Tax (Amendment) Regulations 2003 (SI 2003/605) 242
Landfill Tax Regulations 1996 (SI 1996/1527) 17, 241
Landfill Tax (Site Restoration and Quarries) Order 1999
    (SI 1999/2075) 17

Merchant Shipping (Carriage of Cargoes)
    Regulations 1997 (SI 1997/19) 341
Merchant Shipping (Port Waste Reception Facilities)
    Regulations 1977 (SI 1977/3018) 180
Merchant Shipping (Prevention of Oil Pollution)
    (Amendment) Regulations 2000 (SI 2000/483) 179
Merchant Shipping (Prevention of Oil Pollution)
    Order 1983 (SI 1983/1106) 179
Merchant Shipping (Prevention of Oil Pollution)
    Regulations 1996 (SI 1996/2154) 179
Merchant Shipping (Reporting Requirements for Ships
    Carrying Dangerous or Polluting Goods)
    Regulations 1995 (SI 1995/2498) 179
Motor Fuel (Composition and Content)
    Regulations 1999 (SI 1999/3107) 343
Motor Vehicles (EC Type Approval)
    Regulations 1998 (SI 1998/2051) 403
Motor Vehicles (Type Approval) (Great Britain)
    Regulations 1984 (SI 1984/81) 403
Motor Vehicles (Type Approval) (Great Britain)
    Regulations 1994 (SI 1994/981) 403

National Ceilings Regulations 2002 (SI 2002/3118) 345
Nitrate Sensitive Areas (Designation) Order 1990
    (SI 1990/1013) 155
Nitrate Sensitive Areas Regulations 1994 (SI 1994/1729) 155
Noise Emission in the Environment by Equipment for Use
    Outdoors Regulations 2001 (SI 2001/1710) 407

Pollution Prevention and Control (England and Wales)
    Regulations 2000 (SI 2000/1973) 236, 291, 292, 295, 297, 302
      reg 2 292
      reg 2(1) 293
      reg 4 296
      reg 7 294
      reg 9 293
      reg 9(1) 292
      reg 10 294
      reg 10(3) 296
      reg 10(4) 304
      reg 11 296
      reg 11(2) 296
      reg 11(3) 296
      regs 12–14 297
      reg 12(10) 298
      reg 17 300
      regs 18, 19 298
      reg 21 ....299, 300
      regs 23–25 299
      reg 25 300
      reg 26 ....300, 302
      reg 27 301
      reg 28 ....300, 302
      reg 32 ....300, 301
      reg 32(4) 302
      reg 33 302
      reg 35 303
      Sched 1 293
      Sched 4 ....294, 298
      Sched 5 293
Private Water Supply Regulations 1991 (SI 1991/2790) 169
Producer Responsibility Obligations (Packaging Waste)
    Regulations 1997 (SI 1997/648) 240
      regs 3–11 240
Protection of Water Against Agricultural and Nitrate
    Pollution (England and Wales) Regulations 1996 (SI 1996/888) 156

Quarries Regulations 1999 (SI 1999/2024) 243

Registration of Carriers (Seizure of Vehicles)
    Regulations 1991 (SI 1991/1624)—
      reg 2 251
      reg 5 251
      reg 10 251
      Sched 1 251
Road Traffic (Vehicle Emissions) (Fixed Penalty)
    Regulations 1997 (SI 1997/3058) 344
      reg 61 344
      reg 98 344
Road Vehicles (Construction and Use) Regulations 1986 (SI 1986/1078) 343, 403
Rules of Procedure (Army) (Amendment No 2) Rules 1997 (SI 1997/18) 342
Rules of the Supreme Court—
    Ord 53, r 3(7) 65

Smoke Control Areas (Authorised Fuel)
  Regulations 1991 (SI 1991/1282) 341
Smoke Control Areas (Exempted Fireplaces)
  Order 1991 (SI 1991/2892) 341
Special Waste Regulations 1996 (SI 1996/972) 185, 199–202, 238, 253
  regs 1–17 230
  reg 2(1) 199, 200
  reg 2(2) 199
  reg 2(3) 200, 201
  reg 2(5) 200, 201
  reg 2(6) 200, 201
  reg 4 253
  regs 16, 17 230
  reg 18 ....230, 231
  reg 18(3) 231
  Sched 2 ....199, 200
Statutory Nuisance (Appeals) Regulations 1995
  (SI 1995/2644) 360, 391, 392
  reg 3 361
Surface Water (Abstraction for Drinking Water)
  (Classification) Regulations 1996 (SI 1996/3001) 135
Surface Water Classification Regulations 1989
  (SI 1989/1148) 135
Surface Water (Dangerous Substances) (Classification)
  Regulations 1989 (SI 1989/2286) 135
Surface Water (Dangerous Substances) (Classification)
  Regulations 1992 (SI 1992/337) 135
Surface Water (Dangerous Substances) (Classification)
  Regulations 1997 (SI 1997/2560) 135
Surface Water (Dangerous Substances) (Classification)
  Regulations 1998 (SI 1998/389) 135
Surface Waters (Fishlife) (Classification) (Amendment)
  Regulations 2003 (SI 2003/1053) 136
Surface Waters (Fishlife) (Classification)
  Regulations 1997 (SI 1997/1331) 135, 136
Surface Waters (River Ecosystem) (Classification)
  Regulations 1994 (SI 1994/1057) 135
Surface Waters (Shellfish) (Classification)
  Regulations 1997 (SI 1997/1332) 135

Trade Effluents (Prescribed Processes and Substances)
  (Amendment) Regulations 1992 (SI 1992/339) 165
Trade Effluents (Prescribed Processes and Substances)
  Regulations 1989 (SI 1989/1156) 165

Urban Waste Water Treatment (England and Wales)
  Regulations 1994 (SI 1994/2841) 245

Waste Incineration (England and Wales)
  Regulations 2002 (SI 2002/2980) 237, 239

Waste Management Licences (Consultation and
    Compensation) Regulations 1999 (SI 1999/481) 214
Waste Management Licensing (Amendment) (England)
    Regulations 2003 (SI 2003/595) 212
Waste Management Licensing (Amendment)
    Regulations 1995 (SI 1995/288) 219
Waste Management Licensing (Amendment) (Wales)
    Regulations 2003 (SI 2003/171) 212
Waste Management Licensing Regulations 1994
    (SI 1994/1056) 12, 185, 190–92, 206, 209, 210, 212,
                                            213, 219, 224, 227, 232, 245, 488
    reg 1(3) 192, 205
    reg 3 211
    reg 4 211
    reg 7(1)(b) 220
    reg 9 205
    reg 10 220
    regs 12, 14 213
    reg 15 ....175, 209, 245
    regs 16–18 207
    reg 16(1) 208
    reg 16(1)(a) 244
    reg 17 ....207, 208
    reg 17(4) 207
    reg 18 207
    reg 18(1) 207
    reg 20 ....247, 248
    reg 23 226
    reg 24(8) 192
    Sched 3 ....207, 208
    Sched 4 ....192, 196, 205, 232, 235
Water and Sewerage (Conservation and Recreation)
    (Code of Practice) Order 1989 (SI 1989/1152) 128
Water Protection Zone (River Dee Catchment)
    Designation Order 1999 (SI 1999/915) 154
Water Protection Zone (River Dee Catchment)
    (Procedural and Other Provisions)
    Regulations 1999 (SI 1999/916) 154
Water Resources (Licences) Regulations 1965
    (SI 1965/534) 167
Water Supply (Water Quality) (Amendment)
    Regulations 1989 (SI 1989/1383) 169
Water Supply (Water Quality) (Amendment)
    Regulations 1991 (SI 1991/1837) 169
Water Supply (Water Quality) Regulations 1989
    (SI 1989/1147) 7, 92, 168, 171
    reg 28 169
Water Supply (Water Quality) Regulations 2000 (SI 2000/3184) 169, 176

CHAPTER 1

ELEMENTS OF ENVIRONMENTAL LAW

1.1   INTRODUCTION

In this chapter, we introduce the reader to the legal framework which controls polluting emissions to the three environmental media (air, land and water) in England and Wales. The relevant national law is set in the context of European environmental and international environmental law. We examine the sources of environmental law, the relevant legal and policy principles, and the emergence of alternative methods (to the basic legal framework) to control polluting activities.

1.2   WHAT IS ENVIRONMENTAL LAW?

Before embarking on an explanation of the legal framework which regulates polluting emissions in England and Wales, we suggest that the reader spends a few minutes thinking about his or her answers to the following seven questions which are designed to provide the reader with a 'mindset' (orientation) which will help him or her grasp much of what follows:

(a) What is 'pollution' and what is the 'environment'?

(b) What is environmental law? (What does it comprise?)

(c) What is environmental law for? (What is its function or functions?)

(d) What are the main features of environmental law?

(e) Who uses environmental law and for what purpose(s)?

(f) What are the main driving forces behind the changes in and development of environmental law?

(g) Is the use of legal devices the only available means to control pollution?

1.3   ENVIRONMENTAL LAW: AN OVERVIEW

In this introductory chapter, we provide an outline of environmental law as it relates to the regulation of polluting activities in England and Wales (at the end of the chapter, we provide references to texts which address the law in Scotland and Northern Ireland). At 1.4.1, we consider some preliminary issues, especially the difficulties associated with the concepts of 'pollution' and 'environment', before moving on to discuss the components or elements of environmental law. At 1.4.2, we refer to the persons who frequently use environmental law and their respective objectives. At 1.4.3, we consider the primary functions of environmental law before referring to the forces which are driving its rapid development. At 1.5, we map out the structure of the public regulation of private polluting activities. By this we mean to refer to the regulation of the polluting activities of private legal persons, such as companies and individuals, by public regulatory bodies (such as the Environment Agency and the local authorities). At 1.6, we outline the use of environmental law by private persons to protect private interests, to prosecute and to oversee the fairness and legality of decisions made by public regulators. At 1.7, we summarise the sources of environmental law and at 1.8 the principles which guide its development. Finally, at 1.9, we refer to the emergence of new pollution control tools to supplement the basic command and control framework.

1.4   PRELIMINARY ISSUES

1.4.1 'Pollution' and the 'environment'

Most of us think of 'pollution' in terms of something which is contaminated, unclean, spoilt or irreparably damaged. For example, we may be outraged by the damage to our health caused by atmospheric pollution from a nearby factory, or we may be saddened that the pristine beauty of a local beach has been marred by an oil spill. Implicit in the term 'pollution' is the existence of some element of risk, threat, danger or hazard to ourselves, or some other object such as an important wildlife habitat, which is important to us. We place a high value on the maintenance of a healthy environment. 'Pollution' is therefore a relative term. The level of threat or damage to humans, or some part of the wider environment perceived as important to humans, must be significant enough to trigger a recognition that 'pollution' has occurred. However, what is perceived as pollution by one person (or group or society) may not be perceived as pollution by another. The assessment of what constitutes pollution, in any given set of circumstances, will therefore vary with the values and risk perception of the relevant individual, group or society.

1.4.1.1 Pollution

In environmental law, there is no single, accepted, definition of pollution; however, the Royal Commission on Environmental Pollution (RCEP) (*Pollution in Some British Estuaries and Coastal Waters*, Third Report, Cmnd 5054, 1972) has provided the following helpful definition:

> The introduction by man into the environment of substances or energy liable to cause hazards to human health, harm to living resources and ecological systems, damage to structure or amenity or interference with the legitimate uses of the environment.

Pollution is associated with risks to human health and property, plants, animals, habitats and ecological systems. Pollution is not restricted to the impact of chemical substances upon man or the environment, but may extend to the introduction of energy into the environment, such as the 'hot' cooling water discharged from a power station into a river, or electro-magnetic fields emitted by electrical apparatus, such as power lines.

In an environmental law context, chemical substances and/or energy may be introduced into the environment in any of the following ways:

(a) a legal person (for example, an individual or a company) discharges chemicals and/or energy into the environment in accordance with the conditions of a licence issued by a regulator;

(b) a legal person discharges chemicals and/or energy into the environment in breach of licence conditions;

(c) a legal person discharges chemicals and/or energy into the environment without the benefit of a licence issued by a regulator authorising the discharge.

In the first scenario, there is no pollution within the meaning of the relevant legislation under which the licence was issued. The licence holder will have a defence against regulatory criminal offences alleging pollution of the environment. In the second scenario, the licence holder has caused pollution to occur by exceeding the terms of its licence. A criminal offence has been committed: breach of licence conditions. Readers should note that it is not necessary for the prosecution to prove that environmental harm has occurred as a result of the breach of licence conditions. If the breach is minor, the regulator is likely to exercise its discretion not to prosecute. In the final scenario, whether pollution has occurred will generally depend upon the environmental impact of the substance and/or energy discharged and whether the process emitting the substance and/or energy requires a licence. If the discharge is small and does not result in significant environmental damage, pollution is unlikely to have occurred. However, whether such a discharge amounts to pollution may also depend upon the nature of the process emitting the substance and the identity of the substance itself. Some regulatory regimes (for example, Integrated Pollution Control (IPC)/Integrated Pollution Prevention and Control (IPPC)) insist that a licence is obtained prior to discharge of *any* substance from an IPC/IPPC regulated process. Discharges made without the benefit of a licence will automatically be unlawful. In contrast to IPC and IPPC licences, application for a water pollution discharge consent licence need only be made to the regulator if the substance and/or energy discharged into controlled waters is 'poisonous, noxious or polluting'.

In regard to licensed discharges, Keith Hawkins, in *Environment and Enforcement* (1984, Oxford: Clarendon), observed that: 'Pollution is an administrative creation.' This is a reference to the fact that, because the regulator controls the licensing process, especially the conditions attached to licences, it has the power to determine which discharges will, or will not, amount to pollution because they exceed licence conditions and are therefore unlawful.

1.4.1.2 Environment

In its most general sense, 'the environment' refers to our surroundings. It is often understood to include not only land, air and water, but also the built environment and the condition of the local neighbourhood. The environment can, for others, mean something more specific and refer to the conservation of natural habitats and ecology.

In an environmental law context, s 1(2) of the Environmental Protection Act (EPA) 1990 contains the following definition of the environment which provides a useful guide regarding the issues addressed in this text:

> The 'environment' consists of all, or any of the following media, namely, the air, water and land; and the medium of air includes the air within buildings and the air within other natural or man-made structures above or below ground.

1.4.2   What is environmental law, who is using it and for what purpose or purposes?

Environmental law is primarily a mix of primary legislation (Acts of Parliament), secondary legislation (regulations or statutory instruments), judicial decisions reported in law reports, common law principles, European Community (EC) legislation (mainly in the form of directives) which are transposed into national law (usually in the form of regulations), and international law (found in treaties, conventions and protocols).

The study of environmental law is not confined to a study of the law which is written down in legislation (so called 'black letter' law), but it is also concerned with how the law is used to achieve the objectives of the key environmental stakeholders: the regulators, the regulated (especially businesses), central government, local government, industry associations, pressure groups, local amenity societies and the public. The government and its agencies issue policy documents to public officials and the public, in the form of official guidance, in a never-ending stream of White Papers, Green Papers, consultation documents, guidance notes and circulars. Although this guidance is not law, it is nevertheless important because it guides how the regulators (such as the Environment Agency) will use the law to achieve the regulator's statutory objectives.

It may therefore be helpful to conceive of environmental law not as a collection of separate pieces of legislation and policy documents, but as a 'toolbox' containing a range of legal and policy instruments. Only those legal and policy tools which will achieve the objectives of the specific user will be applied to the problem in hand. Thus, a regulator will use the powers available to it, and which are built into the specific regulatory regime it administers, to enforce the compliance of regulated businesses with the relevant regulatory law. An individual who has sustained pollution damage to his or her property may resort to the common law, for example, using the tort of nuisance, to obtain compensation or other means of redress. An amenity group or society, such as Greenpeace or the Anglers Co-operative, may mount a private prosecution against a polluter in circumstances where a regulator has exercised its discretion not to prosecute. Alternatively, an amenity group, such as Friends of the Earth, may challenge by way of a judicial review application (and subject to 'standing' restrictions discussed in Chapter 12) a regulator's decision to grant a pollution licence to an applicant. In this way, an amenity society may seek to bring a regulator to account for an allegedly unlawful decision. Environmental law is therefore not a simple application of the contents of legislation to particular facts. To understand environmental law properly, we need to be aware of not only the contents of the relevant law and policy, but also how the law and policy will be applied by the regulator, the private litigator or the courts to resolve an environmental problem.

1.4.3   The function of environmental law

Much of environmental law concerns the *regulation* of polluting emissions discharged into the three environmental media – air, water and land. The primary function of environmental law is not to eliminate pollution, except in the case of a relatively few highly toxic pollutants, but to balance the polluting emissions generated by economic activity against the demands of society for a tolerably healthy environment. Polluting emissions must therefore be set, in most cases, by government (or its regulators) at levels which are acceptable to its two major stakeholders: regulated businesses and the public. This balancing task is performed on behalf of government by regulatory agencies such as the Environment Agency and the local authorities. Environmental law also has subsidiary preventive, remedial (clean-up) and compensatory functions.

1.4.4 What is driving the development of environmental law?

The early history of environmental law in England and Wales was characterised by a parochial focus on localised pollution problems. Reliance on the common law, especially the law of torts, to resolve individual disputes over pollution-related property damage was overtaken by the need for legislation to address the gross, and widespread, pollution problems caused by the Industrial Revolution. A series of legislative enactments followed, addressing specific problems: atmospheric pollution from the chemical industry, water pollution controls to prevent rivers becoming effluent channels and the regulation of statutory nuisances.

In the last three decades of the 20th century, the UK's membership of the European Union (EU), together with the recognition of global pollution problems, has marked a turning point in the pace of environmental legal change. Over 200 pieces of European legislation have been passed to date which relate in various ways to the environment. Recent developments in international environmental law, especially regarding 'sustainable development', have helped to influence EC pollution policy and the development of new controls which are then transposed into the legislative systems of the EU's Member States. In addition, the public is both better informed of and is more sensitive to environmental risks. As we have seen, especially in regard to the genetically modified crop protests, the public may be a powerful influence upon the regulation of environmental risks. The pattern of environmental pollution control, with its reliance on Command and Control regulatory regimes, has begun to change. The almost total reliance on the Command and Control regulatory model is giving way to a mixed approach to pollution control incorporating Command and Control and other tools such as eco-taxes, market mechanisms, environmental management systems and self-regulation.

1.5 THE PUBLIC REGULATION OF PRIVATE POLLUTION

Pollution regulation is primarily concerned with the *public regulation of private pollution*. In other words, the State is tasked with the job of setting limits on the polluting activities of private enterprise (companies, firms and individuals). The chief method employed by the State to regulate polluting emissions is the creation of a series of *Command and Control* regulatory frameworks. 'Command and Control pollution regulation' involves 'the "command" of the law and the legal authority of the State' (Hutter, B, *A Reader in Environmental Law*, 1999, Oxford: OUP). It is an approach to regulation which is characterised by several distinguishing features, which are summarised below.

1.5.1   Primary legislation

Command and Control regulatory regimes are dependent upon legislation. Parliament passes an Act of Parliament (also referred to as a statute, enactment or piece of legislation) which creates a broad framework for the control of various types of polluting activity. Implementation of an Act of Parliament is often phased in over an extended period of time and it is the Secretary of State who controls how quickly the individual sections of each statute come into force. Acts of Parliament are scrutinised by both Houses of Parliament prior to their becoming law. The public is not directly consulted in the drafting of new legislation.

1.5.2   Separate and integrated regulation of air, water and land pollution

Command and Control regulatory regimes are often environmentally media-specific responses to problems caused by polluting discharges. For example, the Water Resources Act (WRA) 1991 establishes a regulatory framework to control the discharge of polluting substances and energy into the aquatic environment only. In contrast, the IPC regime (see Pt I of the EPA 1990) regulates all discharges emitted from a limited number of highly polluting activities into *all three* environmental media.

1.5.3   The administrative and 'policing' functions of the regulator

Each Command and Control regime has its own regulatory agency which has the day-to-day responsibility for administering the relevant controls and policing compliance of regulated businesses with the law. Following the creation of the Environment Agency in 1996, the number of regulatory agencies in the UK was reduced (in consequence of the Environment Agency taking over the functions of the National Rivers Authority, the Waste Regulation Authorities and Her Majesty's Inspectorate of Pollution). The Environment Agency, the local authorities and the large, privatised, water and sewage services companies are the main regulatory agencies which we encounter in this textbook.

1.5.4   Licences authorising the discharge of polluting substances into the environment

Many Command and Control pollution statutes compel legal persons, especially businesses, who wish to discharge polluting substances into the environment to obtain a licence authorising such emissions. Pollution licences may be divided into two groups: licences which authorise the discharge of waste products into the environment (for example, a water pollution discharge consent licensing the discharge of wastes into the aquatic environment); and licences which authorise the operational activities of an applicant (for example, a waste management licence or an IPPC licence authorising both the relevant process and the emission of wastes generated by that process). Licences may also be categorised according to whether they are 'anticipatory' (for example, the grant of a planning permission permitting the construction of a waste incinerator) or 'operational' (for example, a waste management licence regulating the day-to-day operational activities of the waste incinerator once it is constructed).

1.5.5 Notice-based and other Command and Control regulatory regimes

Not all Command and Control regulatory regimes require prior licence-based authorisation of polluting activity. Legislation may, as in the case of statutory nuisance, noise and contaminated land controls, impose a dual duty on the regulator to identify pollution problems in its area and ensure the rectification of the pollution problems so identified. After a statutory nuisance, noise or contaminated land problem has been identified, the regulator serves the person responsible for the problem with a notice specifying the necessary remedial works. In the case of air pollution control under the Clean Air Act 1993, where regulatory control is neither licence-based nor notice-based, the 1993 Act lays down strict limits on smoke (and similar) emissions. If these limits are breached, the local authority may prosecute.

1.5.6 Licence conditions

In the water, waste and IPC/IPPC control regimes, each licence issued by the regulator is subject to detailed conditions which apply at the level of the individual polluting plant. The regulator has a wide discretion as to the conditions which it can include in each licence in order to achieve the objectives of the particular Command and Control regime. In addition, the regulator has the power to vary licence conditions. This power ensures that pollution control keeps pace with developments in technology and any new EC or international obligations.

1.5.7 Licence conditions and environmental standards

Licence conditions are set by reference to standards. An increasing number of standards emanate from the EC in the form of directives which are then transposed into national legislation (as regulations). Standards may be set by reference to specific 'objects' which require protection from the adverse impacts of pollution. These object-based or target-based standards are designed to maintain the quality of the three environmental media (air, water and land) upon which the relevant objects (humans, animals, birds, fish, plants, habitats or ecosystems) depend for a tolerably healthy existence. The standards set limits for the presence of various chemical substances in the relevant environmental media – air, water or soil (for example, the Air Quality (England) Regulations 2000, the Bathing Waters Regulations 1991 and the Water Supply (Water Quality) Regulations 1989, as amended). The required environmental quality to sustain life is taken into account when the regulator sets the conditions of individual pollution licences. Alternatively, and more commonly, standards are set by reference to the activity which is responsible for generating pollution. These activity or 'source'-based standards can either be in the form of emission standards (limits on specific chemical substances discharged, via pipe or chimney, from an industrial process) or product standards (for example, the installation of catalytic converters in all new vehicles or the requirement that vehicle engines be able to run on lead free petrol), or process standards (for example, the use of a particular pollution abatement technology in a manufacturing process, or simply specifying the height of a plant chimney discharging pollutants into the atmosphere).

1.5.8   Command and Control regulatory systems are underpinned by criminal law offences

In the case of the licence-based regulatory regimes, failure to apply for a licence, or failure to abide by the terms of a licence once granted, will result in breach of the criminal laws contained in the legislation establishing the regulatory regime. In the case of non-licence-based Command and Control regimes, failure to comply with the relevant remedial notice, or the exceeding of emission limits specified in the legislation, constitutes a criminal law offence. The regulator has a wide discretion as to the enforcement action it may take in these circumstances to bring the polluter back into compliance with the law. The regulator is not obliged to prosecute each and every breach of the law which comes to its attention. In fact, prosecution is the exception rather than the rule.

1.5.9   Licences and legal compliance

Compliance with the terms of a licence entitles the licence holder to discharge substances and energy into the environment in compliance with the law and without fear of prosecution. Possession of and compliance with a licence provides the holder with a defence to any criminal charge relating to the emissions authorised by the licence.

1.5.10 Discretion

Regulatory agencies, such as the Environment Agency, local authorities and the water service companies, are given a wide discretion with regard to how they ensure compliance with the law. For example, a regulator may choose whether or not to prosecute an offending person (usually a business) in order to bring that person's activities back into compliance with the law. Alternatively, a regulator may use its administrative powers (for example, an enforcement notice) to secure the compliance of a regulated business with the terms of its licence, without recourse to mounting a criminal prosecution.

1.5.11 The regulator's powers of investigation

Regulatory agencies are given wide powers to enable them to fulfil their functions. These powers are detailed in the relevant Command and Control framework or other legislation. In particular, the regulator has the following investigatory powers: entry onto premises, examination, investigation, inspection, measurement, testing, recording, photography, removal of items and/or evidence, sampling, installation and operation of monitoring equipment.

1.5.12 Administrative powers

Regulatory agencies are given a range of administrative powers to enable them to fulfil their statutory obligations. These powers are especially important in ensuring that licence holders continue to comply with the terms of their licences. To secure compliance with environmental law, the regulator relies heavily upon the use of a wide range of notices including: Enforcement Notice (EN); Variation Notice (VN); Suspension Notice (SN); Revocation Notice (RN); Works Notice (WN); and Prohibition Notice (PN).

1.5.13 Definition of key legislative terms

The primary legislation establishing the relevant Command and Control regulatory framework uses wide flexible terms, for example, 'pollution' in the WRA 1991 and 'contamination' in the Environment Act (EA) 1995. The definitions of these terms are subsequently interpreted by the regulator, via guidance notes, and by the courts in litigation.

1.5.14 Secondary legislation

Secondary legislation (in the form of regulations and statutory instruments) supplements primary legislation by providing the more detailed and technical content of the relevant regulatory regime. Regulations are generally prepared by the Secretary of State under the authority delegated to him by Parliament. There is little parliamentary scrutiny of the content of secondary legislation as the regulation is merely placed before Parliament for a limited period. The public may comment upon secondary legislation proposals where these are issued as consultation papers by the government. Secondary legislation is frequently used to provide greater detail with regard to the general definitions contained in primary legislation and to provide data on the regulatory standards which are crucial to the setting of individual licences. European environmental legislation is invariably transposed into national law via secondary legislation.

1.5.15 Official guidance

A large volume of policy, in the form of official guidance notes, is issued by government departments and regulatory agencies for the guidance of public decision making bodies. This is used to fill out the details of each pollution regulatory regime. This guidance does not have legal force, in the way in which primary and secondary legislation does, but is important in guiding regulatory decision making. For example, guidance notes set out the procedures concerning applications for licences (discharge consents and operating licences) and appeals against refusals to grant licences. Guidance issued by the Environment Agency details its enforcement and prosecution policy.

1.5.16 Judicial review

A regulator's use of discretion, for example, with regard to the decision to set licence conditions for an industrial plant, or with regard to a decision not to prosecute a polluter, is subject to the supervisory jurisdiction of the courts. The courts, upon a judicial review action by an 'aggrieved person', may strike down a decision arrived at in breach of established procedure, but the court cannot substitute its own decision for that of the regulator. The courts therefore have a 'supervisory' jurisdiction over the decision making activities of the regulators. Judicial review is used by persons with 'standing' (a sufficient interest in the decision challenged) to ensure the accountability of regulators for their decisions. The courts scrutinise decisions for errors in procedure or unreasonableness. Thus, the regulatory agency is responsible for arriving at a decision on the merits of the case taking care to observe the correct procedure.

1.5.17 Appeals

Command and Control regulation is characterised by the right of regulated persons (businesses) to appeal against a wide range of regulatory decisions, such as the refusal to grant a licence, the conditions attached to a licence, the service of an Abatement Notice and the service of an Enforcement Notice.

1.5.18 Public registers

Publicly accessible registers of information are a further facet of Command and Control regulation. Registers contain information on the operation of the relevant licensing regime including: applications for licences, the identity of licence holders, relevant licence conditions, notices served on licence holders, sampling, details of any notices applied for or served in regard to variation, revocation, enforcement, works, etc, appeals, convictions and directions given by the Secretary of State.

1.5.19 Continuous control

Command and Control regulation is the primary tool used by the government to regulate environmental pollution. It provides regulators, in the case of licence-based regimes, with a coherent set of continuous controls which are capable of being tailored to the circumstances of each licence holder. The site licence is the main vehicle through which the government attempts to deliver its environmental policy targets.

1.5.20 The main Command and Control regimes

The main pollution Command and Control statutes are: the EPA 1990 (Pt I of which contains the IPC regime, Pt II waste management and Pt III statutory nuisance), the WRA 1991 (water pollution controls), the Water Industry Acts of 1991 and 1999 (the regulation of discharges to sewers), the Pollution Prevention and Control Act (PPCA) 1999 (containing the IPPC regime which is set to replace IPC by 2007), the EA 1995 (introducing the contaminated land regime which forms Pt IIA of the EPA

1990), and the Control of Pollution Act 1974 (noise). These Command and Control regimes are discussed in detail in Chapters 4–10.

1.5.21 Pollution control, planning control, nature conservation the historic built environment and contaminated land

The licence-based or 'permitting' approach to regulation, evident in water pollution, waste management and IPC/IPPC regulation, is similar in structure to the control of building development, the central feature of which is the issue of a planning permission. In contrast, the protection of animal species, habitat (for example, Sites of Special Scientific Interest), landscape (for example, Areas of Outstanding Natural Beauty) and the historic built environment (Listed Buildings, Conservation Areas and Ancient Monuments) are achieved through a 'listing' process. This form of regulation (listing the 'objects' of the legislation and requiring specific permission for works which may affect or damage their intrinsic importance) has some similarity to contaminated land control. Once the regulator has identified contaminated land, the details of the contaminated site are placed on a public register. In this way contaminated land is, in effect, 'listed'.

1.6   PRIVATE LAW: THE ROLE OF THE INDIVIDUAL, COMPANIES AND NON-GOVERNMENTAL ORGANISATIONS IN THE REGULATION OF POLLUTION

In contrast to Command and Control regulatory regimes (such as the PPCA 1999, which create bureaucracies to regulate whole industries in the public interest), legal persons, especially individuals and companies, also have a role to play in the regulation of pollution. Any person may find it necessary to utilise environmental law in any of the following ways:

(a) to protect property and property-related interests from the threat of environmental damage;

(b) to protect humans from the threat of environmental injury;

(c) to obtain compensation for damage to property and property-related interests;

(d) to obtain compensation for personal injury caused by pollution;

(e) to challenge the decision of a regulator via a judicial review action;

(f) to mount a private prosecution against a polluter.

The reference to 'private law' is intended to convey to the reader the distinction between the role of private persons and the role of 'public' regulators. In the main, private persons are only concerned to advance their own private interests. They do not generally engage in environmental litigation for the greater good of society. Thus, we note that private persons resort to the common law in order to resolve 'one on one' disputes concerning damage to person or property caused by the polluting activities of a neighbouring property owner. The law therefore attempts to balance the competing interests of individual persons. In contrast, Command and Control regulation focuses upon 'the bigger picture'. The polluting emissions of entire industries are regulated in order to safeguard public health and the wider environment. Regulatory law therefore attempts to achieve a balance between the needs of industry to be competitive (and not over-regulated) and the need of society for a tolerably clean environment.

Private persons seeking redress, often in the form of financial compensation, for damage caused to property or person (personal injury) will often resort to civil litigation to achieve their objectives. Such actions will often be based upon common law principles, especially those contained in the law of torts. The outcome of an individual common law action, whilst resolving the dispute between the parties to the litigation, may also set important legal precedents which have widespread application. One such example is the case of *Cambridge Water Co Ltd v Eastern Counties Leather plc* (1994) which drew widespread industry attention to the increased risk of civil liability for damage caused by the escape of polluting substances from land and business premises.

Private persons who wish to challenge the lawfulness of regulatory decisions, such as a decision to issue a licence to an applicant or a decision not to prosecute a polluter, may mount a judicial review challenge in the High Court. The objective of such proceedings is to persuade the court to strike down an unlawful decision which has been arrived at in breach of established procedure or is otherwise unreasonable. The judicial review process is only open to applicants with a sufficient interest ('standing') in the decision which is the subject of the complaint. Private persons may also mount a private prosecution against a polluter, provided the legislation specifying the relevant offence does not exclude the right to launch such a private prosecution.

1.7   THE SOURCES OF ENVIRONMENTAL LAW

1.7.1   The evolution of environmental legislation

Early pollution control legislation in the UK was characterised by: (a) a narrow UK focus; (b) an environmental media focus (air, water and land); (c) reactive creation (especially following industrialisation); and (d) limited scientific input. In the late 20th and early 21st centuries, the identification of inter-State (transboundary) and global pollution problems (climate change, sea level rise, rapid consumption of resources and ozone depletion in the upper atmosphere) has forced all States to adopt a wider focus in their use of environmental law to address the adverse impacts of a rapidly rising population, the consequential pressure on global resources and the resultant pollution problems which occur at national, EC (regional) and global levels.

1.7.2   National sources of UK environmental law

The principle sources of pollution control law in the UK are domestic legislation, EC directives (which are transposed into UK law), the common law and international agreements. Domestic legislation comprises primary legislation (for example, the EPA 1990) and secondary legislation (for example, the Waste Management Licensing Regulations 1994) which establish the pollution control regimes considered in Chapters 4–10 of this text. The common law provides the principles which enable pollution victims to obtain redress (compensation) from the polluters and the means to challenge, via judicial review, the actions and decisions of government and its agencies (for example, the Environment Agency).

1.7.3   EC sources of UK environmental law

Much environmental legislation in the UK (as much as 80% – RCEP Report No 21) arises out of the transposition (conversion) of EC legislation (directives) into UK law. As a Member State of the EU, the UK is bound (see 3.11 regarding the supremacy of EC law) to implement in national law the content of EC directives. EC environmental law comprises the treaties which establish the EC's remit, the legislation passed by the EC institutions, the judgments and principles of the European Court of Justice (ECJ) and the international treaties and agreements to which the EC is a party and which are binding on Member States.

1.7.4   International sources of UK environmental law

International environmental law comprises the body of rules derived both from international agreements and customary international law to which sovereign States have expressly or impliedly (via State practice) consented. Other sources of international environmental law are general legal principles, international case law, and the written analysis and comments of eminent academics and judges.

The principal source of UK environmental law derived from international law is the treaties or other agreements entered into by States on a bilateral or multi-lateral basis. States only incur obligations under international environmental law when they have consented (signing and ratifying treaties and conventions) to them. All States that are recognised under international law are sovereign and equal in their relations with one another. States are, however, not the only participants in the development and use of international law. International organisations, inter-governmental organisations, non-governmental organisations (NGOs), multi-national companies and individuals may also be the subjects of international law. Increasingly, international agreements are characterised by the following features: they are problem-specific; their provisions are detailed and require the taking of adequate enforcement action; the content of the agreements may be amended in the light of new (scientific) information; and there are State requirements regarding identification/delimitation of the relevant problem or issue, monitoring, preventive action and compliance measures.

1.8   LEGAL AND POLICY PRINCIPLES

1.8.1   Principles of environmental law

A number of influential legal and policy principles have emerged from international environmental law and EC environmental law which have important roles to play in guiding the future development of environmental law. These principles relate to both the maintenance of an appropriate balance between development/production on the one hand and conservation of a healthy environment/resources on the other, as well as the allocation of liability for environmental damage.

1.8.2 Sustainable development

International environmental law is important in the following respects:

(a) it focuses attention on the existence of global problems and the need for international solutions to those problems; and

(b) it has pioneered and developed important legal and policy principles (for example, sustainable development) which is so influential that it has been incorporated into the national environmental law and policy of individual nation States and regional communities of States, such as the EC. The UK's participation in the 1992 Rio 'Earth Summit' (the UN Conference on Environment and Development) and the conclusion of 'Agenda 21' led to the emergence of 'sustainable development' as a key component of UK national environmental policy. Several important policy documents were subsequently prepared including: the 1990 White Paper, *This Common Inheritance* (Cm 1200); *Sustainable Development: The UK Strategy* (Cm 2426) in 1994; and *A Better Quality of Life: A Strategy for Sustainable Development for the United Kingdom* (Cm 4345) in 1999. In turn, national policy has led to the incorporation of sustainable development policies at the local level, for example, the appearance of sustainable development policies in local authority town and country planning development plans and in waste management planning.

The most commonly cited expression of the Sustainable Development Principle is to be found in a 1987 United Nations conference on 'Our Common Future' (The Bruntland Report): 'Development that meets the needs of the present without compromising the ability of future generations to meet their own needs.' The principle is clearly anthropocentric – viewing the environment from a human centred, human needs perspective. It also exhibits elements of equality and fairness in its concern for the rights of present day societies, both rich and poor, and for the right of future generations to be able to develop the earth's available resources. The principle has, to a certain extent, moved beyond the status of a pure policy tool and has become incorporated into a number of documents as a legal principle. It forms part of the Signatory States' 'Agenda 21' Earth Summit requirements and, more importantly, is incorporated into Art 2 of the EC Treaty (by the 1997 Treaty of Amsterdam) as a fundamental principle. Thus, the EC now has the task 'to promote throughout the Community harmonious, balanced and sustainable development of economic activities'. The principle has also made an appearance in a UK context, for example, in s 1 of the Natural Heritage (Scotland) Act 1991 and s 4 of the Environment Act 1995 (applying to the Environment Agency). References to sustainable development in UK legislation generally require regard to be had to the principle but do not go so far as to impose any legal obligation to ensure that sustainable development is achieved. The Environment Agency's statutory duties are worded in such a way that the principle is merely a guide to the way in which the Agency should exercise its functions. The importance of sustainable development concerns its impact upon government and regulatory policy by providing targets and tools to monitor progress. These developments in turn affect the Command and Control regulatory regimes discussed in Chapters 4–10. Pollution licence conditions may be tightened to give effect to international agreements.

The concept of 'sustainable development' comprises four subsidiary principles:
(a) inter-generational equity (conservation of natural resources for the use of future

generations); (b) sustainable use (prudent use of natural resources); (c) intra-generational equity (use of resources by one State taking into account the needs of other States); and (d) integration (integration of environmental considerations into development projects, plans and programmes).

The principle is important in that it displays an ethical dimension to the future development of environmental law. What is the value of natural resources from a human centred (anthropocentric) perspective? Should we, in our economic/development-related decisions, value and preserve nature only if it has some utility, especially economic, relevant to humans? What weight should be given to these resources in development-related decisions? What weight does the law require us to give to important natural habitats (Sites of Specific Scientific Interest – see DEFRA Planning Policy PPG 9)? There is a wide spectrum of human perspectives on these issues ranging from the extreme preservationist stance of the 'deep greens' and becoming progressively more pro-development orientated as we encounter the proponents of land ethics, eco-centrism, bio-centrism, animal welfare, non-anthropocentric individualism, extended anthropocentrism, enlightened anthropocentrism and ultimately anthropocentric utilitarianism. These alternative ethical perspectives on the intrinsic value of flora and fauna are discussed in Alder and Wilkinson, 1999 (see the further reading section at the end of the chapter). Perhaps to a large extent our own ethical perspectives reflect our 'hierarchy of needs' (Maslow) so that a father of a hungry family in Africa will have few, if any, qualms about killing apes for food, whereas a well fed citizen in the developed world has less pressing needs and more time to consider the ethical dimension of the plight of the apes (see *Sustainable Development: The UK Strategy*, Cm 2426, 1994).

The Department for Environment, Food and Rural Affairs (DEFRA) has published its 2002 annual report, *Achieving a Better Quality of Life*, on sustainable development (www.sustainable-development.gov.uk/ar2002/index.htm).

1.8.3 The preventive principle

This principle advocates the taking of timely action to eliminate or minimise environmental damage. The principle may be used to prohibit damaging activities, for example, Art 194 of the UN Convention on the Law of the Sea (UNCLOS) of 1984 obliges States to prevent, reduce or control pollution of the marine environment whether within or outside their national waters.

1.8.4 The precautionary principle

This principle enables or requires States to take action where a risk to human health or the environment exists (see the Environmental Impact Assessment Directive and restrictions on hazardous waste transport), but there is evidential uncertainty as to the existence or extent (magnitude) of the risk. A number of versions of the principle include a cost/benefit test (Principle 15 of the Rio Declaration of 1992) designed to limit the potentially far-reaching consequences of a strict application of the principle (for example, a prohibition on an activity until such time as the persons engaging in the activity can prove that it poses no threat to man or the environment).

Principle 15 of the Rio Declaration provides that:

... where there are threats of serious or irreversible damage lack of full scientific certainty shall not be used as a reason for postponing cost effective measures to prevent environmental degradation.

This definition may be compared with those in Art 2(2)(a) of the Paris Convention and Art 3(3) of the Climate Change Convention of 1992 (see pp 49–52 of Sunkin, Ong and Wight: see the further reading section at the end of the chapter).

From a UK perspective, it is important to note that EC environmental policy and ultimately EC law incorporates the precautionary principle (Art 174(2) of the EC Treaty (as amended)). The principle has been applied in both EC and UK contexts. In *UK v Commission* (Case C-157/96 and Case C-180/99), the ECJ upheld the Commission's decision to impose an export ban on UK beef in order to reduce the risk of transmitting BSE to cattle in other countries.

The UK case of *R v Secretary of State for Trade and Industry ex p Duddridge and Others* (1995) concerned the possible link between the exposure of children to EMF radiation, via high voltage electricity power cables, and the development of leukaemia. The applicants unsuccessfully argued that the Secretary of State should take precautionary action (lowering the voltage) to prevent the risk arising. It seems that the mere possibility of serious harm occurring is not sufficient to justify the government taking precautionary action.

It is clear that the UK government will be minded to take precautionary action only if: (a) the risk is serious; (b) there is good reason to believe that prompt action at comparatively low cost will avoid the greater expense of remedying the damage at a later stage; and (c) irreversible damage is likely if timely action is not taken (see paras 1.17 and 1.18 of *This Common Inheritance*, 1990).

1.8.5   The polluter pays principle

This principle envisages that polluters (for example, the manufacturing and service sectors) should internalise the costs of the pollution which they generate so that the cost of their goods and services reflect the true costs of the measures which primarily the State adopts to eliminate, reduce and treat the polluters' emissions. An alternative, and more limited, version of the principle is that it enables the State to charge the cost of rectifying environmental damage to the relevant polluter, provided the polluter can be identified (see ss 85 and 161 of the WRA 1991 and ss 33, 59 and 73(6) of the EPA 1990). The UK policy-based interpretation of the principle contained in *This Common Inheritance*, 1990, para 1.25 refers to the government's aim to make those responsible for causing environmental damage responsible for 'the costs of control in full without subsidy'. Are these costs limited to the regulator's costs in monitoring compliance with licence conditions and undertaking the occasional prosecution?

1.9   ALTERNATIVES TO THE COMMAND AND CONTROL APPROACH TO POLLUTION REGULATION

1.9.1   Emerging regulatory mechanisms

Recognition of the fact that Command and Control licence-based pollution controls are never going to be the complete answer to environmental pollution regulation has led to greater interest in using the market to provide incentive-based pollution controls. Market mechanisms (otherwise referred to as economic instruments) are not generally as expensive to set up and run as a standard Command and Control regulatory regime. A 'market mechanism' is any tool which uses fiscal incentives or deterrents in order to achieve environmental objectives. These mechanisms do not involve the use of the law to compel companies or individuals to act in a particular way. They are persuasive rather than coercive.

The government, in resorting to market mechanisms, aims to send a 'signal' to consumers and manufacturers encouraging them to behave in ways which will reduce the environmental damage they cause. Thus, a motorist may be faced with progressive rises in petrol prices designed to encourage him or her to use public transport. Similarly, a manufacturing company may be faced with increased waste disposal costs, due to the landfill tax, designed to encourage waste minimisation through recycling. Annex A to the 1990 White Paper, *This Common Inheritance* lists the government's preferred pollution control tools: charging schemes, subsidies, deposit/refund schemes, enforcement incentives and markets in pollution credits.

1.9.2 Eco-taxes

The objective of eco-taxes is to persuade businesses to reduce the environmental impact of their activities via the use of financial incentives. Such 'economic instruments' not only save businesses money but they are also attractive to the government because they are perceived as a more economically efficient and cheaper tool than the creation of Command and Control pollution control regimes.

Currently, the best example in the UK of an eco-tax is the landfill tax. The Finance Act 1996, supplemented by the Landfill Tax Regulations 1996, created this eco-tax regime under the control of HM Customs and Excise with effect from October 1996. The tax is paid by operators of landfill sites on the waste deposited in the relevant landfills. The tax paid by the landfill site operators is recovered from waste depositors via 'gate' fees (at the entrance to the landfill). There is a differential rate of tax payable: £2 per tonne for inert wastes (for example, construction waste) and a higher figure for active waste (for example, waste which produces methane). Active waste currently costs £14 per tonne to tip in a landfill. The price of disposal has risen at the rate of £1 per annum, but will reach the maximum taxable cost of £15 per tonne in 2004.

The substances which qualify as waste, and are therefore subject to the tax, are not subject to quite the same degree of problems as the legal definition of waste. The tax applies to materials in transport to the landfill as well as when it is actually tipped (finally disposed of) at the landfill site (see *Customs and Excise Commissioners v Darfish Ltd* (2001) and *Customs and Excise Commissioners v Parkwood Landfill Ltd* (2002)).

The tax is subject to exemptions (see ss 43–46 of the Finance Act 1996), including dredged materials, mining and quarry wastes and reclaimed material from contaminated land sites. In regard to the contaminated land exemption, the power in s 46 of the 1996 Act was used by the Treasury to amend the original scheme to provide exemption for reclaimed deposits from contaminated sites (see ss 43A and 43B). In addition, the Landfill Tax (Site Restoration and Quarries) Order 1999 (SI 1999/2075) exempts inert wastes used to infill a quarry or restore a landfill (see ss 43A and 43C).

In the late 1990s, the House of Commons Environment Select Committee undertook an investigation into the operation of the landfill tax (*The Operation of the Landfill Tax*, HC 150 (1998–99)). Overall, the Report was favourable, although the Committee noted an increase in fly-tipping since the introduction of the tax.

Other forms of tax-related economic instrument include the aggregate levy, the tax/price differentials between unleaded and more polluting fuels, and the reduced level of Vehicle Excise Duty (the road fund licence fee) on vehicles of up to 1400cc engine capacity.

The Aggregates Levy has been set up by virtue of the Aggregates Levy (Registration and Miscellaneous Provisions) Regulations 2001 (SI 2001/4027) and the Aggregates Levy (General) Regulations 2002 (SI 2002/761). The levy aims to address, via an eco-tax, the environmental costs of quarrying (noise, dust, visual intrusion, loss of amenity and damage to biodiversity).

DEFRA has published the 1st annual review of the UK Emissions Trading Scheme launched in April 2002 (www.defra.gov.uk/environment/climatechange/trading).

1.9.3   Tradeable pollution permits (emissions trading)

This regulatory mechanism is designed to create a market in pollution credits. Such schemes are operational mainly in the USA, Canada and in some European States. Currently, emissions trading is focused on creating markets in 'greenhouse' gas emissions from power-generating plants burning fossil fuels. Such schemes fix an upper ceiling for emissions of specified chemical substances (for example, carbon dioxide) and firms operating in the industries emitting these substances bid for pollution credits. Over time, the regulator reduces the number of credits in circulation and this results in an increase in the price of the credits. This provides a financial incentive for participating firms to reduce their need for credits by developing less polluting methods of production.

Section 3(5) of the EPA 1990 enables the Secretary of State for the Environment to establish tradeable pollution permit schemes in the UK. The concept could be applied to water pollution discharges to controlled waters from point sources, such as discharge pipes. It is difficult to see how the concept could apply to power generation in the UK where there are very few generators and therefore no opportunity to create a viable market. One of the key texts in this area is Pearce and Barbier, *Blueprint for a Sustainable Economy*, 2000, Earthscan.

Just as this book was going to press, the government was finalising the details of an emissions trading scheme. The voluntary scheme forms part of the government's strategy (*Climate Change: the UK Programme*, November 2000) to meet its Kyoto Protocol target of a 12.5% reduction on 1990 emission levels of the six main greenhouse gases (see p 347 below regarding the Kyoto Protocol) by 2010. It is estimated that the emissions trading scheme will deliver an annual reduction of two million tonnes of carbon by 2010.

The scheme is open to virtually all private and public sector organisations whose activities result in the emission of the six greenhouse gases either directly into the environment or indirectly (via the use of electricity). There are two main participants in the scheme: (a) Agreement Participants. These are organisations covered by a climate change levy agreement negotiated between the government and the relevant industry; and (b) Direct Entry Participants. These organisations are not covered by a climate change levy agreement and must meet reduction targets set as a condition of entry into the trading scheme.

Details of the proposed emissions trading scheme are to be found on the DEFRA website.

The Environment Agency published in 2002 a discussion paper regarding the establishment of NO_x and SO_2 emission trading schemes (www.environment-agency.gov.uk/commondata/105385/schemes.pdf).

1.9.4 Charging schemes

This approach to pollution regulation involves the recovery of the costs of operating a Command and Control regulatory regime. Licence fees charged by the regulator may be designed to recover all or part of the regulator's operational costs, such as the administrative costs involved in processing licence applications, pollution monitoring and enforcement action. Higher fees may be charged to polluters whose emissions cost more to process, treat and monitor. The fees currently charged for waste, water and IPC/IPPC licences are examples of this approach. The Environment Agency is currently testing an 'enforced self-regulation' scheme in the waste management industry called 'OPRA' (operator pollution risk appraisal). Licence holders who score consistently well in Environment Agency risk assessment visits will be visited less frequently and the savings in monitoring costs made by the Environment Agency will be reflected in reduced annual licence fees. Licence holders who have an accredited environmental management scheme in place, such as ISO 14001, will find that their environmental risk 'score' is reduced. The lower the score, the less often the Environment Agency will visit the licence holder's premises.

1.9.5 Enforcement incentives

Regulators, such as the Environment Agency, may use their enforcement powers in ways that encourage licence holders to comply with the terms of their licences. The threat of prosecution offers a dual incentive: not only the financial penalties and legal costs which a court may impose upon conviction of an environmental offence, but also the damage to a licence holder's reputation as an environmentally responsible business as the progress of a court case is reported in the media. Large companies are more likely to comply with the law, not in consequence of the financial impact of a fine, but as a result of the damage which adverse media coverage may have on sales and company image. The Environment Agency publishes details of companies it wishes to 'name and shame' on its website. The regulator may also use its powers of remediation, for example, s 161 of the WRA 1991 and s 59 of the EPA 1990, to recover the cost of clean-up from the polluter. The use of these powers is not dependent upon a linked criminal prosecution and the costs of remediation may far exceed any fine imposed by a court for breach of environmental law. In addition, the regulator has administrative powers, for example, Anti-Pollution Works Notices, to compel licence holders to install costly water pollution prevention devices.

Polluters must also have regard to the risk of civil actions commenced by individuals whose property or health has been damaged by the polluters' activities. Victims of pollution incidents may use the torts of negligence, nuisance, trespass and the rule in *Rylands v Fletcher* to recover compensation for their losses. For example, the *Cambridge Water Co* case involved a claim of £1 million.

1.9.6   Subsidies and grants

Grants may be made available by government departments as an incentive towards the cost of installation of pollution prevention devices. For example, grants are available for the construction of plant to treat silage effluent and management agreements provide for payments to farmers who agree, by contract, to certain restrictions on their farming methods in environmentally sensitive areas such as Sites of Special Scientific Interest and nitrate sensitive areas.

1.9.7   Deposit and refund schemes

Perhaps the most famous of these schemes was established by a Danish law (the full details of which are examined in Case 302/86, *Commission v Denmark* (1988)) requiring beer and soft drinks containers to be returnable (see p 101 below). The ECJ upheld the relevant law, even though it interfered with the operation of the common market, because the scheme was justifiable on environmental protection grounds.

1.9.8   Environmental contracts (environmental covenants)

Governments, whether national, regional or local, and industry associations may enter into contracts with one another to regulate pollution. Several countries, but not as yet the UK, have made use of this tool. For example, the Rotterdam municipality (local authority) in the Netherlands has concluded an environmental contract with the German chemical industry relating to the pollution of the mouth of the River Rhine. The mouth of the Rhine has been contaminated with heavy metals. These contaminants form part of the silt lying on the river bed of the estuary. When the Rotterdam municipality dredges the navigation channels in the river, the silt it collects is too contaminated to dump at sea. A special containment facility (the *schlufter*) has therefore been built to store the contaminated silt. The environmental contract provides that the German chemical industry will reduce heavy metal discharges to agreed limits by 2005. If the terms of the agreement are breached, the Rotterdam municipality will sue the German chemical industry for the costs involved in constructing the *schlufter* and any future extension of that facility (see ENDS 1992 (205 and 211) and 1993 (224)).

1.10   FURTHER INFORMATION

Further reading

Environmental encyclopaedias

Encyclopaedia of Environmental Health Law, Sweet & Maxwell.

Encyclopaedia of International Environmental Law, Kluwer.

Garner's Environmental Law, Butterworths.

Payne, S (ed), *Commercial Environmental Law and Liability*, Longman.

Slater, J (ed), *EC Environmental Law*, Sweet & Maxwell.

Tromans, S (ed), *Encyclopaedia of Environmental Law*, Sweet & Maxwell.

Casebooks

Elworthy, S and Holder, J, *Environmental Protection: Text and Materials*, 1997, Butterworths.

Sunkin, M, Ong, D and Wight, R, *Sourcebook on Environmental Law*, 2nd edn, 2001, Cavendish Publishing.

Textbooks

Bell, S and McGillivray, D, *Environmental Law*, 5th edn, 2000, OUP.

Franklin, D, Hawke, N and Lowe, M, *Pollution in the UK*, 1995, Sweet & Maxwell.

Hughes, D, Jewell, T, Lowther, J, Parpworth, N and de Prez, P, *Environmental Law*, 4th edn, 2002, Butterworths.

Thornton, J and Beckwith, S, *Environmental Law*, 1997, Sweet & Maxwell.

Woolley, J *et al* (eds), *Environmental Law*, 2000, OUP.

Other books

Alder, J and Wilkinson, D, *Environmental Law and Ethics*, 1999, Macmillan.

Dobson, A, *Fairness and Futurity: Essays on Environmental Sustainability and Social Justice*, 2000, OUP.

Dobson, A, *Green Political Thought*, 3rd edn, 2000, Routledge.

Dobson, A, *Justice and the Environment: Conceptions of Environmental Sustainability and Theories of Distributive Justice*, 1998, OUP.

Markham, A, *A Brief History of Pollution*, 1994, Earthscan.

Maslow, AH, *Motivation and Personality*, 1954, Harper Row.

O'Riordan, T, *Environmental Science for Environmental Management*, 1999, Longman.

Sagoff, M, *The Economy of the Earth: Philosophy, Law and the Environment*, 1998, CUP.

Yearbook of European Environmental Law.

Yearbook of International Environmental Law.

Books covering Scotland and Northern Ireland

Reid, C, *Green's Guide to Environmental Law in Scotland*, 1997, W Green and Son.

Smith, C, Collar, N and Poustie, M, *Pollution Control: The Law in Scotland*, 2nd edn, 1997, T&T Clark.

Turner, S and Morrow, K, *Northern Ireland Environmental Issues*, 1996, Gill and Martin.

Statute books

Duxbury, R, *Statutes on Environmental Law*, 2002, OUP.

Duxbury, R and Morton, S, *Statutes on Environmental Law*, 4th edn, 2002, OUP.

Fry, M, *A Manual of Environmental Protection Law*, 1997, Clarendon.

Waite, A, *Butterworths Environmental Law Handbook*, 3rd edn, 2001, Butterworths.

Statute collections

Annotated Statutes (a yearly chronological record of all primary legislation in England and Wales with explanatory notes for each section), Sweet & Maxwell.

Halsbury's Statutes, Butterworths.

Journal articles and government papers

Bailey, PM, 'The creation and enforcement of environmental agreements' (1999) EELR 170.

Biekart, JW, 'Environmental covenants between government and industry: a Dutch NGO's experience' (1995) RECIEL 141.

Commission of the European Communities, *Communication on Environmental Agreements*, 1996, COM/96/500.

Commission of the European Communities, *Environmental Taxes and Charges in the Single European Market*, 1997, COM/97/9.

Commission of the European Communities, *The Precautionary Principle*, 2000, COM/2000/1.

Commission of the European Communities – the Sixth Action Programme of the European Community, *Environment 2010: Our Future, Our Choice*, 2001, COM/2001/31.

Common Market Law Review.

Department of the Environment, *This Common Inheritance: Britain's Environmental Strategy*, 1990, Cm 1200, HMSO.

Department of the Environment, *A Better Quality of Life*, 1999, Cm 4345, The Stationery Office.

Department of the Environment, *Economic Instruments in Relation to Water Abstraction*, 2000, DoE.

Department of the Environment and Environmental Resources Ltd, *Market Mechansims: Charging and Subsidies*, 1990.

ENDS Report (Environmental Data Services).

Environment Action (Environment Agency publication available free to applicants also available via the Agency's website).

Environmental Law and Management (Lawtext).

Environmental Law Review.

Environmental Liability (Lawtext).

European Environment Agency, *Environmental Taxes: Implementation and Environmental Effectiveness*, 1996, EEA.

European Environment Agency, *Environmental Taxes*, Environmental Issues Series Number 18, 2000, EEA.

European Environmental Law Review.

European Foundation for the Improvement of Living and Working Conditions, *Employment and Sustainability: The UK Landfill Tax*, 1998.

HM Customs and Excise, *Review of Landfill Tax*, 1998.

House of Lords Select Committee on the European Communities (1989–90 Session), *Paying for Pollution*, 25th Report, HMSO.

House of Lords Select Committee on the European Communities (1991–92 Session), *Carbon /Energy Tax*, 8th Report, HMSO.

Jewell, T, 'Setting environmental standards' (1999) ELM 31.

Jewell, T and Steele, J, 'UK regulatory reform and the pursuit of sustainable development: the Environment Act 1995' [1996] JEL 283.

Journal of Environmental Law and Planning (Sweet & Maxwell).

Journal of Environmental Law (OUP).

Organisation for Economic Co-operation and Development, *Economic Instruments for Environmental Protection*, 1989.

Organisation for Economic Co-operation and Development, *Taxation and the Environment*, 1993.

Organisation for Economic Co-operation and Development, *Environment and Taxation*, 1994.

Organisation for Economic Co-operation and Development, *Managing the Environment: The Role of Economic Instruments*, 1994.

Organisation for Economic Co-operation and Development, *Environmental Tax and Green Tax Reform*, 1997.

Organisation for Economic Co-operation and Development, *Reforming Environmental Regulation*, 1997.

Rose-Ackerman, S, 'Market models for water pollution control: their strengths and weaknesses' [1977] Public Policy 383.

Royal Commission on Environmental Pollution, *Setting Environmental Standards*, 21st Report, 1998, Cm 4053, The Stationery Office.

Stone, C, 'Should trees have standing?: towards legal rights for natural objects' (1972) Southern California Law Review 450.

Stone, C, 'Should trees have standing? revisited. How far will law and morals reach – a pluralist perspective' (1985) Southern California Law Review 1.

Tietenberg, T, 'Economic instruments for environmental regulation' (1990) Oxford Review of Economic Policy 17.

United Nations, *Policy, Effectiveness and Multilateral Environmental Agreements*, United Nations Environment Programme Environment and Trade Paper 17, 1998, UNEP/98/6.

Water Law (Lawtext).

World Commission on Environment and Development, *Our Common Future*, 1987, OUP.

Law reports

Environmental Law Reports.

Environmental Health Law Reports.

European Environmental Law Reports.

Common Market Law Reports.

Online sources of information

Note that some of the following sites may require a subscription before you may access the relevant material. University students should check their library home page to confirm which of the following sources of information their library subscribes to.

www.environment-agency.gov.uk

This is perhaps the most important website you will need to refer to. Use the search facility on the agency's homepage to access specific information, for example, prosecution policy. The site also includes NETREGS (accessible directly via www.netregs.environment-agency.gov.uk). This is a collection of legislation in force aimed at small and medium-sized enterprises that wish to keep up to date with legislation which affects their businesses. The agency's site also includes information on pollution incidents and a range of reports – annual report, corporate plan, environmental vision for the future, annual environmental report, half year operational report and customer charter.

www.hmso.gov.uk/legis.htm
UK Acts of Parliament from 1988 and statutory instruments from 1987.

www.official-documents.co.uk
Government policy papers (White and Green Papers).

WESTLAW and LEXIS/NEXIS
These are databases of case reports, legislation and academic articles. Students will require the allocation of an Athens Password to access them.

www.bailli.org
A site operated by British and Irish lawyers containing cases and legislation.

www.lawtel.co.uk
Site containing case summaries and other information.

www.venables.co.uk
Website containing environmental information.

http://library.ukc.ac.uk/library/lawlinks
Kent University Law Department website.

www.casetrack.com
Casetrack site.

http://193.118.187.160
Current Legal Information website.

www.cchnewlaw.co.uk
CCH New Law website.

www.ends.co.uk/envdaily
ENDS daily news.

www.ends.co.uk/report/index.htm
ENDS report website.

www.defra.gov.uk
The Department of Environment, Food and Rural Affairs. An important government site for environmental information such as the GM crop debate.

www.dtlr.gov.uk
The Department of Transport, Local Government and the Regions.

www.echr.coe.int
The European Court of Human Rights.

www.homeoffice.gov.uk/hract
Home Office Human Rights Unit.

www.rcep.org.uk

The Royal Commission for Environmental Pollution. The RCEP has authored a number of highly influential reports on various aspects of the UK environment.

www.clickso.com

Official information available in the UK.

www.open.gov.uk

Open Government website. Index of central and local government bodies. See also www.ukonline.gov.uk

www.statistics.gov.uk

UK national statistics.

www.coi.gov.uk

Central Office of Information.

http://europa.eu.int

Europa: the main website of the EU.

http://europa.eu.int/comm/environment

The website of DG XI – European Environmental Directorate of the Commission.

www.eea.dk

The European Environment Agency.

www.europarl.eu.int

The European Parliament.

http://europa.eu.int/comm/eurostat

EC statistics.

www.un.org

The United Nations.

www.unep.org

United Nations Environment Programme.

www.johannesburgsummit.org

Earth Summit and subsequent developments.

www.foe.co.uk

Friends of the Earth (UK)'s website.

www.greenpeace.org

Greenpeace's website.

www.transport2000.org.uk

Transport 2000.

www.sd-commission.gov.uk/index.htm
The Sustainable Development Commission.

www.elflaw.org.uk
The Environmental Law Foundation.

www.ukela.org.uk
The United Kingdom Environmental Law Association.

www.foe.co.uk/campaigns/safer_chemicals/resource/factory_watch
Friends of the Earth Factory Watch website.

www.butterworths.co.uk/butterworths.htm
Legislation Direct website of full text legislation of UK and Scottish primary and secondary legislation. Chart the progress of legislation by consulting the 'Is it in force?' search facility.

www.hmso.gov.uk/acts.htm
The Stationery Office website. Full text of all statutes after 1996 but not updated with amendments.

To read commentary on Acts of Parliament, see *Halsbury's Laws of England* (see Butterworths website).

www.parliament.the-stationery-office.co.uk/pa/cm/cmwib.htm
The House of Commons Weekly Information Bulletin, which allows you to check the progress of parliamentary Bills.

www.hmso.gov.uk/stat.htm
This site provides full text of statutory instruments from 1997 (see also Lawtel and Legislation Direct).

To access Command Papers, use www.ukop.co.uk for UK official publications (see also Lawtel).

For electronic access to law reports (case law), visit www.justis.com electronic law reports, the Weekly Law Reports and the All England Law Reports (see Butterworths website).

Note also the journal indexes: Legal Journals Index, European Legal Journals Index, Index to Foreign Legal Periodicals, Index to Legal Periodicals and Lawtel articles index.

www.europa.eu.int/comm/dgs/environment/index_en.htm
The EU Directorate General homepage.

www.europa.eu.int/pol/env/index_en.htm
The policy index of the EU homepage.

www.asser.nl/EEL/index.htm
The University of Maastricht environmental law website.

www.keele.ac.uk/depts/ge/teaching/MA/Lawlaw_links.htm
The University of Keele website.

www.law.ecel.uwa.edu.au/intlaw/environment.htm
The Australian website of international environmental law materials.

CHAPTER 2

THE ADMINISTRATION AND ENFORCEMENT OF ENVIRONMENTAL LAW

2.1 INTRODUCTION

As we noted in the previous chapter, the main vehicle which the government uses to regulate pollution in the UK is the Command and Control regulatory model. To be effective, Command and Control regimes require the creation of administrative organisations capable of fulfilling two essential tasks: (a) the bureaucratic task of processing paperwork relating to the issue of licences to pollute (applicable to water, sewage, waste, Integrated Pollution Control (IPC) and Integrated Pollution Prevention and Control (IPPC) regimes) and notices to take action regarding pollution problems identified by the regulator (applicable to statutory nuisance, noise and contaminated land controls); and (b) 'policing' compliance with the relevant licences, notices and other regulatory controls. This latter role involves the regulator in monitoring and enforcement roles.

Because of the historically reactive nature of pollution regulation in the UK, where successive governments responded to pollution issues with the creation of layer on layer of Command and Control regimes in the period 1863–1972, UK pollution control laws presented a picture of a fragmented, complex and unwieldy patchwork of separate controls. The last three decades of the 20th century have witnessed concerted government efforts to achieve a more integrated and coherent set of regulatory controls. It is against this backdrop that we now turn to consider the role of the Environment Agency, and its forerunners, in the administration and enforcement of environmental law. In addition, we shall outline the role of the courts in the adjudication of disputes arising out of the administration and enforcement of environmental law and summarise the roles of other relevant bodies.

On 8 July 1991, the former Prime Minister, John Major announced the government's intention to create a new authority with overall responsibility for the protection of the environment. The principal aim of the government was to create a unified body which would have responsibility for the protection of the environment as a whole, bringing together the key regulatory pollution control functions affecting air, land and water. In order to do this, the government enacted the Environment Act (EA) 1995 which established the Environment Agency (which became fully operational in April 1996). Prior to the establishment of the Environment Agency, responsibility for various aspects of environmental protection and pollution control was largely divided between Her Majesty's Inspectorate of Pollution (HMIP), the National Rivers Authority (NRA), the Waste Regulation Authorities (WRA) and the local authorities, each exercising control under different statutory provisions. (The functions of HMIP, the NRA and the WRAs were transferred to the Environment Agency in April 1996 and each of these regulatory bodies ceased to exist from that date.)

The fragmentary system of control, which existed prior to the creation of the Environment Agency, reflected the way in which environmental legislation had developed in this country, largely in a piecemeal fashion and often in response to pollution problems or incidents. The pre-Environment Agency system of control was often criticised because it did not respect the cross-media integrity and indivisibility of the environment and also because it was unnecessarily confusing to those subject to it. As a consequence, the government took the view that the time was right for the creation of a new unified body, which would effectively provide not only greater co-ordination of environmental protection but would also provide a 'one stop' approach to pollution control, thus simplifying the burdens on industry.

Despite the creation of the Environment Agency in 1996, regulatory control is not entirely unified and it is still the case that some controls are exercised by the local authorities and the large water and sewerage companies. Local authorities still play a key role in environmental protection, indirectly through the planning system and also more directly in relation to air pollution, hazardous substances, statutory nuisances and now contaminated land. Their role is considered more fully at 2.5, below.

Because of the relatively recent creation of the Environment Agency, this chapter is broken down into four parts. First, it considers the system of regulatory control that was in operation prior to the EA 1995. The next section considers the reasons behind the creation of the Environment Agency. The chapter will then consider the structure, role and powers of the Environment Agency, the local authorities and other bodies that still play a role in environmental protection. Finally, the chapter will consider the role of the courts in the administration of environmental law.

2.2   THE SYSTEM OF POLLUTION CONTROL PRIOR TO THE ENVIRONMENT ACT 1995

Prior to the enactment of the EA 1995 and the creation of the Environment Agency, the system of pollution control was exercised by the following regulatory bodies:

(a) HMIP;

(b) the NRA;

(c) the WRAs;

(d) the local authorities;

(e) the water services companies responsible for the sewerage system.

2.2.1   Her Majesty's Inspectorate of Pollution

In a sense, HMIP was a forerunner of the Environment Agency in that it was established to provide a co-ordinated system of pollution control. Prior to its formation in 1987, control of pollution was the responsibility of a number of central government inspectorates: the Alkali Inspectorate (which was formed in 1863 and which was later called the Industrial Air Pollution Inspectorate); the Radiochemical Inspectorate; the Hazardous Waste Inspectorate; and the Water Pollution Inspectorate. (The functions of the Water Pollution Inspectorate were transferred to the NRA by the Water Act (WA) 1989.) HMIP was designed to provide a more co-ordinated system of pollution control, particularly through its administration of the system of Integrated Pollution Control (IPC) established by Pt I of the Environmental Protection Act (EPA) 1990.

HMIP, unlike the NRA, was part of the Department of the Environment (DoE). HMIP operated on a regional basis with seven regions although it had a central office based in the DoE in London. The Head of HMIP was the Chief Inspector. Regional responsibilities were handled through the regional offices which employed in total over 430 staff. In addition, HMIP also contained a Technical Guidance Branch and a Monitoring Branch. In outline, HMIP was responsible for the following:

(a) regulation of the most seriously polluting processes through the system of IPC introduced by Pt I of the EPA 1990;

(b) regulation of sites which use, store or dispose of radioactive material under the Radioactive Substances Act (RSA) 1993;

(c) responsibilities under the Health and Safety at Work Act (HSWA) 1974 in relation to the air emissions of IPC processes;

(d) duties under the Water Industry Act (WIA) 1991 to act on behalf of the Secretary of State with regard to special category effluents discharged into the sewers;

(e) research on pollution control and also on radioactive waste disposal;

(f) acting as a statutory consultee in environmental impact assessments;

(g) oversight of the work of local WRAs;

(h) maintenance of the public register on IPC authorised processes.

In carrying out these functions, it appeared that HMIP was meant to serve the government, industry and also the citizen. In addition to these various roles, HMIP provided expert advice and support to government departments on a wide range of environmental issues. HMIP officials were involved in European Community (EC) working groups and other international bodies.

HMIP drew its powers from a number of statutory provisions including:

(a) the Alkali etc Works Act 1906 (repealed);

(b) the HSWA 1974;

(c) the EPA 1990;

(d) the Water Resources Act (WRA) 1991;

(e) the RSA 1993.

HMIP's main activity was the administration and enforcement of the system of IPC established under Pt I of the EPA 1990. During its period of office, HMIP was responsible for regulating over 200 categories of industry, 5,000 major industrial plants and 8,000 premises storing radioactive material. Once an industrial process had been authorised by HMIP, the Inspectorate was responsible for ensuring compliance with the conditions and standards it had laid down in the authorisations (licences). Usually any authorisation granted would require the holder to carry out routine monitoring and to report the results to HMIP on a regular basis. These monitoring results, plus any obtained directly by HMIP inspectors, were placed on the public register. In addition to this, HMIP inspectors carried out their own site inspections, either on a regular or *ad hoc* basis or in response to any complaints received. In recognition of the significant role that monitoring played, a new monitoring branch of HMIP was established in August 1991.

In terms of enforcement, HMIP had the power to revoke authorisations granted and also to halt a process where there was an imminent risk of serious pollution. In addition, it had the power to bring prosecutions against offenders, which, if upheld in the magistrates' court, could lead to a fine of up to £20,000 or, on indictment in the Crown Court, to an unlimited fine and/or a period of up to two years' imprisonment. To assist HMIP in the process of enforcement, its inspectors enjoyed considerable powers of investigation, particularly under s 17 of the EPA 1990 to enter premises and take samples. However, HMIP was often criticised for its poor prosecution record, particularly in contrast with the NRA which appeared much more willing to prosecute offenders. The following statistics illustrate the number of HMIP prosecutions during the period 1987–92:

HMIP prosecutions:

1987–88	3
1988–89	2
1989–90	4
1990–91	1
1991–92	11

In its publicity material (*Protecting Britain's Environment – The Work of HMIP*), it was stated that 'breaches of authorisations are normally dealt with quickly and effectively with the co-operation of the operator. But where this does not produce the necessary results, HMIP uses its powers of enforcement and prosecution'. Most critics of HMIP's 'poor' prosecution record failed to take account of the extensive array of enforcement powers that were available to HMIP to ensure that regulated businesses complied with the terms of their pollution licences. These powers, such as Enforcement Notices, Prohibition Notices and Revocation Notices, were potentially so draconian that the threat of their use was more effective in achieving compliance than the comparable threat of prosecution.

In order to assist both industrialists and the chief inspectors, HMIP published a considerable amount of guidance material. Following the introduction of IPC, HMIP also began the process of publishing a new series of guidance notes covering all IPC processes. These guidance notes give advice on matters such as the best available technology for the particular process, pollution abatement techniques, operating procedures and, importantly, the emission standards to be achieved. The guidance notes are still relevant, albeit that the system of IPC is no longer administered by HMIP.

One of the government's stated ambitions for HMIP was that it should be self-financing, recovering its costs from charges made for authorisations, variations, etc, of IPC processes. This reflects the notion that the polluter should pay, not just for remedying pollution, but also for the costs of pollution control. A charging scheme was introduced in April 1990. HMIP was required by the EPA 1990 to set fees and charges so that income and relevant costs balance 'so far as practicable'. However, HMIP never managed to become completely self-financing.

The Environment Agency is now responsible for administering the system of IPC and the system of IPPC (which will replace IPC by 2007). The system of control is largely the same although the powers of inspection are now to be found in s 108 of the EA 1995.

2.2.2 The National Rivers Authority

The NRA was the main regulatory body with responsibility for controlling pollution of water, although it shared responsibility with HMIP in relation to those industrial processes subject to the IPC regime established under Pt I of the EPA 1990.

The NRA was set up by the WA 1989, at the same time as water privatisation, to provide integrated management of river basins and the water environment in England and Wales. It took over the functions previously exercised by the Water Authorities. Although the NRA was established by the WA 1989, its constitution, function and powers were later to be governed by the WRA 1991 and all the following section references relate to the 1991 Act. The NRA exercised a range of functions beyond pollution control, for example, it was also responsible for flood protection. In the context of environmental protection, the record shows that the NRA was regarded by many as a strong regulator, willing to prosecute if necessary.

The NRA was established as an independent public body and did not enjoy Crown immunity. However, it was nevertheless accountable to the Secretary of State for the Environment. The Secretary of State had the power to issue directions to the NRA, although only after consultation with the authority, unless the direction was issued in an emergency situation. Details of any directions issued by the Secretary of State were published in the authority's annual report. The NRA was identified by the DoE as the 'competent body' to implement the requirements of numerous EC directives concerning water quality.

Unlike HMIP, the NRA was a non-departmental body. The NRA had its national headquarters in Bristol, but was structured on a regional basis with the regions corresponding to the catchment boundaries of the former regional Water Authorities. In 1993, NRA Northumbria and NRA Yorkshire were amalgamated and NRA South West and NRA Wessex Regions were merged to form NRA South Western. The NRA was assisted by a number of regional advisory committees that were required to act in a consultative role to the authority, providing advice on those areas within their spheres of influence. These committees were established under s 7 of the WRA 1991. There were three main advisory committees that operated in each region:

(a) Regional Rivers Advisory Committees;

(b) Regional Flood Defence Committees;

(c) Regional Fisheries Advisory Committee.

In addition, there was an Advisory Committee for Wales. The advisory committee structure still exists and supports the Environment Agency in its water pollution functions.

When the NRA was established in 1989, it inherited the functions of the Water Authorities relating to pollution control, water resource management, flood defence, fisheries, navigation and conservation and recreation. The functions of the NRA (which have now been transferred in full to the Environment Agency) were laid down in s 2 of the WRA 1991 and covered the following areas:

(a) maintaining and improving water quality in controlled waters;

(b) regulating discharges into controlled waters;

(c) monitoring the extent of water pollution;

(d) managing and safeguarding water resources (abstraction);

(e) conserving amenity and promoting recreation;

(f) flood defence and land drainage;

(g) regulating fisheries (under the Salmon and Freshwater Fisheries Act 1975).

NRA inspectors, often referred to as the 'river police', enjoyed various powers by virtue of ss 169–73 of the WRA 1991. (As in relation to HMIP, the Environment Agency's pollution control powers of inspection are now to be found in s 108 of the EA 1995 which repealed s 169 of the WRA 1991.)

The WRA 1991 placed the NRA under a number of statutory duties which it was required to have regard to when exercising its various functions. The NRA was required by s 16 of the WRA 1991 generally to promote (to the extent that it considered desirable) the conservation and enhancement of the natural beauty and amenity of inland and coastal waters and of land associated with such waters; the conservation of flora and fauna which are dependent on the aquatic environment; and the use of such waters and land for recreational purposes. The NRA also had a duty to consider water supply issues and by virtue of s 15 it had to have regard, when exercising any of its powers, to the duties that are imposed on any water undertakers or sewerage undertakers by Pts II–IV of the WIA 1991. The Environment Agency has similar duties in respect of water and these are discussed more fully at 2.4.8 below.

The policy of the NRA was to provide strong effective regulation in order to secure real environmental improvements of controlled waters. However, it did not view regulation as the only means at its disposal. The NRA placed an emphasis on changing attitudes and, hopefully, behaviour. As part of its pollution prevention campaign, the NRA produced a short promotional video entitled *Pollution Prevention Pays*. The video was made widely available to businesses promoting the benefits of compliance and good practice. Nevertheless, since its creation in 1989, the NRA showed itself to be more willing to prosecute offenders than HMIP. Although prosecution figures are not conclusive of a strong enforcement policy, the statistics are telling. Between 1989 and the end of 1994 the NRA had made over 2,200 successful prosecutions. These resulted in over £5 million in fines.

2.2.3 The Waste Regulation Authorities

WRAs were created by Pt II of the EPA 1990 as part of the overall reform of the waste regulatory regime. The functions of the WRAs were carried out by the county councils, or in metropolitan areas the district councils. Special waste regulation authorities were created in Greater London, Greater Manchester and Merseyside. The WRAs were responsible for administering and enforcing the provisions under Pt II of the EPA 1990 relating to waste management and in particular the waste licensing system. WRAs were responsible for:

(a) preparation of waste disposal plans;

(b) control over the waste management licensing system;

(c) supervision of licensed activities;

(d) inspection of licensed land and landfill sites;

(e) maintaining public registers;

(f) reporting to the Secretary of State.

The functions of the WRAs were transferred to the Environment Agency in 1996 and the WRAs ceased to exist.

2.3   REASONS FOR CHANGE

The government identified several reasons for change. On the one hand, it was argued that there was a need to create a unified regulatory agency which would facilitate a more coherent approach to environmental control. For example, in relation to water pollution, two systems of control operated, regulated by two different bodies. The system of IPC established by Pt I of the EPA 1990 is concerned with controlling the emissions of waste to air, land and water in order that pollution is controlled in a manner which will achieve the best practicable environmental option.

Therefore, HMIP, as the body responsible for regulating processes subject to IPC, was responsible for authorising discharges made into controlled waters as well as air and land. However, the NRA was the body responsible generally for regulating water pollution and enforcing the water pollution control provisions under the WRA 1991. Consequently, HMIP was required to consult the NRA before it set any conditions pertaining to discharges to controlled water. This meant effectively that the NRA had the power indirectly to determine any conditions which should be attached. Clearly, bringing control of water pollution and IPC under the auspices of one unified agency negated the need for this consultation. The problem of overlap was not confined to water pollution. A further example relates to the WRAs which were required also to consult closely with the NRA before setting any waste management licence conditions (under Pt II of the EPA 1990) in order to prevent any contamination of groundwaters from any leachate from a landfill site.

A further and very cogent reason for change was to simplify the system of control for those subject to it, namely the polluting industries and activities regulated under the various statutory provisions. It was not only the government that advocated the creation of a unified regulatory agency; the idea was supported by many quarters of industry. It is worth considering the way in which the system of regulation, pre-Environment Agency, operated in order to grasp what was perceived in some quarters as a regulatory maze.

2.3.1   The regulatory authority maze – pre-Environment Agency

(This section relates to the variety of Command and Control regulatory regimes which were in existence prior to 1 April 1996.)

For any new or expanding industrial development, it is necessary to obtain planning permission from a local planning authority before the development can go ahead. However, the developer may also need to seek further authorisations from the local authority depending on the nature of the project. For example, it may be necessary for the developer to obtain a noise consent from the local authority for the noise generated during the construction period. An industrial development may need to obtain a waste management licence or register with the WRA, which would normally be the county council. It may need to obtain Local Authority Air Pollution Control (LAAPC) authorisation if the development is a Part B prescribed process (under Pt I of the EPA 1990). There may be a need to obtain chimney height approval from the local authority or possibly even a hazardous substances consent.

In addition, an industrialist or industrial developer may need to obtain a consent from the NRA to discharge into water. Alternatively, if the process is prescribed for central control (a Part A Process), it would require IPC authorisation from HMIP. If there were a need to abstract water from a local river, NRA approval would, however, still be required. There may be a need to discharge trade effluent into the drains and in these circumstances the consent of the sewerage undertaker must also be obtained. In short, a business may have to deal with several environmental protection bodies.

It becomes clear from looking at a hypothetical scenario such as this that any industrial developer had to understand the statutory controls that regulated the development and also know which regulatory bodies were responsible for controlling the various aspects of the development. Failure to obtain the correct permissions could (and still can) result in a criminal prosecution. Fines may be unlimited and the Crown Court has the power to impose a custodial sentence of up to two years. Reported cases suggest that the courts are becoming more willing to impose large fines and exercise the option of imprisonment. Additionally, both s 217 of the WRA 1991 and s 157 of the EPA 1990 provide that prosecutions may also be brought against company directors, managers, secretaries or other such officials if the offence was committed with their consent, connivance or negligence.

In the light of the complexity of the regulatory system and the consequences of breaching the regulatory controls, it really came as no surprise that industry and business supported the government's call for the creation of a unified regulatory agency which would reduce the amount of bodies that a business might have to deal with.

2.3.2   The desire to achieve the best practicable environmental option

It is not only from the point of view of the industrialist that the picture was confusing. With so many organisations involved in various aspects of environmental protection, it was often difficult to establish an overview of what polluting activities were going on and where, or more importantly to be certain that each body was exercising its functions in a manner which would benefit the environment as a whole. This respect for the integrity and indivisibility of the environment is at the heart of the decision to create a unified Environment Agency. Although HMIP was established in 1987 with the aim of achieving a more coherent approach to pollution control through the system of IPC, there was clearly still the need for a more integrated approach to pollution control. Whilst the authorities themselves were very active in publicising their work and increasing public awareness of their respective roles, the picture was still not entirely free of confusion.

The government therefore saw the new Environment Agency as a means to develop a consistent and uniform approach to environmental protection, which would at the same time provide a more transparent system of control, more understandable to those subject to it. This desire to have a more co-ordinated approach to environmental protection was also generally supported by the environmentalists and pressure groups, many of whom believed that this unified approach would assist government in integrating environmental concerns into other government policies.

2.3.3   Options for change

The desire to establish a unified approach to environmental control is not entirely new and it is clear that the government was considering such an option as early as 1990 when it considered the possibility of creating an 'umbrella' organisation for overseeing the work of HMIP and NRA in *This Common Inheritance*, 1990. In July 1991, the then Prime Minister, John Major, made the first announcement that it was his government's intention to create an Environment Agency. The process of bringing together HMIP, NRA and the WRAs has been a long drawn out and complex one, subject to much debate and consultation. In October 1991, the government issued a consultation paper, *Improving Environmental Quality: the Government Proposals for a New Independent Environment Agency*. This suggested four options and sought views from all interested parties. The options suggested were as follows:

(1) The creation of an environmental agency and the retention of the NRA. The Environment Agency would assume the responsibilities of the WRAs and HMIP, less HMIP's water functions. The NRA would exercise control over all aspects of water pollution including HMIP's water pollution functions. The main criticism of this option was that it still did not provide an integrated approach to pollution control.

(2) The environmental agency would be simply an umbrella organisation overseeing and co-ordinating HMIP and the NRA. Although this might secure a greater degree of co-ordination, it would still not provide a unified approach for industry.

(3) The environmental agency would take over the functions of HMIP, NRA and the WRAs (the option finally selected).

(4) The environmental agency would take over HMIP and the WRAs and would also assume the NRA's water pollution functions, but the NRA would continue to exist and exercise its remaining controls over matters such as fishing, flood defence and drainage.

The government invited consultation on all four options. Much of the debate centred on options 3 and 4 and the real issue was whether to retain the NRA, given its very wide-ranging functions. Interestingly, the NRA did not favour a separation of its functions and its preferred option was full integration into the environmental agency.

2.4   THE ENVIRONMENT AGENCY

In November 1994, the Environment Bill was introduced before Parliament, its principal purpose being the creation of a new Environment Agency for England and

Wales and a Scottish Environmental Protection Agency (SEPA) (in addition, the EA 1995 introduced new provisions relating to contaminated land, abandoned mines and national parks). The Environment Agency was established in July 1995 and became operational on 1 April 1996.

2.4.1   The structure of the Environment Agency

Section 1(1) of the EA 1995 established the new Environment Agency as a body corporate. The Agency consists of between eight and 15 members, of whom three are appointed by the Minister for Agriculture, the remaining members being appointed by the Secretary of State. In appointing members, both the Minister and the Secretary of State must have regard to the desirability of appointing a person who has experience of, and has shown some capacity in, some matter relevant to the functions of the Environment Agency.

Like the former NRA, the Environment Agency is an independent body. HMIP, on the other hand, was part of the DoE. Although it is independent, the Environment Agency is accountable to Parliament through the Secretary of State. The Environment Agency does not have Crown immunity. In terms of staffing, most of the employees of the Environment Agency have been drawn from HMIP, NRA and the WRAs, thus retaining the expertise which had developed in those bodies.

2.4.2   Regional structure and regional environmental protection advisory committees

The Environment Agency is based upon a regional structure and this is augmented by the regional advisory committees under s 12 of the EA 1995 and the Welsh Advisory Committee under s 11. The regional boundaries are complicated. In terms of water management purposes, the regional boundaries correspond exactly with the eight regional boundaries of the NRA, which were drawn up on river catchment areas. As far as pollution control functions are concerned, the regional boundaries are those eight regions, modified to fit the local authority boundary which is closest to the water management boundary.

The Welsh Advisory Committee, which must meet at least once a year, is made up of members appointed by the Secretary of State. Its function is to advise the Secretary of State on matters affecting or connected with the carrying out of the Environment Agency's functions in Wales (s 11(1)). During the passage of the Environment Bill, there were calls for a separate Environment Agency for Wales similar to the Scottish Environmental Protection Agency for Scotland. These calls were, however, dismissed, largely on the grounds that this would be an inefficient and wasteful use of resources.

Section 12 provides for the establishment of regional environmental protection advisory committees in both England and Wales (therefore note that in Wales there is a Welsh Advisory Committee and a regional environmental protection committee). By virtue of s 12(2), the Environment Agency is required to consult the relevant advisory committee as to any proposals relating generally to the manner in which the Agency carries out its functions in that region and also to consider any representations made to it by the advisory committee. The committee consists of a chairman appointed by the Secretary of State and other members appointed by the Agency. In addition to the regional environmental protection advisory committees, s 13 of the EA 1995 provides for the establishment of regional and local fisheries advisory committees on a similar basis.

The Environment Agency is under a duty to consult the relevant committee on any proposals relating generally to the manner in which it carries out its functions in that region.

2.4.3   Transfer of functions

On 1 April 1996, the Environment Agency became fully operational. Section 2 of the EA 1995 provides specifically for the transfer to the Environment Agency of the following:

(a) the functions exercised by the NRA under the WRA 1991 and the Land Drainage Act 1991 and various other statutory provisions such as the Salmon and Freshwater Fisheries Act 1975. As a consequence, the NRA was abolished. Thus, the Environment Agency has inherited the NRA's water resource management functions, pollution control functions and also its operational functions relating to flood defence, land drainage, navigation and fisheries;

(b) the waste management functions exercised by the WRAs under Pt II of the EPA 1990 and the Control of Pollution (Amendment) Act 1989;

(c) HMIP's responsibilities under Pt I of the EPA 1990. It should be noted here that the LAAPC controls exercised by local authorities under Pt I are retained by the local authorities;

(d) HMIP's functions relating to radioactive substances under the RSA 1993;

(e) certain enforcement functions under Pt I of the HSWA 1974;

(f) certain functions of the Secretary of State (these are listed in s 2(2) of the EA 1995).

As a consequence of this transfer of functions, Sched 22 to the EA 1995 has made a large number of amendments to most of the environmental protection legislation discussed in this book, notably the EPA 1990 and WRA 1991, in order that the legislation now refers to the Environment Agency rather than the NRA, HMIP or the WRAs. Section 3 of the EA 1995 makes provisions for the transfer of property rights and liabilities specifically of the NRA and the WRAs.

In addition to the transfer of functions, the EA 1995 conferred certain new functions on the Environment Agency arising out of new provisions introduced in the Act. These are:

(a) functions relating to contaminated land under s 57 of the EA 1995. The Agency has specific powers relating to certain contaminated sites which have been designated as 'special sites' by a local authority. In addition, the Agency has the power to give guidance to local authorities in respect of the latter's role in relation to contaminated land. For a further discussion of the contaminated land provisions, see Chapter 7;

(b) functions relating to air quality under Pt IV of the EA 1995. The Agency acts as a statutory consultee in relation to the Secretary of State's proposals for a national air quality strategy and also in relation to any regulations which he or she issues relating to air quality. For further discussion, see Chapter 8.

2.4.4   Aims of the Environment Agency

The principal aims and objectives of the Environment Agency are laid down in s 4 of the EA 1995. Section 4(1) states that it shall be the 'principal aim of the EA (subject to and in accordance with the provisions of [the] Act or any other enactment and taking into account any likely costs) in discharging its functions so to protect or enhance the environment, taken as a whole, as to make the contribution towards attaining the objective of achieving sustainable development …'. It is clear from this therefore that the government envisaged that the Environment Agency should be guided by the objective of achieving sustainability. However, it is also very clear that this is not an absolute objective in so far as the principal aim of the Environment Agency is qualified in two ways. First, the aim is subject to and in accordance with any other provisions of the EA 1995 or any other enactment. Therefore, in situations where the EA 1995 or any other enactment places the Environment Agency under a duty to have regard to particular considerations, or instructs the Environment Agency to fulfil actions, then these other provisions will overrule the principal aim. Secondly, the Environment Agency is required to take into account any likely costs of discharging its functions in the attainment of this aim. This includes the likely costs to any person and to the environment (s 56(1)). This latter qualification is considered more fully at 2.4.11 below.

The Secretary of State can issue guidance to the Environment Agency on any further objectives which are considered to be appropriate for the Environment Agency to pursue (s 4(2) of the EA 1995) and in particular the guidance must include advice on how, having regard to the Environment Agency's responsibilities and resources, it is to attain the objective of sustainable development (s 4(3)). Once again, the reference to resources appears in the guidance given to the Environment Agency. Before issuing this guidance, the Secretary of State must consult with the Environment Agency and any other appropriate bodies or persons (s 4(5)).

2.4.5   Sustainable development

Given that the principal aim of the Environment Agency is to use its powers to attain the objective of sustainable development, it is worth considering how the government defined this all important concept. A widely accepted definition of sustainable development is to be found in the 1987 Bruntland Report (*Report of the World Commission on Environment and Development 1987*):

> … development that meets the needs of the present without compromising the ability of future generations to meet their own needs.

The EA 1995, however, fails to provide a definition and sustainable development remains to be defined in the guidance notes referred to above.

The concept of sustainable development, considered at 1.8.2 above, seems to place an important emphasis on the education of stakeholders (government, regulators, companies, NGOs, and individuals) in order to minimise the damaging impacts of human activity upon the planet. The Environment Agency perceives itself, in part, as an educator and advocator of current best environmental practice. Licence holders and others are provided with guidance (for example, Pollution Prevention Guidance Notes (see 4.13.2), pollution prevention campaign information (see 4.13.2) and NETREGS (see www.environment-agency.gov.uk/netregs/?=_e)) to enable them to comply with the law.

2.4.6   General functions of the Environment Agency with respect to pollution control

The general functions of the Environment Agency are defined in s 5 of the EA 1995. Section 5(1) states that the Environment Agency's pollution control functions shall be exercisable for the purpose of preventing or minimising, or remedying or mitigating, the effects of pollution of the environment. The EA 1995 does not, however, provide a definition of 'pollution of the environment' and it has been suggested that the definition as provided in the EPA 1990 (Pt I, s 1(3) and Pt II, s 29(3)) should be used. In order to carry out these functions, or to establish a general picture about the state of the environment, the Environment Agency must compile information which it has either gathered itself or which has been obtained from some other source. Section 5 goes on to list several other functions of the EA, including:

(a) carrying out assessments of the environmental effect or likely effect of existing levels of pollution of the environment;

(b) reporting to the Secretary of State on the ways in which the Environment Agency considers it can prevent, minimise, remedy or mitigate the effects of pollution and reporting on the costs and benefits of such options (s 5(3)(ii));

(c) following developments in technology and techniques for preventing, minimising, remedying or mitigating the effects of pollution of the environment. This clearly relates to the Environment Agency's functions in respect of IPC under Pt I of the EPA 1990 and IPPC under the Pollution Prevention and Control Act (PPCA) 1999.

2.4.7   Duties of the new Environment Agency

The Environment Agency is placed under certain statutory duties which it must have regard to when exercising any of its functions. Section 6 of the EA 1995 deals specifically with those duties pertaining to water, s 7 deals with the Agency's general environmental and recreational duties and s 8 deals with its duties with respect to sites of special interest. Section 39 provides that the Environment Agency is under a general duty to have regard to the costs and benefits in exercising its powers. This has already been referred to in relation to the general aims of the Environment Agency and is considered more fully at 2.4.11 below.

2.4.8   Section 6 – duties in respect of water

In the same way that the NRA was under a similar duty under the WRA 1991, the Environment Agency has specific duties regarding water. The Agency is obliged, to the extent that it considers desirable, generally to promote:

(a) the conservation and enhancement of the natural beauty and amenity of inland and coastal waters and land surrounding them;

(b) the conservation of flora and fauna which are dependent upon the aquatic environment;

(c) the use of such waters and land for recreational purposes, taking into account the needs of the chronically sick or disabled.

In terms of water resources, the Environment Agency is also obliged to take all such action, as it may from time to time consider necessary in accordance with any directions issued by the Secretary of State, to be necessary or expedient to conserve, redistribute or generally augment water resources in England and Wales and also to secure the proper use of water resources. These duties are described as being 'without prejudice' to the Environment Agency's other duties under s 7 of the EA 1995.

2.4.9 Section 7 – general environmental duties

Section 7 deals with the general environmental duties placed upon the Secretary of State and the Environment Agency and in doing so draws a distinction between the Environment Agency's pollution control functions and non-pollution control functions.

When formulating or considering any proposals relating to any non-pollution control functions, the Secretary of State and the Environment Agency are under a duty to 'exercise any power' in respect of such proposals so as to further the conservation and enhancement of natural beauty and the conservation of flora, fauna and geological or physiographical features of special interest (s 7(1)(a)). This duty applies to such proposals made by the Agency so far as may be consistent:

(a) with the purpose of any enactment relating to the functions of the Environment Agency;

(b) with any guidance given under s 4.

In the case of the Secretary of State, this duty applies to him or her so far as it is consistent:

(a) with the objective of sustainable development;

(b) with his or her general duties regarding the water industry under the provisions of s 2 of the WIA 1991.

Where the proposals relate to the Environment Agency's pollution control functions, the duty is worded differently (s 7(1)(b)). Here, the Secretary of State and the Environment Agency must 'have regard' to the desirability of conserving and enhancing natural beauty and of conserving flora, fauna and geological or physiographical features of special interest. Clearly, the duty to have regard to these matters is less onerous than in relation to s 7(1)(a) above where the duty is to exercise any powers to further these matters. This difference was the subject of a great deal of criticism during the passage of the Environment Bill.

In addition, s 7(1)(c) requires the Secretary of State and the Environment Agency, when formulating or considering any proposals relating to any functions of the Environment Agency:

(a) to have regard to the desirability of protecting and conserving buildings, sites and objects of archaeological, architectural, engineering or historic interest;

(b) to take into account any effect which the proposals would have on the beauty or amenity of any rural or urban area or any such flora, fauna, features, buildings, sites or objects; and

(c) to have regard to any effect which the proposal would have on the economic and social well being of local communities in rural areas.

In addition to the above duties laid down in s 7(1), s 7(2) requires the Secretary of State and the Environment Agency, in formulating or considering proposals relating to any functions of the Environment Agency, to:

(a) have regard to the desirability of preserving for the public any freedom of access to areas of woodland, mountains, moors, heathlands, downs, cliffs, the foreshore and other places of natural beauty;

(b) have regard to the desirability of maintaining the availability to the public of any facility for visiting or inspecting any building, site or object of archaeological, engineering or historic interest; and

(c) take into account any effect which the proposals would have on any such freedom of access or on the availability of any such facility.

Section 7(3) applies s 7(1) and (2) in relation to the Environment Agency's duties to water and sewerage undertakers.

2.4.10 Section 8 – environmental duties with respect to sites of special interest

The provisions of s 8 of the EA 1995 are based on the provisions of s 17 of the WRA 1991 which were repealed by the EA 1995. Under s 8(1), the Nature Conservancy Council for England (now known as English Nature) or the Countryside Council for Wales may designate land as being of 'special interest' and notify the Environment Agency accordingly if it is its opinion that any area of land:

(a) is of special interest by reason of its flora, fauna or geological or physiographical features; and

(b) may at any time be affected by schemes, works, operations or activities of the Environment Agency or by an authorisation given by the Agency.

The consequence of designating a site as being of special interest is that the Environment Agency is required to consult with the notifying body before carrying out or authorising certain works which are likely to affect the land. The requirement to consult does not operate in relation to anything done in an emergency (s 8(4)).

2.4.11 Section 39 – duty to have regard to costs and benefits

One of the underlying features of the Environment Agency, and probably one of the most contentious issues surrounding it, is the obligation placed on it to have regard to the costs and benefit of exercising any of its powers. Section 39 of the EA 1995 provides that both the Scottish Environmental Protection Agency and the Environment Agency shall, in considering whether or not to exercise any power conferred upon by any legislation, or even in deciding the manner in which to exercise *any* such power, take into account the likely costs and benefits of the exercise, non-exercise or manner of exercise in question. This duty does not apply if, or to the extent that, it is unreasonable in view of:

(a) the nature or purpose of the power; or

(b) in the circumstances of the particular case.

In addition, s 39(2) provides that the duty does not affect the Environment Agency's obligation to discharge any duties, comply with any requirements or pursue any objectives imposed upon it or given to it otherwise than under s 39. Reference to costs and benefits also appears in relation to the principal aims of the Environment Agency. It should be noted that s 56(1) provides that the definition of costs includes both costs to any person and also cost to the environment. The essence of this duty was described by the Secretary of State during the second reading stage of the Bill where he asserted that 'we cannot deliver on environmental demands unless we take into account the costs and ensure that they are proportionate to the benefits that we gain'. Hence, an evaluation of the costs and the benefits that accrue from taking a course of action must be assessed.

This is an entirely new duty which was not imposed on the Environment Agency's predecessors. As stated above, this has been one of the most controversial provisions in the EA 1995 and has led to widespread criticism from environmentalists. In particular, many have suggested, in opposition to this duty, that it will lead to judicial review challenges by either industrialists or environmental protection groups who believe that the Environment Agency has not properly considered either the costs or the benefits of taking (or failing to take) a particular course of action.

2.4.12 Codes of practice with respect to environmental duties

Section 9 of the EA 1995 empowers the Secretary of State and the Minister of Agriculture to approve codes of practice which have as their purpose the provision of practical guidance to the Environment Agency concerning any of the duties detailed in ss 6(1), 7 and 8 and also to promote other practices which the Minister considers desirable for the Environment Agency to carry out. The codes of practice are made by statutory instrument and may be modified or withdrawn. In carrying out its duties under ss 6(1), 7 and 8, the Environment Agency must have regard to any code of practice issued. In drafting any code, the Minister or Secretary of State must, however, first consult the Environment Agency, the Countryside Agency, English Nature or the Countryside Council for Wales, the Historic Buildings and Monuments Commission for England, the Sports Council and other such persons as he considers appropriate to consult.

2.4.13 Powers of inspectors

The powers of Environment Agency inspectors are set out in s 108 of the EA 1995 (previously s 17 of the EPA 1990). The powers conferred on the Environment Agency are also conferred on local authorities exercising their LAAPC functions under Pt I of the EPA 1990. The purpose of s 108 of the EA 1995 is to streamline the powers of entry and inspection across the range of pollution control functions now exercised by the Environment Agency, and these powers apply equally to pollution control functions under Pt II of the EPA 1990 (waste management) and the WRA 1991 (water discharge consents). Section 108 combines powers previously exercised by HMIP, the NRA and the WRAs.

It is essential that inspectors have adequate powers of entry and inspection in order to ensure compliance with the licences granted and also to identify instances where processes are being carried on without the appropriate licence. The powers listed in s 108 of the EA 1995 may be exercised for one or more of the following purposes:

(a) determining whether any pollution control legislation is being or has been complied with;

(b) exercising or performing pollution control functions;

(c) determining whether and, if so, how such a function should be exercised or performed.

Section 108 refers to persons authorised in writing. In practice, this will be the inspectors employed by the Environment Agency (or the relevant local authority officers). An inspector has the following powers of entry and inspection:

(a) to enter at any reasonable time premises which he or she has reason to believe it is necessary for him or her to enter. This should normally be at any reasonable time unless there is an emergency, in which case entry is permitted at any time and, if need be, by force;

(b) on entering premises, to take with him or her any other person duly authorised by the Environment Agency, and a policeman. The latter may be needed in situations where the inspector has reasonable cause to apprehend any serious obstruction in carrying out his or her duties;

(c) to take any equipment or materials required for any purpose for which the power of entry is being exercised;

(d) to make such examination and investigation as may in any circumstances be necessary;

(e) to instruct that the premises or any part of them, or anything in them, be left undisturbed. The inspector may require that the premises or the part of the premises under investigation are not disturbed for as long as is reasonably necessary to enable him or her to carry out any examination or investigation;

(f) to take such measurements and photographs and make recordings as he or she considers necessary;

(g) to take samples, or instruct samples be taken, of any articles or substances found in or on the premises and also from the air, water or land in, on or in the vicinity of the premises. Specific provisions relate to the possession, safekeeping and use in evidence of such samples;

(h) in the case of any article or substance found in or on premises which appears to him or her to be an article or substance which has caused or is likely to cause pollution of the environment, or harm to human health, to cause it to be dismantled or subjected to any process or test (but not so as to damage or destroy it unless that is necessary);

(i) to require information from any person – the inspector can require any person whom he or she has reasonable cause to believe to be able to give any information relevant to any examination or investigation to answer such questions as the inspector thinks fit to ask. The person answering the questions will be required to sign a declaration of truth to the answers (note the application of the privilege against self-incrimination discussed at pp 488–90 below);

(j) to inspect any information and to take copies – the inspector can require the production of any information that he or she considers necessary, including information held on computer. He or she also has the right to inspect and take copies of such information or any entry in the records;

(k) to require facilities and assistance – here, the inspector can require any person to afford him or her such facilities and assistance with respect to any matters or things within that person's control or in relation to which that person has responsibilities. So, for example, the inspector can require an engineer on the premises to show him or her how the monitoring and testing equipment is working (or not working as the case may be);

(l) any other powers conferred by regulation by the Secretary of State. Certain information can be withheld from the inspector if it is subject to legal professional privilege. This covers correspondence between clients and their solicitors or legal professional advisors.

It is an offence not to comply with the requirements of the inspector or to obstruct him or her in carrying out his or her duty save for offences involving special waste, Environment Agency officials have no power of arrest.

2.4.14 Environmental criminal offences

Command and Control regulation uses the criminal law to help enforce compliance with the provisions of the relevant regulatory regime. A range of criminal offences is built into and forms an intrinsic part of the legislation which created the relevant Command and Control regulatory framework. These criminal law offences and the sanctions associated with them are designed to provide the regulator with the 'muscle' to secure compliance with the law.

Typically, these offences fall into the following categories:

Causing or knowingly permitting pollution	(This is a widely drafted offence which is applicable to both licence holders and non-licensed dischargers.)
Breach of licence conditions	(Targeted at licence holders.)
Breach of statutory duty	(For example, breaching the duty of care with respect to waste.)
Non-compliance with administrative notices issued by the regulator	(Aimed at licence holders who are required to take action in response to an administrative notice served upon them by the regulator. Typically, the regulator will serve an Enforcement Notice requiring full compliance with licence conditions. Alternatively, this offence is relevant to offenders who fail to comply with the terms of an Abatement or similar Notice, such as an Anti-Pollution Works Notice.)

Personal liability of senior company officers, such as directors and managers who consent to or connive in the commission of an offence by their employing company. Liability also extends to offences committed by the company which are attributable to the neglect of a senior company officer.	(It is not possible to imprison a company or similar organisational entity.)

Most of these offences are offences of 'strict liability'. This phrase refers to the fact that the regulator does not need to establish that the polluter knew that what he or she was doing was wrong and would lead to a pollution incident.

Criminal prosecutions are, in practice, sparingly used by the Environment Agency.

2.4.15 Enforcement and prosecution policy

Enforcement is the process by which the regulator ensures that the law, as set out in the relevant Command and Control regulatory regime, is complied with. Enforcement primarily entails the regulator 'policing' the activities regulated by the relevant regime, be they compliance with the terms of a pollution licence or compliance with the terms of an Abatement Notice. Compliance activities also extend to controlling unlicensed polluting activities. Through regular monitoring and inspection visits, the regulator assures itself that the terms of licences and notices are being complied with. In contrast, unlicensed discharges are often identified as a result of information received from the public. These incidents are investigated and dealt with in ways appropriate to the particular circumstances (for example, by issuing a warning, caution, prosecution or requiring the offender to apply for a licence).

The regulator has a discretion (that is, choice) as to how it will enforce compliance with the relevant Command and Control regulatory regime. It has a range of 'tools' available to it to achieve the objectives of the relevant pollution control regime. It may prosecute any person who breaches environmental law or it may use its extensive range of administrative powers to assure compliance with the law. It may not even have to resort to the use of criminal or administrative sanctions since the threat of prosecution and the attendant bad publicity, or the threat of the use of its administrative powers, may be sufficient of themselves to ensure the offender's future observance of the law.

The general public would undoubtedly find it surprising to learn that the regulator does not automatically prosecute each and every violation of environmental law it identifies. In fact, prosecution is the exception rather than the rule. However, the regulator's marked reluctance to prosecute should not be equated with a failure to perform its statutory duties. The regulator aims to ensure a tolerably clean environment and in pursuance of that aim it will choose the tool which it believes is best suited to achieving that end.

Any person who is aggrieved that the regulator has exercised its discretion not to prosecute a polluter will, in most instances, have the option to mount a private prosecution. It is a feature of most UK environmental law that enforcement of the law is not the exclusive province of the regulator; however, relatively few private prosecutions are launched because of a number of practical considerations. Litigation is expensive: in addition to the costs involved in hiring lawyers must be added the cost of gathering evidence to prove the commission of an offence. Expert witnesses are often expensive. The scientific evidence required to prove a case may be complex and contested. If the private prosecutor loses his or her case, then the defendant's costs may be awarded against him or her. Even if the private prosecutor wins the case, the sanction imposed by the courts may be disappointing. In certain circumstances, the threat of mounting a private prosecution may exert sufficient pressure upon the regulator to persuade it to prosecute. It has been suggested that Friends of the Earth's inclination to mount a private prosecution was instrumental in persuading the Environment Agency to prosecute those responsible for the Sea Empress oil pollution (see *Environment Agency v Milford Haven Port Authority and Andrews* (1999)).

The apparent reluctance of regulators to use the formal apparatus of the law to prosecute a polluter may be due to a number of operational constraints. Regulators have limited financial and human resources at their disposal (see Environment Agency annual report and other documents referred to at the end of the chapter as to current resource levels). The regulator may perceive that its resources are better spent in preventive monitoring and the provision of advice and guidance to regulated businesses than in litigation. The regulator may be reluctant to hand over control of the outcome of the case to the courts. This will inevitably happen if a prosecution is launched. Until relatively recently, the courts tended to be lenient in the sanctions which they meted out to polluters. Litigation may also damage the ongoing, co-operational relationship which the regulator has built up, over time, with the licence holder. Finally, regulators possess an increasingly powerful armoury of administrative powers which it is open to them to use to secure the resolution of cases on terms which they, rather than the courts, deem appropriate. Administrative powers such as the service of a Suspension Notice or a Revocation Notice are draconian and have the effect of stopping a business dead in its tracks temporarily or permanently. The use of these powers provides the regulator with flexible tools to control the environmentally damaging impacts of polluters without recourse to the courts.

In 2001, the Environment Agency recorded approximately 34,000 substantiated pollution incidents. There were 118 major incidents (Category 1) and 1,344 significant incidents (Category 2) relating to water and air pollutions. Approximately 32,000 incidents were Category 3 (minor) incidents. The agency served 478 Enforcement Notices and made 1,517 successful charges (one pollution incident may result in several charges). The total penalties in fines amounted to £2.7 million. The average fine per prosecution was £6,410 for companies and £1,290 for individuals. Of the total number of pollution incidents, 13% involved waste management, 11% sewage and the water industry, 10% industry, 8% transport and 7% agriculture.

2.4.15.1 Enforcement styles

Regulators in the UK have traditionally adopted a 'compliance' enforcement policy. The seminal work on compliance enforcement was written by Keith Hawkins in the mid-1980s. In *Environment and Enforcement*, Hawkins explored the foundations of the compliance style of enforcement. Compliance was based on negotiation, conciliation, co-operation and compromise. The regulator, in recognition of the fact that enforcement is an ongoing process, bargained with the polluter to arrive at a solution which 'fixed' the problem which had caused the polluter to breach environmental law in the first place. The objective of the enforcement process was to prevent harm rather than punish wrongdoing. Compliance enforcement is therefore remedial in nature and is chiefly concerned with the attainment of a tolerably clean environment at least cost. Compliance is incremental and recognises that enforcement is not a once and for all response to breaches of environmental law. Over a period of time, the regulator is able to persuade the licence holder to introduce operational improvements which are designed to bring it back into compliance with the conditions of its discharge or operating licence.

Compliance enforcement tends to work precisely because the regulator rarely resorts to prosecution. As Hawkins observed: 'The polluter has goodwill, co-operation and most important, conformity to offer. The enforcement agent may offer in return two important commodities: forbearance and advice.' Generally, only blameworthy breaches of the law result in prosecution. The relevant breach is set in its social context and the blameworthiness of the polluter's conduct is the key to understanding the likely outcome of the enforcement process. Hawkins asserts: 'Pollution control is done in a moral, not a technological world.'

Hawkins identified that a zealous reliance on prosecution could be counter-productive. The regulator was likely to make better progress if it was able to demonstrate an understanding of the polluter's problems and adopted a patient and reasonable stance. In direct contrast to the compliance style of enforcement is the sanctioning, deterrence or penal style of enforcement. The focus here is on coercing the polluter to comply with its legal obligations under threat of prosecution. The law is used to prohibit unacceptable conduct and punish transgressors. Typically, the regulator adopts a confrontational stance in its dealings with offenders. This style of enforcement is common in ordinary policing activities where the prosecutor and offender are unlikely to have an ongoing relationship. In Hawkins' account of compliance enforcement in the water industry, he records a telling comment from a regulatory pollution inspector: 'You can get so much more done by not upsetting people.'

In recent years, a 'third way' enforcement style has emerged which advocates the selection of enforcement tools from both the compliance and sanctioning schools. This enforcement style is captured in Ayres and Braithwaite's *Responsive Regulation*. This approach is based upon a compliance pyramid. At the base of the pyramid are the co-operational tools such as advice and verbal warnings. In the event that the regulator encounters a difficult polluter, it will, over time, increase the pressure on the polluter to comply with its legal obligations by moving up the 'compliance pyramid'. At the apex of the pyramid are criminal prosecutions and the use of administrative notices, such as a Revocation Notice, which will shut the offender down and put him or her out of business.

2.4.15.2 Environment Agency enforcement and prosecution policy

In 1998, the Environment Agency became the first regulatory agency in the UK to publish a publicly accessible enforcement and prosecution policy (the document can be accessed at www.environment-agency.gov.uk). The introduction of the policy will help to standardise the Agency's approach to the enforcement of compliance with the law across all parts of England and Wales. Nevertheless, the existence of the policy will not inhibit the exercise of the Agency's discretion to choose whether or not to prosecute. The Agency will continue to be free to decide on the action which it believes to be an appropriate enforcement response to any breach of the law that it encounters.

The Environment Agency recognises the benefits of using a wide range of enforcement tools including both prosecution and the Agency's administrative powers:

> The use of the criminal process to institute a prosecution is an important part of enforcement. It aims to punish wrongdoing, to avoid a recurrence and to act as a deterrent to others. It follows that it may be appropriate to use prosecution in conjunction with other available enforcement tools, for example, a Prohibition Notice requiring the operation to stop until certain requirements are met. Where the circumstances warrant it, prosecution without prior warning or recourse to alternative sanctions will be pursued [Environment Agency Enforcement and Prosecution Policy, para 19].

The Environment Agency attempts to achieve its mission 'to provide a better environment for England and Wales' by providing education and advice and by regulating activities (para 1).

The Agency states in para 6 of its policy that the purpose of enforcement is to ensure that preventive or remedial action is taken to protect the environment or to secure compliance with a regulatory system.

In deciding the appropriate enforcement action, the Environment Agency is guided by four principles: (a) action will be proportionate to the environmental risks and the seriousness of the breach; (b) whilst like cases should be treated alike (in the interests of consistency) Environment Agency staff will continue to exercise discretion; (c) enforcement action will be targeted at those activities which pose the greatest threat to the environment; and (d) transparency with regard to how the Environment Agency operates and what it expects others to do.

In deciding whether to prosecute, the Environment Agency adopts a two stage test: (a) is the evidence sufficient?; and (b) is a prosecution in the public interest? In regard to the latter limb of the test, the Environment Agency will have regard to the aggravating and mitigating circumstances surrounding the alleged breach. In particular, it will have regard to: the environmental impact of the incident; the foreseeability of the incident; the intent of the offender; the previous history of offending; the attitude of the offender; the deterrent effect of prosecution; and the personal circumstances of the offender.

In regard to offences committed by companies, Environment Agency practice, in most cases, provided it exercises its discretion to prosecute, is to prosecute the company rather than any company employee who was the immediate cause of the offence. Where there is evidence that the offence was committed with the consent of a senior company officer, or the offence was due to a senior officer's neglect, or the senior officer connived at the commission of the offence, then the Environment Agency may also prosecute the senior company officer.

There is a presumption that the Environment Agency will prosecute in any of the following circumstances: incidents or breaches of the law with serious environmental consequences; operating without a licence; excessive or persistent breaches; failure to comply with remedial measures; reckless disregard for management or quality standards; failure to supply information without reasonable excuse or supplying false information; obstructing Environment Agency staff; and impersonating Environment Agency staff.

The Environment, Transport and Regional Affairs Select Committee of the House of Commons criticised the Environment Agency in 2000 for its alleged bias in prosecuting smaller companies rather than larger company polluters.

In 2002, the Agency undertook a consultation regarding a proposal to classify the circumstances in which a licence holder will be adjudged not to be complying with the conditions of its operating licence (see www.environment-agency.gov.uk/commondata/105385/ccsguidance.pdf).

Licences contain two types of conditions: (a) those controlling the amount (that is, numeric limit) of substances that may be discharged into the environment; and (b) other conditions (for example, conditions relating to the operation of the process). The Agency aims to target its enforcement resources on environmentally risky activities rather than instances of trivial non-compliance presenting little or no risk to the environment. Only those instances of non-compliance which cause actual harm (for example, fishkill or detectable smell) will be classified as pollution incidents. Enforcement action will then be guided by the Agency's published Enforcement and Prosecution Policy.

2.4.15.3 Key considerations in enforcement practice

The enforcement style or stance adopted by the regulator in any given case will, to a large extent, depend upon the following factors:

(a) the circumstances surrounding the breach of the law, in particular, the extent of environmental damage, its visibility and the culpability of the polluter. Visible and serious pollution incidents will be picked up by the public and will be reported to the regulator and the media. As regulators function in a political environment, they will be alive to the fact that they need to be perceived as doing their job (as this is perceived by the public – prosecuting polluters) and they will probably prosecute. The more culpable the offender, the more likely it will be that the regulator may have to adopt a sanctioning style of enforcement to punish and deter the offender from future transgressions;

(b) the compliance 'history' of the polluter will be taken into account by the regulator in deciding which enforcement tool to use to bring the polluter back into compliance with the law. If the offender is a problem polluter which shows no inclination to respond to the regulator's previous attempts to help it, the regulator is likely to move up the enforcement pyramid;

(c) the contents of the regulator's publicly available enforcement policy will shape its response to a polluting incident. However, the existence of such a policy can never fetter a regulator's discretion to choose which enforcement tool it prefers to use;

(d) the range and content of the criminal charges available to the regulator is also relevant. The greater the range of offences, the more likely it will be that the regulator will be able to fit the offence to the pollution incident. In addition, as most environmental offences are 'strict liability' offences, the regulator will find it easier to establish liability. Once the regulator has decided to prosecute the polluter, there will be little chance of the polluter successfully mounting a defence. Thus, the threat of prosecution will be a credible threat;

(e) in considering what action to take, especially a prosecution, the regulator will pay attention to the probable consequences of passing the control over the outcome of the case to the courts. Will the sanctions and sentencing options open to the courts have the desired deterrent effect? Are the sanctions available a credible deterrent? Assuming that the regulator has the evidence to establish the offence, it will consider what the outcome of a prosecution is likely to be. It will be unlikely to prosecute if, on conviction, the offender is likely to receive only a minimal fine. Compliance enforcement and the threat of prosecution works better when penalties are credible. Until relatively recently, maximum fines in magistrates' courts (where most cases are heard) were limited to £2,000. These have been increased, for most offences, to £20,000, but the regulator will also bear in mind whether the courts tend to restrict themselves to imposing lower levels of the available maximum. The regulator's view of what would be an appropriate sanction might not reflect the court's view. In addition, the regulator will be influenced by its impressions of the 'environmental awareness' of the courts. Do the courts perceive environmental pollution as morally unacceptable and will they reflect that opprobrium in the sanctions they impose? Too often in the past, the punishment has appeared to the regulator not to fit the crime (see 2.7.3 below on sentencing);

(f) the regulator will have regard to other enforcement tools. The regulator will usually have an extensive range of administrative powers available to it. The impact of an Anti-Pollution Works Notice can be significant – forcing the polluter to acquire and install pollution abatement technology or safeguards. The financial impact of these notices upon the polluter may outstrip the financial impact of the financial sanctions/penalties imposed by the courts. The use of a Notice has certain advantages: (i) the regulator is able to maintain control of the outcome of the case; and (ii) the polluter avoids adverse publicity and is given time to phase in the required improvement. Use of these powers also extends to pro-active preventive measures such as a Works Notice, and remedial powers – clean-up;

(g) there are constraints on the regulator's ability to adopt a sanctioning style of enforcement. Regulators have limited financial and staffing resources (see Environment Agency Corporate Plan 2003–06) which restrict their ability to opt for litigation. Regulators are partly funded from government grants and in the current funding climate large increases in budgets are likely to be minimal. Regulators which adopted a sanctioning enforcement style would soon feel the backlash of industry pressure on government to reign them in;

(h) the extent to which the public, the media, and political parties perceive pollution as a pressing problem impacts upon the regulator's mission. The media report on what concerns the public. Increasingly, pollution is a matter of public concern (see 12.2 below). The more the media reports the adverse impacts of pollution, the more the public becomes sensitised to the issue. This process impacts upon political and legislative processes. Accompanying increases in the public understanding of the causes of pollution are calls for tighter regulation, both at national and EC level. Pollution is no longer perceived as a morally neutral 'quasi-crime' committed by high status white collar criminals. These days, pollution is a crime which attracts just as much opprobrium as street crime. From time to time, the Environment Agency will attempt to harness the damaging impact on businesses of adverse publicity by including the 'worst' polluters in its 'Hall of Shame' (see the Environment Agency website);

(i) the Environment Agency tends to charge the defendant with no more than six offences, unless the circumstances warrant more.

2.4.15.4 *The elements of criminal offences and case law*

In the event that the regulator decides to prosecute a polluter, it must select the relevant offence carefully because it must establish that all the elements of the relevant offence are present before it can hope to secure a conviction. For example, the prosecution of a person for allegedly polluting a watercourse by puncturing a drum of chemicals (raw materials or finished product) and allowing the contents to flow down a bank of a stream and into the stream itself will fail if the prosecutor uses s 85(3) of the WRA 1991 rather than s 85(1). Under s 85(3) of the WRA 1991, it is an offence to discharge trade or sewage effluent into controlled waters. The contents of the drum do not satisfy the 'trade effluent' requirement (unless the contents are waste) and the polluting substance is, arguably, not 'discharged', via a pipe or similar channel, into the stream, so therefore the prosecution must fail. Section 85(1) of the WRA 1991 is a more widely drafted offence, the elements of which would be satisfied by the circumstances described in this example.

Each Command and Control regulatory regime generates a body of case law, some of which is concerned with the interpretation of words and phrases that appear in the primary and secondary legislation establishing the regulatory framework. Each Command and Control regime generates its own case law and great care should therefore be exercised in embarking upon any attempt to apply the judicial reasoning in regard to the meaning of a word or phrase, as it appears in the case law appertaining to one regime, to that of another. Similarly, any word or phrase appearing in a criminal case does not necessarily have the same meaning when the same word appears in a civil case.

2.4.16 Criticisms of the Environment Agency

Most criticisms of the Environment Agency appear to relate to the comparatively small number of prosecutions commenced each year by the Agency against polluters. This could be explained by the fact that many people do not understand the method by which the Agency achieves improvements in environmental quality. As we discussed at 2.4.15.1, the Agency adopts a 'compliance' enforcement policy which views prosecution as a last resort. This is little understood by the general public, which expects the Agency to adopt a penal style of enforcement, using the relevant pollution offences to coerce polluters to comply with environmental law in all pollution incidents investigated.

A number of reports have been critical of the Environment Agency in the following respects: the Agency's poor prosecution record allegedly sending the wrong signal to regulated businesses; the lack of expertise (of staff) in some areas of the Agency's remit; selecting 'easy' targets for prosecution (that is, the smaller companies) rather than the large company polluters with the legal and financial resources to 'take on' the Agency; the failure of the Agency to become the public's environmental champion; and the reluctance of the Agency to enter into debate with the government, business and the public with regard to important environmental debates (for example, the genetically modified organisms (GMO) debate) (see House of Commons Select Committee on the Environment, Transport and Regions, *Inquiry into the Workings of the Environment Agency,* 6th Report, HC 484 (1997–98) and House of Commons Environment Select Committee, *The Environmental Impact of Cement Manufacture,* HC 124 (1996–97)).

A more balanced view of the House of Commons Environment Select Committee would have been obtained by paying attention to the improvements in environmental quality recorded in the Agency's annual report and other corporate documentation.

2.5   THE LOCAL AUTHORITIES

Despite the creation of the Environment Agency, local authorities continue to play a key role in environmental protection. The provisions of the EA 1995 have, however, transferred the functions of the WRAs, previously carried out by the local authorities, to the Environment Agency. Other than that significant transfer of responsibilities, the EA 1995 has done little to affect the overall functions of the local authorities save that local authorities play a key part in the regulation of contaminated land.

Local authorities are involved in various aspects of environmental protection which are described more fully in other parts of this book. This section intends only to provide a brief overview of the main environmental protection functions carried out by local authorities:

(a) local authorities are responsible for the planning control system (under the town and country planning legislation) which requires local planning authorities to take environmental considerations into account in the preparation of development plans and also in respect of planning applications;

(b) district councils are responsible for investigating and abating statutory nuisances under Pt III of the EPA 1990. For many, the statutory nuisance provisions represent the very localised aspect of pollution control, where polluting incidents in their very widest sense (noise, smells, animals) are controlled by the local authorities responding to complaints;

(c) local authorities are responsible under the Clean Air Act (CAA) 1993 for controlling emissions of dark smoke and they also have the power to control smoke emissions through the creation of Smoke Control Areas;

(d) local authorities are responsible for authorising the atmospheric emissions of certain prescribed processes under Pt I of the EPA 1990 and the environmental impacts of Part A2 installations and atmospheric emissions of Part B installations under the PPCA 1999;

(e) local authorities are responsible for identifying areas of contaminated land under the provisions of Pt IIA of the EPA 1990 (inserted into the EPA 1990 by s 57 of the EA 1995). Sites which are designated as contaminated under the provisions of the Act fall under the regulatory control of the local authority unless the authority determines that the site is a special site, in which case the Environment Agency is the relevant enforcing authority. Part IIA of the EPA 1990 empowers local authorities and the Environment Agency to serve Remediation Notices on appropriate persons in order to secure the clean-up of contaminated sites;

(f) county councils, or in the metropolitan areas the district councils or London borough councils, have responsibilities as Hazardous Substances Authorities under the provisions of the Planning (Hazardous Substances) Act 1990.

2.6   OTHER BODIES CONCERNED WITH ENVIRONMENTAL PROTECTION

In addition to the Environment Agency, the large privatised water and sewerage companies, and the local authorities, a number of governmental or statutory organisations play a role in relation to environmental protection either in terms of promoting new legislation, acting in an advisory capacity or dealing with environmental regulation more indirectly. We now consider the role of these organisations.

2.6.1   The Department for Environment, Food and Rural Affairs (DEFRA)

DEFRA (formerly the DoE) has principal responsibility for environmental legislation and policy and also for promoting new environmental legislation. It is responsible for issuing many of the regulations which provide the detailed mechanisms for environmental control. The Department also issues various guidance notes and circulars which are intended to assist either the regulatory authorities or applicants seeking consents from the various bodies.

Organisationally, DEFRA has a number of specialist divisions dealing with the various aspects of environmental law (readers should access the DEFRA website to note changes to DEFRA's organisational structure). These are:

(a) the Directorate of Environmental Policy and Analysis, which is responsible for environmental policy and also provides the main interface with the EU;

(b) the Directorate of Pollution Control and Wastes, which deals with all aspects relating to waste policy and law. The directorate is responsible, in particular, for overseeing the waste management licensing system and provides guidance to the agency and the waste industry;

(c) the Directorate of Air, Climate and Toxic Substances, which is responsible for a wide range of activities, including air pollution (it supervises the activities of the local authorities in respect of their air pollution control activities) and chemical safety;

(d) the Water Directorate, which is responsible for overseeing all aspects of water supply and water quality;

(e) the Rural Affairs Directorate, which deals with wildlife and habitat conservation, National Parks, access to the countryside and Sites of Special Scientific Interest.

The Department's stated aims for environmental protection are to:

(a) promote sustainable development;

(b) ensure prudent use of natural resources and to minimise waste;

(c) prevent and minimise pollution of air, land and water in cost-effective ways;

(d) increase informed public participation in environmental decision making and the involvement of all sectors, especially business;

(e) ensure environmental concerns are reflected in all the government's work both at the national and international level;

(f) reduce the burden of regulation and make markets work for the environment;

(g) protect the environment, and save money, by encouraging better management methods and by promoting the cost-effective use of energy.

2.6.2 The Secretary of State for the Environment, Food and Rural Affairs

A glance through most of the chapters of this book will show that the Secretary of State for the Environment, Food and Rural Affairs plays a key role in regulating environmental protection. This involves, *inter alia*:

(a) dealing with appeals against decisions of the enforcement agencies;

(b) issuing directions, for example, to the Environment Agency concerning applications or to meet various EC legal obligations;

(c) exercising various discretionary powers, for example, in the designation of Special Protection Areas under the Habitats Directive;

(d) reviewing waste disposal plans and waste recycling plans. Following the re-election of the Labour government in 2001, the government restructured a number of government departments. The Department of Environment, Transport and the Regions (DETR) was amalgamated with the Ministry of Agriculture, Fisheries and Food (MAFF) to form the Department of Environment, Food and Rural Affairs (DEFRA). This resulted in the separation of environmental protection and the planning system.

2.6.3 Other government departments

Although DEFRA is the lead department for environmental policy, other government departments have a significant role to play. It is established government policy that all government departments are under a duty to ensure that environmental considerations are taken into account in the development of all policies and programmes.

2.6.4 The Royal Commission on Environmental Pollution

The Royal Commission on Environmental Pollution (RCEP) was established in February 1970 as a standing body to 'advise on matters, both national and international, concerning the pollution of the environment; on the adequacy of research in this field; and the future possibilities of danger to the environment'. It is a permanent body made up of experts in environmental matters who are appointed on the advice of the Prime Minister.

The Royal Commission has played an extremely important role in the development of current environmental legislation, not least because of its expert advice and also because it has had the opportunity to give objective advice on different choices to be made/actions to be taken. The Royal Commission has published a number of reports that provide a valuable insight into a variety of environmental problems and invariably set the agenda for debate and consultation. The reports are intended to give advice to government but, in fact, they have been very influential on UK environmental policy. (All the reports can be accessed via the RCEP's website: see p 26.)

2.6.5 Sewerage undertakers

The sewerage network is operated by the privatised water and sewerage services companies, known as sewerage undertakers. Notwithstanding the fact that they operate as private companies, the sewerage undertakers are responsible for licensing discharges into public sewers through the system of trade effluent consents (see the WIA 1991). The disposal of trade effluent into a sewer (through a drain or sewer) requires a consent under s 118 of the WIA 1991. A consent must be obtained by serving a notice on the sewerage undertaker.

2.6.6 The Office of Water Services

The Office of Water Services (OFWAT) was established in 1989 following privatisation of the water supply industry. Its principal function is to regulate the water supply industry in 'the public interest'. Although OFWAT is not specifically an environmental body, it is required to ensure that the water undertakers have regard to their general environmental duties as laid down in the WIA 1991.

2.6.7 The Health and Safety Executive

The Health and Safety Executive (HSE) is responsible for the administration of the HSWA 1974. However, the boundaries between health and safety of workers and protection of the environment are not always clear and the HSE in fact fulfils a number of functions related to environmental protection. In particular, the HSE is involved in the regulation of certain activities in the workplace which if not carried out properly could have serious environmental consequences. These include the regulation of installations handling hazardous substances such as asbestos. In addition, the HSE acts as a statutory consultee in relation to applications for IPC authorisation and IPPC permits.

2.6.8   English Nature and the Countryside Council for Wales

Part VII of the EPA 1990 created the Nature Conservancy Council for England (known as English Nature) and the Countryside Council for Wales out of the former Nature Conservancy Council. English Nature operates in England and the Countryside Council operates in Wales. English Nature does not have any pollution control powers or means of enforcement. Instead, it acts as the government's statutory scientific advisory body on nature conservation and is responsible for promoting nature conservation generally (especially the designation and regulation of Sites of Special Scientific Interest). The powers of English Nature are mainly contained in the Wildlife and Countryside Act 1981 as amended and the Countryside and Rights of Way Act 2000.

2.6.9   The European Environment Agency

The European Environment Agency (EEA) was set up in 1994 following the adoption by the Council of Ministers in May 1990 of Council Regulation 1210/90 EEC. After considerable debate as to where it should be located, it was eventually decided that it should be based in Copenhagen. The functions of the Agency are as follows:

(a) to provide the Member States with objective, reliable and comparable information about the environment;

(b) to ensure that the public is properly informed about the state of the environment.

The Management Board of the EEA is made up of one representative from each Member State, two representatives from the European Commission and a further two designated by the European Parliament. However, membership of the EEA is not confined to Member States of the European Union (EU) and other non-EU countries may join.

The main criticism of the EEA, as it currently exists, is that it has no role to play in the enforcement of environmental law. Its role is limited essentially to that of gathering and disseminating information on the state of the environment. The EEA is assisted by the European Environment Information and Observation Network which was set up to assist in the collection of information throughout the Member States and effectively links the environmental networks of the Member States into a Community-wide network. (See the EEA website address at the end of Chapter 1.)

2.6.10 Parliamentary select committees (of both the House of Commons and House of Lords)

The primary select committee with an environmental remit is the House of Commons Select Committee on Environment, Food and Rural Affairs. Its function is to scrutinise draft legislation and government environmental policy, and to audit the performance (plus expenditure) of relevant government departments and regulators. Although each select committee controls its own agenda, some criticism has been levelled at them because membership of select committees is controlled by the government.

2.6.11 The Advisory Committee on Business and the Environment

Created in 1991, the Committee informs the government on industry's views on environmental issues, especially where these issues impact upon business performance (for example, the impact of new EC directives). Members of the Committee are appointed by government (by the Secretary of State for Trade and Industry and the Deputy Prime Minister).

2.6.12 Commission on Sustainable Development

The Commission was created in 2000 and comprises 22 members drawn from the government, industry, NGOs and the university sector. It replaces the Round Table on Sustainable Development and the UK Panel on Sustainable Development, and its functions are: (a) to review progress 'across all relevant fields' in regard to the attainment of sustainable development; (b) to promote awareness of sustainable development; (c) to promote agreement amongst stakeholders on sustainability-related issues; and (d) to identify government policies which undermine sustainability and suggest necessary remedial action. (See the website address at p 27 above.)

2.7 THE ROLE OF THE COURTS IN THE ADMINISTRATION AND ENFORCEMENT OF ENVIRONMENTAL LAW

2.7.1 The principal functions

The courts have four principal functions with regard to environmental law and litigation:

(a) an adjudicatory role;

(b) sentencing;

(c) an interpretative role; and

(d) a supervisory role.

2.7.2 Adjudication

The chief function of the courts is to reach decisions on the merits of the cases which come before them. As we endeavour to explain in this book, much of environmental law is about the regulation of human activity and the principal vehicle which is used to regulate activities such as the discharge of polluting emissions and the use of resources (such as land for building purposes) is the Command and Control regulatory regime. Each regulatory regime is underpinned by criminal law offences and, to a lesser degree, civil powers to remediate environmental damage.

The courts are called upon to adjudicate on disputes involving the operation of regulatory regimes, be they prosecutions commenced by the regulators for criminal law offences or the use of civil powers by regulators to force those persons responsible for environmental damage to engage in 'clean-up' operations. The courts also adjudicate upon actions commenced by private persons. These actions may be civil actions, based on the common law, whose function is to compensate the claimant for damage to person or property, or they may comprise challenges to the decisions of regulators. In addition, private persons may take advantage of the criminal laws contained in the legislation establishing regulatory Command and Control regimes to mount their own prosecutions of polluters.

Once the courts have adjudicated upon an environmental dispute, be it a criminal prosecution by the Environment Agency or a civil action brought by a private individual, it will, on conviction in a criminal prosecution, impose a penalty or, in the case of a civil action, make an award of compensation or other relief. The sentencing policy of the courts plays an important part in ensuring compliance with Command and Control regulation and it is to a consideration of this that we now turn.

2.7.3 Sentencing

Criticism has, for many years, been levelled at the minimal penalties imposed on defendants in criminal prosecutions arising out of breaches of environmental law. It is only relatively recently that significant financial penalties have been imposed on some defendants; nevertheless, the perception persists that the courts, especially the magistrates' courts, are too lenient.

2.7.3.1 *Judicial guidance*

In 1998, the Court of Appeal decision in *R v F Howe & Son (Engineers) Ltd* (1999) shed some light on sentencing policy. In *Howe,* the defendant appealed against a fine of £42,000 imposed upon it by the Crown Court on conviction of breaches of s 2(1) of the HSWA 1974 and reg 4(2) of the Electricity at Work Regulations 1989, which caused the death of a workman. The Court of Appeal observed that the level of fines imposed in health and safety cases was generally too low and it went on to set out a number of sentencing guidelines. In particular, the court identified a number of factors which were relevant to fixing an appropriate penalty:

(a) although it is often a matter of chance, in a health and safety incident, whether death or injury results from breach of the law, where death is the consequence, courts should regard death as an aggravating feature of the offence and the penalty imposed on the defendant should reflect public concern at the unnecessary loss of life;

(b) a deliberate breach of health and safety legislation with a view to cutting costs or maximising profits will seriously aggravate the offence charged;

(c) a failure to heed warnings is a seriously aggravating feature of an offence;

(d) mitigating features include a prompt admission of responsibility and guilty plea, prompt action to remedy deficiencies after they are brought to the attention of the defendant, and a good safety record.

The court indicated that the same standards would be expected to be attained regardless of the size and resources of a defendant company. It would also be open to the defendant to make submissions to the court with regard to the level of the financial penalty to be imposed upon conviction and its ability to pay, provided it produced its accounts well before the hearing. Although the *Howe* case is a health and safety case, it is likely to be an influential guideline in the sentencing of environmental crimes.

In *R v Yorkshire Water Services Ltd* (2001), the Court of Appeal refined our understanding of the level of appropriate sanctions in the context of a breach of the law which affected a large number of people. Yorkshire Water had been fined £119,000 by Leeds Crown Court on 17 counts of supplying water unfit for human consumption (smelly and discoloured water) contrary to s 70(1) of the WIA 1991. The court affirmed the use of the sentencing principles in *Howe*. The fine was reduced to £80,000 because the Crown Court should not have used the number of complainants (affected water customers) as a factor in multiplying the penalty imposed. Thus, a single incident, such as supplying unfit water (or a single pollution incident) may give rise to many breaches of the law (for example, unfit water supplied to many individual households or a pollution exceeding several conditions of an operating licence), but the number of breaches may not be aggregated to produce a fine which is, in the circumstances, inappropriate.

R v Friskies Petcare UK Ltd (2000) establishes important guidelines as to the appropriate penalty to impose in the event of a 'guilty' plea. The important facts of the case, including aggravating and mitigating circumstances, are to be agreed by the prosecution and the defence and then presented to the court for sentence in the form of schedules. This clarifies the basis upon which the court imposes the relevant penalty and therefore assists the higher courts in the event that there is an appeal against sentence. In addition, it will assist the magistrates' court in deciding whether to commit the case to the Crown Court for sentence.

The HSE has published a document detailing its policy with regard to the prosecution of individuals. This document is likely to be influential in an environmental context. The document is not yet available on the HSE's website but is available via the website of the Centre for Corporate Accountability (www.corporateaccountability.org/press_releases/2003/Aug18.htm).

2.7.3.2 Sentencing Advisory Panel guidance

It is also significant that the Sentencing Advisory Panel has been actively investigating sentencing policy with regard to a number of pollution offences. These include: polluting controlled waters; treating, depositing or disposing of waste without a waste management licence; carrying out a prescribed IPC process without a licence or in breach of licence conditions; and breach of the packaging recycling and recovery obligations. The Sentencing Advisory Panel recommends that a distinction in sentencing be made between individual defendants and companies. It proposes that the starting point for the sentencing of individuals should be the fine, in recognition of the fact that pollution offences are generally non-violent and often result from the failure to devote adequate resources to preventing a breach of the law. The Panel recommends that the culpability of the defendant be assessed on the basis of how far the defendant's conduct fell below the requisite standard. In determining the culpability of the defendant, it is recommended that the court have regard to: whether the offence was deliberate; whether the defendant broke the law in order to make a commercial profit; whether the relevant breach of the law is part of a pattern of offending; whether the defendant has ignored advice provided by the regulator; whether the defendant ignored concerns expressed by its employees; and whether the defendant has special knowledge of the risks posed by its activities. The Panel has proposed that the fine should reflect the ability of the defendant to pay: 'The fine should be substantial enough to have real economic impact which, together with the attendant bad publicity resulting from prosecution, will create sufficient pressure on management and shareholders to tighten regulatory compliance and change company policy.' With regard to smaller companies, the panel noted that a large fine might have a crippling effect on the company, an adverse impact on the local economy, and might interfere with the company's attempts to bring itself back into compliance with the law. With regard to companies which commit pollution offences, the courts are limited in the sentences they can impose. In virtually all cases, a fine is imposed. In the case of human offenders, in addition to the ubiquitous fine, the courts have a number of other sentencing options at their disposal, including the following: absolute discharge, conditional discharge, community service, probation, suspended sentence, disqualification under the Disqualification of Directors Act 1986 (with regard to company directors) and imprisonment. The use of disqualification is rare but was used in 2000 on the conviction of the managing director of a pharmaceutical company, who was disqualified for four years.

2.7.3.3 Magistrates' courts sentencing guidelines

The Magistrates' Association issued guidance to all magistrates in May 2001 entitled 'Fining Companies for Environmental and Health and Safety Offences'. This guidance is significant as the vast majority of environmental incidents which the courts encounter are dealt with in the magistrates' courts. The guidance draws the attention of magistrates to the much higher public profile of environmental and health and safety offences. This increased level of public concern is reflected in the 'greatly increased' fines which may be imposed on the convicted offender. Magistrates are reminded that their aim should be to ensure that any fine imposed should have equal impact on the convicted offender, bearing in mind the relative financial positions of multi-national companies with huge annual turnovers and individuals. The public must feel confident that convicted companies receive proper and meaningful penalties. Public disquiet at the low level of penalties led the Lord Chancellor to remind magistrates in 1998 that they 'should not flinch' from using maximum penalties if magistrates believed that they were deserved in the particular circumstances.

The guidance refers to the sentencing guidance provided by the higher courts in the cases of *R v Howe and Son (Engineers) Ltd* and *R v Friskies Petcare UK Ltd*, and also to the Sentencing Advisory Panel's advice on sentencing in environmental cases.

If the offence before the magistrates' court is an 'either way' offence (that is, it can be tried in either the magistrates' court or the Crown Court), magistrates must consider whether their sentencing powers are adequate and, if not, the case should be committed to the Crown Court. If the matter is dealt with by the magistrates, the sanction on conviction will usually be a fine. Although environmental offences can cause or risk death, serious injury or ill health, they are 'non-violent' and will generally not pose a continuing threat because the Environment Agency will have used its administrative powers to address these issues. Offences dealt with in the magistrates' court will often be committed in circumstances in which the offender failed to devote adequate resources to prevent a breach of the law and, in such cases, a financial penalty is appropriate.

In assessing an appropriate penalty, magistrates will pay particular attention to the seriousness of the offence. This is 'calculated' by weighing up the aggravating and mitigating features of the offence. The main aggravating factors are: deliberate or reckless breach of the law; action or inaction prompted by financial considerations (profit or cost saving); disregard of Environment Agency warnings or warnings by employees; awareness of the risk leading to a breach of the law; non co-operation with the Environment Agency; the extent of environmental damage; a previous history of offending; adverse human impacts – death, injury or ill health; adverse impacts on flora and fauna; expensive clean-up works required; activities causing unlicensed pollution; and interference with the lawful activities of others. Mitigating factors include: isolated incident/lapse; genuine lack of awareness of wrongdoing (for example, the regulations); the offender playing a minor role in the incident and having little personal responsibility; prompt reporting of the incident to the Environment Agency; co-operating with the Environment Agency; a good previous record; and a timely plea of 'guilty'.

In imposing a fine, magistrates, in line with the principles of the Criminal Justice Act 1991, must have regard to the seriousness of the offence and the defendant's financial circumstances (plus any advice sought from the court clerk). The fine should reflect the culpability of the offender and a high fine is justified even where the damage which actually occurred was less than was the probable result of the offence. The fine will reflect any economic advantage enjoyed by the offender (for example, by failing to expend resources on preventive measures). Where the offender is a company, the finances of the company should receive careful consideration. Turnover, profitability and liquidity should all be considered and the use of expert accountancy evidence may be necessary in order to determine the appropriate penalty. It is essential that companies provide their financial accounts. If they fail to do so, the court is entitled to assume that the offender can pay whatever fine is imposed. With regard to small companies, fines may be paid by instalments if this is necessary to avoid unduly burdening the company. Magistrates are cautioned not to impose a fine which will result in the offending company going into liquidation, with consequent loss of employment.

Whatever the size of the company, the fine should be large enough to make a financial impact on the company. Magistrates may also have regard to the effects of bad publicity upon the company which may pressurise the management and shareholders to improve compliance with the law. In the case of larger companies, magistrates should 'fix' a penalty near the maximum before considering aggravating and mitigating factors.

Other sentencing options include an absolute or conditional discharge, a compensation order of up to £5,000 if a victim of the offence has suffered loss or damage, personal liability of senior company officers (see, for example, s 157 of the EPA 1990 and s 217 of the WRA 1991), and disqualification of directors under the Company Directors Disqualification Act 1986.

In addition to the impact of a fine, the offender will, in most cases, be ordered to pay the prosecution's costs. These costs may be very significant, especially if the offence has involved the Environment Agency in extensive investigation and remediation works. An order of costs must not be disproportionate to the fine imposed. If the fine, compensation (if any) and costs exceed the ability of the offender to pay, the level of costs is to be reduced rather than the fine.

2.7.4 Interpretative role

The courts have an important role in the interpretation of words and phrases which appear in primary and secondary legislation. In addition, they have a similar role with regard to the interpretation and application of common law principles in civil actions.

For example, the House of Lords has given the meaning of 'causing' in s 85 of the WRA 1991 a very strict interpretation in the context of a criminal offence whose purpose is to punish any person who causes pollution of controlled waters (see *Empress Cars (Abertillery) Ltd v NRA* (1998)). Similarly, in *Cambridge Water Co Ltd v Eastern Counties Leather plc* (1994), the House of Lords gave detailed consideration to the application of a civil claim, relating to pollution of an aquifer, based on the common law torts of nuisance and the rule in *Rylands v Fletcher* (1868).

2.7.5 Supervisory role

The High Court, Court of Appeal and House of Lords exercise, with regard to public bodies such as regulators, a supervisory jurisdiction. This entails the consideration of judicial review challenges by persons who are aggrieved by the outcome of decisions made by public bodies. In a judicial review action, the court reviews the process by which the decision was made in order to confirm that it was not made in an unlawful manner. In other words, the court supervises how the relevant administrative decision was arrived at. In an environmental context, judicial review challenges often relate to the granting of licences, such as water pollution discharge consents, or decisions relating to the enforcement of the law (such as the Environment Agency choosing not to prosecute a polluter). Applications for judicial review are usually based on one or more of the following grounds.

2.7.5.1 Illegality

Under this heading, it is alleged that a public body, such as the Environment Agency, has not acted in accordance with its legal powers, either because it has misunderstood them or because it has deliberately ignored them.

2.7.5.2 Procedural flaw

The public body fails to follow the correct procedure in reaching a decision.

2.7.5.3 Relevant and irrelevant considerations

The public body takes into account something which it should have disregarded or it fails to take into account something which it was required to take into account. This applies only where the matters considered or ignored are set out in or implied by statute.

2.7.5.4 Irrationality

This ground applies where no reasonable public body, which understood the relevant law and faced the same set of circumstances, could have acted in the way in which the public body in question has acted.

2.7.5.5 Procedural unfairness

Under this heading, it is alleged that the process by which a decision has been reached by a public body is unfair. This could include failing to allow someone who has a 'legitimate expectation', arising either from an express promise by a public authority or from the existence of a regular practice which the applicant can reasonably expect to continue, to participate in the decision making process, for example, by giving him or her an opportunity to make representations to the public body before it reaches its decision.

2.7.5.6 Improper delegation of powers

The public body has purported to delegate powers to someone which only it can exercise. For example, this might involve the attempted delegation of authority to make decisions relating to the grant or refusal of pollution licences.

2.7.5.7 Who can bring a judicial review action?

In order to bring a judicial review action, a person (individual, company, etc) must demonstrate that he or she has *locus standi* or, in other words, the right to bring the action. The test laid down for 'standing', as it is referred to, appears in Pt 54 of the CPR (formerly Ord 53, r 3(7) of the Rules of the Supreme Court). The applicant must show 'sufficient interest in the matter to which the application relates'. An applicant whose direct personal interests have been affected by the decision of a public body will have standing to challenge the decision. In addition, the court may also allow a challenge by a person, group or organisation acting in the public interest. Whether such a person, group or organisation has standing depends upon a variety of factors, including the importance of the legal issues at stake, the absence of any other responsible challenger, the nature of the alleged breach of duty against which the challenge is made, and the previous involvement and reputation of the applicant with regard to the issue which forms the basis of the challenge. Over the last few years, the High Court has shown an increased willingness to grant standing to environmental organisations to enable them to challenge the decisions of regulators. In *R v HM Inspectorate of Pollution and Another ex p Greenpeace Ltd (No 2)* (1994), the court granted Greenpeace standing to challenge the decision of HMIP to grant a licence authorising the operational activities of a nuclear reprocessing plant because Greenpeace was 'an entirely responsible and respected body with a genuine concern for the environment ... who, with its particular experience in environmental matters, its access to experts in the relevant realms of science and technology not to mention law, is able to mount a carefully selected, focused, relevant, and well argued challenge'.

2.7.5.8 Speed

Applications for judicial review must be made 'promptly'. This requirement means, in most cases, that the application must be lodged with the court within three months of the decision or activity which forms the basis of the complaint. The use of strict time limits enables developments with environmental impacts to proceed without the constant threat of challenge at a late stage in the projects' completion. In *R v Secretary of State for Trade and Industry ex p Greenpeace Ltd* (1998), leave to commence a judicial review action was refused because of undue delay. Laws J observed that 'the courts have very firmly stated that a judicial review applicant must proceed with particular urgency where third party interests are involved'.

2.7.5.9 Relief

Upon a successful challenge, the court may make any of the following orders.

An order of certiorari cancels a decision of a public body which is invalid or has been made improperly. The court may order the matter be sent back to the body which made the original decision so that the matter may be reconsidered using the correct procedure. An order of mandamus compels a public body to carry out specified actions in accordance with the legal duties to which it is subject. An order of prohibition restrains a public body from acting in a particular way.

The court may also make a declaration of the correct legal position and may award damages.

2.7.6   A specialist environmental court?

There has been some debate with regard to the establishment of a specialist court to deal with environmental cases based on the model of the environmental courts which operate in New Zealand and some Australian States. The government appointed Professor Malcolm Grant in the late 1990s to investigate the case for such a court. The Grant Report was published in 2000, since which time the government has shown no desire to take the idea further. This may, to some extent, be due to the fact that most environmental prosecutions are dealt with in magistrates' courts and steps have been taken to bring magistrates up to speed on environmental issues and appropriate penalties to impose on conviction (see 2.7.3.3 above).

The DEFRA funded research report, *Modernising Environmental Justice: Regulation and the Role of an Environmental Tribunal,* has now been published. The report recommends the establishment of a specialist tribunal to hear environmental appeals (see www.ucl.ac.uk/laws/environment and also the 23rd Report of the RCEP – *Environmental Planning*).

2.8   FURTHER INFORMATION

For the Environment Agency's enforcement and prosecution policy, go to the Agency's website (www.environment-agency.gov.uk) and type 'prosecution policy' in the search facility box.

Further reading

Ayres, I and Braithwaite, J, *Responsive Regulation: Transcending the Deregulation Debate*, 1992, OUP.

Baldwin, R and Cave, M, *Understanding Regulation*, 1999, OUP.

Bardach, E and Kagan, R, *Going by the Book: The Problem of Regulatory Unreasonableness*, 1982, Temple UP.

Braithwaite, J, *To Punish or Persuade: Enforcement of Coal Mine Safety*, 1985, New York UP.

De Prez, P, 'Excuses, excuses: the ritual trivialisation of environmental prosecutions' [2001] JEL 65.

Dimento, J, *Environmental Law and American Business: Dilemmas of Compliance*, 1986, Plenum Press.

Gouldson, A and Murphy, J, *Regulatory Realities: The Implementation and Impact of Industrial Environmental Regulation*, 1998, Earthscan.

Grant, M, *Environmental Court Project: Final Report*, 2000, DETR.

Gunningham, N and Grobosky, P (eds), *Smart Regulation: Designing Environmental Policy*, 1998, Clarendon.

Hawkins, K, *Environment and Enforcement: Regulation and the Social Definition of Pollution*, 1984, Clarendon.

Hawkins, K and Tomas, J, *Enforcing Regulation*, 1984, Kluwer-Nijhoff.

Hawkins, K, *Law as Last Resort*, 2001, OUP.

Hilson, C, *Regulating Pollution: A UK and EC Perspective*, 2000, Hart.

House of Lords Select Committee on the European Communities (1991–92 Session), *Implementation and Enforcement of Environmental Legislation*, 9th Report, HMSO.

House of Commons Environment, Transport and Rural Affairs Committee (1999–2000 Session), *The Environment Agency*, 6th Report, The Stationery Office.

Hutter, B, *A Reader in Environmental Law*, 1997, OUP.

Hutter, B, *The Reasonable Arm of the Law*, 1988, Clarendon.

Ogus, A, *Regulation*, 1994, OUP.

Richardson, G, Ogus, A and Burrows, P, *Policing Pollution: A Study of Regulation and Enforcement*, 1982, Clarendon.

Ricketts, M and Peacock, A, *The Regulation Game: How British and West German Companies Bargain with Government*, 1984, Blackwell.

Rowan-Robinson, J and Ross, A, 'The enforcement of environmental regulation in Britain' [1984] JPL 200.

Sandhovel, A, 'What can be achieved by using instruments of self-regulation in environmental policy-making?' (1998) EELR 83.

Steinzor, R, 'Reinventing regulation: the dangerous journey from command to self-control' (1998) Harvard Environmental Law Review 103.

Sinclair, D, 'Self-regulation versus command and control? Beyond false dichotomies' (1997) Law and Policy 529.

Vogel, D, *National Styles of Regulation*, 1986, Cornell UP.

Wilson, W, *Making Environmental Laws Work*, 1999, Hart.

CHAPTER 3

EUROPEAN COMMUNITY ENVIRONMENTAL LAW AND POLICY

3.1 INTRODUCTION

In order fully to appreciate the pace of change and development of environmental law in the UK, we need to consider the role played by European Community (EC) environmental law. The impact of EC environmental law and policy on national environmental law and policy is huge. Over 300 separate measures have been created by the EC which Member States have been obliged to incorporate into their own legal systems. The Royal Commission on Environmental Pollution (RCEP) has established that 80% of environmental law in the UK derives from European law.

In the UK, the significance of the EC is masked because most EC environmental measures take the form of directives which are transposed into UK law by means of statutory instruments. Without doubt, the EC is the most important factor which is 'driving' the development of UK environmental law and, because of its central importance, the student of UK environmental law should study not only the wide range of separate EC-generated environmental laws which currently exist, but also the process by which EC environmental law is created, enforced and challenged.

This chapter examines the institutional arrangements within the EC with reference to the environment; it covers the legislative procedures, enforcement of Community law, the effect of Community law in the domestic legal system and EC environmental policy. These issues are clearly of importance, but it is not appropriate in a textbook on environmental law to include lengthy discussion of all of the issues involved and therefore readers are recommended to consult an EC law textbook for detailed analysis.

This chapter is concerned with EC environmental law and policy and deals with the following issues:

(a) the development of the EC's environmental policy and law. In particular, it considers how the EC has become a key actor in the environment field, although in its early years it had no legal basis on which to do so. Consideration is also given to the relationship between the EC's environmental programme and other areas of EC law, in particular the aim to achieve a common market in which goods and services can move freely. The issue of whether Member States can introduce more stringent environmental laws than those laid down by the EC is also dealt with;

(b) the substantive nature of EC environmental policy and some of the principal features of the Fifth and Sixth Environmental Action Programmes. The chapter highlights some of the key environmental directives which are considered elsewhere in this book.

3.2 THE DEVELOPMENT OF THE EUROPEAN UNION (EU)

The European Economic Community (EEC) was established by the Treaty of Rome in 1957. Since that time, the EU has grown from an initial membership of six

(Belgium, France, West Germany, the Netherlands, Luxembourg and Italy) to 15 following the accession of the UK, Denmark and Ireland in 1973, Greece in 1979, Spain and Portugal in 1986 and Austria, Finland and Sweden in January 1995. Following German reunification in 1989, East Germany was absorbed into the Community, subject to certain special transitional arrangements. It was anticipated that Norway would join at the same time as Austria, Finland and Sweden but following a 'no vote' in the Norwegian referendum, the Norwegian government was not able to proceed to membership.

After successfully growing from six to 15 members, the EU is now preparing for its biggest enlargement ever in terms of scope and diversity. Thirteen countries have applied to become new members. Ten of these countries (Cyprus, the Czech Republic, Estonia, Hungary, Latvia, Lithuania, Malta, Poland, the Slovak Republic and Slovenia) are set to join on 1 May 2004. They are currently known by the term 'acceding countries'. Bulgaria and Romania hope to do so by 2007, while Turkey is not currently negotiating its membership. Enlargement will pose major challenges for the European Union, which has already begun the process of preparing for the arrival of the new members by making the institutional changes necessary for accommodating the new States. One of the criteria for membership is the ability to take on the obligations of membership, including Community laws and policies.

3.2.1   From EEC to EC

Not only has the EC grown in size, it has also considerably increased its spheres of influence by becoming very much more than an association of States pursuing economic goals. The Community can now legitimately take action in a range of areas, including environmental protection, which were never envisaged as Community interests in its formative years. The Treaty of Rome has been amended by the Single European Act (SEA) 1986, the Treaty on European Union (TEU) signed at Maastricht on 7 February 1992 and which took effect in November 1993, the Treaty of Amsterdam (ToA) in 1997 and the Treaty of Nice (ToN) in 2000. The SEA 1986 introduced a number of significant changes to the Rome Treaty designed to speed up the decision making process in Europe so that a programme of over 280 measures could be enacted in order to create the Single European Market by the self-imposed deadline of 31 December 1992. The SEA 1986 also established for the first time that the Community could legitimately take action in the field of environmental protection.

The TEU was an altogether more complex Treaty. On the one hand, it created the EU which essentially is an institutional framework for political inter-governmental co-operation between the Member States. However, the TEU also amended the EEC Treaty itself. Article G of the TEU introduced significant amendments to the EEC Treaty in relation to Community interests, and also procedural changes (the main one being the creation of a new legislative procedure which strengthened the power of the Parliament). A further significant change brought about by the TEU was the change in the name of the EEC to the EC. This change of name is more than symbolic and reflects the fact that the Community had developed to such an extent that it could no longer be regarded simply as an economic community pursuing economic goals.

3.3   THE AIMS OF THE EC

Article 2 of the EC Treaty, which lays down the aims of the EC and as such is pivotal in determining the legal competences of the EC institutions, has been amended by the SEA 1986, the TEU 1993, the ToA 1997 and the ToN 2000. In 1957, the Treaty of Rome stated that the task of the EC was to establish a common market, progressively approximating the economic policies of the Member States to promote throughout the EC a 'harmonious development of economic activities, a continuous and balanced expansion, an increase in stability, an accelerated raising of the standard of living and closer relations between the States belonging to it'. Following the amendments to the Treaty, the aims are now more widely stated:

> The Community shall have as its task, by establishing a common market and an economic and monetary union and by implementing common policies or activities referred to in Articles 3 and 4, to promote throughout the Community a harmonious, balanced and sustainable development of economic activities, a high level of employment and social protection, equality between men and women, sustainable and non-inflationary growth, a high degree of competitiveness and convergence of economic performance, a high level of protection and improvement of the quality of the environment, the raising of the standard of living and quality of life, and economic and social cohesion and solidarity among Member States.

This expansion of EC interests has been one of the key concerns for those who fear the move towards a federal Europe. The TEU stimulated enormous debate and, as a consequence, it did not come into effect until November 1993, following the difficulties of ratification in some Member States. Similar problems of ratification were encountered with the Treaty of Nice, which was signed on 26 February 2001 but did not enter into force until 1 February 2003. Further changes will probably be made to the Treaties as a result of the Convention on the Future of Europe and of the Treaty on the Accession of 10 new Member States, which was signed on 16 April 2003 and which will enter into force on 1 May 2004.

3.4   EC COMPETENCES

The institutions of the EC are entrusted with the power to enact secondary legislation in order to further the aims of the EC. It is Art 3 of the EC Treaty which sets out which actions can be taken in pursuit of those aims. In other words, Art 3 defines what actions can be taken or, to use the jargon, it defines the EC's competences. If the EC institutions take action in an area in which the EC is not legally competent, then any such action may be annulled by the European Court of Justice (ECJ) exercising its powers of judicial review under Art 230 (formerly Art 173). Again, Art 3 has also been subject to positive amendment and now runs to a very wide-ranging list of legitimate actions. Art 3 now states:

1   For the purposes set out in Article 2, the activities of the Community shall include, as provided in this Treaty and in accordance with the timetable set out therein:

    (a) the prohibition, as between Member States, of customs duties and quantitative restrictions on the import and export of goods, and of all other measures having equivalent effect;

(b) a common commercial policy;

(c) an internal market characterised by the abolition, as between Member States, of obstacles to the free movement of goods, persons, services and capital;

(d) measures concerning the entry and movement of persons as provided for in Title IV;

(e) a common policy in the sphere of agriculture and fisheries;

(f) a common policy in the sphere of transport;

(g) a system ensuring that competition in the internal market is not distorted;

(h) the approximation of the laws of Member States to the extent required for the functioning of the common market;

(i) the promotion of co-ordination between employment policies of the Member States with a view to enhancing their effectiveness by developing a co-ordinated strategy for employment;

(j) a policy in the social sphere comprising a European Social Fund;

(k) the strengthening of economic and social cohesion;

(l) a policy in the sphere of the environment;

(m) the strengthening of the competitiveness of Community industry;

(n) the promotion of research and technological development;

(o) encouragement for the establishment and development of trans-European networks;

(p) a contribution to the attainment of a high level of health protection;

(q) a contribution to education and training of quality and to the flowering of the cultures of the Member States;

(r) a policy in the sphere of development co-operation;

(s) the association of the overseas countries and territories in order to increase trade and promote jointly economic and social development;

(t) a contribution to the strengthening of consumer protection;

(u) measures in the spheres of energy, civil protection and tourism.

2   In all the activities referred to in this Article, the Community shall aim to eliminate inequalities, and to promote equality, between men and women.

It is clear from this list that the activities of the EC are wide-ranging, but on closer inspection they are not all necessarily compatible. Whilst activities aimed at protecting the environment, consumer protection and a high level of health protection may be complementary, others are not. There is a potential tension between the aims of securing the strengthening of the competitiveness of EC industry and environmental protection. The need to promote economic growth usually comes at an environmental cost. The creation of new businesses may make the EC more competitive in the global market and may indeed create much needed jobs and opportunities, but there will be environmental consequences and these need to be taken into account. The EC has recognised that the goal of economic growth cannot be pursued without consideration for the environment and that in promoting growth today account needs to be taken of the consequences for future generations. This view is reflected in the current desire to pursue sustainable and non-inflationary growth respecting the environment. More particularly, the EC

Treaty specifically requires in Art 6 that environmental protection requirements must be integrated into the definition and implementation of the Community policies and activities referred to in Art 3, in particular with a view to promoting sustainable development.

3.5   SOURCES OF EC LAW

The EC Treaty is the primary source of EC law since it is from the Treaty that the EC institutions derive their power to enact secondary legislation. The Treaty is often described as *Traité Cadre*, which means that it is a framework treaty which sets out broad general principles and aims, but leaves the institutions to 'flesh out' and implement these aims by means of secondary legislation. The institutions of the EC are entrusted under Art 7 of the Treaty to carry out their respective functions, which include the capacity to enact secondary legislation. However, the institutions must only act within the powers conferred upon them by the Treaty and, as stated above, if they bring forward legislation in areas in which the Community is not legally competent, then such measures may be annulled on the ground of lack of competence (the equivalent of the *ultra vires* doctrine in English law). This is important because it prevents the EC taking action in those areas which are legitimately the domain of Member States and it prevents a transfer of power beyond that which the Member States agreed in the signing of the Treaty.

Therefore, it is clear that all EC secondary legislation must derive from the Treaty and must have a legal basis. This is a particular point which has been of importance in environmental law and will be considered more fully below.

3.5.1 EC secondary legislation

Article 249 (formerly Art 189) of the EC Treaty defines the legislative powers of the institutions and the types of legal instruments available. Because these legislative Acts derive from the Treaty, they are regarded as secondary legislation and are hierarchically inferior to the Treaty which is the primary source of EC law. It is important to be familiar with the distinctions between the types of secondary legislation. However, a note of caution: the classification laid down below is not always straightforward. An Act is not always what it says it is and, consequently, the ECJ will look at the substance rather than the form, and has held that where a regulation fails to lay down general rules it may be a disguised decision (Cases 16 and 17/62, *Confédération Nationale des Producteurs de Fruits et Legumes v Council* (1962)).

3.5.2 Regulations

Regulations have general application, are binding in their entirety and are directly applicable in all Member States. Regulations apply equally to all Member States and can therefore be used to ensure that the law is exactly the same throughout the EC. For this reason, regulations take effect within Member States either on the date specified in the Official Journal of the European Communities (all regulations and directives are published in the Official Journal) or, in the absence of a specified date, the regulation takes effect 20 days after publication. Since regulations are binding in their entirety and directly applicable, there is no need for Member States to implement the regulation in order for it to take effect. In fact, national implementation of regulations has been held in Case 93/71, *Leonesio v Ministero dell'Agricoltura e delle Foreste* (1971) to be incompatible with the aims of regulations.

3.5.3 Directives

Directives differ from regulations in a number of respects. Article 249 (formerly Art 189) states that:

> A Directive shall be binding as to the results to be achieved, upon each Member State to which it is addressed, but shall leave to the national authorities the choice and form of methods.

Although directives are generally addressed to all Member States, it is theoretically possible for directives to be directed to only one or more Member States, and it is equally possible for directives to be addressed to all Member States but with different conditions (such as deadlines for implementation). Directives state the 'aim to be achieved', which is binding upon the Member State, but leave the choice and means of implementation to the discretion of the Member State. Therefore, directives provide that implementation should be within a certain timetable or by a certain deadline. Member States are obliged to ensure that there is effective implementation of the directive within the specified time period. Implementation by means of a government circular will not be sufficient. Member States usually submit a copy of the implementing legislation to the Commission so that the Commission can review whether or not there has been compliance. In the UK, implementation is usually achieved by means of statutory instrument. The European Communities Act 1972 (as amended) provides powers for ministers to introduce delegated legislation giving effect to EC obligations in directives.

The majority of EC environmental 'acts' take the form of directives rather than regulations. This means that Member States play a large part in the implementation of EC environmental law and that they exercise some discretion in terms of how to achieve the aims laid down by the EC. This use of directives rather than regulations has, however, a number of consequences. At the practical level, it means that students and practitioners of environmental law should become familiar with the skills involved in 'tracking' directives and their subsequent implementation. Since this will invariably be by means of statutory instrument, it will necessarily involve finding out whether a statutory instrument has been introduced or not.

However, directives are problematic in another respect in so far as there is clearly the scope for Member States to fail to implement them, either on time or indeed at all. Alternatively, there are cases where implementation takes place in form, but there may not be effective implementation in terms of adequate enforcement or remedies available. Given that environmental legislation (largely in the form of directives) is and will continue to be an important pillar of the Community's approach to achieving its environmental objectives, the Community has come to recognise that there have been significant implementation failures in certain areas of environmental law. The Sixth Environmental Action Programme states that the full application, implementation and enforcement of existing EC environmental legislation is a strategic priority for the Community in the coming decade. Given that directives are prone to such problems, it is reasonable to wonder why they are the principal means of enacting EC environmental legislation. By leaving the choice and form of implementation to the Member States, there will automatically be divergences of approach. Directives provide a flexible means of ensuring harmonised standards whilst taking account of the differing legal and administrative systems within the Member States and, to some extent, reflect the principle of subsidiarity which is so central to the EC Treaty.

Directives have generated considerable case law, both within national legal systems of the Member States and also by the ECJ. The direct effect, or otherwise, of directives is considered more fully below.

3.5.4 Decisions

A decision is an individual act 'binding in its entirety upon those to whom it is addressed'. Decisions can be addressed to Member States but can equally be addressed to individuals and companies. Because it is a binding act, a decision has the force of law and does not require any implementation. Decisions are frequently used by the Commission in the field of competition law but are rarely used in environmental law.

3.5.5 Recommendations and opinions

In addition to regulations, directives and decisions, the EC Treaty also makes provision for recommendations and opinions, which are not legally binding. However, the ECJ held in Case 322/88, *Grimaldi v Fonds des Maladies Professionnelles* (1988) that recommendations and opinions should be of persuasive influence in the decisions of national courts.

3.5.6 Case law of the ECJ

Clearly, where the ECJ gives a ruling in an individual case, that ruling is binding on the parties to the proceedings. However, that decision is also binding in all subsequent cases. National courts are bound to follow rulings of the ECJ by virtue of Art 10 of the EC Treaty, which provides that Member States (which includes the national courts) are bound to ensure fulfilment of the obligations arising out of the Treaty, or resulting from actions taken by the institutions of the EC (which includes the ECJ's decisions). Moreover, s 3(2) of the European Communities Act 1972 requires national courts to take judicial notice of any decision of the ECJ. The case law of the ECJ has provided a rich source of EC law. It is the ECJ which has been responsible for developing the principles of supremacy, direct effect and State liability. As such, the ECJ has been successful in securing the integration of EC law into the domestic legal systems of Member States. In its most active phases, the ECJ has been criticised for judicial law making.

3.6   THE INSTITUTIONAL FRAMEWORK

To understand how environmental policy and legislation has developed in the EC, it is necessary to be aware of the way in which legislation is enacted and the role of the respective EC institutions. This is particularly important when one considers the amount of environmental legislation that the EC has thus far enacted and the way in which influences can be brought to bear to affect its content (or, indeed, existence). It is also important to understand the role of the respective institutions in the enforcement of EC environmental law and the actions that they can take in the event of a breach of the Community laws. The issue of enforcement is of particular importance in the light of what has already been said about the use of directives in the field of environmental law. Since the implementation of most EC environmental law rests with the Member States themselves, the EC must have the means available to ensure that such implementation is both effective and uniformly applied.

3.6.1   The institutions

Within the EC, no one institution is solely responsible for passing legislation; instead, the law making process involves the Council, the Commission, the Parliament and, in some instances, the Economic and Social Affairs Committee and the Committee of the Regions. Neither is there one single law making procedure. Instead, there are several, each of which involves the institutions in a number of different relationships. The Parliament cannot be regarded as the legislative body in the same way in which the UK Parliament is. Instead, the European Parliament participates, in varying degrees, in the overall process of enacting legislation, although in some instances it may play no role at all. The institution with the greatest influence is the Council of the European Union.

3.6.2   The Council of the European Union

The Council of the European Union (formerly called the Council of Ministers prior to the TEU) is made up of 15 representatives from the Member States. The representatives must be Ministers of State who are authorised to commit their respective governments. When Ministers attend Council meetings, they represent their governments and generally pursue national interests. The composition of the Council alters, depending on the subject under discussion: general Council meetings are usually attended by Foreign Affairs Ministers, environment meetings are attended by Environment Ministers and so on. Where high level policy meetings are the subject of discussion, then the Council may consist of Heads of State. However, the Heads of State are also required by the EC Treaty to meet at least twice a year and, when they act in this special capacity, they meet as the European Council. Each Member State takes over the presidency of the Council for a period of six months on a rotating basis.

3.6.3   The functions of the Council of Ministers

The duty of the Council is to 'ensure that the objectives set out in the Treaty are attained' and to ensure the overall co-ordination of the general economic policies of the Member States. The Council, by virtue of Art 202 (formerly Art 145) of the EC Treaty, has the power to take decisions which places it in the most powerful position in terms of enacting legislation (although, as is shown below, it interacts with the other institutions in a variety of ways, depending on the specific legislative procedure that is used).

Because the Council has this power of decision making, the way in which it votes and takes decision on legislative proposals is of utmost significance. Clearly, if decisions were always taken by a simple majority (that is, 8/15) there would be scope for legislation regularly to be enacted despite the disagreement of seven Member States. Therefore, although the EC Treaty specifies that decisions will usually be taken by simple majority unless otherwise provided for, the Treaty does go on to provide otherwise in many instances. The provisions of the Treaty in fact require most decisions to be taken by 'qualified majority'.

3.6.4 Qualified majority voting

In these instances, each Member State has a weighted vote, the weight depending on the size of population. The larger Member States (France, Germany, Italy and the UK) each have 10 votes, Spain has eight, Belgium, Greece, the Netherlands and Portugal carry five votes, Austria and Sweden have four votes, Denmark, Ireland and Finland each have three and Luxembourg, the smallest Member State, has two votes.

Where a qualified majority is required in favour of a proposal, then 62 out of the total of 87 votes must be cast in favour of the proposal. In other words, at least 25 votes are required to block a proposal. The system is complicated by a compromise agreement whereby, if the Member States achieve a total of between 23 and 25 votes against a qualified decision, then the Council is obliged, within certain limits, to try to reach a compromise solution. This system of weighting was introduced by the SEA 1986 essentially to speed up decision making in order to achieve the self-imposed deadline of achieving the single market programme by 1992. It also provides a means of decision making/voting which prevents the larger Member States effectively out-voting the smaller Member States.

Qualified majority voting is used now in relation to the majority of legislation required to complete the single market. Thus, most harmonising measures introduced under Art 95 (formerly Art 100a) of the EC Treaty will require a qualified majority vote by the Council. Qualified majority voting is also used for the majority of environmental protection measures enacted under Art 175 (formerly Art 130s).

3.6.5 Unanimous voting

In certain circumstances, the Treaty still requires that decisions are agreed unanimously. However, the requirement for unanimity generally only applies to the more politically sensitive areas of policy making, for example, the accession of new Member States to the Union, or where the Council is seeking to override the proposals/opinions of the other institutions involved in the law making process. As far as environmental measures are concerned, where the proposed measures concern town and country planning, land use (with the exception of waste management and management of water resources) and energy supply, the Council is required to act unanimously. Where a unanimous vote is required, there is a much greater likelihood that the proposals will be delayed for lengthy periods until a compromise can be reached which satisfies all the Member States. It is not unknown for some proposals to have taken as long as 16 years to be agreed. The Environmental Assessment Directive (85/337/EEC) is a case in point.

3.6.6   The European Commission

The European Commission is made up of 20 Commissioners. Commissioners are appointed by common accord of the governments of the Member States. Once appointed as a Commissioner, an individual must act in the interests of the EC, not taking instructions from any national government. Their independence must be beyond doubt. Each Member State appoints at least one, whilst the larger Member States and Spain put forward two. The Commissioners are appointed for five years and these terms may be renewed. The Commission is headed by a President. Commissioners are each given a specific portfolio for which they are responsible. As a result of the Nice Treaty, the composition of the Commission will alter. From January 2005, every Member State will have one Commissioner. As soon as the Union reaches 27, the number of Commissioners will be reduced to a number smaller than the total number of Member States. The exact number will be determined by the Council of the European Union.

3.6.7   The Commission Services

The Commission Services (the civil service of the EC, based largely in Brussels) is divided into a series of departments which are known as Directorates General (DGs). Headed up by an administrative and permanent Director General, each Director General reports to a specific commissioner.

The Environment DG is one of 36 DGs which make up the European Commission. Its main role is to initiate and define new environmental legislation and to ensure that measures which have been agreed are actually put into practice in the Member States. The Environment DG is based largely in Brussels and has around 550 staff.

3.6.8   The functions of the Commission

The functions of the European Commission are laid down in Art 211 (formerly Art 155) of the EC Treaty. The Commission acts in the capacity of executive and also plays a key role in the formation of legislation. In addition, the Commission exercises considerable powers in relation to the enforcement of EC law, having the right to bring Member States before the ECJ. In this respect, the Commission is regarded as the 'watchdog' of the EC or is sometimes referred to as the 'guardian of the treaties'.

The Commission is responsible for proposing and initiating legislation. Prior to the TEU, only the Commission had this power, albeit that it was not explicitly stated in the Treaty but was implied. The Council can of course suggest proposals to the Commission, but it has no legal power to insist that legislation is brought forward, although it clearly exercises considerable political power. However, since the TEU, the Parliament enjoys the right to request the Commission to propose any legislation that it suggests. The Council can only take legislative action on proposals that have been initiated by the Commission.

3.6.9   The European Parliament

The Parliament was originally called the European Assembly and was made up of representatives from national parliaments. However, in 1979, direct elections to the Parliament were held for the first time and the Assembly changed its name to the European Parliament as required by the SEA 1986. The Parliament is currently made up of 626 directly elected representatives, known as Members of the European Parliament or MEPs. At present, the electoral systems in the different Member States vary, with most States electing by means of proportional representation. The Treaty requires, however, that a uniform electoral system is eventually adopted.

3.6.10 The functions of the European Parliament

The Parliament's functions and powers have grown significantly since 1957. Prior to the SEA 1986, the Parliament acted largely in an advisory and supervisory capacity. Its involvement in the legislative procedure was limited to giving an opinion on proposed legislation, but only in relation to those areas of legislation where the EC Treaty specifically provided that the Parliament should be consulted. In some areas of legislation, the Council could take decisions without the need for any consultation with the Parliament.

The Parliament, as befitting the only directly elected community institution, pressed for greater powers and in particular a greater involvement in the legislative process. Its powers were increased by the SEA 1986, which gave it the right in certain circumstances to be consulted twice in relation to certain proposals and, even more significantly, by the TEU, which introduced the so called co-decision procedure, giving the Parliament, effectively, a right to veto certain legislative proposals. The co-decision procedure, although complex in operation, offers the Parliament the greatest opportunity of influencing the content of legislation. The use of the co-decision procedure was greatly extended by the ToA.

The way in which the Parliament votes in relation to proposals before it is specified in the Treaty. Unless otherwise provided by the Treaty, the normal voting arrangement would be by a simple majority of votes cast. However, the Treaty specifies, particularly in relation to the procedures known as Arts 251 and 252 (formerly Arts 189b and 189c), that in some instances an absolute majority is required.

The Parliament currently exercises a range of functions. Its role in the legislative process is described more fully below. It also acts in a supervisory capacity in relation to the Commission and, to a lesser extent, the Council. The Parliament has the power to dismiss the whole of the Commission with a vote of censure, provided that it can achieve a two-thirds majority in favour of such action. The Parliament also conducts its own version of question time when it requires Commissioners to answer Parliamentary questions, either verbally to the Parliament or in writing. It is in this way that the Parliament exercises a degree of control over the Commission, and this reflects the checks and balances that are built into the institutional framework. The Council of Ministers also reports to the Parliament. At the end of each presidency period, the outgoing President of the Council reports to the Parliament on the achievements during the presidency period.

Since the TEU 1993, the Parliament has had the power to set up a Committee of Inquiry to investigate alleged contraventions or maladministration in the implementation of EC law and has also been required to appoint an Ombudsman for maladministration.

3.6.11 The Parliament and the environment

The political composition of the Parliament is wide-ranging, with large representations from both the left and right of the political spectrum. The Parliament also has its own select Committee on Environment, Public Health and Consumer Protection which has about 50 members. The Parliament receives a number of petitions from environmental pressure groups and these are usually passed on to the Commission to deal with under the Art 226 (formerly Art 169) proceedings (see below). The value of petitioning Parliament is that it can lend a political impetus to the process which may be persuasive when the Commission decides upon enforcement proceedings.

3.6.12 The ECJ

Article 220 (formerly Art 164) of the EC Treaty provides that the role of the ECJ is to 'ensure that in the interpretation and application of this Treaty the law is observed'. Various other Treaty articles deal with its jurisdiction in relation to cases brought by Member States, against Member States, against the institutions themselves and also its relationship with the national courts of the Member States. These will be discussed more fully below in relation to the enforcement of EC law. The ECJ itself is currently made up of 15 judges chosen from people whose independence is beyond doubt. The ECJ is assisted by eight Advocates General who help it by presenting an analysis of the cases before it and also, importantly, their recommendations in the form of an opinion. The ECJ reaches its decisions in private and presents a single judgment known as a collegiate judgment. This means, in fact, that there is no record of any dissenting judgment. It is often very useful when reading judgments of the ECJ to read also the opinion of the Advocate General. Whilst the judges are not bound to follow the Advocate General's recommendations, where they do, the opinion provides a very useful indication of the ECJ's reasoning.

In addition to the ECJ, there is also the European Court of First Instance (CFI), which was created in 1988 to alleviate some of the workload of the ECJ. The CFI consists of 15 members whose qualifications, appointment and legal status are subject to the same requirements as judges of the ECJ. Although, initially, the jurisdiction of the CFI was limited, its jurisdiction has increased so that it is now the court of first instance for all direct actions against Community legal acts brought by natural and legal persons (under Art 230 of the EC Treaty). However, the jurisdiction of the CFI has been significantly extended by the Treaty of Nice (ToN) which, for the first time, has conferred on the CFI the jurisdiction to hear and determine questions referred for a preliminary ruling under Art 234 (formerly Art 177) in specific areas laid down by the Statute of the Court. At the time of writing, these areas had not been determined. In addition, the ToN allows for the creation of judicial panels to hear and determine at first instance certain classes of action or proceedings brought in specific areas. Again, these areas have not yet been determined.

3.6.13 The balance of power between the Member States

The following diagram provides a detailed breakdown of the number of MEPs' votes in Council and Commissioners for each of the 15 Member States.

Member State	MEPs	Votes at Council	Commissioners
Austria	21	4	1
Belgium	25	5	1
Denmark	16	3	1
Finland	16	3	1
France	87	10	2
Germany	99	10	2
Greece	25	5	1
Ireland	15	3	1
Italy	87	10	2
Luxembourg	6	2	1
Netherlands	31	5	1
Portugal	25	5	1
Spain	64	8	2
Sweden	22	4	1
United Kingdom	87	10	2
TOTAL	626	87	20

3.7   THE LEGISLATIVE PROCEDURE

The process of enacting EC secondary legislation is complex; however, there are two underlying fundamental principles which govern it. The first is that, in order to enact EC secondary legislation, the EC Treaty must provide a legal base for such action. The EC institutions have no power to enact legislation that does not serve the aims of the EC. To do so would mean that they were acting unlawfully. However, it should be noted that Art 308 (formerly Art 235) of the EC Treaty provides a residual power to enable the institutions to take action to achieve Community objectives, notwithstanding the absence of an explicit legal basis.

The second point of importance is that the EC Treaty defines how the relevant legislation will be enacted. The legislative procedure that will be employed to enact the secondary legislation depends entirely upon the Treaty article under which the legislation is based. This point is of importance in the field of environmental law, where it is possible to enact environmental legislation either under Art 95 (formerly Art 100a) or under Art 175 (formerly Art 130). Following amendments to the Treaty, measures adopted under both Arts 95 and 175 are to be adopted under the co-decision procedure. Although the law making procedures are the same, there are substantive differences between these two legal bases. The primary objective of legislation adopted under Art 95 is to achieve the approximation of such laws, regulations or administrative provisions of the Member States as directly affect the establishment or functioning of the common market. In essence, the aim is to secure the harmonisation of environmental laws throughout the Community. In contrast, legislation adopted under Art 175 does not need to strive for such harmonisation, but can be adopted purely for securing environmental protection. In this context, legislation adopted under Art 175 may be seen as purely environmental and adopted in pursuance of the Community's environmental protection objectives which are set out in Art 174. To this extent, Community policy must aim at a high level of protection, taking into account the diversity of situations in the various regions of the Community. It must be based on the precautionary principle and on the principles that preventive action should be taken, that environmental damage should as a priority be rectified at source and that the polluter should pay.

3.7.1 Initiation of legislation and the legislative processes

Legislative proposals are initiated by the Commission. In practice, the Commission consults with a variety of groups as to the content of the legislation and it is in this way that environmental pressure groups can influence the content of environmental legislation. Once the proposal has been drafted and agreed by the Commission, it is sent to the Council.

There are a number of ways in which the proposal will be dealt with from this point; however, the main procedures are as follows:

(a) Council legislation without consultation of the European Parliament: where the Council takes a final decision on the Commission proposal without the involvement of the Parliament;

(b) the Consultation Procedure: in this procedure, the Parliament must be consulted before the Council reaches its final decision. The Council must take account of the Parliament's opinion, although the opinion is not binding on the Council;

(c) the Co-operation Procedure: introduced by the SEA 1986, this procedure is strictly called the Art 252 (formerly Art 189c) procedure. The procedure enables the Parliament to have two opportunities to consider the proposal (rather like adding a second reading to the process). The Parliament can suggest amendments to the draft proposal. If the Council does not accept the parliamentary amendments, then it is forced to act unanimously in order to enact the legislative proposal. It is in this way that the Parliament exerts some influence on the content of legislation;

(d) the Co-decision Procedure or Art 251 (formerly Art 189b) procedure was introduced by the TEU and then simplified by the ToA. The procedure is complicated but greatly enhances the role of the Parliament. The effect of the co-decision procedure is to provide for the possibility of a third reading. The procedure follows that of the co-operation procedure until the final stage. Where the Council does not approve parliamentary amendments, a conciliation committee of equal numbers of the Council and the Parliament attempts to agree a joint text. If the joint text cannot be agreed, then the proposed measure fails.

In addition to these main procedures, there are others – such as the Assent Procedure and the Conciliation procedure.

3.8   ENFORCEMENT OF EC LAW

Member States are obliged to fulfil their EC law obligations and not do anything which would jeopardise the attainment of the EC Treaty.

3.8.1   Member States' obligation to comply with EC law (Art 10)

Member States are required by Art 10 to fulfil their obligations as members of the EC. They are specifically required to take all appropriate measures, whether general or particular, to ensure fulfilment of the obligations arising out of the EC Treaty, or resulting from action take by the institutions. Such action embraces both EC policy, secondary legislation and decisions of the ECJ and CFI. In addition, Member States must not take any measures which could jeopardise the attainment of the Treaty objectives.

Failure to fulfil obligations can take many forms:

(a) introducing legislation in contravention to the Treaty: this happened in relation to the Merchant Shipping Act 1988 which contravened the basic principle of non-discrimination on the grounds of nationality and resulted in the *Factortame* litigation and Case 426/89, *Commission v UK* (1989);

(b) failure to implement directives either at all, or on time: the Commission has brought numerous actions against Member States on these grounds. See, for example, Case C-56/90, *Commission v UK* (1993);

(c) partial or incorrect implementation of a directive;

(d) inadequate enforcement of a directive: see, for example, Case C-340/96, *Commission v UK* in respect of the Secretary of State for the Environment's failure to take enforcement actions against water companies.

Member States are under a duty to implement directives effectively and on time. Since EC environmental legislation is largely in the form of directives rather than regulations, the opportunities for Member States avoiding or delaying their obligations under environmental directives are considerable. The non-implementation of environmental directives has given rise to a number of direct actions before the ECJ (see below), for example, in Case C-337/89, *Commission v UK* (1993) concerning non-implementation by the UK of Directive (80/778/EC) on drinking water intended for human consumption. This was the first case in which the UK was found to be in breach of an EC environmental directive. Another example of a direct action against the UK can be found in Case 56/90, *Commission v UK* (1993), where the UK was found to be in breach of its obligation under EC law in respect of the Bathing Water Directive (76/160/EC). In addition to a direct action against a Member State for non-implementation, it is also possible that the failure to implement may be challenged indirectly in the national courts. This happened in the judicial review proceedings brought by Friends of the Earth in *R v Secretary of State for the Environment ex p Friends of the Earth and Another* (1995).

3.8.2   Direct actions against Member States

The main direct sanction against Member States is provided for by Art 226 (formerly Art 169) of the EC Treaty, which enables the European Commission to commence legal proceedings against Member States before the ECJ. Article 226 provides for two pre-litigation stages before court proceedings are taken. If the Commission believes that a Member State is in breach of its Community obligations, it can inform the Member State in question by means of a letter of formal notice, known as an 'Article 226 letter', which sets out the nature of the infringement and the course of action to be taken. This only usually happens after informal negotiations have been exhausted. The letter must state all the grounds for complaint. Member States must then be given an adequate time period to make their observations on the alleged breach. If the Commission is still not satisfied that the Member State is complying with its obligations, then it can take the next step of issuing a 'reasoned opinion'. This formally records the infringement and requires the Member State to take the necessary action to bring the infringement to an end. Normally the Member State will be given a deadline by which it must take appropriate action.

Following these two pre-litigation steps, the Commission can, if it chooses, commence legal proceedings against the Member State before the ECJ (such cases appear as *Commission v UK* or *Commission v Italy* and so on). The number of cases brought before the ECJ under Art 226 are increasing each year. A number of points need to be made in relation to Art 226 proceedings:

(a) the Commission often acts on the basis of complaints made by aggrieved citizens or pressure groups. In addition, the Commission also receives numerous petitions from pressure groups, trade unions and so on. It is in this respect that individuals and pressure groups can exert pressure on the Commission to deal with breaches of environmental law. Complainants do not have to satisfy any legal or sufficient interest in the matter complained of. Therefore, Art 226 provides an inexpensive means by which interested parties can seek to enforce EC law;

(b) the Commission is not bound to investigate or follow through all complaints nor is it bound to commence Art 226 proceedings. In fact, the Commission exercises discretion at all stages. This was confirmed by the ECJ in Case 247/87, *Star Fruit Co v Commission* (1989);

(c) Member States have raised various mitigating factors and defences but these have rarely succeeded. In *Commission v Ireland* (1981), concerning Ireland's failure to implement Directive (77/91/EEC), the ECJ held that a Member State may not plead provisions, practices or circumstances existing in its internal legal system in order to justify a failure to comply with obligations resulting from EC directives.

In addition to Art 226 (formerly Art 169), Art 227 (formerly Art 170) provides for a similar procedure enabling one Member State to bring an action against another Member State. It is very rare for Member States to resort to Art 227. Member States are, in fact, required to ask the Commission to commence proceedings, and only when the Commission has failed to issue a reasoned opinion does this option become available. However, it is more likely that Member States will resolve their differences at the political level through the Council of Ministers rather than resorting to legal action before the ECJ.

3.8.3 Fines

Where a Member State is found to be in breach of its EC obligations, the ECJ will issue a declaration to that effect. Failure to comply with the declaration and remedy the situation will result in the Member State being in breach of both Art 228 (formerly Art 171) and Art 10. Prior to the TEU, the ECJ's powers were limited to issuing a declaration. However, its powers have been enhanced by the TEU and the ECJ now has the power to impose a fine where a Member State continues to breach its obligations after an ECJ declaration. The fine is not automatic; the Commission is required to recommence proceedings against the defaulting Member State before a fine can be imposed. Interestingly, the first occasion in which the ECJ exercised this power to fine a Member State came in an environmental law case (Case C-387/97, *Commission v Greece* (2000)) concerning the repeated failure by the Greek authorities to comply with the provisions of Directives 75/442/EEC and 78/319/EEC regarding waste management. The ECJ ruled that the breaches had been very serious and imposed a fine of 20,000 Euros daily from the date of service of the judgment.

3.8.4 Judicial review of EC law

The EC Treaty also gives the ECJ the jurisdiction to review the acts of the EC institutions and to annul them on specific grounds. The power of the ECJ in this respect is important, because it acts as a check on the other EC institutions which have been given significant powers under the Treaty. Article 230 (formerly Art 173) specifies which 'acts' are reviewable, who may bring judicial review proceedings, the grounds on which review proceedings may be brought and the time limits for bringing such actions.

Judicial review in EC law is complex, particularly in relation to actions brought by aggrieved individuals.

3.8.5 Reviewable acts

The ECJ can review the legality of acts adopted jointly by the European Parliament and the Council, of acts of the Council, of the Commission and of the European Central Bank other than recommendations and opinions. 'Acts' are not defined other than in the negative sense, in that they do not include recommendations or opinions, which, of course, are not legally binding. It is clear therefore that regulations, directives and decisions are 'acts' in this sense and therefore 'reviewable acts'. However, the ECJ has not confined the interpretation of 'acts' to secondary legislation and, in various cases, has held that they include all measures taken by the institutions which are designed to have legal effect irrespective of their nature or form.

3.8.6 Who can bring an action?

Article 230 (formerly Art 173) draws a distinction between the Member States and the institutions on the one hand, and natural and legal persons on the other. Prior to amendments made by the ToN, the Member States, Commission and Council had so called 'privileged applicant' status, in that they could commence judicial review proceedings against any 'act' without having to establish a specific legal interest in the challenged measure. The Parliament had limited standing before the ECJ, only being able to seek review of those acts which infringed the 'prerogatives' of the Parliament. The Nice Treaty has brought the Parliament into line with the other institutions, conferring upon it 'privileged applicant' status.

The position with regard to natural and legal persons, a classification which encompasses environmental pressure groups, is unfortunately much more complex and restrictive.

Article 230 states that any natural or legal person may institute proceedings against 'a Decision addressed to that person, or a Decision which, although in the form of a Regulation or a Decision addressed to another person, is of direct and individual concern to himself'.

In essence there are three situations where a non-privileged person can bring actions for judicial review:

(a) where the applicant is directly addressed by the decision;

(b) where a regulation is really a disguised decision;

(c) where the decision is addressed to another person, which can include a Member State (Case 25/62, *Plaumann & Co v Commission* (1963)).

In the cases of (b) and (c), the applicant also has to prove that the reviewable act is of direct and individual concern to the applicant. The tests laid down by the ECJ in relation to direct and individual concern have been very restrictive, making it extremely difficult for individuals to overcome this hurdle of standing. There is as yet no automatic right for pressure groups to bring judicial review actions. (See Cases T-585/93 and C-321/95P, *Stichting Greenpeace Council (Greenpeace International) v Commission*.)

3.8.7   Grounds for review

Once an applicant has established that he or she has standing, they must then go on to establish the grounds for review. These are laid down in Art 230(2) and can often overlap in individual cases. They are:

(a) lack of competence;

(b) infringement of an essential procedural requirement;

(c) infringement of the EC Treaty or of any rule of law relating to the application of the Treaty; and

(d) misuse of power.

3.8.8   Time limits

Article 230 contains strict time limits regarding the commencement of judicial review actions. Proceedings must be instituted within two months of the publication of the challenged measure, or of its notification to the claimant or, in the absence of either of these, two months from the date on which it came to the knowledge of the claimant.

3.9   INDIRECT ENFORCEMENT THROUGH THE NATIONAL COURTS

Given that Art 226 proceedings can only be brought by the Commission and that individuals have in practice so little access to the ECJ under Art 230, it is vital to understand how EC law can be enforced within the national legal system by domestic courts. The ECJ has established through its rulings that individuals can raise issues of EC law in the context of legal proceedings in order to secure rights under EC law. So, for example, it is possible to use EC law to establish legal rights (Case 152/84, *Marshall v Southampton AHA* (1986)) or as a defence in criminal prosecutions (Case 148/78, *Publico Ministero v Ratti* (1979)).

In order to ensure that EC law is applied by national courts in a uniform manner, Art 234 (formerly Art 177) provides that the domestic courts can refer matters of interpretation and validity of EC law provisions to the ECJ in order to obtain a ruling. This is known as the preliminary rulings procedure.

3.9.1   The preliminary rulings procedure

The ECJ has jurisdiction to give preliminary rulings concerning the interpretation of the EC Treaty, the validity and interpretation of acts of the institutions of the EC and the interpretation of the statutes of bodies established by an act of the Council. It is worth emphasising that the ECJ can only interpret the Treaty; it cannot, as is the case with secondary legislation, question its validity.

If a question arises in the context of national court proceedings about an issue of EC la, then that court or tribunal may, if it considers that decision is necessary to enable it to give judgment, request the ECJ to give a ruling. This is known as the Art 234 procedure. It enables national courts to refer questions on interpretation of EC law to the ECJ. Once the ECJ gives its preliminary ruling, the national court is bound by it and must apply it to the facts of the case. The ECJ is not deciding on the facts or the outcome of the national court case, neither is it acting as an appeal court. Instead, it is essentially co-operating with the national court in order that the EC law provisions be interpreted correctly. The ECJ is well placed to give this authoritative interpretation of EC law given its 'panoramic view' of the Community and of its institutions (*per* Lord Bingham in *Customs and Excise Comrs v Aps Samex* (1983)). When the national court seeks a preliminary ruling from the ECJ, the court proceedings are suspended until the ECJ has given its ruling.

The ECJ cannot pass judgment on the compatibility of domestic law with EC law. In circumstances where the ECJ has been asked to do this (since it is often in cases involving a conflict between domestic and EC law that questions of interpretation are raised), it frequently rephrases the question from the national court in order to provide the interpretation of the relevant Community law provision.

3.9.2   When should a national court refer a question to the ECJ?

The EC Treaty draws a distinction between courts which may refer a question and courts which shall refer a question to the ECJ. Article 234(3) states that courts from which there is no judicial remedy (no right of appeal) shall refer, whereas other (lower) courts exercise a discretion (that is, may refer). Despite this distinction, a court need only refer if it considers that a decision from the ECJ is necessary in order to enable it to give judgment. Therefore, all courts exercise a discretion in determining whether a referral is necessary. In *Customs and Excise v Aps Samex* (1983), Lord Bingham gave the following guidance:

> ... if the facts have been found and the Community law issue is critical to the court's final decision, the appropriate course is ordinarily to refer the issue to the European Court of Justice unless the national court can with complete confidence resolve the issue itself.

> In considering whether it can with complete confidence resolve the issue itself, the national court must be mindful of the difference between national and Community legislation; of the pitfalls which face a national court when venturing into an unfamiliar field; of the need for uniform interpretation throughout the Community and of the great advantages enjoyed by the Court of Justice in construing Community instruments.

In Case 283/81, *CILFIT v Ministry of Health*, the ECJ issued guidelines to the national courts to help them determine when a preliminary ruling would not be necessary.

3.9.3 A court must refer on questions of validity

The exercise of discretion is qualified in relation to questions concerning the validity of EC law raised in the context of national litigation. In Case 314/85, *Firma Foto-Frost v Hauptzollamt Lübeck Ost* (1988), the ECJ explicitly stated that national courts do not have the power to declare acts of the EC institutions invalid. Therefore, where a question about the validity of EC law is raised, the national court must seek a preliminary ruling from the ECJ.

3.9.4 Importance of the Art 234 procedure

The Art 234 (formerly Art 177) procedure has provided the main vehicle for the ECJ to develop the principles of direct effect, supremacy and State liability, dealt with in the following section. Many individuals have benefited from the Art 234 procedure as a result of the ECJ interpreting various EC provisions in such a way as to deem them directly effective and thus enforceable in national courts. There have been relatively few Art 234 rulings concerning environmental law. In the UK, the first reference on an environmental law matter was made by the House of Lords in the case of *R v Secretary of State for the Environment ex p RSPB* (1995).

3.10 THE EC AS A NEW LEGAL ORDER

Commentators have described EC law as 'unique' in international law terms, largely because of the extent to which EC law penetrates the domestic legal systems of the Member States and confers enforceable legal rights upon individuals. The ECJ has itself stated that the EC:

> ... constitutes a new legal order of international law for the benefit of which the states have limited their sovereign rights, albeit within limited fields and the subjects of which comprise not only Member States but also their nationals.

This statement was made by the ECJ in the leading case of Case 26/62, *Van Gend en Loos v Nederlandse Administratie der Belastingen* (1962). At the time when the ECJ made this statement, the role of the EC was limited. However, since that time, the EC has extended its competences and the transfer of sovereign rights referred to in the judgment extends to less limited fields. The issue of the transfer of power away from Member States has caused major problems for a number of the Member States, particularly when those States sought to ratify and incorporate the new TEU into their domestic legal systems. An expression of this concern came with the Danish 'no' vote in the referendum held on whether the Danish government should ratify the new Treaty. Therefore, a principal amendment to the TEU was the introduction in Art 5 (formerly Art 3B) of the principle of subsidiarity.

3.10.1 Subsidiarity

This provides that in areas which do not fall within the EC's exclusive competence, the EC shall only take action if and so far as the objectives of the proposed action cannot be sufficiently achieved by the Member States and can therefore, by reason of the scale or effects of the proposed action, be better achieved by the EC. Furthermore, any action by the EC shall not go beyond what is necessary to achieve the objectives of the EC Treaty, recognition of another fundamental principle of EC law – the principle of proportionality.

3.10.2 The relationship between EC law and UK law

The relationship between EC law and national law is one which has dominated many articles and textbooks and which is usually covered within the context of most constitutional or public law courses. Therefore, it is not the intention of this section to cover this subject in great detail. However, in view of the volume of EC environmental law that has been introduced, it is necessary to reflect on the way in which EC law is incorporated into the English legal system and, in particular, on the issues arising when there has not been adequate implementation of directives. EC law is incorporated into English law by the European Communities Act 1972 (as amended).

3.11   SUPREMACY OF EC LAW

The EC Treaty does not specifically make reference to the issue of supremacy or the relationship between EC law and national law. However, this relationship is of the utmost importance. The ECJ has in a number of famous decisions made it clear that priority is to be accorded to EC law and that EC law should prevail over conflicting national provisions. To allow otherwise would undermine the very being of the EC and its principal aim of establishing a common market.

As early as 1962, in the case of *Van Gend en Loos* (1962), it was established by the ECJ that the Member States had limited their sovereign rights and that the EC constituted a new legal order. The ECJ went further in Case 6/64, *Costa v ENEL* (1964) when it stated that:

... the transfer by the States ... to the Community legal system of the rights and obligations arising under the Treaty carries with it a permanent limitation of their sovereign rights against which a subsequent unilateral act incompatible with the concept of the Community cannot prevail.

National courts are required to apply provisions of EC law and to give full effect to those provisions and, if necessary, to set aside any conflicting provisions of national legislation, even if adopted after the relevant Community law provision (Case 106/77, *Amministrazione delle Finanze dello Stato v Simmenthal* (1978)).

3.12   EFFECT OF EC LAW

In addition to the principle of supremacy, the ECJ has also addressed the problem of the effect of EC law throughout the Member States. The aim of the EC is to achieve a common market where goods, people, services and capital can move freely. It is therefore necessary to achieve uniformity throughout the EC of the standards and provisions established at EC level. This need to secure uniformity of EC law is evidenced by the nature of regulations and also by the presence of the Art 234 procedure. However, a large amount of EC law, particularly environmental law, takes the form of directives, and directives do not guarantee immediate uniformity in the same way that regulations do. The failure by a Member State to implement a directive can distort the standards laid down at Community level and can potentially leave people in one Member State with fewer rights than those in another where there has been full implementation. However, the ECJ has asserted that Member States should not benefit from their failure to implement a directive (see, for example, Case 8/81, *Becker v Finanzamt Munster-Innenstadt* (1982)) and has developed a number of principles which enable Community law to take effect even where there has not been formal implementation by the State.

These are:

(a) *direct effect* – the concept of direct effect allows litigants in national courts to rely directly on the terms of EC measures, notwithstanding that those terms have not been fully implemented into the domestic legal system. However, certain conditions must be satisfied before a measure can be directly effective;

(b) *indirect effect or the duty of interpretation* – the concept of indirect effect stems from the obligations placed on national courts to interpret national law in accordance with EC law;

(c) *damages against the State* – in certain circumstances, damages may be awarded in favour of individuals who have suffered loss as a result of the failure of a Member State to implement EC law properly.

3.12.1 Direct effect of EC law

The concept or principle of direct effect has been developed by the ECJ in a number of cases dealing with Treaty articles, regulations, directives and decisions. It was first established in the *Van Gend en Loos* case in relation to Art 12 (now Art 25) of the EC Treaty. In the course of an Art 234 reference, the ECJ ruled that Art 12 was capable of direct effect and could be relied upon by individuals before national courts and tribunals. The ECJ stated that:

> The objective of the EEC Treaty, which is to establish a common market, the functioning of which is of direct concern to interested parties in the Community, implies that this Treaty is more than an agreement which merely creates mutual obligations between the contracting states.

As a consequence, *Van Gend en Loos* was able to rely on the Treaty article to secure enforceable rights in the Dutch courts.

3.12.2 Conditions for direct effect

The ECJ laid down three conditions which must be satisfied in order for a provision to be directly effective:

(a) the content of the relevant provision must be both clear and precise;

(b) the relevant provision must be unconditional; and

(c) the provision must leave no room for the exercise of discretion by the Member State.

Following the *Van Gend en Loos* case, the ECJ has held a large number of Treaty articles to be directly effective. The criteria laid down have been applied generously and, as a result, even measures which are not particularly clear or precise have been deemed to be capable of direct effect. In addition to Treaty articles, the ECJ has established that EC secondary legislation is also capable of direct effect. Regulations which are described in Art 249 as 'directly applicable' may also be directly effective if they can satisfy the test laid down by the Court.

3.12.3 Direct effect of directives

It was thought that directives, by their nature, could not be capable of direct effect because they could not satisfy the requirement that they leave no room for the exercise of discretion by the Member State. However, the existence of discretion concerning the means of implementation of directives has not prevented them from being directly effective. The ECJ in Case 41/74, *Van Duyn v Home Office* (1974) established conclusively that directives were capable of direct effect and therefore could be enforceable at the suit of individuals in the national courts, providing the provisions of the directive could satisfy the requirements laid down in *Van Gend en Loos*. (It should be noted that these tests are applied not to a directive as a whole but to the relevant provision that is being considered, such as an article of a directive or a particular paragraph.) It follows that directives are only capable of direct effect after the period for implementation by the Member State has expired (Case 148/78, *Publico Ministero v Ratti* (1979)). Until expiry of the implementation period, Member States are free to rely on existing national law, even if it conflicts with the requirements of a directive which is not yet due for implementation.

3.12.4 Direct effect of environmental measures?

It is clearly not possible to state that all EC environmental measures are capable of being directly effective, since many are couched in very vague and uncertain terms and others are dependent on certain criteria being satisfied and will not satisfy the requirement that the provisions are unconditional. However, Ludwig Kramer, a leading author on EC environmental law, suggests that certain types of provisions may be capable of direct effect, in particular directives which lay down specific maximum values for permissible discharges, or provisions which prohibit the use or discharge of certain specified substances. He asserts that certain directives such as the Drinking Water Directive (80/778/EEC) and also the Environmental Impact Assessment Directive (85/337/EEC) are capable of direct effect.

The question of the direct effect of both these directives has been considered in a number of cases. In Case C-337/89, *Commission v UK* (1993), the Commission brought an action against the UK in respect of the Drinking Water Directive (80/778/EEC). The Directive required Member States to set drinking water quality standards not exceeding 'maximum admissible concentrations' (MACs), required formal implementation by 18 July 1982 and required the standards to be met by 18 July 1985. The UK had taken no steps to implement the Directive formally by 1987 and so the Commission commenced proceedings under Art 226 of the EC Treaty. In 1989, the UK implemented the Water Supply (Water Quality) Regulations 1989 (SI 1989/1147), but the Commission continued with the proceedings, arguing that the UK had not fully met the standards set in the Directive in all parts of the UK (specifically that 28 supply zones in England and 17 supply zones in Scotland did not comply with MACs relating to nitrates and lead, and that there had been no formal implementation of the Directive in Northern Ireland). The ECJ found that the UK was in breach of its obligations under the Directive. By way of defence, the UK argued that it had taken all practical steps to secure compliance with the Directive but the ECJ held that this argument could not justify the UK's failure to implement it. The ECJ held that the UK had formally breached the Directive by failing to pass legislation to implement the Directive and had also substantively breached the Directive by failing to achieve the MACs specified in the Directive with regard to nitrates. The ECJ held that the MACs were enforceable obligations and implied as such that they were capable of direct effect, the consequence of direct effect being that the provisions may create legally enforceable rights in the national courts (see *Van Duyn* above). The decision in *Commission v UK* gave rise to further litigation in *R v Secretary of State for the Environment ex p Friends of the Earth and Another* (1995), in which the English Court of Appeal accepted that the MACs laid down in the Directive were capable of direct effect.

The direct effect of the Environmental Assessment Directive (85/337/EEC) has been considered in a number of cases. In *Twyford Parish Council v Secretary of State for Transport* (1992), it was held that the requirement to carry out an Environmental Assessment was directly effective in relation to those projects listed in Annexe 1 of the Directive (Annexe 1 lists projects where an environmental assessment is mandatory whereas Annexe 2 lists projects where an environmental assessment is discretionary).

3.12.5 No horizontal direct effect of directives

As far as directives are concerned, it is well established that litigants in national proceedings can only benefit from the direct effect of a directive in actions against the State or an emanation of the State (Case 152/84, *Marshall v Southampton AHA* (1986)). Therefore, one of the particular problems in relation to directives is that they will not be directly enforceable against individuals (to use the jargon, they are said not to be horizontally directly effective). The ECJ has been consistent in the line that it has taken in relation to directives, maintaining that they can only be directly enforceable against the State or an emanation of the State and that they are not capable of being directly effective against individuals. The consequence of this is that individuals and environmental pressure groups cannot rely on the direct effect of an unimplemented directive against private companies. In 2003, the ECJ delivered a judgment in Case C-320/01, *Busch v Klinikum Neustadt GmbH*, which concerned the provisions of Directive (76/207/EEC) in relation to the protection of pregnant women. In this case, the ECJ appears to have moved significantly away from the strict line it had previously adopted on the lack of horizontal direct effect. The impact of this judgment remains to be seen.

3.12.6 An emanation of the State?

Because of this limitation in relation to the direct effect of directives, it becomes necessary to define what is meant by the State or an emanation of the State. The ECJ has interpreted the phrase widely. In Case C-188/89, *Foster v British Gas* (1991), it was held that bodies responsible for the provision of public services and which have greater powers than are normally accorded to individuals or corporations are to be construed as emanations of the State. The issue was raised in the case of *Griffin v South West Water* (1995).

This case is of particular importance in environmental law because it involved the question of whether South West Water, a privatised water company, could be construed as an emanation of the State. The action concerned a directive relating to employment issues but the decision of the court is of wider significance. Blackburn J held that South West Water was an emanation of the State because the privatised water company was 'a State authority'. He asserted that the relevant question was not whether the body in question is under the control of the State, but rather whether the public service in question is in control of the State. The fact that the overall control of water services is exercised by the State was the relevant factor, not the legal form of the body, nor the fact that the body was a commercial concern. Blackburn J went on to say:

> It is also irrelevant that the body does not carry out any of the traditional functions of the state. It is irrelevant too that the state does not possess day-to-day control over the activities of the body.

The judgment is of particular significance since it paves the way for other directives, in the field of environmental law in particular, to be directly effective against the water companies, as emanations of the State. (See also Cases C-243–58/96, *Kampelmann v Landschafts verband Westfalen-Lippe*, in which the ECJ further considered the definition of an emanation of the State.)

3.13   THE DUTY OF INTERPRETATION APPROACH

Whilst the direct effect doctrine may assist individuals to obtain enforceable legal rights in the national courts in actions against the State or emanations of the State, it will not assist individuals bringing actions against other individuals. This is a clear anomaly but has been justified by the ECJ on the grounds that, because directives are addressed to Member States, they may not of themselves impose obligations on an individual. However, the ECJ has put forward other ways in which individuals can seek to rely on directives, even where the directives are not capable of direct effect (because they cannot satisfy the relevant conditions) or where the action is a horizontal one against another individual. The first of these approaches is sometimes called 'indirect effect', but a more appropriate way of describing it is the 'duty of interpretation'. The approach was first put forward in Case 14/83, *Von Colson v Land Nordrhein-Westfalen* (1983) and later extended in impact in Case C-106/89, *Marleasing SA v La Commercial Internacional de Alimentacion SA* (1989).

In *Von Colson*, the ECJ held that national courts (as emanations of the State and therefore equally bound by Art 10 of the EC Treaty) are under a duty to interpret national law, as far as possible, in the light of the directive which generated the national legislation. In other words, the national legislation should be construed to give effect to the purpose of the directive.

The judgment in *Marleasing*, which affirmed the position in *Von Colson*, was really quite remarkable in that the ECJ came to the view that the duty of interpretation also extended to national provisions whether they were introduced before or after a directive. The ECJ stated that in applying national law:

> ... whether the provisions in question [that is, the national provisions] were adopted before or after the Directive, the national court called upon to interpret it is required to do so, as far as possible, in the light of the wording and the purpose of the Directive in order to achieve the result pursued by the latter ...

The response of the English courts has been mixed. In *Webb v EMO Air Cargo (UK) Ltd* (1993), Lord Keith stated that the ECJ had, in the *Marleasing* decision, only required national courts to construe national legislation to give effect to a directive only if it was possible to do so. He went on to say that it would only be possible to do so where a domestic law was 'open to an interpretation consistent with the directive whether or not it is also open to an interpretation inconsistent with it'. However, in the case of *Wychavon DC v Secretary of State and Others* (1994), the High Court showed itself to be very unwilling to apply this principle. See also *R v Secretary of State for the Environment ex p Greenpeace* (1994).

3.14   STATE LIABILITY

In Cases C-6 and 9/90, *Francovich and Bonifaci v Italian State* (1991), the ECJ extended yet further the impact of directives. The case is important in that it lays down the principle that Member States may be sued for damages as a result of their failure to implement a directive. The ECJ, in its previous judgments, had been clear that Member States should not be able to benefit from their failure to implement directives in actions brought against the State by individuals and that Member States could not plead their failure to implement by way of defence. The *Francovich* judgment was a further extension of this and may well prove to be important in the enforcement of environmental directives.

The facts are as follows: Mr Francovich was owed 6 million lire by his insolvent employers. However, because he was unable to enforce a judgment against them, he brought an action against the Italian government for compensation. Under a Council Directive (80/987/EEC) aimed at protecting employees in the event of the insolvency of their employers, Member States were required to ensure that a system was set up to meet outstanding pay arrears for employees in the event of their employers' insolvency. The Italian government had not implemented the Directive and had not set up any system to act as guarantor in these circumstances. Francovich, however, could not rely on the direct effect of the Directive since it was not sufficiently clear and precise. However, the ECJ held that, subject to three conditions, damages are available against the State for failure to implement the Directive.

3.14.1 The conditions for State liability

The conditions for State liability laid down in *Francovich* were:

(a) the result prescribed by the directive should be the grant of rights to individuals;

(b) it must be possible to identify those rights on the basis of the provisions of the directive; and

(c) there must be a causal link between the breach of the State's obligation and the loss and damage suffered by the injured parties.

The *Francovich* judgment is regarded by many as a further landmark in the development of Community law. By creating the principle of State liability, the ECJ sent out a very loud warning to the Member States about the potential consequences of breaching Community law. Despite previous assertions in the past that Community law did not require the introduction of specific legal remedies, this new principle was seen by many as the creation of a new 'Community law' remedy. However, the decision in *Francovich* left a number of questions unanswered. First, the judgment related specifically to situations where Member States had failed to implement directives; it remained unclear whether the principle would apply to a wider range of breaches. Secondly, the ECJ simply required that there be a 'breach' of Community law (in this case, the failure to implement the directive), but the ECJ did not provide particular guidance on the nature of this breach: whether it should be strict or fault-based. However, it was not long before the ECJ was given the opportunity to examine this principle further in the joined Cases C-46 and C-48/93, *Brasserie du Pêcheur SA v Germany and R v Secretary of State for Transport ex p Factortame Ltd and Others* (1996). These cases concerned the application of the *Francovich* decision to breaches of primary EC Treaty provisions rather than directives. In *Brasserie du Pêcheur SA*, a French company claimed it had suffered loss as a result of German legislation on beer purity which was shown later in Case 178/84, *Commission v Germany* (1987) to be in breach of Art 28 (formerly Art 30). In *Factortame*, a Spanish fishing company was claiming for the losses it incurred as a consequence of the UK's breach of Art 43 (formerly Art 52). The ECJ held that where a Member State has a wide discretion in implementing EC policies (unlike the situation where a Member State has no discretion as to whether it implements a directive), the conditions under which it may incur liability must be the same as those under which the EC institutions incur liability under a comparable situation, which are laid down in Art 288 (formerly 215) of the EC Treaty which deals with the non-contractual liability of the EC. In such circumstances, EC law confers a right to reparation where three conditions are met: the rule of law infringed must be intended to confer rights on individuals; the breach must be *sufficiently serious*; and there must be a direct causal link between the breach of the obligation by the State and the damage sustained by the injured parties. The decisive test for finding that a breach of EC law is sufficiently serious is whether the Member State manifestly and gravely disregarded the limits of its discretion. It is clear from the judgment that the ECJ intends that national courts should be the arbiters as to whether the Member State's breach is sufficiently serious. However, the ECJ laid down a number of factors that the national court should take into account in reaching this determination, including the clarity and precision of the rule breached, the degree of discretion imparted by that rule, whether the infringement and the damage caused was intentional or voluntary, and whether the error of law was excusable or not.

The *Brasserie/Factortame* case thus established that, as a matter of principle, a State may be liable in damages for a wider range of breaches than was previously thought under *Francovich*. The judgment also clarified that only sufficiently serious breaches would give rise to such liability. In relation to the non-implementation of directives, the ECJ held that the failure to implement a directive within the prescribed period would always constitute a sufficiently serious breach because of the mandatory nature of Art 249 (Cases C-178–79/94, *Dillenkoffer and Others v Germany* (1996)). In circumstances where a Member State improperly implements a directive, the national court will have to consider whether this improper implementation constitutes a sufficiently serious breach, having regard to the factors laid down by the ECJ.

As yet, the ECJ or the national courts have not examined the impact of this ruling in the context of the environmental protection Treaty articles or directives. However, in order for a litigant to pursue a claim for damages successfully, he or she will need to establish that the rule that was breached was intended to confer rights; this may be the most difficult obstacle to overcome for many directives other than those that lay down quantifiable quality standards, such as the Drinking Water Directive (see Case C-337/89, *Commission v UK* (1993)) or procedural rights, such as the Environmental Impact Assessment Directive (85/337/EEC).

3.15   THE DEVELOPMENT OF A COMMUNITY ENVIRONMENTAL POLICY

3.15.1 Introduction

When the EEC was formed in 1957 by the Treaty of Rome, the major concern of the founding members was the creation of a common market throughout the six Member States. The Treaty of Rome concentrated primarily on economic issues and there was no specific reference to the environment. It was not until the SEA 1986 that Title VII 'Environment' was incorporated into the Treaty, giving the Community a legal competence in the field of environmental protection for the first time. However, despite the lack of an explicit legal basis, the Community had in the intervening years taken numerous measures to protect the environment. It had also managed to develop its own interventionist environmental policy using other powers under the Treaty, namely Arts 94 and 308 (formerly Arts 100 and 235).

The position today is that the EC has a well developed environmental policy, enjoys specific powers to enact legislation in the environmental field and has enacted over 300 environmentally-related measures largely in the form of directives. In fact, it could be argued that environmental policy has equal standing with economic and social policy. Environmental policy now enjoys a unique status in EC law by virtue of Art 6, which states that environmental protection requirements must be integrated into the definition and implementation of the other Community policies and activities, in particular with a view to promoting sustainable development. The impact of this provision is considered more fully later.

3.15.2 Environmental policy and law before the SEA 1986 (1957–86)

As stated above, the Treaty of Rome made no reference to the environment. The authors of the Treaty and founding members were principally concerned to establish a common market for goods. Article 2 of the Treaty stated the aims of the Community as 'establishing a common market and progressively approximating the economic policies of Member States, to promote throughout the Community a harmonious development of economic activities, a continuous and balanced expansion, an increase in stability, an accelerated raising of the standard of living and closer relations between the States belonging to it'.

Since the institutions of the EC can only legally act within the limits of the powers conferred upon them by the EC Treaty, legislation in the early days of the Community was largely concerned with economic issues and market regulation. However, despite the absence of any specific powers, the Community did in fact introduce a large number of directives which impacted either directly or indirectly upon the environment. As early as 1967, the Community had introduced a directive on the classification, packaging and labelling of dangerous substances. The introduction of the legislation was not aimed specifically at protecting the environment, but rather at harmonising standards in relation to the packaging and labelling of dangerous substances, but it nevertheless had indirect implications for the environment. This early environmental legislation was introduced either under Art 94 (formerly Art 100) or Art 308 (formerly Art 235).

3.15.2.1 Articles 94 and 308 (formerly Arts 100 and 235)

Article 94 provides for measures to be introduced to secure the approximation of laws affecting the functioning of the common market. Environmental measures enacted on the basis of Art 94 were justified on the basis that different levels and standards of environmental protection in the different Member States would interfere with the creation of a common market by distorting competition. In other words, if the standards of environmental protection are low in one Member State compared to another with more rigorous standards, then industrialists in the former State spend less on meeting environmental protection standards than industrialists in the latter Member State. This disparity may give the industrialist in the Member State with the lower standards a competitive edge (in a sense they will be benefiting from a hidden subsidy) and this may distort the patterns of trade. An example of a directive enacted under Art 94 is Directive (78/659/EEC) on the quality of freshwater needing protection or improvement in order to support fish life. Although it is clear that this is an environmental protection measure in its own right, the preamble to the directive states that 'differences between the provisions ... in the various Member States as regards the quality of waters capable of supporting the life of freshwater fish may create unequal conditions of competition and thus directly affect the functioning of the common market'.

Article 308, on the other hand, is a residual power which enables action to be taken by the institutions even where the Treaty has not provided the necessary powers, but where it is 'necessary to attain, in the course of the operation of the common market, one of the objectives of the Community'. Measures such as Council Directive 79/409/EEC on the Conservation of Wild Birds were adopted under Art 308 exclusively. The justification for the Wild Birds Directive in particular was that the conservation of wild birds was necessary to attain the Community's objective of improving living conditions throughout the Common Market. Therefore, the measure was justified rather tentatively by reference to Art 2 of the Treaty of Rome. In a similar way, Art 308 has been used to justify other policy areas such as regional policy, which were not explicitly stated within the Treaty, but which were construed as being Community interests.

3.15.2.2 The Stockholm Conference and the emergence of a Community environmental policy

These early environmental measures were not introduced as part of a coherent strategy on the environment which, at this stage, the Community did not have. However, the early 1970s saw a groundswell in public opinion about the environment and also marked the beginning of the Community's environmental policy. In 1972, a United Nations Conference was held in Stockholm to consider the human environment. The Conference was significant because it marked the beginnings of international co-operation in the field of the environment, and it is from this date that environmental law has become a legitimate and important area of international law. It is also important in Community law terms because it was followed by the Paris Summit in October 1972, when the Heads of State and governments of the Member States of the Community declared:

> Economic expansion is not an end in itself. Its firm aim should be to enable disparities in living conditions to be reduced. It must take place with the participation of all the social partners. It should result in an improvement in the quality of life as well as in standards of living. As befits the genius of Europe, particular attention will be given to intangible values and to protecting the environment, so that progress may really be put at the service of mankind.

3.15.2.3 Environmental Action Programmes

Following this recognition of the importance of protecting the environment, the Commission was requested to draw up an Action Programme on the environment. This first Action Programme for the period 1973–76 was adopted in 1973. Since that time, the Community has produced six Action Programmes:

Action Programmes	Period	Citation
First	1973–76	C112, 20.12.73
Second	1977–81	C139, 13.6.77
Third	1982–86	C46, 17.2.83
Fourth	1987–92	C328, 7.12.87
Fifth	1993–2000	C138, 17.5.93
Sixth	2001–10	L242, 10.9.2002

The Action Programmes are essentially political statements, which outline the Community's intentions for legislation and other activities in the years ahead. The First Action Programme started with a general statement of the objectives and principles of a Community environmental policy and then went on to list the actions that the Commission would bring forward. It also listed 11 principles which are still largely applicable today. The Fifth and Sixth Action Programmes are outlined later in this chapter at 3.15.9.

Although the Community had begun to develop an environmental policy as early as 1973, it still faced the problem that there was no real constitutional basis for that policy. Legislation was still largely enacted on the basis that different standards of environmental protection throughout the Community would distort competition, would hamper the establishment of a common market and had to be justified accordingly. However, the SEA 1986 provided for the first time a specific legal basis upon which the Community could legislate in the field of environmental protection.

3.15.3 The SEA 1986

The SEA 1986 marked a key stage in the development of the EC's environmental protection policy. It resulted in the incorporation of a new Title, specifically on the environment, into the EEC Treaty and in doing so introduced Arts 130r–t (now renumbered as Arts 174–76) into the Treaty.

In addition, Art 100 (now Art 94) was also amended by the SEA 1986 and a new Art 100a (now Art 95) was introduced, which provided that qualified majority voting in the Council of Ministers would be the normal voting procedure in relation to the harmonising measures pursued under this Article. This change was introduced essentially to speed up the decision making process in relation to harmonising measures needed to complete the single market by 1992. A further amendment in relation to the new Art 100a (now Art 95) was the requirement that the Commission would, when making proposals which concerned environmental protection, take as a base a high level of protection. This was significant because it was recognition in the Treaty itself that approximation measures enacted under this Article could legitimately be concerned with environmental protection and was also important in so far as it meant that environmental measures were not exclusively in the domain of Arts 130r–t (now Arts 174–176).

3.15.4 The TEU 1992

The TEU, signed in Maastricht in 1992, gave effect to a number of significant amendments relating to environmental law. These can be briefly stated as follows:

(a) the EEC became the EC, in recognition that it was more than just an economic community;

(b) Art 2 refers to sustainable and non-inflationary growth regarding the environment;

(c) Art 3 established that there should be a policy in the sphere of the environment;

(d) Art 100a (now Art 95) was amended so that the procedure used for harmonising legislation is the co-decision procedure, thus allowing the Parliament the right of veto in relation to such legislation;

(e) Art 130s (now Art 174) was amended and, in particular, changed the legislative procedure so that, with certain exceptions, environmental legislation could now be enacted using the co-operation procedure, thus giving the Parliament a greater degree of control than it had previously. The amended Article also built in the requirement that Community environmental policy should aim at a high level of protection.

3.15.5 The impact of the ToA and the ToN

The significant change brought about by the ToA was the insertion of the 'integration principle' into the more prominent position of Art 3(c) (now Art 6) instead of being included in the Environment Title (Art 130r(2)). The integration principle requires that environmental protection requirements must be integrated into the definition and implementation of the Community policies and activities referred to in Art 3, in particular with a view to promoting sustainable development. This more prominent positioning of the requirement reflects the importance which the Community places on environmental protection as an all-pervading issue. In addition, the ToA further amended Art 2 to provide a new goal of 'promoting a harmonious and balanced and sustainable development of economic activities' as well as 'a high level of protection and improvement of the quality of the environment'.

Amendments made by the ToN were more limited, in that they refined those areas of law making which would be subject to the consultation procedures under Art 175(2).

3.15.6 The ECJ and the development of environmental law

Even before the SEA 1986 was amended to incorporate a Community competence in the field of the environment, the ECJ had recognised that the environment and environmental protection was an 'essential' component of Community policy, even to the extent that protection of the environment could hinder the free movement of goods within the Community, one of the fundamental principles of Community law.

In Case 240/83, *Procureur de la République v ADBHU* (1983), the ECJ stated that there could be no doubt that the protection of the environment constitutes an objective of general interest which the Community could legitimately pursue. The case involved an action in the French courts to dissolve the *Association de défense de bruleurs d'huiles usagées*, an association established in 1980 to defend the interests of manufacturers, dealers and users of heating appliances designed to burn fuel oil and waste oils. In their defence, the Association contested the validity of Directive 75/439/EEC, which aims to protect the environment against the risks from waste oils. The Association contested that the Directive was contrary to the principles of freedom of trade, free movement of goods and freedom of competition. The French court sought a ruling from the ECJ on the interpretation and validity of the Directive, using the Art 234 (formerly Art 177) preliminary rulings procedure. In reaching its decision that the Directive was valid, the ECJ held that:

> The Directive must be seen in the perspective of environmental protection, which is one of the Community's essential objectives.

One of the significant features of the ECJ's judgment in this case is that it came to this conclusion at a time when the Treaty did not provide any specific explicit legal basis for environmental action. The case predated the introduction of Arts 174–76 (formerly Arts 130r–t). The view that environmental protection could constitute one of the Community's essential objectives was reinforced and developed in Case 302/86, *Commission v Denmark* (1988), often known as the *Danish Bottles* case.

3.15.6.1 The Danish Bottles case

The *Danish Bottles* case is important because it raises two very important issues. First, it considered the question of whether Member States could introduce more stringent environmental laws than the rest of the Community; and, second, because it also concerned the related issue of the relationship between environmental protection and the free movement of goods as required by Art 28 (formerly Art 30) of the EC Treaty. It therefore merits detailed attention.

In 1981, the Danish government, concerned about the environmental consequences of litter and waste from discarded metal cans, instituted a system requiring beer and soft drinks to be marketed only in containers that could be reused. The use of metal cans was forbidden. Containers had to meet the requirements laid down and be approved by the Danish National Agency for the Protection of the Environment. In 1984, the legislation was amended so that non-approved containers were permitted subject to very strict limits and also to a deposit and return system. Although the object of the system was to reduce the numbers of discarded metal tins, it had as an effect a potential restriction on competition. Manufacturers of beers and soft drinks outside Denmark could sell their products throughout the Community but not in Denmark unless they could comply with the Danish deposit and return system. Therefore, the Danish manufacturers were in effect protected from external competition.

The European Commission commenced proceedings against the Danish government under Art 226 (formerly Art 169) of the EC Treaty. The Commission alleged that the introduction of a system, under which all containers for beers and soft drinks must be returnable, was contrary to Art 28 of the Treaty. Article 28, which is concerned with the free movement of goods, provides that quantitative measures on imports and all measures having equivalent effect to quantitative restrictions shall be prohibited. Member States are prohibited from introducing quantitative measures such as bans or quotas, or any measure which has equivalent effect. The definition of measures having equivalent effect was provided by the ECJ in Case 8/74, *Procureur du Roi v Dassonville* (1974) as 'all trading rules enacted by Member States which are capable of hindering, directly or indirectly, actually or potentially, intra-Community trade'. The Commission argued that the Danish rules were capable of hindering trade of beer and soft drinks into Denmark and as such were contrary to Art 28.

The ECJ based its decision in this case on an earlier and landmark decision in the case commonly known as the *Cassis de Dijon* case, Case 120/78, *Rewe-Zentral AG Bundesmonopolver-wältung für Branntwein* (1979). In *Cassis*, it was held that, in the absence of Community rules, Member States could introduce certain measures relating to the marketing of products if the measures were necessary to satisfy certain mandatory requirements (known as the 'rule of reason'). The Danish government argued in the *Danish Bottles* case that the mandatory deposit and return system was justified by a mandatory requirement, namely the protection of the environment. The ECJ accepted that the protection of the environment could constitute a mandatory requirement, given the ECJ's previous decision in *Procureur de la République* that the protection of the environment is one of the Community's essential objectives and also given the provisions of the SEA 1986. The question which remained for the ECJ to decide was whether the Danish rules were necessary in order to satisfy the mandatory requirement, or whether the environment could be protected in ways which were less restrictive to trade. In other words, the ECJ had to apply a test of proportionality. The ECJ accepted that the deposit and return system for empty containers was an 'indispensable element of a system intended to ensure the re-use of containers and therefore appears necessary to achieve the aims pursued by the contested rules'. Turning to the system for non-approved containers and the strict limit on the amount of containers that could be imported in non-approved containers (non-approved containers could be used where the quantity of marketed drinks did not exceed 3,000 hecti-litres per year per producer), the ECJ held that the Danish rules were disproportionate. The reasoning was that the system for non-approved containers was also capable of protecting the environment (non-approved containers were subject to a deposit and return system) and, since the quantity of imports was limited, the limitation to 3,000 hecti-litres was excessive.

3.15.7 Environmental legislation after the SEA 1986

It has been established thus far that both the EC Treaty and the ECJ in its case law recognised the importance of Community environmental policy. One would be forgiven for thinking that, after the SEA 1986 and the provisions of Arts 174–76 (formerly Arts 130r–t), the development of Community environmental law from that point in time was simply a matter of developing new environmental initiatives and laws under those Treaty articles. However, the introduction of Arts 174–76 brought with it a number of particular problems. As stated above, prior to their introduction, the Commission had to rely on Arts 94 and 308 (formerly Arts 100 and 235) to justify environmental measures, and sometimes measures were challenged by Member States. The introduction of this new explicit legal base, however, did not mean that from 1987 onwards all environmental legislation would be enacted under Arts 174–76. It is still clearly the case that some legislation is intended to protect the environment *per se*, whereas other legislative acts are intended to approximate standards. The question therefore became: 'which was the correct legal basis for environmental action – Art 95 (formerly Art 100a) or Art 175?'

3.15.7.1 Article 175 or Article 95?

Environmental protection measures can be adopted under either Art 175 or Art 95 of the EC Treaty. These respective Articles determine what action the Community can take. Thus, under Art 175, the Community can take action (that is, adopt legally binding instruments) in order to achieve the specific environmental protection objectives defined in Art 174. On the other hand, under Art 95, the Community can take action to 'approximate' the laws of the Member States in order to establish the internal market. Therefore, it can be seen that the overriding objectives of these two Articles differ. The impact of this can be seen most clearly when considering the extent to which Member States retain the capacity to adopt stricter national measures than those laid down by the Community. This is considered more fully at 3.15.8.2 below.

In addition to providing a legal competence to act, the Articles also define the procedure which must be used in order to bring forward legislation under the relevant article. Thus, for example, Treaty articles specify whether the legislation should be enacted using the co-operation or co-decision procedures. In relation to Arts 175 and 95, the respective law making procedure is the co-decision procedure as laid down in Art 251. This procedure is generally regarded as being the most democratic of the various procedures, since it confers on the European Parliament the power to veto proposed legislation. Thus, it now makes little difference in terms of democratic accountability whether a proposed environmental measure is adopted under Art 175 or Art 95, apart from the fact that, under Art 175, the Council must consult with the Committee of the Regions, but is not required to do so for harmonisation legislation under Art 95. The streamlining of the procedures across these two Articles is welcome. Prior to the amendments made by the ToN, legislation adopted under Art 175 was adopted under the so called co-operation procedure, which effectively gave the Council the greater degree of control over the content of the legislation. The fact that the legislative procedures previously differed between Art 175 and Art 95 generated a number of cases in which the ECJ was called upon to adjudicate the correct legal base (see Case C-300/89, *Commission v Council (Titanium Dioxide)* and Case C-155/91, *Commission v Council (Waste Disposal)*). Although the ToN has effectively ironed out the differences between the law making procedures of these two Articles, the fact remains that the two Articles have very different aims. These can be summarised as follows:

(a) Articles 174–76 allow the Community to adopt legislation specifically to protect the environment. These articles specify, *inter alia*, the objectives of EC environmental policy, the principles upon which such policy should be based, the factors to be taken into account by the Community and the manner in which such legislation should be adopted.

(b) Article 95 allows the Community to adopt measures designed to secure the harmonisation of national laws in order to secure the proper functioning of the common market. A considerable body of law has been enacted under this Article, which seeks to ensure the approximation of environmental standards throughout the European Union. The objective of this legislation is principally to secure harmonisation of standards.

(c) Accordingly, EC environmental protection legislation may have different specific objectives, depending on the Treaty article upon which the legislation is based.

(d) Where legislation has been adopted by the EC under Art 95, then Member States have very little opportunity to develop their own stricter domestic rules.

3.15.8 Stricter environmental rules in Member States and the free movement of goods

The most significant difference between the use of the two Treaty Articles is the extent to which Member States can introduce stricter environmental protection rules than the Community-wide rules or standards. This is an issue of twofold importance.

On the one hand, it is a matter of concern to those Member States that place a particularly strong emphasis upon environmental protection and wish to secure the highest levels of protection. For some Member States, harmonisation suggests harmonising down rather than up, and this is unsatisfactory to them. This is likely to be an important issue to Sweden and Austria, in particular, which have in place certain environmental protection measures which are stricter than prevailing Community-wide measures.

On the other hand, the second and inextricably related issue is the extent to which stricter environmental protection rules can be permitted where they hamper or restrict the free movement of goods required by Art 28 (formerly Art 30). The trade versus environment debate has generated considerable academic debate because it takes place against the backdrop of the shared responsibility for environmental protection between the Member States and the Community.

3.15.8.1 The relationship between environmental protection and the free movement of goods

The free movement of goods throughout the Community is regarded as one of the fundamental cornerstones of EC law. Article 28 (formerly Art 30) of the EC Treaty prohibits Member States from introducing quantitative restrictions and measures having equivalent effect to a quantitative restriction (MEQR). Measures which are introduced by Member States which have the effect of hindering the free circulation of goods across borders are therefore prohibited. Even where measures apply equally to domestic and imported goods (known as indistinctly applicable measures), the measures may still breach Art 28 where they affect inter-State trade. The types of measures which have been held to breach Art 28 range from more obvious measures such as bans and import quotas to 'buy national' campaigns which have the effect of discriminating against imports. Article 28 has been used widely in litigation and its scope has been widely defined by the ECJ (see *Procureur du Roi v Dassonville* (1974)). In environmental terms, it is easy to see how action taken at the national level to preserve and protect the environment or to encourage recycling might fall within the wide scope of Art 28. For example, in Case C-389/96, *Aher-Waggon GmbH v Germany* (1998), German legislation designed to limit noise from aircraft was held to amount to a measure having equivalent effect to a quantitative restriction, contrary to Art 28.

There are of course circumstances in which national rules which *prima facie* breach Art 28 may be justified in the wider public interest. These 'justifications' take the form of specific derogations in Art 30 (formerly Art 36) and also under the growing number of so called mandatory requirements laid down by the ECJ in the famous *Cassis* case. Each of these is considered below.

Article 30 (formerly Art 36) provides a list of six derogations from Art 28 (formerly Art 30) whereby Member States may attempt to justify any measures which breach Art 28. The list is exhaustive. Breaches of Art 28 may be justified on the grounds of public morality; public policy or public security; the protection of health and life of humans, animals or plants; the protection of national treasures possessing artistic, historic or archaeological value; or the protection of industrial or commercial property. However, Art 30 stipulates that measures cannot be justified if they constitute a means of arbitrary discrimination or a disguised restriction on trade between Member States. The ECJ has tended to treat the derogations under Art 30 with a great deal of circumspection by placing, in general terms, a very narrow construction on the six derogations. The ECJ has consistently emphasised the need to preserve as far as possible the fundamental freedom conferred by Art 28 by narrowly interpreting the exceptions to it under Art 30. This is particularly the case where the national measure in question is inherently discriminatory, for example, in relation to an import ban. The burden of proof falls squarely on the Member State pleading the justification to demonstrate the need to adopt such restrictive measures to achieve the stated objective.

In relation to national measures of an environmental protection nature, the obvious justification is the 'protection of health and life of humans, animals or plants'. The ECJ was prepared in Case C-67/97, *Criminal Proceedings against Ditlev Bluhme* (1998) to reach the conclusion that 'measures to preserve an indigenous animal population with distinct characteristics contribute to the maintenance of biodiversity by ensuring the survival of the population concerned. By doing so they are aimed at protecting the life of those animals and are capable of being justified under Article 30 of the Treaty'. The case concerned Danish legislation which was enacted in order to secure the survival of the Læsø brown bee, a bee native to the Island of Læsø. The legislation prohibited the keeping of any bees other than Læsø brown bee. The case involved a criminal prosecution in respect of a breach of this prohibition by B, who argued in his defence that the Danish rule was contrary to Art 28. Having accepted that the prohibition was contrary to Art 28, the ECJ went on to consider whether it could fall within the Art 30 derogation. Presented with various arguments about the importance of maintaining biodiversity, the ECJ accepted that the measure in question was justifiable under the Art 30 derogation.

Whether a measure may be justified under Art 30 also requires a consideration of the type of rule adopted and, in particular, whether it is proportionate to the aims. This was evidenced in Case C-131/93, *Commission v Germany*, in which Germany introduced a total ban on the import of live freshwater crayfish in order to protect native crayfish from disease. Although the ECJ did not challenge the purported aims of the measure, it did accept the Commission's argument that an outright ban was disproportionate and that Germany could have employed less restrictive measures, such as health checks on crayfish coming from other Member States, to achieve the same aim. Thus, this case fell at the proportionality hurdle. However, in practice, it is very difficult for Member States to pass the proportionality test in relation to import bans of this nature.

In addition to the specific heads of derogation under Art 30, the ECJ has developed the so called 'rule of reason' in the case of Case 120/78, *Cassis de Dijon (Rewe-Zentral v Bundesmonopolver-wältung für Branntwein)* (1979). Essentially, the rule of reason operates to 'save' certain national rules/measures which, whilst being capable of hindering trade (that is, they appear to be measures having equivalent effect to a quantitative restriction), are to be 'accepted' in so far as they are necessary to satisfy some overriding wider public interest. These overriding public interests are referred to as 'mandatory requirements':

> Obstacles to movement in the Community resulting from disparities between the national laws relating to the marketing of the products in question must be accepted

in so far as those provisions may be recognised as being necessary in order to satisfy mandatory requirements relating in particular to the effectiveness of fiscal supervision, the protection of public health, the fairness of commercial transaction and the defence of the consumer.

The effect of this is that national rules which are introduced to satisfy these mandatory requirements are 'acceptable' and do not breach Art 28. In the *Cassis* case, the ECJ listed only four mandatory requirements, but this list is not exhaustive and has been expanded through further case law to include, *inter alia*, environmental protection in Case 302/86, *Commission v Denmark (Disposable Cans and Bottles)*, in which the Court held that: '... the protection of the environment is one of the Community's essential objectives, which may justify certain limitations of the principle of the free movement of goods ... it must therefore be stated that the protection of the environment is a mandatory requirement which may limit the application of [Art 28] of the Treaty.' The ECJ applied the same reasoning in Case C-2/90, *Commission v Belgium (Walloon Waste)* (1992) and Case C-389/96, *Aher-Waggon*, where, in relation to German legislation governing the noise levels of aircraft registered in Germany, the ECJ stated that:

National legislation of the kind at issue ... restricts intra-Community trade since it makes the first registration in national territory of aircraft previously registered in [another] Member State conditional upon compliance with stricter noise standards ... Such a barrier may, however, be justified by considerations of public health and environmental protection ...

The fact that a national measure is introduced in order to protect the environment will not necessarily mean that is acceptable under this rule. Some important limitations need be considered. First, the rule of reason only operates to save national rules in the absence of Community measures. Thus, where the EC has adopted a directive, for example, in relation to the level of chemicals acceptable in a given product, then that becomes the norm and Member States may not be able to deviate from this unless, as in Case C-389/96, *Aher-Waggon*, the directive only specifies a minimum acceptable standard. Secondly, national measures must satisfy a proportionality test. The ECJ has made it clear that any national rules which have the effect of hindering trade must be *necessary* to satisfy a mandatory requirement and must not go beyond that which is necessary. As with Art 30, the national measure must be proportionate and will fail if it can be shown that there are other less restrictive ways of achieving the same objective.

Finally, one further limitation of the rule of reason should be considered, particularly since it has been subject to some recent controversy. The traditional position of the ECJ is that the rule of reason is only available when national legislation is 'indistinctly applicable' (Case 788/79, *Gilli & Andres* (1980), and Case 113/80, *Commission v Ireland (Souvenir Jewellery)* (1981)). However, this view has been cast in some doubt following two cases concerning Art 29 of the EC Treaty. Article 29 prohibits Member States from introducing quantitative restrictions or measures having equivalent effect to a quantitative restriction on exports. The ECJ's earlier position was that the rule of reason should never be available in Art 29 cases, because the ECJ has also held that national legislation only breaches Art 29 if it is 'distinctly applicable' (Case 53/76, *Bouhelier* (1977), and Case 15/79, *PB Groenveld BV* (1979)). However, in Case 155/80, *Sergius Oebel* (1981), and Case C-203/96, *Dusseldorp BV* (1998), the ECJ appears to concede that it may be prepared to accept a rule of reason argument in cases where the national legislation is not 'indistinctly applicable' after all. In *Dusseldorp*, Dutch legislation prohibited the export of waste oil filters unless it could be shown that they would be subject to a waste recovery treatment of a higher quality than that available in the Netherlands. The aim of the legislation was to promote the principles of self-sufficiency in waste. On a preliminary ruling, the ECJ held that the ban was contrary to Art 29, but then went on to consider possible justifications for it. Despite the fact that the measure was discriminatory, the ECJ explored the possibility that it could be acceptable under the rule of reason. On the facts, the ECJ held that the 'justifications' in fact were purely economic and thus held that the Dutch rules were incompatible with Art 29. Nevertheless, the ECJ appears to have considered using the rule of reason in respect of a distinctly applicable measure. Thus, the ECJ seems to have blurred the distinction between distinctly and indistinctly applicable measures. Various commentators have argued that, specifically in relation to the environmental protection mandatory requirements, the ECJ should allow the mandatory requirement to be used to save distinctly applicable measures as well as indistinctly applicable measures because, in most cases, it is not possible to distinguish between justifications based on the 'protection of the health and life of humans, animals or plants' (which appears in Art 30) and those based on 'environmental protection' (which is a mandatory requirement). The ECJ appeared to do this in Case C-2/90, *Commission v Belgium (Walloon Waste)*, in relation to a ban on waste imports imposed by the Walloon Region of Belgium. Although the ban was to all intents and purposes discriminatory, because it discriminated against imported non-hazardous waste, the ECJ employed some interesting reasoning to reach the conclusion that it was not distinctly applicable 'having regard to the differences between waste produced in one place and that in another and its connection with the place that it is produced the measures cannot be considered to be discriminatory'. Thus, in consideration of the 'special' character of waste, the ECJ concluded that this ban was not discriminatory and was acceptable to serve the mandatory requirement of environmental protection.

3.15.8.2 Stricter environmental protection measures: Art 176 (formerly Art 130t)

Where the Community has enacted an environmental directive, the extent to which Member States may maintain or even introduce more stringent environmental protection measures than those laid down in the directive will be determined by the legal basis on which the directive was enacted, namely Art 175 (formerly Art 130s) or Art 95 (formerly Art 100a). In relation to legislation adopted under Art 175, the position is clarified in Art 176 (formerly Art 130t). Article 176 provides that the protective measures adopted under Art 175 shall not prevent any Member State from maintaining or introducing more stringent protective measures providing that these measures are compatible with the EC Treaty. In other words, a Member State may maintain or introduce environmental protection measures which go beyond those adopted by the EC under Art 175, but they must be compatible with other Treaty provisions, particularly Art 28. Therefore, Art 176 provides a balance between the Member States' right to adopt measures against the right of the Community to legislate in this area.

Measures introduced under Art 95 are introduced with the intention of approximating laws and, therefore, Member States ought not to apply national measures which differ from EC measures adopted under this Article. However, there is one specific exception provided for in Art 95(4) (formerly Art 100a(4)) whereby Member States may maintain national provisions relating to the protection of the environment or the working environment. The Member State in question must notify the Commission of its intentions and the Commission must within six months either confirm or reject the national provisions. In reaching its decision, the Commission must verify that the national measures in question are not a means of arbitrary discrimination or a disguised restriction of trade between the Member States. Further provision exists for the Commission or any Member State to bring the matter before the ECJ if it believes that a Member State is improperly using the powers provided for in Art 95(4). Such a challenge was mounted by France in the so called *PCP* case.

3.15.8.3 The PCP case

Case C-41/93, *France v the Commission of the EC* (1994) concerned the use of Art 95(4) (formerly Art 100a(4)). Following the adoption of Directive 91/173/EEC, Germany applied for a derogation under Art 95(4). Directive 91/173/EEC was adopted under Art 95 (formerly Art 100a) and concerned the marketing and use of substances and preparations containing pesticide and preservative pentachlorophenol (PCP). At the time of its adoption, Germany had in place much stricter standards, setting lower concentration limits on PCP. The Council of Ministers had reached a decision on the directive by qualified majority vote, with Germany voting against the measure. Germany sought to maintain its own stricter standards and therefore asked the Commission for confirmation under Art 95(4). The Commission granted Germany the derogation, despite strong opposition from France, Italy and Greece who were concerned about the impact of the German measure on imports of their leather goods into Germany. The case involved an action for judicial review under Art 230 (formerly Art 173) of the EC Treaty brought by France against the Commission's decision. The ECJ, accepting that the Commission's decision was a reviewable act, held that Art 95(4) should be interpreted restrictively and that it is up to the Member State seeking the derogation to prove that the measure is both necessary and proportionate, and that there are no other suitable means of achieving the aim pursued in a manner which is less restrictive of the free movement of goods. In the case in hand, the ECJ annulled the Commission's decision but only on procedural grounds: the Commission had failed to justify their position adequately. The Commission subsequently took a second decision, reaffirming its original position but this time ensuring there was sufficient justification.

Article 95(4) refers specifically to the situation where a Member State wishes to maintain existing national measures. Article 95(5), however, allows Member States to introduce national measures relating to the protection of the environment. The right to introduce national laws after the EC has adopted harmonising legislation under Art 95 is circumscribed. First, the Member State must 'deem it necessary' to introduce the rule based on 'new scientific evidence' relating to need, and the national measure must address a problem that is specific to that Member State, the problem having arisen after the adoption of the EC harmonising measure. Clearly, this will have limited application. Once again, the Member State must notify the Commission, which has the power to confirm or accept the national provision. Moreover, where this occurs, the Commission is bound to examine immediately whether to propose an adaptation to the harmonising measure.

3.15.9 The Community's Environmental Action Programmes

The European Community's First Action Programme for the Environment was adopted by the Council of Ministers on 22 December 1973. It set Community-wide objectives to resolve urgent pollution problems concerning water, air and soil. More importantly, it also established 11 principles upon which the Community's environmental policy is based. The Second, Third and Fourth Action Programmes continued in much the same vein as the first, only providing refinements to the Community's objectives. They concentrated upon specific environmental media: air, water and waste. In particular, many of the policy aims, subsequently translated into directives, were concerned with setting emission limits. They were seen largely as 'end of pipe' solutions or 'fire fighting' measures. However, they were not entirely reactive in nature and over the subsequent programmes there was a growing emphasis on prevention rather than cure. The Fifth Action Programme represented a departure and change in thinking. On 26 June 1990, the Heads of State of the Member States called for the Fifth Action Programme to be drawn up on the principles of sustainable development, preventive and precautionary action and shared responsibility.

3.15.9.1 The Fifth Environmental Action Programme – Towards Sustainability

The Fifth Environmental Action Programme covered the period 1993 to 2000 and, to that extent, differed from the previous programmes in that it covered a seven year period rather than five. The programme also marked a more important departure from previous programmes in its approach. Entitled *Towards Sustainability*, the programme did not specifically concern itself with the protection of environmental media, such as air, water or land. Instead, the programme concentrated on five key sectors of activity which have significant impacts on the state of the environment. The five sectors were: industry, energy, transport, agriculture and tourism. In the field of transport, for example, the Commission had produced a Green Paper on transport entitled *Sustainable Mobility*. This recommended the transfer from private transport use to more public transport and considered using fiscal measures such as road pricing and higher fuel prices to reduce demand. Agriculture, as another key sector, is responsible for a significant amount of environmental damage and there was recognition that the Common Agricultural Policy had been responsible for a negative impact on the environment. The aims of the Fifth Action Programme in this regard were to reduce the impact of agriculture on the environment by encouraging farmers to see themselves as 'guardians of the countryside' and to reduce in particular the pollution from nitrates and phosphates.

3.15.9.2 Sustainability

The emphasis in the Fifth Action Programme is sustainable development. One of the best definitions of sustainable development is the one provided in the Bruntland Report, *Our Common Future*, which set the agenda for discussions about the relationship between economic growth and protection of the environment. The Report states that sustainable development is:

... economic development which meets the needs of the present generation without compromising the ability of future generations to meet their own needs.

The TEU introduced the principle of sustainability explicitly into the EC Treaty for the first time in Art 2.

3.15.9.3 Shared responsibility

Another feature of the Fifth Environmental Action Programme was the emphasis that it placed on 'shared responsibility'. Inherent in the Fifth Action Programme was the belief that everyone shares a responsibility towards the environment and that there must be an 'optimum involvement of all sectors of society'. In order to change patterns of behaviour of producers, consumers, government and citizens, the Action Programme called for information campaigns to raise public awareness. Access to environmental information was also seen as a key element in enabling citizens to assist with the monitoring of pollution throughout the Community and also as a means of exercising consumer preferences for 'green' products and producers.

3.15.9.4 Types of environmental measures

The Action Programmes provide the broad policy framework from which the Commission can initiate legislative proposals. However, the Fifth Action Programme recognised that environmental protection could not be secured entirely by legal and regulatory measures. In a review of the measures available to improve the environment, the Commission stated that future environmental policy would be based on four types of measures:

(a) regulatory instruments;

(b) market-based measures;

(c) support measures, such as education, information and research; and

(d) financial support mechanisms.

This theme of using different measures is continued in the current Sixth Action Programme.

3.15.9.5 Review of the Fifth Action Programme

In 1995, the Commission carried out a detailed review of the Fifth Action Programme, as required by the Action Programme itself, given the time period which the programme spans. The review involved wide consultation with various governmental and non-governmental organisations, and concentrated on the latest scientific data and also the results of the Conference on Environment (the Earth Summit) held in Rio in June 1992. Several issues were prominent in the review, a number of which are highlighted below:

(a) *Public awareness, information and education* – the Commission reaffirmed its commitment to extending awareness of environmental issues and has introduced a Community Action Programme specifically aimed at promoting non-governmental organisations active in the field of environmental protection.

(b) *Economic, fiscal and legal instruments* – one of the aims of the Fifth Action Programme was to diversify the range of instruments used beyond legislative measures. One of the principal measures proposed has been the introduction of a tax on carbon dioxide emissions and energy.

(c) *Financial instruments* – the LIFE Programme has been extended to cover the period 1996 to 1999.

(d) *International co-operation* – in 1995, the EU participated in a number of international initiatives including the third Pan-European Conference of Environment Ministers, which brought together ministerial representatives from United Nations and OECD countries, together with several environmental pressure groups.

3.15.9.6 The Sixth Environmental Action Programme

The Sixth Environmental Action Programme proposals are set out in 'Environment 2010: Our Future, Our Choice'. The new programme focuses on the following four priority areas: climate change; nature and bio-diversity; environment and health; and sustainable use of natural resources and sustainable management of wastes.

Objectives have been set for each priority area. In line with Kyoto Protocol commitments, there is a target of an 8% reduction in greenhouse gases, based on 1990 levels of the six main gases, during 2008–12. The programme also sets a target for noise reduction: 10% fewer people suffering from long term high levels of noise by 2010, rising to 20% by 2020. Efforts are to be made to 'protect and restore the functioning of natural systems and halt the loss of biodiversity' and to protect soils against erosion and pollution. Also of note are the following objectives: 12% of total energy use to be derived from renewable sources by 2010; loss of biodiversity to be halted by 2010; only chemicals which do not have significant adverse impacts on man and the environment to be produced and used by 2020; fossil fuel subsidies to be phased out; and economic growth de-coupled from resource usage.

As well as the priority areas, the new action programme details four 'approaches' to be taken in regard to environmental issues. These approaches relate to:

(1) effective implementation and enforcement of environmental legislation in order to set a common baseline for all EU countries;

(2) integration of environmental concerns into other policy areas (in pursuance of the requirements of Art 6 of the EC Treaty);

(3) using of a range of instruments including legal instruments alongside fiscal and educational measures;

(4) the stimulation of participation and action of all actors from business to citizens, NGOs and social partners through better and more accessible information on the environment.

It is anticipated that this will necessitate the introduction of legislation on strategic environmental assessment of policies and plans.

3.15.10 Objectives and principles of EC environmental policy

The environmental policy and programme of the EC is based upon a number of fundamental principles which underpin the legislative framework These principles, like the policy that stems from them, have evolved over time. The First Action Programme listed 11 key principles which, although they have developed since, still form the basis of EC policy. These 11 principles are:

(1) pollution should be prevented at source rather than dealt with after the event;

(2) environmental issues must be taken into account at the earliest possible stage in planning and other technical decision making processes;

(3) abusive exploitation of natural resources should be avoided;

(4) the standard of knowledge in the EU should be improved to promote effective action for environmental conservation and improvement;

(5) the polluter should pay for preventing and eliminating 'nuisances', subject to limited exceptions and transitional arrangements;

(6) activities in one country should not degrade the environment of another;

(7) the EU and the Member States must in their environmental policies have regard to the interests of developing countries and should aim to prevent, or minimise, any adverse effects on their economic development;

(8) there should be a clearly defined long term European environmental policy that includes participation in international organisations and co-operation at both regional and international levels;

(9) environmental protection is a matter for everyone in the EU at all levels; their co-operation, and the harnessing of social forces, is necessary for success. Education should ensure the whole Community accepts its responsibilities for future generations;

(10) appropriate action levels must be established – local, regional, national, Community and international – for each type of pollution area to be protected;

(11) major aspects of national environmental protection policies should be harmonised. Economic growth should not be viewed from purely quantitative aspects.

A number of these principles are of significant importance and have now been incorporated formally into the EC Treaty by Art 174 (formerly Art 130r). The principles discussed below have also shaped UK environmental policy and underpin the framework not only for EC legislation but also UK legislation. Article 174 sets out the basic principles of environmental policy.

3.15.10.1 Article 174: environmental policy and principles

Article 174 (formerly Art 130r) identifies the aims of EC environmental policy and the fundamental principles upon which legislative action should be taken.

The objectives of the EC's environmental policy are that it should contribute to:

(a) preserving, protecting and improving the quality of the environment;

(b) protecting human health;

(c) the prudent and rational utilisation of natural resources; and

(d) promoting measures at international level to deal with regional or worldwide environmental problems.

In addition to the above, Art 174 states that Community environmental policy shall aim at a high level of protection. However, the article also requires that the Community takes into account the diversity of situations in the various regions of the Community. These provisions pose some difficulties, since it is not clear what is exactly meant by a 'high' level of protection. According to Kramer, 2000, the benchmark for determining 'high' would be the environmental standard of those Member States which seek a high level of environmental protection, such as Denmark or Sweden. Clearly, the attempt here is to ensure that Community policy does not aim for the 'lowest common denominator'. However, environmental policy must take into account the diversity of situations in the regions – an implicit recognition that the Member States have different problems and will in fact go at different speeds in pursuance of environmental goals. Already a diverse Community of regions with 15 Member States, it remains to be seen how this provision will operate in a significantly enlarged Union in which some of the new States will face very real difficulties in achieving the 'high' level of protection pursued by the Community.

Community policy is based on the following principles:

(a) the precautionary principle;

(b) the preventive principle; and

(c) the polluter pays principle.

Careful attention to the wording of Art 174 shows that Community *policy* should be based on these principles and not Community legislation. Nevertheless, one would expect that any environmental legislation developed in pursuance of this policy should also be based upon these principles, and may be subject to challenge if these principles are thwarted in some way. Some guidance as to the nature of these principles can be ascertained from Commission communications. For example, in 2000, the Commission issued a communication on the precautionary principle (COM(00)1). This outlines the Commission's approach to using the precautionary principle and suggests that the precautionary principle may inform certain Community actions, but there is nothing in this to suggest that action must be based on the principle.

3.15.10.2 Environmental policy and other EC interests

One of the most unique features about the EC's environmental policy is its status in relation to other policy areas. By virtue of Art 6 of the EC Treaty, environmental protection requirements must be integrated into the definition and implementation of the Community policies and activities referred to in Art 3, in particular with a view to promoting sustainable development. This 'integration' requirement was, prior to the ToA amendments, to be found in Art 174(2). In 1998, the European Council (the Heads of State and government) met in Cardiff, launching the Cardiff Integration Process. By this, the various Council formations responsible for developing Community policy across the span of Community competences are required to integrate environmental considerations into their respective activities. Each Council formation (for example, in relation to agriculture, transport, the internal market) is required to produce its own strategies for integrating the environment into its work. The importance of the integration principle was further substantiated in the Sixth Environmental Action Programme, which stipulates that 'integration of environmental concerns into other policies must be deepened' in order to move towards sustainable development.

3.15.10.3 *International involvement*

Community policy on the environment is required to contribute to promoting measures at the international level to deal with both regional and worldwide environmental problems. In the early days of its environmental policy, the EC was mainly concerned with controlling pollution within the Community. However, it was soon recognised that pollution has no frontiers and that there is a need to co-operate with non-EC countries. Article 174(4) requires that both the EC and the Member States, within their respective spheres of competence, co-operate with third countries and with the competent international organisations such as the United Nations. The Community is party to a number of international conventions such as the Rio de Janeiro Convention on Biological Diversity and Climate Change 1992.

3.15.11 Environmental legislation

The EC has enacted over 300 legislative Acts which are either directly or indirectly concerned with environmental protection. It is clearly not possible within the scope of this book to cover all of this legislation, the majority of which has been incorporated into UK law and is rightly regarded now as domestic law. However, it is possible to identify certain types of legislation and it is clear that the EC has adopted various approaches aimed at combating pollution and protecting various environmental media. The approaches taken may be categorised as follows.

3.15.11.1 *Quality standards approach*

A number of directives set quality objectives and limit values for different media. With regard to water, for example, a number of directives have been adopted which establish water quality objectives for different uses of water. The most important is Directive 75/440/EEC, which establishes the quality required for surface water which is intended for drinking. Directive 80/778/EEC sets standards for water intended for human consumption; 78/659/EEC for fish and 79/923/EEC for shellfish, and note also Directive 76/160/EEC which sets standards for water used for bathing purposes. Directives setting air quality objectives and limit values include 82/884/EEC – lead; and 85/203/EEC – nitrogen dioxide.

3.15.11.2 *Control of dangerous substances*

Another approach that the EC has adopted is to control the use, discharge or emission of dangerous substances. Framework Directive 76/464/EEC is particularly important in this regard since it is concerned with the control of certain dangerous substances discharged into the aquatic environment. This Directive provides a list of dangerous substances which are either to be eliminated (List I substances) or to be progressively reduced (List II substances). Subsequent daughter directives have since been adopted relating to specific discharges of dangerous substances from industrial discharges. These include Council Directives 82/176/EEC and 84/156/EEC – mercury; Directive 83/513/EEC – cadmium; and Directive 84/491/EEC – lindane. Additionally, Directive 86/280/EEC (as amended) deals with certain other dangerous substances. In addition, Directive 91/676/EEC provides protection of waters against pollution caused by nitrates from agriculture.

3.15.11.3 Vehicle emission standards

Directive (70/220/EEC) was introduced to minimise air pollution from car exhaust fumes, and did this by prescribing limit values for certain gaseous emissions. This was followed by a similar Directive 72/306/EEC, in relation to diesel engines. These have been amended by subsequent legislation, increasing the stringency of the controls. Now, all new petrol engine cars must be fitted with a three-way catalytic converter by virtue of Directive 91/441/EEC.

3.15.11.4 Product quality standards

Certain directives aim to restrict the level of polluting substances in products. For example, Directive 78/611/EEC set the maximum content of lead in petrol.

3.15.11.5 Framework directives

In recent years, the Community has established a number of important 'framework directives' which, as the name suggests, provide a framework for Community action in certain fields. The Waste Framework Directive (75/442/EEC) was probably the first directive of this sort, setting out a framework for waste management within the Community and a requirement for the licensing of waste activities as defined in the Directive. More recently, the Community has adopted the Air Quality Framework Directive (96/62/EC) and, in October 2000, the Water Framework Directive (00/60/EC). The Water Framework Directive typifies this new approach to ensuring a sustainable water policy. Although the Community had previously adopted a range of measures in relation to water pollution (as discussed above), there was a growing recognition of the fragmented nature of these measures both in terms of objectives and means. As a result of calls for the need for a more global and combined approach to water pollution, the Water Framework Directive was adopted. The Framework Directive, typical of this new approach, sets out in a single piece of legislation a range of measures and a framework for developing future controls.

3.15.12 Enforcement of environmental legislation

Member States are under an obligation to comply with their Treaty obligations by virtue of Art 10 of the EC Treaty and this clearly includes an obligation to comply with Art 249, which in turn states that directives are binding on Member States. The obligation to implement directives within the time specified in the directive is absolute (see, for example, Case 56/90, *Commission v UK*). Under Art 226, the Commission, as 'guardian of the Treaty', is responsible for monitoring the application of Community law in the Member States (see the earlier discussion in this chapter). Each year, the Commission publishes a General Report on the Activities of the European Union, which includes, *inter alia*, details of the application of Community legislation and enforcement actions against Member States (available online at http://europa.eu.int/abc/doc/off/rg/en/welcome.htm).

The most recent report published is for the year 2002. A review of the statistics for 2002 shows that the ECJ gave more judgments relating to environmental protection and consumers (40) than any other area of Community law. More telling perhaps is the fact that, in 2002, of the 200 direct actions before the ECJ, 57 were in relation to environmental protection and consumers (compared to the next highest figure of 27 for agriculture). Since 1996/97, the Commission has also produced an annual survey on the implementation and enforcement of Community environmental law. The second annual survey covered the period 1998–99. The Commission in this survey emphasised the crucial need for 'timely and correct' transposition of environmental directives. In particular, the survey points to the need for Member States to provide clear details of the transposing measures introduced to implement directives as an essential requirement in achieving transparency. However, Member States are not just required to transpose directives; it is clear that the obligation imposed under a directive is absolute in terms of the practical fulfilment of the objectives. This much is clear in Art 175(4), which states that Member States are responsible for implementing and financing Community environmental policy. This effectively means that Member States are legally and financially responsible for formal legal compliance (transposition), practical implementation and the creation of a regulatory regime to ensure compliance.

3.15.12.1 *Legal transposition of directives*

In Case C-42/89, *Commission v Belgium* (1990), the Commission brought an action against Belgium in respect of its failure to adopt legislation necessary to comply with the provisions of Council Directive 80/778/EEC. The ECJ held in respect of this infringement action that a Member State may not plead practical or administrative difficulties in order to justify non-compliance with the obligations and time limits laid down in Community directives. The same holds true for financial difficulties, which it is for the Member State to overcome by adopting appropriate measures. The fact that a Member State may argue that it already conforms to the directive in practice does not constitute a reason for not transposing that directive into the national legal system. The ECJ held in Case C-361/88, *Commission v Germany* (1991) that legal transposition is necessary to enable individuals to ascertain their rights and obligations. In order to secure the full implementation of directives in law and not only in fact, Member States must establish a specific legal framework in the area in question.

3.15.12.2 *There must be practical implementation as well as formal compliance*

Directives do not just require administrative action. In Case C-337/89, *Commission v UK (re the Drinking Water Directive)*, Advocate General Lenz said there were two obligations under the directive: first, to transpose the directive into national law and, secondly, a further absolute obligation to bring about physical changes to the environment. The ECJ has stated that a failure in practice to achieve standards will be equated with a failure at law. In Case C-214/97, *Commission v Portugal* (1998), the Portuguese authorities had argued that they had made 'serious efforts' to implement Art 4 of Directive (75/44/EEC), which required them to draw up a systematic plan of action including a timetable for the improvement of surface water. The ECJ held that this was not sufficient. This emphasis on full implementation can be seen in Case C-56/90, *Commission v UK (Bathing Water)* (1993), where the ECJ unequivocally rejected the UK's argument that the Bathing Water Directive did not impose an obligation to achieve a result, but merely required Member States to take all necessary steps in order to comply with the Directive. Observing closely the words of the Directive and its permitted derogations, the ECJ held that the Directive required the Member States to take all the steps necessary to ensure that certain results are attained and, apart from those derogations, they cannot rely on particular circumstances to justify a failure to fulfil that obligation. Interestingly, despite this unequivocal ruling, the Commission has not initiated further proceedings against the UK in respect of the continuing breach.

3.15.13 The European Environment Agency

In May 1990, the Council of Ministers adopted Council Regulation (EEC) 1210/90 setting up the European Environmental Agency (EEA). After much debate, the Agency was eventually set up in Copenhagen and became fully operational in 1995. The EEA's main area of activity is data collection, analysis and dissemination of information on the state and trends of the environment at European level. It is supported in this role by an Environmental Information and Observation Network.

The EEA is open to countries that do not belong to the European Union but share its concern for the environment. Iceland, Liechtenstein and Norway have been members from the start, and a further 12 countries joined in 2002.

3.16 FURTHER INFORMATION

Further reading

Doolittle, I, 'After implementation, enforcement? The next challenge for European environmental law' (1999) 11(3) Env Law Management 101–02.

This considers a survey carried out by specialist environmental law firms in EU Member States questioning the implementation and enforcement of EC law throughout the European Union by reference to a number of issues, including the responsibilities of environmental enforcement agencies, the number of court actions concluded by the agencies and the penalties usually imposed. The article concludes with an analysis of the strengths and weaknesses of each environmental regime, and proposals for improvements.

Krämer, K, *EC Environmental Law*, 4th edn, 2000, Sweet & Maxwell.

Notaro, N, 'The new generation case law on trade and environment' [2000] 25(5) EL Rev 467–91.

This provides an in-depth analysis of the trade and environment case law of the Court of Justice since the entry into force of the Treaty on European Union of 1992. In particular, the article considers the replacement of traditional necessity and proportionality tests with a single necessity test and replacement of extra-territorial application of national law with extra-jurisdictional application of national law.

Stokes, E, 'Precautionary steps: the development of the precautionary principle in EU jurisprudence' (2003) 15(1) Env Law Management 8–15.

This gives a detailed examination of the approach of the European Court of Justice to the precautionary principle.

Usui, Y, 'Evolving environmental norms in the European Union' (2003) 9(1) ELJ 69–87.

This discusses the development of EC environmental law and how this law developed in the absence of a specific legal base. It also examines the rights of individuals to enforce EC environmental law.

Wasmeier, M, 'The integration of environmental protection as a general rule for interpreting Community law' [2001] 38(1) CMLR 159–77.

This examines the importance of the protection of the environment objective incorporated into EC law by Art 2 of the EC Treaty and the requirement that environmental protection be an integral part of Community law.

Williams, R, 'Commission's reasoned opinion in Danish Can ban – legal sense, environmental nonsense?' (1999) 11(1 and 2) Env Law Management 57–60.

This examines the provisions of the Packaging Waste Directive and their application by the Commission in infringement proceedings against Denmark.

Websites

http://europa.eu.int

The European Union online. The Europa portal provides access to the websites of the institutions of the EU, including the Commission and the Court of Justice. There is also a vast array of information on EU environmental policy.

http://europa.eu.int/eur-lex

The official European Union website providing access to legislative acts and decisions of the European Court of Justice.

www.curia.eu.int

The official website of the European Court of Justice.

www.eea.eu.int

The official website of the European Environment Agency.

CHAPTER 4

WATER POLLUTION

4.1   INTRODUCTION

This chapter is concerned with the regulation of water pollution and water quality. Without pollution controls, water would become grossly polluted and unusable for a wide range of human and non-human needs. Humans require clean water for drinking and other uses such as manufacturing, food production and agriculture. Once water has been used, it is returned to the aquatic environment as an effluent. These effluent discharges into surface waters and sewers must be regulated so as to maintain a sufficiently high quality of the receiving waters (waters into which effluent is discharged) to meet our needs. These needs vary according to the use which is made of the available surface and groundwaters. Thus, an industrial discharge of effluent into a river will be tightly controlled if there is a fishery downstream of the industrial plant, or water is abstracted from the river for human consumption.

The control of water pollution through Command and Control legislative regulation has a longer history than similar environmental controls over waste disposal or atmospheric pollution; nevertheless, it shares a basic and recognisable structure with other environmental media-based controls. That structure is reflected in the arrangement of the material in this chapter, the majority of which concerns the *public regulation of water pollution generated by businesses and individuals.*

4.2   CONTROL OVER WATER POLLUTION: AN OVERVIEW

The Water Resources Act (WRA) 1991, as amended by the Environment Act (EA) 1995, and the Water Industry Acts (WIA) 1991 and 1999 (plus the regulations which supplement these statutes) provide the main regulatory control framework relating to the prevention and control of water pollution in England and Wales. The Environment Agency is responsible for controlling pollution of 'controlled waters' and for achieving the improvements in water quality necessary to meet statutory water quality objectives.

The control of water pollution is exercised by the Environment Agency through a system of authorised discharge consents (licences). Any *polluting* discharge made into controlled waters must be authorised by the Environment Agency. The system of consents enables the Environment Agency to control, by means of conditions, the nature and volume of contaminants discharged into surface and groundwaters in order to achieve improvements in water quality. Discharges made without consent, provided they are poisonous, noxious or polluting, or in breach of the conditions attached to a discharge consent, constitute criminal offences but prosecution does not automatically follow. The Environment Agency employs inspectors who have wide-ranging administrative powers to secure compliance with the relevant law. In the event that there is a discharge into controlled waters without consent or in breach of consent conditions, the Environment Agency has the power to prosecute.

Various statutory defences exist. The fines for water pollution offences may be unlimited if a case is dealt with by the Crown Court and, indeed, some of the fines have been very high. In addition, under s 161 of the WRA 1991, the Environment Agency has a preventive power to take action to avoid pollution of controlled water and a remedial power to 'clean up' after an incident. It can then recover its reasonable costs from those responsible for the pollution. The costs of clean-up may well far exceed any fine imposed by a court. The pace of legislative change delivering improvements in water quality and water pollution reduction has been profoundly influenced by the UK's membership of the EC.

4.3   POLLUTING SUBSTANCES AND POLLUTING ACTIVITIES

In order to comprehend the development and 'shape' of regulatory water pollution controls, we need to have some understanding of the activities which are chiefly responsible for water pollution and the substances which are discharged by those activities into the aquatic environment. There are four key questions: (a) which activities are the main polluters?; (b) what substances do these activities discharge into the aquatic environment?; (c) what properties do these substances possess which are problematic?; and (d) what factors will affect the impact of such pollutants upon the waters into which they are discharged?

The main water polluters are industry and commerce. According to various estimates, there are between 75,000–100,000 water pollution discharge consents granted to licence holders entitling them to discharge substances into the aquatic environment. In addition to these 'consented', legitimate discharges, industrial activity is associated with a large number of accidental spillages of chemical substances, such as oils and fuels. Every individual is also partly responsible for the discharge of treated sewage, from the numerous sewage treatment works spread throughout the UK, into surface waters. Pollution from agriculture is also problematic, especially with regard to fertilisers and pesticides, which 'run off' the land when it rains, and are carried into our river systems. Run-off from mining waste tips (slag heaps), which are rich in metals, also cause pollution. Pollutants may leach out and escape from the base of waste sites, especially old landfills, and cause contamination of groundwaters. Abandoned mines also cause pollution when old mine workings fill up with water, become contaminated and then discharge into surface waters.

The substances which, when discharged into the aquatic environment, cause pollution are those which have one or more of the following properties:

(a) they deoxygenate water, for example, agricultural slurry and milk;

(b) they cause eutrophication, for example, fertilisers which accelerate algal growth;

(c) they block out light which disrupts plant growth, for example, suspended solids, such as silty water pumped out of a construction site and discharged into a stream;

(d) they are toxic to humans, plants and animals, for example, pesticides and heavy metals;

(e) they cause diseases, for example, water-borne infections such as cryptosporidium;

(f) they damage amenity, for example, dyes from the textile industry and detergents (causing foaming on surface waters); and

(g) they have undergone change, due to the presence of energy, for example, water which is abstracted from a river in order to provide cooling water for a power station. The water is heated in the cooling (energy exchange) process and is then reintroduced into the river where it may have an adverse impact upon the ecology of the river system.

The impact of polluting substances and energy upon the waters into which they are discharged will vary with a variety of factors including:

(a) the rate of flow (to disperse and dilute the pollutant) of the receiving water system;

(b) the volume of the receiving water system;

(c) the geology and topography of the relevant area in which the river system is situated (for example, the impact of an agricultural spillage of slurry, which deoxygenates a river, will be mitigated by the presence of a downstream waterfall which reoxygenates the river);

(d) upstream or downstream uses of a river system (for example, the presence of urban and industrial areas discharging pollutants into a river upstream of a polluter, or the presence of a sensitive area, such as a Site of Special Scientific Interest, downstream of a polluter).

Whilst the public regulatory apparatus of the WRA 1991 has the primary role to play in the control of water pollution, the private regulatory activities of individuals and environmental groups are also relevant. Such persons may use private prosecution, judicial review of regulatory decision making, and common law tortious actions to achieve their objectives. In the context of the 'private' regulation of pollution, it is important to bear in mind the differing aims of the criminal and civil law and the differing aims of the public regulators and ordinary individuals or regulated companies.

Private prosecutions, based on criminal law offences contained in the relevant primary and secondary legislation, are concerned with punishing the polluter and enforcing compliance with the law through the deterrent effect of prosecution. Civil actions are, in the context of environmental pollution, concerned with obtaining compensation for damage to property or person (personal injury) caused by pollution.

Regulatory agencies, such as the Environment Agency and local authorities, 'police' compliance with the law laid down in Command and Control legislation (for example, the WRA 1991, the Environmental Protection Act (EPA) 1990 and the EA 1995). The objectives of individuals, environmental groups and companies in their use of environmental law vary. Environmental groups may mount a private prosecution against a polluter if they disagree with the exercise of regulatory discretion not to prosecute. An individual may commence an action against a polluter, using the tort of nuisance, to compensate him or her for pollution damage to his or her property. A regulated business may wish to challenge, by way of a judicial review action, a decision by the regulator to refuse an appeal against service of an Enforcement Notice.

In a civil law context, possession of and compliance with the conditions of a water pollution discharge consent will not provide a defence to a civil action brought by any person against the holder of a water pollution discharge consent (s 100(b) of the WRA 1991).

4.4   THE HISTORICAL DEVELOPMENT OF THE PUBLIC REGULATION OF WATER POLLUTION

Legislative attempts to prevent and control water pollution date back to the 1860s. Since that time, various government administrations have introduced new controls and have established new criminal offences. The following section is intended to provide a very brief overview of the history of those controls. The first Act of Parliament to attempt to control water pollution was the Rivers (Pollution Prevention) Act of 1876. Although there had been previous Acts which had dealt with water pollution, they were primarily aimed at improving public health (the Public Health Act 1875) or the productivity of fishing (the Salmon Fisheries Act 1861). The Rivers (Pollution Prevention) Act 1876 created several offences in relation to the discharge or dumping of specified solid matter into any stream; the discharge of solid or liquid sewage matter into any stream; and the discharge of poisonous, noxious or polluting liquid from any factory or manufacturing process into surface waters. The Rivers (Pollution Prevention) Act 1876 also introduced a number of defences, including the defence that the 'best practicable means' had been employed to render pollutants harmless. Despite the creation of these offences, the Act was regarded as ineffective.

The Rivers (Pollution Prevention) Act 1876 was replaced by the Rivers (Prevention of Pollution) Act 1951. This Act created the offence of causing or knowingly permitting any poisonous, noxious or polluting matter to enter a stream and it also introduced the first system of discharge consents. It required all new discharge outlets to be licensed. However, any existing discharge outlets were not required to be licensed unless they were altered, or the composition of the discharge itself was altered or increased. The Rivers (Prevention of Pollution) Act 1961 extended the consent procedure to cover certain types of discharges that were operational before the 1951 Act, thus extending the coverage of licensing. The 1961 Act also provided a much stricter regime insofar as it removed certain defences that had been available under the 1951 Act. The Control of Pollution Act 1974 repealed both the 1951 and 1961 Acts.

4.4.1   The 1991 Water Acts

The starting point in considering the current legislative controls is the Water Act (WA) 1989 which, although superseded by consolidating legislation in 1991, was the Act which established the National Rivers Authority (NRA). It also led to the privatisation of water supplies and sewerage services. In 1991, Parliament passed five Acts which consolidated the various legislative provisions relating to all aspects of the water industry and control of water pollution. The main Acts were the Water Industry Act (WIA) 1991 and the Water Resources Act (WRA) 1991. The provisions of the WRA 1991 provide the main framework for control of water quality and quantity and are considered in detail below. The WIA 1991 (and the WIA 1999) contain provisions relating to water supply and sewerage services; however, some provisions are related to environmental protection, particularly in relation to the controls over the quality of drinking water. The EA 1995 transferred the NRA's water pollution functions to the Environment Agency.

4.4.2 Other statutory controls

In addition to the controls within the main water legislation, various other statutes contain provisions which relate to the control and prevention of water pollution or the maintenance of water quality standards. These include:

(a) the EA 1995;

(b) the EPA 1990;

(c) the Salmon and Freshwater Fisheries Act (SFFA) 1975;

(d) the Land Drainage Act 1994; and

(e) the Pollution Prevention and Control Act 1999.

4.5   THE WATER INDUSTRY AND THE WIA 1991

The water industry covers a wide range of diverse activities, all of which share a common involvement in the water cycle, ranging from the collection and treatment of water and its supply to the provision of sewers and sewage works. It also covers those bodies involved in the control of pollution, the regulation and control of fishing, navigation, flood defence, land drainage, conservation and recreational activities.

The water industry has undergone many changes since the 1940s, primarily as a result of reorganisation and privatisation. Before 1948, the responsibility for water supply and also sewage disposal fell to the local authorities. In 1948, the River Boards Act established 32 River Boards which were organised on a catchment area basis. The River Boards acquired responsibility for most water industry activities including water supply and sewage disposal. In 1963, the River Boards were taken over by 27 River Authorities as a consequence of the Water Resources Act (WRA) 1963. The River Authorities had responsibility, among other things, for pollution control. However, it was not really until 1973 that there was any real attempt to achieve an integrated control of the industry. The Water Act (WA) 1973 established 10 Regional Water Authorities which took charge of managing the various water functions in the relevant river basin areas. The WA 1973, however, did permit the continued existence of a number of statutory private water companies.

Although the WA 1973 was intended to provide a more coherent framework for control, it did not tackle one of the main problems that had thus so far existed in the industry. The regional water authorities had responsibility for pollution control but were at the same time themselves major polluters in their capacity as operators of sewage disposal works. This 'gamekeeper and poacher' scenario (role conflict) gave rise to a great deal of criticism of the water industry. Consequently, the industry went through further reorganisation in 1989 with the WA 1989, which led to the privatisation of water supply and sewerage services and the creation of the NRA. In 1991, the government consolidated the legislation controlling the water industry and now the WIA 1991 (plus the WIA 1999) provides for the regulation of water supply and sewerage.

The position today is that the supply of water and the provision of sewerage services rests with privatised water service companies (known as water undertakers and sewerage undertakers). In addition, there are also water companies which are only responsible for the supply of water and play no role in relation to sewerage services. The office of the Director General of Water Services was established to regulate the activities of the privatised water industry.

4.6   CONTROLLED WATERS

The pollution controls contained in the WRA 1991 apply only in respect of waters defined as 'controlled waters' and the Environment Agency *can only exercise its controls over pollution in relation to those waters*. Section 104 of the WRA 1991 provides a definition of controlled waters which includes:

(a) inland fresh waters – including lakes, ponds, rivers or water courses above the fresh water limit;

(b) groundwaters – that is, waters contained in underground strata: wells, boreholes and aquifers;

(c) coastal waters – including all estuarine waters up to the fresh water limits of rivers and water courses;

(d) territorial waters – the seas within the relevant territorial limit.

These terms are defined much more fully in s 104 as follows:

'Inland fresh waters' means the waters of any relevant lake or pond or of so much of any relevant river or watercourse as is above the fresh water limit. 'Relevant lake or pond' means any lake or pond, including reservoirs, which, whether it is natural, artificial, above or below ground, discharges into a relevant river or watercourse or into another lake or pond which is itself a relevant lake or pond. The Secretary of State is empowered to provide by order that any lake or pond which does not discharge into a relevant river or watercourse or into a relevant lake or pond is to be treated as a relevant lake or pond, or to be treated as if it were not a relevant lake or pond as the case may be.

A 'watercourse' includes all rivers, streams, ditches, drains, cuts, culverts, dikes, sluices, sewers and passages through which water flows, except mains and other pipes which belong to the authority or a water undertaker or are used by a water undertaker or any other person for the purpose only of providing a supply of water to any premises.

'Relevant river or watercourse' means any river or watercourse, including an underground river and an artificial river or watercourse, which is neither a public sewer nor a sewer or drain which drains into a public sewer. The Secretary of State has the power to provide by order that a watercourse of a specified description is to be treated for these purposes as if it were not a relevant river or watercourse.

The 'fresh water limit', in relation to any river or watercourse, means the place for the time being shown as the fresh water limit of that river or watercourse in the latest map deposited by the Secretary of State with the authority for that purpose.

'Ground waters' are defined as any waters which are contained in underground strata. An underground strata means strata subjacent to the surface of any land.

'Coastal waters' means waters which are within the area which extends landward from the baselines of the territorial sea as far as the limit of the highest tide or, in the case of the waters of any relevant river or watercourse, as far as the fresh water limit of the river or watercourse, together with the waters of any enclosed dock which adjoins waters within that area. The relevant territorial waters are those waters which extend seaward for three miles from the baselines from which the breadth of the territorial sea adjacent to England and Wales is measured. This definition is subject to the power of the Secretary of State to provide by order that any particular area of territorial sea adjacent to England and Wales is to be treated as if it were an area of relevant territorial waters.

4.7   THE REGULATOR'S STATUTORY WATER POLLUTION RESPONSIBILITIES

4.7.1   The NRA

Between 1989 and 1 April 1996, the NRA was the main regulatory body with responsibility for controlling water pollution, although it shared responsibility with Her Majesty's Inspectorate of Pollution (HMIP) in relation to those industrial processes that are governed by the IPC regime under Pt I of the EPA 1990. By virtue of s 2(1)(a)(i) of the EA 1995, the water-related (including pollution control) functions of the NRA were transferred to the Environment Agency and the NRA ceased to exist, as did the IPC functions of HMIP which were also transferred to the Environment Agency. Consequently, the Environment Agency is now the primary regulatory body which is concerned with water pollution; nevertheless, it is useful to consider at this juncture the role of the NRA during the period 1989 to 1996.

The NRA was set up in 1989 by the WA 1989 to provide integrated management of river basins and the aquatic environment in England and Wales. The constitution, functions and powers of the NRA were prescribed by the WRA 1991. The NRA was a body corporate, unlike HMIP which was part of the Department of the Environment (DoE). When the NRA was established, it inherited the functions of the water authorities relating to pollution control, water resource management, flood defence, fisheries, navigation and conservation and recreation. The responsibilities of the NRA as laid down in s 2 of the WRA 1991 were as follows:

(a) water resources (Pt II of the WRA 1991);

(b) water pollution (Pt III of the WRA 1991);

(c) flood defence and land drainage (Pt IV of the WRA 1991 and other enactments);

(d) fisheries (Pt V of the WRA 1991 and other enactments);

(e) navigation authority, harbour authority and conservancy authority which were transferred to the NRA by virtue of Chapter V of Pt III of the WA 1989 (and other provisions);

(f) functions assigned to the NRA by any other enactment.

The NRA was required by s 16 of the WRA 1991 to promote the conservation and enhancement of the natural beauty and amenity of inland and coastal waters and of land associated with such waters; the conservation of flora and fauna which are dependent on the aquatic environment; and the use of such waters and land for recreational purposes. The way in which the NRA was required to carry out this duty was described in the Code of Practice on Conservation, Access and Recreation which was issued pursuant to s 18(1) of the WRA 1991, and also in the Water and Sewerage (Conservation and Recreation) (Code of Practice) Order 1989 (SI 1989/1152). The NRA also had a duty to consider water supply issues and by virtue of s 15 it had to have regard, when exercising its powers, to the duties that are imposed on any water undertakers or sewage undertakers by Pts II–IV of the WIA 1991. During its period of operation, the NRA established itself as a strong regulator, willing to prosecute offenders where necessary.

4.7.2   The Environment Agency

By virtue of s 2 of the EA 1995, the functions of the NRA under the WRA 1991 and various other statutory provisions were transferred to the Environment Agency. In addition, the water pollution control functions exercised by HMIP under the IPC regime (Pt I of the EPA 1990) were also transferred to the Environment Agency, giving the Environment Agency overall control over water resources and water pollution. For a further discussion of the details of the transfer of functions and the reasons for the establishment of the Environment Agency, see Chapter 2.

4.7.3   Environment Agency duties in respect of water

Section 6 of the EA 1995 (see also s 19 of the WRA 1991) obliges the Environment Agency, to the extent that it considers desirable, generally to promote:

(a) the conservation and enhancement of the natural beauty and amenity of inland and coastal waters and land surrounding them;

(b) the conservation of flora and fauna which are dependent upon the aquatic environment;

(c) the use of such waters and land for recreational purposes, taking into account the needs of the chronically sick or disabled.

With regard to water resources, the Environment Agency is also obliged (s 20 of the WRA 1991) to take all such action as it may from time to time consider (in accordance with any directions issued by the Secretary of State) to be either necessary or expedient to conserve, redistribute or generally augment water resources in England and Wales and also to secure the proper use of water resources. This duty is described as being 'without prejudice' to the Agency's other environmental duties under s 7 of the EA 1995. The performance of the Agency's water resource management duties remains subject to its principal aims and objectives (see s 4 of the EA 1995). Sections 20–23 of and Sched 5 to the WRA 1991 relate to the Agency's duty to devise, in conjunction with water undertakers, water resource management schemes. The Agency has the power to produce and submit draft statements to the Secretary of State for approval in respect of minimal acceptable flows of inland waters. Minimal acceptable flows are those which meet the needs of existing authorised users (industry, agriculture and domestic (potable) consumption) as well as safeguard public health. Schedule 5 contains the relevant provisions relating to publicity, consultation and procedure prior to obtaining the Secretary of State's approval of the draft statement (taking into account any representations received).

4.8   DISCHARGE CONSENT LICENCES

The licence is the primary vehicle through which the quality of the aquatic environment is regulated. A licence, issued by the Environment Agency (and referred to as a 'discharge consent'), is required to authorise the following activities:

(a) discharging trade or sewage effluent into 'controlled waters';

(b) discharging trade or sewage effluent through a pipe from land into the sea beyond the relevant territorial limit;

(c) discharging trade or sewage effluent into controlled waters which are subject to a s 86 of the WRA 1991 prohibition.

The licensing system is underpinned by a range of administrative powers, plus the criminal law offences contained in s 85 of the WRA 1991.

The Environment Agency is empowered to issue consents in relation to any discharge of trade or sewage effluent into controlled waters. The practical reality of these provisions is that a discharger must obtain a consent for each discharge. Many discharge consents relate to sewage treatment works. The WRA 1991 provides that a person will not have committed an offence under s 85 of the WRA 1991 if the discharge is carried out in accordance with the conditions included in the consent. The detailed provisions relating to the granting of discharge consents are contained in Sched 10 to the Act. (It should be noted that the EA 1995 (Sched 22) amended Sched 10 entirely.)

4.8.1   Applying for a discharge consent licence

Section 88 of the WRA 1991 provides that applications for discharge consents are to be made in accordance with Sched 10 to the Act and the Control of Pollution (Applications, Appeals and Registers) Regulations 1996 (SI 1996/2971). The provisions of Sched 10 have been replaced with a completely new Sched 10 by the EA 1995.

An application for a discharge consent under the WRA 1991 has to be made to the Environment Agency on the prescribed form accompanied by any such information that the Environment Agency may reasonably require or any information prescribed by the Secretary of State. Supplying false information is a criminal offence (s 206 of the WRA 1991). If the Environment Agency requires any further information from the applicant, it can serve a notice on the applicant to that effect. Section 1(3) of the Schedule states that a failure to provide information requested will not invalidate the application; however, s 3(3) states that where a person has failed to comply with his obligation to provide further information, the Environment Agency may refuse to proceed with the licence application. The Environment Agency has four months from the date on which the application was submitted to reach a decision unless a longer period is agreed with the applicant. If a decision is not reached within four months or the agreed period, then the application is deemed to have been refused.

4.8.2   Consultation and publicity requirements

Schedule 10 to the WRA 1991 also deals with consultation and publicity requirements. Previously, details of applications were required to be published by the NRA in both the *London Gazette* and in a local newspaper. Schedule 10, as amended by the EA 1995, states that applications must be advertised by, or on behalf of, the applicant in such a manner as may be prescribed in regulations made by the Secretary of State. The relevant regulations are the Control of Pollution (Applications, Appeals and Registers) Regulations 1996.

The 1996 Regulations specify that the application must be advertised in a local newspaper and in the *London Gazette*. In addition, the applicant must notify relevant local authorities and water service companies. The Environment Agency has a discretion to dispense with publicity where it appears that the discharge will have 'no appreciable effect' on the controlled waters into which the substance or substances are to be discharged. DoE Circular 17/84 provides guidance on the circumstances in which a discharge will have no appreciable effect on the receiving waters.

The Environment Agency has to allow a period of six weeks for consultees specified in the WRA 1991 to submit their representations to the Agency, which is then required to consider any representations made, including any made by the public. The Secretary of State has the power to exempt any class of application from these consultation requirements.

4.8.3 Discharge consent conditions

On receipt of an application for a discharge consent, the Environment Agency is under a duty (s 88 of the WRA 1991) to consider whether the application should be granted, either unconditionally or subject to conditions, or refused. As stated above, a decision should normally be given within four months. The Environment Agency may refuse to deal with an application if the applicant has not provided all the required information or if the application is not accompanied by the appropriate fee. As far as fees are concerned, a charge is made in respect of each discharge (with the exception of minor discharges below certain thresholds; see ss 41–42). Fees, based on charging schemes devised by the Environment Agency and approved by the Secretary of State, are designed to reimburse the agency's administrative costs (in particular, application and monitoring). Such costs vary with the intrinsic polluting quality of the substances discharged and the quality of the receiving waters. Consents may be granted subject to such conditions as the Environment Agency thinks fit.

Conditions may relate to:

(a) the composition of the proposed discharge, especially in regard to Biochemical Oxygen Demand (BOD), toxicity and suspended solids;

(b) volume;

(c) rate of flow;

(d) times at which discharges take place;

(e) means adopted to minimise the polluting impact of discharges;

(f) position and design of discharge pipe/outlet;

(g) provision of monitoring and metering equipment;

(h) sampling and recording, and provision of that information to the Environment Agency.

The conditions contained in each discharge consent will reflect the quality of the waters into which the effluent is discharged. Therefore, conditions will be strict if there is a fishery or drinking water abstraction point downstream of the discharge point.

Currently, discharge consent conditions tend to fix maximum numerical limits on the substances which make up the effluent discharge; however, at some point in the future, discharge consents may be based on the toxicity (that is, the toxic impact of the discharge on the receiving waters) of the discharge.

Any breach of the numerical limits detailed in the discharge consent conditions will be an offence (s 85(6) of the WRA 1991), but it is unlikely that the Environment Agency will prosecute isolated, 'technical' breaches of discharge consent conditions.

It is possible for the Environment Agency to specify, via a condition, the installation of abatement technology to pre-treat the effluent before it is discharged into controlled waters. The use of discharge consent conditions to compel pre-treatment of the discharge is rare, but note the biological pre-treatment required by the Urban Waste Water Treatment Directive, and the policy preference for the discharger to have 'ownership' and control of the technology employed to meet consent conditions.

In reaching a decision upon whether or not to grant a discharge consent, and the conditions to be included in the consent, the Environment Agency must have regard to all relevant considerations. If the Environment Agency fails to do this, its decision may be challenged by way of a judicial review application although, in practice, an appeal is more likely and is cheaper. The considerations which the Environment Agency must have regard to include:

(a) any relevant water quality standards and water quality objectives (see s 83 of the WRA 1991), with regard to the waters into which substances are to be discharged;

(b) the impact of the discharge on downstream users (for example, a water company abstraction point where water is abstracted for drinking use, agricultural uses such as irrigation, fisheries and any sensitive ecological sites such as Sites of Special Scientific Interest);

(c) the 'cocktail' effect of the discharge when combined with upstream and downstream discharges;

(d) the Environment Agency's general and specific (water pollution) environmental duties contained in the EA 1995 and the WRA 1991;

(e) the responses received by the Environment Agency from consultees and members of the public in regard to the discharge consent application;

(f) any relevant European Community (EC) standards relating to both the nature of the proposed discharge and the quality of the receiving waters;

(g) any relevant EC directive, such as the Hazardous Substance Directive (76/464/EEC), concerning the elimination or minimisation of certain substances discharged into the aquatic environment.

Discharges which are made 'under and in accordance with' the relevant consent will be able to take advantage of the s 88 of the WRA 1991 defence; however, if any discharge contains substances not specified in the consent, this will constitute a breach of s 85(6) of the WRA 1991. Most consents include conditions excluding, and therefore outlawing, the discharge of any substance not referred to in the consent.

Where such a condition applies to a sewerage consent (a consent relating to a sewage works), the condition will be ineffective except to the extent that it was 'reasonably practicable' for the sewerage undertaker to exclude non-consented substances. This reflects the special problems encountered by sewerage undertakers where the design of the sewerage system itself prevents the undertaker from controlling all substances which are present in, and discharged into, the sewage treatment system. For example, where a torrential downpour causes an overflow of the sewage treatment system which results in untreated sewage entering controlled waters, or an unconsented substance which the undertaker had never agreed to treat is, due to its illegal introduction, present in the sewerage system, then the undertaker may take advantage of the special defence for sewerage undertakers provided by s 87(2) of the WRA 1991.

Sections 41–42 provide the Secretary of State with a 'call in' power enabling him (whether or not in response to a representation) to call in an application for his own determination. The Secretary of State may order a local inquiry or hearing to be held regarding the application (and must do so if requested by the applicant or the Environment Agency). At the conclusion of the inquiry or hearing, the Secretary of State may refuse the application, grant it with or without conditions, or grant it subject to the conditions which he deems appropriate.

4.8.4 Appeals

Appeals against Environment Agency licensing decisions are made to the Secretary of State (s 91 of the WRA 1991). Appeals are generally heard by Planning Inspectors (s 114 of the EA 1995) and the Secretary of State is only personally involved in important appeals. An applicant can appeal to the Secretary of State against the Environment Agency's refusal to grant a consent, the conditions in the consent, a variation or revocation. The Secretary of State has four months within which to determine the appeal and failure to make a decision within that period will mean that the appeal is deemed to have been refused. Appeals are complete rehearings of the original Environment Agency decision. The relevant appeal procedures are detailed in the Control of Pollution (Applications, Appeals and Registers) Regulations 1996.

As to the outcome of an appeal, the Secretary of State may affirm the Environment Agency's decision on the original application or, in the case of a refusal to grant or vary a consent, he can direct the Agency to grant or vary the consent. Where the appeal relates to consent conditions, the Secretary of State can quash (cancel) as many of the conditions as he considers appropriate. Where the Environment Agency has revoked a consent, he may quash or vary the revocation. During the time it takes to conclude an appeal relating to a revocation, variation of conditions or the imposition of conditions on an unconditional consent, the original decision of the Environment Agency is suspended pending the conclusion or withdrawal of the appeal (s 91(2F) of the WRA 1991). However, no suspension will occur if the Agency reasonably believes that its original decision on the application is necessary: (a) to prevent/minimise the entry of poisonous, noxious or polluting matter and solid waste into controlled waters; and (b) to prevent harm to human health (s 91(2G) of the WRA 1991). If the Agency's belief is challenged by a consent holder and is found by the Secretary of State to be unreasonable, the suspension will immediately take effect and the Agency must then compensate the consent holder for any loss sustained whilst the suspension was not effective (s 91(2H) of the WRA 1991).

4.8.5 Reviewing discharge consents

Paragraph 7 of Sched 10 to the WRA 1991 states that the Environment Agency *may* from time to time review a discharge consent. Where the Environment Agency has reviewed a consent, it has, if necessary, the power to vary the conditions of the consent, revoke the consent, vary the consent or impose conditions on consents which have been granted unconditionally.

4.8.6 Revocation and variation of discharge consents

The original consent will state a period, which must not be less than four years, within which the Environment Agency cannot vary or revoke the consent. Prior to the amendments contained in the EA 1995, a consent could not be varied within a two year period. Variation or revocation within that stated period can only occur with the agreement of the consent holder. However, after that period, both the Environment Agency and the licence holder can apply to vary or revoke a consent. The Secretary of State also has the power to direct the Environment Agency to vary or revoke a consent (see Sched 10, para 9). At any time, the Secretary of State may direct the Environment Agency to carry out a comprehensive review of the consents which it has granted. The Secretary's power to direct the Agency to review and vary the conditions of consents also extends to the following circumstances: where changes in EC law or international law make it necessary to vary consents; where variation is necessary to protect public health; or where variation is necessary to protect the flora and fauna in controlled waters.

Generally, no compensation is paid upon variation or revocation of a discharge consent, but compensation is payable if the Secretary of State makes a direction requiring a variation because of human health or nature conservation considerations.

The power to vary discharge consents is necessary for the following (non-exhaustive list of) reasons: to take account of changes in scientific knowledge which reveal new risks; to take account of the presence of new businesses discharging pollutants into controlled waters; and to take account of changes in the law, such as the introduction of a new EC directive. The Environment Agency has the power to revoke a consent which has not been used in the year prior to revocation. The consent holder may apply to the Agency, giving a minimum of 21 days' notice (see Sched 10) for the transfer of a consent to a new discharger.

4.8.7 Weaknesses in the discharge consent licensing system

One of the main weaknesses of the discharge consent scheme under the WRA 1991 is that it only applies to specific identifiable discharges from a known spot, that is, through a pipe. Other more diffuse sources of pollution such as agricultural run-off and accidental spillages cannot easily be controlled by the discharge consent system, although criminal liability may occur in such circumstances (because poisonous, noxious or polluting matter has entered controlled waters).

4.8.8   Section 86 Prohibition Notices

The Environment Agency can serve notice (under s 86 of the WRA 1991) on a person who is discharging substances into controlled waters but who does not require a licence to authorise the discharge, prohibiting the discharge or prohibiting the continuation of the discharge. Alternatively, the notice may prohibit the discharge unless certain conditions are observed. It is an offence to discharge in contravention of the terms of a Prohibition Notice. This device is used to regulate selected discharges which do not require, in most cases, to be controlled by the licensing process. Prohibition Notices may be used to control the following discharges: soakaways from trade premises, discharges from storm drains and substances prescribed by regulations.

4.8.9   Water quality and discharge consent licences

The ability to assess and classify (categorise) the quality of controlled waters is an important aspect of the WRA 1991 regulatory regime since it provides the Environment Agency with a benchmark which will enable it to plan any necessary changes in discharge licence conditions.

The quality of the waters into which a polluting substance is discharged will form a key consideration with regard to the exact conditions incorporated into an individual water pollution discharge consent. If the quality of the receiving waters is high and downstream users require that quality standard to be maintained, for example, because they own fishing rights, then the conditions attached to the consent will be strict.

In the late 1970s, the National Water Council (NWC) developed a non-statutory water classification scheme as a guide to the setting of river water quality objectives (see below). This scheme has been superseded by a statutory scheme (see ss 82–84 of the WRA 1991) but provides a useful insight into the link between water quality and water usage.

4.8.9.1 The NWC water classification system

The NWC water classification system reflected potential uses of water and provided for the following broad classes:

(a) Good Quality – class 1a – water of high quality suitable for potable (drinkable) supply abstractions; game or other high class fisheries; high amenity value.

(b) Good Quality – class 1b – water of less high quality than class 1a but usable for substantially the same purposes.

(c) Fair Quality – class 2 – waters suitable for potable supply after advanced treatment; supporting reasonably good coarse fisheries; moderate amenity value.

(d) Poor Quality – class 3 – waters which are polluted to an extent that fish are absent or only sporadically present; may be used for low grade industrial abstraction purposes; considerable potential for further use if cleaned up.

(e) Bad Quality – class 4 – waters which are grossly polluted and are likely to cause nuisance.

4.8.9.2 Statutory water quality standards

It was in fact the WA 1989 which introduced a system for setting statutory water quality standards and objectives, but the relevant provisions are now to be found in ss 82–84 of the WRA 1991.

Section 82 of the WRA 1991 enables the Secretary of State to make regulations which classify controlled waters into categories which reflect the standard of quality and the uses to which the water can be put, for example, drinking, bathing and fishing. The regulations specify the standard the waters must attain in order to fall within each classification. In accordance with this power, and also to implement EC directives in this area, a number of regulations have already been made, but the system is by no means complete. The classification of water is necessary before water quality objectives (under s 83) can be established. The criteria specified in regulations made under s 82 in relation to any classification of water must consist of one or more of the following requirements:

(a) general requirements as to the purpose for which the waters to which the classification is applied are to be suitable (in other words, water may be classified according to the use to which it will be put);

(b) specific requirements as to the substances that are to be present in or absent from the water and as to the concentrations of substances which are or can be present in the water;

(c) specific requirements as to the other characteristics of those waters.

The following regulations have been introduced under s 82:

(a) the Surface Waters (Classification) Regulations 1989 (SI 1989/1148) and the Surface Waters (Abstraction for Drinking Water) (Classification) Regulations 1996 (SI 1996/3001). These regulations give effect to the EC Abstraction Directive (75/440/EEC) and prescribe a system for classifying waters according to their suitability for abstraction as drinking water (waters are classified into bands DW1–DW3);

(b) the Surface Waters (Dangerous Substances) (Classification) Regulations 1989, 1992, 1997 and 1998 (SI 1989/2286, SI 1992/337, SI 1997/2560 and SI 1998/389), which give effect to the EC Dangerous Substances Directive (76/464/EEC) and its daughter directives by prescribing a system for classifying inland, estuarine and coastal waters according to the presence in them of concentrations of certain dangerous substances (waters are classified into bands DS1–DS7). The regulations list a number of dangerous substances and state the concentration of each which should not be exceeded in fresh or marine waters;

(c) the Bathing Waters (Classification) Regulations 1991 (SI 1991/1597), which give effect to the Bathing Waters Directive (76/160/EEC) and which prescribe a system for classifying relevant territorial waters, coastal water and inland waters which are bathing waters;

(d) the Surface Waters (River Ecosystem) (Classification) Regulations 1994 (SI 1994/1057). The regulations lay down a system of classifying inland freshwaters (waters are classified into bands RE1–RE5);

(e) the Surface Waters (Fishlife) (Classification) Regulations 1997 (SI 1997/1331) and the Surface Waters (Shellfish) (Classification) Regulations 1997 (SI

1997/1332), which prescribe systems for classifying freshwater fish waters and shellfish waters. The Surface Waters (Fishlife) (Classification) (Amendment) Regulations 2003 (SI 2003/1053) have amended the Surface Waters (Fishlife) (Classification) Regulations 1997.

4.8.9.3 Statutory water quality objectives

Once a range of classifications has been established under s 82 of the WRA 1991, the Secretary of State will, as required by s 83, set a Statutory Water Quality Objective (SWQO) for the relevant stretch of controlled waters. The Secretary of State serves a notice on the Environment Agency detailing a SWQO and maintains a five yearly review of progress. The Agency is given at least three months' notice of the proposed SWQO whilst other interested persons are made aware of the SWQO via publicity. All representations received are taken into account by the Secretary of State before he confirms or varies the SWQO. Section 84 obliges the Environment Agency and the Secretary of State to use their water pollution powers to achieve a SWQO. Together, ss 82–84 and 102 (a power to make regulations) enable the UK to comply with its EC and international legal obligations relating to water quality and water pollution. The SWQO established for each body of controlled waters will incorporate a water classification (and the water quality standards referred to in the classification regulations) as a target to be attained by the Environment Agency. In turn, the Environment Agency is under a duty (s 84 of the WRA 1991) to exercise its functions, especially in regard to discharge consents, to achieve and maintain SWQOs. The Environment Agency risks a judicial review challenge if it does not exercise its powers (for example, in regard to the grant and variation of discharge consents) in ways which will achieve the SWQOs as far as practicable.

4.8.9.4 River quality improvements

Studies carried out in 1999 reveal continuing improvements in the quality of surface waters in the UK. Ninety-five per cent of Britain's rivers are rated good or fair. These statistics represent a 3% improvement on 1990 studies. (See the Environment Agency Corporate Plan 2003–2006.)

4.8.10 Powers of inspection

The powers of inspection and entry by Environment Agency staff are now contained within s 108 of the EA 1995. These powers have been dealt with more fully in Chapter 2. The powers listed in s 108 are exercisable in respect of the Environment Agency's water pollution functions and can be used for one or more of the following purposes:

(a) determining whether any pollution control legislation has been complied with;

(b) exercising or performing its pollution control functions;

(c) determining whether, and if so, how such a function should be exercised.

The powers include the following:

(a) to enter at any reasonable time (or in an emergency at any time) any premises which the inspector believes it is necessary for him or her to enter;

(b) to make such examination and investigation as may be necessary in the circumstances;

(c) to carry out inspections, measurements, tests;

(d) to take photographs and make recordings as necessary;

(e) to remove samples of water, effluent, land or articles;

(f) to carry out experimental borings;

(g) to install and operate monitoring equipment.

The original tripartite sampling procedure contained in s 209 of the WRA 1991 (in which the sample was immediately divided into three parts – one part was given to the licence holder, one part was retained by the NRA and the final part was sent for analysis) has been replaced by s 111 of the EA 1995. Information obtained by licence conditions (requiring the installation of sampling equipment by the licence holder) is admissible in evidence in proceedings brought against the licence holder or any other person. Information so obtained includes data from automatic effluent sampling equipment and therefore a licence holder will be convicted on evidence which the licence holder has itself supplied. Apparatus recording relevant data is presumed to be accurate and failure to record data is treated as admissible evidence of breach of condition.

4.9   WATER POLLUTION OFFENCES

4.9.1 Criminal liability underpins the WRA 1991

The WRA 1991 discharge consent licensing system is underpinned by a number of offences, the majority of which are contained in s 85 of the WRA 1991. The offences are targeted at two types of polluting activity: (a) discharging polluting matter into controlled waters in circumstances in which the discharger has no licence authorising its discharge; and (b) discharges which are in breach of the conditions of the discharger's licence.

Strictly speaking, the WRA 1991 regulatory regime *does not require* all persons who discharge substances into the aquatic environment to obtain a discharge consent prior to making the discharge. The regulatory system uses the criminal law, especially the threat of prosecution, as a tool to encourage dischargers to obtain licences authorising their discharges into controlled waters. Thus, if you have obtained a discharge consent licence from the Environment Agency and are complying with its terms, you will have a complete defence to a s 85 prosecution. If you have not obtained a licence, then your only hope is likely to be that your discharge was not 'poisonous, noxious or polluting'.

4.9.2 Section 85 of the WRA 1991

A person contravenes s 85 of the WRA 1991 if he causes or knowingly permits:

(a) any poisonous, noxious or polluting matter or any solid waste matter to enter controlled waters;

(b) any matter, other than trade effluent or sewage effluent, to enter controlled waters by being discharged from a drain or sewer in contravention of a prohibition imposed under s 86 of the WRA 1991;

(c) any trade effluent or sewage effluent to be discharged into any controlled waters or from land (in England and Wales) through a pipe, into the sea outside the seaward limits of controlled waters;

(d) any trade effluent or sewage effluent to be discharged in contravention of any prohibition imposed under s 86 of the WRA 1991, from a building or from any fixed plant either onto or into any land or into any waters of a lake or a pond that are not inland fresh waters;

(e) any matter whatever to enter any inland fresh waters so as to tend to impede the proper flow of the waters in a manner leading, or likely to lead to substantial aggravation of pollution due to other causes or the consequences of such pollution.

Paragraphs (a)–(e) correspond to sub-ss (1)–(5) of s 85 of the WRA 1991. Breach of the conditions of a discharge consent is also an offence under s 85(6) of the WRA 1991.

The majority of these offences (the ones referring to 'causing' and also s 85(6) of the WRA 1991) are offences of strict liability. This means that it is irrelevant whether the defendant intended to cause the offence. The defendant's state of mind is not one of the elements of the offence which the prosecution must establish. As long as the defendant did the act which was a cause of the pollution incident, he will be guilty. In contrast, the 'knowingly permitting' offences require the prosecution to prove that the defendant was aware that a pollution incident had taken place but took no action to bring the incident to an end. Each of the sub-sections containing the words 'causing or knowingly permitting' in effect contain two separate methods of committing the offence (see *McLeod v Buchanan* (1940)) – 'causing' the pollution and 'knowingly permitting' the pollution. The main offences (those most frequently used by the Environment Agency in mounting a prosecution) are s 85(1), (3) and (6) of the WRA 1991 and s 4 of the Salmon and Freshwater Fisheries Act (SFFA) 1975.

Section 85(1) of the WRA 1991 is a widely drafted general offence covering an array of circumstances in which polluting substances may enter controlled waters. The term 'entry' covers situations in which polluting matter enters controlled waters from both point (for example, a pipe channel or conduit) and non-point or diffuse (for example, field 'run-off') sources. Section 85(3) of the WRA 1991 is limited to trade and sewage effluents which are discharged into controlled waters usually via a pipe or channel.

It is not uncommon for the Environment Agency to prosecute a polluter for both s 85(1) and (3) offences, provided the elements of each offence can be established. More than one person may have caused a single pollution incident and the Environment Agency has a discretion to prosecute any of those persons.

Section 85(6) of the WRA 1991 is limited to discharge consent licence holders. As the offence is an offence of strict liability, the discharge does not have to be poisonous, noxious or polluting. All that the Environment Agency is required to prove is that the licence holder exceeded the conditions of its licence.

4.9.3   Elements of the s 85 of the WRA 1991 offences

If the Environment Agency decides to prosecute, it must be able to establish that each element of the relevant offence is present before it can prove its case to the satisfaction of the court. A number of the key words or phrases used in each of the s 85 offences are not defined in the WRA 1991 (or the earlier incarnations of this legislation) and so we must consider the judicial interpretations of these terms which appear in case law.

4.9.3.1 Causing

The leading cases on the meaning of 'causing' water pollution are the House of Lords decisions in *Alphacell Ltd v Woodward* (1972) and *Empress Car Co (Abertillery) Ltd v NRA* (1998). In the *Alphacell* case, the defendant paper manufacturer was charged with an offence, under s 2 of the Rivers (Prevention of Pollution) Act 1951, of causing polluting matter to enter a river. This offence is similar to s 85(1) of the WRA 1991. Settling tanks in the paper factory overflowed when vegetation clogged up the pumps which maintained the level of effluent in the tanks. The tanks filled up and overflowed, causing polluting matter to enter a river. An overflow channel led directly from the tanks to the river. Although the factory had a discharge consent (licence), this could not save the defendant company from prosecution because the conditions attached to the licence were breached when the settling tank effluent entered the river. Alphacell argued unsuccessfully that it had not caused the polluting matter to enter the river; rather, the presence of vegetation (a natural cause or natural event) in its settling tanks was the real cause of the incident. Rejecting Alphacell's submission, the court held that the act of constructing and operating the effluent tanks was a positive and deliberate act which led to the overflow which caused the pollution of the river. Lord Wilberforce stated:

> In my opinion, 'causing' here must be given a common sense meaning and I deprecate the introduction of refinements such as *causa*, effective cause or *novus actus*. There may be difficulties where acts of third parties or natural forces are concerned but I find the present case comparatively simple. The appellants abstract water, pass it through their works where it becomes polluted, conduct it to a settling tank communicating directly with the stream, into which the polluted will inevitably flow if the level rises over the overflow point.

The test set out in the *Alphacell* decision relating to the meaning of 'causing' water pollution simply requires the defendant to carry on an activity which gives rise to a pollution incident. Provided the defendant's activities could be said to be intentional, all that was necessary to prove liability was to establish a link between the defendant's activities and the pollution of controlled waters.

Alphacell has been applied in Scotland (*Lockhart v NCB* (1981)), Australia (*Marjury v Sunbeam Corp Ltd* (1974)), and in a number of English cases, including *FJH Wrothwell v Yorkshire Water Authority* (1984) and *Southern Water Authority v Pegrum* (1989).

In the period 1975–95, some dilution of the original *Alphacell* interpretation of 'causing' water pollution occurred. In *Price v Cromack* (1975), a farmer contracted with a company to allow the storage of liquid animal waste (slurry) in lagoons erected on the farmer's land. One lagoon wall failed and a serious water pollution incident occurred. The farmer was acquitted of causing water pollution as he had only permitted the accumulation of polluting matter and had done nothing positive to cause the pollution.

Eighteen years later, in *Wychavon District Council v NRA* (1993), the defendant local authority successfully appealed against its conviction for causing water pollution (contrary to s 107(1)(a) of the WA 1989). The defendant had entered into a contract with Severn Trent Water Authority to operate and maintain part of Severn Trent's sewerage system. A blockage occurred in one of the pipes which the defendant did not promptly discover and rectify. This resulted in a pollution incident. The High Court found the defendant 'not guilty' of causing the pollution, because what the defendant had done (failing to detect and repair a blockage) was not a positive act which could be said to have caused the pollution. Similarly, in *NRA v Welsh Development Agency* (1993), the defendant escaped liability because it was held not to have actively caused the pollution despite the fact that it had designed, constructed and maintained the industrial estate drainage system which conducted polluting substances (which had escaped from one of the units on the industrial estate) into controlled waters.

The tide in favour of a strict interpretation of 'causing' began to turn in the mid-1990s. In *NRA v Yorkshire Water Services Ltd* (1995), the prosecution argued that the law had taken a wrong turning by insisting that a positive act by the defendant causing the pollution was an essential prerequisite of liability. Although the House of Lords did not overrule *Wychavon*, it confined it to its particular facts. In the same year, the Court of Appeal in *Attorney General's Reference (No 1 of 1994)* (1995) held that: (a) 'causing' offences could be committed by more than one person where each person's act had formed part of the causal chain; (b) a defendant (sewage treatment company) which, due to a defect in its pumping system, accepted and disposed of polluting matter into controlled waters had caused a pollution, since what it had done amounted to a chain of operations which was a cause of the pollution; and (c) the failure properly to maintain the sewage treatment system, despite the fact that someone else had undertaken responsibility for its day-to-day running, entitled a jury to find the defendant guilty of causing the relevant offence. The return to *Alphacell* occurred three years later in the House of Lords in *Empress Car Co (Abertillery) Ltd v NRA* (1998).

The decision in *Empress Cars* in 1998 concerned the prosecution of a car sales company for causing red diesel fuel to enter controlled waters contrary to s 85(1) of the WRA 1991. The defendants maintained a fuel storage tank on their site. The tank was protected by a bund (a barrier built around a tank to contain spillages) wall. Standing outside the bund was a much smaller drum which was connected to the tank by a rubber hose. From time to time, the defendants would take fuel from the drum. The open/close valve on the tank was not lockable and site security was poor. A trespasser entered the site and opened the valve on the tank. Red diesel flowed from the tank to the drum which rapidly filled up and overflowed. The escaped fuel found its way into the surface water drains and from there entered controlled waters. The defendant argued that it had not caused the resultant pollution but had merely created the circumstances whereby a trespasser could enter the site, turn on the open storage tank valve and cause the pollution. The defendant submitted that the act of the trespasser broke the chain of causation linking the defendant to the pollution and absolved it of liability. The House of Lords rejected this argument and found the defendant guilty.

Lord Hoffmann gave the leading judgment of the court in which he laid down five key guides for judges and magistrates who might be faced with determining the question who or what had caused a pollution. First, the relevant court should require the prosecution to identify what it was that the defendant had done to cause pollution. If the defendant had not done anything at all, then the prosecution for 'causing' must fail. The prosecution need not prove that what the defendant did was the *immediate* cause of the pollution. Maintaining the storage tank was doing something, even if the immediate cause of the pollution was lack of maintenance, a natural event, or the act of a third party, such as a trespasser. Once it had been established that the defendant had done something, the court must then decide whether what the defendant had done was a cause of the pollution. It was quite conceivable that a single pollution incident would have several causes. If the defendant had done something which had produced a situation in which a polluting substance could escape into controlled waters, but a necessary precondition of that escape was the act of a third party or a natural event, then the court had to consider whether that act or event *was a normal fact of life or was something extraordinary*. If it was a matter of ordinary occurrence (something normal), it would not break the chain of causation and the defendant would be liable for causing the pollution. Only extraordinary or abnormal events act to break the chain of causation.

The *Empress Cars* case has important ramifications for defendants charged with causing water pollution. Liability has been extended to situations in which the defendant fails to take appropriate steps to guard against the actions of trespassers and other third parties, equipment failure or natural events. The Hoffmann test for events which operate to break or interrupt the causal chain has created a situation in which s 85(1) of the WRA 1991 creates almost absolute liability for escapes of pollutants into controlled waters. The prospect that a defendant will be able to establish that an extraordinary event has occurred is very slim indeed. It is also clear from the judgment of Lord Clyde that a failure to take precautions in relation to the risk of an escape of polluting substances will amount to 'doing something' for the purposes of establishing liability.

The very strict judicial approach to liability will be tempered by Environment Agency enforcement and prosecution policy limiting the number of prosecutions commenced. However, a very strict rule of liability may act as a disincentive to businesses who take their environmental management responsibilities seriously. They may be disinclined to invest in pollution prevention if the courts will hold them strictly liable for causing water pollution irrespective of the efforts they have made to control polluting emissions.

The Hoffmann test may be difficult to apply in practice. A terrorist bomb which damages storage tanks and causes a pollution incident may well be an extraordinary event if it occurs in rural North Yorkshire but may not be extraordinary in Northern Ireland. The test is a 'fact and degree' test (that is, it depends on the particular circumstances). The *Empress* decision has been applied in at least two decided cases. In *Environment Agency v Brock plc* (1998), the failure of a valve on a hose during a pumping operation caused leachate from a landfill site to spray out and enter controlled waters via a ditch. The defendant was convicted of the s 85(1) offence, irrespective of the fact that the immediate cause of the pollution was defective equipment. There was no evidence that the defendant had been in any way negligent. The escape of polluting substances had occurred due to a latent defect (pipework seal failure) (see the similar case of *CPC (UK) Ltd v NRA* (1995)). It is submitted that the defendant was rightly convicted because the design of the landfill leachate collection system was something which was under the defendant's control. The failure of the hose seal, although a rare occurrence, was not an extraordinary event. In *Environment Agency v British Steel plc* (1999), the defendant was charged with causing polluting matter (mill coolant) to enter controlled waters contrary to s 85(1) of the WRA 1991. The defendant submitted that the combined failure of a hose, which had been poorly installed by one of its employees, and the failure of a sub-contractor's employee (a security guard in the employ of RCO, a security company) to act appropriately in response to alarms (audible and visual alarms were ignored) warning of an impending pollution was an extraordinary event absolving the defendant of liability. The stipendiary magistrate who heard the case applied the Hoffmann test and convicted the defendant. It is clear from this decision that the court was not diverted by the fact that the immediate cause of the pollution incident was the failure of the defendant's agent to respond to an alarm.

4.9.3.2 Intervening acts of third parties and vicarious liability

In the event of an escape of polluting substances from company premises or other land into controlled waters, the company cannot escape conviction for causing a water pollution offence by blaming an employee who was the immediate cause of the pollution (provided the employee was acting within the terms of his employment contract). The defendant company is *vicariously* liable for the acts or omissions of its employees and on the authority of *NRA v McAlpine Homes East Ltd* (1994), it is not necessary for the prosecution to prove that the controlling officers of the company were directly involved in the incident. It is sufficient that an employee was responsible for the act or omission which caused the pollution.

Prior to the *Empress Cars* decision, it was possible for a defendant to escape liability in circumstances in which a third party, such as a trespasser, vandal or independent contractor, had intervened to break the causal chain linking the defendant to the pollution. Such third party acts are not defences, but operate to negate the 'causing' element of the relevant offence. In such circumstances, the third party's act has supervened the defendant's act and relegated it to one of the background circumstances. In *Impress (Worcester) Ltd v Rees* (1971), a vandal entered Impress's premises at night and opened a valve on an unbunded fuel tank which allowed fuel to escape from the site, enter and pollute a river. The defendant company's conviction was quashed (cancelled) by the High Court on the ground that the defendant's conduct (operating the premises) was not a cause at all, but was merely part of the surrounding circumstances (see also *Welsh Water Authority v Williams Motors (Cymdu) Ltd* (1988) and *NRA v Wright Engineering Co Ltd* (1994)). The House of Lords in *Empress Cars* has overruled *Impress* and has drastically restricted the circumstances in which third party acts will operate as a supervening cause to absolve the defendant of legal liability (see the discussion relating to Lord Hoffmann's distinction between normal and extraordinary acts or events at p 141 above).

4.9.3.3 Knowingly permitting

Water pollution offences such as those under s 85(1) of the WRA 1991, s 85(3) of the WRA 1991 and s 4(1) of the SFFA 1975 may be 'knowingly permitted'. Liability is established in circumstances in which the defendant has knowledge of ongoing pollution yet fails to act to put a stop to it. As it is necessary to establish the defendant's knowledge of water pollution, this offence is not an offence of strict liability. This may well explain the few prosecutions brought by the Environment Agency and its predecessors. In *Schulmans Inc v NRA* (1993), Schulmans was charged with two 'knowingly permitting' offences (under s 107(1)(a) of the WA 1989 and s 4(1) of the SFFA 1975). Fuel oil from a tank standing on the defendant's premises escaped into a nearby brook. The defendant was acquitted of the charges because there was no proof that the defendant could have acted sooner than it did to prevent the pollution occurring. The prosecution could not establish that: (a) the defendant was aware of the spillage of fuel oil; (b) the polluting matter had entered the surface water drainage system which discharged into controlled waters; (c) unless prompt action was taken, a pollution would occur; and (d) (with regard to s 4(1) of the SFFA only) the defendant was aware of the extent of the pollution.

Price v Cromack (1975) provides a useful illustration of the difference between the 'causing' offence and the offence of 'knowingly permitting'. A farmer was charged with 'causing' pollution when a lagoon on his land failed and waste animal products were released into a river. The farmer had a contract with an animal products firm which allowed the firm to discharge animal waste products into the lagoons on the farmer's land. The farmer was acquitted of the 'causing' charge on the basis that he had not caused the pollution. Whilst he had permitted the build up of the waste on his land, he could not be said to have caused the pollution. Had he been charged with knowingly permitting pollution, then the verdict would probably have been different. Following the *Empress Cars* decision, the courts would convict the defendant in *Price v Cromack* for causing a water pollution incident.

4.9.3.4 Entry

The term 'entry' in s 85(1) of the WRA 1991 refers to a wide range of scenarios in which polluting matter may enter controlled waters. The term 'enter' covers situations in which polluting matter is deliberately introduced into controlled waters, such as the deliberate pouring of the contents of a drum of pesticides into a stream, accidental spillages of polluting matter into surface drains, leaky pipes and tanks which cause polluting matter to escape into groundwaters, and 'run-off' from farmers' fields entering a river over a wide area. 'Entry' covers the introduction of polluting substances into controlled waters from point (pipe) and diffuse (run-off) sources.

4.9.3.5 Discharge

The term 'discharge' in s 85(3) of the WRA 1991 has a more restricted meaning than 'entry' and refers to discharges from pipes, channels, or similar features into controlled waters. It is possible that polluting matter from a single incident could both enter and be discharged into controlled waters. If an unprotected (for example, a tank with no protective surrounding barrier or bund) oil storage tank were to rupture on an industrial site situated adjacent to a river or canal, some of the escaping oil could flow into the surface drains of the industrial estate and be discharged into controlled waters, whilst a further quantity of oil could flow down the river or canal bank and enter controlled waters.

4.9.3.6 Poisonous, noxious or polluting

This term has a wide meaning. Poisonous matter entering or discharged into controlled waters is often associated with large fish kills and is therefore largely unproblematic. 'Polluting' may cover the discharge of dyes or detergents into controlled waters in quantities which do little damage to the ecology of the receiving waters but are polluting in the sense that they damage the amenity of controlled waters. Streams will be discoloured by the presence of dyes and banks of foam, caused by the presence of detergents, are unsightly. In *NRA v Egger (UK) Ltd* (1992), the court held that the term 'polluting' requires the substance which has entered controlled waters to have the likelihood or capability of causing harm to humans, animals and plants. In *R v Dovermoss Ltd* (1995), the defendant argued that slurry which had contaminated a spring could only be 'polluting matter' if actual harm had resulted from its introduction into controlled waters. The Court of Appeal held that the definition of 'polluting' should be based on the *Oxford English Dictionary's* definition – 'to make physically impure, foul or filthy; to dirty, stain, taint, befoul'. Polluting material was the 'sort of material which, if introduced into the water reduces the quality of the water'. On this basis, the court held that there was no need to prove harm. The question was whether the matter was capable of causing or likely to cause harm to controlled waters. Whether or not a substance has polluted water is a question of fact.

4.9.3.7 Controlled waters

Although the term 'controlled waters' is defined in s 104 of the WRA 1991, this definition is not comprehensive and the courts have been active in expanding our understanding of this term.

In *R v Dovermoss Ltd* (1995), the Court of Appeal was asked to interpret the meaning of the term 'controlled waters'. In this case, Welsh Water had received a number of taste complaints from consumers whose drinking water had been supplied from a spring. It was discovered, following investigations, that the water contained excessive amounts of ammonia which were traced back to two fields adjacent to a stream. The fields were owned by Dovermoss Ltd. Slurry had been spread on these fields. As a result of a heavy rainfall, the stream had deviated from its normal course and ran over the slurry covered fields into the spring, thus causing contamination. Dovermoss was charged and convicted with causing polluting matter to enter controlled water contrary to s 85 of the WRA 1991. Dovermoss appealed on a number of grounds. One of its arguments was that the water, which had been diverted from its normal course, was no longer controlled waters within the meaning of s 104 of the WRA 1991. The Court of Appeal held that the term 'controlled waters' included 'waters of any watercourse', not, as it was argued, water *in* any watercourse. The court went further and stated that the term 'watercourse' refers to the channel rather than the water itself. Consequently, waters from a watercourse (such as the stream) remain controlled waters even where the water has departed from its normal course

In *Environment Agency v Brock plc* (1998), the court held that a man-made ditch could fall within the definition of controlled waters provided the ditch connected to and drained into controlled waters.

4.9.3.8 Discharge

The term 'discharge' is synonymous with the entry of substances into controlled waters via a pipe, channel, or conduit from a point source. Arguably a 'discharge' would also include liquid poured from a drum or similar receptacle into controlled waters.

4.9.3.9 Effluent, substance, sewage effluent and trade effluent (see s 221 of the WRA 1991)

(a) 'Effluent' means any liquid, including particles of matter and other substances in suspension in the liquid.

(b) 'Substance' includes micro-organisms and any natural or artificial substance or other matter, whether it is in solid or liquid form or in the form of a gas or vapour.

(c) 'Sewage effluent' includes any effluent from the sewage disposal or sewerage works of a sewerage undertaker but does not include surface water.

(d) 'Trade effluent' includes any effluent which is discharged from premises used for carrying on any trade or industry, other than surface water and domestic sewage. For the purposes of this definition, any premises wholly or mainly used (whether for profit or not) for agricultural purposes, fish farming, scientific research or experiment, are to be deemed to be premises used for carrying on a trade.

4.9.4 Section 85(6) of the WRA 1991

Breach of any of the conditions of a discharge consent is an offence of strict liability. In the case of a minor breach, the Environment Agency is unlikely to prosecute, unless breaches are persistent. A separate s 85(6) offence is committed on each occasion a breach of condition occurs (*Severn Trent Water Authority v Express Foods Group Ltd* (1988)). Consents may contain a condition banning the discharge of any substances not specifically referred to in the discharge consent. It is most unlikely, in view of the Court of Appeal's decision in *R v Ettrick Trout Co Ltd v Baxter* (1994), that in a s 85(6) prosecution the defendant will evade liability by challenging the validity of the discharge consent conditions in s 85(6) of the WRA 1991 criminal proceedings. In *Ettrick*, the defendants, who ran a fish farm, were alleged to have breached a condition of their discharge consent (exceeding the volume of effluent which could be discharged into controlled waters in any 24 hour period) and they attempted to challenge the validity of the relevant condition. They argued that the condition had been unlawfully imposed for water abstraction control purposes rather than pollution control. The Court of Appeal rejected this submission and held that this type of collateral challenge was clearly an attempt to bypass the judicial review and statutory appeal procedures, and was an abuse of process (see *R v Wicks* (1998) and *Boddington v British Transport Police* (1999)).

4.9.5   Criminal liabilities of directors and other third parties

Section 217 of the WRA 1991 extends liability for water pollution offences to senior company officials. Section 217 states that where a body corporate is guilty of an offence under the Act, then any director, manager, secretary or other similar officer may also be personally liable and be guilty of that offence. However, in order to secure a conviction under s 217, it is necessary to prove that the offence was committed with the consent or connivance of, or is attributable to any neglect on the part of, that person. In practice, the regulatory authorities have rarely prosecuted company officials under s 217 of the WRA 1991 (or s 157 of the EPA 1990), although the fact that individuals cannot hide behind the company veil should provide some deterrent against negligent environmental management. A successful s 217 prosecution is more likely in small companies where the senior officers are intimately concerned with the day-to-day running of the business. Unlike larger companies, they are not shielded by several layers of middle management.

4.9.6   Section 90 of the WRA 1991

It is an offence: (a) to remove, without the Environment Agency's permission, from the channel or bed of any inland freshwater any deposit accumulated by a dam, weir or sluice in circumstances where the act of removal causes the deposit to be carried away in suspension; and (b) to cause or permit vegetation to be (i) cut or uprooted (plus failure to remove it) and (ii) cut or uprooted near inland waters so that the vegetation falls into inland waters (plus failure to remove it). Section 90A (see s 120 of and Sched 22 to the EA 1995) details the requirements (for example, publicity, etc) of the Environment Agency before it will grant permission. Permission is required to satisfy s 89(4), s 90(1) and s 90(2) of the WRA 1991. The Environment Agency has the power to serve an Enforcement Notice if it believes that any consent required by s 90 is being contravened or is likely to be contravened (s 90B(1)).

4.10   STATUTORY AND OTHER DEFENCES

4.10.1 Authorised discharges

Section 88 of the WRA 1991 provides that a person will not be guilty of an offence under s 85, in respect of the entry or discharge of matter into controlled waters, if the entry or discharge is made under and in accordance with a consent granted by the Environment Agency under the WRA 1991. In addition to consents under the WRA 1991 (and prior legislation), it will also be a defence if the entry or discharge is made under and in accordance with:

(a) an IPC authorisation for a prescribed process control led under Pt I of the EPA 1990;

(b) an IPPC permit granted pursuant to the Pollution Prevention and Control Act (PPCA) 1999;

(c) a waste management licence or a waste disposal licence granted under Pt II of the EPA 1990 (there are exceptions where the offence is of discharging trade or sewage effluent or where a prohibition is in force);

(d) a licence granted by the Ministry of Agriculture under Pt II of the Food and Environment Protection Act 1985 (authorising the deposit of waste at sea);

(e) s 163 of the WRA 1991 or s 165 of the WIA 1991 (concerned with discharges for works purposes);

(f) any local statutory provision or statutory order (for example, a drought order) which expressly confers power to discharge effluent into water; or

(g) any prescribed enactment (primary or secondary legislation).

The WRA 1991 in general, and s 88 in particular, does not include what is commonly referred to as a 'due diligence' defence. An example of such a defence is to be found in s 33(7)(a) of the EPA 1990. A defendant may avail itself of this defence with regard to prosecution for the waste offences detailed in s 33 of the EPA 1990 if the defendant can establish that it has taken all reasonable precautions and exercised all due diligence to avoid the commission of an offence. The absence of such a defence in the WRA 1991 has attracted criticism (McFarlane, 1998). One commentator has suggested that the basis of the s 85 of the WRA 1991 liability could be changed to give effect to this criticism (Stanley, 1999).

4.10.2 Other defences

In addition to the defence that a discharge is authorised under the provisions listed above, the WRA 1991 also provides a number of other defences in s 89.

A person will not be guilty of an offence under s 85 of the WRA 1991 in respect of an entry of any matter into any waters or any discharge if:

(a) the entry is caused or permitted, or the discharge is made, in an emergency in order to avoid danger to life or health; and

(b) that person takes all such steps as are reasonably practicable in the circumstances for minimising the extent of the entry or discharge and of its polluting effects; and

(c) particulars of the entry or discharge are furnished to the Environment Agency as soon as reasonably practicable after it occurs (s 89(1)(c) of the WRA 1991). Section 89(1)(a) implicitly refers to danger to man rather than danger to flora and fauna.

In *Express Dairies Distribution v Environment Agency* (2003), the High Court considered the circumstances in which the statutory defence to a s 85 prosecution could apply. Under s 89(1)(a) of the WRA 1991, it is a defence to a s 85 charge if the pollution is caused in order to avoid danger to life or health.

The defendant's milk tanker suffered a tyre 'blow out' on the M5 and the incident damaged a delivery pipe, causing 4,000 litres of milk to escape and enter controlled waters (when the driver pulled onto the hard shoulder and the milk entered surface drains). The driver took prompt action to stop the spillage and contacted the emergency services. The defendant was convicted of a s 85 offence (an offence of strict liability) in the relevant magistrates' court. The magistrates rejected the defendant's submission that the driver had pulled onto the hard shoulder to avoid danger to life or health, preferring to view the cause of the pollution as the 'blow out'. The defendant appealed against its conviction to the High Court by way of case stated. The question the High Court was required to consider was: 'whether the s 89 statutory defence is available in circumstances in which the entry [of the pollutant into controlled waters] is caused or permitted or the discharge is made as a result of an emergency in which a person acts so as to avoid danger to life or health or whether the statutory defence is limited to circumstances in which the entry or discharge is itself the emergency occasioned to avoid danger to life or health.'

Hale LJ allowed the appeal. Although, in the opinion of the court, there was no break in the causal chain from the blow out to the pollution (that is, no 'extraordinary event' to break the causal chain), nevertheless, the defence applied. The court was entitled to focus on the latter part of the causal chain (that is, the driver's decision to pull onto the hard shoulder) rather than the immediate cause (the blow out) of the incident (which the magistrates had done). Thus, the driver's actions fell within the wording of the statutory defence.

In addition to the above defences, a number of discharges made in a number of specific situations are exempted from the provisions of the Act. A person will not be guilty of an offence under s 85 by reason of:

(a) causing or permitting any discharge of trade or sewage effluent from a vessel (s 89(2)) (these discharges are regulated by bylaws);

(b) depositing the solid refuse of a mine or quarry on any land so that it falls or is carried into inland freshwater if the deposit is authorised by the Environment Agency, no other site for the deposit is reasonably practicable, and he takes all reasonable steps to prevent the refuse from entering those inland freshwaters. (This defence does not apply except in respect of the entry of any poisonous, noxious or polluting matter into any controlled waters (s 89(4)).)

A Highway Authority or other person entitled to keep open a drain by virtue of s 100 of the Highways Act 1980 will not be guilty of an offence under s 85 by reason of its causing or permitting any discharge to be made from a drain kept open by virtue of that section unless the discharge is made in contravention of a prohibition imposed under s 86 (s 89(5)).

Section 87 of the WRA 1991 contains defences relating to the privatised water companies (referred to as sewerage undertakers) which run the sewage treatment and disposal systems. It is the responsibility of sewerage undertakers to ensure, through the WIA 1991 licensing system relating to sewers, that it can effectively treat the trade and sewage effluent it has licensed to receive and treat in its sewage works. This is given legal effect to by s 87(1) of the WRA 1991. This provision deems a sewerage undertaker to have caused pollution of controlled waters in circumstances where it cannot treat the effluent it has itself licensed to accept and, in consequence, it breaches its own discharge consent granted by the Environment Agency for each of its sewage treatment works. The position is different, however, in circumstances where the sewerage undertaker receives unlicensed effluent to treat. In this case, the sewerage undertaker may avail itself of the benefit of the s 87(2) defence and escape liability for causing water pollution (see *NRA v Yorkshire Water Services Ltd* (1994)).

Farmers who act in accordance with best agricultural practice may escape liability if a water pollution incident occurs. Although farmers have no due diligence defence, their adherence to best agricultural practice will be taken into account when the Environment Agency exercises its discretion whether to prosecute.

4.11 PROVING WATER POLLUTION

In carrying out their investigations, Environment Agency inspectors have the power to take samples of water or effluent, which may later be used as evidence in court to substantiate a criminal case (s 108 of the EA 1995). Evidence of pollution must be 'sufficient' if the Agency is to commence a criminal prosecution (see 2.4.15.2).

4.12 ENFORCEMENT

4.12.1 Environment Agency enforcement powers

The Environment Agency has various powers (including the service of an Enforcement Notice) at its disposal which enable it to ensure that authorised dischargers comply with consent conditions, to investigate any breaches of consents and also to detect and investigate pollution incidents. The Environment Agency can exercise control through the consent system, using its power to prohibit certain discharges or by varying or revoking a consent. The Environment Agency may also decide to bring criminal proceedings against a person who contravenes the provisions of the WRA 1991. In deciding what action to take, the Agency will be mindful of its s 39 of the EA 1995 cost/benefit duty.

4.12.2 Enforcement policy

Whether the Environment Agency will choose to enforce compliance with the law by means of a prosecution will, to a large extent, depend upon the Environment Agency's 1998 enforcement and prosecution policy (see 2.4.15). Essentially, the Environment Agency bases its decision whether or not to prosecute upon the aggravating and mitigating circumstances surrounding the commission of the relevant offence. Of particular significance will be the severity of environmental damage resulting from the pollution incident.

The Environment Agency divides water pollution incidents into the following categories based on their severity:

• Category 1 – major incidents resulting in any of the following impacts: extensive fish kill; major and/or frequent breach of consent conditions; closure of potable (drinkable) water abstraction point; extensive remediation required; actual and/or potential persistent effect on water quality and/or aquatic life; significant adverse affect on amenity; and significant effect on an important conservation site.

• Category 2 – significant incidents resulting in any of the following: significant fish kill; water abstractors notified (water companies, farms, industry, etc); readily observable affect on aquatic invertebrates; stock watering ban necessary;

watercourse bed contamination; and amenity value reduced (odour, appearance, etc) to downstream users.

- Category 3 – minor incidents with localised impacts.
- Category 4 – incidents with no environmental impact.

There is a presumption of prosecution with regard to Category 1 incidents. Category 2 incidents usually result in prosecution or warnings. Category 3 incidents usually entail a warning only.

The Environment Agency's pollution statistics for 2001 (see the Agency's website) reveal that there were 118 Category 1 (major) incidents in 2001. This was a significant increase on the figures for 2000 (77) and 1999 (90). There were 860 Category 2 incidents in 2001, although overall the Agency asserts that the long term trend reveals a steady decrease in the number of incidents.

The total number of reported incidents rose in 1999 and subsequent years because the Agency has changed its reporting methods. Before 1999, Category 4 incidents were not included in the total number of substantiated pollution incidents, but now Category 4 incidents are those which relate to substantiated pollution incidents (incidents with regard to which there is evidence of pollution) with no environmental impact.

In 2001, the most common incidents involved the following activities: agriculture (174), sewage and the water industry (171), and industry (142). The largest case concerned the prosecution of United Utilities for a variety of water pollution offences relating to the discharge of raw sewage into the River Waver estuary in Cumbria. The defendant company was fined a total of £70,500.

The Environment Agency's enforcement policy (para 28) confirms that it will normally prosecute in the case of 'incidents or breaches which have significant consequences for the environment' and therefore there is a presumption of prosecution in the case of Category 1 (major) incidents.

In 1998, the Environment Agency successfully prosecuted 262 cases (of which 185 incidents actually occurred in 1998) representing about 1% of the total number of substantiated water pollution incidents occurring in 1998. The strict liability nature of many water pollution offences ensures that there is little prospect of the defendant being able to mount a successful defence. In the vast majority of cases, approximately 93%, the Environment Agency secures a conviction.

4.12.3 Penalties for water pollution offences

A person who contravenes the provisions of Pt III of the WRA 1991, or the conditions of any consent given under the Act, will be guilty of a criminal offence and will be liable (s 85(6) of the WRA 1991):

(a) on summary conviction (in a magistrates' court), to imprisonment for a term not exceeding three months, or to a fine not exceeding £20,000, or to both;

(b) on conviction on indictment (in a Crown Court), to imprisonment for a term not exceeding two years or to a fine (of unlimited amount), or to both.

The average fine imposed by the courts in respect of water pollution convictions in 1998 (excluding the Welsh Region of the Environment Agency whose statistics were distorted by the £4 million fine, reduced to £750,000 on appeal, imposed on the defendant in the Sea Empress prosecution) was £3,335. This is in line with the gradual upward trend in the level of fines for water pollution offences, but is some way short of the £20,000 maximum financial penalty which may be imposed in the magistrates' court. Interestingly, there is some evidence of an increased willingness, on the part of the Environment Agency, to make greater use of the Crown Court's ability to impose higher penalties than the magistrates' court. The imposition of a financial penalty by the courts to deter water polluters appears to be the rule in the criminal courts. Only rarely will a custodial penalty be imposed. Custodial penalties may not be imposed on companies and similar organisations.

4.13   PREVENTIVE APPROACHES TO WATER POLLUTION CONTROL

4.13.1 Introduction

The WRA 1991 contains provisions which enable the Environment Agency to take a more preventive approach to water pollution, whereby harm is prevented by means of anticipatory action. Section 161 of the WRA 1991 in particular empowers the Environment Agency to take action to avoid pollution of controlled waters. This section also equips the Environment Agency with extensive clean-up powers. In addition to s 161, ss 92–95 of the WRA 1991 contain provisions relating to the prevention of pollution. These provisions are particularly useful in relation to more diffuse sources of pollution such as run-off arising from agricultural activities. However, we begin our examination of the preventive role of the Environment Agency by reference to the advisory documents which it has produced.

4.13.2 Pollution advice and information

The Environment Agency produces a range of documents and other media to educate and guide licence holders and others as to best environmental management practice to minimise the risk of substances escaping containment to pollute controlled waters.

Prior to the creation of the Environment Agency, the NRA produced, and issued on request, a free pack of information, comprising leaflet and video, entitled *Pollution Prevention Pays*. This initiative formed part of a campaign to highlight common errors in operational practice which were often the real causes of pollution incidents. The key features of the initiative are summarised below:

(a) site drains – distinguish between surface drains (draining into controlled waters) and foul drains (draining to sewer); colour code drainage systems; drainage plans should be accessible;

(b) deliveries – label maximum content of storage tanks; gauges should be installed to give a visual display of tank levels; build bund walls; isolate delivery areas from drains; pipes should be above ground or placed in 'sleeves'; install automatic cut-off valves to prevent overfilling; install high level alarms in storage tanks; and ensure the supervision of unloading and loading operations;

(c) storage – check bund walls in good repair with no valves in bund wall to drain rain water; drum storage areas should be bunded and roofed; use sturdy drums and label appropriately; install oil interceptor pits on surface drains to minimise the risk of pollution of controlled waters;

(d) security – ensure adequate perimeter security through proper fencing; CCTV surveillance; and install locks on open/close tank valves;

(e) training and emergency planning – ensure adequate staff training and prepare contingency plans.

This initiative demonstrates the link between poor environmental management practice and the increased probability that the Environment Agency will exercise its discretion to prosecute should a pollution incident occur on a poorly managed site.

The Environment Agency has also produced a range of 20 Pollution Prevention Guidance notes (PPGs) which are provided free on request to enquirers (not to be confused with planning PPGs). Environment Agency staff will draw the attention of businesses to relevant PPGs as part of its rolling programme of routine site inspection visits. The PPGs cover the following topics:

PPG 1 – general guide to the prevention of pollution of controlled waters;

PPG 2 – above ground oil storage tanks;

PPG 3 – the use and design of oil separators in surface water drainage systems;

PPG 4 – disposal of sewage where no main drainage is available;

PPG 5 – works in, near or liable to affect water courses;

PPG 6 – working at demolition and construction sites;

PPG 7 – fuelling stations: construction and operation;

PPG 8 – safe storage and disposal of used oils;

PPG 9 – pesticides;

PPG 10 – highway depots;

PPG 11 – industrial sites;

PPG 12 – sheep dip;

PPG 13 – the use of high pressure water and steam cleaners;

PPG 14 – boats and marinas;

PPG 15 – retail premises;

PPG 16 – schools and other educational establishments;

PPG 17 – dairies and other milk handling operations;

PPG 18 – control of spillages and fire fighting run-off;

PPG 19 – garages and vehicle service centres;

PPG 20 – dewatering underground ducts and chambers.

Adherence by farmers to agricultural best practice with regard to the water pollution risks identified in *The Water Code Revised*, 1998 is an important factor which the Environment Agency takes into account when deciding whether to prosecute a farmer for causing a water pollution incident.

The government published in 2003 a strategic review of *Diffuse Water Pollution from Agriculture* (see www.defra.gov.uk/environment/water/dwpa/index.htm). The function of the review is to create an action plan to help reduce diffuse water pollution from agricultural sources. This type of pollution is a significant barrier to compliance with the terms of the Water Quality Framework Directive (2000/60/EC) by 2012–15. The publication of the strategy follows publication of *The Government's Strategic Review of Diffuse Water Pollution from Agriculture in England: Initial Thinking on the Problem and Solutions* in June 2002 and the *Strategy for Sustainable Farming and Food*.

The Environment Agency has placed on its website (www.environment-agency.gov.uk), chiefly for the benefit of small and medium-sized enterprises, information relating to the primary and secondary legislation affecting business (access NETREGS via the search facility on the home page of the Agency's website).

4.13.3 Section 92 of the WRA 1991

Under s 92 of the WRA 1991, the Secretary of State has the power to make provisions (by means of regulations) for:

(a) prohibiting a person from having custody or control of any poisonous, noxious or polluting matter unless prescribed works and prescribed precautions and other steps have been taken for the purpose of preventing or controlling the entry of the matter into any controlled waters;

(b) requiring a person who already has custody or control of, or makes use of, poisonous, noxious or polluting matter to carry out such works for that purpose and to take precautions and other steps for the same purpose as may be prescribed.

Using these powers, the Control of Pollution (Silage, Slurry and Agricultural Fuel Oil) Regulations were introduced in 1991. These Regulations require persons with custody of silage, livestock slurry or fuel oil to carry out works and take precautions, and other steps, for preventing pollution of controlled waters.

Essentially, s 92 and the regulations made under it are designed to minimise the risk of highly polluting substances escaping containment and causing water pollution. The regulations may specify, as a condition of being allowed to store and handle such substances, that farmers adhere to a range of controls and standards relating to the design, construction, and operation of manufacturing and storage facilities, especially relating to silage making, slurry lagoons and agricultural fuel and oil stores. Regulations made pursuant to s 92 may create criminal offences and administrative remedies which will be similar to the water pollution discharge consent system.

The Control of Pollution (Oil Storage) (England) Regulations 2001 (SI 2001/2954) came into force in March 2002. The Regulations apply to persons having custody or control of oil (that is, storage) and require the taking of precautions to prevent oil-related water pollution incidents. Compliance with the Regulations is required by 2005, save that the Environment Agency can insist on earlier compliance if there is a significant risk of an oil pollution. The Regulations apply to and set technical standards for storage tanks, valves, pipes, gauges, drums and secondary containment (bunds).

The Regulations do not apply to below ground tanks in view of the powers available to the Environment Agency in the Groundwater Regulations 1998 and the Anti-Pollution Works Notices Regulations 1999.

4.13.4 Water Protection Zones: general zoning control

A further mechanism for preventing water pollution is contained in s 93 of the WRA 1991 and allows for the designation of Water Protection Zones (WPZs). Where, upon the application of the Environment Agency (Sched 11), the Secretary of State, after consultation with the Minister of Agriculture, considers that it is appropriate to prohibit or restrict the carrying on in a particular area of activities which he considers are likely to result in the pollution of any controlled waters, he may by order make provision:

(a) designating an area as a WPZ; and

(b) prohibiting or restricting the carrying on in the designated area of such activities specified or described in the order.

Section 93 orders may themselves prohibit or restrict specific activities or alternatively they can establish a system under which the Environment Agency is empowered to decide which activities are prohibited or restricted. They are especially useful in controlling diffuse pollution such as agricultural run-off which falls outside the ambit of the discharge consent pollution controls. Similar to the discharge consent licensing system, s 93 orders can establish procedures for obtaining consent to engage in restricted activities and provide for criminal offences for breach of the relevant provisions. The detailed procedure for making a s 93 order is contained in Sched 11 to the WRA 1991. An example of a designated WPZ is the River Dee (Water Protection Zone (River Dee Catchment) Designation Order 1999 (SI 1999/915)). The special regulatory regime on the Dee controls the use and storage of a number of polluting substances in order to safeguard drinking water abstracted from the Dee. It is mainly applicable to industrial sites (IPC/IPPC sites, farms, retail premises, and construction sites are exempt) and the content of each consent is dependent upon the outcome of a risk assessment. Carrying out the activities specified in the relevant order without a consent or in breach of consent conditions is an offence (to cause or knowingly permit a contravention of WPZ controlled activity). A 'controlled activity' refers to the keeping or use of controlled substances within a site in the WPZ. 'Controlled substances' include: dangerous substances; fuels; lubricants; liquid industrial solvents and spirits; liquid (animal) food or feed; and inorganic fertiliser. The Water Protection Zone (River Dee Catchment) (Procedural and Other Provisions) Regulations 1999 set out the procedure to obtain a WPZ consent. In order to process the application, the Environment Agency requires: a site map, emergency plan, controlled substances location plan, information relating to controlled substances such as density, solubility and quantity, and details of storage (for example, in tanks). The Agency must consult downstream abstractors and affected local authorities before determining the application. The Secretary of State has a 'call in' power and the applicant has a right of appeal to him. A due diligence defence is available as well as a defence based upon the defendant's ability to prove that it was not aware of the regulated activity itself or was not aware of the extent of the storage or use of regulated substances.

4.13.5 Nitrate Sensitive Areas: specific control

In addition to the designation of WPZs, areas may also be designated as Nitrate Sensitive Areas (NSAs) under s 94 of the WRA 1991. (Nitrate pollution cannot be controlled under the mechanisms of the WPZs.) Upon the application of the Environment Agency (Sched 12) and subject to the consent of the Treasury, the Secretary of State for Environment and the Minister for Agriculture (or National Assembly for Wales) acting together have the power to designate areas as Nitrate Sensitive Areas in order to prevent or control the entry of nitrate into controlled waters (as a result of the use of any land for agricultural purposes). Designation of an area is made by order and the order may:

(a) require, prohibit or restrict the carrying on, either on or in relation to any agricultural land in the area, of specified activities; and

(b) provide for specified or determined amounts to be paid in compensation in respect of the obligations imposed as a result of the designation.

Where an area has been designated as an NSA and the relevant minister considers it appropriate, he may enter into an agreement (s 95) to allow for payments to be made to the owner of the freehold interest in any agricultural land in the area (or with the permission of the freehold owner, or any other person having another interest in the land) where that person accepts obligations with respect to the management of the land (especially regarding the application of fertilisers) or other obligations imposed under the agreement. Management agreements run with the land and bind successors in title. In contrast to WPZs, NSA orders may include positive obligations such as constructing bund walls.

NSA orders can only be made at the request of the Environment Agency, rather than at the request of other interested parties such as an environmental organisation, and can only be applied for if the Environment Agency is of the opinion that its other regulatory powers are inadequate. An order is required to identify both the agricultural land from which nitrate is likely to emanate and the controlled waters which will be affected. There are three types of NSA: (a) NSAs where mandatory controls apply; (b) NSAs where mandatory controls apply and compensation is payable; and (c) NSAs where controls are voluntary.

In total, 32 NSAs have been designated. The first 10 NSAs were designated under the Nitrate Sensitive Areas (Designation) Order 1990, which provided for both a basic scheme agreement restricting the use of inorganic nitrogen fertiliser and a premium scheme relating to the cessation of arable farming and its replacement with grassland. The premium scheme was subsequently amended so that increased payments could be made to farmers. The remaining 22 NSAs were designated after the introduction of the 1994 NSA Regulations (see SI 1994/1729 and EC Regulation 2078/92). These NSAs were of three types: basic, premium arable and premium grass. Following the introduction of the 1994 Regulations, further schemes came into effect applying to arable woodland and set aside. Following amendments in 1998 to the 1994 Regulations, no further applications were processed after September 1998. All NSA agreements will end by 2004.

4.13.6 Nitrate Vulnerable Zones

The ability of the government to designate Nitrate Vulnerable Zones (NVZs) arose out of the Protection of Water Against Agricultural and Nitrate Pollution (England and Wales) Regulations 1996 which gave effect to the Nitrates Directive (91/676/EEC). The twofold objective of the Nitrate Directive was: (a) to reduce levels of water pollution caused by the agricultural use of nitrate; and (b) to prevent new sources of water pollution causing further damage. EC Member States were obliged to identify water catchments in which the amount of nitrate in surface and underground waters exceeded 50 parts per million and designate them as NVZs. To date, 68 NVZs have been designated in England and Wales, including all NSAs.

In contrast to some Member States (for example, Germany, the Netherlands and Denmark), the UK has not designated all of England and Wales as an NVZ and has adopted a selective policy of designation. The UK's implementation of the Directive was judicially reviewed in *R v Secretary of State for the Environment and MAFF ex p Standley and Metson* (1997) on the ground that the correct approach required the UK government to have regard to the sources of nitrate pollution before identifying *only* those waters containing nitrate levels in breach of the directive due to solely *agricultural inputs*. The UK government's approach consisted of: (a) identifying the waters containing levels of nitrate in excess of the Directive's limits; (b) identifying the NVZs which drained into those waters; and (c) assessing whether agricultural inputs were a significant, but not exclusive, source of nitrate pollution in the NVZs. The High Court referred the issue to the ECJ, which held that the approach adopted by the UK government was not in conflict with the Directive.

Once a NVZ has been designated, the Secretary of State produces an action plan for each NVZ to reduce and/or prevent nitrate water pollution (Action Programme for Nitrate Vulnerable Zones (England and Wales) Regulations 1998 (SI 1998/1202)). The Action Programme details the measures which farmers in the NVZs must take to reduce the levels of nitrate in surface and groundwaters. The 1998 Regulations ban: (a) the application of organic and inorganic fertilisers at certain times; (b) the application of nitrate fertilisers on steeply sloping fields; and (c) the application of nitrate fertilisers to waterlogged, flooded, snow-covered or frozen fields. In addition, detailed records must be kept of the place, times and quantities of fertiliser applied to the NVZ land and the quantities of each type of livestock manure moved off each farm in the NVZ. In contrast to NSAs, NVZs are mandatory, as provided by the Directive, and compensation is not payable.

In 2002, following the decision of the ECJ in Case C-69/99, *Commission v UK* that the UK had failed to comply fully with the Nitrates Directive (91/676/EC), DEFRA issued a consultation paper entitled *How Should England Implement the 1991 Nitrates Directive?*. A summary of this document has been circulated to all English farmers, since the outcome of *Commission v UK* is a requirement for farmers to apply Action Programmes to limit the use of nitrate-based fertilisers and manure spreading. DEFRA has a choice: apply Action Programmes to all farms in England or extend NVZ designations to cover at least 80% of England.

4.14   THE PREVENTION AND REMEDIATION OF POLLUTED WATER

4.14.1 Anti-Pollution Works Notices and clean-up operations

Section 161 of the WRA 1991 provides the Environment Agency with an important set of powers which enable it to take (a) preventive action where it identifies a pollution risk, and (b) post-incident remedial action following a pollution.

Under s 161(1), where it appears to the Environment Agency that any poisonous, noxious or polluting matter or any solid waste matter is likely to enter or has entered any controlled waters, the Environment Agency is entitled to carry out remedial works to clean up the pollution. The section provides that the following works and operations may be carried out:

(a) preventing any matter entering controlled waters;

(b) removing or disposing of polluting matter;

(c) remedying or mitigating any pollution caused by the presence of the matter in the waters; or

(d) so far as it is reasonably practicable to do so, restoring the waters, including any flora and fauna dependent on the aquatic environment of the waters, to their state immediately before the matter became present in the waters.

The Environment Agency is entitled to carry out and recover the costs of any investigations in order to establish the source of the matter and also the identity of the person who caused or knowingly permitted it to be present in controlled waters or at a place from which it is likely to enter controlled waters.

The EA 1995 (Sched 22) inserted a new provision (s 161(1A)) which provides that the power to carry out works (not the power to carry out investigations) is only exercisable in cases where:

(a) the Environment Agency considers it necessary to carry out the works forthwith; or

(b) it appears to the Environment Agency, after carrying out a reasonable enquiry, that no person can be found on whom to serve a Works Notice (WN) under s 161A.

Section 161(3) provides that where the Environment Agency carries out any such works or operations as are mentioned in s 161, it will be entitled to recover the expenses reasonably incurred in doing so. Expenses may be recovered from any person who caused or knowingly permitted the matter in question to be present at the place from which it was likely to enter any controlled waters or who caused or knowingly permitted the matter in question to be present in any controlled waters. In *Bruton and NRA v Clarke* (1993), the NRA sought recovery of its costs under s 161(3) of the WRA 1991 in remediating the damage to the ecology of the River Sappiston caused by the entry of three million gallons of agricultural slurry. The High Court limited the recovery of costs to £90,000 because not all the NRA's surveys directly related to the remediation. The Environment Agency can exercise its s 161 powers *independently* of any criminal proceedings which it has the power to initiate.

The Environment Agency has issued guidance on the circumstances in which it will use its s 161 power: *Environment Agency Policy and Guidance on the Use of Anti-*

Pollution Works Notices. Section 161 may not be used by the Environment Agency to override the authority of a discharge consent authorising the discharge of substances into controlled waters. In such circumstances, the Environment Agency must apply for a variation of the discharge consent.

4.14.2 Works Notices

Section 161 of the WRA 1991 is a powerful enforcement tool in view of the fact that the cost of clean-up is likely to far exceed any penalty imposed by the courts with regard to any linked prosecution. The Environment Agency now has the power to compel polluters to take (and bear the cost of) preventive or remedial action themselves, rather than relying upon the Environment Agency's power to undertake the clean-up works itself and then attempt to recover the relevant costs from the person responsible. Under ss 161A–D, the Environment Agency may serve a Works Notice (WN) on the polluter, or potential polluter, requiring it either to remedy the pollution or take specified preventive action to stop pollution occurring. The WN procedure is not applicable in circumstances where immediate action is required or where the polluter cannot be found.

Section 161A, inserted into the WRA 1991 by the EA 1995, provides a new procedure for the serving of WNs. The Environment Agency may serve a WN on any person who caused or knowingly permitted the poisonous, noxious or polluting matter, or solid waste matter in question to be present either in any controlled waters or at the place from which it is likely to enter any controlled waters. The WN is a legal notice which requires the person on whom it is served to carry out the works or operations specified in the notice. Typically, the WN will require the recipient of the notice to: (a) remove and/or dispose of the relevant polluting matter; (b) remedy and/or mitigate the effects of the polluting matter; or (c) so far as reasonably practicable, restore the waters and flora and fauna to their pre-pollution state. A WN must specify the time period within which the recipient of the notice must comply. Section 161A(4) provides that before serving a WN, the Environment Agency should endeavour to consult the person concerning the works that are to be specified in the Notice. A WN may not be served on the person responsible for polluting matter which enters controlled waters from an abandoned or partly abandoned mine (provided the abandonment occurred before 2000). The Anti-Pollution Works Regulations 1999 (SI 1999/1006) detail the form and content of WNs and the requirements for consultation. With regard to preventive works, the Regulations require that the WN contain details of the risk, the controlled waters likely to be affected and the location of the land from which the polluting matter is likely to enter controlled waters. With regard to post-pollution remediation, the WN must detail the nature and extent of pollution, the controlled waters affected and the necessary remedial works. A WN will contain the Environment Agency's reasons for serving the notice, rights of appeal, the Environment Agency's entitlement to have its reasonable costs reimbursed and the consequences of failure to comply with the Notice.

A WN may include conditions which require the person served with the Notice to carry out works or operations in relation to land or waters even where he or she has no legal right to do so, for example, where the land is outside his or her ownership or control. Section 161B provides that any person whose consent is required before any works or operations are carried out *shall* grant, or join in granting the necessary rights in relation to any land or waters, thus enabling the person served with the WN to carry out the required works. For example, a WN might require A to go onto B's land in order to carry out necessary clean-up works and B must grant A the right to go onto his or her land and carry out those specified works. Section 161B(5) provides that a person who grants such rights is entitled to compensation from the person on whom the WN is served. The written application must be made within one year of the date the rights were granted under s 161B, save where an appeal is in progress.

Section 161C provides for the right of appeal to the Secretary of State against a WN within 21 days of the Notice being served. The Secretary of State may confirm, vary or quash (cancel) the WN. As well as specifying the relevant grounds of appeal, the WN will draw attention to the choice of appeal (full hearing or written representations).

4.14.3 Offences

It is an offence to fail to comply with any of the terms of a WN (s 161D). The maximum penalties on conviction are: (a) a fine of up to £20,000 and/or a three month gaol term in the magistrates' court; and (b) an unlimited fine and/or gaol term of up to two years in the Crown Court. In addition, the Environment Agency may carry out the work detailed in the WN and recover its reasonable costs from the convicted defendant. Under s 161D(4), the Environment Agency has the power to apply to the High Court for an injunction to enforce compliance with the WN where it considers that a prosecution for failure to comply with the terms of the WN will provide an ineffective remedy (for example, where the recipient of the WN has previously breached a WN). A conviction for breach of s 161D is entered on the public register (Control of Pollution (Applications, Appeals and Registers) Regulations 1996 (SI 1996/2971)).

4.15   ACCESS TO INFORMATION (s 83 OF THE WRA 1991)

The Environment Agency is required to maintain (see the Control of Pollution (Applications, Appeals and Registers) Regulations 1996) a publicly accessible register of data relating to the regulation of controlled waters (s 190 of the WRA 1991, as amended by Sched 22 to the EA 1995). The register contains details of applications for water pollution discharge consents (that is, pollution licences); pollution licences granted (and the relevant conditions); information provided by the licence holder as a condition of its pollution discharge consent; sampling information; applications for variation of conditions; appeals (s 91); Enforcement Notices (s 90B); Revocation Notices (Sched 10, para 7); Works Notices (s 161 as amended); convictions of the licence holder for WRA offences; directions given by the Secretary of State; and water quality objectives (s 83).

Application may be made by the discharge consent holder to exclude information from the public register which (a) is commercially confidential, or (b) affects national security. Inspection of the registers at the Environment Agency's offices at reasonable times is free. Copies of register entries may be taken subject to payment of a reasonable fee. The contents of the register have, on occasion, been used as both evidence in criminal prosecutions and civil actions. Sections 51–52 of the EA 1995 require the Environment Agency to prepare an annual report and to supply the Secretary of State with relevant information. In addition, s 202 obliges the Environment Agency to supply government ministers with advice and assistance regarding their water pollution functions. Both the Environment Agency and ministers may serve on any person a notice requiring the provision of water pollution-related information. Failure to comply with a request is an offence. Section 203 requires the Environment Agency and water companies, subject to the restrictions in s 204, to exchange information relating to water quality and water pollution incidents.

4.16   THE PRIVATE REGULATION OF WATER POLLUTION

Individuals with 'riparian rights' (that is, property owners whose land adjoins a watercourse and who therefore own the bed and banks of the relevant river or stream, but not the waters flowing in them) are often well placed to take action against polluters who damage their property and property-related interests. They have the right to receive water in its natural state, subject only to reasonable use by upstream users (*Chasemore v Richards* (1859)). Any interference with the quantity and quality of the water the riparian owner receives is actionable, based on the tort of nuisance.

4.16.1 The common law and water pollution

The law relating to the rights of riparian owners appears to be well settled. A riparian owner is entitled to:

> ... have the water of the stream, on the banks of which his property lies, flow down as it has been accustomed to flow down to his property, subject to the ordinary use of flowing water by upper proprietors, and to such further use, if any, on their part in connection with their property as may be reasonable under the circumstances. Every riparian proprietor is thus entitled to the water of his stream, in its natural flow, without sensible diminution or increase and without sensible alteration in its character or quality [*John Young & Co v Bankier Distillery Co* (1893), *per* Lord McNaughton].

In the *John Young* case, a whisky distillery obtained an injunction, in an action based on private nuisance, because the activities of an upstream mine owner had changed the chemistry of the water and so had unreasonably interfered with the whisky manufacturer's riparian right to receive the water in its natural state. A riparian owner can bring an action for damages or can seek an injunction. Interference with fishing rights can also give rise to an action in nuisance. In *Cook v South West Water plc* (1992), the plaintiff, Cook, owned three-quarters of a mile of riparian salmon and trout fishing rights. During 1990, South West Water, which operated three sewage works upstream from the plaintiff's stretch of river, discharged detergent and phosphates into the river which damaged the river's ecosystem and also seriously interfered with fishing. The plaintiff brought an action in nuisance against South West Water seeking both damages and an injunction.

More recently, in *Marcic v Thames Water Utilities Ltd* (2001), a householder successfully sued his sewerage services provider in nuisance due to repeated flooding of his property with foul water from the sewerage system.

In addition to a claim in nuisance, it may be possible for a riparian owner to make a claim in trespass. The tort of trespass on land has many functions and its application for environmental purposes is a more recent and limited development. Trespass involves the unjustifiable physical interference with land, arising from intentional or negligent entry onto the land. The key issues which must be present in order for an action in trespass to be brought are that the trespass was direct, that the act was intentional or negligent and that there is a causal link between the directness of the act and the inevitability of the consequences. An example of a successful claim in trespass in relation to water pollution can be found in the case of *Jones v Llanrwst UDC* (1911) in which it was held that sewage, which had been released into a river and which had passed downstream and settled on the plaintiff's land, was a direct interference and amounted to trespass.

The tort of negligence may also have application in water pollution cases. In *Scott-Whitehead v National Coal Board* (1987), the defendant, a regional water authority, was found to be negligent for failing to advise a farmer that the water he was abstracting from a stream (in accordance with an abstraction licence granted by the water authority) to irrigate his crops contained a strong chlorinated solution. The farmer's potato crop was damaged as a consequence of using the chlorinated water and the court held that the water authority was liable in negligence.

The case of *R v South West Water Authority* (1991) illustrates the relevance of the tort of public nuisance in a drinking water context. The case arose out of the Camelford Disaster, when a large quantity of aluminium sulphate was accidentally introduced into the water supply system of a Cornish town. The defendant water company was slow to respond to customer complaints about the taste of the water and slow to take remedial action. Approximately 5,000 people suffered varying degrees of injury, including memory loss, vomiting and temporary changes in hair colour. The defendant was found guilty of causing a public nuisance and was fined £10,000 and ordered to pay £25,000 costs.

4.16.2 Private prosecutions

Unless specifically restricted by the relevant legislation, any individual has the right to commence a private prosecution to enforce the criminal law, including regulatory offences (such as a breach of s 85 of the WRA 1991). This right is useful where the regulator declines to prosecute a polluter. Early environmental legislation tended to restrict this right by requiring the private prosecutor to obtain the consent of the Attorney General (AG) or the Director of Public Prosecutions (DPP) (for example, using s 6(3) of the Control of Pollution Act (COPA) 1974). Some restrictions continue to apply (see s 211 of the Water Industry Act 1991 and s 7(4) of the WIA 1991). Private prosecutions are usually commenced by the more litigious NGOs, such as Greenpeace; however, an unsuccessful private prosecution will carry a financial risk. In the mid-1990s, Greenpeace brought an unsuccessful action against ICI (*Greenpeace v ICI* (1994)). Greenpeace brought this private prosecution under s 85(1) of the WRA 1991 and the case illustrates one of the dangers faced by private prosecutors. Greenpeace was required to pay over £28,000 towards ICI's legal costs. Clearly, only large environmental pressure groups such as Friends of the Earth or Greenpeace can afford to run the financial risks of losing legal actions. However, in addition to traditional environmental pressure groups, the Anglers Associations have availed themselves of these rights as well as resorting to common law actions to secure injunctions or obtain damages. Readers may wish to refer to Chapter 12 for general coverage of private prosecutions and access to evidence of breach of the law contained in public registers.

4.17   DISPOSAL OF WASTES INTO SEWERS

The disposal of effluent (industrial effluent and human sewage) into sewers is inextricably linked to pollution of controlled waters (see *NRA v Yorkshire Water Services Ltd* (1995)). Industrial processes generate enormous quantities of waste which is either discharged on land as solid waste, emitted into the atmosphere or, in the case of liquid wastes, either discharged into controlled waters or released into the sewers. The discharge of trade effluent into sewers is controlled directly by the sewerage undertakers, exercising their powers under the WIA 1991, but also indirectly by the Environment Agency. Sewerage undertakers grant consents for the disposal of trade effluent into the sewers but they are then required to obtain consent from the Environment Agency to release the final treated effluent into controlled waters. The WIA 1991 regulates the discharge of trade effluents into sewers and s 87 of the WRA 1991 deals with the discharge of sewage effluent into controlled waters.

4.17.1 Discharges of sewage into controlled waters

The 10 privatised water companies which operate as both water and sewerage undertakers are responsible for discharging large quantities of treated effluent from sewage treatment plants into controlled waters. The sewerage undertakers receive trade effluent through the sewers which they then treat and finally return, after treatment, into controlled waters. The sewerage undertakers are therefore effectively responsible for all discharges made from their sewers or treatment plants into controlled waters. The sewerage undertakers control the trade effluent disposed of into the sewers by means of trade effluent consents which they grant under s 118 of the WIA 1991.

Although the sewerage undertakers treat waste from other sources, they are, like other industrial polluters, subject to the provisions of the WRA 1991. Since s 85 of the WRA 1991 makes it an offence to discharge sewage effluent into controlled waters, sewerage undertakers are themselves required to obtain a water discharge consent from the Environment Agency in order legally to discharge treated sewage from each of their sewage treatment plants.

Although it has been stated that the sewerage undertakers are subject to the same provisions as other licensed dischargers under the WRA 1991, they do nevertheless benefit from an additional defence under s 87 of the WRA 1991 that is not available to other persons. Section 87 of the WRA 1991 deals specifically with discharges into and from public sewers. Under s 87, a sewerage undertaker will not be guilty of an offence under s 85 if the discharge is in breach of consent conditions where:

(a) the breach is attributable to a discharge which another person caused or permitted to be made into the sewer (that is, an illegal discharge into the sewers);

(b) the sewerage undertaker was not bound to receive the discharge into the sewer (that is, the discharge was not authorised by a licence); and

(c) the undertaker could not reasonably have been expected to prevent the discharge into the sewer (this may be due to the design of the sewage treatment process).

This defence recognises that sewerage undertakers deal with effluent from a variety of sources which are treated and then discharged from the sewer or works under the terms of a discharge consent into controlled waters. If the final discharge from the sewerage works is in breach of consent conditions, the undertaker will not be guilty of an offence if the reason for the breach was the unauthorised discharge of effluent into the sewer (providing it can be shown that the undertaker could not reasonably have expected the unauthorised discharge into the sewer). The availability of this defence was considered in the case of *NRA v Yorkshire Water Services Ltd* (1995). In this case, an unidentified person discharged iso-octonal, an industrial solvent, into a sewer. The water company had not granted any consent to any person to discharge this substance into the sewers and therefore the initial discharge by the unknown person was unlawful. The iso-octonal travelled by means of gravity through the sewer system into a sewage treatment plant, which it disabled, and iso-octonal was discharged in an almost undiluted state into controlled waters. Yorkshire Water Services were charged with discharging poisonous, noxious or polluting water (that is, the discharge of the mixture of iso-octonal and untreated sewage) into controlled waters contrary to s 85 of the WRA 1991. The House of Lords held that there was sufficient evidence for a court to find that the water company had caused the discharge from the sewerage works (reaffirming the strict test of 'causing' laid down in *Alphacell v Woodward* (1972)). However, on the facts, the House of Lords held that the water company could rely on the special defence available in s 87(2) of the WRA 1991. The water company could not reasonably have been expected to prevent the discharge of the iso-octonal into the sewer.

4.17.2 Discharges of trade effluent into the sewers

Given that sewerage undertakers are subject to the same controls as any other discharger (subject to the availability of the additional defence, discussed at 4.17.1 above), they are required to maintain a tight control on the effluent they are prepared to accept into the sewers and, for this reason, the disposal of trade effluent into a sewer requires a separate consent from the sewerage undertaker under s 118 of the WIA 1991.

4.17.3 Trade effluent consents: s 118 of the WIA 1991

The disposal of trade effluent into a sewer requires a trade effluent consent under s 118 of the WIA 1991 and it is an offence to discharge any trade effluent from trade premises otherwise than in accordance with the conditions of a consent obtained from the sewerage undertaker. The definitions of 'trade effluent' and 'trade premises' are contained in s 141 of the WIA 1991. Trade effluent means any liquid, which is partly or wholly produced in the course of any trade or business, but does not include domestic sewage. Trade premises include premises used for industry or any trade, research and agriculture.

The application for a consent is made by means of serving a trade effluent notice on the sewerage undertaker. At least two months' notice must be given of an intention to discharge and the notice has to provide details of the proposed discharge, including information about the proposed quantity and composition of the trade effluent and the maximum daily volume of the discharge. Following the service of a notice, the sewerage undertaker has to decide whether or not to grant the consent and the relevant conditions to attach. Failure to determine the notice within two months constitutes a deemed refusal enabling the applicant to appeal.

Section 121 of the WIA 1991 gives the sewerage undertaker wide discretion as to the conditions that can be imposed. Conditions may relate to the time of day during which effluent may be discharged into sewers, temperature, acidity or alkalinity, inspection of sewers, testing and monitoring of effluent and the keeping of records. When framing conditions of WIA 1991 licences, the sewerage undertaker must have regard to the conditions in its own water discharge consent, issued by the Environment Agency, under the WRA 1991. In addition, a condition will be imposed which sets out the amount payable to the undertaker for receiving the trade effluent. In setting trade effluent consent conditions, sewerage undertakers should have regard to the criteria in *Trade Effluent Discharged to the Sewer* (1986) which specify the key objectives or purposes of trade effluent control. These include:

(a) the protection of the integrity of the sewage system (that is, the conducting pipes);

(b) the protection of personnel;

(c) the protection of sewage treatment works (from substances and objects which will cause damage);

(d) the protection of the environment from the impact of treated sewage; and

(e) to ensure that dischargers pay a reasonable charge for sewage treatment.

Consent conditions are set by reference to the ability of the sewer system to treat the proposed discharge. Substances, such as metals or solvents, which the sewage treatment works cannot cope with will be excluded from the terms of the discharge consent. In such circumstances, the discharger must pre-treat its effluent to remove the banned substances.

The sewerage undertaker has various powers in respect of trade effluent consents. The consent may be varied on two months' notice, although the undertaker can only do so after two years from the grant of the consent. This power is essential so that the sewerage undertaker can respond to the tightening by the Environment Agency of the terms of the discharge consent licences of its sewage treatment works. A variation of the consent is possible within the two year period, but compensation will be payable unless the need for the variation has resulted from circumstances which were not foreseen when the consent was last varied. In contrast to the WRA 1991, there is no provision in the WIA 1991 relating to the revocation of trade effluent discharge consents. A person aggrieved by a consent condition or variation has the right of appeal to the Director General of Water Services under s 122 of the WIA 1991. The discharger and sewerage undertaker may enter into an agreement under s 129 of the WIA 1991 as an alternative to the trade effluent discharge consent licensing process. The terms of such an agreement enable the discharger to pay the capital costs involved in constructing a new sewage treatment plant where the existing works are already at maximum capacity.

4.17.4 Special consents

Certain types of effluents, known as 'special category effluents', require a special consent because they are potentially harmful and are difficult to treat. The Trade Effluents (Prescribed Processes and Substances) Regulations 1989, as amended (by SI 1992/339), prescribe the particular substances that fall into this category.

In cases where the trade effluent is special category effluent, the sewerage undertaker must consult the Environment Agency and ask whether the discharges should be prohibited or, if not, whether the Agency requires any specific conditions to be imposed (s 120(1) of the WIA 1991). The sewerage undertaker commits a criminal offence if it fails to comply with this duty.

4.18   WATER ABSTRACTION

The quality of water is not simply determined by what is discharged into it. Water quality is inextricably linked to water quantity. If water levels are low, there is less water available to dilute waste and effluents and this may cause a reduction in water quality. Therefore, it is appropriate in a chapter on water pollution to consider the legal controls that exist in relation to the abstraction of water. The Environment Agency is under a statutory duty to secure the proper use of water resources. Under s 19 of the WRA 1991, the Environment Agency is under a duty to conserve and increase the available water resources. The Agency therefore has to assess the need for new developments and ensure that the most appropriate schemes are licensed, taking into account the environmental impact of new developments on existing users. The system of water abstraction licensing controls is set to undergo a major overhaul in the Water Bill (see 4.19.2 below).

Before legislation was enacted to control the use of water, the common law had developed various rules which determined the rights of riparian owners to abstract water. These have largely been superseded by the legislation but need to be considered.

4.18.1 Riparian rights

Owners of property adjoining a river, known as riparian owners or occupiers, have the right to what the courts called the 'ordinary use of water flowing past their land'. In *Miner v Gilmore* (1859), Lord Kingsdown stated that:

> By the general law applicable to running streams, every riparian proprietor has a right to what may be called the ordinary use of water flowing past his land; for instance to the reasonable use of the water for his domestic purposes and for his cattle, and this without regard to the effect which such use may have, in case of a deficiency on a proprietor lower down the stream.

Not only does this view have potentially detrimental consequences for riparian owners further downstream, it clearly takes no account of any environmental consequences of such actions. However, the position is qualified to the extent that uses which may be regarded as extraordinary can only be carried out if they do not cause harm to lower riparian occupiers. Therefore, if one riparian owner wished to use water for what would be described as an extraordinary use, he or she could only do so if it would not harm the rights of others. This was the view taken in the case of *Rugby Joint Water Board v Walters* (1967), where the court stated that the water removed must either have no effect on the river or it must be returned to it substantially undiminished in quantity or quality. This more recent decision appears to reflect the changing attitude to the environment in so far as the decision is couched in terms of the quality of the river in its own right.

4.18.2 Statutory controls over water abstraction

Growing concern about the problems of over-abstraction, water shortages, rivers drying out and the consequent loss of natural habitat led to the creation of legislative controls to control the abstraction of water. The WA 1945 provided some limited controls over water abstraction. However, it was the WRA 1963 that provided the first comprehensive control over water abstraction, prohibiting the abstraction of water without an abstraction licence.

When the requirement for an abstraction licence was first introduced, many industrial companies had already been abstracting water for use in their industrial processes for many years. Section 33 of the WRA 1963 provided a special entitlement for such users, automatically granting a Licence of Right to any person who was entitled to abstract water from a source or supply in a river authority area at the date that s 33 came into force, or to a person who had a record of five years' continuous abstraction. These Licences of Right are presumed to be lawful by the WRA 1991; however, such licence holders are now required to pay for their abstraction rights.

Together, s 6 of the EA 1995 and ss 19–20 of the WRA 1991 (subject to s 4 of the EA 1995) impose the following water resource management duties on the Environment Agency: (a) the promotion of the conservation and enhancement of the natural beauty of inland and coastal waters; (b) the promotion of the conservation of the flora and fauna which are dependent upon the aquatic environment; (c) the promotion of inland and coastal waters for recreational purposes, taking into account the needs of the chronically sick and disabled; (d) to conserve, redistribute, manage and secure the proper use of water resources in England and Wales; and (e) to make water resource management schemes in conjunction with the large privatised water companies in order to implement (d).

Under s 21 of the WRA 1991, the Environment Agency has the power to prepare and submit to the Secretary of State for approval draft statements regarding the minimum acceptable flows of inland waters (the term 'Inland Waters' include rivers, streams, lakes, ponds, channels, creaks, bays, estuaries, docks and natural and man-made watercourses). In preparing each minimum acceptable flow statement, the Environment Agency must have regard to SWQOs and its general environmental duties (see Chapter 2). Proposed flows must safeguard public health and meet the needs of current lawful users of inland waters. Schedule 5 to the WRA 1991 contains the relevant publicity and consultation (with privatised water companies, drainage boards, harbour authorities and conservancy authorities) requirements. The Secretary of State may approve the draft flow statements (s 21(7) and Sched 5) and he may, of his own volition, direct the Environment Agency to consider the minimum acceptable flow of any inland waters (s 22).

Under s 23, the Environment Agency has a power to consider the level or volume of inland waters in addition to or in substitution for the flow under consideration.

4.18.3 Abstraction licences authorised by the WRA 1991

Abstraction licences are granted by the Environment Agency. Abstraction without a licence is prohibited (s 24), subject to limited exceptions, for example, land drainage (s 28). To apply for an abstraction licence (s 34), it is necessary to be either:

(a) an occupier of the land adjacent to the inland water; or

(b) an occupier of land above the underground strata from which the water is drawn.

The licence (which confers a right on the holder (s 48)) is issued to the occupier of land. Once his or her occupation ceases, the licence will lapse and the new occupier must notify the Environment Agency if he or she wishes to take over the licence (succession rights are governed by ss 49–50, as amended). Water undertakers are required to apply for a licence for the water which they abstract from water courses. Sections 27 and 29 of the WRA 1991 provide various exceptions to the need to obtain an abstraction licence. Owners of the land through which water flows may use for domestic or agricultural purposes a maximum of 20 cubic metres each day without the need for a licence.

An application for an abstraction licence is made to the Environment Agency in accordance with the Water Resources (Licences) Regulations 1965 (as amended) (s 38). The application must be accompanied by a fee. Notice of the application is publicised by the applicant in the *London Gazette* and a local newspaper (s 37). The Environment Agency is required when considering an application for an abstraction licence to consider:

(a) representations made in response to publicity;

(b) representations made arising from consultation with bodies such as water undertakers, drainage boards and English Nature;

(c) the effect of the proposed abstraction on other existing licence holders;

(d) the effect on other users of the supply (exempt users).

(e) the reasonable requirements of the applicant; and

(f) the need to maintain a minimum acceptable flow irrespective of whether a minimum flow has been determined.

The form and content of licences are detailed in ss 46–47.

4.18.4 Water abstraction licence conditions

The Environment Agency may attach conditions to abstraction licences which may require the abstractor to return the water to the relevant watercourse after use. Monitoring of the amounts of water abstracted will usually be required as a condition of the licence. When considering whether to grant a licence or the conditions to be attached to it, the Environment Agency must consider whether the grant of licence will prevent another current licence holder, or someone extracting water for domestic or agricultural purposes, from abstracting their full entitlement. If the proposed abstraction will affect existing abstractors in this manner, then the Environment Agency must refuse to grant a licence unless the person affected agrees to the grant of the new licence. The Secretary of State has the power (ss 41–42) to 'call in' an application for his own decision.

An abstraction licence may be varied either by the Environment Agency acting on its own initiative or at the request of the licence holder (ss 51–53). If the Environment Agency decides that it intends to vary a licence, then a licence holder has a right of appeal to the Secretary of State (ss 43–45). If the holder suffers damage as a result of the Secretary of State's decision, he or she may recover compensation from the Environment Agency (s 61). Once a licence is granted, the Environment Agency is not able to derogate from the grant of the licence.

4.18.5 Drought-related powers

The serious drought affecting West Yorkshire in 1995 (see the Uff Report) provided a timely reminder of the vulnerability of water supplies and the utility of Drought Orders, Emergency Drought Orders and Drought Permits (see Pt II, Chapter III of the WRA 1991). Schedule 8 to the WRA contains the procedural requirements regarding the making of these orders and permits. Under s 73(1), the Secretary of State has the power to make an 'Ordinary Drought Order' upon receipt of an application from the Environment Agency or a water undertaker (large privatised water company). This Order is used where an exceptional shortage of rain has brought about or threatens to bring about a serious deficiency of water supply or deficiency in flow or level of inland waters, posing a serious threat to the flora and fauna dependent on the relevant inland water. Under s 73(2), the Secretary of State has the power, subject to receipt of an application from the Environment Agency or a water undertaker, to make an 'Emergency Drought Order' to address serious supply deficiencies due to low rainfall which is likely to impair the economic or social well being of the public. Emergency Drought Orders enable water companies to supply water via stand pipes and bowsers (water tanks). The terms of a drought order (s 78) may provide the Environment Agency or a water undertaker with the power to enter land to carry out works. Compensation is payable to 'injuriously affected' owners, occupiers and interested persons (s 79 and Sched 9). Under s 80, it is an offence either to take, abstract or use water in contravention of the terms of a drought order, or to discharge water except in accordance with the terms of a Drought Order. Under s 79A, the Environment Agency may issue Drought Permits upon the application of a water undertaker, authorising the applicant to take water from the sources specified in the permit. A Drought Permit suspends or restricts the operation of any Drought Order relating to the relevant inland waters. Drought Permits, intended for use when a drought exists or is pending, last for six months unless extended by application to the Environment Agency (subject to a maximum duration of 12 months). Section 79 and Scheds 8 and 9 detail the relevant procedural, publicity and financial requirements regarding the making of a Drought Permit.

4.19   CONTROLS RELATING TO DRINKING WATER

The WIA 1991 provides the regulatory framework concerning water quality and sufficiency of water supplies. Under s 67, the Secretary of State may make regulations specifying the criteria relating to 'wholesome water' (that is, water which is safe and pleasant to drink – see *McColl v Strathclyde Regional Council* (1984)).

The relevant regulations giving effect to the EC Drinking Water Directive (80/778/EEC) are the Water Supply (Water Quality) Regulations 1989 (SI

1989/1147), as amended by SI 1989/1383 and SI 1991/1837. The Regulations specify the substances which may be present in water, the characteristics of the water (taste, odour, etc), sampling, and the mandatory standards regarding water used for drinking, washing, cooking and food production. The Regulations make provision for the keeping of publicly accessible registers of water quality information and reporting requirements. A water undertaker may apply to the Secretary of State to relax the Regulations subject to the right of local authorities to make representations or objections. The 1989 Regulations are set to be superseded in 2004 by the Water Supply (Water Quality) Regulations 2000 (SI 2000/3184)

The quality of private water supplies such as wells is regulated by the Private Water Supply Regulations 1991 (SI 1991/2790). Private water supplies are divided into domestic supplies (Category 1) and food production (Category 2). Local authorities have a duty to sample these supplies and if they are found to be unwholesome or insufficient, the authority may by notice specify remedial works or other action to improve the supply.

Under s 68 of the WIA 1991 and the Drinking Water (Undertakings) (England and Wales) Regulations 2000 (SI 2000/1297), water undertakers have a duty to ensure that water supplied to premises for domestic or food production purposes is wholesome at the time of supply and, so far as is reasonably practicable, to ensure that (with regard to each source of supply or combination of supplies) there is no deterioration in the quality of supply. The Secretary of State has the power (s 18 of the WIA 1991) to enforce these drinking water-related duties.

4.19.1 Section 70 of the WIA 1991

It is an offence under s 70 for a water undertaker to supply water which is unfit for human consumption. Only the Secretary of State or the DPP may prosecute. In *Drinking Water Inspectorate v Severn Trent Water* (1995), the Crown Court convicted Severn Trent of supplying unfit water. The court drew a distinction between 'fitness' and 'wholesomeness' and held that water could be unfit for human consumption, although it was wholesome within the meaning of the Drinking Water Supply Regulations and did not pose a public health risk.

The heightened concern with health risks (see 'public concern' in Chapter 12) is apparent in the case of *Secretary of State for Wales v Dwr Cymru* (1995), in which the defendant, Welsh Water, was convicted of breaching reg 28 of the Water Supply (Water Quality) Regulations 1989. Although there was no evidence that the breach (consisting of failure to obtain consent to line water pipes with a particular material (epoxy resin)) had affected drinking water quality, the defendant was nevertheless convicted, for it was not certain that its actions had not exposed its customers to any risk.

In *R v Yorkshire Water Services Ltd* (2001), the court set out sentencing guidelines relating to breach of s 70. In assessing an appropriate fine, the court should have regard to the following factors: the severity of the damage, culpability, previous convictions, the attitude of the defendant, the defendant's post-incident response, and the balance between a censorial penalty and the impact of a large fine on the water company's water supply responsibilities (see 2.7.3 above for further coverage of sanctions).

4.19.2 The Water Bill

The Water Bill received its first reading in the House of Lords in early 2003 and contains reforms relating to the current system for abstracting water for drinking and other uses from both surface and groundwaters. The Bill addresses the shortcomings of the current system: (a) licences which were granted with insufficient thought with regard to their environmental impacts; and (b) the large number of statutory exemptions from licensing control. In addition, the Bill is designed to enable the UK to comply with the EC Water Framework Directive which requires the regulation of the abstraction of fresh surface water and groundwater, the regulation of the impoundment of fresh surface water, prior authorisation (licensing) of abstractions, and the setting up of abstraction registers. The Water Framework Directive must be transposed into UK legislation by the end of 2003.

Once the Bill comes into force, there will be three types of new abstraction licence: (a) temporary licences for fewer than 28 days' abstraction; (b) a transfer licence; and (c) a full licence applying to one source of supply. Each licence must state the purpose for which the water is intended to be abstracted and the date the licence will expire (expected to be fixed at 12 years, except for water companies, which require longer licences, for example, hydropower operators). Licences will specify a 'minimum value' which is the minimum amount of water which can be extracted without payment of compensation by the Environment Agency. The Bill lifts the threshold for exemptions from licensing from five cubic metres per day to 20 cubic metres (subject to the Secretary of State's power to raise or lower this limit with regard to areas of the country or classes of licence holder. This power will not apply until new licences have been in existence for 12 years and the Secretary of State is satisfied that the exercise of the power is necessary to protect the availability of water in the source of supply to which the licence relates). Therefore, approximately 20,000 of current licence holders (48,000 in total) will no longer need to obtain an abstraction licence. Existing statutory exemptions are to be phased out over a period of years.

Only full licence holders, subject to exceptions relating to 'protected rights', will be protected against the Environment Agency granting new licences which derogate from existing abstraction rights. The Environment Agency will be required to set up registers of non-licensed protected right holders. The Bill contains important powers of revocation and variation of licences *without payment* of compensation. After 2012, the Secretary of State will be able to revoke or vary existing licences (granted before the Bill becomes law) without compensation provided that this is necessary to protect any waters or underground strata, or any flora or fauna dependent on them, from serious damage.

Section 48 of the WRA 1991 (licence holder's defence to legal action, except in the case of negligence and breach of contract, based on possession of a licence) is to be amended by the Bill. A duty will be imposed on abstractors not to cause loss or damage to other persons, and possession of a licence will not be a defence to actions commenced by claimants. The Environment Agency is to be granted a power to serve an Enforcement Notice (EN) (provided unlicensed abstraction is causing or is likely to cause significant environmental damage) on any person abstracting water without the benefit of a licence (or exemption). The power to serve an EN will also extend to persons constructing abstraction machinery to abstract groundwater.

The Bill will have the greatest impact on water companies, food and drink manufacturers, industrial and agricultural abstractors and users of private water supplies.

4.20 THE INTERFACE OF THE WRA 1991 AND WIA 1991 WITH OTHER STATUTORY WATER POLLUTION CONTROLS

Section 69 of the WIA 1991 empowers the Secretary of State to make regulations (for monitoring, recording, analysis, etc) relating to the s 68 duty of water undertakers to supply wholesome water (see the Water Supply (Water Quality) Regulations 1989).

4.20.1 Offences

Under s 71 of the WIA, it is an offence to cause or permit any underground water to run to waste from any well, borehole or other work, and to abstract water from a well, borehole or other work in excess of requirements.

Under s 72 of the WIA, it is an offence to commit any act of neglect whereby water in any water works (to be used for domestic or food production purposes) is likely to be polluted. Note the provision of exemptions relating to agriculture (complying with best husbandry practice) and highway authorities using tar on public roads.

Under s 73 of the WIA, it is an offence for an owner or occupier of premises to cause or permit, whether intentionally or negligently, any of his water fittings to be in disrepair or misused so as to result in contamination or waste of water (the Secretary of State may make regulations addressing this issue under s 74).

If, in the opinion of a water undertaker, a serious water deficiency exists or is threatened, it may introduce a hosepipe ban (s 76 of the WIA).

4.20.2 Local authority functions regarding water supply

Under s 77 of the WIA 1991, local authorities must be provided with information regarding the wholesomeness and sufficiency of water supplies. Regulations (SI 1989/1147) require water undertakers to provide local authorities and health authorities with information regarding threats to water supplies which may result in serious risks to health. The Secretary of State has power to make regulations regarding the provision of information (s 77(3)).

Section 78 of the WIA 1991 requires local authorities to inform water undertakers of anything which suggests that any water supply is, or has been, or is likely to be: (a) unwholesome or insufficient for domestic use; (b) so unwholesome or insufficient as to be likely to endanger life or health; and (c) likely to lead to breach of the suppliers' duty to supply wholesome water. Local authorities have no power to control the remedial action taken by water undertakers with regard to public water supplies. Any concerns which local authorities have with regard to remedial action must be referred to the Secretary of State.

Local authorities enjoy their most extensive powers with regard to private water supplies. If a local authority believes that a private water supply is unwholesome or insufficient, it may serve a notice (a private supply notice (PSN)) on the owners and occupiers of the relevant land detailing the necessary remedial works (s 80). The PSN may specify that the local authority will undertake the remedial works or that a water undertaker or some other person will provide a supply of wholesome water. Sections 81–85 set out: (a) the Secretary of State's powers to hold a local inquiry and to confirm, vary, or quash a PSN; (b) the powers of local authorities to obtain information and enter premises; and (c) provisions relating to the variation and enforcement of PSNs.

4.20.3 Part I of the EPA 1990

In addition to the controls under the WRA 1991 and the WIA 1991 discussed above, Pt I of the EPA 1990 also provides controls which relate to water pollution. Part I introduced IPC as a system for controlling pollution from the most seriously polluting processes which are prescribed by the Act. Processes which are subject to IPC are also controlled by the Environment Agency, which seeks, under the IPC system, to control pollution discharged into all environmental mediums, including water, in order to achieve the best practicable environmental option. In other words, for the most seriously polluting processes subject to IPC, the controls over water pollution are not seen in isolation but are dealt with by considering the impact of the prescribed activity on the environment as a whole.

4.20.4 The PPCA 1999

The PPCA 1999 has introduced IPPC which will replace IPC controls completely by 2007. The licences issued under the PPCA 1999 control all environmental impacts of licensed installations, including discharges to controlled waters.

4.20.5 Part II of the EPA 1990

Additionally, Pt II of the EPA 1990, which is concerned with waste management, is also relevant. Before granting a waste management licence under Pt II of the EPA 1990, the Environment Agency must consider the likely effect of a waste deposit on groundwater.

4.20.6 Part IIA of the EPA 1990

Part IIA of the EPA 1990 establishes the contaminated land regime. The pollution pathways regulated under Pt IIA of the EPA 1990 include contamination of groundwaters.

As regards the overlap between water pollution controls and contaminated land, the Water Bill will alter the test for determining when land is contaminated so that less property is stigmatised for what is, in effect, minor pollution. Currently, land is contaminated under Pt IIA of the EPA 1990 if it is in such a state that 'pollution of controlled waters is being or is likely to be caused'. The change proposed in the Water Bill will only trigger contaminated land remediation where 'significant pollution of controlled waters is being caused or there is a significant possibility of such pollution being caused'.

4.20.7 The Salmon and Freshwater Fisheries Act (SFFA) 1975

In addition to the offences established by the WRA 1991, s 4(1) of the SFFA 1975 provides that it is an offence where a person 'causes or knowingly permits to flow, or puts, or knowingly permits to be put, into waters containing fish or into any tributaries of waters containing fish, any liquid or solid matter to such an extent as to cause the waters to be poisonous or injurious to fish or the spawning grounds, spawn or food of fish'. Although the WRA 1991 provides the main provisions relating to water pollution, charges may be brought under s 4 of the SFFA 1975 where fish or their spawning grounds are damaged.

4.21 WATER POLLUTION: THE EC AND THE PACE OF REGULATORY CHANGE

The UK's membership of the EC has had important consequences for the UK with regard to improvements in water quality and the regulation of water pollution. The European Commission has been very active in drawing up a series of water-related directives which, when passed by the European Parliament, must then be transposed into national law. These directives have sought to set standards for the regulation of a wide range of activities, including:

(a) discharges of dangerous substances into the aquatic environment (surface waters and groundwaters);

(b) bathing water quality;

(c) regulation of nitrate levels;

(d) sewage effluent treatment processes;

(e) drinking water quality;

(f) water quality for freshwater fish and shellfish.

These directives establish clear parameters and objectives and their effects are channelled through to individual dischargers, via (primary and secondary legislation transposing the directives into UK law) the discharge consent licensing system. Most water directives fall into two types:

(a) those, such as the Dangerous Substances Directive, which set emission limits (emission standards); and

(b) those, such as the Bathing Water Directive, which set quality objectives linked to actual or intended use of the relevant waters (quality objectives of receiving waters).

The EC has had, and continues to have, a major impact on water quality and water pollution control in the UK. Over the last three decades, the EC has passed a range of directives designed to prevent discharges of pollutants into the aquatic environment and also to establish quality standards for waters which are used for drinking, bathing and fishing. Often, the EC adopts a 'framework directive' to set up a specific control regime and then, over time, supplements this with 'daughter directives' which set limits for the presence of chemical substances in different types of waters (that is, drinking, bathing and fishing). Member States are given a set period of time to transpose the relevant EC directive into national law and achieve actual compliance with the specific provisions of the directive.

Water directives have established a coherent system of control of pollution and water quality. Directives are often characterised by the following features: Member States must set up regulatory bodies to 'police' compliance with the obligations contained in each directive; some directives set quality standards – these may be of two types: mandatory, imperative, 'I' guides or target 'G' guides; Member States have limited discretion as to the waters which are designated for different uses (and therefore the EC-based controls which apply to those waters); and the original standards (and other contents of the directive) may be tightened to keep pace with technological and scientific advances.

4.21.1 The Dangerous Substances Directive (76/464/EEC)

The dual objectives of this framework directive are: (a) to *eliminate* the discharge (and presence) of highly toxic substances (the 'Black List'– List I) in the aquatic environment; and (b) to *reduce* the discharge (and presence) of other chemical substances (the 'Grey List' – List II) in the aquatic environment (note the comparable lists of hazardous substances referred to in the 1974 Paris Convention on the Prevention of Marine Pollution from Land Based Sources). Black List substances are hazardous because of their toxicity, persistence and their bio-accumulative and carcinogenic properties (for example, mercury, cadmium, organophosphorous, mineral oils, hydrocarbons, etc).

The EC favours the use of daughter directives to set limit values (maximum allowable concentrations – MACs) for these substances.

List II substances are those which have an adverse impact on the aquatic environment but the severity of the relevant impacts varies with the location and characteristics of the receiving waters. These substances (for example, lead, zinc, some biocides, etc) have adverse effects on receiving waters with regard to such matters as taste and odour of water sources used for human consumption or food production.

The Dangerous Substances Directive requires Member States to set up 'competent authorities', for example, the Environment Agency, to oversee the elimination and/or reduction of Black and Grey List substances via licensing systems. Authorisation of the discharge of substances on both lists must be obtained before discharges commence. Licence conditions must include provisions relating to duration and the quality and quantity of the substances discharged. The limit values (MACs) for some Black List substances are set by daughter directives, although Member States are allowed to set stricter standards. As an alternative to the limit value approach with regard to Black List substances, the EC allows Member States (notably the UK) to achieve compliance with EC law by focusing on the quality of the receiving waters into which listed substances are discharged. The UK sets SWQOs, taking into account listed substances discharged into the relevant waters. Grey List substances are controlled via discharge licence conditions linked to SWQOs in Member States. The regulation of Grey List substances is chiefly the responsibility of Member States, because States develop their own SWQOs subject to timescales set by the EC.

4.21.2 The Groundwater Directive (80/68/EEC)

The objective of this Directive is to prevent, reduce or eliminate pollution of groundwater due to the presence of listed substances. The contents of Lists I and II of this Directive are similar to the Dangerous Substances Directive. The Groundwater Directive regulates both direct and indirect (for example, percolation from landfill sites) discharges. Direct discharges of List I substances are banned whilst indirect discharges must be authorised by the Environment Agency after investigation (comprising hydrogeological investigation and an assessment of whether the discharge is a satisfactory environmental solution – see reg 15 of the Waste Management Licensing Regulations 1994 (SI 1994/1056)). 'Groundwater' is defined as water below the surface of the ground, in the saturation zone, and in direct contact with the ground or sub-soil. Pollution of groundwater occurs where a discharge of listed substances (direct and indirect) results in danger to human health, water supplies, harm to living resources or aquatic ecosystems and interference with legitimate water use.

Regulation of indirect List I substances and indirect and direct List II substances is licence-based. Licences contain conditions relating to place of discharge, method of discharge, maximum quantity, monitoring arrangements and precautionary measures. Licences are subject to a mandatory four yearly review. The Groundwater Directive will, in due course, be replaced by the Water Framework Directive.

4.21.3 The Surface Waters Directive (75/440/EEC)

This Directive aims to maintain and, via treatment, improve the quality of surface waters, especially those waters from which water is abstracted for human consumption. Surface waters are classified (A1–A3) according to the measures necessary to produce potable (drinkable) water. The Directive contains a mix of mandatory standards and guideline standards relating to various aspects of water quality.

4.21.4 The Bathing Waters Directive (76/160/EEC)

This Directive is designed to protect public health by maintaining the quality of bathing waters (freshwaters and seawaters). The directive specifies the necessary micro-biological and physio-chemical characteristics of bathing waters. Both waters authorised for bathing and those which, although not authorised, are used by large numbers of bathers are covered by the directive. All Member States were required to identify the relevant waters and put the relevant standards in place by the end of 1985; however, the UK was held to be in breach of the directive (see Case C-56/90, *Commission v UK* (1993)) because of its failure to designate Blackpool, Southport and Formby as bathing waters falling within the terms of the Directive. Bathing waters will comply with the standards laid down by the Directive provided sampling confirms that mandatory (Imperative – I values) standards are achieved in 95% of samples and guide standards (G values) are achieved in 90% of samples. All Member States are subject to reporting requirements (that is, reporting to the Commission).

4.21.5 The Freshwater Fish Water Directive (78/659/EEC), as amended by Directive 91/692/EEC

The dual objective of this Directive is to designate relevant waters and set quality objectives for waters capable of supporting freshwater fish. Designations may either be 'salmonid' (capable of supporting salmon and trout) or 'cyprinid' (capable of supporting coarse fish). The Directive (a) sets mandatory 'I' and guide 'G' standards, (b) requires Member States to set up pollution reduction programmes with the aim that designated waters achieve 'I' and 'G' standards within five years of the date of designation, and (c) sets out sampling and reporting (three yearly) obligations.

4.21.6 The Shellfish Waters Directive (79/923/EEC)

This Directive has the same objectives as the Freshwater Fish Water Directive, save that it sets water quality objectives for waters which support shellfish (bivalve and gastropod molluscs). Designated waters include coastal and brackish waters.

4.21.7 The Drinking Water Directive (80/778/EEC)

This Directive sets quality standards for drinking waters and waters used in cooking. The relevant standards, mandatory and guide, are located in Annexe 1. Mandatory standards, whether maximum allowable concentrations (MACs) or minimum required concentrations (MRCs), must be achieved, but States have some flexibility in the actions they may take to achieve guide value standards. Derogations (permitted delays in achieving the target standards) may be permitted due to exceptional climatic conditions (floods and droughts), the condition of the ground which is the source of water supply (aquifer contamination), the existence of an emergency, and in circumstances in which a State experiences compliance problems (see Arts 9, 10 and 20). The Directive is to be replaced in late 2003 by Directive 98/83/EC, which has been transposed into UK law by the Water Quality (Water Supply) Regulations 2000 (SI 2000/3184).

4.21.8 The Detergents Directives (73/404/EEC) and (73/405/EEC), amended by Directives 82/242/EEC, 82/243/EEC and 86/94/EEC

The purpose of these Directives is to protect water quality from the adverse impacts, including photosynthesis, oxidation, and damage to sewage treatment processes, of detergents. The Directives set biodegradability standards.

4.21.9 The Titanium Dioxide Directive (78/176/EEC), amended by Directives 82/883/EEC and 83/29/EEC

Whilst titanium dioxide is an important constituent of paints, the waste from the manufacturing process poses problems when dumped, stored or injected into the earth. The Directive requires Member States to licence the disposal of waste from the industry. Before granting permission to discharge, dump, store or inject waste, the Environment Agency will: (a) in the case of existing plants, undertake an assessment of the method of waste disposal. The Environment Agency must be satisfied that the method of disposal adopted poses no deleterious aquatic consequences and there is no better way of dealing with the waste; and (b) in the case of a new plant, require an environmental impact assessment and undertakings from the operator to use the least damaging environmental techniques and raw materials. The directive contains provisions relating to the establishment of waste reduction programmes, monitoring and reporting. Directive 89/428/EEC bans the dumping of wastes, including titanium dioxide wastes, into inland waters and marine waters.

4.21.10 The Urban Waste Water Treatment Directive (91/271/EEC)

This Directive sets standards for the treatment of waste waters (by sewage treatment systems) generated by urban centres large enough to require sewage collection and treatment systems. Stricter standards apply to 'sensitive areas'. Member States are free to define these areas, but typically they are: (a) coastal waters and freshwaters prone to eutrophication (algal blooms associated with high nitrate content of coastal or inland waters); and (b) surface waters from which drinking water is abstracted, which are at risk of exceeding the nitrate levels in Directive 75/440/EEC.

From 1998, the disposal of sewage sludge, whether by dumping or pumping, into surface waters (including coastal waters) has been banned. This has resulted in major sewerage infrastructure expenditure.

4.21.11 The Water Framework Directive (2000/60/EC)

This Directive, in force from December 2000, provides a framework for the protection of inland surface waters, groundwaters and transitional waters (river mouth/estuary waters which change from fresh to saline).

The Directive aims to: (a) halt deterioration in the quality of these waters; (b) improve the quality of aquatic ecosystems and terrestrial systems which depend upon water and wetlands; (c) promote sustainable water use to protect water resources in the longer term; (d) mitigate the impacts of floods and droughts; (e) eliminate 'priority' hazardous substances; and (f) contribute to reducing concentrations of substances in the marine environment which equate to naturally occurring background levels.

The Directive will by 2013 replace several directives including the Dangerous Substances Directive (save for Art 6), the Groundwater Directive, the Surface Waters Directive and the Freshwater Fish and Shellfish Directives.

The Directive adopts a river basin focus to water resource management and pollution control. This will require Member States to co-operate with non-EU States and will lead to greater integration of resource management and pollution control. The Directive imposes the following duties on Member States:

(a) to identify river basins (small basins are to be combined into a river basin district);

(b) to create a regulatory body;

(c) to assign a river basin which is shared with two or more Member States to an international river basin district;

(d) to endeavour to co-operate with a non-EU State where a river basin in the Member State is shared with a non-EU State (to achieve compliance throughout the entire basin);

(e) by 22 December 2004, and thereafter annually, to analyse the characteristics of the river basin, review human impacts on ground and surface waters, and carry out an economic analysis of water use.

By 2020, Member States must ensure that water pricing policies provide adequate incentives to ensure the efficient use of water resources. The Commission will, in due course, identify a list of 'priority' hazardous substances (based on risk assessments: see Regulation (EEC) 793/93, Directive 91/41/EEC and Directive 98/8/EC) and submit proposals for controlling such substances (via the phasing out of discharges of these substances over a 20 year period). Implementation of the Directive in the UK will involve some amendment to existing legislation.

The House of Commons Environment, Food and Rural Affairs Select Committee published its 4th Report, *The Water Framework Directive*, HC 130 I and II (2002–03) in 2003. The Report is critical of the apparent lack of urgency on the part of the government to implement the Directive properly within the relevant time limits (transposition into UK law is due on 21 December 2003). In addition, the Committee draw attention to: the amount of work yet to be completed to finalise the relevant criteria and definitions regarding ecological water quality; the lack of information regarding the extent of UK waters which will comply with the Directive; and the current threats to water quality posed by over-abstraction, flood defence, drainage works and eutrophication. The Committee has recommended the setting up of a scientific steering group to commission research, clarification of the roles of DEFRA and the Environment Agency, the provision of adequate resources to the Environment Agency, and an assessment of the legislative impact of the Directive on the current national legislative framework.

4.22 MARINE POLLUTION

Coverage of water quality and water pollution in England and Wales would not be complete without some mention of marine pollution. The main human-related marine environmental problems appear to be: discharge of hazardous substances into the aquatic environment (for example, oil pollution discharges from oil tankers, pipelines or oil rigs, and the discharge of toxic substances from manufacturing and other human activity) especially if such substances are bioaccumulative and get into the food chain (for example, fish and shellfish contaminated with mercury); waste dumping; chemical 'run-off' which flows from rivers into the seas and results in eutrophication in coastal zones (algal blooms); resource depletion (overfishing); and the impact of climate change on oceanic currents (such as *El Niño*).

For centuries, waste substances were poured into surface waters and found their way into the marine environment, where their effects were diluted; however, international recognition that the practice of treating oceans as 'free' dustbins must be regulated led, in the late 20th century, to the conclusion of a series of important multilateral treaties (although customary international law is still highly relevant: see *Nicaragua v United States (Merits)* (1986), *Lake Lanoux Arbitration* (1957) and *The Trail Smelter Arbitration* (1940)).

Perhaps the most significant treaty is the UN Convention on the Law of the Sea (UNCLOS), which was concluded in 1982 and came into force in 1994 (ratified by the UK in 1997). Part XII of UNCLOS contains important obligations of contracting parties regarding marine protection and preservation. Contracting States are subject to a general duty to protect the marine environment, plus obligations relating to monitoring, exchange of information, scientific and technical co-operation and enforcement.

In regard to oil pollution, the key international treaty is the International Convention for the Prevention of Pollution from Ships (MARPOL) of 1973 (plus the London Protocol of 1978). MARPOL was drafted by the International Maritime Organisation (IMO) – a UN agency with responsibility for the safety of shipping and marine oil pollution). By 2001, the vast majority of the world States with large shipping fleets had ratified the Convention, which is designed to eliminate and/or minimise the pollution of international waters by oil or other harmful substances. Annexes I (oil pollution provisions) and II (noxious liquids) are compulsory (that is, they automatically bind contracting States), whereas Annexes III–VI are optional (and relate to the regulation of packaged harmful substances, sewage and waste dumping from ships, and air pollution from ships).

International treaties, conventions and agreements are concluded between contracting States but do not automatically bind the citizens of the contracting State, hence the need to enact domestic legislation (primary or secondary legislation) to give effect to the terms of the relevant international agreement. In the UK, the key provisions of MARPOL, contained in Annexe I, are implemented by the Merchant Shipping (Prevention of Oil Pollution) Order 1983 (SI 1983/1106), the Merchant Shipping (Prevention of Oil Pollution) Regulations 1996 (SI 1996/2154), the Merchant Shipping (Prevention of Oil Pollution) (Amendment) Regulations 2000 (SI 2000/483) and the Merchant Shipping (Reporting Requirements for Ships Carrying Dangerous or Polluting Goods) Regulations 1995 (SI 1995/2498). The 1996 Regulations contain the key provisions and apply to all ships in UK territorial waters and UK registered vessels wherever they are. The Regulations ban discharges of oil and oily water (most often routine discharges resulting from cleaning a tanker's cargo tanks), whether a deliberate disposal or accidental escape. A number of exemptions apply. Any ship is exempt if it has embarked on a voyage, is not within a special marine area at the time the discharge takes place (for example, the Mediterranean or Baltic Seas), the oil content of the discharge does not exceed 15 parts per million (ppm), and the vessel is operating the oil filtering and monitoring equipment specified in the Regulations. Additional restrictions apply to UK tankers. UK tankers must be at least 50 miles from land at the time the discharge takes place, the rate and quantity of the discharge must comply with the Regulations and 'control systems' (that is, cleaning the oil tanks) must be in operation. Exemptions also apply: (a) if the discharge was necessary for ship safety or for saving life; (b) the discharge was due to damage to the ship or its equipment; and (c) the discharge was made to combat pollution.

UK tankers of over 150 gross registered tonnage (similar provisions relate to UK offshore installations) are required to undergo a full survey every five years and annual and intermediate surveys, following which, if satisfactory, an International Oil Pollution Prevention Certificate will be issued to the vessel. Accidents or incidents affecting the integrity of the vessel or its equipment must be reported without delay to the relevant UK marine authority. Records must be kept of the movements of oil and oil tank cleaning operations.

The Secretary of State has power to refuse entry to UK ports of non-compliant tankers which represent an unreasonable threat of harm to the marine environment. The Secretary of State also has the power to detain any vessel suspected of breaching the Regulations.

Under s 131 of the Merchant Shipping Act (MSA) 1995, it is an offence to discharge oil (crude oil, fuel oil, some diesel oils, etc) into navigable territorial waters. A defence is available to dischargers if the escape of oil, or the delay in discovering the escape, was not caused by lack of reasonable care and remedial actions were taken as soon as practicable. Harbour Masters have the power (s 144) to detain vessels believed to have committed a s 131 offence.

Under s 136 of the MSA 1995, discharges or escapes of oil or oily water into any UK harbour must be reported to the Harbour Master. Failure to report, subject to certain exceptions, is an offence. The provision of 'reception facilities' (port disposal) for waste oil and oily water arising from cargo tank cleaning is governed by the Merchant Shipping (Port Waste Reception Facilities) Regulations 1977 (SI 1997/3018). The provision of such facilities will clearly reduce the need to discharge wastes at sea.

In the event of a tanker accident which threatens to cause significant pollution of UK waters, the Secretary of State (see s 137) is empowered to give directions to any of the following persons (the tanker owner, the master, the pilot or the salvor) to prevent and/or minimise pollution (s 138A enables a s 137 direction to be given in the case of threatened pollution due to hazardous substances other than oil). A s 137 direction may, for example, order the moving of a tanker, the removal of its cargo and the carrying out of salvage operations. Furthermore, if the Secretary of State believes that his powers are insufficient, he can order the destruction of the vessel. It is an offence to fail to comply with a s 137 direction subject to due diligence and emergency action defences. Section 141 enables the Secretary of State to give directions to non-UK vessels sailing in non-UK waters but in a UK pollution zone (for example, the area around a damaged UK oil tanker).

Section 100A enables the Secretary of State to create a temporary exclusion zone around a wrecked or damaged tanker (or offshore oil/gas rig) in UK waters or outside UK waters but within a UK pollution zone. The direction will specify the restrictions applying within the zone. Exclusion zones may only be created where significant harm may be caused by the wreck and an exclusion zone is necessary to prevent/reduce the actual/potential harm.

The EC Commission has proposed a Directive on Ship Source Pollution (COM(2003)92 Final, dated 5 March 2003). The Commission is concerned that, despite international law (see MARPOL, Rules 73/78), deliberate discharges of waste oil and cargo residues continue to occur at an unacceptable rate. Whilst MARPOL focuses on the provision of compensation to victims of oil pollution, the proposed Directive aims to deter and punish offenders. The draft Directive incorporates the relevant international legal rules relating to discharges of wastes and then sets out criminal offences and guidance on the sanctions to impose on convicted offenders.

The Prevention of Oil Pollution Act 1971 regulates polluting discharges from marine oil pipelines and oil exploration operations irrespective of the location of the relevant pipeline.

The main agreements regulating and/or banning waste dumping at sea are the London Convention of 1972 and the 1998 OSPAR Convention. The Convention on the Prevention of Marine Pollution by Dumping of Wastes and Other Matter (the London Convention) came into force in August 1975. The key objectives of the Convention are: (a) to control all sources of pollution entering the marine environment; and (b) to take all practicable steps to prevent dumping-related pollution likely to create hazards to man and marine life, taking into account the capacity (technical, scientific and economic) of each contracting State to achieve the relevant objectives. The Convention bans the dumping of certain highly toxic wastes (for example, mercury and radioactive wastes) and the dumping of other wastes must be licensed. The regulatory bodies in each contracting State which license dumping must keep records of the waste dumped (type of waste, quantity, location, when dumped and ('how') method of dumping). The Convention was amended by an important Protocol in 1996 requiring contracting States to adopt a precautionary approach to wastes licensed to be dumped. Annexe I of the Protocol lists the categories of wastes which may be dumped (including sewage sludge, fish processing waste, dredged material, inert inorganic material, natural organic material, iron, steel, concrete and other non-harmful materials from islands with no other disposal option) subject to the grant of a licence. Consequently, the disposal of all other wastes by dumping is banned.

The Convention for the Protection of the Marine Environment of the North East Atlantic (OSPAR) entered into force in early 1998. It is intended that OSPAR will supersede the Oslo and Paris Conventions. OSPAR regulates all land-based and other (that is, off-shore) sources of marine pollution within the limited geographical remit of the Convention. The need for effective regional co-operation underpins the Convention. Contracting States bind themselves to take all possible steps to prevent and/or eliminate all sources of marine pollution (contrast the 'listing'-based regulatory approach of the Paris Convention). 'Pollution' is widely defined: the introduction by man, directly or indirectly, of substances or energy into the maritime area which results, or is likely to result, in hazards to human health, harm to living resources and marine eco-systems, damage to amenities or interference with other legitimate uses of the sea (note the similarity of this definition with the RCEP's definition of pollution on p 2).

Part II of the Food and Environmental Protection Act (FEPA) 1985, as amended, implements the UK's obligations stemming from the London and OSPAR Conventions. Under s 5 of the FEPA 1985, any waste deposition (dumping) in UK waters must be licensed. Licences are also required for UK vessels with regard to (a) waste dumping in any sea, and (b) waste incineration at sea. Under the FEPA 1985, it is the Fisheries Minister who is the licensing authority. In deciding whether to grant or refuse a licence application, the Minister must have regard to marine ecosystem needs, human health and legitimate uses of the sea.

The disposal of offshore rigs (oil and gas) such as the Brent Spar is, in international law, governed by a combination of the London Convention, the 1996 Protocol to the London Convention, the OSPAR Convention and the OSPAR Decision 98/3 concerning the disposal of redundant offshore installations. The OSPAR Decision prohibits the disposal of rigs by dumping at sea save that dumping may be permitted (licensed) following an assessment (as required by Annexe 2 of the OSPAR Decision) if there are significant reasons why disposal at sea is preferable to re-use of the facility, recycling or disposal on land. In the UK, these obligations are implemented by Pt IV of the Petroleum Act 1998.

4.23   FURTHER INFORMATION

Further reading

See Chapter 3 of Sunkin, M, Ong, D and Wight, R, *Sourcebook on Environmental Law*, 2nd edn, 2001, Cavendish Publishing. This contains extracts from the WRA 1991 (the more important sections), coverage of the *Empress Cars* and *Cambridge Water Co* cases, EC Directives (Water Framework, Groundwater, Drinking Water, Quality of Surface Freshwater, Bathing Water, Urban Waste Water Treatment and Nitrate Pollution) and international conventions (UNCLOS).

See also the Environment Agency report, published each year, entitled *Water Pollution Incidents in England and Wales* (see the Agency's website at www.environment-agency.gov.uk).

Ball, S, 'Causing water pollution' [1993] JEL 128.

Ball, S, '*Cambridge Water*: what does it decide?' (1994) WLAW 61.

Bates, I, 'Water quality: the new regime' (1990) LMELR 156.

Bates, J, *Water and Drainage Law*, looseleaf publication, 1990, Sweet & Maxwell.

Bell, S, 'Commentary on the report of the *Empress* case' [1998] Env LR 412.

Birch, *Poison in the System*, 1988, Greenpeace.

Byatt, I, 'The impact of EC Water Directives on water customers in England and Wales' (1996) JEPP 665.

Department of the Environment, *Review of Water Abstraction Licensing*, 1998.

Department of the Environment, *The Shellfish Waters Directive*, 1998.

Department of Environment, Food and Rural Affairs, *How Should England Implement the 1991 Nitrates Directive?*, 2001, DEFRA.

Department of Environment, Food and Rural Affairs and the National Assembly for Wales, *First Consultation Paper on the Implementation of the EC Water Framework Directive 2000/60/EC*, 2001, DEFRA/National Assembly of Wales.

Elworthy, S, *Farming for Drinking Water*, 1994, Avebury.

Elworthy, S, 'Finding the causes of events or preventing a "state of affairs"?: designation of nitrate vulnerable zones' [1998] JEL 92.

Environment Agency, *Policy and Guidance on the Use of Anti-Pollution Works Notices*, 1999, Environment Agency.

Environment Agency, *Water Pollution Incidents in England and Wales* (yearly publication), Environment Agency.

Forster, M, 'Nitrate sensitive areas: too voluntary a settlement?' (1990) LMELR 48.

Friends of the Earth, *Slippery Customers*, 1997, Friends of the Earth.

Hilson, C, '*Cambridge Water* revisited' (1996) WLAW 126.

House of Commons Environment Committee (1996–97 Session), *Water Conservation and Supply*, 1st Report, The Stationery Office.

House of Lords Select Committee on the European Communities (1994–95 Session), *Bathing Water Revisited*, 7th Report, The Stationery Office.

House of Lords Select Committee on the European Communities (1997–98 Session), *Community Water Policy*, 8th Report, The Stationery Office.

Howarth, W, 'Water pollution: improving the legal controls' [1989] JEL 25.

Howarth, W, 'Reappraisal of the Bathing Water Directive' (1991) WLAW 51.

Howarth, W, 'Poisonous, noxious and polluting' (1993) 56 MLR 171.

Howarth, W, 'Making water polluters pay – in England and Wales' (1994) Env Liability 29.

Howarth, W, 'Accommodation without resolution: emission controls and environmental quality objectives in the proposed EC Water Framework Directive' [1999] Env LR 6.

Howarth, W, 'Self-monitoring, self-policing, self-incrimination and pollution law' (1997) 60 MLR 200.

Howarth, W and McGillivray, D, *Water Pollution and Water Quality Law*, 2001, Shaw and Sons.

Howarth, W and Somsen, H, 'The EC Nitrates Directive' (1991) WLAW 149.

Jordan, A, 'European Community water policy standards: locked in or watered down?' (1999) 37(1) JCMS 13.

Kinnersley, D, *Coming Clean: The Politics of Water and the Environment*, 1994, Penguin.

McFarlane, S, 'The *Empress* case: a plea for common sense' (1998) WLAW 104.

McGillivray, D, 'Discharge consents and the unforeseen' (1995) WLAW 72 and 101.

Maloney, W and Richardson, J, *Managing Policy Change in Britain: The Politics of Water*, 1995, Edinburgh UP.

Ministry of Agriculture, Fisheries and Food, *Code of Good Agricultural Practice for the Protection of Water*, 1998, MAFF.

National Rivers Authority, *Discharge Consents and Compliance: the NRA's approach to Control of Discharges to Water*, NRA Water Quality Series No 17, 1994, National Rivers Authority.

National Rivers Authority, *EC Freshwater Fish Directive: UK Implementation*, Water Quality Series No 20, 1994, National Rivers Authority.

National Rivers Authority, *Bathing Water Quality*, Water Quality Series No 22, 1994, National Rivers Authority.

O'Quinn, J, 'Not-so-strict-liability: a foreseeability test for *Rylands v Fletcher* and other lessons from *Cambridge Water Co v Eastern Counties Leather plc*' (2000) Harvard Environmental Law Review 287.

Organisation for Economic Co-operation and Development, *Agriculture, Pesticides and the Environment*, 1997, OECD.

Parpworth, N, 'The offence of causing water pollution: a New South Wales perspective' [1997] JEL 59.

Parpworth, N, 'Causing water pollution and the acts of third parties' [1998] JPL 752.

Poustie, M, 'The demise of coal and causing water pollution' (1994) ELM 95.

Royal Commission on Environmental Pollution, *Freshwater Quality*, Cm 1966, 1992, The Stationery Office.

Ryan, 'Unforeseeable but not unusual: the validity of the *Empress* test' [1998] JEL 356.

Shelbourn, C, 'Historic pollution: does the polluter pay?' [1994] JPL 703.

Somsen, H, 'EC Water Directives' (1990) WLAW 93.

Stallworthy, M, 'Water quality: the capacity of the European Community to deliver' (1998) WLAW 127.

Stanley, N, 'The *Empress* decision and causing water pollution' (1999) WLAW 37.

Warn, T, 'Discharge consents: how they are set and enforced' (1994) ELM 32.

Wilkinson, D, 'Causing and knowingly permitting pollution offences: a review' (1993) WLAW 23.

Wilkinson, D, '*Cambridge Water v Eastern Counties Leather*: diluting liability for continuing escapes' (1994) MLR 799.

Van Dunne, J, *Non-Point Source River Pollution*, 1996, Kluwer Law International.

CHAPTER 5

WASTE MANAGEMENT

5.1 INTRODUCTION

Part II of the Environmental Protection Act (EPA) 1990, as amended by the Environment Act (EA) 1995, and supplemented by the Waste Management Regulations 1994, the Special Waste Regulations 1996 and the Controlled Waste (Registration of Carriers and Seizure of Vehicles) Regulations 1991, as amended, comprise the main planks of the regulatory regime relating to the management of solid wastes arising in England and Wales. The EPA 1990 has introduced a stricter and more extensive regulatory framework than had previously existed under the Control of Pollution Act (COPA) 1974. In particular, the EPA 1990 has introduced a statutory duty of care which creates 'cradle to grave' responsibility applying to all persons in the waste chain who handle waste from the time it is created to the time it is finally disposed of. The definition of 'waste' has been amended, as a result of European Community legislation, so that a greater range of wastes are now subject to regulatory control. In addition, additional controls apply to wastes which are 'special' because they are particularly dangerous or difficult to handle.

Waste management licensing controls have been transferred to the Environment Agency which is equipped with a wide range of administrative powers and criminal law offences to enable it to enforce compliance with the terms of waste management licences and waste management law.

Progressive waste policy, largely driven by EC policy developments, has brought about a planned and proactive approach to solid waste regulation with an emphasis on waste reduction and recycling. In contrast to the COPA 1974, the EPA 1990 focuses upon the management of waste throughout its lifecycle (cradle to grave) rather than concentrating simply upon its disposal.

The EPA 1990 is an example of a Command and Control regulatory regime which requires those persons (usually companies) who engage in waste management operations (waste treatment and waste disposal) to obtain waste management licences authorising, controlling and legitimising those activities. There are, however, a significant number of activities which are exempt from the legal obligation (in s 35 of the EPA 1990) to obtain a waste management licence. These controls represent a coherent and integrated response to the problems associated with the high level of waste production in an industrialised society.

5.2 THE PROBLEM OF WASTE

Since the Industrial Revolution, pollution of the landscape has been associated with the accumulation of unwanted solid waste materials. England and Wales is estimated to generate around 400 million tonnes of waste, divided as follows: 35% industry and commerce; 25% mining; 18% agricultural; and 5% household. Today, the constant increase in wastes has become a cause for major concern. The UK, Germany, France and Italy produce 85% of the total volume of wastes in the

European Union and 78% of the dangerous substances. In addition to the increased volume of waste, there has been a significant change, since the 1950s, in the nature of waste generated. Although the volume of domestic waste has increased, the weight and density has decreased. Domestic waste is no longer largely cinders and ash, but contains more packaging materials, particularly plastics. This has resulted in the need for bigger dustbins and more frequent collections. Some evidence suggests that the use of larger dustbins results in the generation of more waste! About 90% of all household rubbish is tipped as landfill.

5.2.1   Methods of disposal

In the UK, waste is largely disposed of by means of landfill (approximately 70–85% of regulated waste is disposed of in landfill). Other means of disposal include incineration and chemical treatment. Only a small percentage of waste is incinerated. All methods of disposing of waste raise objections, either from environmental protection groups or from residents who object to the disposal of waste in their locality. The NIMBY (not in my back yard) philosophy is one which causes problems especially for the development of new waste incinerators and landfills (see 'public concern' in Chapter 12). Inevitably, the disposal of waste will become more and more problematic as the amount of waste increases and the land available for landfill decreases.

5.2.2   Landfill and co-disposal

One of the particular problems faced in the UK arises out of the practice of co-disposal of waste (the mixed disposal of active and inert waste in the same landfill). The UK now has a large number of abandoned landfill sites which historically, when operational, accepted a wide range of differing types of wastes including inert solids, chemical and organic wastes. Often, the exact composition of landfill sites is unknown. Surface water and groundwater contamination by leachate discharges is a particular problem. Equally, the effect that these sites have on the environment is not known. Modern landfills are monitored with regard to methane and leachate production and the offsite migration of these substances.

The current predominance of landfill as the preferred waste disposal option reflects the fact that, in most parts of the UK, it is by far the cheapest method of disposal. Landfilling does, however, have a number of disadvantages:

(a) even in well engineered sites, contaminants may leach into the ground to cause pollution of groundwaters;

(b) it adversely impacts upon the amenity of people living nearby because of the smell, noise, traffic, vermin, flies and litter associated with the operation of a landfill;

(c) there is a risk of methane build-up and explosion;

(d) methane is a greenhouse gas which contributes to global warming;

(e) landfilling generates public concern with regard to its impacts upon man and the environment (odour, noise, dust, birds, flies, vermin, litter, vehicle movements and adverse impacts on property prices).

The volume of waste currently landfilled is set to be considerably reduced as a result of the waste reduction targets contained in the Landfill Directive and the introduction of the landfill tax.

5.2.3   Incineration and other methods of disposal

Incineration as a means of waste disposal is not widely practised in the UK as compared to other European countries. According to the 17th Report of the Royal Commission on Environmental Pollution, UK incinerators only account for the disposal of 7% of wastes. In 1991, there were over 200 incineration plants in the UK licensed by Waste Regulatory Authorities. Thirty of these were municipal incinerators; most of the remaining incinerators were for clinical waste or were privately owned. Clinical waste incinerators had been exempt from pollution controls and waste licensing because they benefited from Crown immunity. This was removed in 1991 following recommendations of the Royal Commission on Environmental Pollution in its 11th Report.

There are considerable differences of opinion about the desirability of incineration as a means of waste disposal. Incineration has a number of advantages over landfill. Unlike landfill, it does not produce leachate and methane, and it is able to cope with the disposal of some hazardous wastes which are unsuitable for landfilling. Incineration greatly reduces the volume of solid waste requiring final disposal. The new breed of Energy from Waste incinerators produce electricity as a byproduct of the incineration process.

Conversely, incineration is more expensive than landfill. Incinerators have high capital costs and their construction may be considerably delayed by opposition to such developments encountered in the town and country planning process. Incinerators require a minimum throughput of waste in order to function properly. Disposal contracts, entered into by the local authority and the operator of the incinerator, generally have lifespans of approximately 30 years, thereby reducing flexibility in waste management policy. Whilst incinerators do reduce the volume of material which requires disposal on or in land, they produce residues, such as bottom ashes and liquid effluent from the gas scrubbers (which clean the gases discharged to air), which will require careful disposal.

Air pollution is, however, the most significant problem associated with incineration of waste. Incineration may produce dioxins and other hazardous atmospheric pollutants which cause high levels of public concern.

Although there are concerns about the polluting effects of incinerators, there are rigorous controls over their operation. Incinerators are controlled under the following regimes:

(a) the town and country planning regime (see *Gateshead MBC v Secretary of State for the Environment* (1993));

(b) the waste management licensing system (Pt II of the EPA 1990);

(c) Integrated Pollution Control (IPC) and Integrated Pollution Prevention and Control (IPPC).

Incinerators must meet the standards laid down in Directives 89/369/EEC, 89/429/EEC and 94/67/EEC, which relate to the incineration of hazardous waste.

In addition to landfilling and incineration, waste may be disposed of by the following methods which fall outside the ambit of the EPA 1990:

(a) landraise – this form of solid waste disposal (for example, the construction of slag heaps) is usually associated with the disposal of mine or quarry wastes;

(b) discharge of waste to sewers;

(c) discharge of waste to controlled waters;

(d) landspreading of wastes to 'condition' agricultural land;

(e) burying wastes (such as radioactive wastes).

5.3   THE HISTORICAL DEVELOPMENT OF STATUTORY WASTE CONTROLS

5.3.1 Public health protection

The system of waste regulation in this country has its roots in public health controls. Before 1972, there was no legislation primarily concerned with waste production and disposal. There were some basic provisions in the Public Health Acts of 1848 and 1936 which enabled local authorities to remove house and trade refuse and to require removal of any 'accumulation of noxious matter'. The Public Health Act 1936 placed local authorities under a statutory duty to inspect their areas to detect 'statutory nuisances' including 'any accumulation or deposit which is prejudicial to health'. (These provisions are now contained in ss 79–82 of the EPA 1990.) However, the aim of this early legislation was to protect public health from the problems of disease and vermin associated with the Industrial Revolution (crowded towns, poor housing and poor sanitation) rather than dealing with the environmental problems associated with solid waste creation.

5.3.2 Town and country planning controls

The Town and Country Planning Act (TCPA) 1947 provided the first preventive legislation requiring new developments, including waste disposal sites, to obtain planning permission (that is, a planning permit or licence). The deposit of waste on land is 'development' within the terms of the town and country planning regime and requires planning permission. Certain waste facilities may now require an environmental assessment to be carried out as part of the planning process. Current planning controls relating to waste are now to be found in the TCPA 1990.

5.3.3 The Control of Pollution Act (COPA) 1974

Growing concern in the early 1970s about the detrimental environmental effects of waste led the government to set up two working groups on refuse disposal and toxic waste. The reports of these two groups provided the impetus for the COPA 1974. However, prior to that legislation, the government introduced the Deposit of Poisonous Wastes Act 1972 in response to a series of incidents concerning indiscriminate dumping of toxic wastes. The 1972 Act is now repealed, but it was the first attempt at statutory control of industrial waste disposal in the UK.

The COPA 1974 attempted to achieve a degree of *comprehensive* pollution control in the UK. It introduced the requirement for local authorities to make plans regarding waste generated in their areas and also introduced a system of licensing to control sites where waste was deposited. The Act required all Waste Disposal Authorities (WDAs) (which were the county councils in England and the district councils in Wales and Scotland) to draw up a plan for the disposal of all household, commercial and industrial waste generated in its area. These plans were to be reviewed and modified by the WDA where appropriate. The authorities were placed under a statutory duty to publicise the draft plans, giving the public an opportunity to make representations. In addition, there was a requirement that the WDAs consult with the water authorities, other levels of local government and other relevant bodies. Waste plans had to include information on the types and quantities of waste estimated to arise in the area or to be brought into it during the period of the plan, the methods of disposal and the provision of waste sites. The WDAs were also under a statutory duty to consider what arrangements could reasonably be made for reclaiming waste materials.

5.3.4   The COPA 1974 – site licensing

The COPA 1974 introduced a comprehensive licensing system for the disposal of waste on land, over and above the existing planning controls. It made it an offence to deposit household, commercial or industrial waste on land, unless the land in question was licensed by a WDA. In May 1994, the site licence provisions of the COPA 1974 were superseded by the waste management licence system under Pt II of the EPA 1990. Existing COPA 1974 licences were automatically transferred into the EPA 1990 waste management licences. As many existing licence holders obtained their licences under the COPA 1974 regime, it is necessary to compare the two systems of waste regulation.

5.3.5   Defects in the COPA 1974

The COPA 1974 was the first comprehensive piece of legislation to tackle environmental pollution in an integrated way, and regulated air pollution, noise nuisance and waste on land. In fact, the COPA 1974 was used as a model for the EC Waste Framework Directive (75/442/EEC). However, the COPA 1974, despite its worthy aims, was defective in the following respects:

(a) the relevant regulatory bodies were responsible for both waste regulation and waste disposal operations and this gave rise to a conflict of interest (that is, the poacher turned gamekeeper issue);

(b) the regulatory bodies had very limited powers to refuse a licence application or control the transfer of licences;

(c) only those licence conditions which related specifically to the licensed activity, that is, the deposit of waste, could be enforced. Conditions relating to the management of sites and monitoring, for example, were unenforceable;

(d) licences could be surrendered at will. Disreputable licence holders could surrender licences to avoid obligations and liabilities arising from the licensed site.

5.4   PART II OF THE THE EPA 1990

Waste management regulation in this country has undergone substantial reorganisation in recent years. Part II of the EPA 1990 was enacted to provide a more effective and comprehensive regime for dealing with waste on land, and also to address some of the defects of the COPA 1974. The EPA 1990, as amended by the Environment Act (EA) 1995, created a regulatory framework which has been supplemented by detailed secondary legislation. In May 1994, the Waste Management Licensing Regulations were introduced, bringing into force the provisions relating to the licensing system.

The EPA 1990 did far more than re-enact the provisions of the COPA 1974. It introduced a number of very significant changes in the whole of the waste chain. In particular, it shifted the focus from the concept of waste disposal upon which the provisions of the COPA 1974 were based to the concept of waste management. The imperative behind the 1990 Act was that the legislative controls should relate to waste at all points in the waste chain creating a 'cradle to grave' system of control. The main changes introduced by the EPA 1990 are summarised below:

(a) it introduced a much stricter licensing system, particularly in relation to the qualifications of licence holders, licence conditions and surrender of licences;

(b) it established a statutory duty of care applicable to anyone who imports, produces, carries, keeps, treats or disposes of controlled waste;

(c) it reorganised the functions of the regulatory authorities to avoid the poacher turned gamekeeper scenario that existed under the COPA 1974.

5.4.1   The Environment Act 1995

The Environment Act (EA) 1995 introduced a new definition of 'directive waste' to give effect to the EC Waste Framework Directive (75/442/EEC), as amended. The principal change brought about by the EA 1995 was the transfer of the waste regulatory functions of the Waste Regulation Authorities (WRAs) to the newly established Environment Agency. The EA 1995 also made a number of amendments to the waste management licensing system, for example, the Environment Agency's enforcement powers were strengthened. The EA 1995 repealed s 61 of the EPA 1990 (concerned with closed landfills). On a more strategic level, s 92 of the EA 1995 inserted s 44A into the EPA 1990 which empowered the Secretary of State with responsibility for producing a national waste strategy and ss 93–95 of the EA 1995 introduced new provisions concerning producer responsibility for waste.

5.5   WHAT IS WASTE?

The statutory definition of waste, contained in Pt II of the EPA 1990 as amended by the EA 1995, is crucial to understanding the remit of waste management controls in the UK. The definition distinguishes those substances, materials and articles which fall within the statutory definition and are therefore regulated by the Command and Control regulatory regime contained in Pt II of the EPA 1990, and those which fall outside the regime and are therefore not subject to EPA 1990 controls.

The original definition of waste contained in the EPA 1990 and the Waste Management Regulations 1994 has been amended to take account of EC Directives 75/442/EEC and 91/156/EEC. Before we turn to examine the rather complex statutory definition, the following introductory remarks are called for.

It is helpful to think of a waste substance, material or article from the perspective of the person who wishes to dispose of it. A substance, material or article will, as a general rule, be waste if the intention of the person who produced it, or who is currently in possession of it, is to rid (that is, dispose) himself or herself of it. The substance, material or article is 'waste' regardless of any commercial value it has. For example, a sawmill will produce large quantities of sawdust as a byproduct of its timber cutting operations. This material may be of no further use to the sawmill and the owner of the sawmill will desire to rid himself of it. The sawdust is 'waste' and continues to be so despite the fact that it may be sold, as a raw material feedstock, to a fibreboard manufacturer. This aspect of the definition of waste is reflected in government policy guidance. Department of the Environment (DoE) Circular 11/94 draws attention to the critical issue: 'Has the substance or object been discarded so that it is no longer part of the normal commercial cycle or chain of utility?'

5.6   THE LEGAL DEFINITION OF WASTE

5.6.1   Controlled waste

The provisions of Pt II of the EPA 1990 refer to 'controlled waste'. Section 75(4) to (7) of the EPA 1990 defines the wastes which are 'controlled'. The definition of controlled waste in s 75(4) of the EPA 1990 refers to 'household, industrial or commercial waste or any such waste'. This definition has been amended by the Waste Management Licensing Regulations 1994 which amend the provisions of the Controlled Waste Regulations 1992 (SI 1992/588) so that anything which is not 'directive waste' (see 5.6.2) shall not be treated as controlled waste. Although controlled waste is broken down into three categories (see below), it is nevertheless directive waste. The classification of controlled wastes into three broad heads reflects the relative strictness of licensing controls relating to the types of premises which generate the waste:

- *Household waste* includes waste from domestic properties, caravans, residential homes, educational establishments, hospitals and nursing homes (subject to regulations).

- *Industrial waste* means waste from any of the following premises: factories (see the Factories Act 1961); public transport premises; premises used to supply gas, water, electricity, sewerage, postal or telecoms services. Waste from construction or demolition operations is also termed industrial waste, as is waste from contaminated land. Industrial waste is sometimes referred to as trade waste.

- *Commercial waste* includes waste from premises used wholly or mainly for the purposes of a trade or business or for the purposes of sport, recreation or entertainment, except household, industrial, mining, quarrying and agricultural waste, or any other waste specified in regulations.

Not all types of waste are 'controlled'. For example, waste from agricultural premises, waste from mines and quarries, explosive or most radioactive waste fall outside the ambit of the Pt II of the EPA 1990 regulatory controls.

5.6.2 Directive waste

Section 75(2) and (3) of the EPA 1990 provides the original statutory definition of waste, referred to in the statute as 'controlled waste', which determined which substances and objects were subject to the waste management controls in Pt II of the EPA 1990. These provisions have been amended by Sched 2B to the EPA 1990 and regs 1(3) and 24(8) and Sched 4, para 9 of the Waste Management Licensing Regulations 1994 to provide us with a new definition of waste: 'directive waste'. Directive waste is defined in Art 1(a) of the Waste Framework Directive (75/442/EEC), as amended by Directive 91/156/EEC, as 'any substance or object in the categories set out in Annexe 1 (of the Directive) which the holder discards, or intends to discard, or is required to discard'.

The definition of 'directive waste' comprises a two stage test. Directive waste is:

(a) a substance or object falling within the 16 categories in Annexe 1 of the Directive (the 16 categories are reproduced in full in Sched 4 of Pt II of the Waste Management Regulations 1994);

which

(b) the holder discards, intends to discard, or is required to discard.

The 16 categories of substances or objects referred to in the Waste Management Regulations 1994 are summarised below:

(1) production or consumption residues not otherwise specified below;

(2) off specification products (for example, rejects);

(3) products whose 'sell by' date has expired;

(4) materials which have been spilled, lost or have undergone other mishap (for example, materials contaminated by accident);

(5) materials contaminated or soiled as a result of planned actions (for example, residues from cleaning operations, packing waste materials, waste containers, etc);

(6) unusable parts (for example, reject batteries, exhausted catalysts, etc);

(7) substances which no longer perform satisfactorily (for example, contaminated acids and solvents);

(8) residues from industrial processes (for example, metal smelting slags and still bottom residues);

(9) residues from pollution abatement processes (for example, scrubber sludges, baghouse dusts and spent filters);

(10) machining or finishing residues (for example, lathe turnings and mill scales);

(11) residues from raw materials extraction and processing operations (for example, mining residues and oil field slops);

(12) adulterated materials (for example, oils contaminated with PCBs);

(13) any materials, substances or products whose use has been banned by law;

(14) products for which the holder has no further use (for example, agricultural, household, office, commercial and shop discards);

(15) contaminated materials, substances or products resulting from land remediation (for example, contaminated soils);

(16) any materials, substances, or products which are not contained in the above categories (a miscellaneous 'catch-all' provision).

This list is an illustrative guide to the type of substances or objects which will fall within the definition of directive waste provided they are discarded. They are not the final word on what will, or will not, fall within the definition of directive waste.

In determining whether a substance falls within the legal definition of waste, it is essential to focus upon the intention of the current holder of the relevant material. Is the holder's intention to rid himself (that is, dispose or discard) of the substance or material? Is the holder intending to discard or is he required to discard the substance or material? In answering these questions, it is irrelevant that the substance or material has a commercial value (because it can be re-used immediately or after treatment (recovery) or recycled) and can be sold to a buyer.

Problems of definition tend to arise because the EC waste regulatory regime requires many types of disposal and recovery operations to be regulated and it is not always easy to determine when a substance or material is consigned to a regulated recovery operation or whether it is subjected to ordinary industrial processes which are not recovery operations and are therefore not subject to regulatory control (licensing).

At what point in time does a substance or material change its status and become waste? When the waste creator or holder resolves to discard it? What if the waste generator subjects the substance or material to a waste recovery process? Has the substance or material been discarded in these circumstances? Is the substance or material waste if it has been: (a) discarded by disposal (that is, sent to a landfill site or to an incinerator); or (b) consigned to a waste recovery operation (for example, waste oil or solvent cleaning process)? Does a substance or material handed over to a waste disposal or waste recovery process listed in the Waste Framework Directive automatically fall within the definition of 'waste'? Do waste substances, or materials which have been subjected to a waste recovery process, ever cease to be waste? The case law of the ECJ and the UK courts is complex and answers to the questions which we have posed are not always easy to decipher from the judgments of the relevant courts.

5.6.3 Case law

Substances which are capable of being recycled and have a commercial value may nevertheless be waste (see *R v Rotherham Metropolitan Borough Council ex p Rankin* (1990) and joined Cases C-206/88 and C-207/88, *Vessoso v Ministere Public of Italy* and *Zanetti v Ministere Public of Italy* (1990)).

In the *Tombesi* litigation (1998), the ECJ held that the Waste Framework Directive, based on a 'purposive' (inclusive) interpretation, was intended to apply to all substances or objects discarded by the original waste creator or current holder (despite any commercial value the substance might have if recycled, reclaimed or re-used) and consignment of a substance to a recovery operation could amount to discarding it; in those circumstances, the substance could be waste.

The *Tombesi* decision has been subject to further judicial consideration. In *Inter-Environment Wallonie ASBL v Regione Wallonie* (1998), the court held that a substance consigned to a recovery operation could be distinguished from ordinary or normal industrial treatment of raw materials. Consigning a substance to an Annexe IIB recovery operation would usually indicate that the substance was intended to be discarded. Thus, the Waste Framework Directive could still apply to waste recovery operations which were part of a larger process. The question, however, remained: what is the distinction between an ordinary industrial process and an Annexe IIB recovery operation? This question was considered by the UK High Court in *Mayer Parry Recycling Ltd v Environment Agency* (1999). The issue before the court was whether scrap metals which were then smelted and re-used were waste. Carnwath J stated that 'discard' is synonymous with 'get rid of' and, therefore, materials which had ceased to be required for their original purpose were waste (because they were no longer suitable for their original purpose, or were unwanted or were surplus). Conversely, substances or materials which may be re-used without being subjected to a recovery operation were not waste. If such substances were subjected to a recovery operation, then the substance ceased to be waste at the end of the recovery process. More recent guidance on this ongoing issue is provided by the ECJ in Cases 418–19/97, *ARCO Chemie Nederland Ltd v Minister van Volkshuisvesting and EPON* (2000). This case concerned the use of a manufacturing byproduct (for example, waste solvent) as a fuel in a separate (for example, cement) manufacturing process. The ECJ was of the opinion, in regard to the definition of waste, that the key determinant was whether the byproduct had been discarded and not whether the substance was consigned to an Annexe IIB waste recovery process. The factors which the ECJ paid particular attention to in deciding that the substance had been 'discarded' were: whether the material was generally regarded as waste; whether the use of the byproduct was considered to be 'recovery'; whether the substance or material was really a process byproduct; whether there was no other use for the substance, except disposal; and the extra precautions necessary to use the substance as a fuel. This decision has added another layer of complexity to the definition of waste, for the decision means that: (a) it is not automatically the case that substances which may be re-used without being subjected to a recovery process fall outside the definition of waste; and (b) the substance produced by a recovery process ceases to be waste.

The *ARCO Chemie* decision, when applied in a UK context, will be read subject to our own waste policy which addresses the knotty problems of waste definition. In particular, DoE Circular 11/94 contains a practical, 'common sense' approach to such issues. Can the substance, material or object be immediately used as a raw material? If it can, then it is not waste because there is no intention to discard.

In Case C-114/01, *AvestaPolarit Chrome Oy* (2003), the ECJ considered whether Art 2(1)(b) of the Waste Framework Directive (75/442/EEC) applied to waste sand and rock left over from ore extraction and ore dressing operations in Finland. Under Art 2(1)(b), mineral extraction waste is exempt from the definition of waste if it is 'already covered by other legislation'. The ECJ considered whether the reference to 'other legislation' included national legislation and, if so, (a) whether that legislation had to be in force at the time Directive 75/442/EEC entered into force; and/or (b) whether the legislation had to comply with the environmental protection requirements of the Directive. In the opinion of Advocate General Jacobs, the Directive envisaged the possibility of other EC legislation entering into force after Directive (75/442/EEC) (rather than national legislation) and whilst mining wastes were covered by Finnish legislation, these wastes were not excluded by Art 2(1)(b) because there was as yet no EC legislation specifically covering mining wastes.

Confusion with regard to the definition of waste in EC law continues. In Case C-9/00, *Palin Granit Oy v Vemassalon kansanterveystoyn kuntayhtyman hallitus* (2002), a Municipal Board in Finland granted a licence to Palin Granit Oy (PGO) to operate a quarry. The licence relating to quarrying operation could not, under Finnish law, authorise landfilling; however, the operating management plan for the quarry contained a proposed use (a filling material) for the stone left over from the quarrying operations. The issue in this case was whether the leftover stone was 'waste'. A Finnish administrative court had ruled that the material was waste, but PGO challenged that ruling on the grounds that (a) the waste stone was identical in composition to the rock from which it had been quarried, and (b) it posed no threat to human health or the environment. PGO contended that the site where the leftover stone was stored was not a landfill site, but a deposit of reusable materials.

The ECJ held that there was no definitive test to determine whether a substance was waste; there were only indicators. It was not decisive that the material was capable of economic use. More important was the fact that the material was a production residue. Advocate General Jacobs stated, 'According to its ordinary meaning, waste is what falls away when one processes a material or an object and is not the end product which the manufacturing system directly seeks to produce'. The ECJ held that, having regard to the principle established in earlier cases, 'waste' should be interpreted widely so as to limit the substance's inherent risks and pollution. In determining whether the material or substance was waste, the fact that the material was a production residue was significant, as was the likelihood that the material could be re-used without reprocessing. If there was financial advantage in the operator re-using the material, so that re-use was highly likely, and the substance was not a burden for the operator so that the operator would not wish to discard it, then the material was to be regarded as a product. In the circumstances of the *PGO* case, the only foreseeable use of the leftover stone was in the construction of harbour walls and breakwaters. This would necessitate long term storage, which would impose a burden on PGO, and could potentially cause the type of pollution which the Waste Framework Directive sought to avoid. Re-use of the leftover stone was not certain and only foreseeable in the long term. In these circumstances, the material was waste.

This case has implications for residues produced by other industries such as power generation and waste incineration. Surprisingly, the ECJ, in contrast to previous cases, took into account the economic value of the leftover stone as a factor in deciding whether this particular production byproduct was waste.

5.6.4 What is meant by 'discarded'?

DoE Circular 11/94 (a government policy document) suggests a number of questions that should be answered in order to determine whether something is waste or not. These are:

(a) Has the item been discarded so that it is no longer part of the normal commercial cycle or chain of utility?
- If the answer is no, the matter is probably not waste.

(b) Has the item been consigned to a disposal operation?
- If the answer is yes, it is almost certainly waste.

(c) Has the item been abandoned or dumped?
- If the answer is yes, it is probably waste.

(d) Has the item been consigned to a specialised recovery operation?
- If the answer is yes, it is waste.

(e) Can the item be used in its present form without being subjected to a specialised recovery operation?
- If the answer is yes, then the item may well not be waste.

(f) Does the owner have to pay for the item to be taken away?
- If the answer is yes, this would usually suggest the matter is waste, although there are exceptions.

(g) Will the person who receives the item regard it as something to be disposed of rather than a useful product?
- If the answer is that the item is a useful product, it may nevertheless be waste.

(h) Has the item been reprocessed such that it can now re-enter the commercial cycle?
- If the answer is yes, it is probably no longer waste.

5.6.5 What constitutes a disposal operation and what constitutes a recovery operation?

Disposal operations (listed in Sched 4, Pt III of the Waste Management Licensing Regulations 1994) include:

(a) landfill or land raising;
(b) land treatment of waste such as biodegradation of sludge in soil;
(c) deep injection;
(d) surface impoundment;
(e) incineration;
(f) permanent storage.

Recovery operations (listed in Sched 4, Pt IV of the Waste Management Licensing Regulations 1994) include:

(a) solvent recovery;
(b) recycling/recovery of organic substances which are not used as solvents;

(c) recycling/reclamation of metals and their compounds;

(d) recovery of waste oil;

(e) spreading waste on land for agricultural purposes.

Substances consigned to a recovery operation will not automatically be waste. There is a distinction, however, between recovery operations and specialist recovery operations. Waste consigned to a specialist recovery operation will always be waste. Unfortunately, no definition of specialist recovery operations is provided. However, it is apparent that a specialist recovery operation is one in which waste materials are recovered or recycled for re-use in a way which removes or reduces the threat posed by the original waste and which results in a new raw material.

DoE Circular 11/94 gives various practical examples of waste; however, as stated earlier, the Circular is neither definitive nor legally binding.

In February 2003, the ECJ set out the principles to determine whether the operation of waste incinerators or cement kilns (both generating energy) constituted waste recovery or waste disposal operations. The relevant cases, Case C-458/00, *Commission v Luxembourg* (2003) and Case C-228/00, *Commission v Germany* (2003) related to transboundary shipments of waste for incineration with energy recovery in another State. The shipments were described as being for the purposes of waste recovery, but both Luxembourg and Germany were of the opinion that the processes to which the wastes were to be subjected were waste disposal operations. The Commission rejected these opinions and claimed that there had been a contravention of the Waste Shipments Regulation (EC) 259/93. The Luxembourg shipment comprised municipal waste which was to be incinerated (with energy recovery), whereas the German shipment comprised waste which was to be incinerated in cement kilns whilst the energy produced was to be used in the cement manufacturing process to replace (fully or partially) ordinary kiln fuel.

The ECJ relied on Case C-6/00, *ASA Abfall Service AG v Bundesminister für Umwelt, Jugend und Familie* (2002) as authority for holding that the incineration of waste is a recovery operation if the principal objective of incineration is that the waste can fulfil a useful function (energy generation), replacing the need to use a primary source of energy (that is, normal fuel). Annexes IIA and IIB of the Waste Framework Directive (75/442/EEC) list the main categories of waste disposal and waste recovery operations. The Annexes refer to categories D10 'incineration on land' and R1 'use principally as a fuel or other means to generate energy', and the Commission argued that both shipments were R1 waste recovery operations. In determining whether the shipments were designed for R1 processes/operations, the ECJ had regard to the following criteria: (a) the main purpose of an R1 process was to use waste to generate energy; (b) there must be a reason to believe that the waste is to be used to generate energy (the energy generated by the process is greater than the energy consumed and part of the surplus energy is immediately used as heat or, after processing, as electricity); and (c) the term 'principally' referred to the fact that the majority of the waste had to be consumed and the majority of the energy generated recovered and utilised. Thus, the use of the German waste in a cement kiln was an R1 waste recovery process, but the use of the Luxembourg waste was a waste disposal operation because the reclamation of heat was only a secondary effect of a process whose main function was waste disposal.

Approximately one month later, the ECJ in Case C-116/01, *SITA EcoService Nederland BV v Minister van Volkshuisvesting, Ruimtelijke Ordening en Milieubeheer* (2003) gave further guidance on distinguishing between waste recovery and waste disposal operations. The issue in this case was whether a process comprising distinct stages was a waste recovery or waste disposal process for the purposes of the Waste Shipments Regulation 259/93. SITA intended to ship waste for use as fuel in cement kilns and the ash from the incineration of the fuel was to be used in the production of clinker. The Dutch courts asked the ECJ to rule on the matter. Should all the stages of the process be viewed as a single comprehensive process or should they be treated as separate? The ECJ had regard to the fact that it was not uncommon for a process to comprise several successive stages of recovery or disposal. and ECJ held that, for the purposes of the Waste Shipments Regulation, only the first operation that the waste was subjected to after shipment determined whether it was a waste recovery or waste disposal operation. In this case, the first operation was combustion of the waste. The Dutch court would therefore have to take into account the three criteria in Case C-228/00, *Commission v Germany* in deciding whether the process was a D10 disposal operation or an R1 recovery operation.

5.6.6 Special waste

5.6.6.1 *Introduction*

Special waste, like all other directive waste, is subject to waste management regulation under Pt II of the EPA 1990 but, because special waste is dangerous and/or difficult to dispose of, it is subject to additional controls. Special wastes include acids, alkalis, asbestos, pesticides and flammable solvents. Special wastes are 'special' because of their harmful properties. For example, they may be flammable, irritant, corrosive, infectious, toxic or carcinogenic.

5.6.6.2 *The Control of Pollution (Special Waste) Regulations 1980*

The original definition of special waste was contained in the Control of Pollution (Special Waste) Regulations 1980 (SI 1980/1709). The Regulations were commonly known as s 17 Regulations because they were enacted under the provisions of s 17 of the COPA 1974. The 1980 Regulations provided a definition of special waste and also established a detailed system of written documentation which would accompany the transfer of special waste, known as the consignment note system. The purpose of the Regulations was to control the movements of those special wastes. The definition of special waste under the 1980 Regulations was by means of an inclusive list and set of criteria. The term 'special waste' applied to all prescription only medicinal products (as defined by s 130 of the Medicines Act 1968) and any controlled waste which consisted of or contained any substances listed in Sched 1 to the Regulations, if it was also dangerous to life or had a flash point of 21ºC or less. This definition was subject to some criticism on the basis that the criteria laid down defined special waste not by reference to possible environmental damage, but by reference to the possible effect of such substances on human health.

5.6.6.3 The Special Waste Regulations 1996 and the definition of special waste

The 1980 Regulations were replaced in 1996 by new regulations introduced under the auspices of s 62 of the EPA 1990. The Special Waste Regulations 1996 (SI 1996/972) came into force on 1 September 1996. The 1996 Regulations give effect to the provisions of the EC Hazardous Waste Directive (91/689/EEC). The 1996 Regulations provide a new definition of special waste and in doing so extend the controls over wastes which were not previously defined as special. In addition, the 1996 Regulations modified the system of consignment notes established in the 1980 Regulations.

The provisions of the EPA 1990 dealing with the waste offences, licensing system and duty of care apply equally to special waste. However, since special waste is by definition dangerous and difficult to dispose of, any offences involving special waste will tend to attract higher sanctions.

The definition of waste as provided in the 1996 Regulations essentially has two component parts. Effectively, the definition covers waste on the hazardous waste list (reg 2(1)), as required by the EC Directive, but also includes a further catch-all provision (reg 2(2)) to ensure that wastes which were previously defined as special under the 1980 Regulations continue to be defined as special waste under the 1996 Regulations. The definitions are complex and reference should be made to Sched 2 to the Regulations but, as a general guide, 'special waste' includes wastes on the EC hazardous wastes lists, medicinal products, but not household waste.

5.6.6.4 Official guidance

The 1996 Regulations are supported by official guidance, *Special Wastes: A Technical Guidance Note on their Definition and Classification* (DETR, 1999).

Of particular significance in the Regulations are the provisions which relate to:

(a) the requirement for special waste holders to give a minimum of three days' notice to the Environment Agency before moving a consignment of special waste. There are limited exceptions to the requirement to pre-notify the Environment Agency of special waste movements (for example, lead acid batteries, movements of waste for storage purposes between companies in the same company group, and defective products which are returned to manufacturers or suppliers). Notification is effected by the special waste consignment note system which obviates the need to complete a waste transfer note (see 5.21 below). A fee is payable per consignment;

(b) a ban on waste carriers and consignees (i) mixing special waste with normal directive waste, unless mixing is necessary to ensure the safe disposal of special waste, and (ii) mixing certain classes of special waste;

(c) consignment notes which provide improved descriptions of special waste, especially its hazardous properties;

(d) improvements in record keeping. In addition to the special waste consignment note system, any person who deposits special waste is required to keep details of the location of each deposit. Generally, this information will be recorded on a map of the relevant site. Records must be maintained throughout the lifetime of the site (for example, a landfill site) and must be passed on to the Environment Agency at the time the site licence is surrendered or revoked;

(e) simplification of procedures with regard to regular special waste movements;

(f) periodic regulatory inspections of the premises of special waste producers;

(g) the introduction of 14 hazard criteria (see Sched 2, Pt II of the Special Waste Regulations 1996) to determine when regulated directive waste is also 'special waste'.

5.6.6.5 Waste on the Hazardous Waste List

Regulation 2(1) of the Special Waste Regulations 1996 states that (subject to the provisions of reg 2(5) and (6) – see below) special waste is any controlled waste (directive waste) to which a six digit code is assigned in the list set out in Pt I of Sched 2 to the 1996 Regulations. The list is far too long to reproduce in a text of this nature; however, the following extract gives an example of what the list looks like:

Waste Code	Description
05	wastes from petroleum refining natural gas purification and pyrolitic treatment of coal
0501	oily sludges and solid wastes
050103	tank bottom sludges
050104	acid alkyl sludges
050105	oil spills
050107	acid tars
050108	other tars

Inclusion in the list does not necessarily mean the waste is special waste. Regulation 2(1) states that the waste must also demonstrate any of the properties specified in Pt II of the Schedule (subject to the provisions in reg 2(3)), which provides a list of hazardous properties as follows:

H1	Explosive
H2	Oxidising
H3-A	Highly flammable
H3-B	Flammable
H4	Irritant
H5	Harmful
H6	Toxic
H7	Carcinogenic
H8	Corrosive
H9	Infectious
H10	Teratogenic
H11	Mutagenic
H12	Substances or preparations which release toxic or very toxic gases in contact with air, water or land

| H13 | Substances or preparations capable by any means, after disposal, of yielding another substance, eg, a leachate, which possesses any of the characteristics listed above |
| H14 | Ecotoxic |

Each of these properties is defined. For example, in relation to H1, 'Explosives' are substances and preparations which may explode under the effect of flame or which are more sensitive to shocks or friction than dinitrobenzene.

Regulation 2(3) deals with the determination of whether or not a waste displays certain of the properties (toxic, very toxic, harmful, corrosive, irritant or carcinogenic) mentioned in Pt II.

5.6.6.6 Other wastes which are special waste

In addition, special waste is (subject to the provisions in reg 2(6) – see below) any controlled waste (that is, directive waste) which:

(a) displays any one of the following properties:

- H3 – 'highly flammable': liquid substances and preparations having a flash point below 21ºC;
- H4 – 'irritant': non-corrosive substances and preparations which, through immediate, prolonged or repeated contact with the skin or mucous membrane, can cause inflammation;
- H5 – 'harmful': substances and preparations which, if they are inhaled or ingested or if they penetrate the skin, may involve limited health risks;
- H6 – 'toxic': substances and preparations (including very toxic substances and preparations) which, if they are inhaled or ingested or if they penetrate the skin, may involve serious, acute or chronic health risks and even death;
- H7 – 'carcinogenic': substances and preparations which, if they are inhaled or ingested or if they penetrate the skin, may induce cancer or increase its incidence;
- H8 – 'corrosive': substances and preparations which may destroy living tissue on contact;

(b) is a medicinal product as defined in s 130 of the Medicines Act 1968 of a description, or falling within a class, specified in an order under s 58 of that Act (medicinal products on prescription only).

5.6.6.7 Exceptions

Certain wastes which fall within the definition of special waste are excepted, by virtue of reg 2(5) and (6). Household waste is excepted unless it comprises clinical waste, asbestos, synthetic oils and greases, and minerals (reg 2(6)). Also, there are exceptions where a quantity of waste comprises less than 3% special waste (reg 2(5)).

5.6.7 Radioactive wastes

The Waste Management Regulations 1996 apply to radioactive wastes which fall outside the ambit of s 78 of the EPA 1990. Section 62 of the EPA 1990 empowers the Secretary of State to make regulations which provide for the control of radioactive wastes under the special waste control regime. Such controls will only apply to radioactive wastes which have harmful properties characteristic of special wastes.

5.7   THE SYSTEM OF WASTE REGULATION

By virtue of the EA 1995, the Environment Agency was tasked with the responsibility for the waste management licensing system under Pt II of the EPA 1990. The Environment Agency not only has responsibility for waste management licensing, but is also responsible for waste carrier licensing, special waste licensing and 'policing' the duty of care. Prior to the establishment of the Environment Agency, the system of waste regulation was administered by WRAs. The WRAs ceased to exist on 1 April 1996 when the Environment Agency took over their functions. Since the system of waste regulation has undergone significant change in recent years, it is useful at this point to consider briefly some of those changes and to comment on the role fulfilled by the WRAs during their period of operation between 1990 and 1996.

5.7.1   Part II of the EPA 1990 prior to the EA 1995 amendments and the creation of the Environment Agency

Part II of the EPA 1990 was introduced in part to address some of the deficiencies of the COPA 1974 and to introduce a much stronger licensing system and system of waste regulation. Under the regulatory system established by the COPA 1974, local authorities were placed in the position of being both waste regulators, issuing waste disposal licences, and operating their own waste disposal sites. This type of situation is often referred to as a 'poacher turned gamekeeper' scenario and often gives rise to conflicts of interest. The reasoning behind the administrative changes in the EPA 1990 was that local authorities should no longer be able to act as both regulators and operators of waste facilities and the EPA 1990 sought to provide for a division of responsibilities. Another principal reason for change was to ensure that waste disposal operations were no longer subsidised but run on a proper economic basis with charges reflecting the full economic cost of running the operation. In other words, the intention was to make waste disposal operations more competitive and subject them to market forces.

The EPA 1990 therefore created three different levels of waste authority, each with a different role in relation to waste management. These were defined in s 30 of the EPA 1990 as:

(a) Waste Regulation Authorities (WRAs);

(b) Waste Disposal Authorities (WDAs);

(c) Waste Collection Authorities (WCAs).

WDAs and WCAs continue to operate, but the functions of the WRAs have been transferred in full to the Environment Agency.

The waste-related functions of the Environment Agency comprise: waste licensing, licensing exemption registration, waste carrier registration, 'policing' compliance of licensed sites, enforcement, removing illegal waste deposits, monitoring the movement of special wastes and 'policing' the s 34 of the EPA 1990 duty of care.

5.7.2   WRAs (now replaced by the Environment Agency)

In non-metropolitan local authorities, the WRAs were the county councils. In metropolitan areas, the WRAs were the district councils, with special authorities established for Greater London, Greater Manchester and Merseyside. WRAs were intended to 'regulate' the waste industry and had no operational responsibilities. Where a local authority was both a WRA and a WDA, then provisions in the EPA 1990 required the local authorities' WDA functions to be carried out 'at arm's length'. Section 30(7) made it the duty of each authority which was both a WRA and a WDA to make administrative arrangements for keeping these functions separate. This meant that the actual operational functions of the WDA were not carried out by the authority itself but by a 'waste disposal contractor'. Section 30(5) defines a 'waste disposal contractor' as a person who in the course of business collects, keeps, treats or disposes of waste, being either:

(a) a company formed for all or any of these purposes by a waste disposal authority; or

(b) a company, partnership or individual (sole trader).

5.7.3   WDAs

The WDA is normally the county council in non-metropolitan areas and the district council in metropolitan areas. Special arrangements exist in London, Manchester and Merseyside. The functions of the WDA are:

(a) making arrangements for the disposal of controlled waste collected in the area by WCAs;

(b) formation of waste disposal companies;

(c) provision of municipal waste sites for household waste to be deposited by residents (civic amenity sites);

(d) provision of waste transfer stations;

(e) waste recycling.

Section 51 of the EPA 1990 obliges a WDA to dispose of the waste collected in the WDA's area. Facilities (civic amenity/waste sites) are provided for residents to dispose of household waste at no charge (typically items which the waste collection contractors refuse to take). Sections 32 and 51 and Sched 2 enable WDAs to enter into contracts with waste disposal contractors for the disposal of waste collected. Contracts may be arranged with either private contractors or Local Authority Waste Disposal Contractor (LAWDCs) (WDA-owned waste disposal businesses operated at arm's length) (see Annexe C of DoE Circular 8/91). Schedule 2 regulates the waste disposal contract competition which WDAs must conclude with a private contractor or LAWDC. Each contract is put out to tender, must be advertised widely and attract a minimum of four tenders (often by invitation). In appointing a waste disposal contractor, the WDA is subject to a number of duties: (a) to create a competitive market in which private companies and LAWDCs compete on equal terms; (b) to establish a LAWDC; and (c) to have regard to environmental considerations in discharging its functions (see *R v Avon County Council ex p Terry Adams Ltd* (1994)). A WDA is not obliged to accept the cheapest tender and is entitled to have regard to all the relevant factors (especially environmental impacts) including the WDA's favoured disposal option (see *R v Cardiff City Council ex p Gooding Investments Ltd* (1995)).

5.7.4 WCAs

WCAs are the district councils or London boroughs. Their functions are:

(a) to arrange for the collection of household waste in their area;

(b) to arrange for the collection of commercial or industrial waste on request;

(c) to provide bins/receptacles;

(d) to collect waste and to deliver for disposal as directed by the waste disposal authority;

(e) to investigate, draft plans and make arrangements for recycling.

WCAs are placed under a statutory duty (s 45) to collect household waste free of charge (except where the waste is not reasonably accessible and acceptable alternative arrangements are made). In certain circumstances, WCAs can charge for household waste collection (see Sched 2 to the Controlled Waste Regulations 1992). They include large items, garden waste and other difficult wastes or waste produced from commercially run residential premises.

The WCAs also have a duty, if requested by the occupier of premises in its area, to collect commercial waste, and may charge a reasonable sum for the collection and disposal of the waste unless the authority considers it inappropriate to do so.

If requested by the occupier of premises, WCAs may collect, subject to the consent and reasonable charges of the WDA, industrial waste. WCAs also have a discretion to collect sewage waste from occupiers of premises equipped with septic tanks and similar apparatus.

The WCAs are required by s 48 of the EPA 1990 to deliver the waste collected to such places as directed by the WDAs unless the WCAs intend to recycle any household or commercial waste collected. If the WCAs keep the waste for recycling purposes, they will still need to secure the consent of the WDAs, since WDAs have the power to buy and sell waste for recycling purposes. A WDA may withhold its consent where it has contracted with a waste disposal contractor to recycle all or part of the waste.

WCAs are obliged (s 49 of the EPA 1990) to prepare waste recycling plans regarding household and commercial waste collected (see 5.19).

5.7.5 Waste carriers – the Control of Pollution (Amendment) Act 1989

The requirements of Art 12 of the Waste Framework Directive have been implemented in the UK by the Control of Pollution (Amendment) Act (COP(A)A)

1989. Businesses which transport controlled (directive) waste in England and Wales are obliged to register with the Environment Agency (and re-register every three years). Transporting waste without a licence is an offence (s 1(1)) and carries a maximum fine of £5,000 on conviction in a magistrates' court. A limited number of defences are available: (a) the transport of waste in an emergency, provided the Environment Agency is informed; (b) the carrier (vehicle driver) did not know and had no reasonable grounds to suspect that he was transporting controlled (directive) waste and (i) was acting in accordance with his employer's instructions, or (ii) took reasonable steps to check what he was carrying; (c) the carrier was transporting waste (i) within the same premises, (ii) from the place of importation in England and Wales to the first point of arrival, and (iii) to the place from which the waste is to be exported.

The Environment Agency is required to carry out periodic checks on waste carriers (regs 1(3) and 9 of and Sched 4 to the Waste Management Licensing Regulations 1994). The Regulations provide the Environment Agency with the power (see s 5 of the COP(A)A 1989) to carry out off-road inspections of carriers' vehicles whilst the police have off-road and on-road inspection powers. In addition, the Environment Agency has a power of vehicle seizure (see s 6 of the EPA, s 6 of the COP(A)A 1989, and regs 20–25 of the Controlled Waste (Regulation of Carriers and Seizure of Vehicles) Regulations 1991 (SI 1991/1624), as amended).

The following are exempt from registration (see s 1(3) of the COP(A)A 1989 and reg 2 of the 1991 Regulations): the Environment Agency (as waste regulator), WCAs, WDAs, a waste producer carrying waste (except construction and demolition waste) in its own vehicles, and charities and voluntary organisations. Registration as a waste carrier may be refused by the Environment Agency, applying a two-stage test, if: (a) the applicant, or one of its employees, has been convicted of a relevant offence; and (b) a company of which the applicant is or was an officer has been convicted of a relevant offence (reg 1(2) of and Sched 1 to the 1991 Regulations) and the Environment Agency considers it undesirable that the applicant be registered (reg 5(1)). In deciding whether to register an applicant, the Environment Agency takes into account the circumstances surrounding the commission of the relevant offence (see *Scott v Berkshire County Council* (1984)). Carriers may appeal against refusals to register or re-register.

5.7.6 Waste brokers

Waste brokers (individuals, businesses, or companies such as environmental consultants (see Annexe 8 of DoE Circular 11/94)) who arrange for the disposal or recovery of controlled/directive waste on behalf of others will be exempt from registration if they are subject to, or exempt from, any other requirement to license themselves with the Environment Agency.

5.8   THE WASTE MANAGEMENT LICENSING SYSTEM

The requirement for a waste management licence to legitimise directive waste disposal operations and directive waste recovery operations lies at the heart of the waste regulatory regime established by the EPA 1990. The acquisition of a waste management licence and compliance with its conditions will shield the licence holder from liability for s 33(1)(a) and (b) of the EPA 1990 offences. Nevertheless, activities which are carried out in accordance with the terms of a waste management licence may still constitute a criminal offence under s 33(1)(c) of the EPA 1990.

The Environment Agency is responsible for regulating the waste management licensing regime and is equipped with a range of enforcement powers to ensure that licence holders comply with their licences. The current regime is a considerable improvement on the former waste management licensing system contained in the COPA 1974.

The system of waste management licences came into force in May 1994 by virtue of the Waste Management Licensing Regulations 1994 (SI 1994/1056), as amended. The Regulations were enacted some four years after the EPA 1990, although this should be seen as an improvement on the COPA 1974, where some of the provisions took over 10 years to come into effect (and others never came into effect!). COPA 1974 licensed sites automatically became EPA 1990 licensed sites on 1 May 1994. The new system is complex and all waste producers need to determine, by reference to the Waste Management Licensing Regulations 1994, whether or not they need to obtain a waste management licence or whether they are exempt. In the latter case, they will still need to register with the Environment Agency.

The main changes in the licensing system introduced by Pt II of the EPA 1990, as amended, are as follows:

(a) applicants for licences must satisfy the 'fit and proper person test';

(b) all aspects of the licence are enforceable at all times, that is, not only when the disposal operations are in progress;

(c) the Environment Agency must agree any proposed licence transfer;

(d) new arrangements were introduced in respect of surrender of licences.

The effectiveness of the waste management licensing regime is also improved by:

(a) a range of widely drafted criminal offences (many of them offences of strict liability) to underpin the EPA 1990;

(b) a range of administrative enforcement powers which provide the Environment Agency with an alternative mechanism (to prosecution) to enforce compliance with the terms of licences;

(c) a duty of care, breach of which constitutes a criminal offence, applying to everyone in the 'waste chain', and which ensures that directive waste is properly handled from 'cradle to grave'.

The Environment Agency proposes to change its approach to consideration of licence applications, licence transfers and applications for registration as waste carriers and brokers. The Environment Agency would like to target its enforcement powers on poor quality operators at the point of application for licences. Licences are unlikely to be granted to applicants with criminal records causing the Environment Agency serious concern unless the application is accompanied by a credible post-conviction plan setting out measures to improve the applicants' performance (see www.environment-agency.gov.uk/commondata/105385/relevant_convictions.pdf).

5.8.1 Definition of a waste management licence

Section 35 of the EPA 1990 defines a waste management licence as a:

> ... licence granted by a waste regulation authority authorising the treatment, keeping or disposal of any specified description of controlled waste in or on specified land or the treatment or disposal of any specified description of controlled waste by means of a specified mobile plant.

(Section 35 must now be interpreted by reference to the fact that licensing relates to both directive disposal and directive recovery operations and that the Environment Agency is the relevant waste authority.)

When the Environment Agency grants a licence, it will include any conditions that it thinks are appropriate. There are two different types of waste management licence: the site licence and the mobile plant licence. The site licence is granted to the person in occupation of the land. Occupation is not defined but will be someone who has some degree of control associated with or arising from his or her presence on or use of land. The mobile plant licence is granted in respect of mobile plant which is defined under s 29(9) (subject to a power to refine the definition by regulation) as 'plant which is designed to move or to be moved, whether on roads or other land'.

5.8.2 Exemptions and exclusions from licensing

The combined effect of regs 16–18 of and Sched 3 to the Waste Management Regulations 1994 is to exempt a range of activities from waste licensing control. Sites operating exempt activities are nevertheless required to register with the Environment Agency, and supply details of the activity, the place it is being carried on, and the exemption relied upon. Under reg 18(1), it is an offence to carry on an exempt activity without registration, save that this requirement does not apply to private individuals. Exemptions granted by Member States' legislation must be compatible with the need to attain the objectives of the Waste Framework Directive (regs 18 and 17(4)). Except in very limited circumstances, detailed in Sched 3, there is no exemption from licensing in the case of special waste.

The main exempt activities referred to in reg 17 of and Sched 3 to the Waste Management Regulations 1994 are:

(a) temporary storage (for example, in a skip) of directive waste at the place of production pending disposal or recovery. 'Temporary' is not defined and will depend upon the particular circumstances;

(b) temporary storage of special waste by the waste producer at the place of production, subject to limitations, including quantity and security arrangements;

(c) activities related to recovery and re-use such as bailing, compacting and shredding;

(d) the storage or deposit of demolition and construction waste for construction-related use at the place of demolition/construction;

(e) the deposit of organic materials to 'condition' land;

(f) a wide range of recycling activities including the collection of metals, paper, cardboard, plastics, glass, textiles and drink cans.

Also exempt is the disposal of waste within the curtilage (that is, the small area of land around a building) of a dwelling house (s 33(2)).

Exempt activities (reg 17 and Sched 3), except for the household waste exemption, are still subject to the prohibition contained in s 33(1)(c) of the EPA 1990 but are free of the requirements of s 33(1)(a) and (b). Further guidance on exemptions is given in Annexe 5 of Circular 11/95.

The power to exclude certain activities from the licensing regime is given to the Secretary of State by s 33(3) and (4) of the EPA 1990. The Secretary of State can make regulations, excluding certain activities involving the deposit, keeping, treatment or disposal of waste from the need to have a licence. Council Directive 91/156/EEC permits exemptions from the licensing system providing there are other adequate controls. This is reflected in s 33(4) which states that the Secretary of State when exercising his or her powers in respect of exemptions should have regard to the expediency of excluding from the controls imposed by the waste management licensing system:

(a) any deposits which are small enough or of such a temporary nature that they may be so excluded;

(b) any means of treatment or disposal which are innocuous enough to be excluded;

(c) cases for which adequate controls are provided by other legislation (s 33(3) and reg 16(1)).

The main licensing exclusions under reg 16(1) relate to: (a) the deposit, recovery or disposal of waste (except the final disposal of waste by deposit) on an IPC or LAAPC licensed site; (b) substances (liquid wastes) discharged to controlled waters, licensed under the WRA 1991; and (c) the disposal or recovery of waste licensed under the Food and Environmental Protection Act 1985.

There is some evidence that exempt sites are being used to dispose of directive waste which would ordinarily have been consigned to a landfill site, for example, by diverting inert materials for landscaping use (golf courses). In view of this, the Environment Agency is likely to press for changes in waste management law. In particular, the Agency would benefit from powers to inspect exempt disposal operations, to charge for inspections and to require annual exemption registrations. It is understood that the Agency would also like to see greater specificity with regard to the types of waste which benefit from exemption and changes in planning law to ensure that some exempt sites acquire planning permission authorising such development.

The High Court case of *Environment Agency v Newcomb and Son Ltd and Another* (2002) has examined the powers of the Environment Agency with regard to waste management licensing exemptions. The case related to the carrying out of waste management and disposal activities on land owned by Newcomb and Son Ltd consisting of the deposit of inert waste (block-making and wood chipping wastes exempt from licensing under Sched 3 to the Waste Management Licensing Regulations 1994), as part of the construction of a football pitch and car park. The Environment Agency agreed to the carrying out of the exempt activities provided at least 95% of the waste imported onto the development was block waste destined for use in the development's foundations. The Agency stressed that the deposit of biodegradable waste was to be avoided. Evidence emerged that biodegradable waste had been deposited and the company and one of its directors were charged by the Environment

Agency with knowingly causing or permitting the deposit of controlled waste on land (where no waste deposit licence was in force) contrary to s 33 of the EPA 1990. In the magistrates' court, the defendants were acquitted on the ground that, although there was waste on the development which fell outside the exemptions in the 1994 Regulations, that waste was within the 5% specified by the Environment Agency as acceptable. Subsequently, in the High Court, Newman J, allowing the Environment Agency's appeal, held that the Agency had no power to vary the exemptions detailed in the 1994 Regulations and the magistrates had been wrong to take the Agency's letter into account. Section 33 banned the making of unauthorised waste deposits and, as each of the charges related to a specific deposit made by the respondents, each deposit constituted a criminal act. The onus was on the prosecution to prove that the facts of the case established that the terms of the relevant exemption had been exceeded, resulting in a deposit or deposits prohibited by s 33.

5.8.3   The applications procedure

Applications for a waste management licence must be made in writing to the appropriate regional office of the Environment Agency accompanied by the fee payable under s 41 of the EPA 1990. There is now a standard application form which must be completed by all applicants. Where the applicant fails to provide the Environment Agency with any information required, the Agency has the right to refuse to proceed with the application (s 36(1)(a) of the EPA 1990). Section 36 deals with the applications procedure and determines the considerations that the Environment Agency must take into account. The Agency's discretion (s 74(4)) to grant or refuse a licence is subject to an important limitation in s 36(3) (see below).

The making of false statements in any waste management licensing application (and in any applications for licence modification, transfer, or surrender) is an offence: s 44 of the EPA 1990. The maximum penalty on summary conviction in a magistrates' court is a £5,000 fine; however, on conviction in the Crown Court, the maximum penalty is an unlimited fine and/or gaol term of up to two years. There is, in such cases, a presumption of prosecution.

By virtue of s 36(3) of the EPA 1990, the Environment Agency must reject an application if:

(a) the applicant is not a fit and proper person;

(b) the rejection is necessary to prevent pollution to the environment, harm to human health or serious detriment to the amenities of the locality.

The Environment Agency must reject a waste management licence application if the relevant site does not have the benefit of planning permission (see 5.8.3.5 above) or if direct or indirect discharges (including the tipping of waste falling outside the waste management regulatory regime) from the site will adversely affect groundwaters (see s 36(2) of the EPA 1990, reg 15 of the Waste Management Regulations 1994 and 5.8.3.4 below).

The Environment Agency must either grant a licence or give notice of rejection within four months of receiving the application, unless an extension is agreed in writing with the applicant. Failure to deal with the application in the prescribed time is deemed a rejection (except where the delay is due to the applicant's failure to supply information requested by the Environment Agency to process the relevant application).

5.8.3.1 Charges

As in other pollution control regimes discussed in this book, 'polluters' are required to pay for the system which controls them. The application of the 'polluter pays' principle in this instance means that charges are levied by the Environment Agency for the following:

(a) applications for waste management licences;

(b) applications for modification of the licences;

(c) transfers;

(d) surrender;

(e) subsistence, to cover the costs of the Environment Agency's supervision of the licence.

Charges for waste management licences are provided for by s 41 of the EA 1995.

5.8.3.2 Consultation and publicising the application

If the Environment Agency is minded to grant a waste management licence, it must consult with a variety of public bodies and consider any objections or representations it receives. The Agency must consult the Health and Safety Executive (s 36(4)) and the appropriate planning authority. In certain protected areas (for example, a Site of Special Scientific Interest), the application must be referred to the Nature Conservancy Council for England (English Nature) or the Countryside Council for Wales. The period for consultation is 28 days. If there is any disagreement arising out of the consultation, then the matter must be referred to the Secretary of State for his decision. In reaching its decision on a waste management licensing application, the Environment Agency must have regard to official guidance (s 35(8)). The relevant advice is largely contained in Waste Management Paper No 4, *Licensing of Waste Facilities*, and Circular 11/94.

Arguably one significant weakness in the licensing process is the lack of effective public participation, although the Environment Agency has tried out a new procedure for the licensing of contentious sites. Waste management licensing applications are not required to be advertised in the local press. Currently, central government views public participation in the waste management licensing process as superfluous on the basis that the public was provided with the opportunity to make representations and objections at the planning application stage.

The Environment Agency is also required by the Waste Management Licensing Regulations 1994 to have regard to the protection of groundwater when determining a licence application. The Regulations give effect to the Groundwater Directive (80/68/EEC). A new s 36A of the EPA 1990 was inserted by the EA 1995. Where the Environment Agency proposes to impose a licence condition which requires the licence holder to carry out works or do anything on land which he or she is not legally entitled to do (for instance, requiring the licence holder to take soil samples on neighbouring land), then the Environment Agency must serve a notice on the person who owns or occupies the relevant land (s 36A(3)). The notice will set out the relevant conditions, indicate the nature of the works that are to be carried out and specify a date by which representations are to be made to the Environment Agency. The Environment Agency must consider any representations made. Similarly, if the

Environment Agency proposes to vary a waste management licence and impose such conditions, it must also consult the owner occupier of the relevant land.

5.8.3.3 The fit and proper person test (s 74 of the EPA 1990)

The Environment Agency has a discretion whether or not to grant a waste management licence in circumstances where the applicant is not a 'fit and proper person'. This is an entirely new requirement introduced by the EPA 1990 and specifically addresses one of the principal defects in the COPA 1974 system, namely that almost any person could obtain a waste disposal licence irrespective of his or her 'track record' in waste management.

Section 74(3) of the EPA 1990 provides that a person shall be treated as not being a fit and proper person if it appears to the Environment Agency:

(a) that he or she or another relevant person has been convicted of a relevant offence;

(b) that the management of the activities which are to be authorised by the licence are not or will not be in the hands of a technically competent person; or

(c) that the person who is to hold the licence has not made and has no intention of making or is no position to make financial provision adequate to discharge the obligations arising from the licence.

There are three elements to the test: the first relates to previous convictions for relevant offences; the second to the technical competence of the applicant; and the third to the applicant's financial position:

(1) *The relevant offences* – these are set down in reg 3 of the Waste Management Licensing Regulations 1994 and include offences contained in the EPA 1990, the WRA 1991 and the COP(A)A 1989. Offences relating to planning law and dishonesty are excluded. However, s 74(4) of the EPA 1990 provides that, if the Environment Agency considers it proper to do so in any particular case, it may treat a person as a fit and proper person notwithstanding that he or she has been convicted of a relevant offence. The Environment Agency will clearly have to take into account matters such as the gravity of any previous offences and whether or not it was a one-off offence, possibly with mitigating circumstances. The fit and proper person test in this particular regard does not simply concern the applicant but also relates to other 'relevant persons' which includes (s 74(7)):

  (a) any employee of the applicant who has been convicted of a relevant offence; or

  (b) a company of which the applicant was a director, manager, secretary or similar officer and which has been convicted of a relevant offence; or

  (c) where the applicant is a company, any current director, manager, secretary or similar officer of the company who has been convicted of a relevant offence, or was an officer of another company when that company was convicted of a relevant offence. (See *R v Boal* (1992) and *Woodhouse v Walsall Metropolitan BC* (1994) as to who is a 'manager' for the purposes of the Act and the fit and proper person test.)

(2) *Technical competence* – the management of the licensed facility must be in the hands of technically competent persons (see reg 4 of the Waste Management Licensing Regulations 1994). A person is technically competent if he holds one of

the certificates awarded by the Waste Management Industry Training and Advisory Board (WAMITAB) or a Certificate of Technical Competence. The precise qualification is determined by reference to the type of waste facility and waste that it accepts. Transitional provisions concern 'existing managers'. These are persons who registered with WAMITAB before 10 August 1994, and were employed as managers in the year prior to registration. Managers of sites licensed under previous legislation, such as the COPA 1974, are presumed to be competent.

(3) *Financial resources* – the Environment Agency will need to be certain that the licence holder is in a position financially to be able to discharge the obligations arising from the licence. This means that the licence holder will need to show that he or she has adequate financial resources to comply with the conditions of the licence and to meet any liabilities or remedial action if a pollution event occurs, for example, through insurance, bank guarantee or contingency fund. Waste Management Paper (WMP) No 4, *Licensing of Waste Management Facilities* provides useful guidance on all these aspects of the fit and proper person test. In particular, the guidance in WMP 4 refers to specific stages in the life of a waste management site where adequate financial provision is critical: acquisition, preparation, operation, restoration, landscaping and aftercare (especially monitoring). These stages in the lifecycle of a site should be reflected in the applicant's business plan for the site.

DEFRA issued in April 2003 a draft of a new version of WMP 4. The proposed guidance suggests that amendments are required to take account of the variety of risks posed by differing waste management activities (see www.defra.gov.uk/corporate/consult/wasteman/index.htm).

The Environment Agency has proposed that non-landfill waste sites (for example, waste transfer stations, civic amenity sites, recycling facilities and mobile waste management plants) should not require the same stringent financial provisions as landfills. Specific monies to cover potential liabilities may therefore not need to be put aside (see www.environment-agency.gov.uk/commondata/105385/financial_provision.pdf).

If the fit and proper test is satisfied, the Environment Agency is under a duty to grant a waste management licence to the applicant (s 36(3)). The Rehabilitation of Offenders Act 1974 applies to 'spent' convictions.

The Waste Management Licensing (Amendment) (England) Regulations 2003 (SI 2003/595) and the Waste Management Licensing (Amendment) (Wales) Regulations 2003 (SI 2003/171) introduce changes to the 'fit and proper' person requirement for a waste site manager (see s 74 of the EPA 1990 and reg 4 of the Waste Management Regulations 1994).

5.8.3.4 Rejection necessary to prevent pollution

Even if an applicant is deemed to be a fit and proper person, the Environment Agency must not grant a licence if it is satisfied that rejection is necessary to prevent pollution of the environment (pollution of the environment is defined in s 29 of the EPA 1990) or harm to human health. In most cases, this will not be an issue and the Environment Agency should be able to impose sufficiently rigorous conditions to ensure that the activity does not harm the environment or human health.

The Environment Agency can refuse an application if the activity would cause serious detriment to amenities of the locality, but it cannot have regard to this particular aspect if the activity in question has planning permission. The justification for this is that questions of amenity will already have been taken into account by the planning authority.

Section 36(3) is particularly relevant to the risk of groundwater contamination posed by waste management sites. The Waste Management Licensing Regulations 1994 provide guidance on the conditions which the regulator should include in a waste management licence to prevent or minimise the risk of escape of dangerous substances into controlled waters. One key condition will be the installation of an impermeable membrane or liner to reduce the risk of substances leaching out of the base of the site (for example, a landfill) into groundwater.

5.8.3.5 Planning and waste

The Environment Agency must refuse an application for a waste management licence if planning permission, or a certificate of lawful use or development, or an established use certificate is required for the activity which the applicant proposes to carry on (s 36(2)) and the site does not have the benefit of such permission.

5.9   LICENCE CONDITIONS

The objective of the licensing system is to regulate the day-to-day operation of waste facilities. This should be achieved by unambiguous conditions which leave the operator in no doubt as to what the required standards are and how they are to be met. Each condition should be necessary, comprehensive, unambiguous and enforceable otherwise it will be unreasonable and challengeable. In *AG's Ref (No 2 of 1988)* (1990), the Court of Appeal struck out a site licence condition requiring a waste site to be operated so as not to cause a nuisance to adjacent property owners. The condition did not relate to the purposes of the COPA 1974 (the forerunner to Pt II of the EPA 1990) and was therefore unlawful. The main focus of licence conditions is the protection of the environment, human health and property. Guidance issued by the Secretary of State in Waste Management Papers (see WMP 4) assists the Environment Agency with regard to the choice of appropriate conditions. Conditions attached to a waste management licence should not duplicate planning conditions relating to the use of the site for waste management purposes. The Secretary of State also has the power to prescribe in regulations the conditions to be attached to a licence, by virtue of s 35(6) and (7) of the EPA 1990. For example, reg 12 of the Waste Management Regulations 1994 prohibits the imposition of conditions designed purely to secure health and safety at work objectives. Regulation 14 prescribes conditions to be included in a waste management licence to comply with the Waste Oils Directive (75/439/EEC).

Section 35(3) of the EPA 1990 provides that a waste management licence will be granted on such terms and subject to such conditions as appear to the Environment Agency to be appropriate, and these conditions may relate to the activities authorised, the precautions to be taken and the works to be carried out. In practice, conditions will be set which cover fundamental issues such as the site infrastructure and site operation. They will also stipulate monitoring and record-keeping requirements, security and methods of avoiding nuisances. In practice, many of the conditions set in the licence will primarily be the outcome of negotiation between the Environment Agency and the applicant.

Although the Environment Agency has a wide discretion as to the conditions it may include in a licence, its power to impose such conditions as it thinks fit is limited by the Waste Framework Directive, which obliges Member States to include conditions relating to 'technical matters' in waste management licences. A licence may be set aside if it does not properly address these issues (see *Guthrie v SEPA* (1998)).

The conditions that can be included in a licence can cover matters before the site becomes operational (that is, site preparation and insurance cover), during operation and, importantly, can include conditions after the waste operation has ceased (such as the monitoring of methane emissions and leachate production). The conditions may also extend to waste other than controlled (directive) waste (s 35(5)). The conditions will detail the types and quantities of waste that can be treated, kept or disposed of. They will also specify detailed operational matters such as methods of receiving waste, security arrangements, monitoring arrangements and after-care of the site.

One condition which may be attached is particularly important: s 35(4) enables a condition to be set on a new application and also on a modification or suspension of an existing licence, requiring the holder to carry out works or do other things even though he is not generally entitled to do them. For example, a licence holder may be required to carry out sampling or monitoring on neighbouring land owned by another person. Section 35(4) further provides that any person whose consent would be required should grant or join in granting the holder of the licence such rights in relation to land as will enable the holder to comply with such a condition (although, as noted above, a person has the right to be consulted and make representations under s 36A). WMP 4 suggests that this power will be used sparingly and only when absolutely necessary. Provisions exist for compensation to be payable where conditions of this sort are imposed (Waste Management Licensing (Consultation and Compensation) Regulations 1999 (SI 1999/481)). Finally, it should be noted that the Secretary of State has the power to make regulations specifying conditions to be attached to licences.

The Environment Agency is under a duty (s 35(8)) to have regard to guidance issued by the Secretary of State, such as WMP 4, entitled *The Licensing of Waste Facilities* and Circular 11/94. According to the Circular, licence conditions must be proportionate to the relevant risks and be cost-effective. Licence-related offences are set out in s 35(7)(A), (B) and (C).

5.9.1 Compensation to third parties

In the light of the provisions of s 35(4) of the EPA 1990 discussed above, s 35A of the EPA 1990 (inserted by Sched 22 to the EA 1995) provides that any person whose consent would be required under ss 35(4) and 38(9A) and who has granted the licence holder any rights in relation to land is entitled to be paid compensation by the licence holder. By s 36A(4) of the EPA 1990, the Secretary of State has the power to issue regulations prescribing a scheme of compensation (see the Waste Management Licences (Consultation and Compensation) Regulations 1999).

The Environment Agency has been granted significant administrative powers to 'police' licence holders' compliance with the terms of their waste management licences. These powers are important because they enable the Environment Agency to retain control of the outcome of the enforcement process without resorting to prosecution and thereby handing control over the outcome of the case to the courts. As we shall see, these powers are potentially draconian, because they enable the Environment Agency to put persistently poor operators out of business, either temporarily or permanently. Licence holders are not entitled to compensation when their operating licences are varied, suspended or revoked (unless the relevant notice is successfully appealed).

5.10 ADMINISTRATION AND ENFORCEMENT POWERS

5.10.1 Operator and Pollution Risk Appraisal (OPRA)

The Environment Agency has adopted a risk-based approach to regulation of waste and the IPC regime. OPRA is a tool which the Agency uses to assess the environmental risks posed by waste sites and the competence of the site operator to manage those risks properly. Agency field staff visit sites and allocate scores for various aspects of the risks posed by the site and the performance of the operator (the lower the score, the better). The relevant scores are then used to help assess the number of compliance visits Agency staff will make in that year. The current OPRA methodology was published in 2000 and is subject to continuous refinement.

OPRA comprises two types of appraisal: the Environmental Appraisal of the site and the Operator Performance Appraisal. The Environmental Appraisal focuses on the following factors: (a) the type of facility; (b) the type and quantity of waste received; (c) the control and containment measures on site; (d) the sensitivity of 'receptors' (that is, how close houses are to the site boundary); (e) groundwater sensitivity (is the site in a groundwater protection zone?); and (f) location of surface waters from the site and their sensitivity to contamination. The Operator Performance Appraisal comprises: (a) operator assessment – the operator's ability to manage the site in accordance with licence conditions. A zero score (for each criterion on the waste inspection score sheet) indicates compliance with licence conditions, whereas the maximum score of 15 indicates an emergency situation; and (b) operator management – the level of management control. No control mechanism equals a score of 10, whereas a score of 1 equals an accredited management system in operation (for example, ISO 14001).

5.10.2 Variation of licences (s 37)

Waste management licences can, in contrast to planning permissions, be varied by means of a Variation Notice (VN) either by the Environment Agency or at the request of the licence holder (s 37 of the EPA 1990). The Environment Agency is under a duty to vary the conditions of the licence where it is necessary to ensure licensed activities 'do not cause pollution of the environment or harm to human health or become seriously detrimental to the amenities of the locality affected by the activities' (s 37(2)) or to comply with regulations made by the Secretary of State under s 35(6)). Alternatively, the Environment Agency may choose to serve a

Revocation Notice (RN). Where the Environment Agency wishes to vary the licence because it considers a variation is desirable, then it may only vary the conditions if a variation is 'unlikely to require unreasonable expense on the part of the holder' (s 37(1)(a)). Consultation is required if the Environment Agency serves a VN. Where the variation requires the licence holder to carry out works on someone else's land, then the Environment Agency is required to consult with the relevant landowner, and as noted above at 5.9.1, compensation may be payable. The Secretary of State also has the right to direct the Environment Agency to modify conditions. Any variation of a licence must be effected by a notice served on the licence holder. Section 37A provides for consultation before variation in similar terms to s 36A where the variation will require the grant of rights by a third party. However, by virtue of s 37A(9), consultation may be postponed in the event of an emergency.

Alternatively, the licence holder may wish to seek a variation of the licence, for example, to accommodate different types of wastes. There is no restriction regarding the extent of a proposed variation (*Guthrie v SEPA* (1998)). A licence holder must apply to the Environment Agency for a variation and pay the appropriate fee. Failure to determine an application to vary a licence within a period of two months, unless the period has been extended by agreement in writing, will result in the Environment Agency being deemed to have rejected the application. A licence holder can appeal to the Secretary of State against the decision of the Environment Agency to refuse the variation application.

5.10.3 Transfer of licences

Waste operations are businesses run on commercial lines. Many are very profitable. Like all businesses, the ownership and control of the business can change hands. It is therefore necessary in such circumstances for there to be a transfer of the licence to the new owner/operator. Section 40 of the EPA 1990 deals with the right of transfer. A licence may be transferred on the joint application of present holder and transferee using the prescribed form and on payment of the prescribed fee. However, the Environment Agency can only agree to the transfer if it is satisfied that the transferee is a fit and proper person. As in the other provisions relating to licences, a right of appeal exists to the Secretary of State. If the Environment Agency fails to determine an application for transfer within a period of two months (unless applicants agree in writing to extend the period), the application will be deemed to have been rejected by the Environment Agency. Licences may be transferred even if they are subject to partial suspension or revocation.

5.10.4 Revocation and suspension of licences

The powers of revocation and suspension (provided in s 38(3) and (4) of the EPA 1990) available to the Environment Agency are dependent upon certain circumstances. A licence may be revoked in whole or in part, although it can only be partially revoked if the reason is the lack of technical competence of the management. The partial revocation of the licence allows for continuing obligations to be imposed on the licence holder even if operation of the site is no longer permitted. Partial revocation may occur where the Environment Agency revokes only that part of a licence which authorised the reception and management of special waste. Complete revocation is unlikely, in most cases, because the Environment Agency will require after care licence conditions to remain in force.

The Environment Agency has a discretion whether to serve a Revocation Notice (RN). The Notice will specify when the revocation is to take effect and which activities the notice applies to. Revocation can take place if:

(a) the licence holder ceases to be a fit and proper person as a result of a relevant offence (s 38(1) of the EPA 1990) or the management is no longer in the hands of a technically competent person (s 38(2));

(b) continuation of the licensed activities will cause pollution of the environment or harm to human health or serious detriment to amenities in the locality (s 38(1)) and these cannot be avoided by modifying conditions;

(c) the licence holder fails to comply with a s 42 notice requiring compliance with a condition of the waste management licence (s 42(6)); or

(d) the licence holder fails to pay the annual subsistence charge (s 41(7)).

The Environment Agency may suspend the licence in the following circumstances (s 38(6)):

(a) the licence holder is no longer a fit and proper person on the grounds of technical competence;

(b) the licensed activities have caused or are about to cause serious pollution of the environment or serious harm to human health;

(c) continuation of the licensed activities will continue to cause serious pollution of the environment or serious harm to human health;

(d) the licence holder fails to comply with the terms of a condition of the waste management licence (s 42(6)).

The Environment Agency has a discretion whether to serve a Suspension Notice (SN). If it chooses to serve an SN, the Notice will specify the dates when the suspension will commence and cease. SNs will only suspend site activities and will not affect precautionary measures designed to prevent contaminants escaping from the site.

Compensation may be payable by the Environment Agency to the site operator if, on appeal against the service of an SN, the Secretary of State rules that the Environment Agency acted unreasonably in suspending the waste management licence (s 43(7)).

Whilst a suspension is in effect, the licence has no effect and therefore does not authorise the activities specified in the licence. However, notwithstanding suspension, the Environment Agency may require the licence holder to carry out works to deal with or avert pollution or harm (s 38(9)). The measures which the licence holder could be required to take under s 38(9) may extend beyond the ambit of the pre-suspension licence conditions. Again, like s 35(4), the Environment Agency may require the licence holder to do works on land which he or she is not otherwise entitled to do. For example, the Environment Agency may require the licence holder whose licence has been suspended to carry out clean-up operations on neighbouring land. Any person whose consent would be required must grant the licence holder such rights as will enable him or her to fulfil the Environment Agency's requirements. A person should normally be consulted under s 36A, but the Environment Agency may postpone the service of a notice or consideration of any representations in emergency (s 38(9C)) situations. A licence holder who fails without reasonable excuse to comply with any requirements under s 38(9) commits a criminal offence. The maximum penalty on summary conviction in the magistrates' court is a fine of £5,000. On conviction in the Crown Court, the maximum penalty is an unlimited fine and/or a gaol sentence of two years. In the case of special waste offences, a maximum six month term of imprisonment may be imposed in the magistrates' court and a five year gaol sentence in the Crown Court. Section 38(1)–(13) allows the Environment Agency to take enforcement proceedings in the High Court in order to obtain an injunction forcing the person whose licence has been suspended to carry out the required works. This is a provision which greatly strengthens the enforcement powers of the Environment Agency.

5.11   SURRENDER OF LICENCES (s 39)

It is in relation to the surrender of licences that the EPA 1990 makes some very significant changes to the COPA 1974. A fundamental flaw of the COPA 1974 waste regime was that licence holders could surrender their licences and walk away leaving the local authority with the problem of cleaning up a poorly run site. In point of fact, this is precisely what happened to many licensed sites in the months and weeks before the EPA 1990 came into force in May 1994. Many COPA licence holders surrendered their licences to avoid an automatic transfer to an EPA waste management licence and the more stringent responsibilities that that entailed. In particular, operators taking this rather radical course of action were aware of the difficulties they would face in surrendering a waste management licence. In short, the EPA 1990 provisions, concerning the surrender of licences are much stricter than the COPA 1974 counterparts and it is no longer possible for licence holders to give up their licences at will (except in the case of mobile plant licences).

A waste management mobile plant licence may be surrendered at any time by its holder but, in the case of a site licence, the licence can only be surrendered with the agreement of the Environment Agency. If the Environment Agency accepts the application for surrender, it will issue the licence holder with a 'certificate of completion'. However, the Environment Agency can only accept the surrender if it is satisfied that the condition of the relevant land whether or not permitted is unlikely to cause pollution of the environment or harm to human health. In order to come to a decision about surrender, the Environment Agency must first inspect the land and consider any information provided by the licence holder about the state of the land. The information which the licence holder will be asked to supply includes: site location, details of all activities carried out on site and their respective locations, the times during which various activities were being carried out on site, the quantity of waste handled, hydrogeology, methane production and leachate production. In view of the fact that landfills, even those fitted with impermeable liners, create ongoing gas and leachate problems, it is unlikely that the Environment Agency will be keen to issue certificates of completion. It is safer to require licence holders of closed sites to continue monitoring and reporting the results to the Environment Agency. The Environment Agency has three months to determine the application or a longer period if agreed in writing with the applicant. The Environment Agency may, however, determine within that period that it cannot accept the surrender until certain information is supplied about the site or until it has undergone remedial works. For this reason, the licence holder should always keep accurate and detailed records about the wastes that have been deposited in order to facilitate the process of surrender. The stricter EPA 1990 regime is not completely watertight and problems have arisen in regard to the status of the licence if the licence holder dies or goes into liquidation (if a company). In *Official Receiver v Environment Agency, Re Celtic Extraction Ltd* (2000), the Court of Appeal held that if a waste management company becomes insolvent, then the licence may qualify as 'onerous property' within the meaning of that term in the Insolvency Act 1986, and may be disclaimed by the Official Receiver. The court observed that there were no clear words in the EPA 1990 which were intended to exclude the effect of the Insolvency Act 1986. The Environment Agency conceded in the course of the proceedings that a licence ceases to have effect when a licence holder dies. Once a licence expires, the Environment Agency has no power to regulate; however, in such circumstances, the waste site may be subject to local authority control via the statutory nuisance or contaminated land regimes. In the event that the licence holding company becomes insolvent but the licence is not disclaimed, the Environment Agency retains regulatory control. If the Environment Agency wishes to commence a prosecution against an insolvent licence holder, it must obtain the consent of the court before commencing any prosecution relating to breach of licence (see *Environment Agency v Clarke, Re Rhondda Waste Disposal Co Ltd* (2000)). The fact that a financial penalty imposed on the insolvent company will adversely affect creditors will not necessarily lead to the Environment Agency refraining from prosecuting.

The Environment Agency has issued a draft guidance on landfill completion criteria for comment. The Environment Agency may only accept the surrender of site licences (both waste management and IPC/IPPC licences) if it considers that the relevant site poses no pollution risk. The draft sets out the suggested approach to risk assessment of such sites (see www.environment-agency.gov.uk/yourenv/consultations).

5.12   RIGHTS OF APPEAL (s 43)

In all of the various provisions discussed above, it has been noted that the applicant (for a waste management licence) or licence holder has a right of appeal. Section 43 of the EPA 1990 provides a right of appeal to the Secretary of State against a determination by the Environment Agency in the following instances:

(a) an application for a licence or a variation of the conditions of a licence is rejected;

(b) a licence is granted subject to conditions which are unacceptable to the applicant;

(c) the conditions of the licence are varied;

(d) a licence is suspended;

(e) a licence is revoked;

(f) an application to surrender a licence is rejected;

(g) an application to surrender a licence is not decided upon within three months; or

(h) an application for the transfer of a licence is rejected.

An appeal must be made within six months of the relevant decision. Details of appeal procedures are to be found in the Waste Management Licensing Regulations 1994 (SI 1994/1056), as amended by the 1995 Regulations (SI 1995/288). There is no right of appeal where the Secretary of State has 'called in' the matter for his or her own determination. Nevertheless, the opportunity to make a judicial review application is available (*R v Vale of Glamorgan Borough Council and ABP ex p James* (1996)).

The appellant and the Environment Agency may choose whether an appeal proceeds by way of a full hearing or by written representations (a paper-based appeal). Appeals are generally heard by inspectors appointed by the Secretary of State and drawn from the ranks of the planning inspectorate. The Secretary of State will decide major or contentious appeals.

There are no specific grounds of appeal, as in the case of statutory nuisance, but applicants are guided by Annexe 10 of Circular 11/94.

Appeals normally suspend the effect of modification and revocation applications (s 43(4) of the EPA 1990) pending the outcome of the appeal unless the Environment Agency indicates, by notice, that the effect of a modification or revocation should not be suspended because of the overriding need to prevent pollution of the environment or harm to human health (s 43(6)). Suspension Notices are unaffected by appeals (s 43(5)). Any waste management licence holder who is aggrieved by the Environment Agency's use of its s 43(6) power or its s 38 suspension power may request the Secretary of State to rule on whether the Environment Agency has acted unreasonably. If the Secretary of State rules in favour of the licence holder, the Environment Agency may be ordered to pay compensation (s 43(7)).

5.13   PUBLIC REGISTERS (s 64)

The Environment Agency maintains a publicly accessible register of waste licensing information (s 64 of the EPA and reg 10 of the Waste Management Licensing Regulations 1994). Section 64(6) requires 14 types of information to be noted on the register including the grant of a licence, licence conditions, monitoring data (whether collected by the Environment Agency or by the licence holder as a licence condition), licence applications, Variation, Suspension and Revocation Notices, and relevant convictions. Information may, by application to the Secretary of State, be excluded from the register due to commercial confidentiality and national security considerations (s 65), subject to a right of appeal against a decision of the Secretary of State not to allow exclusion (s 65(5) and reg 7(1)(b) of the Waste Management Licensing Regulations 1994).

5.14   SUPERVISION AND MONITORING (s 42)

The Environment Agency has a general duty to monitor and supervise all licensed activities (s 42). It must take the necessary steps to ensure that the licensed activities do not cause pollution of the environment, harm to human health or serious detriment to the amenities of the locality. The Environment Agency must also take steps to ensure that licence holders comply with licence conditions.

In addition, the Environment Agency will also carry out inspections of its area to ensure that there are no unlicensed activities such as fly-tipping. Unlicensed waste disposal constitutes a breach of s 33 of the EPA 1990.

5.14.1 Powers of Environment Agency officials

In order to carry out its functions, the Environment Agency employs inspectors to inspect and monitor sites, thereby ensuring compliance with the relevant legislation.

The powers of inspection and entry, contained in ss 108–10 of the EA 1995, enable an Environment Agency inspector:

(a) to enter at any reasonable time premises which he or she has reason to believe it is necessary for him or her to enter. This should normally be at any reasonable time unless there is an emergency, in which case entry is permitted at any time, and if need be, by force;

(b) on entering premises to take with him or her any other person duly authorised by the Environment Agency, and a policeman. The latter may be needed in situations where the inspector has reasonable cause to apprehend any serious obstruction in carrying out his or her duties;

(c) to take any equipment or materials required for any purpose for which the power of entry is being exercised;

(d) to make such examination and investigation as may in any circumstances be necessary;

(e) to instruct that the premises or any part of them, or anything in them, be left undisturbed. The inspector may require that the premises or the part of the premises under investigation are not disturbed for as long as is reasonably necessary to enable him or her to carry out any examination or investigation;

(f) to take such measurements and photographs and make such recordings as he or she considers necessary;

(g) to take samples, or instruct samples be taken, of any articles or substances found in or on the premises and also from the air, water or land in, on or in the vicinity of the premises. Specific provisions relate to the possession, safekeeping and use in evidence of such samples;

(h) in the case of any article or substance found in or on premises which appears to him or her to be an article or substance which has caused or is likely cause pollution of the environment, or harm to human health, to cause it to be dismantled or subjected to any process or test (but not so as to damage or destroy it unless that is necessary);

(i) to require information from any person – the inspector can require any person whom he or she has reasonable cause to believe to be able to give any information relevant to any examination or investigation to answer such questions as the inspector thinks fit to ask. The person answering the questions will be required to sign a declaration of truth to the answers;

(j) to inspect any information and to take copies – the inspector can require the production of any information that he or she considers necessary, including information held on computer. He or she also has the right to inspect and take copies of such information or any entry in the records;

(k) to require facilities to afford assistance – here the inspector can require any person to afford him or her such facilities and assistance with respect to any matters or things within that person's control or in relation to which that person has responsibilities. So, for example, the inspector can require an engineer on the premises to show him or her how the monitoring and testing equipment is working (or not working as the case may be);

(l) any other powers conferred by regulation by the Secretary of State. Certain information can be withheld from the inspector if it is subject to legal professional privilege. This covers correspondence between clients and their solicitors or legal professional advisors.

5.14.2 Requests for information (s 71)

Section 71 empowers the Environment Agency to serve a request for information on any person in order to obtain information relevant to the performance of the Environment Agency's statutory responsibilities. Failure to provide such information or knowingly providing false information is a criminal offence. There is a defence of 'reasonable excuse' but this does not apply to a refusal based on a violation of the rule against self-incrimination (see *R v Hertfordshire CC ex p Green Environmental Industries Ltd* (2000)). The s 71 power may only be used by the Environment Agency if it already has sufficient information which will form the basis of the s 71 request (see *JB and M Motor Haulage v London Waste Regulation Authority* (1993)). The maximum penalty on summary conviction in the magistrates' courts for breach of s 71 is a £5,000 fine. If the matter is committed to the Crown Court, the maximum penalty is an unlimited fine and/or a gaol sentence of two years. (See Chapter 12 regarding the privilege against self-incrimination and human rights.)

5.14.3 Seizure of vehicles (s 6)

Section 6 of the EPA 1990 empowers the Environment Agency to seize any vehicle which has been used for specified illegal activities. If the Environment Agency has been unable, through its informational powers, to obtain details of the ownership of vehicles suspected of being involved in illegal waste operations, the Environment Agency may make an application to a magistrate for seizure of the relevant vehicle. (See also regs 20–25 of the Controlled Waste (Registration of Carriers and Seizure of Vehicles) Regulations 1991 (SI 1991/1624).)

5.15   CLEAN-UP POWERS (s 59)

Section 59 of the EPA 1990 gives the Environment Agency and the Waste Collection Authorities power to require the removal of controlled (directive) waste (via the service of a Waste Removal Notice (WRN)) where the waste has been deposited in contravention of the conditions of a waste management licence or in breach of s 33(1)(c) of the EPA 1990. The relevant authority may serve a notice on the occupier of land, requiring the waste to be removed or specifying the steps to be taken to mitigate the consequences of the deposit. At least 21 days must be allowed to comply with the notice, during which time the recipient has a right to appeal to the magistrates' court. Such an appeal must be allowed if the court is satisfied that the appellant occupier neither deposited nor knowingly caused nor knowingly permitted the deposit, or if there is a material defect in the notice (s 59(3)).

The Environment Agency may serve a WRN on a mortgage lendor who repossesses property upon which an illegal deposit of waste has taken place (*Devonshire WRA v Roberts, Warren and Snow* (1995)).

If the occupier fails to take necessary action, then the authority can do so and recover its costs from the occupier (s 59(6)) or, in appropriate cases, from the person who deposited or knowingly caused or knowingly permitted the deposit of waste (provided the person can be traced).

In the event of an emergency occurring at a waste management site, the Environment Agency has the power (s 42(3)) to carry out works and recover its costs from the licence holder.

The Environment Agency may, in circumstances in which immediate action is necessary to prevent pollution of the environment or harm to man, remove illegally deposited waste or take other steps if the occupier of the land was not responsible for the deposit, or if the occupier cannot be traced (s 59(7)). The Environment Agency may only recover costs which were necessarily incurred from the person or persons who deposited, or knowingly caused, or knowingly permitted, the illegal waste deposit (s 59(8)). Where more than one person is responsible for the deposit, as long as the Environment Agency acts reasonably, it does not have to apportion its costs between the unlawful depositors (*Berridge Incinerators v Nottinghamshire County Council* (1987)).

The s 59 remedial power may be used in conjunction with a s 33 prosecution or it may be employed independently of any prosecution.

Lodging an appeal will suspend the operation of the WRN until the appeal is determined (s 59(4)). Failure to comply with a WRN constitutes a criminal offence, but any prosecution may only be heard in the magistrates' court (s 59(5)). The maximum penalty on conviction of the offence is a £5,000 fine. The offence is a 'continuing' offence which attracts a further penalty of a maximum fine of £500 for every day the offence continues after conviction.

5.15.1 Statutory civil liability for the deposit of waste (s 73(b) of the EPA 1990)

In addition to s 59 of the EPA 1990, which empowers the Environment Agency to require the removal of waste deposited in contravention of the conditions of a waste management licence, s 73(6) imposes *civil liability* on the person or persons responsible for damage caused by the deposit of controlled (directive) waste in contravention of s 33(1) or s 63(2) of the EPA 1990. Damages may be claimed by any person sustaining property damage or personal injury. Section 73(6) liability is strict and an action may be commenced by any person. In addition, such persons have the option of commencing a common law tortious action against the person responsible for the damage (see the tort of nuisance discussed in Chapter 11).

Section 63(2) of the EPA 1990 provides that it is an offence for any person to deposit or knowingly cause or knowingly permit the deposit of non-controlled waste (that is, waste which is not regulated because, for example, it is exempt) if the relevant waste has special waste characteristics (that is, it is dangerous or difficult to dispose of) and is deposited without a licence, in breach of licence conditions or without some other form of permission.

The circumstances giving rise to an unlawful deposit of waste include:

(a) the deposit of wastes which are not in accordance with the conditions of a waste management licence;

(b) waste deposited in a manner likely to cause pollution of the environment or harm to human health;

(c) the deposit of exempt wastes which constitute an unlawful disposal.

The person who deposited the waste which caused the damage will be liable, save in those circumstances in which the injured party was totally at fault or chose to run the risk of incurring damage. In those cases, where the defendant was not totally to blame, contributory negligence issues arise.

In addition to the person who deposited the relevant waste, liability may extend to any person or persons who knowingly caused or knowingly permitted the waste deposit (such as the person who arranged with a fly-tipper to dispose of the waste).

5.16   WASTE OFFENCES

The regulation of waste is identical to other Command and Control pollution control regimes in that it is underpinned by a range of criminal offences. The main offences are contained in s 33(1); however, these offences must take account of the changes to the definition of waste, contained in the Waste Management Regulations 1994 and implementing the EC Waste Framework Directive (91/156/EEC). Section 33(1) of the EPA 1990, as amended by the Waste Management Regulations 1994, contains the key waste offences.

5.16.1 Section 33 offences

Section 33(1) of the EPA 1990 (which refers to controlled waste) provides that it is an offence to:

(a) deposit controlled (directive) waste, or knowingly cause or knowingly permit controlled (directive) waste to be deposited in or on any land, unless a waste management licence authorising the deposit is in force and the deposit is in accordance with the licence (s 33(1)(a) of the EPA 1990); this offence applies to all deposits, whether temporary or permanent. The deposit of waste is not limited to directive disposal or directive recovery operations;

(b) treat, keep or dispose of controlled (directive) waste, or knowingly cause or knowingly permit controlled (directive) waste to be treated, kept or disposed of:

  (i) in or on any land; or

  (ii) by means of any mobile plant;

  (iii) except under and in accordance with a waste management licence (s 33(1)(b) of the EPA 1990). This offence is restricted to directive disposal operations and directive recovery operations;

(c) treat, keep or dispose of controlled (directive) waste in a manner likely to cause pollution of the environment or harm to human health (s 33(1)(c) of the EPA 1990). This offence applies to any person whether or not he or she holds a waste management licence. It is especially useful in dealing with 'fly-tippers' (see s 35).

Section 33(1)(a) and s 33(1)(b) each comprise a combination of alternative ways of committing the relevant offence. For example, the offence in s 33(1)(a) may be committed by someone who deposits directive waste (an offence of strict liability), or it may be committed by someone who knowingly causes or knowingly permits a deposit of waste (see *R v Leighton and Town and Country Refuse Collections Ltd* (1997)).

5.16.1.1 Elements of the s 33 offences

(1) 'Knowingly causing' and 'knowingly permitting'

The offences of 'knowingly causing' or 'knowingly permitting' contained in s 33(1)(a) and s 33(1)(b) are strict even though they require some degree of knowledge on the defendant's part. In *Shanks and McEwan (Teeside) Ltd v Environment Agency* (1997), a waste company was prosecuted by the Environment Agency for knowingly permitting the deposit of controlled waste (directive waste) in contravention of a condition of its waste management licence. The defendant argued, unsuccessfully, that although it knew that a deposit of waste had occurred, it was not aware that the deposit had breached a condition of its operating licence. The court held that the defendant's knowledge of the deposit was sufficient to establish liability and it was unnecessary for the prosecution to prove that the defendant knew that the deposit would breach the conditions of its operating licence. Knowledge of a deposit may be inferred from the facts (see *Kent CC v Beaney* (1993)).

The very act of operating a landfill site will be interpreted by the courts as constructive knowledge, on the part of the site operator, that deposits are taking place and it is not necessary for the prosecution to demonstrate knowledge of individual breaches of licence conditions (see *Shanks* above). This interpretation of 'knowingly causing' or 'knowingly permitting' in effect imposes strict liability for breaches of waste management licence conditions.

The inclusion of 'knowingly causing' appears to have been inserted into s 33(1)(a) and s 33(1)(b) to cover the situation where one person orders another to deposit waste (for example, a waste producer contracts a carrier to transport waste to the nearest suitable landfill site, but the carrier fly-tips the waste on waste ground) and the waste consignor is unaware that the consignee deposits the waste illegally.

(2) 'Pollution of the environment' and 'harm to human health'

Section 33(1)(c) makes it an offence to treat, keep or dispose of controlled (directive) waste in a manner likely to cause pollution of the environment or harm to human health. It makes no reference to knowingly causing or knowingly permitting, nor does it make it a defence to be operating in accordance with a waste management licence. It is possible for a person to be operating in accordance with a waste management licence and yet still be committing an offence under s 33(1)(c). All that is required is that the treatment, keeping or disposal is likely to cause pollution of the environment or harm to human health. 'Pollution of the environment' refers to harm to flora and fauna, whilst 'harm' refers to both harm to living organisms and ecological systems.

5.16.2 Meaning of 'deposit'

The word 'deposit' has an extended meaning primarily to counter arguments by waste producers and waste handlers that the presence of waste on site does not constitute a 'deposit' because the waste has not reached its final destination. This argument has been raised, unsuccessfully, in order to evade liability for s 33 offences. In *Leigh Land Reclamation Ltd v Walsall Metropolitan Borough Council* (1991), the court held that 'deposit' referred to the tipping and burying of the waste at a landfill site so that the waste became incorporated into the site so that there was 'no realistic prospect of further examination'. In *R v Metropolitan Stipendiary Magistrate ex p London Waste Regulation Authority* (1993), the High Court adopted a wider meaning of the term and held that 'deposit' covered both temporary (at waste transfer station) and permanent deposits of waste. Furthermore, 'deposit' includes the continuing activities on a waste management site. In *Thames Waste Management Ltd v Surrey CC* (1997), the defendant waste management company was convicted of breaching the terms of its waste management licence and therefore committing an unlawful deposit of waste. One of the licence conditions required waste, which had been deposited on the site, to be covered over on the day of deposit. The defendant argued, unsuccessfully, that the failure to cover the waste occurred after the waste had already been deposited. The court held that the word 'deposit' could cover continuing activities specified in the waste management licence. Thus, the 'deposit' continued until it was covered over. Section 33 offences at a landfill site may not only be committed by the site operator breaching the terms of its licence but also by waste carriers (with regard to breach of s 33(b), see *Shanks & McEwan (Teeside) Ltd v Environment Agency* (1997)).

5.16.3 Other waste offences

In addition to the main offences created by s 33(1), the EPA 1990 also creates a number of other specific offences such as:

(a) s 33(6) – contravening any condition of a waste management licence (this is an offence of strict liability);

(b) s 33(5) – where controlled (directive) waste is carried in and deposited from a motor vehicle, the person who controls or is in a position to control the use of the vehicle shall be treated as knowingly causing the waste to be deposited, whether or not he or she gave any instructions for this to be done. This provision is designed to address the problem of the illegal fly-tipping of waste. Section 33(5) should be read in the light of the Environment Agency's s 6 power relating to the seizure of vehicles used for unlawful waste-related activities. If the Environment Agency is unable to obtain information, through its s 7 and s 71 powers, with regard to any vehicle suspected of being used for fly-tipping, it can apply to a magistrates' court for a warrant to seize the vehicle. After seizure, the Environment Agency may publicise the seizure and, if no one comes forward to claim the vehicle, it may dispose of it (reg 23 of the Controlled Waste (Registration of Carriers and Seizure of Vehicles) Regulations 1991). The issue of what constitutes 'control' of a vehicle for the purposes of the s 33(5) 'fly-tipping' offence has been considered in *Environment Agency v Melland* (2002). The Environment Agency alleged that Melland had knowingly caused controlled waste to be deposited on land where no waste management licence was in force, contrary to s 33(1)(a) and 33(6) of the EPA 1990. At the hearing in the magistrates' court, it was established that the registered keeper of the vehicle, at the time of the alleged offence, was a company under which Melland was trading. Prior to the hearing, the Environment Agency had served on Melland a request for information under s 71 of the EPA 1990 in reply to which Melland stated that he had been the owner and registered keeper of the vehicle at the relevant time. Melland argued that there was no case to answer because there was insufficient evidence (that is, the mere fact that his company was the registered keeper) to prove that he was in control of the vehicle at the relevant time the offence was alleged to have been committed. The magistrates dismissed the Environment Agency's case on the basis that the person controlling the vehicle (driving it) was not Melland and therefore control by him had not been established. On appeal, by way of case stated, the Environment Agency argued that the issue of 'control' was one of fact and common sense and vehicle ownership carried with it the ability to control its use. Once ownership had been established, there was evidence to demonstrate control and there followed an irresistible inference of control in the absence of evidence to the contrary.

Harrison J held that evidence of vehicle ownership was capable of amounting to *prima facie* evidence (that is, an initial evidential inference) that the vehicle owner controlled, or was in a position to control, the use of a vehicle. Each case was dependent upon its facts and evidence could be presented (for example, the vehicle had been loaned to someone or stolen) which rebutted the inference the court was entitled to make. In this case, the owner and keeper of the vehicle was Melland, Melland ran a waste (skip hire) business, and waste had been unlawfully deposited from the vehicle. It could therefore be inferred that Melland controlled or was in a position to control the vehicle at the relevant time. This was sufficient evidence to convict Melland in the absence of evidence to the contrary. The Environment Agency was not required to produce evidence linking Melland and the driver of the offending vehicle, although the burden of proof remained with the prosecution. This judgment was consistent with the object of s 33(5) to make prosecution for fly-tipping easier where some of the relevant circumstances might be obscure;

(c) s 34(6) – breach of the duty of care (see 5.21 below);

(d) s 44 – making false statements when applying for a waste management licence is an offence;

(e) s 60 – interfering (scavenging) with a licensed waste site and receptacle for waste (a skip) provided by a WCA, WDA, or waste disposal contractor unless that person has the consent of the relevant authority, contractor or other person;

(f) s 63(2) – depositing waste other than controlled (directive) waste in certain circumstances (see 5.15.1 above);

(g) s 157 – offences by senior company officers (see 5.16.7 below).

5.16.4 The household waste exemption

The main exemption from the waste offences is in relation to household waste. The offences contained in Pt II of the EPA 1990 do not apply in relation to household waste from a domestic property which is treated, kept or disposed of within the curtilage of the dwelling by or with the permission of the occupier of the dwelling (s 33(2)). It should be noted that the following will not be treated as household waste for the purpose of this exception: any mineral or synthetic oil or grease; asbestos; or clinical waste. The Waste Management Licensing Regulations 1994 exempt certain activities relating to household waste from the s 33(1)(a) and (b) offences.

5.16.5 Defences

It is clear from the wording of s 33(1)(a) and s 33(1)(b) of the EPA 1990 that an offence will not be committed if the deposit, treatment, keeping or disposal of controlled (directive) waste is in accordance with a waste management licence (it is in accordance with the conditions attached to the licence). Therefore, compliance with a waste management licence and all its conditions will provide a defence to these two offences. Compliance with the terms of a waste management licence, however, affords no defence in relation to a s 33(1)(c) offence.

Section 33(7) also provides a number of additional defences. To succeed in defending a s 33 prosecution, a person charged must prove that:

(a) he or she took all reasonable precautions and exercised all due diligence to avoid the commission of the offence. This defence is often associated with the defendant proving that he or she has set up an adequate system to avoid the commission of an offence. For example, in *Durham County Council v Peter Connors Industrial Services Ltd* (1993), a waste carrier who was contracted to make regular visits to a waste producer's premises to collect waste in an awaiting skip was not allowed to take advantage of the s 33(7)(a) defence. The waste carrier had not checked the contents of the skip on every occasion it had *collected a skip from the waste producer's premises* and the court held that the waste carrier had not done enough to inform itself of the nature of the waste which was being collected. To avail itself of the defence, a specific enquiry had to be made of any person who knew what the waste was and whether a deposit of the waste would be unlawful; or

(b) he acted under instructions from his or her employer and neither knew, nor had reason to suppose, that the acts done by him or her constituted a contravention of s 33(1); or

(c) the acts alleged to constitute the contravention were done in an emergency to avoid danger to human health. However, to rely on this defence, it is necessary to fulfil two further criteria, namely that the person seeking to rely on the defence took all such steps as were reasonably practicable in the circumstances for minimising pollution of the environment and harm to health and that, as soon as reasonably practicable after these actions were taken, particulars of the incident were given to the Environment Agency. Section 33(7)(c) restricts this defence to circumstances in which emergency action was taken to avoid danger to the public but not danger to the environment. The onus is on the defendant to prove that the circumstances constituted an emergency and the court will employ an objective test in deciding whether the circumstances constituted an emergency (see *Waste Incineration Services Ltd v Dudley Metropolitan Borough Council* (1993)).

The courts will determine as a question of fact whether a person can rely on any of these defences.

5.16.6 Penalties

A person committing an offence could be liable to an unlimited fine or even imprisonment for a period of up to two years. Section 33(9) of the EPA 1990 details the penalties as follows:

(a) on summary conviction (in a magistrates' court), to imprisonment for a term not exceeding six months or a fine not exceeding £20,000 or both; and

(b) on conviction on indictment (in a Crown Court), to imprisonment for a term not exceeding two years or an unlimited fine or both.

Persons who commit waste offences range from individuals to companies (a company is a legal person who may be prosecuted and sued). Whilst an individual may be fined *and* sent to gaol, it is not possible to imprison a company, although it is possible to imprison senior company officers.

The penalties are more serious if special waste is involved (up to a maximum gaol term of five years (s 33(9)). Prison sentences are relatively rare for environmental crimes, but the courts have imposed terms of imprisonment on convicted waste offenders in several instances.

In most cases, the penalty for a waste offence will be a fine (plus costs, which may be considerably higher than the fine imposed). Although the fine may not always be that great in relation to the company's resources, the poor publicity arising from a prosecution may be more damaging. With regard to senior company officers, the court may order that they be disqualified from holding office (Disqualification of Directors Act 1986).

5.16.7 Personal liability

Section 157 of the EPA 1990 opens up the possibility of making company directors and managers personally liable for waste offences. Where a waste offence has been committed by a company, the senior management may also be personally liable for the offence. However, it has to be proved that the offence was committed with their consent or connivance or was attributable to their neglect.

Whilst it is clear from company records who the directors are, there has been considerable debate with regard to who is a 'manager' for the purposes of s 157 of the EPA 1990 and similar offences (for example, s 217 of the WRA 1991, s 210 of the WIA 1991 and s 37 of the Health and Safety at Work etc Act 1974). The courts have developed and applied a 'controlling officer' test to determine who is a 'manager' for the purposes of s 157 of the EPA 1990 and similar offences. In *R v Boal* (1992), the defendant was the assistant general manager of a large bookshop. The defendant took charge of the bookshop whilst the general manager was on holiday. During the time he was in charge, serious breaches of the Fire Precautions Act 1971 came to light. The defendant was prosecuted and acquitted. The court held that, although the defendant was fourth in the seniority in the company, he was not a manager within the 1971 Act. In *Woodhouse v Walsall Metropolitan Borough Council* (1994), the defendant was the general manager of a waste management company. He was prosecuted, under the COPA 1974, for breaches of the company's waste management site licence. The court held that Woodhouse was not a manager for the purposes of the COPA 1974. Although he was a site manager, he was not in a position of *real authority* regarding the overall running of the company and was not in a position to *guide or control company policy*. In the Scottish case of *Armour v Skeen* (1976), the Director of Roads of Strathclyde Regional Council was convicted of health and safety offences which led to the death of an employee. In reaching its verdict, the court referred to the fact that the defendant had responsibility for implementing the local authority's health and safety policy and as such was of sufficient seniority to be a 'director, manager, secretary or similar officer'. This case will be of interest to any senior public or private sector manager who has responsibility for devising and implementing an environmental policy.

Section 157 of the EPA 1990 and other similar offences not only apply to registered companies but also to other organisations such as local authorities and universities (incorporated by Royal Charter).

Offences such as those covered in s 157 of the EPA 1990 are not offences of strict liability and the prosecution must prove that:

(a) the defendant consented to the commission of the offence; or

(b) the defendant connived at the commission of the offence; or

(c) the offence was attributable to the defendant's neglect.

Consent requires some affirmative act or approval (see *Huckerby v Elliott* (1970)). The defendant must be aware that an environmental offence is being committed and acts in a way which indicates that he or she is giving positive approval to the breach (for example, a company's plant malfunctions resulting in a breach of the terms of the company's pollution or operating licences, and a director orders production to continue). Connivance suggests acquiescence in conduct which is likely to lead to the commission of an offence (for example, a director is aware of some illegality and, whilst he or she does not actively encourage the breach, he or she allows it to continue, says nothing about it and chooses not to make any enquiry). Neglect has been defined as 'a failure to perform a duty which the person knows or ought to know' (see *Re Hughes* (1943)). Whether any particular director has been guilty of neglect will depend upon the nature and extent of the director's duties. Managers should therefore be wary of accepting responsibilities relating to the environment and health and safety unless they are provided, by their employing organisation, with sufficient resources to carry out their responsibilities.

5.17   SPECIAL WASTE OFFENCES

Regulation 16 of the Special Waste Regulations 1996 requires any person who makes a deposit of special waste in or on any land to record the location of the deposit. Records must be kept until the person surrenders his or her waste management licence. The site records will comprise either a site plan marked with a grid or a site plan with overlays on which deposits are shown in relation to the contours of the site. Regulation 17 prohibits any establishment or undertaking which carries out the disposal or recovery of special waste, or which collects special waste, from mixing different categories of special waste, or from mixing special waste with waste which is not special waste.

5.17.1 Offences – reg 18

It is a criminal offence for any person (other than a member, officer or employee of the Environment Agency) to breach any of the provisions in regs 1–17. In addition, it is also an offence to furnish any false information or to make a false entry in any record or register. A person who commits an offence under the Special Waste Regulations 1996 is liable to a fine not exceeding level 5 (£20,000) on the standard scale if the case is dealt with by the magistrates' court. On indictment, the penalty may be an unlimited fine or imprisonment of up to five years, or both. The Regulation also makes special provision for the personal liability of a director, manager, secretary or other similar officer of a company if the offence was committed with their consent, connivance or was attributable to their negligence. Regulation 18, however, does provide a defence. Regulation 18(3) states that it shall be a defence for a person charged with an offence if he can prove that he or she was not reasonably able to comply with the provision in question by reason of an emergency or grave danger and that he or she took all reasonable steps as were reasonably practicable in the circumstances for:

(a) minimising any threat to the public or the environment;

(b) ensuring that the provision in question was complied with as soon as reasonably practicable after the event.

5.17.2 Proposed changes to special waste controls

New regulations are proposed and are expected to come into force in the near future. It is proposed that the phrase 'special waste' be replaced with the phrase 'hazardous waste' to bring the current special waste provisions into line with the Hazardous Waste Directive (91/689/EEC). In effect, this would introduce a new definition of 'hazardous waste' and such waste would comprise: (a) any waste listed as hazardous in the European Waste Catalogue (published in the Official Journal of the European Communities on 16 January 2001); (b) any waste which is not listed but which displays the hazardous properties listed in Annexe II of the Directive; and (c) all prescription medicines.

Other changes which are likely to be implemented relate to:

(1) a duty on the Environment Agency to inspect hazardous waste producers and hazardous waste facilities on a regular basis;

(2) compulsory registration of hazardous waste producers. Such persons would be required to identify the types and amounts of hazardous waste they intend to consign during the year, provide an estimate of the number of consignments and the intended treatments or disposal sites for waste streams produced;

(3) the end of the requirement to pre-notify the Environment Agency of hazardous waste movements;

(4) a requirement that hazardous waste producers supply the Environment Agency with quarterly information relating to hazardous waste consignments;

(5) a requirement on hazardous waste management sites to provide quarterly information on hazardous wastes received;

(6) changes in the consignment note system relating to multiple consignments;

(7) changes to the fee structure to reflect the need to recycle more waste;

(8) an obligation to separate wastes where this is technically and economically viable;

(9) a reduction in the household waste exemption to bring the controls in line with the Hazardous Waste Directive.

5.18   WASTE STRATEGY FOR ENGLAND AND WALES

5.18.1 National waste policy

Until the dawn of the 1990s, there was no coherent national waste policy in the UK. Waste policy was largely a local authority concern due to the ready availability of landfill sites across the UK. However, amendments made to the EC Waste Framework Directive (91/156/EC) in 1991 coincided with central government recognition of the need for a more coherent and planned strategy to deal with the ever increasing quantity of waste produced in the UK and the need for better methods of waste management and disposal.

During the period 1990–2000, the government produced several key policy documents: *This Common Inheritance* (Cm 1200, 1990), DoE Circular 11/94 establishing the 'waste hierarchy', *Making Waste Work* (Cm 3040, 1995, DoE), *Less Waste: More Value* (1998, DETR), *A Way With Waste* (1999, DETR) and *Waste Strategy for England and Wales* (Cm 4693, 2000, DETR). These policy documents revealed the government's key waste objectives:

(a) to reduce the amount of waste generated;

(b) to make the best use of waste;

(c) to give preference to waste management options which minimise the immediate and future risk of pollution of the environment and harm to human health.

Together, these objectives represent a sustainable waste strategy for the 21st century reflecting EC environmental policy objectives. As part of its national strategy, the government has set national waste reduction, waste recovery and waste recycling targets. The government intends to achieve these targets by a combination of regulatory licence-based controls, eco-taxes, planning controls and information and education initiatives (the first two of these reflecting the EC's 'polluter pays' principle).

Whilst *This Common Inheritance* introduced the concept of the 'waste hierarchy' in 1990, ranking the waste management options in descending order of preference (minimisation, recycling, recovery and disposal), practical progress, at local level, in achieving the government's waste policy vision has been somewhat slow. The use of s 50 of the EPA 1990 to achieve national coverage of waste management plans, as required by the Waste Framework Directive, was not particularly successful and the WRAs had made rather 'steady' progress in the preparation of waste disposal plans in an attempt to comply with the requirements of the Directive (see 5.19.1 below).

In 1994, the objectives contained in the Waste Framework Directive, as amended, were transposed into national law by the Waste Management Regulations 1994 (see Sched 4 to the 1994 Regulations). Section 50 of the EPA 1990 was repealed and replaced by ss 44A and 44B (inserted by the EA 1995) requiring the Secretary of State to prepare a *national* waste strategy replacing the previous system of local authority waste disposal plans.

The National Waste Strategy requires the Secretary of State to prepare a plan for England and Wales which will contain policies in relation to the recovery and disposal of waste in England and Wales. The strategy details the policies for attaining the objectives set out in Sched 2A to the EPA 1990. Schedule 2A sets out the two key objectives of the strategy:

(1) waste should be recovered or disposed of without endangering human health and without using processes or methods which could harm the environment and in particular without:

(a) risk to water, air, soil, plants or animals;

(b) causing nuisances through noise or odours; or

(c) adversely affecting the countryside or places of special interest, and

to secure the implementation of the strategy so as (with regard to waste disposal only) to secure an integrated and adequate network of waste disposal installations taking account of the best available technology not entailing excessive costs; and

(2) ensuring self-sufficiency in waste disposal (having regard to location, need, and the availability of appropriate facilities), encouraging the prevention or reduction of waste production, and encouraging the recovery of waste by recycling, reuse or reclamation.

The strategy includes provisions relating to each of the following:

(a) the type, quantity and origin of waste to be recovered or disposed of;

(b) general technical requirements; and

(c) any special requirements for particular wastes.

In preparing the national strategy, the Secretary of State has consulted with the Environment Agency, local authorities and industry (and any other bodies or persons that he considers appropriate). The strategy's broad objectives will have major impacts on local authority waste-related responsibilities.

The actual preparation of the national waste strategy for England and Wales (and similar plans for Scotland and Northern Ireland) has taken time to come to fruition largely due to informational uncertainties in waste arisings. The strategy was completed and published in May 2000. 'Waste Strategy 2000 for England and Wales' is the national plan for the purposes of the Waste Framework Directive. The strategy sets the following waste reduction targets, which are to be reviewed at five-yearly intervals:

(a) to reduce the amount of waste (industrial and commercial) going to landfill by 85% of 1998 levels by 2005;

(b) to recover value from 40% of municipal waste (EfW incineration generating electricity) and 25% of household waste by 2005. A House of Commons Research Paper on Waste Incineration (Library Research Paper 02/34, 9 May 2002) contains a useful discussion on the role of incineration in meeting the objectives of the National Waste Strategy. Of particular relevance is the discussion on public health concerns from incinerators (see discussion of 'public concern' on pp 457–64 of this text);

(c) to recycle/compost 30% of household waste and 45% of municipal waste by 2010.

The national strategy has been criticised by the House of Commons Environment, Transport and Regional Affairs Select Committee for failing to provide guidance on how its targets are to be achieved (see 'Delivering Sustainable Waste Management').

Since the waste management licensing system is not the ideal vehicle to address waste minimisation and waste recycling targets, the strategy incorporates the use of eco-taxes (such as the landfill tax) and producer responsibility obligations (such as the Packaging Directive). These non-licence-based regulatory tools are designed to provide the necessary financial incentive to bring about greater waste minimisation and waste recovery efforts.

The House of Commons Environment, Food and Rural Affairs Select Committee has recently published its report, *The Future of Waste Management* (8th Report, HC 385 I and II (2002–03), summarised in [2003] JPL 1120–24). The Committee is critical of government waste policy, especially the lack of direction evident in DEFRA and the under-funding of Environment Agency enforcement. The main criticisms include the following issues: over-reliance on a single eco-tax (landfill tax) which could be developed further and other taxes introduced (for example, a household waste collection charge); the adoption, by the government, of a passive role with regard to the formulation of new waste directives; the failure to provide timely guidance on new directives; poor communication between government and local authorities regarding the role of local authorities with regard to attaining the objectives of the government's waste hierarchy; confusion of waste policy responsibility between DEFRA, the Office of the Deputy Prime Minister and the Department of Trade and Industry; Environment Agency delays in processing waste management licensing applications; government reticence with regard to waste incineration as a waste management option; and the failure of WDAs and WCAs to work together.

5.18.2 The significance of EC waste policy

EC waste law and policy has had, and will continue to have, a profound impact upon the UK. The EC's waste strategy, set out in the Commission's 'A Community Strategy for Waste Management' ([1990] OJ L122) and rooted in the waste hierarchy (see 5.18.1), details the relevant concerns and priorities of the Commission (which largely reflect UK waste policy). Waste management is also a key 'priority area' of the EC's Sixth Action Programme, *Environment 2010; Our Future, Our Choice* (COM(2001)31 Final), the central theme of which is waste prevention and greater efficiency in the use of raw materials (resources) which will minimise waste generation.

The Commission has identified waste policy as one of the seven priority policy thematic strategies in its Sixth Action Programme in its *Communication Towards a Thematic Strategy on the Prevention and Recycling of Waste* published in May 2003 (COM(200)301). The Commission invites discussion from Member States on several issues, including: identifying areas where there is the potential for waste prevention; exchanging best practice; evaluating the relative merits of voluntary and mandatory waste prevention planning; assessing the waste prevention potential of the IPPC Directive; the development of materials based recycling targets; and placing the onus on producers to recycle waste. The strategy is likely to be finalised in 2004.

5.18.3 The Waste Framework Directive

The 1975 Waste Framework Directive (75/442/EEC) as amended in 1991 by Directive 91/156/EEC has influenced the shape of UK waste law and policy in the following ways:

(a) the original definition of 'controlled waste' in the EPA 1990 has been amended to reflect the waste definition favoured by the EC – 'directive waste' (Directive 91/156/EEC);

(b) EC waste policy created the need for a centralised national waste strategy (Art 6);

(c) the EC goal of self sufficiency in the treatment and disposal of waste (Art 5) has influenced national waste strategy;

(d) the creation of a 'waste management hierarchy' of waste policy objectives drives EC and Member State national waste policy (Arts 3 and 4).

The relevant EC policy objectives are:

(a) the prevention of and/or reduction of waste (see Art 174(2) of the EC Treaty);

(b) the recovery of waste produced;

(c) the recovery or disposal of waste without endangering human health or the environment.

To a marked degree, the Waste Framework Directive reflects the regulatory structure created by Pt II of the EPA 1990. For example, the Waste Framework Directive:

(a) imposes a duty of care (Art 8 and s 34 of the EPA 1990) on all persons in the waste chain;

(b) obliges all waste disposal and waste recovery operations to be licensed (Arts 9 and 10 and ss 35–42 of the EPA 1990);

(c) obliges waste producers, handlers, recoverers, and disposers to keep proper records (Art 14 and the s 34 of the EPA 1990 duty of care waste transfer note system).

The Waste Framework Directive objectives were transposed into UK law by the Waste Management Regulations 1994 (see Sched 4). Whilst the Regulations form part of national law, they do not create legal rights and obligations of benefit to non-decision makers and cannot therefore be relied upon directly by individuals. These objectives are therefore not 'directly effective' in litigation before national courts (see Case C-236/92, *Comitato Di Coordinamento per la Difesa della Cava v Regione Lombardia* (1994)).

In *R v Bolton Metropolitan BC ex p Kirkman* (1998), the Court of Appeal held that the Waste Framework Directive expressed objectives rather than legal requirements. The court went on to hold that the effect of transposing the objectives into national law was to create a separate legal duty, applying to regulators, to *ensure* the attainment of the Sched 4 objectives. There is some debate as to how strict this duty will be in practice. For example, does the duty merely require the regulatory decision maker to have regard to the attainment of the objectives in determining questions which concern the Sched 4 objectives? Are the waste objectives just one of several issues which must be taken into account in regulatory decision making, but leaving the final weighting of the factors to the discretion of the regulator? Alternatively, does the duty oblige the regulatory decision maker to achieve the Sched 4 objectives thereby restricting the extent of the decision maker's discretion and elevating the Sched 4 objectives above other considerations? In *R v Leicestershire CC, Hepworth Building Products and Onyx (UK) Ltd ex p Blackfordby and Boothcorpe Action Group* (2001), the judge viewed the Waste Framework Directive objectives as a factor which the decision maker must take into account, but the weight which had to be accorded to the objectives was a matter entirely within the discretion of the decision maker.

To hold otherwise would be to give the Sched 4 objectives an 'indeterminate' status – higher than material considerations, but not an absolute obligation. The subsequent decision in *R v Daventry District Council* (2002) seems to accord greater weight to an 'obligatory' objective than other material considerations, without going so far as to establish a hierarchy of relevant considerations, placing the Sched 4 objectives at the top.

5.18.4 The Landfill Directive

In July 1999, the EC issued legislation relating to the harmonisation of landfill standards (the Landfill Directive (99/31/EC)). The Directive was required to be transposed into national law by July 2001. The Directive's main objective is to bring about a reduction in the amount of methane producing, biodegradable household and municipal waste which is disposed of in landfill sites.

Article 5 of the Directive has set the following reviewable reduction targets based on 1995 waste arisings:

(a) a 25% reduction by 2006;

(b) a 50% reduction by 2009;

(c) a 65% reduction by 2016.

The deadlines for achievement of these targets may be extended where more than 80% of household and municipal waste was landfilled in 1995. Since waste disposal in the UK falls into this category, the UK has been granted an extra four years to achieve each target. The conditions of all waste management licences and some IPPC permits will require amendment to enable the national targets to be achieved.

The Landfill Directive is set to have major impacts upon national landfilling practice. The more important of these impacts is that: disposal of liquid, corrosive, clinical and infectious wastes to landfill is banned, as is the disposal of most types of tyres. The Directive divides landfill sites into three categories: those licensed to accept (a) hazardous wastes, (b) non-hazardous wastes, and (c) inert wastes.

The Directive:

(a) requires all waste to be pre-treated (for example, sorting and compacting) before disposal;

(b) bans the co-disposal of wastes (for example, the practice of landfilling hazardous (special) wastes with household wastes);

(c) requires waste sites to install technology to control landfill gas and leachate (for example, collecting methane and using it to produce electricity);

(d) requires proper financial provision to deal with site after care.

The Landfill (England and Wales) Regulations 2002 (SI 2002/1559) came into force on 15 June 2002 and implement the Landfill Directive (99/31/EC). In Pt I of the Regulations, reg 3 details their scope, reg 5 requires planning authorities to have regard to the location requirements of the Regulations when dealing with planning applications for landfills, reg 6 amends the Pollution Prevention and Control (PPC) Regulations 2000 so that all landfills are Part A(1) installations (regulated by the PPCA 1999 and requiring a permit under the PPC Regulations). Part II controls landfill permit (licence) conditions. Of particular note is reg 7, which requires the Environment Agency to classify landfills into sites licensed to accept (a) hazardous waste, (b) non-hazardous waste, and (c) inert waste. Waste acceptance criteria and monitoring procedures are detailed in Sched 1 to the Regulations. Regulation 16 concerns closure notices (for Environment Agency use to accept completion and closure of a landfill). Part III contains relevant offences (reg 17) such as acceptance of waste in contravention of para 3 of Sched 4. Sites which are unable to comply with the Regulations will close.

The Landfill Directive (99/31/EC) regulates the types of waste which are to be accepted at the relevant landfill types (hazardous, non-hazardous and inert). The Commission, in furtherance of the Directive, has published a decision (Decision 2003/33/EC) which sets out the rules on waste acceptance procedures for landfills. The Landfill (England and Wales) Regulations 2002 require operators to demonstrate that they have procedures in place which enable them to accept waste in accordance with licence conditions and the waste acceptance procedures.

All current landfill sites should have put in place a 'site conditioning' plan by April 2002. Site operators must monitor their closed landfills for methane emissions and migration of leachate for up to a maximum of 30 years. The Directive requires Member States to improve landfill regulation in the following areas: (a) checking and accepting wastes; (b) monitoring; (c) passing on the full operating costs to customers via gate fees; and (d) providing adequate after care and financial provisions to address post closure problems.

Following the introduction of the Landfill Regulations 2002, the Environment Agency has consulted, especially with the waste industry, with regard to new best practice guidance on the monitoring of leachate, groundwater and surface water at landfill sites (including closed sites). The new guidance (to replace the 2001 Environment Agency, *Guidance on Landfill Leachate Monitoring*) takes account of the Environment Agency's draft guidance notes (*Guidance on Hydrogeological Risk Assessments for Landfills and Derivation of Groundwater Control and Trigger Levels*).

The IPPC regime (see Chapter 6) is set to apply to approximately 1,000 large landfill sites by 2007. The remaining 900 or so smaller landfills will remain subject to the current waste management licensing controls (although the transfer of these sites to a simplified IPPC regime has been discussed). The government is considering introducing a landfill tradable pollution credit scheme to provide additional 'muscle' to achieve the municipal waste reduction targets in the Landfill Directive (see *Tradable Landfill Permits*, 2001, DETR).

The application of the Landfill Regulations 2002 and the Waste Incineration Regulations 2002 are both dependent upon correctly identifying the substances which fall within the definition of 'waste'. Thus, the definition of 'controlled waste' (see s 75(4) of the EPA 1990) is amended by para 88 of Sched 22 to the EA 1995 to include the list of substances listed in Sched 2B to the EA 1995 (that is, controlled waste includes directive waste). Agricultural waste now falls within both sets of Regulations.

The case of *Blackland Park Exploration Ltd v Environment Agency* (2003) is an interesting and novel examination of the question of what constitutes a landfill site. A mixture of oil and water was extracted from underground strata at Whisby in Lincolnshire. The oil was separated out and the water was then reinjected into the ground together with imported hazardous liquid wastes. Oil production was IPC regulated (licensed) whilst the waste disposal process was covered by a waste management licence. Following the introduction of the Landfill Regulations 2002 (SI 2002/1559), the Environment Agency informed the site operator that the disposal of the liquid wastes constituted a landfill operation and that the site would have to be reclassified as a hazardous waste landfill. It followed that, under reg 9 of the

Landfill Regulations 2002, liquid wastes could no longer be disposed of to landfill. The site operator disputed the Agency's view and sought a ruling on its legal position. The High Court held that the site was a landfill within reg 3(2) of the Landfill Regulations 2002. Blackbourne J rejected the submission (a) that the word 'deposit' implied placing wastes into a controlled (that is, static) medium (as in the case of normal landfilling operations), and (b) that the reinjection of water and waste constituted a 'discharge' into groundwaters regulated by the Groundwater Regulations 1998 (SI 1998/2746). Blackbourne J stated that: 'The site is operated as a waste disposal site. That activity forms a major and distinct part of the claimants' operations at the site. Since the waste is deposited onto or into land it follows that the site is a landfill within the meaning of the Landfill Regulations.'

5.18.5 Other waste directives

In addition to the general waste controls set out in the Waste Framework Directive, other directives regulate specific wastes. The Hazardous Waste Directive (78/319/EEC), as amended by Directives 91/689/EEC and 94/31/EEC, is a 'daughter' directive of the Waste Framework Directive and is concerned with the management of wastes which have properties which make the wastes dangerous or difficult to handle. These properties are specified in the Annexes to the Directive (for example, toxicity). Much of the Directive has been implemented in UK law by the Special Waste Regulations 1996. The EC is responsible for compiling the list of hazardous substances, based on the capacity of substances to cause harm, which are to be subject to tighter control than other directive wastes. The Hazardous Waste Directive requires Member States to prepare and make publicly accessible hazardous waste management plans and to provide the Commission with information relating not only to implementation, but also to the number and type of facilities available in each Member State for the recovery or disposal of hazardous waste. It is the Commission's intention to set up a European network of hazardous waste facilities.

Movements of waste into, within and out of EC Member States is controlled by Directive 84/631/EEC and the directly effective Regulation (EC) 93/259. The UK has put in place its own controls (the Special Waste Regulations 1996) which ban the export of waste for the following purposes: (a) disposal; and (b) recovery, in non-OECD States. The objective of the EC is to tailor waste movement controls to the health and environmental risks posed by the waste and also the ability of Member States to transport, treat and dispose of it. Regulatory control is based upon a system of prior notification of proposed waste movements. The waste mover/exporter notifies both 'recipient' States and 'transient' States (States through which the waste will be transported). Following receipt of the relevant notice of the proposed consignment, transient and recipient States may: (a) request further information from the exporting State; (b) impose conditions on the waste shipment; or (c) refuse permission. Exporting States must ensure that proper financial provisions regarding shipping, treatment and disposal of the waste are in place before the waste is shipped.

Directives 89/369/EEC and 89/429/EEC ('daughter' directives of the Air Framework Directive (84/360/EEC) on air pollution from industrial plant) regulate the operation of municipal waste incinerators, whilst hazardous waste incineration is dealt with by the Hazardous Waste Incineration Directive (94/67/EC).

The Waste Incineration Directive (2000/76/EC) was passed in order to limit the emission of dioxins from waste incinerators. The Directive has been implemented in England and Wales by the Waste Incineration (England and Wales) Regulations 2002 (SI 2002/2980). The new Regulations, which came into force on 28 December 2002, apply (a) immediately to all new plant, and (b) from late December 2005 to existing incinerators, and set a limit of 1 part in 10 billion on dioxin emissions to air from waste incinerators/co-incinerators. The Regulations apply to approximately 950 incinerators/co-incinerators (including the 13 large municipal incinerators, cement kilns and clinical waste incinerators). The aim of the Regulations is to prevent and/or limit, as far as practicable, the negative impacts upon humans and the environment of atmospheric emissions. Operators of incinerators must obtain a permit (licence) authorising their operations.

The Waste Incineration Directive (2000/76/EC) details stringent operating conditions for new incinerators (from the end of December 2002) and for existing incinerators (from the end of December 2005). The Directive consolidates previous EC incinerator directives into one single Directive. The new Directive applies to a much wider range of incinerators (approximately 2,600), including incinerators burning waste oils. DEFRA has concluded a consultation on the relevant implementing regulations.

The Waste Incineration Regulations 2002 came into force in late December 2002 implementing Directive 2000/76/EC. DEFRA concluded a consultation exercise in May 2003 with regard to a guidance note on the new Regulations. The guidance includes commentary upon the definitions of 'waste', 'incineration' and 'co-incineration' (co-incineration is the use of waste fuel to generate energy) (see www.defra.gov.uk/environment/ppc).

Directive 86/278/EEC controls the regulation of sewage sludge disposal. Until the mid-1980s, it was common practice to spread sewage sludge on farmland; however, as many sewage treatment plants treat both human and industrial wastes, the processed sludge may contain high levels of heavy metals. The heavy metal content may be so high that the waste will be classified as 'special waste' and must be disposed of appropriately (for example, in a landfill licensed to accept sewage sludge). The Directive requires sewage sludge with high levels of heavy metals to be pre-treated before it can be used on farmland. It also sets limits on the number of times annually that sludge may be spread on the same fields.

Directive 75/439/EEC regulates the collection and disposal of waste oils. Facilities which collect, keep or dispose of more than 500 litres of waste oils per year are required to keep records of their activities. To avoid harm to human health and the environment, the Directive bans the discharge of: (a) waste oils into watercourses and drains; (b) waste oils on land resulting in damage/harm to soils; and (c) uncontrolled discharges of process residues, and waste oil processing causing atmospheric pollution in excess of the limits detailed in the Directive.

The Titanium Dioxide Directive (78/176/EEC) regulates the disposal of waste from the titanium dioxide industry. Titanium dioxide is an important constituent of paints.

The Batteries and Accumulators Directive (91/157/EEC) regulates the risks relating to the heavy metal content of waste batteries and accumulators.

Directive 76/403/EEC regulates the disposal of waste PCBs and PCTs. Uncontrolled discharges/disposal of these substances are banned. Methods of treatment and disposal must avoid harming human health or the environment.

5.18.6 Producer responsibility

Section 93 of the EA 1995 enables the Secretary of State to introduce regulations which oblige manufacturers to recycle, recover, or reuse products or materials. The intention is to impose waste reduction targets on business sectors to enable national waste reduction targets to be met and EC legislation to be complied with.

The principal example of a producer responsibility initiative is the 1994 Packaging Directive (94/62/EEC), transposed into national legislation by the Producer Responsibility Obligations (Packaging Waste) Regulations 1997 (SI 1997/648). The function of the Directive is threefold: (a) to minimise the environmental impacts of packaging waste; (b) to harmonise packaging waste regulation within the EC; and (c) to ensure the free movement of packaged goods within the EC. Article 6 of the Directive sets the following reviewable (in 2006) recovery and recycling targets: (a) 50–65% (by weight) of packaging waste to be recovered by mid-2001; and (b) 25–45% of the packaging waste in (a) to be recycled with a minimum of 15% per packaging type.

The UK waste packaging producer responsibility scheme is subject to a number of restrictions: (a) the burdens imposed by the scheme must be the minimum necessary to achieve the anticipated benefits; (b) the persons subjected to the burdens of the scheme must be those most able to contribute towards the attainment of national waste reduction targets; (c) environmental benefits (such as increased re-use of materials) will result from the scheme's implementation; and (d) the environmental benefits are 'significant' when compared to costs. The UK scheme adopts a similar definition of 'packaging waste' to that which appears in the Directive and includes all products to contain, handle, protect, deliver and present goods (for example, jars, bottles, boxes, shrinkwrap and pallets). Packaging may consist of 'primary' packaging (the packaging a consumer receives with his goods), 'secondary' packaging (the packaging removed by retailers before goods are placed on retailers' shelves) and 'tertiary' packaging (bulk handling packaging such as shrinkwrap).

Member States are required to provide infrastructure for the collection and recovery of packaging waste from the consumer. Member States must also ensure that each type of packaging waste reaches the most appropriate waste facility (for re-use, recovery, treatment or disposal). The 1997 Regulations are based on the concept that the responsibility for meeting the national target will be shared amongst the producers of packaging materials and the retail users of the producers' products. Businesses (producers) which fall within the ambit of the packaging regulations (regs 3–11) register with the Environment Agency and purchase packaging recovery notes (PRNs) from other businesses which recover and recycle packaging waste. In this way, each business is able to meet the recycling and recovery targets set for it by the Environment Agency. Businesses who engage in the following activities: the manufacture of cardboard, cardboard box manufacturing, the filling or packing of cardboard boxes, and the sale of cardboard packaged goods to retailers, are subject to the producer responsibility obligations provided each business produces, handles, or supplies more than 50 tonnes of packaging each year and has an annual turnover of £2 million. Businesses which satisfy these criteria must register with the Environment Agency and supply data upon which the Environment Agency bases its calculation of the volume of waste packaging that must be recycled. Alternatively, any business may join a 'compliance scheme' where several businesses are aggregated together for administrative convenience. Each business certificates its own compliance with the targets set by the Environment Agency.

Recycling includes reprocessing the materials so that they can be used again, either for their original purpose or an alternative purpose. Recovery refers to processes which recover some benefit from the waste, such as burning the waste in an energy from waste incinerator to produce electricity.

The main packaging offences are failing to register with the Environment Agency and failing to take 'reasonable steps to achieve the recycling or recovery target set for the relevant business'. The maximum fine in the magistrates' court on summary conviction is £5,000. Conviction on indictment in the Crown Court is punishable by an unlimited fine.

The European Commission has proposed a directive to amend the Packaging Waste Directive (94/62/EC) which is intended to clarify the definition of packaging in Art 3(1). Currently 'packaging' is divided into three types of packaging waste (primary, secondary and tertiary); however, the proposal would add a fourth limb to the definition. This draft fourth limb contains a further three criteria and a list of illustrative examples of items which are packaging (or which are not within the definition of packaging). Paper or plastic carrier bags, disposable cups and plates, clingfilm, sandwich bags and aluminium foil are packaging waste, whereas flower pots (intended to remain with the plant), tool boxes, tea bags, sausage skins, cheese wax and disposable cutlery are not. The proposed directive sets new targets for the recovery of packaging waste. By 2009, 60% (by weight) of packaging waste is to be recovered and 55–80% recycled (including 60% of glass, 60% of paper and board, 50% of metals, 15% of wood and 22.5% of plastics).

5.18.7 Landfill tax

In 1996, the government introduced a tax on waste going to landfill (see the Finance Act 1996, the Landfill Tax Regulations 1996, the Landfill Tax (Qualifying Materials) Order 1996 and the Landfill Tax (Contaminated Land) Order 1996). The landfill tax reflects the government's principal aim, namely the reduction of waste by taxing waste going to landfill. Landfilled 'active' waste (for example, organic methane producing waste) currently attracts a tax of currently £15 a tonne, whilst 'inactive' waste (for example, construction waste) is taxed at £2 a tonne. Certain wastes are exempt. The tax is paid by landfill companies who pass on the tax, collected via landfill gate fees, charged to waste producers and carriers.

There is some evidence that the introduction of the tax has led to an increase in fly-tipping and diversion of inert or inactive wastes to activities which are exempt, such as landscaping.

The creation of a Landfill Tax Credit Scheme enables landfill operators to claim a tax credit for any payments they make to approved environmental organisations. Environmental projects which have been approved under the scheme include amenity improvement schemes, sustainable management education projects, and reclamation and restoration of contaminated land.

The Landfill Tax (Amendment) Regulations 2003 (SI 2003/605) are now in force. The Regulations reduce the level of credit given to landfill operators regarding the contributions they make to approved bodies for environmental purposes. Landfill Tax Credit is reduced from 20% to 6%.

5.19   WASTE PLANNING

5.19.1 Waste disposal plans and the national waste strategy

Section 99 of the EA 1995 places specific responsibility upon the Secretary of State to produce a national waste strategy complying with the Waste Framework Directive (75/442/EEC). The Directive imposes an obligation on Member States to produce a national waste plan. Prior to the introduction of the EA 1995, it was originally planned that this would be done through the duty of local authorities to prepare waste disposal plans (s 50 of the EPA 1990). Section 50 of the EPA 1990 required each WRA to prepare a waste disposal plan. In order to do this, the WRAs were required to carry out an investigation to decide what arrangements were needed for treating or disposing of controlled (directive) waste within their area so as to prevent or minimise pollution of the environment or harm to human health. Waste disposal plans had to specify the kinds and quantities of controlled (directive) waste the WRA expected to find in its area, or to be transported in or out of the area; methods of disposal; licensing policy; the sites and disposal methods in use and expected to come into use; and the expected costs, for the period of the plan. The WRA was also under a duty to have regard to the desirability, where reasonably practicable, of giving priority to recycling waste. Section 50 was repealed by the EA 1995 and replaced by the national waste strategy (s 44A of the EPA 1990 and see 5.18.1 above).

Despite the demise of waste disposal plans, waste recycling plans continue to be of relevance.

5.19.2 Development control, development plans and the waste local plan

The town and country planning system controls the geographical siting of all waste management sites. A planning permission (licence) must be obtained to authorise the use of land for waste management activities (s 55 of the Town and Country Planning Act (TCPA) 1990 and s 36(2) of the EPA 1990).

Local authorities are responsible for much of the administration of the planning system. The decision (often referred to as 'development control') to grant planning permission for a waste management site is the responsibility of the County Planning Authority (or metropolitan or unitary authority) (see Sched 1 to the TCPA 1990). Planning permission is required to 'develop' land. 'Development' is defined in s 55(1) of the TCPA 1990 and includes both 'operational' development (for example, building a waste incinerator) and a 'material change of use' of land (for example, using a redundant quarry as a landfill site). Section 55(3)(b) provides that 'development' includes the deposit of refuse or waste materials on land if (i) the area of the deposit is extended, or (ii) the height of the deposit is extended and exceeds the level of the land adjoining the site. Such activities constitute a material change of use (as does a change in the waste disposal operations carried out on the site; see *Roberts v Vale District Council* (1997) and *Northavon District Council v Secretary of State for the Environment* (1980)).

The decision whether to grant or refuse a planning application for a new waste incinerator, landfill site or waste transfer station will be taken by the County Planning Authority (or metropolitan or unitary authority) on the basis of the policies contained in the relevant development plan and any material considerations (which include government policy guidance contained in planning policy notes PPG 10 (*Planning and Waste Management*) and PPG 23 (*Planning and Pollution Control*), the national waste strategy, and the Art 4 objectives of the Waste Framework Directive). The content of policies contained in the development plan will, in the light of s 54A of the TCPA 1990, have an important effect on the outcome of the application. Development plans will include policies concerning waste-related developments.

The waste policies which are relevant to a planning application for a landfill or other waste site may be scattered amongst a range of documents. In those parts of the country where the main local authority administrative unit is the county, the relevant waste policies will be found in the County Structure Plan, the Waste Local Plan (prepared by local authority district councils) or a combined minerals and waste plan. In metropolitan areas, the structure plan and local plan are combined into a unitary plan.

The General Permitted Development Order (GPDO) 1995 authorises planning permission for some categories of mining-related waste management activity. For example, Class C, Pt 20 of the GPDO 1995 authorises the construction of waste tips at coal mines. Additional controls apply to such waste tips (see the Mines and Quarries (Tips) Act 1969 and the Quarries Regulations 1999).

Any conditions attached to a waste-related planning permission should only be imposed for a planning purpose such as access to the site, restoration of the site after closure (especially gas and leachate monitoring), the extent of tipping, the phasing of operations, adverse impacts of the proposed development on adjoining land uses (odour, litter, dust, vermin, birds, visual impact, vehicle movements, hours of operation, contamination of groundwater and gas disposal via flare) and future land uses in the area ('blight' deterring future development proposals). Conditions should not be imposed which duplicate the operational conditions the Environment Agency may choose to impose when determining a waste management licensing application for the same site (see PPG 23). Typically, such conditions relating to operational matters include the duration of the waste management activities on the site, the types of wastes which are to be tipped and record keeping.

County planning authorities are required by s 38 of the TCPA 1990, as amended, to prepare a waste local plan or, at least, to combine a waste local plan with a minerals local plan. The waste local plan addresses the land use implications of the authority's waste policies. Therefore, it deals with issues such as the need for sites and waste facilities and where these should be located, having regard to geological and hydrological considerations. The waste local plan should not be confused with the now defunct local authority waste disposal plan.

Once granted, planning permission (including conditions) cannot be withdrawn unless compensation is paid to the landowner, and the permission continues to attach to and benefit the land even if ownership changes. In contrast, waste management licences are personal to the licence holder and may only be transferred with the Environment Agency's consent (s 40 of the EPA 1990).

5.19.3 Waste recycling policy and waste recycling plans

In 1990, the government set targets for the recycling of household waste (25% of household waste) to be met by the year 2000. However, according to government statistics, the current average recycling rate for household waste is just under 6%. Although s 49 of the EPA 1990 requires WCAs to prepare recycling plans to ensure that government targets are met, very few local authority recycling targets have been met.

Waste recycling is largely the responsibility of the WCAs, although the WDAs have certain powers and duties in this regard. The main provisions relating to recycling are contained in the following sections of the EPA 1990:

(a) s 49 – WCAs are under a duty to investigate what arrangements can practicably be made for recycling household and commercial waste. They must prepare a waste recycling plan and keep it under review;

(b) s 46(2) – WCAs can require household waste to be placed in separate receptacles if certain wastes are going to be recycled (multi-bin schemes and kerbside collection);

(c) s 52 – a system of recycling credits to encourage recycling was introduced.

Each WCA is required by s 49 to prepare a waste recycling plan. The WCA in preparing the plan has to consider the effect that recycling proposals will have on the amenities in the locality and also the likely cost or saving (benefit) to the authority. A copy of the plan should be made available for the public to inspect.

5.20   THE INTERFACE BETWEEN THE WASTE MANAGEMENT REGIME AND OTHER REGULATORY POLLUTION CONTROLS

5.20.1 IPC

The recovery or disposal of directive waste, providing it forms an integral part of an IPC licensed process, is exempt from the need to obtain a waste management licence (reg 16(1)(a) of the Waste Management Regulations 1994). Section 28(1) of the EPA 1990 provides that it is not possible to include a condition in an IPC authorisation regulating the final disposal of directive waste in or on land.

5.20.2 IPPC

The IPPC Directive introduces integrated controls over waste disposal sites, such as landfill sites with effect from 2007. Approximately 900 large landfill sites (that is, those capable of accepting over 710 tonnes of waste per day and with a total capacity of over 25,000 tonnes) fall within the IPPC regime. The smaller landfills continue to be controlled under the waste management licensing provisions of Pt II of the EPA 1990 until such time as the government transfers regulatory control to a simplified version of IPPC. All waste management installations which are subject to IPPC will also be subject to the requirements of the EC Waste Framework Directive and therefore operators of IPPC licensed waste management installations must be fit and proper persons in order to be granted an IPPC permit.

5.20.3 Water pollution

Liquid effluent is not waste which falls to be regulated by the waste management licensing regime in Pt II of the EPA 1990 and the Waste Management Licensing Regulations 1994. Waste in liquid form is controlled by a combination of the Water Resources Act 1991, the Water Industry Act 1991, the Urban Waste Water Treatment Directive (91/271/EEC) and the Urban Waste Water Treatment (England and Wales) Regulations 1994.

With regard to the threat of groundwater pollution from waste disposed of (but not waste recovery activities) to landfill, reg 15 of the Waste Management Licensing Regulations 1994 provides that a waste management licence will only be granted if the Environment Agency is satisfied that adequate measures exist to prevent pollution of groundwaters by the substances listed in List I and II of the Groundwater Directive (80/68/EEC). In such circumstances, the landfill site will be exempt from the Groundwater Regulations 1998.

5.20.4 Contaminated land

The contaminated land remediation notice procedure does not apply (see s 78YB(3) of the EPA 1990) where contamination results from an illegal deposit of waste (for example, an illegal deposit of waste in an unlicensed landfill rather than contamination caused by pollutants escaping from an underground storage tank) and the power to require the removal of the waste is available to the Environment Agency under s 59 of the EPA 1990.

5.20.5 Town and country planning

Before the Environment Agency can issue a waste management licence, it must be satisfied that the waste management operation has planning permission (s 36(2) of the EPA 1990). The applicant will need to demonstrate that either he or she has a full planning permission certificate of lawful use or development or an established use certificate.

5.20.6 Statutory nuisance

Statutory nuisances may arise in relation to waste in two instances. The deposit of controlled (directive) waste could amount to an accumulation, prejudicial to health or a nuisance under s 79(1)(e) of the EPA 1990. Alternatively, the resultant smell from the waste could, if prejudicial to health or a nuisance, constitute a statutory nuisance under s 79(1)(d).

5.20.7 The Planning (Hazardous Substances) Act 1990

Additional controls are available under the Planning (Hazardous Substances) Act 1990. Prior to the introduction of the 1990 Act, the control of developments under the town and country planning regime could exert little control over the use of hazardous substances in developments. It was possible for factories and manufacturers to introduce new hazardous products and uses without requiring the need for further planning consent.

The Planning (Hazardous Substances) Act 1990, which was brought into force on 1 June 1992, requires that the keeping of any hazardous substance on, over or under land, beyond small quantities, will require the consent of the Hazardous Substances Authority (usually the London boroughs, the district councils in metropolitan counties and the district planning authorities elsewhere). Before a 'hazardous substances consent' is granted, the Hazardous Substances Authorities consider whether the proposed storage or use of a hazardous substance is appropriate in a given location.

5.21 THE DUTY OF CARE

One of the most significant features of the EPA 1990 was the introduction of a statutory duty of care (on 1 April 1992) in relation to the handling of waste. In its 11th Report, *Managing Waste: The Duty of Care* (1985), the Royal Commission on Environmental Pollution recommended that a duty of care be placed on everybody involved in the waste chain establishing 'cradle to grave' responsibility for the waste:

> The producer [of waste] incurs a duty of care which is owed to society, and we would like to see this duty reflected in public attitudes and enshrined in legislation and codes of practice.

The objective of s 34 of the EPA 1990 is to ensure that all persons in the waste chain who produce, handle, treat or dispose of directive waste take reasonable steps to:

(a) store the waste properly;

(b) package the waste in adequate packaging or containers;

(c) describe the contents of packaged or containerised waste properly so that the next person in the waste chain can handle it safely;

(d) hand the waste over only to an authorised person;

(e) complete a waste transfer note recording details of the consignment of the waste to the next person in the waste chain;

(f) check that the waste is properly disposed of.

Thus, every person in the waste chain, from waste producer to final waste disposer, is obliged to act responsibly with regard to waste, especially at the point when the waste is handed over (consigned) to the next person in the waste chain. The s 34 duty of care creates statutory 'cradle to grave' responsibility for waste.

Failure to observe the s 34 duty is a criminal offence (s 34(6)). This offence is a 'relevant offence' for the purpose of ascertaining who is a fit and proper person to operate a waste management facility and hold a waste management licence.

The duty of care is set out in s 34 of the EPA 1990 and is supplemented by regulations made under s 34(5), the Environmental Protection (Duty of Care) Regulations 1991 (SI 1991/2839), as amended, and official guidance in the form of a code of practice. The code of practice, initially issued in 1991, was revised in 1996 to take account of the revised statutory definition of waste and the extension of the duty of care to scrap metal facilities. Any person who fails to comply with the duty imposed by s 34 or with the Regulations commits a criminal offence (s 34(6)). It is not necessary for any environmental damage to have been caused for there to be a breach of s 34. All that is required is that there has been a breach of the duty. There is no statutory provision allowing for a civil action where damages have been caused as a result of a breach of s 34. On summary conviction in a magistrates' court, a breach of the duty of care can lead to a maximum fine of £5,000 or, on indictment (in the Crown Court), an unlimited fine.

According to the code of practice, the duty of care is designed 'to be an essentially self-regulating system which is based on good business practice'. For example, the code states that if a waste holder is certain that waste he or she handles is being wrongly managed by another person, then he or she should, at first instance, refuse to deal with that other person (for example, refuse to transfer waste to that person). The code goes on to say that it may not always be possible to take such a course of action, and that, if appropriate, a person should bring the matter to the attention of the Environment Agency.

Section 34 creates a form of self-regulation underpinned by the criminal law sanction of a s 34(6) prosecution. Any waste producer, broker or waste holder who transfers waste to a 'dodgy' waste carrier who undercuts the going rate charged by legitimate carriers for waste carriage may not only face prosecution for breach of the duty of care (s 34(6)), but also prosecution for knowingly causing the deposit of waste (s 33) if the waste carrier illegally deposits (fly-tips) the waste on an unlicensed site. Furthermore, civil liability may also be incurred with regard to damage caused by the illegal deposit of waste (s 73(6)).

5.21.1 The duty applies to waste holders

Section 34(1) of the EPA 1990 applies to any person who imports, produces, carries, keeps, treats or disposes of controlled (directive) waste or, as a broker, has control of such waste. Essentially, this means any person in the waste chain from producer to final disposer. (DoE Circular 19/91 uses the shorthand term 'waste holder' to refer to all persons who are subject to the duty.) Section 34(2) provides the only exception to the duty: occupiers of domestic premises who produce household waste on their property.

A waste broker is a person who may exercise control over waste, but may not necessarily hold it (such as an environmental consultant). For the purposes of the duty, he or she can be considered as sharing responsibility for any transfer of waste that he or she arranges with the actual parties who effect the transfer.

Regulation 20 of the Waste Management Regulations 1994 brings waste brokers and waste dealers within the waste management regulatory regime. Waste brokers and waste dealers must register with the Environment Agency and failure to do so constitutes a criminal offence (reg 20). The Environment Agency has a discretion to refuse registration based on the applicant's previous record of relevant offences.

Holders of waste management licences, discharge consent licences, WCAs, WDAs, registered charitable and voluntary waste carriers are exempt.

5.21.2 What does the duty of care involve?

Any person bound by the duty must:

> ... take all such measures applicable to him in that capacity as are reasonable in the circumstances:
>
> (a) to prevent any other person committing the offences in s 33;
>
> (b) to prevent the escape of the waste from his control or that of any other person;
>
> (c) to ensure that if the waste is transferred, it is transferred only to an 'authorised person' or to a person 'for authorised transport purposes'; and
>
> (d) when waste is transferred, to make sure that it is accompanied by a written description of the waste which will enable other persons to avoid a contravention of s 33 of the Act and to comply with the duty under s 34(1)(b) to prevent the escape of waste.

5.21.3 Elements of the duty of care

5.21.3.1 *To take all such measures applicable to him in that capacity as are reasonable in the circumstances*

Section 34(1) requires any person to whom the duty applies to take 'all such measures as are applicable to him in that capacity as are reasonable in the circumstances' to avoid a breach of the statutory duty.

This requirement limits the duty of care in two respects. First, waste holders are only required to take all measures that are applicable to them in their respective capacities. Second, such measures need to be reasonable in the particular circumstances. The responsibility of the individual waste holder is limited and the duty is a subjective one and depends in part upon the holder's relationship to the waste.

The extent of the waste holder's responsibility under s 34(1) will vary with the capacity of the waste holder and extent of control the waste holder has over the waste. The waste holder will therefore be expected to take different measures to comply with the duty of care varying with his capacity as a waste producer, importer, carrier, keeper, treater, disposer, dealer, or broker. For example, the waste producer will bear primary responsibility for ensuring that the waste is accurately described.

A waste holder is also only expected to take measures that are reasonable in the circumstances. It is here that the code of practice is of importance, since it provides guidance for waste holders on the measures that are reasonable in different circumstances. The circumstances which affect what is reasonable will include:

(a) what the waste is;

(b) the dangers it presents in handling and treatment;

(c) how it is dealt with;

(d) what the holder might reasonably be expected to know or foresee.

5.21.3.2 *To prevent any other person committing offences under s 33*

The first element of s 34 comprises a duty to prevent any other person committing offences under s 33. A waste holder must not only take steps to ensure that he or she does not breach s 33, but he or she must take reasonable steps to ensure that any other person who has control of his or her waste does not breach s 33. For example, a waste producer's s 34 responsibilities do not end with the transfer of the waste to a waste carrier. Not only must the waste producer check the waste carrier's credentials (carrier's registration certificate), but it is also the waste producer's responsibility to ensure that the waste arrives at the waste management site specified in the transfer documentation.

The code of practice advises waste transferors (consignors) to halt any waste transfer if the waste holder suspects that the waste will not be dealt with properly if handed over to the consignee. Such a situation might arise if a waste carrier arrives at the consignor's premises, very soon after carrying away an initial load of waste, to load up for a second time and arousing the consignor's suspicions that the first consignment of waste has been illegally disposed of (fly-tipped). The waste holder must act responsibly, as judged by an objective (reasonable man) standard, having regard to the waste holder's resources and knowledge. In the circumstances outlined above, the waste holder should first check the position with the waste carrier and, if the explanation given is unsatisfactory, inform the Environment Agency. Higher standards will be expected of the big waste operators in view of their greater resources. Clearly, it is for the waste holder to draw up a contract with a carrier/waste manager which incorporates provisions that enable the waste producer periodically to check the site (for example, a waste transfer station site), check that records and transfer notes are being kept and allow for termination of the contract in the event of the waste manager losing his or her licence. The contract should require the waste disposal contractor to comply with all of the relevant laws and licence requirements and should ideally cover matters of liability, ownership of the waste, insurance and indemnities against liability. In practice, many arrangements are made without any written contract or are made by means of a standard contract which does not adequately cover all of the important issues.

The code of practice provides practical advice on complying with this element of the duty. However, it should be emphasised that compliance with the code does not ensure that the duty of care is being complied with.

5.21.3.3 *To prevent the escape of waste from his control or that of any other person*

In order to prevent the escape of waste, producers of waste should label it properly and package it in such a way as to prevent escape and leakage whilst on site, in transit or in storage. Consideration should also be given to preventing any escape in subsequent transfer or transfers and up to the final treatment or disposal. Since escape can occur in a variety of circumstances, care will need to be taken to address all possibilities. For example, escape may occur where there is a spillage or where containers have been overfilled; it can occur when adverse weather conditions result in waste being blown away or washed down storm drains. Vandals may cause waste to escape, hence the need for adequate security as well as containerisation. The waste producer, in particular, should take into account the time it will take for the waste to reach its final destination and the mode in which it will be carried or stored at a waste transfer station. Containerisation should be adequate for all of these different situations. For example, black bin bags will almost certainly be inadequate. The suitability of packaging is particularly important where the wastes include flammable or corrosive substances.

5.21.3.4 To transfer the waste only to authorised persons and for authorised transport purposes

To comply with the duty of care, it is also essential to ensure that waste is only transferred to authorised persons or to a person for authorised transport purposes. These are defined respectively in s 34(3) and (4) of the EPA 1990.

Section 34(3) states that the following are authorised persons:

(a) a WCA;

(b) a holder of a waste management licence;

(c) persons exempted by regulations made by the Secretary of State under s 33(3);

(d) a registered carrier (registered under s 2 of the Control of Pollution (Amendment) Act 1989);

(e) any person not required to be registered under the Control of Pollution (Amendment) Act 1989.

Transferors of waste should make sure that they are only transferring their waste to an authorised person. If waste is being transferred to a carrier, then the carrier must be registered under the Control of Pollution (Amendment) Act 1989. Subject to limited exceptions (prescribed in the Controlled Waste (Registration of Carriers and Seizure of Vehicles) Regulations 1991 and 1998 (SI 1991/1624 and SI 1998/605)), any person carrying waste in the course of a waste transport business, or in any other way for profit, must be registered with the Environment Agency. It is an offence under s 1(1) of the 1989 Act to carry controlled (directive) waste without registering with the Environment Agency as a waste carrier. The offence may only be dealt with summarily in the magistrates' court and the maximum penalty is a £5,000 fine. Anyone intending to transfer waste to a carrier should check that the person is registered (or exempt from the need to register) with the Environment Agency. The Environment Agency maintains a register of waste carriers which is open to public inspection. It is necessary for the person handing over the waste to a carrier to check the actual certificate of registration since photocopies are not proof of registration (official duplicates of the original certificate are available from the Environment Agency). Moreover, the transferor should also carry out regular checks to ensure that the registration has not lapsed (for example, due to revocation).

5.21.3.5 Exemptions

Under reg 2 of the Registration of Carriers (Seizure of Vehicles) Regulations 1991, exemptions are granted to a variety of waste carriers including:

(a) a waste producer who uses its own vehicles to transport waste (except demolition and construction waste);

(b) local authorities, charities, and voluntary groups.

The 1989 Act and 1991 Regulations are targeted at carriers who transport waste as a commercial venture. Therefore, the incidental carriage of waste, on a non-profit basis, by private individuals falls outside the ambit of the legislation.

5.21.3.6 Rejection of registration applications

The Environment Agency may refuse to register any applicant whom it believes not to be a desirable carrier. A carrier will not be desirable if:

(a) the carrier, or a person closely connected with the carrier, has been convicted of a relevant offence (listed in Sched 1 to the 1991 Regulations); and

(b) the Environment Agency considers it undesirable that the carrier be authorised to carry controlled (directive) waste (reg 5).

The provisions of the Rehabilitation of Offenders Act 1974 apply to any 'spent' relevant offence.

5.21.3.7 Revocation

The Environment Agency may revoke a carrier's registration certificate where the carrier ceases to be a desirable carrier (reg 10), for example, a carrier who is convicted of a 'relevant offence', such as illegally fly-tipping waste contrary to s 33(5) of the EPA 1990.

5.21.3.8 Appeals

There is a right of appeal to the Secretary of State against a refusal to grant a carriers' registration certificate (licence) or regarding the Environment Agency's decision to revoke an existing registration certificate.

5.21.3.9 Renewal and surrender

Waste carriers' licences (certificate of registration) are of three years' duration and must be renewed if the carrier wishes to operate lawfully. A carrier may surrender its registration certificate at any time.

5.21.3.10 Stop and search

Section 5(1) empowers both the Environment Agency and the police to stop and search vehicles which are reasonably believed to be transporting waste but which are not covered by a waste carriers' registration certificate.

5.21.3.11 Authorised transport purposes

Section 34(4) lists the following as authorised transport purposes:

(a) the transport of controlled (directive) waste within the same premises and between different places in those premises;

(b) the transport to a place in Great Britain of controlled (directive) waste which has been brought from a country or territory outside Great Britain not having been landed in Great Britain until it arrives at that place;

(c) the transport by air or sea of controlled (directive) waste from a place inside Great Britain to a place outside Great Britain.

5.21.3.12 The written description

Waste producers are responsible for ensuring that, when they transfer waste, the waste is accompanied by an adequate written description. This description should provide sufficient information to enable all persons who might foreseeably come into contact with the waste to ensure that they can handle the waste safely. The description must be sufficient to ensure that other waste holders in the waste chain can avoid committing offences under s 33. The level of detail necessary in the transfer note will vary with the properties of the waste.

The Environmental Protection (Duty of Care) Regulations 1991 (made under s 34(5)), which came into force on 1 April 1992, established a system of transfer notes and record keeping of waste transfers to help waste holders comply with this element of the duty of care. However, the transfer note does not necessarily provide the full written description. Neither does the transfer note have to accompany the waste, although it is safer if it does so. The Regulations place responsibilities on the transferor and transferee of waste to keep detailed records of all waste transfers. On completion of the transfer of waste, both the transferor and transferee must complete and sign a transfer note. The transfer note provisions contained in these Regulations do not apply, by virtue of reg 2(3), to transfers of special waste where a consignment note system operates. (The consignment note system is described in more detail below.) Under the Regulations, a transfer note must include details of the following:

(a) identification of the waste;

(b) quantity;

(c) whether it is loose or in a container at time of transfer;

(d) place and time of transfer;

(e) name and address of both the transferor and transferee;

(f) whether the transferor is the producer or importer;

(g) if the transferee is authorised for transport purposes.

All parties involved in the transfer must keep a copy of the transfer note and the written description for at least two years. The Environment Agency may serve a notice demanding copies of transfer notes and these must be supplied within seven days. While all transfers of waste must be documented, the Regulations do not require each individual transfer to be separately documented. It is possible for a single transfer to cover multiple consignments transferred at the same time or over a period not exceeding a year. However, this can only apply where the description is provided before the first consignment and all the other consignments covered by the note are the same.

5.21.4 The consignment note system for special waste

The Control of Pollution (Special Waste) Regulations 1980 introduced a detailed consignment note system in relation to special waste. This system remains but it has been slightly simplified by the Special Waste Regulations 1996. The purpose of the consignment note system is to enable the Environment Agency to control and monitor the movements of special waste, through a system of pre-notification and transfer documentation, enabling control of special waste at every stage, from production to final disposal. The consignment note system also fulfils the requirements of the duty of care in respect of special waste. Therefore, only one set of documentation is required.

5.21.4.1 Pre-notification

The Special Waste Regulations 1996 provide for a mandatory system of consignment notes which must be prepared by the producer of special waste *before the waste may be removed* from the premises at which it is produced. Producers of special waste are under a statutory duty to comply with the consignment note procedure.

The 1996 Regulations provide for three different procedures:

(a) the standard procedure;

(b) the procedure for repeat shipments of the same waste;

(c) the procedure for a carrier's round.

Regulation 4 of the 1996 Regulations introduces a system of coding of consignment notes. The Environment Agency is required to supply, to any person who requests, or to a carrier, a code which will be used in relation to the consignment of waste. The code may consist of letters, numbers, or symbols or even a barcode which would enable the consignment or carriers to be identified electronically. When the Environment Agency assigns a code, there is a fee to pay (unless the consignment consists entirely of lead acid motor vehicle batteries, in which case the fee is reduced).

5.21.4.2 The standard procedure

The 1996 Regulations require five copies of a standard form, known as the consignment note to be prepared by the special waste producer:

(a) the producer must complete Pts A and B on each of the copies. The producer will give full details of the nature of the waste and the consignment. The producer will also use the code provided by the Environment Agency;

(b) the producer must send one copy to the Environment Agency in whose area the waste is to be disposed of. The note must be sent not more than one month and not less than three working days before the waste is moved;

(c) the waste carrier completes Pt C on each of the remaining four copies. The carrier has to certify that the waste has been collected and also that the details provided by the producer in Pts A and B are correct;

(d) the waste producer must then fill in Pt D on each of the remaining four copies. The producer certifies that the waste carrier is either a registered carrier or is exempt from registration;

(e) the waste producer then has to keep one of the four copies on a register. The producer is required to keep records of consignment notes for at least three years;

(f) the waste carrier takes the remaining three copies and these travel with the consignment of special waste;

(g) when the waste is delivered, the waste carrier gives the operator of the disposal site (known as the consignee) the three copies. The consignee then has to complete Pt E on each of the three copies, certifying that the consignee is licensed to receive the waste. The consignee retains one copy on a register. The register is maintained until the licence is surrendered;

(h) the consignee returns one copy to the waste carrier who must also retain this copy on a register for a period of at least three years;

(i) the remaining copy is sent to the Environment Agency.

Thus, it can be seen from these requirements that a record of all the waste transfers is retained and that the Environment Agency can keep track of all special waste movements. A simplified procedure operates in instances where several identical consignments of waste are sent from the same waste producer to the same disposal site over a period of 12 months.

5.21.4.3 *Procedure for a carrier's round*

In addition, there is an alternative procedure where the same waste carrier regularly collects similar consignments of waste from a series of different waste producers over a period of 12 months. This only operates where the waste carrier takes the waste to the same disposal or recycling facility. The intention of this alternative procedure is clearly to reduce the amount of paperwork that the carrier has to complete.

5.21.5 The code of practice

In 1991, the Secretary of State issued a code of practice which provided practical guidance on how to discharge the duty of care (*Waste Management, The Duty of Care, A Code of Practice*). The 1991 code was replaced with a new code in 1996. The code recommends a series of steps which would normally be enough to satisfy the requirements of the duty. Its importance, however, is reflected in the fact that, by virtue of s 34(10), the code of practice shall be admissible in evidence and, if any provision of the code appears to the court to be relevant to any question arising in the proceedings, it shall be taken into account in determining that question. It is therefore important that all those who are subject to the duty of care are familiar with the code. The code is not law but ranks as important administrative guidance.

5.21.6 Breach of the duty of care

Any person who fails to comply with the duty of care, or the documentation requirements laid down in the Environment Protection (Duty of Care) Regulations 1991, commits a criminal offence and will be liable, on summary conviction (in a magistrates' court) to a fine not exceeding £5,000. On indictment, the Crown Court can impose an unlimited fine. Once again, directors and senior management may be personally liable for a breach of s 34. It is therefore in the interests of management to ensure that adequate training programmes and systems are in place to ensure that all relevant staff understand the requirements of the duty of care at all times.

Finally, breach of the duty of care could result in a person being deemed not to be a fit and proper person for the purposes of obtaining, maintaining or revoking a waste management licence.

5.21.7 Civil liability

It has already been noted that the EPA 1990 (under s 73(6)) provides a statutory civil remedy for any person who has suffered damages as a consequence of another person's breach of s 33. However, no such statutory remedy exists in relation to a breach of the duty of care. Damages may be available through common law actions such as nuisance (see Chapter 11).

5.21.7.1 EC Directive on Civil Liability for Damage Caused by Waste

Although the duty of care as currently defined does not apply strict liability to waste producers, it may be amended in the future, should the proposed EC Directive on Civil Liability for Damage Caused by Waste be adopted. This Directive will radically alter the current liability of waste producers and waste controllers (that is, anyone who handles waste). The Directive, if adopted in its current form, will make a producer or controller of waste liable under civil law for damage or injury caused by the waste, irrespective of fault on their part. In addition, the draft Directive also contains proposals concerning liabilities arising out of co-disposal (see COM(89)282, COM(91)219).

5.22   FURTHER INFORMATION

Further reading

See Chapter 4 of *Sourcebook on Environmental Law*, 2nd edn, 2001, Cavendish Publishing. The chapter contains important sections from the EPA 1990, case reports relating to *Celtic Extraction Ltd, Shanks & McEwan v Environment Agency, Mayer Parry Recycling Ltd v Environment Agency*, the government's Waste Strategy 2000, the definition of waste, EC Directives (Landfill, Packaging Waste, Waste Shipments, Hazardous Waste and Waste Framework) and international conventions (the BASEL Convention (and Protocol) on Transboundary Movements of Hazardous Wastes).

Abbot, C, 'Waste management licensing: benefit or burden?' [2000] JPL 1003.

Bates, J, *UK Waste Law*, 2nd edn, 1997, Sweet & Maxwell.

Cheyne, I and Purdue, M, 'Fitting definition to purpose: the search for a satisfactory definition of waste' [1995] JEL 149.

Commission of the European Communities, *Strategy for Waste Management*, 1989, CEC(89)934.

Department of the Environment, *Planning, Pollution, and Waste Management*, 1992, DoE.

Department of the Environment, *Packaging Waste*, 1998, DoE.

Department of the Environment, *Waste Strategy for England and Wales 2000*, Cm 4693, 2000, The Stationery Office.

Department of the Environment Waste Management Papers (especially Waste Management Paper 4 – *Licensing of Waste Management Facilities*, 1994, and 26B, *Landfill Design, Construction and Operational Practice*, 1995).

DETR, *Limiting Landfill*, 1999.

Fluck, J, 'The term "waste" in EU law' [1994] EELR 79.

Garbutt, J, *Waste Management Law: A Practical Handbook*, 2nd edn, 1995, Wiley.

Harris, R, 'The Environmental Protection Act 1990 – penalising the polluter' [1992] JPL 515.

House of Commons Environment Select Committee (1988–89 Session), *Hazardous Waste Disposal*, HMSO (see also government response to the House of Commons Select Committee Report, Cmnd 679).

House of Lords Select Committee on Science and Technology (1988–89 Session), *Hazardous Waste Disposal*, 4th Report, HMSO.

House of Lords Select Committee on the European Communities (1997–98 Session), *Sustainable Landfill*, HL Paper 73, HMSO.

House of Lords Select Committee on the European Communities (1998–99 Session), *Waste Incineration*, 11th Report, The Stationery Office.

Kitson, A and Harris, R, 'A burning issue: planning controls, pollution controls and waste incineration' [1994] JPL 3.

Laurence, D, *Waste Regulation Law*, 2000, Butterworths.

Parpworth, N, 'The draft EC Landfill Directive' [1999] JPL 4.

Pocklington, D, *The Law of Waste Management*, 1997, Shaw and Sons.

Pocklington, D, 'The utility of the concept of waste' (1996) Env Liability 94.

Pocklington, D, 'Waste holder liability' [1996] ELM 101.

Purdue, M and van Rossem, A, 'The distinction between using secondary raw materials and the recovery of waste: the directive definition of "waste"' [1998] JEL 116.

Royal Commission on Environmental Pollution, *Incineration of Waste*, 17th Report, Cm 2181, 1993.

Royal Commission on Environmental Pollution, *Managing Waste: The Duty of Care*, 11th Report, Cmnd 9675, 1985.

Salter, J, 'The meaning of waste in European Community law' (1997) EELR 14.

Smith, J, 'The challenges of environmentally sound and efficient regulation of waste' [1993] JEL 91.

Tromans, S, 'The difficulties of enforcing waste disposal licence conditions' [1991] JEL 281.

Tromans, S, 'EC waste law – a complete mess?' [2001] JEL 133.

Vaughan, D, *Environment and Planning Law*, 1991, Butterworths.

Wilkinson, D, 'Time to discard the concept of waste?' [1999] Env LR 172.

CHAPTER 6

INTEGRATED POLLUTION CONTROL AND INTEGRATED POLLUTION PREVENTION AND CONTROL

6.1 INTRODUCTION

Integrated Pollution Control (IPC) and Integrated Pollution Prevention and Control (IPPC) are typical Command and Control regulatory regimes in that they use 'licensing' as the primary pollution control mechanism. They differ from other regulatory regimes in that they are designed to control polluting discharges from a relatively narrow range of highly polluting industries. In contrast to the single environmental medium focus of the water pollution controls contained in the Water Resources Act (WRA) 1991 and the waste management controls contained in Pt II of the Environmental Protection Act (EPA) 1990, the IPC and IPPC regimes are designed to regulate polluting emissions, discharged by industrial processes, into *all three environmental media* (air, water and land). Thus, industrial sites subject to IPC or IPPC generally require only one licence authorising all polluting discharges from that site. IPC and IPPC are 'one stop shops' and it is not necessary for the site operator to obtain separate licences in respect of polluting discharges to water, air and land from the regulators who police each of those statutory regimes. IPC and IPPC adopt an *holistic* perspective, paying attention to the polluting impacts of the emissions discharged by industries into the environment as a whole. Any licence issued under the IPC regime will only authorise discharges into the environmental media (air, water or land) which cause the least damage to the environment. This is the 'best practicable environmental option' (BPEO) principle which guides IPC regulatory decision making in respect of sites which are discharging pollutants into more than one environmental medium. The BPEO principle is not specifically referred to in the IPPC controls, but its influence has helped shape the contours of the IPPC controls.

IPC regulates a range of polluting processes (fuel and power, chemicals, minerals, metals, waste disposal and miscellaneous industries such as paper mills) and polluting substances (such as sulphur dioxide and carbon dioxide emissions into air, DDT and mercury discharges to controlled waters, and solvents discharged onto land). Several processes which require authorisation under the IPC regime may be carried on from the same premises. Whilst IPC focuses on the control of polluting emissions into the three environmental media, IPPC is concerned with a wider range of environmental impacts caused by the operation of predominantly industrial installations. The focus of IPPC extends beyond polluting emissions and includes energy use and efficiency, raw material usage, waste minimisation, noise, vibration, heat effects and accident prevention measures.

The IPC regime had only been in existence for some six years when, as a result of European Community (EC) legislation, it began to be superseded by the new IPPC regime in the late 1990s. The IPPC regime, introduced in the UK by the Pollution Prevention and Control Act (PPCA) 1999 to implement the Integrated Pollution and Control Directive (96/61/EC), is intended to replace IPC controls by 2007. Consequently, it is necessary to understand how both regulatory regimes function. Many businesses will continue to be regulated by the IPC regime for some time to come but new businesses, and substantial changes to existing businesses, will, in many cases, be immediately subject to IPPC controls. The first part of this chapter will examine the existing IPC regime as it effects some 1,800 *industrial* processes. The new IPPC regime will be examined towards the end of this chapter.

6.2 THE DEVELOPMENT OF AN INTEGRATED APPROACH TO POLLUTION CONTROL

The historical development of IPC has its roots in the Industrial Revolution. The creation of the Alkali Inspectorate, by the Alkali Act 1863, was the first attempt to regulate the toxic byproducts of the emergent chemical industry. This regime addressed, somewhat ineffectively, only one aspect of the pollution problems associated with industrial production. Meanwhile, smoke and other pollutants were being pumped into the atmosphere at an alarming and unregulated rate.

From the 19th century to well into the 20th century, the standard UK response to pollution problems was to create separate regulatory regimes to deal with problems reactively, as and when they arose. This created a complicated and fragmented jigsaw of overlapping regulatory regimes. Regulated industries experienced difficulties in keeping abreast of the different investigatory and enforcement powers available to the various regulatory authorities. One of the most significant drawbacks of this reactive and piecemeal approach to pollution control was the failure to focus on the environment as a whole. A more sanction orientated enforcement policy by one regulator might have the undesired effect of encouraging businesses to divert their wastes into less tightly regulated environmental media. This situation was not helped by the absence of environmental quality standards which could provide benchmarks in regard to which the terms of Command and Control licences could be set. Regulatory regimes had an 'end of pipe' focus which took a very narrow view of the impact of environmental pollution on the environment. The 'environment' was essentially the environmental media (air, water and land) into which pollutants were discharged and regulated by the particular regulatory regime. The general public had difficulty identifying the correct regulatory authority to complain to and this reduced the accountability of some regulators.

In 1976, the Royal Commission on Environmental Pollution (RCEP) referred to some of the shortcomings of UK pollution control in its 5th Report on air pollution (Cmnd 6731). In particular, it recognised the need for a comprehensive regulatory body which could integrate the existing disparate and fragmented legal controls policed by a multitude of regulatory bodies.

The RCEP asserted the need for an integrated approach to pollution control to replace the single environmental medium approach that had developed in the UK. The Report stated that:

> The reduction of emissions to the atmosphere can lead to an increase in wastes to be disposed of on land or discharged to water. If the optimum environmental solutions are to be found, the controlling authority must be able to look comprehensively to all forms of pollution arising from industrial processes where different control problems exist.

In practical terms, this means that where a manufacturer selects a manufacturing process which reduces or eliminates the need to discharge into water, this may have a knock-on effect in terms of the emissions it makes into the atmosphere or the amount of solid waste that needs to be disposed of. The single medium approach, which had developed in a largely piecemeal fashion in this country, could not take account of this interrelationship between different environmental media.

The RCEP Report also referred to the 'transferability of pollution':

> The three principal forms of pollution – of air, water and land – are often very closely linked. In order to reduce atmospheric pollution, gases or dusts may be trapped in a spray of water or washed out of filters. This means polluted water, if not discharged to a sewer or direct to a river or the sea, can be piped into a lagoon to settle and dry out, leaving a solid waste disposal problem. The pollutant may even go full circle by blowing off the lagoon as dust.

The Report identified other examples of the transferability of pollution, such as water seeping through refuse tips and smoke from the incineration of rubbish or sludge. The absence of a co-ordinated view, and the fragmented approach to pollution control that had developed in the UK, meant that this interrelationship was largely ignored. Decisions on water discharges taken by the water authorities were largely taken in isolation of decisions made by the waste disposal authorities, the local authorities exercising their clean air functions or the Alkali Inspectorate. The RCEP could find little evidence of co-ordination between the various agencies. This lack of co-ordination meant that, in practice, industries that had been prevented from releasing hazardous substances into a particular medium could choose another means of disposal – for example, burning or burying – and effectively divert the wastes into another medium where the regulatory regime and rules were less stringent. The RCEP therefore recommended the need for a more co-ordinated approach or a cross-media approach so that pollutants were not simply transferred from one medium to another. There was clear evidence of the need for a new regulatory authority which could control the whole process and achieve the 'best practicable environmental option'. Her Majesty's Inspectorate of Pollution (HMIP) was established in 1987 to provide a more co-ordinated and integrated system of pollution control and was given specific responsibility under Pt I of the EPA 1990 to administer the new system of IPC created under that Act. The functions of HMIP were transferred to the Environment Agency in April 1996 by s 1 of the Environment Act (EA) 1995, demonstrating the continued desire to provide a more co-ordinated system of pollution control.

6.3   IPC: ACHIEVING THE BEST PRACTICAL ENVIRONMENTAL OPTION

The EPA 1990 established a system of pollution control which aimed to fulfil the recommendations of the RCEP. The system is known as Integrated Pollution Control or IPC and was initially controlled by HMIP but is now regulated by the Environment Agency. To implement the RCEP's recommendations, the system of IPC was established to prevent or minimise pollution of the environment due to the release of substances into any environmental medium (and thus takes a cross-media approach). IPC does not cover all industrial processes but concentrates only on the most seriously polluting processes. These seriously polluting processes are regulated by a means of prior approval in which the process obtains an authorisation (that is, a licence) from the Environment Agency. In deciding whether to grant approval, the Environment Agency must consider the impact of the process on all three environmental media and determine the means of operation that would result in the BPEO.

In its 12th Report in 1988, the RCEP dealt with the issue of the 'best practicable environmental option' (BPEO) and defined it in the following way:

> The selection of BPEO requires a systematic approach to decision-taking in which the practicability of all reasonable options is examined and in which environmental impact is a major factor in the final choice.

For a discussion of BPEO in the context of a variation of an authorisation, see *R v The Environment Agency and Redland Aggregates Ltd ex p Gibson* (1999).

There is therefore a requirement that the Environment Agency considers the process as a whole and authorises the option that provides the most benefit or the least damage to the environment as a whole, at acceptable cost.

6.4   OVERVIEW OF IPC

Part I of the EPA 1990 establishes two systems of pollution control:

(a) IPC for the most seriously polluting processes which were originally regulated by HMIP but which are now regulated by the Environment Agency (known as Part A processes); and

(b) Local Authority Air Pollution Control (LAAPC) for those processes which should not be allowed to operate without an authorisation, but are not so seriously polluting as to fall within the central control of the Environment Agency. Local authorities regulate these less seriously polluting processes with regard solely to their atmospheric emissions (known as Part B processes).

Section 6 of the EPA 1990 requires that certain *prescribed processes* must not be carried on, or certain *prescribed substances* must not be released into any environmental medium, without prior authorisation from either the Environment Agency or the relevant local authority. To carry on a prescribed process or discharge a prescribed substance without an authorisation is a criminal offence (s 23(1)(a) of the EPA 1990). Regulations prescribe two lists of processes: those in the 'A' list to be controlled by the Environment Agency, and those in the 'B' list to be controlled by the local authority in whose area the process takes place.

Where a process is prescribed for central control by the Environment Agency, then it regulates, by means of an authorisation (licence), releases into all environmental media. The Environment Agency must take into account the process as a whole in terms of the releases into air, water and land. In reaching its conclusions about the levels of discharges and emissions, it is required to have regard to achieving the BPEO. Where the process is designated for control by a local authority, the local authority can only regulate any emissions that such a process makes into air. That does not mean, of course, that processes designated for LAAPC only discharge into air. It means that such processes must seek an authorisation from the relevant local authority (which will be the district council or London borough council) for the atmospheric emissions and, if they discharge into controlled waters, they will be required to seek a separate consent from the Environment Agency under the WRA 1991. Therefore, for these 'less seriously polluting' processes, there is no 'IPC'.

For the purposes of Pt I of the EPA 1990, the definition of environment is 'all, or any, of the following media, namely the air, water and land; and the medium of air includes the air within buildings and the air within other natural or man-made structures above or below ground' (s 1(2)).

The Secretary of State has issued regulations prescribing those processes and substances which should be subject to control under Pt I of the Act and which should be subject to either IPC or LAAPC (see the Environmental Protection (Prescribed Processes and Substances) Regulations 1991 (SI 1991/472), as amended). If a process falls into one of the categories listed in the Regulations, then it must obtain an authorisation as specified in the Regulations, that is, from either the Environment Agency or the local authority, depending on whether the process is an 'A' list process or a 'B' list process. The Regulations do provide for a small category of exemptions. Authorisations from the Environment Agency or the local authority may either be refused or granted subject to conditions and it is a criminal offence to operate a process in contravention of any specific condition or general conditions attached to such authorisations such as the 'best available techniques not entailing excessive cost' (BATNEEC) condition (s 7(2)).

One of the features of Pt I of the EPA 1990 is the degree to which it is supplemented by further regulations which lay down the detailed provisions relating to applications, the operation of authorisations, public consultation, public registers, powers of inspectors, enforcement powers and appeals (see the Environmental Protection (Applications, Appeals and Registers) Regulations 1991 (SI 1991/507)). It is estimated that some 1,800 processes are subject to IPC control and 12,500 processes subject to LAAPC.

The provisions in Pt I of the EPA 1990 relate to both the Environment Agency and local authorities; the Act refers to them as the 'enforcing authorities'. However, reference will usually be made in this chapter to the Environment Agency only. Where there are differences between the IPC and LAAPC procedures, then specific mention will be made.

6.5   PRESCRIBED PROCESSES AND SUBSTANCES

6.5.1   What is a process?

The definition provided in Pt I of the EPA 1990 (s 1) is that a process means any activities carried on in Great Britain, whether on premises or by means of mobile plant, which are capable of causing pollution of the environment. 'Activities' are further defined as industrial or commercial activities or activities of any other nature whatsoever (including, with or without other activities, the keeping of a substance). There may be several processes carried on in a plant at the same time. The term 'process', therefore, has been given a very wide meaning and it is clear from the definition that even storage (keeping a substance) may constitute a process if it is capable of causing pollution. The definition of 'process' was considered in *HMIP v Safety Kleen UK Ltd* (1994). Safety Kleen were prosecuted by HMIP in respect of an incident in which some 13,000 litres of 'cemfuel' (a fuel produced from waste solvents) escaped from a tanker which was parked overnight at the company's premises. Large quantities of the fuel ended up in controlled waters. Safety Kleen had an IPC authorisation in respect of its solvent recovery plant and this expressly excluded the release of substances into controlled waters. At first instance, the defendant company argued that it was not guilty of breaching conditions since the parked tanker was not a prescribed process and was therefore not subject to any conditions. However, the magistrates' court held that the description of the prescribed process in the authorisation included any other process carried on at the same location by the same person as part of that process. The court accepted therefore that the definition of process included the keeping of a substance in a tanker and found the defendant guilty. The company was fined £7,500 after it put forward mitigating arguments concerning their speedy response to the incident and the subsequent implementation of measures to avoid future similar incidents.

6.5.2   Pollution of the environment

Pollution of the environment is central to the definition of a 'process'. It is defined in s 1(3) of the EPA 1990 in terms of the release into any environmental medium from any process of substances which are capable of causing harm to man or any other living organism. Harm is defined in s 1(4) as harm to the health of living organisms or other interference with the ecological systems of which they form a part. In the case of man, this includes offence to any of his senses or harm to his property.

Since it is an offence to 'carry on' a prescribed process without an authorisation, there may be a question as to what constitutes carrying on. Cases which have considered this question (albeit not within the context of the EPA 1990) suggest that there must be an element of repetition or series of acts and that the person carrying on the process must have control and direction of it.

6.5.3   The Prescribed Processes and Substances Regulations 1991

Using his powers under s 2 of the EPA 1990, the Secretary of State has enacted the Environmental Protection (Prescribed Processes and Substances) Regulations 1991 (SI 1991/472), which have been amended and further amended on numerous occasions.

Schedule 1 to the Regulations contains the descriptions of *processes* prescribed for control, and Scheds 4–6 prescribe the *substances* subject to control. Schedule 1 to the Regulations is broken down into chapters, each dealing with a broad industrial sector. Within each of these broad sector headings, there is a more detailed list of industrial processes. These are further sub-divided into Part A processes and Part B processes. Part A processes are subject to IPC and Part B processes are subject to LAAPC.

6.5.4 Industrial sectors

Schedule 1 is sub-divided into chapters which relate to the following broad industrial sectors:

Chapter 1 – Fuel Production Processes, Combustion Processes (including power generation);

Chapter 2 – Metal Production and Processing;

Chapter 3 – Mineral Industries;

Chapter 4 – The Chemical Industry;

Chapter 5 – Waste Disposal and Recycling;

Chapter 6 – Other Industries.

Within each of these chapters, there is a further sub-division into more detailed industrial processes, so, for example, within Chapter 4 on the Chemical Industry, the following processes are included:

(a) petrochemical processes;

(b) the manufacture and use of organic chemicals;

(c) acid processes;

(d) inorganic chemical processes;

(e) chemical fertiliser production;

(f) pesticide production;

(g) pharmaceutical production;

(h) the storage of chemicals in bulk.

For each of these processes, there is more detailed description and also a breakdown between those activities which are classified as a Part A process (IPC) or a Part B process (LAAPC). The following example best demonstrates this:

Chemical fertiliser production:

- Part A:

  (a) the manufacture of chemical fertilisers;

  (b) the conversion of chemical fertilisers into granules.

- Part B:

  Nil.

6.5.5 How to find out whether a process is prescribed for IPC or LAAPC

In order to determine whether a process falls under Pt A or Pt B, it is necessary to find the description of the relevant process in the Regulations. So, for example, if you are trying to determine whether a factory that manufactures ink is subject to IPC or LAAPC, you would first of all need to determine which broad industrial sector it falls into. Since it is not obvious which broad industrial grouping it falls into, the best starting point is the chapter on Other Industries (Chapter 6). From there, one can find s 6.6 'the manufacture of dyestuffs, printing ink and coating materials'. Under this sub-section, the manufacture and formulation of printing ink is determined to be a Part B process. However, the process will only need an authorisation from the relevant local authority where the carrying on of the process is likely to involve the use of 100 tonnes or more of organic solvents in any 12 month period at the location in question.

6.5.6   What happens when a plant operates more than one process?

Many companies operate large industrial plants where a number of different industrial processes are carried out at the same location. In these circumstances, the company may have applied for one or more authorisations in respect of the different processes. In the event that there is a dispute, or it is not clear which category (or indeed categories) a particular plant should fall into, Sched 2 to the Regulations assists with a number of rules of interpretation. The issue of which category a plant falls into is more than academic and has practical implications for the plant concerned. An application for an authorisation from the Environment Agency is considerably more expensive than one from the local authority. The rules of interpretation provide for situations where a process appears to fall into two categories or where a plant undertakes a number of different processes falling into several categories. The rules are lengthy, but the most important one covers situations where a particular plant operates a process which falls within both Part A and Part B of the same section. In such circumstances, the whole process will be controlled centrally as an IPC process by the Environment Agency.

6.5.7   Prescribed substances

By virtue of s 2(5) of the EPA 1990, the Secretary of State can also prescribe certain substances for control and, accordingly, the release of the prescribed substances requires authorisation under s 6. The list of prescribed substances can be found in Scheds 4, 5 and 6 to the Prescribed Processes and Prescribed Substances Regulations 1991 (as amended). Substances are prescribed in relation to the environmental medium in which they are released:

(a) *Schedule 4: Substances released into the air*:

　　Oxides of sulphur and other sulphur compounds;

　　Oxides of nitrogen and other nitrogen compounds;

　　Oxides of carbon;

　　Organic compounds and partial oxidation products;

　　Metals, metalloids and their compounds;

　　Asbestos (suspended particulate matter and fibres), glass fibres and mineral fibres;

　　Halogens and their compounds;

　　Phosphorous and its compounds;

　　Particulate matter.

(b) *Schedule 5: Substances released into water*:

　　Mercury and its compounds;

　　Cadmium and its compounds;

All isomers of hexachlorocyclohexane;

All isomers of DDT;

Pentachlorophenol and its compounds;

Hexachlorobenzene;

Hexachlorobutadiene;

Aldrin;

Dieldrin;

Endrin;

Polychlorinated Biphenyls;

Dichlorvos;

1,2–Dichloroethane;

All isomers of trichlorobenzene;

Atrazine;

Simazine;

Tributyltin compounds;

Triphenyltin compounds;

Trifluralin;

Fenitrothion;

Azinphos-methyl;

Malathion;

Endosulfan.

(c) *Schedule 6: Substances released on to land*:

Organic solvents;

Azides;

Halogens and their covalent compounds;

Metal carbonyls;

Organo-metallic compounds;

Oxidising agents;

Polychlorinated dibenzofuran and any congener thereof;

Polychlorinated dibenzo-p-dioxin and any congener thereof;

Polyhalogenated biphenyls, terphenyls and naphthalenes;

Phosphorous;

Pesticides;

Alkali metals and their oxides and alkaline earth and their oxides.

6.5.8 Exemptions

The 1991 Regulations, as amended, provide for a number of situations where a process is exempt from the need to obtain an authorisation. These exemptions apply to those processes where the amount of any prescribed substance released is trivial. In particular, by virtue of reg 4, a process cannot be taken to be a Pt A process if the process cannot result in:

(a) the release to air of prescribed substances, or there is no likelihood that it will result in the release to air of any such substance except in a quantity which is so trivial that it is incapable of causing harm, or its capacity to cause harm is insignificant; and

(b) the release of prescribed substances into water except in a concentration which is no greater than the background concentration, or in a quantity which does not, in any 12 month period, exceed the background quantity by more than the amount specified in Sched 5 to the Regulations;

(c) the release onto land of any prescribed substances, or there is no likelihood that it will result in the releases on to land of any such substance, except in a quantity which is so trivial that it is incapable of causing harm, or its capacity to cause harm is insignificant.

A process cannot be a Part B process unless it will, or there is a likelihood that it will, result in the release into the air of one or more of the prescribed substances, unless the quantity which is released is so trivial that it is incapable of causing harm or its capacity to cause harm is so insignificant.

In *Tandridge DC v P&S Civil Engineering Ltd* (1995), the district council prosecuted the defendant company on the ground that the company was operating a prescribed process, a tarmac production plant, without authorisation. The defendant contended that the district council had not proved that the exceptions under reg 4 did not apply. The question of where the burden of proof lies in respect of these exceptions was considered by the Divisional Court by way of case stated. The Divisional Court held that the burden of proving exceptions was clearly on the defendant and that this is clearly stated in s 101 of the Magistrates' Court Act 1980. On the facts, the defendant had not produced any evidence regarding the discharge levels and it was not able to benefit from the exceptions. Thus, it is clear that anyone wishing to benefit from these exceptions must clearly establish that they fall within the exceptions. There are a number of additional specified exceptions. These include processes carried on in working museums which are intended to demonstrate matters of historical interest, processes carried on in schools for educational purposes and domestic processes which are incidental to the use of a private dwelling. The running of aircraft, hovercraft, cars, trains and ships are also excluded. The list of exceptions is contained in reg 4 of the 1991 Regulations.

6.6 LICENSING: THE NEED FOR AN AUTHORISATION

Section 6 of the EPA 1990 provides that:

> No person shall carry on a prescribed process after the date prescribed or determined for that description of process by or under Regulations under s 2(1) ... except under an authorisation granted by the enforcing authority and in accordance with the conditions to which it is subject.

Once it has been determined whether a process is a prescribed process or is a process which is discharging a prescribed substance, an application for an authorisation for that process must be made to the appropriate enforcement agency. It is only an offence for a person to carry on the prescribed process without an authorisation after the date prescribed or determined. Such dates were prescribed by regulations issued under s 2(1) and these regulations prescribed a timetable for applications to be made to avoid an enormous influx of applications once the provisions came into force (see 6.6.1 below).

An IPC authorisation is required to operate:

(a) any process subject to IPC;

(b) any proposed new process in any IPC category;

(c) any existing process in any IPC category where a 'substantial change' in the process is proposed.

The s 6 obligation to obtain an IPC authorisation should now be interpreted in the light of the provisions of the PPCA 1999. These provisions are considered later in this chapter.

An application for IPC authorisation is made to the relevant regional office of the Environment Agency. It should be noted here that, where the process is prescribed for LAAPC, the application for authorisation is made to the local authority in whose area the prescribed processes are (or are to be) carried on. LAAPC applications may also be made for prescribed processes carried on by means of mobile plant, in which case the application is made to the local authority in whose area the person carrying on the business has his or her principal place of business.

6.6.1 Phasing in IPC

Part I of the EPA 1990 was implemented in April 1991. At the time the EPA 1990 came into force, many plants were operating under authorisations from previous legislation but they were still required to obtain an IPC authorisation from HMIP. However, given the large number of plants concerned and the time it would take to process all of the applications, the government recognised that it needed to include provisions for a phased programme of applications. Consequently, a rolling programme of applications was established, which required applications to be made on a sectoral basis by deadlines, specified in Sched 3 to the Environmental Protection (Prescribed Processes and Substances) Regulations 1991. As noted above, these Regulations have since been amended by further regulations to take account of delays in the system.

The first sector to be covered under this phased-in programme was the combustion processes. This was necessary in order to meet the deadline of an EC Directive (88/609/EEC) concerned with large combustion plants (that is, power stations). The phased-in programme was completed in 1996. A similar phasing-in process is now being adopted in relation to the IPPC regime which should be complete by 2007.

6.6.2 New processes

As far as new processes were concerned, the phased-in programme was not applicable. An authorisation had to be obtained before operation began. This usually occurred at the same time as planning permission was sought for the development. The Environment Agency could agree to a staged application for new developments, enabling it and the operator to discuss the proposal at the design stage and moving on later to the detailed application.

6.6.3   Processes undergoing substantial change

There were also specific provisions for existing plants which had undergone a substantial change. An existing plant was defined as one which had operated for the previous 12 months. Where modifications or alterations to the plant were proposed, which were deemed to amount to a substantial change, then the operator was required to obtain an immediate authorisation, irrespective of the deadlines stated in the programme of applications. Substantial changes to existing IPC licensed processes will now trigger IPPC controls. Consequently, those processes which are currently subject to IPC but seek to make a substantial change to the process will need to apply for an IPPC permit ahead of the deadline stated in the PPC regulations. On the other hand, existing IPC processes which make minor modifications to the process will continue to be regulated under Pt I of the EPA 1990, but may need to seek a variation of the authorisation (under s 11) in order to avoid breaching the conditions of the IPC authorisation. See the discussion of *R v Environment Agency and Redland Aggregates Ltd ex p Gibson* (1999) at 6.10 below.

6.6.4   What amounts to substantial change?

Substantial change is defined in s 10(7) of the EPA 1990 as 'substantial change in the substances released from the process or in the amount or any other characteristic of any substance so released'. If a Process Guidance Note (that is, official guidance issued by HMIP/Environment Agency) is available for the prescribed process, this will provide examples of changes which are either substantial or not. Changes which are not substantial may still require a variation of the conditions of the authorisation. Once again, it is advisable to seek the advice of the Environment Agency.

6.7   IPC APPLICATIONS

With the phased introduction of the IPPC regime, which began in 2000 and should be complete by 2007, no new IPC applications should now be made. However, given that some 1,800 processes are currently subject to IPC, it is worthwhile considering the process that they had to go through in order to obtain the IPC authorisation.

Schedule 1 to the EPA 1990 provides details about the form of the licence application and the information that it must contain. It also deals with publicity requirements. In addition, the form and content of applications is specified in the Environmental Protection (Application, Appeals and Registers) Regulations 1991, as amended.

Applications to the Environment Agency for authorisations to operate IPC processes required a substantial input from the applicants. A search through the IPC registers held by the Environment Agency will reveal that some of the applications are supported by many hundreds of pages of documentation. It is estimated that most applications take between 100 and 500 man hours to prepare and, indeed, many are prepared on behalf of companies by specialist consultants.

Applications had to be made on the appropriate form, together with relevant supporting information. The following information was required:

(a) the name and address of the applicant;

(b) if the applicant was a company, the registered number and office;

(c) the address of the premises where the prescribed process was being (or would be) carried on;

(d) a map or location plan;

(e) a description of the prescribed process;

(f) a list of prescribed substances used in connection with or resulting from the prescribed processes;

(g) a list of any other substances used in connection with or resulting from the prescribed processes and which might cause harm if released into any environmental medium;

(h) a description of the techniques to be used for preventing the releases into any environmental medium of such substances, for reducing the releases of such substances to a minimum and for rendering harmless any such substances which were released;

(i) details of any proposed releases of such a substance into any environmental medium and an assessment of the environmental consequences;

(j) proposals for monitoring the release of substances and the environmental consequences of such releases;

(k) details of how the process would comply with 'any specific conditions' and how the process would operate, using the best available techniques not entailing excessive cost;

(l) any other additional information that the applicant wanted the enforcing authority to take into account when considering the application.

The information provided in the application had to be clear, comprehensive and, of course, accurate. The Environment Agency had the power to serve a notice on the applicant requiring further information to be supplied by a specified date. The application procedure for IPC licences has now been repealed by the PPCA 1999. Although the details concerning the applications procedure for IPC are largely of historical interest, some of the important elements, such as fees and charges and public consultation, merit further attention.

6.7.1 Fees and charges

One of the government's intentions when HMIP was created in 1987 was that it should eventually become self-financing through a system of fees and charges levied on applicants. One justification for this cost recovery scheme was that it would be an application of the 'polluter pays' principle, with those processes polluting the environment paying for the system of regulation that controls their activities. However, the charging scheme was controversial and HMIP was never able to generate sufficient income from fees and charges to become self-financing.

This desire for self-financing is continued in relation to the Environment Agency. Section 8 of the EPA 1990, which covered fees and charges in respect of IPC and LAAPC processes, now only concerns LAAPC. Section 41 of the EA 1995 details the

Environment Agency's charging scheme. An application to the enforcing authority must be accompanied by the requisite fee. The charging scheme for IPC is detailed in a document produced by the Environment Agency, *Charging Scheme for Integrated Pollution Control*, which is produced annually. The charging scheme operates on the basis of the following categories of charges:

(a) an application fee to cover the costs of considering each application;

(b) a subsistence charge payable annually for the holding of each IPC authorisation to cover:

    (i)   the ongoing costs of inspection, monitoring and enforcement by enforcing authority staff,

    (ii) a contribution to recouping previous years' under-recovery,

    (iii) the costs of independent monitoring;

(c) a supplementary charge where applicable;

(d) a substantial variation fee, to cover the costs of considering an application for subsequent variation of an authorisation.

Charges are not made in respect of processes. In order to relate the size of IPC fees and charges to the amount of regulatory effort involved, payments due on particular processes are linked to the number of defined 'components' which the process contains. The definitions of components for each category of process are set out in the Appendix to the charging scheme.

The fees and charges for LAAPC authorisations are lower. The penalties for not paying the annual subsistence charge are serious. If the authorisation holder fails to pay the relevant annual subsistence fee, the enforcing authority can serve a written notice on the holder of the authorisation revoking the authorisation or can take other enforcement action (s 8(8) of the EPA 1990).

6.7.2 Processing the application

On receipt of an IPC application, the enforcing authority could either grant the authorisation, subject to any conditions required, or refuse the application. The enforcing authority could not grant an authorisation if it considered that the applicant would not be able to carry on the process in compliance with the conditions attached to the authorisation. There is no requirement within Pt I of the EPA 1990 that the applicant be a fit and proper person in the same way that there is in relation to waste management licences contained within Pt II of the Act. The Secretary of State has the right, if he or she thinks fit, to intervene in the processing of an application and issue directions to the enforcing authority as to whether or not they should grant the authorisation.

Once an application was received, it would normally be decided upon within a period of four months. However, the period could be extended with the agreement of the applicant. In an attempt to speed up the process, and also to ensure greater consistency between applications, the Environment Agency could issue 'template' authorisations which were described as generic authorisations which could be applied to many industrial processes with the minimum of modification.

6.7.3 Consultation

Consultation was an important part of the process of dealing with IPC applications and continues to be so in the IPPC regime. Before reaching a decision on an application, the Environment Agency was required to carry out a consultation exercise and seek the views of a number of bodies. In all cases, the views of the Health and Safety Executive had to be sought. In addition, the following organisations were consulted:

(a) the Ministry of Agriculture, Fisheries and Food (where the process was in Wales, the Secretary of State for Wales);

(b) the sewerage undertaker, where the prescribed process involved or might involve the releases of any substance into a sewer;

(c) the Nature Conservancy Council for England (English Nature) or the Countryside Council for Wales, where the process might involve releases of any substance which might affect a Site of Special Scientific Interest;

(d) the harbour authority, where the process involved a release of any substance into a harbour;

(e) the district council in whose area the process would be carried on;

(f) the local fisheries committee, where the process involved a release of any substance into relevant territorial waters or coastal waters.

6.7.4 Advertising

In addition to the consultation exercise, there were also provisions for the advertising of applications in order to ensure that other interested parties, such as local residents, had the opportunity to comment on the application. An advert had to be placed in a local newspaper providing details about applications (for authorisation or variation), and also in the *London Gazette* if the process was subject to IPC. Details relating to consultation and advertising were contained in the Environmental Protection (Applications, Appeals and Registers) Regulations 1991 (SI 1991/507), as amended.

6.8 CONDITIONS

Authorisations can either be granted subject to conditions or refused. The conditions imposed in an authorisation are the principal mechanism by which the enforcing authorities can control or prevent the releases of substances into the environment and by which the UK can not only abate pollution, but fulfil its obligations under European Community law and other international treaties.

In deciding upon conditions, the Environment Agency and the local authorities are guided by s 7 of the EPA 1990 which deals specifically with conditions. As such, s 7 is of vital importance since it spells out what considerations the Environment Agency and the local authorities must take into account and, importantly, what the objectives of the conditions are. It also introduces the concepts of BATNEEC and BPEO. Section 7 provides that both the Environment Agency and the local authorities must include conditions which they consider appropriate for achieving certain stated objectives. In particular, conditions must be included which:

(a) the enforcing authority considers appropriate for achieving the objectives laid down in s 7(2) – BATNEEC;

(b) comply with any directions given by the Secretary of State for the implementation of obligations under EC or international law;

(c) comply with any limits or requirements, and achieve any quality standards or quality objectives, prescribed by the Secretary of State;

(d) comply with any requirements applicable to the grant of authorisations specified by or under a plan made by the Secretary of State under s 3(5) of the EPA 1990 (see below);

(e) comply with any other directions given by the Secretary of State in relation to all authorisations, certain types of authorisation or an individual authorisation;

(f) appear to the enforcing authority to be appropriate.

Whatever conditions are included in the authorisation, it is important to note that they are all subject to administrative law principles – they must be necessary, they should be clear and, of course, they must be lawful. In addition, no conditions can be imposed for the purposes only of securing the health of the people who work at the plant where the process is being carried on.

In setting conditions, not only must the enforcing authority take into account directions given by the Secretary of State, they must also set conditions which meet the objectives laid down in s 7(2), known as the BATNEEC conditions. Before considering the BATNEEC provisions in detail, it is important to consider the role that the Secretary of State plays in giving directions and making plans.

6.8.1   The role of the Secretary of State

Section 7 refers to directions issued by the Secretary of State, to quality standards and objectives prescribed by him and also to plans. The Secretary of State is empowered to make such plans, directions and regulations by virtue of s 3.

Section 3 empowers the Secretary of State to make regulations which establish standards, objectives or particular requirements in relation to particular prescribed processes, or particular substances, and also to develop strategic plans aimed at reducing pollution. This power is significant in that it enables the Secretary of State to comply with obligations laid down in EC directives.

Using s 3, the Secretary of State can make regulations which lay down quality objectives or quality standards in relation to any substance which may be released in any medium. Regulations may also prescribe standard limits for the concentration of substances, the amount, or the amount in any period, which may be released, or even any other characteristic of that substance in any circumstance in which it may be released.

6.8.2   Plans

The Secretary of State can also, under s 3, make plans for:

(a) establishing limits for the total amount, or the total amount in any period, of any substance which may be released into the environment in the UK or any area within it;

(b) allocating quotas, as regards the release of substances, to persons carrying on processes in respect of which any such limit value is established;

(c) establishing limits so as progressively to reduce pollution of the environment;

(d) the progressive improvement in the quality objectives and quality standards established by the above mentioned regulations issued under s 3.

The system of IPC enables the Environment Agency to ensure that the UK complies with its obligations under EC law. In particular, the Environment Agency is required to ensure that, in drawing up conditions of authorisations, the UK satisfies any quality standards or quality objectives laid down in EC directives. Certain directives are particularly relevant in this context, such as Directive 88/609/EEC on the limitation of emissions of certain pollutants into the air from large combustion plants and Directive 84/360/EEC on the combating of air pollution from industrial plants.

6.8.3 Specific conditions

In the light of what has been said above, specific conditions will be imposed which state expressly the quantities and compositions of substances that can be released, when and where they can be released, and the duration of the releases.

6.9   THE BATNEEC CONDITION

In setting conditions, both the Environment Agency and the local authorities are required by virtue of s 7 of the EPA 1990 to comply with the directions issued by the Secretary of State, discussed above, and also to meet the objective laid down in s 7(2).

This objective is to ensure that, in carrying on a prescribed process, the best available techniques not entailing excessive cost will be used for:

(a) preventing the release of substances prescribed for any environmental medium into that medium or, where that is not practicable, by such means for reducing the release of such substances to a minimum and for rendering harmless any such substances which are so released; and

(b) rendering harmless any other substances which might cause harm if released into any other environmental medium.

This section is of the utmost importance. It introduces the concept of BATNEEC and requires that, in setting the specific conditions, the 'best available techniques not entailing excessive cost' are employed to prevent releases or to render them harmless. The BATNEEC requirement applies to the specific conditions laid down by the Environment Agency. However, in addition to those aspects which are specifically covered by a condition in the authorisation, s 7(4) states that there is also an implied general condition in every authorisation that, in carrying on the process, the person carrying it on must use BATNEEC to achieve the same purposes. The specific and implied general conditions relating to BATNEEC are considered in detail below.

In a number of recent cases, the courts have considered the nature of the Environment Agency's responsibilities under s 7 of the EPA 1990 in relation to conditions and have shown a marked reluctance to interfere with the discretion of the Agency. In *Levy v Environment Agency* (2003), the Divisional Court held that the Environment Agency was obliged to consider achieving the statutory objectives, not as a specific requirement that had to be achieved, but as ends to be aimed at. The Agency had to carry out a balancing exercise in deciding what conditions were appropriate. Moreover, the court showed itself unwilling to interfere with a decision which called upon the Agency to exercise sophisticated, specialised scientific knowledge and expertise and which, accordingly, had a wider margin of appreciation than that in the average case.

6.9.1 What are the 'best available techniques not entailing excessive cost'?

The concept of BATNEEC is of vital importance. BATNEEC is to be used both in relation to expressly stated conditions and also as a general implied condition.

The purpose of using BATNEEC is to prevent the release of substances into the environment or, where that is not practicable, to reduce the release to a minimum and render any releases harmless. In the context of IPC and LAAPC, the types of conditions that fulfil the requirements of BATNEEC can relate to such things as:

(a) the actual technology and machinery used;

(b) the qualifications, training and supervision of the workforce;

(c) the design, layout and maintenance of the factory;

(d) the amounts, compositions, etc, of the substances used in the process.

BATNEEC is not a fixed standard; it will alter over a period of time. For example, those processes which were in operation prior to the introduction of IPC in 1990 were invariably allowed to phase in the BATNEEC requirement over time, allowing for a phased programme of investment and improvements. Authorisations would generally require a timetabled upgrade programme, allowing the operator to achieve the prescribed BATNEEC conditions over a period of time and, importantly, allowing the operator to spread the costs of achieving this. Where a process is a new one, a different view will be taken of what constitutes excessive cost and an applicant will be expected to meet BATNEEC immediately. This is made clear in the Department of the Environment Guidance on the interpretation of BATNEEC. It should be noted that the local authorities and the Environment Agency are under a statutory duty (s 4(9)) to follow developments in technology and techniques for preventing or reducing pollution of the environment in relation to relevant processes.

6.9.2 BATNEEC: the implied condition

Any aspect of a process that is not regulated by a specific condition is nevertheless subject to an implied BATNEEC condition (see s 7(7) of the EPA 1990). In general, the Environment Agency has sought to make the conditions as clear and as specific as possible in order to minimise any reliance on the implied general condition.

In order to achieve some degree of consistency between regions with regard to the interpretation of BATNEEC across a particular industry, sector or process, a number of technical sectoral guidance notes have been issued. These are accessible on the Environment Agency website.

6.9.3 Guidance notes

The local authorities and the Environment Agency inspectors are assisted in their IPC and LAAPC work by a number of published technical guidance notes issued by the Secretary of State. They are under a duty to have regard to the guidance provided. For IPC processes, industry guidance notes have been published covering the fuel and power sector, metal industry, mineral industry, chemical industry and the waste disposal industry. These provide general guidance for the industry sector. They contain information on the processes that fall within that sector, relevant EC directives and information about available abatement technologies and techniques, sampling and monitoring. In practice, the content of the guidance notes indicates the approach that the Environment Agency or local authority is likely to take in the authorisation.

Local Authority Air Pollution Guidance Notes have also been issued providing guidance on Part B processes. General guidance notes are available and provide very useful information on general matters such as the applications procedure, public registers and the appeals procedure. These are supported by specific process guidance notes which give advice in particular on the techniques appropriate for the control of air pollution for individual processes. In addition, the Secretary of State has issued a further guidance note for local authorities on upgrading of existing processes and this adds to the information already provided in the process guidance notes. See *United Kingdom Renderers Association Ltd, John Pointon and Sons Ltd v Secretary of State for the Environment, Transport and the Regions* (2002).

6.9.4 Failure to comply with conditions

Failure to comply with the conditions attached to an authorisation is an offence (s 23 of the EPA 1990). This includes failure to comply with any of the specific conditions and also failure to comply with the implied BATNEEC condition. In the event that legal proceedings are brought concerning a failure to satisfy the BATNEEC condition, the burden of proof falls squarely on the operator. It must prove that there was no better available technique that could be used without entailing excessive cost.

6.10   BATNEEC AND THE BEST PRACTICAL ENVIRONMENTAL OPTION (BPEO)

The important feature of IPC is that it replaces the single medium approach to pollution control with an approach that takes into account the environment as a whole. When the Environment Agency is considering a process prescribed for central control, it must have regard, when drawing up the conditions of the authorisation, to all of the environmental media involved. Section 7(7) of the EPA

1990 makes a specific connection between BATNEEC and BPEO. It specifically requires that where a process is subject to IPC and the process involves the release of substances into more than one environmental medium, then the BATNEEC conditions should include the objective of ensuring that BATNEEC will be used for minimising the pollution that may be caused to the environment as a whole (*the holistic approach*), having regard to the best practicable environmental option (BPEO) concerning the substances that may be released. In other words, the aim is to minimise pollution by the application of BATNEEC, having regard to BPEO.

Unfortunately, the EPA 1990 does not provide a definition of what is meant by BPEO. It is clear that it will involve a balancing exercise, taking into account ways in which, for example, a slight increase in air emissions might radically reduce discharges to water, and weighing up what is 'best' for the environment as a whole. Using this example, although emissions to air might be greater than if there were a single medium approach, the small increase in atmospheric emissions is more than offset by the reduction in water pollution. The RCEP definition serves as a useful guide as to what is intended:

> A BPEO is the outcome of a systematic consultative and decision-making procedure which emphasises the protection and conservation of the environment across land, air and water. The BPEO procedure establishes, for a given set of objectives, the option that provides the most benefit or least damage to the environment as a whole, at acceptable cost, in the long term as well as the short term.

This statutory duty to ensure that BATNEEC is used, having regard to BPEO, was considered by the Divisional Court in *R v Environment Agency and Redland Aggregates Ltd ex p Gibson* (1999). The case concerned three separate applications for judicial review of the Environment Agency's decision to grant variations to existing IPC authorisations so as to allow the burning of substitute liquid fuels (SLF) in three separate manufacturing processes. The applicants claimed that the Agency was obliged to carry out a thorough examination of all of the practicable options and the available techniques relating to the process as a whole and, because the Agency had merely selected the preferred option from a list of two, it had not selected the *best* option. The case very much concerned the fact that what was at issue was the terms of a variation of an IPC authorisation, as opposed to the granting of one. Nevertheless, in the context of the variation, the court held that although the Agency was under a duty to ensure that the terms of a variation to an existing authorisation complied with the statutory objectives of s 7, this did not mean that there was a duty to carry out an exhaustive examination of all practical options and techniques regardless of the circumstances. The extent of this duty to assess BATNEEC and BPEO in an application for a variation was a matter of 'fact and degree' which was dependent upon all the circumstances of the particular case.

For further consideration of BPEO in the context of waste management licensing, see *R v Bolton MBC ex p Kirkman* (1998); *R v Derbyshire County Council ex p Murray* (2001).

6.11   PUBLIC REGISTERS

As in other parts of the EPA 1990, and other environmental legislation, there is a requirement that information pertaining to IPC and LAAPC processes is maintained on public registers. Section 20 of the EPA 1990 requires the Environment Agency and the local authorities to maintain public registers which contain information on:

(a) LAAPC/IPC applications;

(b) LAAPC/IPC authorisations;

(c) Variation, Enforcement and Prohibition Notices issued;

(d) revocations of authorisations;

(e) emission monitoring results provided to the enforcing authority;

(f) details of any enforcement action taken by the enforcing authority against operators;

(g) details of any convictions for offences under s 23(1);

(h) details of any appeals;

(i) details of any directions from the Secretary of State.

6.11.1 Exemptions from publicity requirements

There are only two exceptions to the requirement for information to be publicly available. By s 21, information may be excluded if it affects national security and, by s 22, a more widely used provision, information may be excluded on the grounds of commercial confidentiality.

6.11.2 Exclusion on the grounds of national security

Under s 21, the Secretary of State may issue directions requiring information to be left off the register:

> ... if, and so long as, in the opinion of the Secretary of State, the inclusion in the register of that information, or information of that description, would be contrary to the interests of national security.

Where the Environment Agency excludes information on this ground, then it must inform the Secretary of State that it has done so. It is possible that an applicant may wish information to be excluded on the grounds that he or she believe its inclusion would be contrary to the interests of national security. If this is the case, the person seeking to rely on s 21 should give notice to the Secretary of State, specifying the information and indicating its apparent nature. The person must notify the Environment Agency that he or she has done this and, as a consequence, the information cannot be included on the register until the Secretary of State has determined that it should be included.

6.11.3 Exclusion on the grounds of commercial confidentiality

It is much more likely, and indeed more common, that a company will want to exclude information from the public registers because they do not want the public generally, or competitors specifically, to have access to such information. For example, a company may have pioneered a new process or product or may not want to reveal what raw materials are used. Provision is made for information to be excluded on the basis that the information is 'commercially confidential'. Section 22(11) defines commercially confidential information as information which, if it were contained in the register, would 'prejudice to an unreasonable degree the commercial interests of that individual or person'.

If a company wishes information to be excluded on this ground, then it must apply to the Environment Agency for a determination. The Environment Agency must reach a decision within a period of 14 days beginning with the date of the application for exclusion. Failure to make a determination within 14 days will result in the information being deemed to be commercially confidential.

6.12   TRANSFER OF AN AUTHORISATION

Once an authorisation has been granted, it is possible to transfer the authorisation to another person. In the event that a company or business is sold, or is taken over, it will be necessary for the new owner to obtain an authorisation if he or she wishes to carry on the process. Before entering into a contract for the sale of the business, the prospective owner would be well advised to establish that the business has the relevant authorisation, otherwise he or she might enter into a situation where he or she is themselves 'carrying on the process' and, consequently, acting in breach of s 6 by operating a prescribed process without authorisation.

Section 9 makes specific provision for the transfer of authorisations and allows the holder of an authorisation to transfer the authorisation to another person who intends to carry on the process. The new holder must notify the Environment Agency within 21 days of the transfer taking place. There is no requirement that the Agency is consulted before the transfer takes place. This contrasts with the situation in relation to waste management licences, where the Agency would need to be satisfied that the new licensee was a fit and proper person. However, it would clearly be extremely prudent for the transferee to check the position with the Agency beforehand, since the Environment Agency has the power to revoke a licence if it considers that the holder cannot comply with the conditions.

6.13   MONITORING OF AN IPC AUTHORISATION

The Environment Agency ensures compliance with the standards laid down by a number of means including:

(a) regular site visits;

(b) analysis of monitoring data;

(c) investigation of problems and complaints;

(d) specifying online monitoring by the process operator.

All IPC authorisations will include conditions which require the process operator to monitor discharges and emissions from the prescribed process in order to ensure compliance with conditions. Moreover, the authorisation will usually contain a condition that, where there is a breach of condition, the process operator will inform the Environment Agency. Failing to tell the Agency that there has been a breach of condition constitutes a further breach. As stated above, the Environment Agency, through its inspectors, will respond to complaints from the public and it operates a 24 hour telephone line for the public to call if they become aware of any polluting incident.

The Environment Agency is guided by an enforcement and prosecution policy, which was discussed more fully in Chapter 2. The policy clearly makes reference to monitoring as this is an integral part of overall enforcement. For instance, the policy states that inspection should be targeted primarily towards those whose activities give rise to the most serious environmental damage or pollution, or where the hazards are less well controlled.

6.13.1 Reviewing authorisations

The Environment Agency is under a duty to review the conditions of the authorisations that it has granted. The EPA 1990 requires that this happens 'from time to time' but in any event at least every four years. The Secretary of State has the right to alter this period.

6.14 POWERS OF ENFORCEMENT

The EPA 1990 arms the Environment Agency and the local authorities with a wide range of investigatory, administrative enforcement, criminal prosecution and remedial powers to enable them to enforce compliance with the conditions of the authorisations that they have granted, and also to take action against processes that are operating without authorisation. The powers of enforcement include the following actions:

(a) variation and revocation of authorisations;

(b) Enforcement Notices (ENs) and Prohibition Notices (PNs);

(c) powers to secure compliance with the above notices;

(d) power to enter property;

(e) power to carry out examinations and investigations;

(f) powers of seizure;

(g) power to take steps to remedy harm.

6.14.1 Variation of authorisations

It has already been noted that the Environment Agency is under a statutory duty to review all authorisations at least every four years. As a consequence of that review, the Environment Agency may decide that it is necessary to alter or vary the conditions of the authorisation. A variation of an authorisation may be necessary to comply with new quality objectives or standards, or directions issued by the Secretary of State. Alternatively, the person carrying out the process may wish to make changes to the authorised process. For example, it might be the case that changes are made to the actual process or the substances handled or discharged, in which case it may be necessary for the authorisation holder to seek a variation of the authorisation. Sections 10–11 make provision for variation of authorisations by the Environment Agency (s 10) or at the instigation of the authorisation holder (s 11).

6.14.2 Variation by the Environment Agency

Section 10 enables the Environment Agency (or the local authority) to vary an authorisation at any time in order to incorporate new conditions in order to comply with the requirements of s 7. To vary the notice, the Environment Agency must serve a written Variation Notice on the holder of the authorisation, specifying the variations it has decided to make and the date or dates from which the new conditions will have effect. Variation takes effect from the date specified in the notice. The authorisation holder will be required by the Variation Notice to inform the Environment Agency, within a specified period, of what action it proposes to take to comply with the varied conditions. The authorisation holder will also be required to pay a variation fee. Sometimes, a variation will result in a substantial change to the process that is authorised. Where the Environment Agency is of the opinion that, as a result of requiring variations, there will be a substantial change, it must notify the authorisation holder of that opinion. Section 10(3) of the EPA 1990, inserted by the EA 1995, provides that the Environment Agency may serve a further notice which varies a Variation Notice. Substantial changes to IPC licensed processes will now trigger IPPC controls.

6.14.3 Variation by licence holder

Section 11 deals with situations where the authorisation holder applies for a variation in the authorisation. The procedure is described in Pt II of Sched 1 to the EPA 1990. An application may be made at any time by an authorisation holder requesting that the authorisation be varied. The application for the variation must be made on the prescribed form and must be supported by information prescribed in regulations and any other information that the Environment Agency requires. When the Environment Agency receives a request to alter or change a process, it must consider the following:

(a) whether the proposed change would involve a breach of any of the conditions of the existing authorisation;

(b) if it would not involve such a breach, whether the Agency would be likely to vary the conditions of the authorisation as a result of the change;

(c) if the variation does involve a breach of the authorisation, whether or not the Agency would consider varying the authorisation so that the change may be made; and

(d) whether the change would involve a substantial change in the manner in which the process is being carried on.

The Environment Agency must, after taking these considerations into account, notify the applicant of its decision and the variations that it would consider making. The position then depends on whether the proposed changes amount to a substantial change or not. If they do not, then the applicant may apply for the relevant variations. If, on the other hand, the Environment Agency determines that the proposed change would amount to a 'substantial change' and notifies the applicant accordingly, then the applicant must apply for a variation if he or she wishes to proceed with the changes. This differs from the former situation where the applicant has a choice of whether or not to apply for a variation. However, in practice, if the Environment Agency has determined that a variation is required for a proposed change and the authorisation holder proceeds with the change without seeking the appropriate variation, the authorisation holder lays open the possibility of enforcement action by the Environment Agency. The Secretary of State has the power, by virtue of the EA 1995 (Sched 22), to call in applications for variations, in the same way that he or she can call in applications for authorisations.

6.14.4 Revocation of authorisations

The Environment Agency can serve a written notice of revocation on the holder of an authorisation where the holder fails to pay the necessary charges associated with the authorisation. In addition, the Environment Agency is also empowered to revoke an authorisation at any time, by virtue of s 12, and can revoke an authorisation where it has reason to believe that the prescribed process has not been carried on at all or for a period of 12 months. The Secretary of State may also issue a direction to the Environment Agency as to whether the Environment Agency should revoke an authorisation.

Revocation of an authorisation is clearly an important enforcement tool, since it means that, once the revocation becomes effective, the prescribed process cannot continue to be carried on without an offence being committed under s 6. Therefore, it is important that the authorisation holder has adequate notice of revocation and the right of appeal. Section 12(1) provides that notice of revocation must be served in writing on the person holding the authorisation, and s 12(3) provides that it shall have effect from the date specified in the notice. The authorisation holder must have at least 28 days' notice from the date the notice is served and the date specified in the notice. The Environment Agency can withdraw the Revocation Notice (RN), or vary the date specified in it, at any time up until the date that the revocation takes effect.

An appeal against a decision of the Environment Agency to revoke an authorisation must be made to the Secretary of State. Where an appeal is made, the revocation will not take effect until the final determination of the appeal or the withdrawal of the appeal (s 15(8)).

6.14.5 Enforcement Notices

Section 13 provides the Environment Agency with the power to serve an Enforcement Notice (EN) in two circumstances:

(a) if, in the opinion of the Environment Agency, the person carrying out the prescribed process under an authorisation is contravening any condition of the authorisation; or

(b) that person is likely to contravene any such condition.

Therefore, the Environment Agency is equipped to deal with situations where there has been a breach of the authorisation or it can take anticipatory action where it is of the opinion that a breach is likely to occur.

Procedurally, the Notice must state that the Environment Agency is of this opinion, it must specify the matters which constitute the contravention or which make a contravention likely, and it must also specify the steps that must be taken to remedy the situation and the date by which such steps must be taken. Once again, the Secretary of State has the power to issue a direction to the Environment Agency as to whether it should exercise its powers under s 13. Failure to comply with an EN is an offence (s 23). A new s 13(4) of the EPA 1990, incorporated by the EA 1995, enables the Agency to withdraw an EN.

6.14.6 Prohibition Notices

Prohibition Notices (PNs) are different from ENs in that they are not aimed at dealing with situations where there has been, or is likely to be, a breach of an authorisation. The aim of the PN is to enable the Environment Agency to take action in situations where the carrying on of the process involves an imminent risk of serious pollution.

Section 14 provides:

If the enforcing authority is of the opinion, as respects the carrying on of a prescribed process under an authorisation, that the continuing to carry it on, or the continuing to carry it on in a particular manner, involves an imminent risk of serious pollution of the environment the authority shall serve a notice (a 'prohibition notice') on the person carrying on the process.

There is no requirement for there to be a contravention of the authorisation. Section 14(2) specifically states that the PN may be served whether or not the manner of carrying on the process in question contravenes a condition of the authorisation. As with ENs, the PN must state the Environment Agency's opinion, specify the risks involved, specify what steps are to be taken to remove the risk and the period of time in which such steps should be taken. Where the Notice applies only to a part of the prescribed process, then it may also apply conditions to that part of the process. The Secretary of State can issue direction to the Environment Agency as to whether a Notice should be served and what matters it should specify in it.

6.14.7 Power to secure compliance with Enforcement Notices and Prohibition Notices

Failure to comply with an EN or PN is an offence triable either way in the magistrates' court or the Crown Court (s 23(1)(b)). Under s 24 of the EPA 1990, the Environment Agency can also seek an injunctive remedy from the High Court to secure compliance with a Notice if it feels that a criminal prosecution will not provide an effective remedy.

6.14.8 Powers of Environment Agency inspectors

The powers of inspectors are wide and are now provided for in a lengthy s 108 of the EA 1995 (previously s 17 of the EPA 1990). The powers conferred on the Environment Agency are also conferred on local authorities exercising their LAAPC functions under Pt I of the EPA 1990. The purpose of s 108 was to streamline the powers of entry and inspection across the range of pollution control functions now exercised by the Environment Agency, and these powers apply equally to control functions under Pt II of the EPA 1990 (Waste Management) and the WRA 1991 (water discharge consents). Section 108 combines the powers previously exercised by HMIP, the NRA and the WRAs.

It is essential that inspectors have these powers of entry and inspection in order to ensure compliance with the authorisations granted and also to identify instances where processes are being carried on without the appropriate authorisation. The powers listed in s 108 of the EA 1995 may be exercised for one or more of the following purposes:

(a) determining whether any pollution control legislation is being or has been complied with;

(b) exercising or performing pollution control functions;

(c) determining whether and, if so, how such a function should be exercised or performed.

Section 108 refers to persons authorised in writing. In practice, this will be the inspectors employed by the Environment Agency (or the relevant local authority officers). An inspector has the following powers of entry and inspection:

(a) to enter at any reasonable time premises which he or she has reason to believe it is necessary for him or her to enter. This should normally be at any reasonable time unless there is an emergency, in which case entry is permitted at any time and, if need be, by force;

(b) on entering premises to take with him or her any other person duly authorised by the Environment Agency, and a policeman. The latter may be needed in situations where the inspector has reasonable cause to apprehend any serious obstruction in carrying out his or her duties;

(c) to take any equipment or materials required for any purpose for which the power of entry is being exercised;

(d) to make such examination and investigation as may in any circumstances be necessary;

(e) to instruct that the premises or any part of them, or anything in them, be left undisturbed. The inspector may require that the premises or the part of the premises under investigation are not disturbed for as long as is reasonably necessary to enable him or her to carry out any examination or investigation;

(f) to take such measurements and photographs and make recordings as he or she considers necessary;

(g) to take samples, or instruct samples be taken, of any articles or substances found in or on the premises and also from the air, water or land in, on or in the vicinity of the premises. Specific provisions relate to the possession, safekeeping and use in evidence of such samples;

(h) in the case of any article or substance found in or on premises which appears to him or her to be an article or substance which has caused or is likely cause pollution of the environment, or harm to human health, to cause it to be dismantled or subjected to any process or test (but not so as to damage or destroy it unless that is necessary);

(i) to require information from any person – the inspector can require any person whom he or she has reasonable cause to believe to be able to give any information relevant to any examination or investigation to answer such questions as the inspector thinks fit to ask. The person answering the questions will be required to sign a declaration of truth to the answers;

(j) to inspect any information and to take copies – the inspector can require the production of any information that he or she considers necessary, including information held on computer. He or she also has the right to inspect and take copies of such information or any entry in the records;

(k) to require facilities and assistance – here, the inspector can require any person to afford him or her such facilities and assistance with respect to any matters or things within that person's control or in relation to which that person has responsibilities. So, for example, the inspector can require an engineer on the premises to show him or her how the monitoring and testing equipment is working (or not working as the case may be);

(l) any other powers conferred by regulation by the Secretary of State. Certain information can be withheld from the inspector if it is subject to legal professional privilege. This covers correspondence between clients and their solicitors or legal professional advisors.

Section 23 of the EPA 1990 makes it an offence not to comply with the requirements of the inspector or to obstruct him or her in carrying out his or her duty.

6.14.9 Powers to remedy harm

Where a process has been operating without authorisation, in breach of conditions or in breach of an EN or PN, then the Environment Agency has the power (s 27) to remedy any harm that may have occurred. In this respect, remediation work can be carried out by the Environment Agency and any costs incurred by it can be recovered from the offender. In addition, s 26 makes provision for the court to make an order for a person convicted of these particular offences to remedy the matter. The court can choose to do this in addition to, or instead of, imposing a fine.

6.15   OFFENCES

Section 23 sets out the offences in relation to IPC and LAAPC processes. These include:

(a) operating a process without authorisation;

(b) failure to comply with an authorisation condition;

(c) failure to comply with an EN or PN;

(d) obstructing an inspector;

(e) failure to comply with the requirements of an inspector;

(f) providing false information on any records that are required to be maintained as a condition of the authorisation.

Through its monitoring and as a result of inspections, the Environment Agency inspectors are usually able to detect breaches of authorisations, either as a result of public complaints or because there has been a pollution incident. The Environment Agency relies on information received from complainants and, to this extent, pressure groups and citizens can play a role in securing the enforcement of environmental law.

Section 157 of the EPA 1990 provides that where an offence is committed by a company, it is possible that any director, manager, secretary or other similar officer (or a person who was purporting to act in such a capacity) of the company may also be guilty. However, in order to establish this personal criminal liability, it has to be proved that the offence was committed with that person's consent or connivance or to have been attributable to any neglect on his or her part. Section 158 also provides that where an offence has been committed by any person due to the act or default of some other person, that other person may be charged with and convicted of the offence. The effect of this provision is that it could expose senior company officials to the risk of prosecution.

6.15.1 Enforcement policy

The Environment Agency's enforcement and prosecution policy is considered in detail in Chapter 2. The Environment Agency's policy does not apply to the local authorities which also have responsibility in terms of enforcing the provisions of Pt I of the EPA 1990 in respect of Part B prescribed processes (LAAPC).

In general terms, it is clear that the intention is that breaches of authorisation standards and other problems should be dealt with quickly and effectively with the co-operation of the operator. However, it is also very clear that the Environment Agency will strive to avoid problems occurring in the first instance by providing advice and assistance to those subject to the system of IPC control.

Notwithstanding this, the Environment Agency does have a number of enforcement tools at its disposal, notably ENs and PNs, which have already been discussed, warning, caution and, ultimately, prosecution. However, it is also worth noting that before taking any of these steps, an inspector may often write a letter to an alleged offender which sets out any remedial action which the Environment Agency expects to be taken. Where an inspector sends out such a letter, it must set out in clear terms what needs to be done, why, within what period, and what relevant law applies. It should also explain to the recipient that he or she has 10 working days to make any representations to the Environment Agency if it is thought that the action required is not justified. The Environment Agency should not take formal enforcement action during the 10 working day period, unless immediate action is justified by the risk. Thus, it can be seen that the Environment Agency can seek to resolve problems or deal with breaches of the law in an informal manner which gives the 'polluter' the opportunity to comply before any formal action is taken.

As far as prosecution is concerned, the Environment Agency's enforcement policy makes it clear that this is an issue for its discretion. Clearly, a breach of IPC authorisation does not result in automatic prosecution and the Environment Agency will consider the circumstances of each case and what would be gained by a prosecution.

6.15.2 Penalties

Section 23 of the EPA 1990 lays down the various penalties for the offences created in the same section. The offences of carrying on a prescribed process without an authorisation or failing to comply with an EN or PN can result in a maximum fine of up to £20,000 in the magistrates' court or six months' imprisonment or both. On conviction on indictment in the Crown Court, the penalty can increase to an unlimited fine or to between two and five years' imprisonment.

Evidence suggests that the magistrates are willing to impose sizeable fines for offences committed under IPC. For example, in a case brought by HMIP against Southern Refining Services (SRS) (*HMIP v Southern Refining Services Ltd* (1994)), Newbury magistrates imposed a fine of £12,000 for an air pollution incident caused by SRS's procedures for dealing with residues from a distillation process. In addition, the magistrates made an award of costs against SRS of over £6,000. The case concerned an air pollution incident which occurred as a result of an operator mistakenly adding quantities of the biocide sodium dichloroisocyanurate to a process, instead of sodium carbonate. This resulted in the release of noxious fumes, including chlorine gas. The release lasted for 10–15 minutes. As a result of the incident, more than 20 of the company's workforce had to be treated for eye irritation. The company showed itself willing to co-operate with HMIP during the subsequent investigation. The company was charged with, and pleaded guilty to, a breach of an IPC authorisation under s 23(1) of the EPA 1990. Three breaches were identified by HMIP: failure to take all practicable means to prevent fugitive emissions; failure to provide staff with appropriate written operating instructions; and failure to label drums correctly. The case is interesting because the magistrates, unusually, took the turnover and the profitability of the company into account when determining the level of fine. The turnover of the company was reported to be £500,000 and its profit between £80,000 and £100,000.

6.16   RIGHTS OF APPEAL

Section 15 of the EPA 1990 provides various rights of appeal in relation to all parts of Pt I and, as such, it should be remembered that this is equally applicable to LAAPC. In addition to s 15, the Environmental Protection (Application, Appeals and Registers) Regulations 1991 (SI 1991/507) provide detailed information about the appeals procedure. An appeal must be brought within two months of the relevant decision or determination.

A right of appeal lies with the person seeking the authorisation or the authorisation holder against the following:

(a) refusal to grant an authorisation;

(b) the conditions attached to an authorisation;

(c) refusal to grant a variation of an authorisation sought by the authorisation holder (under s 11);

(d) revocation of an authorisation;

(e) a Variation Notice (VN), EN or PN.

No appeal may be brought against a decision which implements a direction made by the Secretary of State.

In addition, s 22 allows a right of appeal concerning exclusion of commercially confidential information from the register.

In the following actions in appeal cases, the Secretary of State can:

(a) affirm the decision taken by the Environment Agency or local authority;

(b) where the decision was a refusal to grant an authorisation or a variation of an authorisation, direct the Environment Agency or local authority to grant the authorisation or vary it accordingly;

(c) quash all or any of the conditions of an authorisation;

(d) quash a decision to revoke an authorisation;

(e) give directions as to the conditions to be attached to authorisations;

(f) quash, affirm or modify a VN, EN or PN.

6.16.1 The form of appeal

Although the appeal is to the Secretary of State, the Secretary of State has the power, by virtue of s 114 of the EA 1995, to delegate the hearing of appeals to chief inspectors. Alternatively, the Secretary of State may direct that the hearing takes the form of a local inquiry. As stated above, the details of the appeals procedure are laid down in SI 1991/507.

6.17   THE INTERFACE BETWEEN IPC AND OTHER POLLUTION CONTROLS

One of the principal reasons for establishing the Environment Agency was to achieve a degree of uniformity across the environmental protection regimes thus far regulated by different bodies. The creation of the Environment Agency has removed the need for HMIP, the NRA and the WRAs to consult each other on areas of shared concern and therefore a number of statutory provisions requiring that consultation have been repealed. For example, HMIP was required by Pt I of the EPA 1990 (s 28) to consult the NRA regarding any discharges to controlled water from IPC processes before granting an IPC authorisation. Nevertheless, the system of IPC described in this chapter does not provide a completely integrated system for controlling all polluting activities. The system sits alongside other control mechanisms and so it is worth considering the relationship between IPC and other legislative controls.

6.17.1 Waste

Processes that operate under an IPC authorisation are exempted from the waste management licensing system. However, the Environment Agency cannot attach any conditions to an IPC authorisation concerning the final disposal by deposit in or on land of directive waste. Where an IPC process involves the final disposal of controlled (directive) waste deposited in or on land, then it is also subject to the licensing controls under Pt II of the EPA 1990. A person or business carrying on the process may then need to obtain a waste management licence in addition to the IPC authorisation.

6.17.2 Statutory nuisance

Section 79 in Pt III of the EPA 1990 deals with the relationship between the controls under Pt I of the Act and the statutory nuisance provisions under Pt III. A local authority cannot institute summary proceedings without the consent of the Secretary of State in respect of a nuisance falling under s 79 if proceedings could be instituted under Pt I of the EPA 1990. However, this provision does not prevent a citizen commencing his or her own action under s 82, or a local authority from serving an Abatement Notice under s 80.

6.17.3 Discharges into sewers

Many IPC processes will involve the discharge of trade effluent into the sewers. Although the IPC authorisation will attach conditions concerning the discharge, the process operator will still require a trade effluent consent from the sewage undertaker by virtue of s 118 of the Water Industry Act 1991. Where it is proposed that special category effluent is discharged into the sewer, the sewerage undertaker is duty bound to consult the Environment Agency before granting a trade effluent consent. In fact, it is a criminal offence if the undertaker fails to consult the Environment Agency.

6.17.4 IPC and contaminated land

Land which is being used, or has been used, for the operation of an IPC process (and in the future an IPPC installation) may be classed as contaminated if the local authority is satisfied that it falls within the statutory definition under Pt IIA of the EPA 1990. In practice, it seems likely that land subject to the types of industrial processes falling under IPC/IPPC will at least have substances present on it. The determining factor will be whether the substances pose a significant possibility of harm. Where land subject to an IPC process/IPPC installation is contaminated, then it will be classed as a 'special site' by virtue of reg 2(1)(d) of the Contaminated Land (England) Regulations 2000 (SI 2000/227). However, even where the land is classed as a special site, it does not follow that remediation will be required under Part IIA of the EPA 1990. The Environment Agency, as the enforcing authority for special sites, cannot serve a Remediation Notice in relation to the site if the powers of clean-up under s 27 of the EPA are exercisable (see s 78YB(1) of the EPA 1990). Section 27 allows the Agency to take steps to remedy harm where harm has been caused as a result of the breach of an IPC consent or breach of an Enforcement or Prohibition Notice. It should be noted that remediation operations may constitute regulated processes under IPC/IPPC.

6.18   IPC AND IPPC

6.18.1 Introduction

In late 1996, the EC passed the Integrated Pollution Prevention Control Directive (96/61/EC) which required all Member States to set up a Command and Control licensing system of regulation with regard to the activities listed in Annexe 1 of the Directive. The IPPC control regime as detailed in the Directive is similar, in many respects, to IPC except that the primary objective of IPPC is to regulate environmental impacts of highly polluting industrial activities, rather than the IPC focus on the regulation of all environmental emissions from highly polluting industrial processes.

The IPPC Directive was transposed into national legislation by the Pollution Prevention and Control Act (PPCA) 1999. The legislative framework contained in the 1999 Act is supplemented by the Pollution Prevention and Control (England and Wales) Regulations 2000 (PPC Regulations 2000) (SI 2000/1973), as amended. IPPC controls are to be phased in over the period 1999–2007. Activities commenced after 31 October 1999 are immediately subject to IPPC, as are substantial changes to existing processes which are currently subject to IPC control.

The IPPC Directive obliges Member States to prevent or, where prevention is not possible, reduce pollution *and* environmental impacts from the range of installations listed in Annexe 1 of the Directive in order to achieve a high level of protection of the environment as a whole. A licensing system is used to regulate the activities of the listed installations.

Each IPPC licence (referred to as a 'permit') is designed, not only to regulate environmental emissions discharged to all three environmental media (air, water and land) but also the environmental impacts of the following: energy use and efficiency, raw material consumption, noise, vibration, accident prevention measures and heat (thermal effects). Regulatory control, as specified in permit conditions, extends beyond day-to-day operational controls to include after-care and site remediation. In contrast to a number of other EC directives, the IPPC Directive requires permits to be set by reference to local conditions and any applicable environmental quality standards. The UK has taken advantage of the terms of the Directive to extend the scope of IPPC control to include activities which are currently regulated under Pt I of the EPA 1990 as Part B processes (that is, local authority air pollution control). It has been necessary to extend IPPC control to Part B processes since the entire IPC regime will be phased out by 2007 and processes subject to local authority air pollution control would otherwise be left unregulated.

IPPC replaces the dual system of IPC controls (regulating the highly polluting emissions from Part A processes, regulated by the Environment Agency, and less polluting emissions to the atmosphere, regulated by the local authorities) by a 'single' system of control applying to the *installations* listed in Annexe 1 of the IPPC Directive. Under the IPPC regulatory regime, the Environment Agency regulates the highly polluting installations (Part A(1) installations). However, in contrast to their previously limited LAAPC responsibilities, local authorities now have a greater regulatory role under IPPC: they are responsible for regulating Part A(2) installations with regard to *all environmental impacts*, and Part B installations regarding atmospheric emissions only (rather than atmospheric impacts).

IPPC controls, like their IPC counterparts, use process standards to determine licence conditions. In particular, 'best available techniques' (BAT) must be employed by installation operators to prevent and/or reduce the environmental impacts of regulated installations.

6.18.2 IPPC distinguished from IPC

Not only does IPPC have a wider focus than IPC, regulating environmental impacts rather than environmental emissions, but its ambit is also significantly wider. The Environment Agency has asserted that whilst the IPPC regime builds upon IPC, it would be 'wrong to view it as IPC with an added "P"'. Like IPC, it covers emissions to air, land and water, but IPPC goes further and covers noise and vibration, energy efficiency, waste minimisation, environmental accidents and site protection. There are approximately 7,000 'listed' installations subject to IPPC control as opposed to the 2,000 Part A and 12,500 Part B processes subject to IPC control. In particular, IPPC has extended control to large landfill sites, intensive agricultural production units, and food and drink factories.

IPPC regulates 'installations' rather than 'prescribed processes'. IPPC regulation is therefore a site, or plant-based, method of regulation. This avoids the potential complexity of IPC regulation where several individually licensed processes are all undertaken on the same site.

IPPC provides a greater role for local authorities who have assumed responsibility for the regulation of the environmental impacts of Part A(2) installations to all three environmental media, in addition to their existing Part B regulatory role. Thus, for the first time, local authorities extend their remit beyond 'policing' atmospheric emissions from Part B processes. In contrast to IPC, IPPC provides no exemptions from the need to obtain an IPPC permit.

IPPC's adoption of a BAT standard for all installations contrasts with the BATNEEC condition incorporated in IPC authorisations but, in reality, the two standards are similar since, when determining IPPC permits, the regulator must have regard to the 'proportionality principle' requiring it to take the economic viability of the BAT standard into account.

Under IPC, the Environment Agency and the local authorities are required to review authorisations at least once every four years. IPPC does not specify a mandatory timetable for reviewing permits although official guidance may recommend timetables for each industry sector.

6.19 IPPC PERMITS

Regulation 9(1) of the PPC Regulations 2000 states that no person shall operate an installation or mobile plant after the prescribed date, except under and in accordance with a permit granted by the regulator, and it is an offence under reg 32 of the PPC Regulations 2000 to contravene this provision.

In deciding whether or not to grant a permit, the Environment Agency or local authority must take into account the statutory objectives of IPPC: to achieve a high level of protection for the environment taken as a whole by, in particular, preventing, or reducing, emissions into the air, water and land.

'Pollution' (see reg 2 of the PPC Regulations 2000) has a wider meaning under IPPC than its equivalent IPC definition (s 1(3) of the EPA 1990) and includes emissions which may be harmful to human health or environmental quality. The term also extends to activities which cause offence to human senses, damage to property, or impair or interfere with amenities and other uses of the environment. The largely anthropocentric (human-centred) definition of pollution is clearly intended to focus attention upon the wide range of environmental impacts caused by human activity. These impacts are commonly referred to as 'externalities'. The definition reflects the wider IPPC focus on impacts rather than a narrower range of polluting emissions. Readers should note that the emission-focused BPEO concept is not relevant to IPPC regulation.

6.19.1 'Listed' activities which are subject to IPPC

Schedule 1 to the PPC Regulations 2000 lists and divides 'activities' into six chapters:

(1) energy industries;

(2) production and processing of metals;

(3) minerals industries;

(4) chemical industry;

(5) waste management;

(6) other activities.

Each of the six industry chapters is subdivided into a further set of groupings. Finally, each industry grouping is split into two smaller groups reflecting the regulatory body responsible for 'policing' the relevant installation. Part A(1) activities are regulated by the Environment Agency and Part A(2) and B installations are regulated by the local authorities.

The six industry chapters include activities which were not previously subject to IPC. Of particular note is the inclusion of large waste management facilities, food and drink manufacturing and intensive agricultural production units. Annexe 1 of the IPPC Directive contains details of thresholds. Activities falling below the thresholds are excluded, for example, small landfill sites.

6.19.2 Installations

The term 'installation' (see reg 2(1)) refers to any stationary technical unit where a prescribed activity is carried out. It also includes any other directly associated activities carried out on the same site which have a technical connection with the prescribed activities and which could have an effect on pollution. Although that specific definition of installation appears to exclude mobile plant, it is apparent from the Regulations that mobile plants are within the scope of the regime. For example, reg 9 specifies that no person shall operate an installation or mobile plant except under authorisation. A 'mobile plant' is defined as a plant which is designed to move or be moved whether on roads or otherwise and which is used to carry out one or more activities listed in Pt I of Sched 1.

6.19.3 Listed substances and permit conditions

Schedule 5 to the PPC Regulations 2000 lists substances which might be discharged by installations into air or water. Where significant amounts of these substances are to be discharged from an installation, the IPPC permit must include conditions which set either limit values or environmental quality standards for the relevant substances.

6.19.4 Exemptions

There is no exemption from the necessity of obtaining a permit if the relevant installation falls within the parameters of IPPC. Installations which have only 'trivial' ('trivial' is a term which has no statutory definition and, as yet, no official guidance) environmental impacts will require a permit, but the permitting process will be simpler.

6.19.5 Applying for a permit

The application process is detailed in regs 7 and 10 of and Sched 4 to the PPC Regulations 2000.

An application (accompanied by the relevant fee) must contain the following essential information:

(a) condition of the site (information is required regarding any pollution risks posed by the site. The applicant may use any Environmental Impact Assessment (EIA), prepared with regard to a linked planning application for the site, to help satisfy this requirement. Details relating to site condition will be used, at the time of site closure, for the purpose of comparing the relative condition of the site before and after the cessation of activities);

(b) raw materials and energy usage relevant to the proposed activity;

(c) waste minimisation and waste prevention measures;

(d) emissions and environmental impacts;

(e) technology and techniques to reduce emissions and impacts which are currently incapable of elimination;

(f) accident prevention;

(g) monitoring proposals;

(h) a non-technical summary of the foregoing information.

The Environment Agency, in an effort to secure quality applications, has produced guidelines for applicants on how to produce a 'good' application. This information is available on the Environment Agency's website.

6.19.6 Advertising the permit application

Any applicant who requires a permit or who operates an existing permitted facility but is planning a substantial change to the relevant installation must advertise details of the application in a local newspaper and, in the case of Part A(1) and Part A(2) installations, in the *London Gazette* (see Sched 4 to the PPC Regulations 2000). The relevant press notice must contain the following information:

(a) the applicant's name and address;

(b) a brief description of the proposed activities;

(c) a reference to any public register containing relevant information relating to the applicant;

(d) an invitation to make representations to the relevant regulator (Environment Agency or local authority) within 28 days of the appearance of the press notice.

This procedure is similar to planning applications since it provides an opportunity for the general public to participate in the licensing process.

6.19.7 Consultation and participation

As in the case of IPC, IPPC permit applications are subject to consultation with a number of statutory bodies including:

(a) the Health and Safety Executive;

(b) the relevant health authority;

(c) the Nature Conservancy Council (if emissions could affect a Site of Special Scientific Interest);

(d) the relevant water service company;

(e) the relevant sewerage undertaker;

(f) the relevant planning authority (regarding proposed waste management sites);

(g) an EC Member State (where the Secretary of State is 'aware' that the application, if granted, is likely to have significant effects on the relevant Member State).

In addition to the statutory consultees, the Environment Agency and local authorities consult one another regarding Part A(1) and Part A(2) applications.

The consultation process is administered by the regulator responsible for the relevant installation. Within 14 days of receipt of the permit application or variation application, the regulator is required to notify the consultees (with the exception of affected Member States) of the application and provide a minimum 28 day period (which may be extended) within which the consultee can make representations. Responses received from consultees are material considerations which the regulator must have regard to in reaching a decision on the application. Normally, the application should be decided within four months of the date it was lodged with the regulator, but this period may be extended by agreement.

On 18 January 2001, the European Commission put forward a proposal for a directive providing for public participation in respect of the drawing up of certain plans and programmes relating to the environment, which would amend the IPPC Directive (96/61/EC) in order to bring it in line with Art 6 of the Aarhus Convention (see http://europa.eu.int/scadplus/leg/en/lvb/l28056.htm). The article on public participation is amended, *inter alia*, to require Member States to ensure that the public concerned are given early and effective opportunities to participate in the decision making procedure for granting permits. In addition, a new annexe is introduced which sets out detailed provisions on public participation, including a requirement for competent authorities to inform the public of the contents of their decisions (a copy of the permit and any conditions) and of the grounds and considerations on which those decisions are based. The proposal for a directive stipulates that the public concerned must have access to legal review procedures which are expeditious, are not prohibitively expensive and which make it possible to challenge the legality of any act or omission covered by the provisions of the Aarhus Convention relating to public participation.

6.19.8 The considerations which are material to the permit decision

The decision to grant an application for a permit (with conditions) or refuse it will be taken by the regulator (Environment Agency or local authority) on the basis of the information submitted by the applicant, the representations made by consultees and the public, matters specified in the PPC Regulations 2000 and any other material considerations, such as official guidance relating to what constitutes BAT for the relevant installation.

In most cases, it is anticipated that, like planning applications, the decision will be made on the merits of each individual application. However, the option exists to decide applications on the basis of 'general binding rules'. This is a decision process which will probably apply to simple installations, such as intensive agricultural installations, and would set standard permit conditions in accordance with the relevant set of general binding rules.

The regulator (Environment Agency or local authority) is under a duty to refuse the application if it considers that the applicant will not be able to comply with the permit conditions which would be included were the application to be approved (reg 10(3)). It is quite likely that this IPPC duty will enable the regulator to take into account whether the applicant is fit to carry on the activities detailed in the application, bearing in mind the applicant's compliance history. Where the application relates to a waste management site, the regulator will be compelled to reject the application if (a) the applicant is not a fit and proper person (reg 4), or (b) no planning permission authorising waste management usage for the site exists. This reflects the requirements of the waste management licensing regime under Pt II of the EPA 1990.

6.19.9 The permit conditions: general principles

Regulation 11 lays down some general principles which the regulator must take into account when determining the conditions of a permit. Regulation 11(2) specifies the general principle that installations and mobile plant should be operated in such a way that all appropriate measures are taken against pollution, in particular through application of the best available techniques and that no significant pollution is caused. This means that the regulator must, in determining applications, prescribe conditions which do not permit *significant* pollution to be caused. In addition to this, reg 11(3) also lays down further general principles which relate only to Part A installations and mobile plant. These are that the installation or mobile plant should be operated in such away as to minimise waste production (in accordance with the Waste Framework Directive (75/442/EEC)) or, where minimisation is not possible, to ensure that waste is recovered or disposed of whilst avoiding or reducing any impact on the environment; and that the installations should use energy efficiently and take the necessary measures to prevent accidents and limit their consequences. Thus, the widened scope of this regime is expressed here in terms of general principles which must be taken into account by the regulator. They are not expressed in terms of duties and it seems clear that, providing the regulator takes these principles 'into account', it retains considerable discretion as to the weight accorded to them. No doubt, as the regime becomes more fully operative, the courts will be given the opportunity to examine the status of these principles.

6.19.10 Best available techniques

Material to the permit decision are the IPPC objectives which require all applicants to operate their installations in ways which use best available techniques (BAT) to prevent pollution of the environment.

The requirement for IPPC permit holders to employ BAT is detailed in regs 12–14. The BAT obligation is applicable not only to the technology employed in operating the installation, but also encompasses the design, construction, maintenance and decommissioning of the installation. Official guidance, in the form of 'BREF' (BAT reference) notes and other guidance will provide supplementary information on what is considered to be BAT in each industry sector subject to IPPC.

Bearing in mind that IPPC is applicable to all EC Member States, in contrast to IPC which has a UK remit, guidance as to what will constitute BAT is now an EC matter. Under Art 16(2) of the IPPC Directive, the EC Commission has established a pan-European forum for the exchange of information on BAT. The IPPC Information Exchange Forum will publish its findings tri-annually. The Forum will have an important input into the final form of BREF guidance notes, especially concerning what BAT can achieve with regard to reductions in emissions, energy consumption, and raw material usage. BREF notes will be material to both individual permit applications and what is considered to be BAT in each of the six industry sectors subject to IPPC.

In contrast to the equivalent IPC BATNEEC requirement, BAT does not itself include any reference to cost/benefit considerations in determining the techniques which fulfil the BAT test. Nevertheless, cost/benefit considerations are relevant because of the applicability of the EC proportionality principle. Under the BATNEEC test, not only were the costs and benefits of a particular technique taken into account, but also the capacity of each industry sector to buy in the relevant technique. BAT differs from BATNEEC with regard to the materiality of the economic viability of an industry sector as a relevant consideration.

6.19.11 The meaning of BAT

The PPC Regulations 2000 provide much of the detail on what constitutes BAT. A summary of the key points is provided here.

6.19.11.1 Best

This term refers to the effectiveness of any technique to be employed by an applicant to achieve a high level of environmental protection. There may be several techniques which could be employed to achieve the requisite level of environmental protection and in such circumstances they will all satisfy the 'best' criterion.

6.19.11.2 Available

This term refers to the availability of techniques. Techniques are available if they have been developed on a sufficiently large enough scale which enables the applicant to acquire and install/implement them. This is a stricter criterion than the equivalent term in the BATNEEC test. Techniques will not be treated as available in any of the six industrial sectors subject to IPPC control if economic or technical conditions in the relevant industry prevent the technique being viable. Material to the question of whether a specific technique is available will be its costs and benefits, and its current manufacture and/or use in the UK.

6.19.11.3 Techniques

This term is wider than 'technology' and includes considerations such as the design, construction, maintenance and decommissioning of the relevant technique.

In the guidance issued by the Environment Agency, it is suggested that applicants must demonstrate how they intend to operate the installation and why such operation represents BAT. There must be a reasoned justification that the techniques employed represent BAT. It is only sufficient simply to state that the chosen option represents BAT if it corresponds with that specified as indicative BAT in the technical guidance. However, where the operator opts to employ an alternative option, then he will presumably have to provide this reasoned justification. In the same way that s 7(4) of the EPA 1990 does in relation to IPC, reg 12(10) of the PPC Regulations 2000 introduces an implied BAT condition. There is implied in every permit a condition that, in operating the installation or mobile plant, the operator shall use the best available techniques for preventing or, where that is not practicable, reducing emissions from the installation or the mobile plant.

6.19.12 'Call in' power

The Secretary of State has the power to 'call in' an IPPC permit application for his own decision (Sched 4, para 14 of the PPC Regulations 2000). Where an application is called in, the Secretary of State cannot make the decision himself on the application but he directs the regulator as to whether it should grant or refuse the application. In the event that he directs that the application should be granted, he has the power to direct the conditions which are to be included in the permit. Before directing the regulator as to the outcome of the permit application, the Secretary of State will either hold a public inquiry or an informal hearing into the application.

6.19.13 The transfer and surrender of IPPC permits

Regulation 18 of the PPC Regulations 2000 details the procedure to apply for a transfer of all or part of the activities authorised by the installation permit to another person (usually the company which is in the process of acquiring the permit holders' business). A joint application by the existing and proposed permit holder is necessary specifying the date on which the transfer is required to take effect. The regulator may only reject the application if it considers that the proposed permit holder would not be able to comply with the permit conditions or, in the case of the proposed transfer of a waste management installation permit, that the proposed permit holder is not a fit and proper person.

The regulator has two months to determine the application but this period may be extended by agreement. Somewhat unusually, a failure by the regulator to deal with the application within the relevant timescale will lead to a deemed transfer rather than a deemed refusal.

The provisions relating to the surrender of IPPC permits are similar to those contained in s 39 of the EPA 1990 relating to the surrender of waste management licences. In this respect, they represent a much stricter approach to environmental regulation than is currently found in Pt I of the EPA 1990. Under reg 19 of the PPC Regulations 2000, the regulator is not permitted to accept a surrender of an existing permit unless it is satisfied that any necessary clean-up works have been satisfactorily completed. A Part A(1) and A(2) installation permit holder must make a specific application to the regulator regarding a proposed surrender of its permit. The application can relate to all or part of the authorised activities at the relevant installation. The application must include the following information:

(a) the name and address of the permit holder;

(b) a plan of the installation indicating whether the whole or part of the installation is subject to the application;

(c) a site report specifying the present condition of the site and any changes which have occurred since the permit was originally granted;

(d) details of the precautionary steps taken to avoid pollution and any remedial action taken to return the installation to a satisfactory state.

The regulator must be satisfied that the installation does not pose any pollution risk before it can accept the surrender. The onus falls squarely on the permit holder to provide the regulator with sufficient information which will convince the regulator that the installation is in a satisfactory condition, poses no risk of pollution and therefore the regulator can safely accept the surrender. The permit holder is presumed to be responsible for any material difference in the condition of the installation as revealed in the pre-permit report and the present condition of the installation.

The regulator has three months to reach a decision on the surrender application, although this period may be extended by agreement. Failure to determine the application within the relevant timescale results in a deemed refusal.

6.20 ENFORCEMENT POWERS

6.20.1 Administrative enforcement powers

IPPC regulators (the Environment Agency and local authorities) have an extensive array of enforcement powers at their disposal to ensure that the permit holder complies with the terms of its permit (regs 21 and 23–25 of the PPC Regulations 2000). These powers enable the regulators to retain tight control over authorised activities without having to resort to prosecution as a control mechanism.

The regulator is subject to a duty (reg 23 of the PPC Regulations 2000) to supervise authorised activities. The regulator is required to take any steps which are necessary to ensure that the permit holder complies with the conditions attached to its permit. How the regulator chooses to secure compliance with permit conditions is a matter for regulatory discretion. The following administrative powers are the most significant.

6.20.2 Enforcement Notice (EN)

The regulator may serve an EN on a permit holder if the regulator believes that the permit holder has breached, or is likely to breach, any permit condition (reg 24 of the PPC Regulations 2000). An EN will specify the breach, the remedial action required and the timescale during which the remedial action must be completed.

Failure to comply with an EN is a criminal offence (reg 32 of the PPC Regulations 2000).

6.20.3 Revocation Notice (RN)

The regulator may revoke all or part of the activities authorised by the permit via service of an RN (reg 21 of the PPC Regulations 2000). With regard to waste management installations, an RN may be served where the permit holder ceases to be a fit and proper person. As the service of an RN is a rather heavyweight enforcement option, it is only likely to be used in the face of persistent non-compliance. An appeal against an RN suspends the operation of the notice pending the outcome of the appeal hearing.

6.20.4 Suspension Notice (SN)

The regulator has a duty to serve an SN if it considers that the operation of an installation involves an imminent risk of serious pollution (reg 25 of the PPC Regulations 2000). If such a risk exists, an SN must be served irrespective of whether permit conditions have been observed. The duty to serve an SN does not apply in circumstances in which the regulator intended to take action in any event under reg 26 of the PPC Regulations 2000. An SN may be used to suspend all or part of the permitted activities.

6.20.5 Variation Notice (VN)

The regulator has a discretion to review permits at any time (reg 17 of the PPC Regulations 2000) subject to official guidance relating to the permit review process. The VN power enables the regulator to tighten permit conditions in response to changes in circumstances, such as changes in industry sector BAT, or the emergence of new environmental risks. IPPC permit holders are obliged to inform the regulator of changes made to the installation which may have environmental impacts. The receipt of such information may act as a trigger and prompt the regulator to review and vary the current permit conditions. VNs may also be served in two further instances: (a) where the permit holder wishes to vary the terms of the permit; and (b) where the Environment Agency specifies new conditions applicable to Part A(2) installations which the local authorities must implement.

A VN application must include the following information:

(a) the name, address, and telephone number of the permit holder;

(b) the address of the installation;

(c) the proposed changes and their environmental impacts.

The regulator has the power to require the permit holder to provide further information to enable the regulator to process the VN application.

6.20.6 Powers to acquire information

The regulator and the Secretary of State have the power by virtue of reg 28 of the PPC Regulations 2000 to serve a notice on any person requiring him or her to provide the information specified within the notice and by the deadline also specified in it. This provision is widely stated, in that the regulator can serve such a notice on 'any person'. It is a criminal offence not to comply with such a notice without reasonable excuse.

6.21 APPEALS AND PUBLIC REGISTERS

Appeals are dealt with in reg 27 of the PPC Regulations 2000 which states that IPPC permit holders have a right of appeal to the Secretary of State against the following:

(a) the service of an RN, VN, EN or SN;

(b) a refusal to grant or a refusal to vary or suspend a permit (refusals include deemed refusals);

(c) the permit conditions;

(d) the regulator's decision that information relating to the permit is not commercially confidential and should be included on the public register.

Appeals must be lodged within six months of the regulatory decision appealed against except in the case of appeals against ENs, SNs and VNs (where the time limit is two months from the date of the relevant notice), RNs (where the appeal must be lodged before the notice takes effect) and appeals against commercial confidentiality (where the time limit is 21 days from the relevant decision). Only in the case of RN appeals is the operation of the notice suspended provided the appeal is lodged in time. Appeals may be heard by way of a full hearing or written representations (that is, a paper-based appeal) and the Secretary of State has the power to order that an appeal proceed by way of a full hearing, in public, irrespective of the wishes of the applicant. On determining an appeal, the Secretary of State may, *inter alia*, either affirm the decision of the regulator, direct the regulator to grant or vary the conditions or quash all or any of the conditions.

6.21.1 Public registers

The IPPC regime makes provision for a public register of information in much the same way as the current IPC regime. Where information of any description is excluded from the register because it is commercially confidential then the register must include a statement to that effect.

6.22 CRIMINAL LAW ENFORCEMENT

In common with other Command and Control licence-based regulatory regimes, IPPC is underpinned by a number of criminal offences (reg 32 of the PPC Regulations 2000). These offences are not expected to be used frequently given the extensive range of administrative enforcement powers available to regulators. Amongst the criminal offences listed in reg 32, it is a criminal offence to:

(a) operate an IPPC installation without a permit;

(b) breach permit conditions;

(c) fail to give notice of a change in the operation of that installation;

(d) fail to comply with an EN or SN;

(e) fail without reasonable excuse to provide the information required by the register under reg 28;

(f) intentionally make false entries in official records.

6.22.1 Sentencing

All offences may be summarily tried in the magistrates' court or on indictment in the Crown Court. The penalties vary depending upon the offence; however, in relation to the offences (a), (b) and (d) listed above, the maximum penalty in the magistrates' court is a fine of up to £20,000 or to imprisonment for up to six months or both. The maximum penalty in the Crown Court is an unlimited fine and/or a prison sentence of up to five years.

The PPC Regulations 2000, like the provisions relating to IPC in the EPA 1990, provide for the personal liability of 'management' in the event that a company is prosecuted under these Regulations. Specifically, reg 32(4) of the Regulations provides that where an offence has been committed by a company and is proved to have been committed with the consent or connivance of (or attributable to the neglect on the part of) any director, manager, secretary or other similar officer (or a person who was purporting to act in any such capacity), he or she will also be liable. This regulation makes it plain that the regulator can proceed against both the company and the individual in such circumstances and both shall be punished accordingly.

6.22.2 Injunctions

Where a permit holder has failed to comply with an EN or SN, the regulator may apply for an injunction provided that it can establish that enforcement of the relevant criminal law would fail to secure adequate compliance with the EN or SN (reg 33 of the PPC Regulations 2000).

6.22.3 Remedial powers

Both the regulator and the courts have powers in relation to the remediation of environmental damage. Under reg 26 of the PPC Regulations 2000, the regulator may take steps to remedy the effects of the pollution caused when an operator has operated without a permit, has operated in contravention of the permit conditions or has failed to comply with an EN or SN. Where the regulator does this, it must give the operator seven days' notice of this intention and it may recover the costs of taking those steps from the operator concerned. However, in circumstances where the regulator is of the opinion that the operation of an installation or mobile plant, or the way in which it is being operated, involves an imminent risk of serious pollution, the regulator can arrange for immediate steps to be taken to remove that risk and there is no need for the seven day notification. Again, the regulator can seek to recover its costs except where the operator can prove that there was no imminent risk of serious pollution. In relation to either of these situations, it appears from the wording of the regulation that the operator is not required to pay any costs which have been caused 'unnecessarily' by the regulator.

In circumstances where a person has been convicted for operating without a permit, for contravening the permit conditions or for failure to comply with an EN or SN, then the courts also have the power to make an order requiring that any environmental damage resulting from the offence be remedied by the defendant (reg 35 of the PPC Regulations 2000). The court may do this either as an alternative or in addition to imposing any fine/custodial sentence.

6.23   THE INTERFACE OF IPPC WITH OTHER REGULATORY CONTROLS

There are a number of regulatory regimes whose remits overlap with IPPC. The more important of these regulatory controls are referred to below.

6.23.1 Waste management

IPPC will take approximately 900 landfill sites out of the waste management licensing regime in Pt II of the EPA 1990. Small landfill sites (defined by the volume of waste received in any day and the total capacity of the site) will continue to be licensed and regulated under the EPA 1990.

The application of IPPC regulation to large landfill sites is expected to be phased in by the end of 2003. What constitutes BAT for these installations is detailed in the Landfill Directive. Certain waste disposal and waste recovery operations, subject to the thresholds referred to in the regulations, fall within IPPC control.

6.23.2 Contaminated land

Site contamination which precedes IPPC control may be dealt with either under the contaminated land controls (Pt II of the EPA 1990) or under s 27 of the EPA 1990 relating to IPC controls and breach of an IPC authorisation.

The standard of clean-up required under the IPPC regime (to accord with the condition of the site before commencement of the activities authorised in an IPPC permit) is higher than the standard required under the contaminated land regime ('suitable for use'). This has ramifications for an applicant who wishes to apply for an IPPC permit. An applicant who fails to identify any pre-existing site contamination before commencement of IPPC regulated activities will almost certainly be required to clean up all contamination discovered irrespective of whether the contamination relates to the permit holders' IPPC activities or not.

6.23.3 Water pollution

Since local authorities have no experience of issuing water pollution discharge consents, it was recognised that the regulation of Part A(2) installations might be problematic for local authorities with regard to aquatic discharges. To address this potential problem, the Environment Agency has been tasked to supervise the imposition of water-related permit conditions for Part A(2) installations. The Environment Agency has power to notify local authorities of the minimum conditions, relating to aquatic discharges, which the Environment Agency requires to be included in any Part A(2) permit. The Environment Agency also has a discretion to require the imposition of stricter conditions to take account of local circumstances. Compliance with an IPPC permit will provide a statutory defence to any s 85 of the WRA 1991 prosecution.

6.23.4 Sewer discharges

There is an overlap of regulatory controls in regard to discharges from IPPC installations to sewers. All discharges to sewers must be licensed by the relevant sewerage undertaker under the WIA 1991. Since such discharges have environmental impacts, they may be the subject of IPPC permit conditions.

6.23.5 The town and country planning system

In practice, planning and IPPC controls may overlap with regard to the type of conditions which are appropriate to impose in both planning permissions and IPPC permits. Decision makers in the planning system (local planning authorities and planning appeal inspectors) are required to focus on the land use implications of a proposed development and should avoid imposing conditions which would be replicated in the IPPC permitting process. How far 'land use' considerations extend into and overlap with both the IPC and IPPC regimes will depend upon the circumstances of each case and it is therefore difficult to indicate with any degree of certainty where planning regulation ends and IPC and IPPC begin. What is clear, however, is the fact that a decision maker in the planning system cannot refuse to have regard to the polluting impacts of a proposed development when determining a planning application.

In relation to IPPC applications for specified waste management activities, the regulator cannot grant the permit unless the applicant has secured the relevant planning permission for the activity on that site (reg 10(4) of the PPC Regulations 2000).

Readers should note that the IPPC Directive and the EIA Directive make provision for the interchange of information. Thus, the Environmental Statement, produced for the purposes of a planning application, may be used to provide information on site condition and environmental impacts of the installation as part of the IPPC permit process.

6.23.6 Statutory nuisances

Since IPPC regulation focuses upon environmental impacts, IPPC permits will include, if relevant, conditions relating to noise, vibration and similar environmental impacts. Local authorities are barred from using their statutory nuisance powers in Pt III of the EPA 1990 to deal with noise and other problems which the IPPC regulator can address, using the relevant IPPC enforcement powers. Local authorities may nevertheless use their statutory nuisance powers on an IPPC installation in circumstances where the relevant nuisance falls outside the remit of IPPC controls.

Irrespective of the limitations on local authority power to take statutory nuisance action against an IPPC permit holder, an individual may use s 82 of the EPA 1990 to lodge a complaint against an IPPC permit holder in respect of an alleged nuisance.

6.24   FURTHER INFORMATION

Further reading

Allot, K, *Integrated Pollution Control: The First Three Years*, 1994, Environmental Data Services Ltd.

Henshawe, I, 'The EC Directive on Integrated Pollution Prevention Control: implications for the United Kingdom' [1996] Env Liability 29.

Lea, A, 'BATNEEC, BPEO and the variation of IPC consents – a review of a recent High Court decision concerning the burning of alternative fuels' [1998] JPL 913–18.

Mehta, A, 'The benefits of IPC: views from industry' (1988) 10(4) ELM 190–96.

This article considers the commercial benefits to firms of an IPC regime.

Royal Commission on Environmental Pollution Reports: *Air Pollution Control, An Integrated Approach*, Fifth Report, Cmnd 6371, 1976, HMSO; *Best Practicable Environmental Option*, Twelfth Report, Cmnd 310, 1988, HMSO.

Tromans, S, 'Pollution prevention, skeletons and the Stuarts' (1999) 149 NLJ 634–35.

Stephen Tromans examines the powers contained in the Pollution Prevention and Control Bill 1998–99 (written prior to royal assent) and considers whether the provisions contained in the Bill confer too much power on ministers.

Websites

www.environment-agency.gov.uk

The Environment Agency website includes a wide range of official information relating to both IPC and IPPC, including Technical Guidance Notes and information about infringements of the EPA 1990 and recent applications under the Pollution Prevention and Control Act 1999.

www.defra.gov.uk/environment/index.htm

Official information about IPC and IPPC.

www.rcep.org

Royal Commission on Environmental Pollution reports are accessible from this site.

CHAPTER 7

CONTAMINATED LAND

7.1 THE CONTAMINATED LAND LEGACY

7.1.1 Introduction

The Industrial Revolution and subsequent manufacturing activity in the 20th century has left the UK with a significant contaminated land legacy. However, the problem of Britain's 'Badlands', although recognised for many years, has only recently begun to be addressed with the introduction of the contaminated land regulatory regime in Pt IIA of the Environmental Protection Act (EPA) 1990. The delay in tackling contaminated land may be due to the low visibility of the issue. Contamination of the land is literally out of sight and out of mind. In addition, the introduction of licence-based controls over many aspects of present day industrial pollution, for example, Integrated Pollution Control (IPC), has deflected attention away from historic contamination of the land.

7.1.2 Activities typically associated with land contamination

Many old industries which existed in the 19th and early 20th centuries have either been swept away or have adapted to modern production methods. Whilst the land upon which these old industries stood has been redeveloped, and old buildings replaced with modern ones, it is probable that, in some circumstances, historic contamination of the soil and sub-soil remains as a ghostly legacy. This is especially true of contaminants which are not biodegradable.

The following activities are typically linked to historic land contamination: gas and coking works which produced tars and other residues; closed landfill sites with leachate and methane emission problems; tanning works which used solvents to degrease animal skins; metal works smelting toxic metals such as lead; plating works; heavy engineering works; chemical works using powerful acids and alkalis; petro-chemical works; asbestos production; premises which handled and stored hazardous substances, for example, docks, railways and Ministry of Defence property; and factories which manufactured pesticides.

7.1.3 Specific incidents

The evacuation of an entire community, whose homes had been built on a former hazardous waste site, at Love Canal in North America in the late 1970s, and a similar incident in Lekkerkerk in the Netherlands, helped to focus international attention upon the health implications of the redevelopment of contaminated land. In 1976, methane which had migrated from a closed landfill at Loscoe in Derbyshire caused an explosion which destroyed a bungalow. This is just a brief sample of the incidents which helped to draw attention to the problem of historic land pollution.

7.1.4   The risks associated with contaminated land

Contaminated land, containing toxic chemicals, poses a threat to the health of humans, plants and animals. Harmful chemicals can enter the food chain via crops grown in contaminated soil. These crops, or the animals which feed upon them, are then eaten by humans and toxic substances are ingested. Alternatively, chemicals, such as solvents or pesticides, may leach out of closed landfills and enter groundwaters. Groundwaters (that is, aquifers) are commonly used to supply water for human consumption. The dust from buildings insulated with asbestos may be inhaled with serious consequences to health.

Many chemical substances, which are present in and contaminate land, are either not biodegradable or take many years to break down into less harmful chemicals. The *Cambridge Water* case, which is discussed in detail in Chapter 11, illustrates the persistence and longevity of solvents and their ability to migrate, through underground strata, over significant distances.

The chemicals which are present in contaminated land may cause damage to crops and livestock. They may even, if they are corrosive, damage building foundations and service pipes and cables.

Contaminated land may also result in property blight and property stigma. Residential developments erected on closed landfills may be blighted if methane enters sub-floor areas. If a risk of explosion exists, the property will either become unsaleable or the price must be reduced to reflect that risk. Property stigma occurs in cases where contamination has been remediated but the fact that the land on which the property stands was contaminated causes the market price of the property to be depressed. The stigma associated with nuclear waste contamination is apparent in the case of *Blue Circle v Ministry of Defence* (1999).

7.1.5   Growing recognition of the problem of contaminated land and the government's initial response

In comparison to other environmental problems, such as waste and water pollution, the issue of contaminated land is a relative newcomer in terms of the recognition of the problem and the identification of the means to address it. Since the 1970s, various governments sought to examine ways of tackling the problem, but encountered significant difficulties in terms of reaching agreement about how to define contaminated land legally and how to procure the remediation of contaminated sites without resulting in a significant property blight. In 1989, the House of Commons Select Committee on the Environment recommended that 'urgent attention [must] be given to the question of creating statutory liability for damage caused by contamination to land'. The Committee also accepted that the establishment of a statutory regime would raise complex questions as to retrospection, insurance cover and limitation periods. As a result of this recommendation, in the following year, the Committee undertook a report on contaminated land (1990). The Committee examined the issue of contamination in detail. Its main recommendations were that records of contamination should be created and open to the public and that a comprehensive framework of regulation should be established. This recommendation led to the inclusion in the Environmental Protection Act (EPA) 1990 of the ill-fated s 143 registers.

The EPA 1990, as originally drafted, contained a provision which, if it had ever been brought into force, would have required local authorities to maintain public registers of land in their area 'subject to contamination'. This was the first statutory attempt specifically aimed at addressing the issue of contaminated land. It was also highly controversial. One specific problem related to the definition of land subject to contamination, which the government proposed would be 'land which is being or had been put to a contaminative use', that being 'any use of land which may cause it to be contaminated with noxious substances'. Thus, land would be deemed to be contaminated because of the use to which it had been or was being put regardless of whether the land was capable of causing harm to humans or property. The government carried out extensive consultations with regard to the proposed registers (see *Let the Buyer be Better Informed*) but, in view of the strength of objections, it decided to abandon the s 143 registers. On 24 March 1993, the government announced that the registers would not be introduced, but that a further detailed review of responsibility for contaminated land would be undertaken.

7.1.6 Reasons for abandonment

The principal reasons given by the government for abandoning the s 143 registers were as follows:

(a) the proposed registers were based on the use to which the land had been put regardless of whether or not the use had actually caused the land to be contaminated; this would have led to some sites which were not actually contaminated being included whilst missing other sites which were actually contaminated but by uses not contained on the prescribed list of contaminative uses;

(b) there was no system for removing a site from the register once it had been cleaned up; and

(c) inclusion on the register did not address the potential problem of remediation or the issue of liability for remediation.

As a result of the abandonment of the registers in 1993, the government formed an inter-departmental group to begin a wide-ranging review of the problems of contamination. The task of the review group was to investigate, *inter alia*, 'the powers and duties of public authorities which relate to the identification, assessment and appropriate treatment or control of land that could cause pollution of the environment, or harm to human health' (see *Hansard*, 24 March 1993, col 634). Following this, the then Conservative government published two wide-ranging consultation documents in March and November 1994 (*Paying for Our Past*, March 1994 and *Framework for Contaminated Land*, November 1994). Following this extensive consultation exercise, the government enacted the new statutory regime by s 57 of the Environment Act 1995, which inserted a new Part IIA into the Environmental Protection Act 1990. Part IIA includes 26 sections from s 78A to s 78YC.

7.1.7　Government objectives and standard of remediation required

In the 1994 consultation paper, *Paying for our Past*, the government set out the principles and objectives on which the contaminated land regime was intended to operate:

(a) the government recognised that it was necessary to bring large tracts of contaminated land back into beneficial use;

(b) the standard of clean-up of contaminated land would be based on a 'suitable for use' concept. Clean-up works to remediate the land would only be necessary if the contamination present in the land posed actual or potential risks to man or the environment which were considered to be unacceptable. In assessing what, if any, remediation works were required, it was necessary to have regard to the actual (that is, current) or intended use of the contaminated land. Thus, if planning permission was sought to redevelop a site for housing, the extent of clean-up works would reflect that intended use and its attendant risks, especially to humans. The 'suitable for use' concept is therefore distinguishable from the 'polished earth' approach of the 'Superfund' legislation in the USA (Comprehensive Environmental Response Compensation and Liability Act 1980) or the similar, and now discontinued, 'multifunctional' approach in the Netherlands which required contaminated land to be cleaned up so that it was fit for any use;

(c) the contaminated land regime would target, prioritise and address the most serious cases of contamination first;

(d) the financial impact of the contaminated land regime on the economy and specific industries and landowners would be taken into account;

(e) the creation of a contaminated land regime would clarify responsibility for the clean-up of contaminated land and enable contaminated land to be bought and sold under proper market conditions.

7.2　THE CONTAMINATED LAND REGIME

7.2.1　Introduction

In contrast to the majority of the 'Command and Control' regulatory controls discussed in this book, the regulation of contaminated land is not licence-based. The damage, in the main, has already been done and the law responds reactively by: (a) identifying the relevant parcels of land which are 'contaminated'; (b) identifying the person or persons responsible for the contamination; and (c) allocating the cost of clean-up between the responsible person or persons.

The main function of the contaminated land regime is to address the problem of historic pollution, but the relevant controls do recognise and take account of the fact that current industrial and other activities may cause contamination. Thus, the regime is both retrospective and prospective.

7.2.2 Defining contaminated land

Of great significance to the ambit of the contaminated land regime is the method by which 'contaminated' land is distinguished from uncontaminated land. Section 78A(2) of the EPA 1990 defines contaminated land as:

> ... any land which appears to the local authority in whose area it is situated to be in such a condition, by reason of substances in, on or under land, that:
>
> (a) significant harm is being caused or there is a significant possibility of such harm being caused; or
>
> (b) pollution of controlled waters is being, or is likely to be, caused.

It is important to note that the definition refers to the central role of 'significant harm' in identifying contaminated land. Land may be polluted but if the presence of the pollutants does not, or is not likely to, cause significant harm to humans or the environment, then no remedial action is necessary and the land will not be 'contaminated' so as to fall within the ambit of s 78A(2) of the EPA 1990.

Section 78(4) defines 'harm' as:

> ... harm to the health of living organisms or other interference with the ecological systems of which they form part and, in the case of man, includes harm to his property.

The combined effect of these provisions is to clarify that it is only unacceptable (that is, significantly harmful) risks to man or the environment which convert polluted land into 'contaminated land'. This requires the regulator to undertake a risk assessment to determine whether the risks posed by the land are unacceptable and, to do this, the regulator (referred to as the 'enforcing authority') must 'act in accordance' with the official guidance relating to the meaning of 'contaminated land' when exercising its statutory functions (see DETR Circular 2/2000, *Contaminated Land: Implementation of Part IIA of the EPA 1990*). The fact that the regulator is obliged to act in accordance with the guidance, to the extent that it addresses the meaning of 'contaminated', will curtail the regulator's discretion as to the identification of which parcels of land fall within the contaminated land control regime.

Circular 2/2000 must be consulted to gain a fuller understanding of the criteria which are employed to determine whether land is contaminated. Whilst s 78A(2) refers to 'significant harm' and the 'significant possibility of such [significant] harm', the statute does not define how the authority assesses the issue of the significance of harm (for example, what does significant harm to man mean?) nor does it deal with the assessment of risk. These phrases can only be understood by reference to Annexe III of DETR Circular 2/2000.

There are essentially two distinct steps in the determination of contaminated land. It is essential to establish that:

(a) a pollutant linkage is present; and

(b) the pollutant linkage is causing significant harm or is significantly likely to cause such harm. In which case, the pollutant linkage becomes a 'significant pollutant linkage'.

7.2.3   The pollutant linkage

Although the statute makes no reference to a pollutant linkage, it is clear from the guidance that this concept is central to the definition. Unless a pollutant linkage exists, there is no possibility of land being 'legally' contaminated.

A pollutant linkage is the link between:

(a) the presence of a substance in, on or under the ground;

(b) a 'receptor', such as a human or a Site of Special Scientific Interest; and

(c) a 'pathway' via which the substance comes into contact with and harms the receptor.

One thing that is made very clear is that before a local authority determines that any land appears to be contaminated land, it must as a first step be satisfied that the above three elements have been identified with respect to the land. Theoretically, it is possible for land which contains very hazardous substances to fall outside this legal definition because there are no targets/receptors present, or there is no pathway by which the receptors can be exposed to the contaminants. There may also be more than one pollutant linkage, depending on the contaminants in the land. The local authority must make the determination that a pollutant linkage is present, and in doing so must act in accordance with the guidance. A pollutant linkage may arise as a result of substances which are naturally occurring; a pollutant linkage may also arise because substances (such as asbestos) are present in buildings or drains.

7.2.4   A significant pollutant linkage (risk assessment)

The presence of a pollutant linkage does not mean that the land is legally contaminated. The guidance requires that the pollutant linkage is resulting in:

(a) significant harm being caused;

(b) a significant possibility of significant harm being caused;

(c) pollution of controlled waters being caused;

(d) pollution of controlled waters likely to be caused.

If one of these situations arises, then the 'pollutant linkage' becomes a 'significant pollutant linkage'.

Whether any given set of circumstances constitutes 'a significant pollution linkage' will depend upon the vulnerability of the receptor, the magnitude of the threat posed by the contaminating substance(s), the timescale during which there is exposure to harm and the probability that the contaminant will escape along the envisaged pathway. When combined, these criteria comprise the components of a risk assessment.

Although the statute provides in s 78A(4) a broad definition of harm, the Act leaves it to the statutory guidance to deal with the more difficult issue of what harm is to be regarded as significant. When one turns to the guidance, it becomes immediately clear that only harm, of a certain type, to certain receptors is to be regarded as significant. The guidance is given in Table A.

Table A adopts a restricted interpretation of 'receptor': man, nature conservation sites subject to protective legislation, buildings and other property (for example, crops and livestock). With regard to the type of harm envisaged, triggering the relevant controls, the Circular details these on a receptor by receptor basis. As regards damage to crops and buildings, the Circular requires a substantial reduction in crop value or substantial building damage. With regard to nature conservation sites, the Circular specifies the requirement of irreversible or substantial adverse changes in ecosystem functioning affecting a substantial part of the nature conservation site. In the case of harm to humans, the Circular refers to death, serious injury, birth defects, and reproductive impairment.

In circumstances where significant harm has not yet occurred but the regulator is required to assess whether a 'significant possibility' of such harm exists, the circular (in Table B) draws the regulator's attention to the primary importance of the magnitude of the relevant threat. A 'significant possibility' of harm to humans will exist if the relevant risk is medically unacceptable. In contrast, in the case of non-human receptors, a significant possibility of harm will arise if the risk assessment reveals that it is more likely than not that there will be a significant possibility of harm. The guidance is both technical and complex and it is clear that the enforcing authority is going to have to make some very difficult decisions based upon the advice of experts from various disciplines.

A 'balance of probabilities' risk assessment also applies to contaminants which pose a threat to controlled waters. The harm envisaged is the damage caused by the entry of contaminants which have a poisonous, noxious or polluting impact upon controlled waters (see s 78(9)).

The regulator is entitled to take into account the combined impact, or 'cocktail effect', of more than one parcel of land in assessing whether land is contaminated. The combined effect of two or more parcels of land may satisfy the definition of contaminated land where, treated separately, each parcel on its own would not (see s 78X(2)).

7.3 THE STATUTORY FRAMEWORK OF THE CONTAMINATED LAND REGIME

7.3.1 Overview of the contaminated land regulatory framework

Part IIA of the EPA 1990 (introduced by the Environment Act (EA) 1995), supplemented by the Contaminated Land (England) Regulations 2000 (SI 2000/227), the Contaminated Land (Wales) Regulations 2001 (SI 2001/2197) and Circular 2/2000 (*Contaminated Land: Implementation of Pt IIA of the EPA 1990*), together comprise the current contaminated land regulatory regime controls.

Local authorities (borough councils, district councils and unitary authorities) have been allocated the major responsibility for the identification and remediation of contaminated land. The Environment Agency is, however, the enforcing authority in relation to the most severely contaminated sites (known as Special Sites), the provision of technical guidance, and the preparation (with local authority input) of a periodic report on contaminated land in England and Wales (s 78U).

The contaminated land regime shares some similarities with statutory nuisance controls under Pt III of the EPA 1990: each regime is largely a reactive form of control; each regulator has a statutory duty to inspect its area; regulation is not licence-based but revolves around the service of a notice specifying the remedial works which are required to be completed within a set timescale; non-compliance with the Remedial Notice is a criminal offence; the local authority has responsibility for the administration of the regulatory regime (although the Environment Agency regulates the more severely contaminated sites); extensive rights of appeal are available; and details of the Remedial Notice, and other information, is placed by the regulator on a publicly accessible register of information.

7.3.2 The duty to identify and 'list'

Section 78B(1) obliges local authorities to inspect, from time to time, their areas to identify contaminated land. With regard to the more severely contaminated sites (known as 'special sites'), the Environment Agency is the enforcing authority. Each local authority is tasked with the complex job of assessing whether any land in its area satisfies the relevant contaminated land criteria. Once it is satisfied that a parcel of land is contaminated land, the authority must serve a Remediation Notice on the person or persons who have been identified as being liable for the remediation of the land. Since details of the Remediation Notice are entered on a public register, the authority, in effect, 'lists' contaminated land. Once listed, there is no mechanism to 'de-list' or remove details of the land from the public register.

Local authorities are required to take a strategic approach to the inspection of contaminated land. Authorities are not expected to undertake random inspections; instead they should adopt a rational, ordered and efficient approach, concentrating on those areas where contamination is most likely to be identified. These strategies are published and are therefore open to public scrutiny. As such, they should provide a useful reference point for lawyers involved in commercial transactions of potentially contaminated land. However, see *Maile v Wigan Metropolitan Borough Council* (2001), in which the Divisional Court held that a database of information complied by WMBC for the purposes of identifying potentially contaminated sites within the borough was exempted from the access to information provisions of the Environmental Information Regulations 1992 on the grounds that the information was still in the course of completion (an exempted category under the Regulations). However, where a strategy document or report is complete, then the public will have the right to access this documents under the terms of the 1992 Regulations. Applying the strategy will result in the identification of particular areas or sites where it is likely that a significant pollutant linkage exists.

In the course of investigating whether land is contaminated, the local authority has identical investigatory powers to those of the Environment Agency contained in s 108 of the Environment Act 1995. The more important of these powers include: entry, inspection, experimental boring and sampling. These powers will be available to the regulator if other avenues of information have not been sufficient to establish whether the land is contaminated.

It is not necessary for there to be an intrusive site investigation. The local authority may make a determination following an inspection, which is based purely on the collation and assessment of documentary information from other bodies, such as the Environment Agency. Clearly, this is the least costly type of inspection. Moreover, under the provisions relating to Remediation Notices, the authority can require the appropriate persons to carry out a more detailed and intrusive site investigation as part of a remediation action, as the definition of remediation provided by s 78(7) includes the 'doing of anything for the purposes of assessing the condition of the land in question'.

However, before the authority has 'sufficient' information to reach a conclusion about the state of the land, it must have evidence of the actual presence of the pollutant. It is difficult to see how the authority can obtain this evidence without an intrusive investigation, unless it is relying on Environment Agency records.

With regard to potentially contaminated land which could cause actual or threatened harm to nature conservation sites, the local authority must consult with and take into account any comments made by English Nature or the Environment Agency. These comments should assist the local authority in deciding whether the land is contaminated.

7.3.3 Special sites

Having satisfied itself (and formally recorded its decision) that the land it has investigated is contaminated land, the authority must then decide whether the land qualifies as a special site. The definition of 'special site' is contained in the Contaminated Land (England) Regulations 2000 and with regard to which the Environment Agency is the relevant enforcing authority. In general terms, special sites are those: (a) on which the actual or threatened contamination is serious by virtue of the substances used on the land or the harm caused by the land; and (b) which would benefit from the Environment Agency's expertise. The Regulations include the following within the definition of special sites: IPC/IPPC sites, nuclear industry sites, Ministry of Defence sites and land causing the pollution of controlled waters where the receiving water is intended to be used for the supply of drinking water or breaches of any water quality standards classified under s 82 of the Water Resources Act 1991.

The local authority consults the Environment Agency before designating the site as a special site. Details of the fact that the site is a special site are entered on the public register. The local authority has a duty (s 78C) to notify the Environment Agency, the owner and/or occupier and any other person who might be responsible for the cost of remediation that the site has been designated as a special site. The Environment Agency retains its (s 108 of the EA 1995) investigation powers with regard to special sites (s 78Q). Interestingly, the Environment Agency has the power to de-list special sites, but the site will nevertheless remain listed as contaminated land. Where a special site is de-listed, the local authority resumes its role as the enforcing authority.

7.3.4 Duty to notify and consult

As soon as the local authority has decided that a parcel of land fulfils the statutory land criteria, it has a legal obligation (see s 78B) to notify the following persons that the land has been formally designated or listed as contaminated land:

(a) the owner;

(b) the occupier;

(c) any other person who appears to the local authority to be liable for all or part of the remediation costs;

(d) the Environment Agency. Notification to the Environment Agency triggers consultation on whether the site qualifies as a special site.

Except in those cases where the contaminated land poses an imminent danger of serious harm or pollution of controlled waters (s 78N(3)), mandatory provision is made for a minimum three month period of consultation between the local authority and the person or persons who are thought to be responsible for the cost of clean-up (s 78H). These provisions are designed to provide the opportunity to reach a negotiated agreement on the extent of and responsibility for remedial works. Even if agreement cannot be reached, it is envisaged that the consultation device will help narrow down areas of dispute between the enforcing authority and the persons responsible for remediation of the contamination. If agreement is reached, the person or persons responsible for remedial works sign an undertaking, referred to as a remediation statement, detailing the necessary works and the relevant timescale. These details are then entered onto the public register (s 78H(7)). Provision may be made for the phased completion of the remedial works. Where, on a cost/benefit basis, the enforcing authority concludes that remedial works are not justified, the authority is required to note this on the public register in the form of a remediation declaration (s 78H(6)). Despite the existence of a remediation declaration, the land remains listed as contaminated land.

7.3.5 The standard of remediation

Central to the government's aims is that the remediation that is undertaken on the land is 'suitable for use'. The definition of remediation is provided in s 87A(7) of the EPA 1990 and is much wider than simply 'clean-up'. The Remediation Notice may require the recipient to undertake remediation in the form of assessing the condition of land; the doing of works, carrying out of operations, taking of steps and also the making of subsequent inspections. The guidance refers to these in turn as 'assessment actions', 'remediation treatment actions' and 'monitoring actions'.

When deciding what is required by way of remediation, the enforcing authority must take into account s 78E(4) and (5) of the EPA 1990. In short, remediation may only comprise those things that the authority considers reasonable, having regard to likely cost and seriousness of harm in question. This section does not prevent an authority from serving a Remediation Notice; it simply limits what the authority might require by way of remediation. The authority must have regard to the guidance in deciding what is reasonable in the circumstances. DETR Circular 2/2000 identifies the procedural approach to be taken in identifying a remediation scheme which fulfils the requirements of s 78E(4) and (5). In particular, the circular reiterates the government's intention that any remediation should result in land being 'suitable for use'. The aim of any remediation should be to ensure that the circumstances of the land are such that, in its current use, it is no longer contaminated land. 'Current use' is defined as the use to which the land is currently being put or is likely to be put under any *existing* planning permissions. (Where land is subject to development proposals and planning permission is sought, then the contaminated land regime has no application, since the regime only applies to current use.) See below for the relationship with town and country planning regime.

In terms of how the land is remediated, the guidance requires that the 'best practicable techniques' are used.

7.3.6 Remediation Notice

Where the consultation period has elapsed without the successful conclusion of a voluntary agreement and remediation statement, the enforcing authority must, by virtue of s 78E, serve a Remediation Notice on the 'appropriate person or persons' who is or are responsible for bearing the cost of clean-up. The Remediation Notice is similar in format to a statutory nuisance Abatement Notice. It will specify the works and the relevant timescale to complete them (s 78E(1)).

The enforcing authority may not serve a Remediation Notice in the following circumstances:

(a) where it appears to the enforcing authority that imminent danger of serious harm or water pollution exists and the authority has the power to carry out the remediation under s 78N;

(b) where remediation may be effected under other regulatory controls;

(c) where the authority is satisfied that, having had regard to the costs and benefits of remediation, it is not reasonable to serve a Remediation Notice under s 78E(4) and (5) (s 78H(5)(a));

(d) where the remedial works are undertaken voluntarily pursuant to a remedial statement (s 78H(5)(b));

(e) where the enforcing authority is the owner of contaminated land or has caused contamination (s 78H(5)(c));

(f) where the enforcing authority is satisfied that it has the power to carry out the remediation itself under s 78N;

(g) where, in the case of pollution of controlled waters, the appropriate persons are owners or occupiers.

Despite the fact that the enforcing authority is precluded from serving a Remediation Notice in the circumstances detailed above, the authority has a discretion to undertake the works itself and then endeavour to recover its costs from the responsible person.

7.4 THE APPROPRIATE PERSON

The selection of the person or persons responsible for the remediation of contaminated land and the just application of the relevant cost of clean-up between two or more responsible persons is one of the more contentious aspects of the contaminated land regime. The division of liability for remedial costs depends upon the concept of 'the appropriate person'. Section 78F(2) defines the appropriate person as 'the person, or any of the persons, who caused or knowingly permitted the substances, or any of the substances, which have been the cause of the contamination to be in or under the land'. Section 78K makes it clear that the appropriate person may also be the person from whose land substances have escaped which has caused the contamination of someone else's land.

In essence, this definition seeks to apply the 'polluter pays' principle by placing primary responsibility on the person(s) who polluted the land. The authority is charged with making 'reasonable inquiry'. If after such reasonable inquiry no such persons can be found, then the liability for the remediation will switch to the 'owner or occupier for the time being of the contaminated land', who will become the appropriate person (s 78F(4)). The guidance seeks to distinguish between these two separate categories of appropriate persons by classifying them as Class A persons (the polluter) and Class B persons (the owner and occupier). Thus, primary responsibility rests with the so called Class A person or persons (known as the Class A liability group), but will switch to the Class B persons if the enforcing authority cannot identify the Class A person. It is important to note that the liability of the Class A person is referable only to the particular substances which the person has caused or knowingly permitted to be present. This means that the remedial action to be required is to be taken by the appropriate person *only* in relation to the substances he or she contributed (s 78F(3)).

7.4.1   Causing or knowingly permitting contamination

Liability for causing or knowingly permitting contamination is strict but, with regard to the allocation of the cost of remediation between the appropriate persons, the contaminated land regime does provide mechanisms to mitigate the potential financial impact of liability. Significantly, there is no defence to causing contamination based on the use of 'best practice' (otherwise referred to as 'a state of the art' defence). It seems likely that 'causing contamination' will be interpreted in much the same way as causing water pollution. The 'appropriate person' in s 78F(2) will be someone who has engaged in, or is engaging in, an active operation which has caused, or is causing, contamination. Maintaining tanks, pipes and cables from which contaminants have escaped will therefore all be active operations attracting liability. More than one person can cause contaminants to be present in or under land (for example, a contractor who negligently installs an underground storage tank resulting in contamination of the site). Once contaminated land has been identified by an enforcing authority, it is presumed that the owner or occupier of the site, at the date the contamination occurred, caused the contamination. If this presumption does not accord with the facts, the onus is on the owner or occupier to establish that someone else caused the contamination.

It seems probable that the phrase 'knowingly permitted' in s 78F(2) refers to the dual requirement that the owner or occupier knew that contamination existed and had the power to prevent contamination (for example, by removing the contaminating substances from the site). Thus, the owner and occupier must be aware not only that the substance is present on site but also that the substance has the capacity to cause contamination if it escapes containment. In view of the purpose of the legislation and the extent of contamination, in a national context, it seems likely that the owner or occupier will not be able to escape liability because of any subjective ignorance of the risks which would have been obvious to a reasonable site owner or occupier. Thus, the presence of storage tanks on site should alert a potential purchaser or leaseholder (that is, owner or occupier) to the risk of contamination. A purchaser acquiring contaminated land in such circumstances effectively permits the presence of contaminants and is therefore liable. A prudent purchaser would have recognised the risk of contamination and addressed this in the terms of the property acquisition deal (through warranties and indemnities). Whether someone caused or knowingly permitted contamination will be decided on the balance of probabilities (that is, more likely than not).

7.4.2 Liability of site owners and occupiers

The contaminated land regime contains fairly complex arrangements for identifying which past or present owners and/or occupiers of contaminated land are liable for all or part of the remediation costs. Primary responsibility, according to Circular 2/2000, rests with 'Class A persons'. Class A persons are those who have caused or knowingly permitted the presence of contaminating substances in or under land. In the event that the current owner or occupier is not a Class A person, they will only be liable, as a Class B person, if, after reasonable inquiry, no Class A persons can be found (s 78F(4)).

The term 'owner' is defined in s 78A as the person who is entitled to receive the market rent for the property, but mortgagees not in possession and insolvency practitioners are not owners (s 78X(3)). 'Occupier' is not defined.

Where land is contaminated with several substances, it will be necessary to establish whether the current owner or occupier is responsible for all or only part of the contamination. If the owner or occupier is only responsible for the presence of some of the substances which are present, then the owner or occupier will be liable as a Class A person with regard to the contamination he or she caused. With regard to other contaminating substances on site, the owner or occupier may also be liable as a Class B person if the relevant Class A person or persons cannot be found.

7.5   ALLOCATING THE COST OF REMEDIATION

Having identified the responsible 'appropriate person or persons', the enforcing authority must then determine the extent of each person's liability for clean-up. The enforcing authority's discretion in the allocation of liability is tightly constrained by the Circular 2/2000 guidance.

The enforcing authority allocates liability by undertaking the following sequential tasks:

(a) it identifies the significant pollutant linkages on the land. There may be more than one significant pollutant linkage;

(b) it makes reasonable inquiry to identify the Class A persons. Liability as a Class A person is referrable only to the particular substances which the person has caused or knowingly permitted to be present. There may be more than one significant pollutant linkage and more than one Class A liability group;

(c) it identifies, in the absence of Class A persons, the Class B liability group for the relevant significant pollutant linkage;

(d) it applies the Class A and Class B exclusion tests to the liability groups;

(e) it apportions the remediation costs between the remaining (non-excluded) liable persons.

Exclusion tests are applicable where a Class A or B liability group has more than one person in the relevant liability group. The function of the test is to exclude from liability those persons who are not especially blameworthy and therefore should not, in fairness, be burdened with liability.

7.5.1 The Class A exclusion tests

Before examining these exclusion tests, it is necessary to recall that there is a significant limitation to the liability of a Class A person and that is that such a person is *only* liable in respect of those substances which they are actually responsible for having caused or knowingly permitted to be present on the land. This is sometimes referred to as the 'referability exclusion'. However, where the enforcing authority has identified a group of Class A persons, it will need then to examine whether any members of this group should be excluded from liability by virtue of s 78F(6). The enforcing authority must do this in accordance with the guidance, which in turn lays down six exclusion tests which must be applied sequentially. In applying these tests, the enforcing authority cannot exclude all of the members of the group; in other words, at least one member of the Class A group must remain. The six tests are summarised as follows:

(1) Test 1: the purpose of this test is to exclude persons who fall within the Class A liability group because of the performance of certain excluded activities. The list of excluded activities is lengthy, but principally includes mortgage lenders and other providers of finance, insurance underwriters and persons who have provided technical, legal or scientific advice.

(2) Test 2: this test excludes persons who have already made payments for the remediation of the land. Such a payment would normally occur when land is transferred (sold) and the vendor either reduces the price to account for the cost of the remediation or makes a payment to the purchaser to cover the costs.

(3) Test 3: the purpose of this test is to exclude from liability those who sold the contaminated land with information regarding the contamination so that it is reasonable to expect the purchaser to bear the costs of the remediation. The test includes an interesting retrospective provision in relation to land transactions where the buyer is a large commercial organisation or public body. In transactions since the beginning of 1990 where the buyer was a large commercial organisation or public body, permission from the seller for the buyer to carry out his or her own investigations of the land should normally be taken as sufficient indication that the land was sold with information.

(4) Test 4: this excludes persons from liability in situations where the person has caused substances to be present on the land, but those substances have only formed a significant pollutant linkage because of the unforeseeable introduction of substances by another person at a later date.

(5) Test 5: this test excludes a person from liability where it can be shown that the land has become contaminated because of the escape of substances from some other (presumably adjoining) land and that another member of the liability group caused that escape.

(6) Test 6: this test excludes a person from liability where he or she is only liable because of the subsequent introduction by others (such as later developers) who have introduced a relevant pathway or receptors.

The exclusion tests are detailed and complex and, particularly in relation to exclusion tests 2 and 3, there are many conditions to be satisfied before a person can reliably benefit from the test.

7.5.2 Class B exclusion tests

Class B persons are excluded from liability if they are occupiers or tenants paying a market rent but have no long term financial interest in the land which would benefit from clean-up works.

The exclusion tests may not be used to exclude the liability of all persons in a liability group. In the event that a liability group reaches agreement on the allocation of their respective liabilities and informs the enforcing authority of the voluntary agreement, the terms of the agreement prevail over any other allocation favoured by the enforcing authority except to the extent that the agreement is a sham device intended to avoid liability. This situation could arise if the terms of the agreement purported to transfer liability to a group member who would, in consequence, suffer hardship, thus preventing the enforcing authority serving a Remediation Notice on that person.

In liability groups whose members include two or more related companies, those companies will be treated as one person for the purpose of applying the exclusion tests.

In the interests of justice, the financial standing of each member of a liability group is irrelevant for the purpose of applying the exclusion tests.

7.5.3 Allocating costs between appropriate persons

Once the exclusion tests have been applied, the enforcing authority will apportion remediation costs in accordance with the relative responsibility of each remaining appropriate person. The enforcing authority will, in arriving at its allocation, have regard to the duration of the period during which each responsible person was in occupation of the land and was using contaminating substances. An accurate assessment will, in most cases, largely depend upon the availability of reliable information. In default of receiving a reasonable amount of information upon which to base an assessment, the enforcing authority may apportion the remediation costs equally between the non-excluded members of the relevant Class A or B liability group.

7.6   THE REMEDIATION NOTICE

Once the allocation and apportionment processes are concluded, the enforcing authority is subject to a legal duty to serve a Remediation Notice on the appropriate person or persons (s 78E(1) of the EPA 1990 and reg 4 of the Contaminated Land (England) Regulations 2000).

Remediation Notices must contain sufficient information including:

(a) a description of the work which is required to be undertaken;

(b) the identity of the person required to do the work;

(c) the proportion of the costs each person must bear;

(d) the timescale within which the work must be completed;

(e) the identity of each appropriate person;

(f) the reason(s) for serving the notice; and

(g) rights of appeal.

A further Remediation Notice may be served, even if the original notice has been complied with, if it transpires (as a result of the original remediation work) that further works or different works are necessary.

Upon successful completion of the remedial works, the enforcing authority is obliged to enter details of the remediation work on the public register. In appropriate circumstances, it may indicate on the register that no further remedial work is anticipated.

7.6.1 Failure to comply with a Remediation Notice

Non-compliance with a Remediation Notice without reasonable excuse is an offence (s 78M). The offence is a 'summary' offence and therefore may only be heard in a magistrates' court. Penalties reflect the distinction between the contamination of industrial and other land. In the case of industrial, trade, or business premises, the maximum financial penalty is £20,000 and a further daily penalty of up to £2,000 for every day the Remediation Notice is not complied with. In the case of other land, the maximum fine and daily penalty are £5,000 and £500 respectively (s 78M(3) and (4)).

7.6.2 Completion of remediation works

The enforcing authority has the power to complete the remediation, specified in the Notice, where the Notice has not been complied with (s 78N), and the authority is entitled to recover its reasonable costs (s 78P), unless this will cause hardship.

The enforcing authority's costs may be secured by means of a legal charge on the legal title of the contaminated land. A person served with a charging order notice has a right to lodge an appeal in the county court within 21 days of receipt of the notice (s 78P(8)).

7.6.3 Appeals

A right of appeal against the service of a Remediation Notice is contained in s 78L(1). The appeal must be lodged within 21 days of receipt of the Notice and will suspend the operation of the Notice. Appeals relating to special sites are dealt with by the Secretary of State, otherwise appeals are dealt with by magistrates' courts.

With regard to special site appeals, the Secretary of State may hold a public inquiry into the appeal (which will allow third parties to participate in the appeal process), but in most cases he or she is likely to transfer the appeal to the Planning Inspectorate. Interestingly, planning inspectors may be assisted by assessors who have relevant expertise. In contrast, appeals to the magistrates' court will be dealt with by a stipendiary magistrate, who, whilst legally qualified, is unlikely to have any expertise in contaminated land issues.

The grounds of appeal are detailed in reg 7 of the Contaminated Land (England) Regulations 2000, and include:

(a) appeals based on submissions that the land is not contaminated;

(b) that the recipient of the Remediation Notice is not an appropriate person;

(c) that the appellant should have been excluded from liability;

(d) that the notice is unreasonable; and

(e) that the enforcing authority failed to act in accordance with the guidance contained in Circular 2/2000.

In a magistrates' court appeal, the winner will be entitled to reasonable costs. Costs are generally not available in appeals heard by planning inspectors. Given the complex subject matter of these appeals, it has been argued that the period within which the appeal must be lodged is woefully inadequate and also that the magistrates' court does not have the technical expertise to deal with such complex issues.

7.6.4 The public register

The contaminated land register, maintained by each enforcing authority, contains details of: Remediation Notices, remediation statements, declarations, notices, appeals, convictions, remediation work (see s 78R of and Sched 3 to the Contaminated Land (England) Regulations 2000).

7.6.5 Tax incentives

The Finance Act 2001 has introduced a valuable tax incentive which is designed to encourage the remediation of contaminated land. The Act is targeted at companies which have purchased land that was in a 'contaminated state' at the time of purchase and which incur 'qualifying land remediation expenditure' after 10 May 2001. The amount of tax relief is 150% of the qualifying expenditure which is offset against corporation tax.

7.7   INTERFACE WITH OTHER CONTROLS

7.7.1 The subsidiary role of contaminated land controls

The interface between contaminated land controls and other regulatory regimes is particularly important in that the contaminated land regime is designed to 'kick in' only when other statutory controls are unable to tackle contamination effectively.

The clean-up powers built into other regulatory regimes, for example, water pollution, waste management and IPC/IPPC, have several significant advantages over contaminated land controls. These powers are quicker, less complex (no complicated liability rules to apply), and more accessible than their contaminated land counterparts. Clean-up powers in the licence-based regimes have the key advantage of 'joint and several liability' application. In other words, the regulator can choose which one of several polluters is pursued to bear the cost of remediation. If land contamination occurs on a site subject to licence-based regulatory controls, the clean-up powers contained in the relevant statute may be used to remedy completely the damage caused by the contamination, without the restriction, as in the case of contaminated land, of limiting the extent of the remedial works to the current use of the land.

7.7.2   Water pollution

One of the key pollution concerns of the contaminated land regime is the risk of contaminated land causing pollution of groundwaters. An overlap exists between s 161 of the WRA 1991 (Works Notice powers) and the remediation procedure in the contaminated land controls. The s 161 of the WRA 1991 clean-up power applies to situations where pollution has occurred or is likely to occur. It may be used proactively and reactively.

The Environment Agency has published guidance addressing the potential conflict between the two regimes (see *Environment Agency Policy on the Use of Anti-Pollution Works Notices*). The guidance advises that where land has been formally 'listed' as contaminated land, the contaminated land controls will apply because the enforcing authority is legally obliged to serve a Remediation Notice. Where land has not been formally listed as contaminated, the s 161 of the WRA 1991 power will apply.

7.7.3   Waste management

In the case of contamination of waste management sites caused by breach of licensed activities, priority is given to the use of the clean-up powers contained within the waste management regime. Section 78YB(2) precludes the enforcing authority from serving a Remediation Notice in such circumstances. In addition, the waste management regime has priority where contamination arises as a result of the unlawful deposit of directive waste (s 78YB(3)). In such circumstances, the regulator will use its s 59 of the EPA 1990 clean-up powers.

7.7.4   IPC and IPPC

The contaminated land Remediation Notice procedure may not be used to address contamination which has arisen as a result of the licensed activities of IPC and IPPC processes (s 78YB(1)). If contamination occurs, the regulator will use its s 27 of the EPA 1990 powers to deal with the problem. Land upon which an IPC or IPPC process is being carried on may be listed as contaminated land if it fulfils the relevant contaminated land definition. In this regard, the baseline assessment prepared for the purposes of obtaining an IPPC permit will provide valuable information to the enforcing authority on the question of whether the land is contaminated.

7.7.5   Statutory nuisance

Statutory nuisance abatement controls do not apply where land is in a 'contaminated state' (Sched 2, para 89 of the EA 1995). Statutory nuisance controls do not apply even where the relevant land in a contaminated state does not pose significant harm to man or the environment (s 78A(2)). Thus, land which is in a contaminated state, but is not posing a risk of significant harm to man or the environment, falls outside the remit of statutory nuisance controls and contaminated land controls. This creates something of a lacuna in the law.

7.7.6 Town and country planning

There is some degree of overlap of planning controls with contaminated land regulation at the strategic planning and individual planning decision levels. The content of development plans provide an important mechanism enabling planning authorities (the local authorities) to plan the appropriate redevelopment of 'brownfield' sites which may also be contaminated. The government has set a target of 60% of new housing to be constructed on brownfield sites and 100% of contaminated land to be brought back into beneficial use by 2030.

Contamination is a 'material consideration' in individual planning applications and must be taken into account in reaching a decision upon the application. The local planning authority, if it grants planning permission for development on contaminated land, may impose planning conditions to address risks to man and the environment posed by the presence of contaminants on site. For example, a condition requiring the venting of methane from sub-floor areas if residential development on a closed landfill is contemplated.

Government planning advice relating to contaminated land appears in Circular 1/95 and Planning Policy Guidance Note 23.

7.8   FURTHER INFORMATION

Further reading

CLR7, *Assessment of Risks to Human Health from Land Contamination: An Overview of the Development of Soil Guidelines and Related Research*, March 2002.
> This can be accessed at: www.environmentagency.gov.uk/subjects/landquality/113813/274663/274683/ ?version=1&lang=_e

DETR Circular 02/2000, Department of the Environment Planning Policy Guidance 23, Planning and Pollution Control, Annexe 10, Contaminated Land (February 1997).

Edwards, M, *Contaminated Land: Property Transactions and the New Regime*, 2000, CLT Professional.

Harris, S, 'What shall we do with the contaminated site?' [1992] JPEL 809.

Hellawell, T, *Blackstone's Guide to the Contaminated Land Regime*, 2000, OUP.

Langhalm, R, 'Contaminated land – the legal aspect' [1993] Journal of Planning and Environment Law 807.

Tromans, S and Turrall-Clarke, R, *Contaminated Land: The New Regime*, 2000, Sweet & Maxwell.

Woolley, D, 'Contaminated land – the real world' (2002) Journal of Planning and Environment Law 5–11.

Websites

www.environment-agency.gov.uk

An enormous amount of information on the contaminated land regime can be accessed via the Environment Agency's website at the above address. In particular, you can access via this site (by searching for 'contaminated land') a copy of the Agency's first annual report on the contaminated land regime.

The Agency's report on the state of contaminated land in England gives an overview of progress made in identifying and remediating contaminated land in England since the Pt IIA regime was introduced in April 2000.

www.defra.gov.uk/environment/landliability/circ2-2000/2.htm

The DEFRA web page contains a significant amount of information about the contaminated land regime, including a summary of the Act and the statutory guidance.

www.claire.co.uk/aboutframes.html

CLAIRE provides a link between the main players in contaminated land remediation in the UK, to catalyse the development of cost-effective methods of investigating and remediating contaminated land in a sustainable way.

CHAPTER 8

ATMOSPHERIC POLLUTION

8.1   INTRODUCTION

Atmospheric pollution in England and Wales is regulated by legislative controls which reflect the historic development of the law as it has moved away from a localised, reactive, response to pollution problems to a more integrated and planned response to pan-European and global threats associated with airborne pollutants.

The three main air pollution controls comprise:

(a) the Integrated Pollution Control (IPC) and Integrated Pollution and Control (IPPC) licence-based controls relating to a range of highly polluting industries detailed in Pt I of the Environmental Protection Act (EPA) 1990 and the Pollution Prevention and Control Act (PPCA) 1999;

(b) the criminal sanction-based controls over the emission of smoke and other particulate matter from chimneys and furnaces detailed in the Clean Air Act (CAA) 1993; and

(c) controls relating to vehicle emissions. These controls encompass engine efficiency standards, the chemical composition of fuels, the mandatory use of catalytic converters, eco-taxes, price differentials between different types of fuel and the use of traffic management powers.

These controls are supplemented by the Environment Act (EA) 1995, which has enabled the Secretary of State to create a national air quality strategy and local air quality zones. Due to the inherent mobility of atmospheric pollution and its transboundary impacts, the development of the law is largely driven by a combination of international and European Community (EC) responses to the global threat of climate change.

8.2   PROBLEMS CAUSED BY AIR POLLUTION

Atmospheric pollution poses three major threats:

(a) the *threat to human health*, particularly respiratory illnesses, such as bronchitis and asthma caused by airborne pollutants, skin cancer and eye disorders (cataracts) linked to ozone layer depletion in the upper atmosphere. There is some judicial authority for asserting the right of a State in customary international law not to be subjected to damaging transnational boundary emissions from another State;

(b) the *threat to ecosystems*, particularly the damage caused by acid rain – acid rain is created by the release of the following gases into the atmosphere: sulphur dioxide, nitric oxide, nitrogen dioxide, ammonia, ozone and hydrocarbons; and

(c) the *threat of severe climatic disruption* caused by global warming of the atmosphere with excessive levels of greenhouse gases – global warming has not only been linked to the increasing incidence of storms, droughts, desertification, forest fires, floods, and attendant crop and property damage, but there has also been research which suggests that global warming may lead to the disruption of the ocean current systems upon which the world's climatic patterns depend for their stability. Ironically, in the long term, the main consequence of heating the atmosphere may be the onset of a new ice age. It is therefore imperative that effective and timely steps are taken to control the production of greenhouse gases. The problem is compounded by the short-termism of party political systems and the unwillingness of governments to take unpopular decisions.

8.3   HISTORIC CONTROLS

The problems associated with air pollution are not new. Legislation aimed at controlling acidic emissions from alkali works dates back to 1863 (see the Alkali Act 1863). The 1863 Act, like so many that followed it, was reactive; it was introduced following the recommendations of a Royal Commission regarding pollution from alkali works, especially the very damaging emissions of hydrochloric acid gas. The 1863 Act was extended in scope by the Alkali Act of 1874, and both were consolidated in 1906 in the Alkali Works Regulation Act 1906. The provisions of the 1906 Act were repealed by the EA 1995.

Legislation aimed at controlling smoke and similar atmospheric emissions was later introduced by the Public Health Acts of 1875 and 1936 and the Public Health (Smoke Abatement) Act 1926. These Acts were not successful in dealing with the problems of smoke pollution, and it was not until the Clean Air Act (CAA) 1956 that there was a comprehensive attempt to control all smoke emissions from domestic fires and commercial and industrial premises.

The CAA 1956, like the earlier legislation, was introduced as a reactive measure to combat an existing air pollution problem. In London in 1952, some 4,000 people lost their lives as a result of the 'great smog'. Smogs, which occur frequently now in places like India, occur when fog combines with smoke particles. The result is that the fog is very dense (smog is a very apt description; it is really a smoke-filled fog), visibility is reduced and breathing is impaired. The CAA 1956 was extended in scope by the CAA 1968 and the provisions have now largely been consolidated in the CAA 1993, which is considered in more detail below.

8.4   GOVERNMENT POLICY

The government's 'early' policy in relation to air pollution was set out in *This Common Inheritance* in 1990. This expression of government policy was, in part, concerned with the protection of public health. In the second year report on the government's programme outlined in the 1990 report, there was a commitment to further action to reduce air pollution. In particular, it was suggested that, in addition to traditional legal controls, the government would also explore the use of economic instruments, for example, measures to ensure that charges incurred by transport users reflect the full costs of their journeys. The landfill tax in relation to waste is a further example of how economic and fiscal measures can be employed to reduce pollution or encourage recycling.

8.4.1   Air quality: meeting the challenge

In March 1994, the Department of the Environment (DoE) published a discussion paper, *Improving Air Quality*, which was followed in January 1995 by *Air Quality: Meeting the Challenge – the Government's Strategic Policies for Air*, which set out the government's policies for air quality management. The 1994 discussion paper recognised that the existing approach to air quality was somewhat fragmented and also that there should be a move to what was described as a more 'effects-based' approach, with revised air quality standards based principally on human health effects. *Meeting the Challenge* put forward the following proposals:

(a) a new framework of national air quality standards and targets. Two main levels of air quality were proposed:

   (i) the first is a long term target in which nine key pollutants will be rendered harmless to health and the environment. The following were the nine pollutants of greatest concern:

   ozone, benzene, 1.3-butadiene, sulphur dioxide (SO_2), carbon monoxide (CO), nitrogen dioxide (NO_2), particles (especially PM10 emitted from diesel engines), polycyclic aromatic hydrocarbons (PAHs) and lead.

   This target will be achieved through measures such as the introduction of less polluting raw materials, production processes and products;

   (ii) the second level is essentially a trigger or an alert threshold which indicates when air quality in parts of England and Wales is so poor that an immediate response would be justified to prevent serious damage to health. Such measures might include banning cars from city centres. Local authorities already have legal powers to impose traffic restrictions, but whilst, as yet, they have not used these powers to protect air quality by imposing traffic bans, London has, from March 2003, introduced a congestion charging scheme (Transport Act 2000) which should bring about improvement of air quality in London.

(b) The establishment of a framework for local air quality management and, in particular, concentrating action on areas where progress is slow. Local authorities will be responsible for reviewing air quality and they will be under a duty to designate Air Quality Management Areas (AQMAs) if they are not attaining the relevant air quality targets. AQMAs are to be controlled in a similar fashion to smoke control areas (see below) and will centre upon an Air Quality Plan prepared by the relevant local authority.

   Local authorities will be required to draw up air quality management plans which set out their proposals for meeting air quality targets.

(c) Vehicle emissions are seen as a major contributor to air pollution and the strategy suggests an action plan to reduce the contribution of road transport to air pollution, particularly in urban areas. In AQMAs, local authorities will be required to appraise their development and transport policies against an air quality assessment. Planning Policy Guidance Note 23 on Planning and Pollution Control has been revised to reflect these changes. Planning Policy Guidance Note 13 on Planning and Transport already recognises the relationship between planning transport uses and air quality; however, it is not clear to what extent its recommendations are currently being delivered through the system of development plans.

8.5   THE ENVIRONMENT ACT 1995

Part IV of the EA 1995 contains provisions which are intended to implement the policies set out in *Air Quality: Meeting the Challenge*. Part IV includes provisions aimed at securing a national air quality strategy and also provisions concerned with local air quality management. In particular, it provides a framework for ensuring that the UK meets a number of objectives in reducing and controlling the nine pollutants listed above. Improvements in ambient air quality will help to protect human health.

8.5.1   National Air Quality Strategy (NAQS)

Section 80 of the EA 1995 imposes a duty on the Secretary of State to prepare and publish a National Air Quality Strategy. The 1997 Strategy contains policies designed to attain air quality obligations under EC law or international agreements. The Secretary of State is under a duty to review the National Air Quality Strategy (s 80(4)) from time to time, consulting with the Environment Agency, industry, experts, and the public (via a draft strategy).

The NAQS comprises:

(a) standards relating to the quality of air;

(b) objectives for the restriction of levels at which particular substances are present in air; and

(c) measures which are to be taken by local authorities and other persons for the purpose of achieving those objectives.

The current NAQS is detailed in *Air Quality Strategy for England, Wales, Scotland and Northern Ireland*, Cm 4548, 2000.

The Secretary of State is under a duty to: (a) determine a base (target) air quality standard, to be achieved by 2005; and (b) set 'alert thresholds' for particular pollutants (see below) which, if exceeded, will result in the adoption of remedial measures via the designation of an AQMA. The relevant standards set for SO_2, CO, ozone, particulates, benzene and 1.3-butadiene have been attained in the UK. The current regulations are the Air Quality (England) Regulations 2000 (SI 2000/928). Draft regulations have been issued by DEFRA to implement Directive 99/30/EC (setting pollutant limit values) and Directive 96/62/EC (setting ambient air quality assessment and management provisions). The most recent EC proposal covering the period 2005–10 tightens the targets for most pollutant thresholds and includes a new standard for polycyclic aromatic hydrocarbons (PAHs). The Environment Agency is required by s 81 of the EA 1995 to have regard to the national strategy when exercising its functions.

8.5.2   Local Air Quality Management Areas (AQMAs)

Part IV of the EA 1995 places particular responsibilities on the local authorities to achieve, at a local level, the national air quality strategy. Although the provisions that are about to be discussed place additional burdens on local authorities, they have generally been welcomed by local authority associations, such as the Association of Metropolitan Authorities. However, it remains to be seen how quickly local authorities will be able to respond to the new demands placed upon them and whether they have sufficient resources to fulfil their obligations.

Section 82 of the EA 1995 places each local authority under a duty (the 'appraisal' duty) to carry out a review from time to time of the present and likely future air quality within its area. Where a local authority carries out such a review (an AQR), it must also assess whether air quality standards or objectives are being achieved, or are likely to be achieved within the relevant period. If it appears that any air quality standards or objectives are not being achieved, or are not likely to be achieved, the local authority must identify the parts of their area where this is the case.

Section 83 makes provision for the establishment of the local air quality management areas. Where it appears that any air quality standards or objectives are not being achieved, or are not likely to be achieved, the local authority *must* designate, by order, the relevant area as an AQMA (referred to in the 1995 Act as a 'designated area'). Financial assistance regarding AQMAs is available from DEFRA and advice from the Environment Agency. Following a subsequent air quality review, the order may be varied or revoked, in the latter case only if it appears that the air quality standards and objectives are being achieved, or are likely to be achieved within the relevant period.

Once an order has been made to designate an area as an AQMA, the local authority (whether district or unitary) is under a duty to exercise its powers in order to reduce the relevant pollutants. Section 84 deals with the duties of local authorities in relation to designated areas. These are as follows:

(a) to carry out a further detailed investigation and assessment of local air quality;

(b) to prepare a report regarding the outcome of the detailed assessment referred to above within 12 months of the order becoming operational;

(c) to prepare a written action plan (air quality plan) which details how and when the local authority intends to exercise its powers to achieve the relevant air quality standards and objectives. If the plan is made by a district council, then the relevant county council can make recommendations. These recommendations must be taken into account when finalising the plan (s 86). In the event of disagreement, the matter can be referred to the Secretary of State. The Secretary of State enjoys a reserve power to carry out the review and assessment stages, either directly or through a third party (such as the Environment Agency) (see s 85);

(d) to provide regular information to the public regarding air quality;

(e) to prepare contingency plans regarding air quality emergencies.

In drawing up its air quality plan, a local authority is obliged to consult government (DEFRA and the Department of Transport, Local Government and the Regions), adjoining local authorities, industry and the general public. The government may provide: (a) financial assistance towards the carrying out of air quality assessments; (b) access to government data; (c) best practice guidance; and (d) research. The preparation of air quality plans will require local authorities to adopt a more holistic perspective, similar to the wide ambit of Development Plans, and have regard to local pollution control, transport and development policies. The costs falling on the local economy, especially the transport and industry sectors, must be proportionate to plan objectives and be cost-effective. Air Quality Plans may include traffic management controls. Vehicles may be deterred from entering city centres via the use of congestion charging schemes (now operational in London), increasing the number of pedestrianised areas, the provision of park and ride schemes, the introduction of multi-occupancy express vehicle lanes, resident-only parking zones and banning vehicles from city centres at times when air quality is especially poor. Alternative transport measures could include the introduction of cycle lanes, supertrams (light railways) and bus-only lanes.

8.5.3 Powers of the Secretary of State (ss 85, 87 and 88 of the EA 1995)

8.5.3.1 Section 85

The Secretary of State has the power to direct a local authority (s 85(5) of the EA 1995) to take actions designed to enable the UK to comply with its EC and international obligations. Local authorities are duty bound to comply with the directions which the Secretary of State gives (s 85(7)). The actions of local authorities designed to respond to air pollution affecting more than one authority will be co-ordinated by government departments via their regional offices.

8.5.3.2 Section 87

In addition to the power to resolve disputes, the Secretary of State is given considerable power under s 87 to make regulations for the following purposes:

(a) implementing the national air quality strategy;
(b) implementing EC or international legal obligations;
(c) prescribing air quality standards;
(d) prescribing objectives for the restriction of levels at which particular substances are present in air;
(e) conferring or transferring powers to local authorities;
(f) controlling the details of reviews; and
(g) regarding procedural steps.

8.5.3.3 Section 88

Before issuing such regulations, the Secretary of State is required to consult with the Environment Agency, local authorities, industry and other appropriate bodies or persons. In addition, s 88 enables the Secretary of State to issue guidance to local authorities which they are obliged to take into account with regard to any relevant matter.

8.6   OTHER LEGISLATIVE CONTROLS

The local authorities (the district councils, London borough councils, the metropolitan districts and unitary authorities), through their environmental health departments and officers, play a key role in controlling air pollution. They are involved in other areas of air pollution control:

(a) providing authorisation (licensing) for industrial processes governed by the Local Authority Air Pollution Control (LAAPC) regime contained in Pt I of the EPA 1990 and equivalent IPPC regulatory controls contained in the PPCA 1999;

(b) enforcing the provisions of the Clean Air Act (CAA) 1993;

(c) enforcing the provisions of Pt III of the EPA 1990 in relation to those statutory nuisances which have an impact on the quality of air (see Chapter 9);

(d) designating AQMAs under Pt IV of the EA 1995 (as described above).

Emissions into the air are also controlled by the Environment Agency through the system of IPC and IPPC (described in Chapter 6).

The town and country planning system regulates the siting of new sources of atmospheric pollution. Policies, including those relating to air quality contained within local authority Development Plans, may guide polluting development to appropriate locations whilst the siting decision itself is based upon a consideration of both Development Plan policies and 'other material considerations' (a list of factors relevant to planning and relevant to the particular application for development) (note the decision making legal duties in ss 54A and 70(2) of the Town and Country Planning Act 1990). 'Material considerations' include policy documents which set out national air pollution policy, and the result of consultations with regulators responsible for the day-to-day regulation of activities which discharge pollutants into the atmosphere (for example, the Environment Agency and local authorities regarding IPC and LAAPC).

Following the introduction of the NAQS, all local authorities must take account of air quality considerations and standards when updating their Development Plans (see PPG 23 Planning and Pollution Control). A persistent and knotty problem regarding the grant of planning permission for developments which will discharge pollutants to atmosphere is the extent to which a decision maker (the planning committee of the local authority or an appeal inspector) may impose conditions (see DoE Circular 11/95), on the grant of permission, which impinge upon and duplicate the conditions which could be imposed by the regulator responsible for licensing the operational aspects of the development. The leading case here is *Gateshead Metropolitan Borough Council v Secretary of State for the Environment and Northumbrian Water* (1995). The developer applied for planning permission to construct a clinical waste incinerator. The planning committee of the local authority refused to grant permission largely because it believed that the applicant had paid too little attention to the air pollution impacts of the proposal. The planning committee thought that, were it to grant planning permission for the development, HMIP was unlikely to refuse to grant it an IPC licence, and the committee was not convinced that the IPC regime would adequately safeguard the public from environmental damage arising from the operation of the incinerator. In the Court of Appeal, it was accepted that there was an overlap between the planning control and pollution control regimes and that pollution was a material consideration in the planning decision. The court held that the planning committee was entitled to refuse planning permission if, after consulting HMIP (now the Environment Agency), it was clear that an IPC licence application would be refused by HMIP. In other cases, pollution control was a matter to be left to HMIP because HMIP could not issue a licence if the applicant could not satisfy HMIP that the process would comply with the IPC BATNEEC condition and thereby ensure an acceptable degree of environmental protection. Current best practice is to obtain the Environment Agency's views on the acceptability of the proposal at the planning application stage.

In attempting to resolve concerns relating to the harmful atmospheric impacts of development proposals, planning conditions and planning agreements (and unilateral planning obligations) may be employed to address such reservations. By way of example, the applicants' agreement to accept a planning condition providing for a totally enclosed drum unloading facility, thereby drastically reducing the risk of the escape of malodorous chemical substances, in *Envirocor Waste Holdings Ltd v Secretary of State for the Environment* (1995) was a crucial issue which the planning inspector failed to appreciate fully when he refused permission for a proposed waste transfer station.

Crop residue (stubble) burning is regulated by a combination of s 152 of the EPA 1990 and the Crop Residues (Burning) Regulations 1993 (SI 1993/1366). The Regulations prohibit, subject to exemptions and restrictions, the burning of cereal straw (hay), oil seed rape, peas and beans. Breach of the Regulations is an offence punishable by a fine in the magistrates' court.

Sections 161 and 161A of the Highways Act 1980 prohibit the lighting of fires on, over or off a highway which injure, interrupt or endanger road users.

Other controls exist under:

(a) the Health and Safety at Work Act 1974;

(b) EC legislation (see below);

(c) international conventions and protocols.

8.7 LOCAL AUTHORITY AIR POLLUTION CONTROL (LAAPC)

Local authorities are responsible for controlling the atmospheric emissions of certain prescribed industrial processes. Usually, it will be the district council or the London borough council that exercises these powers. Part I of the EPA 1990 establishes a two tier system of control over certain prescribed industrial processes. Processes are prescribed for control under either system by the Secretary of State by means of regulations. The Environmental Protection (Prescribed Processes and Substances) Regulations 1991 (SI 1991/472), as amended, identify those processes which fall under the central control of the Environment Agency (Part A processes) or the control of the relevant local authority (Part B processes).

Where a process falls into Pt B of the Regulations, it must be authorised by the local authority in whose area the process is based. Local authorities are required to regulate the process so as to prevent or minimise the pollution of the environment due to the release of prescribed substances into the air. The system of LAAPC only permits the local authority to control atmospheric emissions, whereas the central system of IPC enables the control of substances into more than one environmental medium to secure the Best Practical Environmental Option (BPEO) (see 6.10).

In regulating these prescribed processes, local authorities have the power to set down conditions in authorisations (licences) which secure the objectives laid down in s 7 of the EPA 1990. In particular, processes should use the Best Available Techniques Not Entailing Excessive Costs (BATNEEC) to prevent the release of substances into the air or, where that is not practicable, to reduce the release to a minimum and to render harmless any substances that are released.

The LAAPC responsibilities of the local authorities are currently being phased out and replaced by equivalent responsibilities under the PPCA 1999. Chapter 6 examines the transition from LAAPC to IPPC in detail. Under the IPPC regime, local authorities are responsible for regulating Part A(2) installations with regard to all environmental impacts and Part B installations with regard to atmospheric emissions only.

8.8   THE CLEAN AIR ACT (CAA) 1993

Whilst the first legislative controls over atmospheric emissions date back to the Alkali Act 1863, nevertheless, this early legislation did not control the emissions of smoke from all industrial processes. The use of coal and the consequent emissions of smoke and grit particles from both houses and factories resulted in serious pollution and health problems. However, it was not until the Clean Air Acts of 1956 and 1968 that there was any comprehensive attempt to control emissions of smoke, dust and grit from industrial and domestic premises. (The earlier Public Health (Smoke Abatement) Act 1926 proved to be an ineffective control of domestic smoke.) The CAA 1956 was introduced to prohibit the emission of dark smoke from any domestic or industrial chimney. A chimney was defined as any structure or opening through which smoke is emitted. Its scope was extended by the CAA 1968 which prohibited emissions of dark smoke from any industrial or trade premises, even though the emission was not made from a chimney. These Acts have now been consolidated into the CAA 1993. Enforcement of the CAA 1993 is the responsibility of the local authorities, which may act both with regard to smoke arising within their areas or affecting their areas.

8.8.1 Definition of 'smoke'

'Smoke' includes soot, ash, grit and gritty particles emitted in smoke, any visible non-carbonaceous vapour (for example, water vapour) and visible fumes (but not invisible gases). For 'dark smoke', see 8.8.4 below and for 'grit, dust and fumes', see 8.8.10.

A government report, *Transboundary Air Pollution: Acidification, Eutrophication, and Ground Level Ozone in the UK 1999–2001*, published by DEFRA, contains data regarding the range of pollution challenges facing the UK (acid rain, surface ozone and concentrations of the main pollutants). Overall, there appears to be a general decline in levels of atmospheric pollutants, but high levels of NO_x, CO, ozone, volatile organic compounds (benzene) and fine particulates (diesel exhaust emissions) continue to cause concern.

8.8.2 Relationship between the CAA 1993, Pt I of the EPA 1990 and the PPCA 1999

Before considering the details of the CAA 1993, it is important to note the relationship between these controls and the controls over atmospheric emissions under Pt I of the EPA 1990 (IPC and LAAPC) and the equivalent IPPC regulatory controls in the PPCA 1999. The provisions of Pts I–III of the CAA 1993 do not apply to any process regulated under Pt I of the EPA 1990. Section 41 of the CAA 1993 excludes IPC and LAAPC processes from the date of authorisation. Similarly, the CAA 1993 does not apply to installations regulated by the PPCA 1999.

8.8.3 Offences under the CAA 1993

The CAA 1993 prohibits emissions of smoke, dust and grit by means of criminal offences. The following are the main offences:

(a) emission of dark smoke – from a chimney or from industrial premises other than from a chimney;

(b) emission of dust and grit from non-domestic furnaces;

(c) emission of smoke from a chimney in a Smoke Control Area;

(d) various offences relating to the installation of furnaces;

(e) the burning of insulation cable as part of a metal recovery process unless a LAAPC licence has been obtained (s 33 of the CAA 1993).

Prosecutions under most provisions of the CAA 1993 are dealt with in the magistrates' court.

8.8.4 The 'dark smoke' offences (ss 1 and 2)

The CAA 1993 creates numerous criminal offences, including the so called 'dark smoke' offences. Sections 1 and 2 of the 1993 Act prohibit the emission of dark smoke from different categories of premises; s 1 requires the relevant emission of dark smoke to be through a chimney whereas s 2 does not. The offences are strict liability offences, although various activities are exempted from the provisions (see 8.8.8 below) and some statutory defences are available (see 8.8.9 below).

Section 1 prohibits the emission of 'dark smoke':

(a) from the chimney of any building (s 1(1)); or

(b) from a chimney which serves the furnace of any fixed boiler or industrial plant (s 1(2)).

'Building' includes railway locomotives (s 43) and vessels in coastal waters (s 44).

Section 1 applies to emissions of dark smoke from the chimneys of domestic premises as well as industrial or commercial premises. Where an offence has been committed under s 1(1), liability will rest with the occupier of the building from which the dark smoke is emitted. In the case of dark smoke emissions from a chimney serving a fixed boiler or industrial plant (s 1(2)), the person having control or possession of the boiler or plant will be liable if an offence is committed.

A person guilty of an offence under s 1(1) as respects a chimney of a private dwelling is liable to a fine not exceeding level 3 on the standard scale (£1,000), whereas in any other case the fine should not exceed level 5 (£5,000) on the standard scale.

Section 2 prohibits the non-chimney emission of dark smoke from industrial trade premises. Unlike s 1, the s 2 emission need not be through a chimney. Trade or industrial premises are premises which are used for an industrial or trade purpose or premises on which matter is burnt in connection with any industrial or trade purpose. A s 2 offence may be committed either by the occupier of the premises or any other person causing or permitting the emission. In *Sheffield CC v ADH Demolition Ltd* (1984), it was held that premises could include a demolition site. The burning of rubbish on a demolition site amounted to an industrial or trade process because there was a close relationship between the activity (burning the rubbish) and the trade (demolition) and thus the defendant was properly convicted. Section 2(3) is worded in such a way as to catch offenders who attempt to evade the CAA 1993 by burning substances under cover of night-time. A person guilty of an offence under s 2 is liable on summary conviction to a fine of up to £20,000.

8.8.5   What is dark smoke? (s 3 of the CAA 1993)

'Dark smoke' is defined by reference to a device known as the Ringlemann Chart. Smoke which is determined to be as dark or darker than shade 2 on the Ringlemann Chart is 'dark smoke' for the purposes of the 1993 Act. The Ringlemann Chart indicates differing shades of darkness. The Chart consists of a piece of card with cross-hatching in black on a white background so that a known percentage of white is obscured. The Chart needs to be placed at some distance from the observer who will then be able to see that the lines merge into different greyish/black shades. The different shades are numerically categorised: 0 equals white and 5 equals dense black. Shades 2–4 increase by degrees so that shade 1 indicates a 20% obscuration of the white, shade 2 equals 40%, and so on. In order to compare the shades with the smoke, it is necessary to place the card between the observer and the smoke (the chart is usually mounted on a wooden or metal frame). The observer usually stands about 50 ft from the Chart in order to match the smoke colour with the Chart. The matching should normally take place in good daylight conditions.

In any legal proceedings for breach of s 1 or s 2, the court must be satisfied that the smoke falls within the statutory definition of dark smoke. However, there is no requirement for an actual comparison of the smoke with the Chart. It is sufficient that the court is certain that the method was properly applied and that the smoke was thereby determined to be dark.

There is no requirement in the CAA 1993 for the defendant to have caused or knowingly permitted the discharge of dark smoke. The offence is one of strict liability. There are, however, a number of defences and exemptions which are considered below.

8.8.6   Notification that an offence has been committed

An occupier of premises must be notified of an alleged offence by the local authority environmental officer 'as soon as may be'. This will usually mean that an environmental health officer or officer from the local authority advises the occupier verbally. However, the local authority is required to confirm this notification in writing within a period of four days. Failure to give notice will provide the defendant with a defence to any charges made under ss 1, 2 and 20. Unlike other pollution offences discussed in this book, the offence can only be tried in the magistrates' court.

8.8.7   Strict liability and burden of proof

The CAA 1993 presumes that there will have been an emission of dark smoke from industrial or trade premises in any case where material is burned on those premises and the circumstances are such that the burning would be likely to give rise to the emission of dark smoke. The burden of proof falls squarely on the occupier (or any other person causing or permitting the burning) to show that no dark smoke was actually emitted.

8.8.8 Exemptions

Section 1(3) of the CAA 1993 provides certain exemptions from the above offences. These are contained in the Dark Smoke (Permitted Periods) Regulations 1958 (SI 1958/498), which establish the following exceptions whereby no offence is committed if the emissions of dark smoke are made within certain periods:

(a) the emission of dark smoke is permitted for a defined number of minutes (between 10–40) during an eight hour period. The precise number of minutes depends on the number of furnaces which feed into the chimney and whether or not the emission involves the blowing of soot;

(b) in any event, the continuous emission of dark smoke cannot at any time exceed four minutes and the continuous emission of black smoke must not at any time exceed two minutes in any half hour period.

The Clean Air (Emissions of Dark Smoke) (Exemptions) Regulations 1969 (SI 1969/1263) also provide exceptions relating to the burning of certain materials in the open. The following are exempt from s 2 of the CAA 1993:

(a) burning timber and other waste material which results either from the demolition of a building or from the clearance of a site upon which there is building operation or engineering construction;

(b) burning explosive which has become waste and any material which has become contaminated by such explosive;

(c) burning tar, pitch or asphalt and other matter in connection with any resurfacing;

(d) burning animal and poultry carcasses where the animals have died or have been slaughtered due to a disease;

(e) burning containers which have been contaminated by any pesticide or toxic substance used for veterinary or agricultural purposes.

However, for these exceptions to apply, the person seeking to rely on them must satisfy certain conditions. Among other things, there is the requirement that there is no other reasonably safe and practicable method of disposing of the matter. Other conditions relate to the manner in which the burning takes place and that steps are taken to minimise the emission of dark smoke. The burning must be carried out under the supervision of the occupier of the premises.

8.8.9 Defences

Section 1(4) of the CAA 1993 provides that where a breach of the dark smoke provisions occurs, a number of defences may be raised in any proceedings. These defences arise in the following circumstances:

(a) when lighting the furnace from cold; or

(b) when there has been some unforeseeable and unavoidable failure of the furnace or apparatus connected with the furnace; or

(c) when unsuitable fuel has been used when suitable fuel is unobtainable and that the least unsuitable fuel was used.

Garner's *Encyclopaedia of Environmental Law* suggests that the defence of lighting a furnace from cold might only be available in relation to the initial ignition of the furnace and not each time the furnace is restoked after a period (that is, overnight) of being damped down.

These defences are all subject to the important caveat that all practicable steps were taken to prevent or minimise the emission of dark smoke.

As far as the s 2 offence is concerned, s 2(4) provides a defence if it can be proved that the emission was inadvertent and that all practicable steps had been taken to prevent or minimise it. It appears from the statute that both these elements will be required before a defendant can rely on the defence. 'Practicable' is defined here in a similar way to practicable in the context of 'best practicable means'. Therefore, regard must be had to factors such as local conditions and circumstances; financial considerations; and the current state of technical knowledge.

Finally, if the person charged with an offence under either of these sections has not been served with a written notification of the offence from the environmental health department of the local authority within the prescribed four day period, this will provide him with an additional defence (s 51).

8.8.10 Grit, dust and fumes

Section 5 establishes similar offences to the dark smoke offences in relation to grit, dust and fumes emitted from furnaces. Grit is defined by the Clean Air (Emission of Grit and Dust from Furnaces) Regulations 1971 (SI 1971/162), which also prescribe the limits of grit and dust emissions from certain types of furnaces. 'Dust' does not include dust emitted from a chimney as an ingredient of smoke and 'fumes' means any airborne matter smaller than dust.

It is an offence if, on any day, the grit or dust emitted from a chimney serving a specified furnace exceeds the prescribed emission limits laid down in the Regulations. Monitoring equipment is required to measure emissions accurately and the Ringlemann Chart procedure is not applicable. The occupier will be guilty of the offence unless he or she can successfully raise the defence that the *best* practicable means had been used to minimise or prevent the emission. It should be noted here that the defence requires the best practicable means to be employed rather than any practicable means. However, in circumstances where the Regulations do not specify a prescribed limit (that is, certain furnaces are not covered by the Regulations), an offence will still be committed if the occupier fails to use any practicable means to minimise the emission of grit or dust from the chimney.

8.8.11 Control over the installation of non-domestic furnaces

Section 4 of the CAA 1993 provides that, before installing a furnace over a certain size (basically a non-domestic boiler), the person seeking to make the installation must obtain the approval of the local authority. The section also stipulates that all new non-domestic boilers should, so far as practicable, be smokeless. Anyone who installs a furnace in contravention of this requirement is committing an offence, but if the local authority has approved the installation, it is deemed to comply with the requirements of the section.

Additionally, all non-domestic furnaces over a certain energy value must comply with the provisions contained in ss 6–8. Furnaces falling under these sections must be fitted with local authority approved grit and dust arrestment equipment. The arrestors must be properly maintained, if used for the following purposes:

(a) to burn pulverised fuel; or

(b) to burn, at a rate of 45.4 kg or more an hour, any other solid matter (waste); or

(c) to burn, at a rate equivalent to 366.4 kilowatts or more, any liquid or gaseous matter.

There are certain exemptions from these provisions specified in s 7. In particular, the Secretary of State has used his powers under s 7 to prescribe by regulation that furnaces of a certain class (for example, mobile furnaces) may be exempted (see the Clean Air (Arrestment Plant) (Exemption) Regulations 1969 (SI 1969/1262)). Alternatively, it is possible to apply to the local authority for an exemption under s 7. The local authority can only grant an exemption if it is satisfied that the emissions of grit or dust will not amount to a statutory nuisance.

The local authority may also require the occupier of these furnaces to comply with certain monitoring requirements in relation to the measurement of grit, dust and fumes. In turn, the occupier has the right to request that the local authority make and record such measurements and the local authority will be required to do so from time to time. A right of appeal to the Secretary of State is available if the local authority refuses to approve the proposed equipment.

8.8.12 Control over chimney height

Section 14 applies to furnaces connected to a chimney and empowers the local authorities to control the height of chimneys for the purposes of regulating air pollution. These controls are based on the principle of dilute and disperse. Tall chimney stacks are supposed to enable the more effective dispersion of pollution in order to dilute it to harmless levels. The control under s 14 exists in addition to the normal planning controls which the planning authority can exert.

If any person is intending to:

(a) erect a new chimney to serve a furnace;

(b) enlarge an existing chimney to serve a furnace; or

(c) replace a chimney with an increased combustion space,

then he or she must make an application to the local authority for chimney height approval. The local authority will determine the application by reference to the 1981 *Third Memorandum on Chimney Heights* (DoE Circular 25/81), which assists with the calculation on chimney heights. The local authority must take into account various factors (proximity of neighbouring property, topography and current levels of atmospheric pollution) and, in particular, must not grant approval for a chimney unless it is satisfied that its height will be sufficient to prevent, as far as practicable, the chimney emissions becoming prejudicial to health or a nuisance.

The local authority can either approve the chimney height with or without conditions. Once again, there is a right of appeal against the decision of the local authority to the Secretary of State.

8.8.13 Smoke Control Areas

The ability to establish Smoke Control Areas is one of the principal features of the CAA 1993 and provides an important means by which local authorities can control smoke from domestic properties. A local authority has the power (see s 18 of the CAA 1993) to declare all or part of its area as a Smoke Control Area and does so by designating a Smoke Control Order. The relevant steps to create a Smoke Control Area are set out in Sched 1 to the CAA 1993. In addition, the Secretary of State has the power, by virtue of s 19, to order a local authority to designate a Smoke Control Area. Two or more local authorities may combine to declare a larger Smoke Control Area (see s 61(3)). Smoke Control Orders may be varied or revoked at any time.

The Smoke Control Order may designate certain classes of building; it may exempt specific buildings or classes of buildings or fireplaces. It has been suggested that the widespread adoption of Smoke Control Areas has been an important factor in achieving compliance with the Sulphur Dioxide Directive (80/779/EEC).

Once an area has been designated as a Smoke Control Area, then an occupier of a building in the area is guilty of an offence if smoke (note that this includes any shade of smoke) is emitted from a chimney of that building. However, defences are available if:

(a) the emission resulted from the use of an authorised fuel; or

(b) the emission resulted from the use of a fireplace exempted by regulations.

Authorised fuels are defined by the Smoke Control Areas (Authorised Fuel) Regulations 1991 (SI 1991/1282). Various regulations exempt certain classes of fireplace (the Smoke Control (Exempted Fireplaces) Orders).

It is also an offence to buy solid non-authorised fuel for use in a Smoke Control Area (unless of course it is for an exempt fireplace) and it is also an offence to retail unauthorised fuel for unauthorised use in a Smoke Control Area.

8.8.14 Air pollution research and data collection responsibilities of local authorities

Local authorities are empowered (s 34 of the CAA 1993) to undertake or make financial contributions towards the cost of research into air pollution and publication of research results (s 38 of the CAA 1993 and the 1997 Regulations (SI 1997/19)). In furtherance of the s 34 power, authorities may serve notices (s 36) on the occupiers of non-domestic premises requiring the provision of air pollution emissions data. A right of appeal to the Secretary of State exists with regard to service of such a notice (s 37). In the event that the data requested is not forthcoming, local authorities have a power of entry, subject to giving the occupier a minimum of 21 days' notice to take the necessary measurements (s 35(1)(b)). Air pollution emissions data may be recorded by the occupier and supplied to the local authority under the terms of an agreement. The s 35 power of entry does not apply to IPC licensed premises, although the s 36 power may be used to obtain relevant air pollution data which is not already supplied to the Environment Agency under the terms of IPC licences. Similar restrictions apply to Crown property (MOD establishments). Whilst the s 36 power does apply to Crown land, there is no power of entry. Defence research facilities may be exempted (s 36(6) of the CAA 1993 and the 1997 Regulations (SI 1997/18)).

Of considerable importance is the Secretary of State's power (under s 39 of the CAA 1993) to direct, subject to prior consultation, a local authority to acquire and operate air pollution monitoring and recording equipment and to forward the data collected to him. The resultant network of air pollution monitoring stations forms a key component of the government's pollution reduction strategy. The data collected enables the Secretary of State to comply with his duty to provide the public with ozone information.

8.9 STATUTORY NUISANCES RELATING TO AIR QUALITY

Statutory nuisance is considered in Chapter 9. However, in the context of controls over air pollution, it should be noted that the following matters may constitute a statutory nuisance if they are either prejudicial to health or a nuisance:

(a) any premises in such a state so as to be prejudicial to health or a nuisance (this could cover odour emissions from such premises, even though smell is specifically mentioned in (c) below);

(b) smoke, fumes or gas emitted from premises so as to be prejudicial to health or a nuisance;

(c) any dust, steam, smell or other effluvia arising on industrial, trade or business premises.

However, it should be noted that, in relation to (b) above, where the emission of smoke can be controlled under the CAA 1993, the statutory nuisance provisions do not apply. Therefore, this statutory nuisance is largely concerned with smoke which is less than 'dark' from non-domestic premises.

Civil actions, based on the tort of private nuisance, may arise out of activities on the defendant's land which result in air pollution and either consequent physical damage to the claimant's land (for example, airborne acidic deposits or fumes – *St Helens Smelting Co v Tipping* (1865)) or an unreasonable interference with the use or enjoyment of the claimant's property. Nuisance actions relating to odour, smoke, dust and airborne litter occur from time to time (see *Blackburn v ARC Ltd* (1998), in which smells emanating from a poorly managed landfill site gave rise to a successful action). Public nuisance actions are less frequent than private nuisance actions (*Halsey v Esso Petroleum* (1961) – acidic deposits damaging a car parked on the public highway).

8.10 POLLUTION FROM MOTOR VEHICLES

There is no doubt that the emissions from motor vehicles are a major source of atmospheric pollution (especially NO_x, CO_2 and hydrocarbons). Approximately 98% of the UK's benzene emissions arise from vehicle emissions. Eighty-nine per cent of the UK's carbon monoxide emissions, 10% of CO_2, 51% of NO_x, 70% of lead and

36% of hydrocarbons come from petrol and diesel engined vehicles. Linked to these statistics is the further fact that vehicle emissions have increased by 50% since 1970, although there is some evidence of a temporary downward trend since the introduction of cars fitted with catalytic converters. Pollution emission 'gains' linked to improvements in motor vehicle engine efficiency and the development of less polluting fuels have been offset by increases in the number of motor vehicle journeys made and the number of vehicles in circulation (currently 24 million, estimated to rise to over 50 million by 2025). Vehicles are also relatively cheaper now than at any time before. Vehicle emissions are also largely responsible for emissions of other pollutants such as 1.3-butadiene, which has been shown to be linked to increased risks of lymphoma or leukaemia.

Vehicle emission limits relating to NO_x, CO_2 and hydrocarbons are set by the EC according to the age of motor vehicles, with tighter limits being progressively imposed on vehicle manufacturers. The relevant EC Directives (78/665/EEC, 83/351/EEC, 88/76/EEC, 89/458/EEC, 91/441/EEC, 91/542/EEC, 93/59/EEC and 94/12/EC) are implemented in the UK via the Road Traffic Acts (especially the Road Traffic Act (RTA) 1988) and the Road Vehicles (Construction and Use) Regulations 1986 (SI 1986/1078 as amended). Breach of the Regulations is an offence (s 42 of the RTA 1988).

The problem of vehicle emissions was one of the main themes in *Air Quality: Meeting the Challenge* (see 8.5 above) which put forward five proposals. These were:

(a) new technological standards for fuels, vehicle engine efficiency (economy), vehicle exhaust systems (especially particulate filters), catalytic converters and air pollution monitoring, recording and data transmission equipment;

(b) planning policies and local transport strategies aimed at reducing the need to travel and encouraging more environmentally friendly modes of transport;

(c) new environmental partnerships with public service and fleet operators; involving improved consultation with bus service operators, road haulage companies and taxi firms regarding their respective contributions to achieving NAQS and AQMA pollution reduction targets;

(d) stricter enforcement of emissions regulations and, in particular, targeting those vehicles doing the most damage to the environment;

(e) voluntary action and guidance, especially best practice guidance for industry, commerce and the public.

The composition of fuels is an important factor in reducing traffic-related air pollution. Section 30 of the CAA 1993 empowers the Secretary of State to make regulations relating to fuel contents. The Secretary of State may prevent or restrict the production, treatment, importation, distribution, use or sale of fuels. Section 30 imposes an obligation on the Secretary of State to consult the key stakeholders (motor vehicle manufacturers, vehicle buyers and users, fuel companies and air pollution regulators) before introducing new regulations. The current regulations implementing Directives (98/70/EC (petrol)) and (93/12/EEC (diesel)) are the Motor Fuel (Composition and Content) Regulations 1999 (SI 1999/3107). Local authorities have responsibility for enforcing the regulations (s 201 of the Local Government Act 1972). Similar regulations to the 1999 Regulations apply to fuels with high sulphur content (for example, gas oil) used in non-motor vehicle engines and furnaces. The use of kerosene in aircraft and ships is exempt.

It is clear that for many local authorities with heavy traffic flows and congestion problems, vehicle emissions are going to pose the biggest single problem in terms of meeting air quality standards and objectives. Better traffic management and local transport strategies are seen as important in reducing the use of vehicles. In areas which designate AQMAs, the action plan may need to embrace traffic management issues. For example, restricting access to a particular area or roads, regulating traffic flows and speed, and encouraging other transport modes, such as park and ride. Local authorities have the power, under the Road Traffic Regulation Act (RTRA) 1984 in the interest of preserving local amenity, to prohibit, restrict or regulate vehicles, or particular types of vehicles.

The objectives of the NAQS are incorporated into the RTRA 1984 by Sched 22 to the EA 1995. Sections 1, 6 and 122, as amended, enable local authorities (shire counties, metropolitan district authorities, metropolitan borough councils, London borough councils and unitary authorities) to make orders with a view to achieving the national strategy objectives. The Road Traffic (Vehicle Emissions) (Fixed Penalty) Regulations 1997 (SI 1997/3058) enable local authorities to issue fixed penalty notices to road vehicle users who fail to comply with the emission limits set out in regs 61 and 98. Only the police have powers to stop and check vehicles regarding their emissions.

An emergency traffic re-routing power is included in the RTRA 1984, enabling local authorities to divert traffic away from heavily polluted city centres and urban areas when threshold pollution limits have been exceeded.

8.11　EC LEGISLATION

The EC had a relatively slow start in terms of its programme of legislation aimed at controlling air pollution. The first directive establishing air quality standards was not adopted until 1980 (Directive 80/779/EEC). Since then, the EC has adopted various measures aimed at combating atmospheric pollution, particularly in response to acid rain. Generally speaking, EC air pollution measures can be categorised into the following broad types:

(a) *Emissions from large industrial plants*

Of particular importance is the Large Combustion Plant Directive (88/609/EEC (power stations)). This has been implemented in the UK via the IPC regulatory regime. In addition, Directive 84/360/EEC required that new industrial plants use the best available technologies not entailing excessive cost (BATNEEC). Directive 89/369/EEC deals with emissions from municipal waste incineration plants. In 1996, the EC introduced an Integrated Pollution Prevention and Control Directive (96/61/EC) which has been implemented into national law by the PPCA 1999. The IPPC Directive is, in effect, an extension to the existing IPC and LAAPC licence-based controls over a number of highly polluting industries.

Directive 2001/80/EC, applying to large power stations producing energy only (power plants, of all fuel types, with a thermal input of at least 50 MW), replaces Directive 88/609/EC and sets new emission limits for sulphur dioxide, oxides of nitrogen and dust.

(b) *Air pollution affecting the ozone layer*

EC Regulations 3322/88 and 549/91 have now banned the use of CFCs (chlorofluorocarbons) and HFCs (hydrofluorocarbons) (see Regulations SI 1994/199 and SI 1996/506).

(c) *Air quality standards*

The EC passed the Air Quality Framework Directive (96/62/EC) in 1996. This Directive is intended to be supplemented by a number of daughter directives to control 12 pollutants. The first of the daughter directives (99/30/EC) specifies binding limits for lead, sulphur dioxide, nitrogen dioxide, and small particulate matter (PM 10). The remaining pollutants are ozone, carbon monoxide, benzene, polyaromatic hydrocarbons (PAH) and the toxic metals – arsenic, mercury, cadmium, and nickel.

Directive 2001/18/EC, which sets national emission ceiling limits for sulphur dioxide, oxides of nitrogen, ammonia and volatile organic compounds in Member States, has been implemented in the UK by the National Ceilings Regulations 2002 (SI 2002/3118). The Secretary of State must, as of 2010, ensure that emissions of the gases listed above do not exceed the ceiling limits specified in the Schedule to the Directive. In addition, the Secretary of State must prepare plans for the progressive reduction of the relevant gases, require local authorities to take the reduction programme provisions into account when exercising their functions, and prepare annual inventories of the relevant polluting emissions.

(d) *Vehicle emission standards* (see 8.10 above)

The EC has enacted various directives which aim to control vehicle emissions. Initially, the directives in this area were intended to harmonise standards in order to promote the free movement of goods (namely vehicles). In 1991, the EC adopted Directive 91/441/EC which imposed strict standards on emissions from passenger cars and a similar Directive 93/59/EC was adopted in relation to light commercial vehicles. However, since then, emission limits have been tightened via further directives relating to passenger cars (94/12/EEC). In addition to setting emission limits, the EC has also sought to control the content and composition of fuels in order to reduce emissions of lead and sulphur. These are dealt with below. It is worth noting that the Commission recognises that the problem of vehicle emissions cannot simply be addressed by legislative measures. The Commission has also proposed a variety of other measures concerned with traffic management. The Commission's Green Paper on impact of transport on the environment (COM(92)46 Final (1992)) considers the impact that vehicle emissions will have on the environment by the year 2010 and suggests actions which are required to be taken.

(e) *Product quality standards*

A variety of directives have been concerned with improving product quality standards particularly in relation to fuel products. Examples include Directive 76/716/EEC and Directive 99/32/EC on the sulphur content of liquid fuels and Directive 98/70/EC on the chemical composition of fuels.

(f) *Atmospheric pollution and waste reduction*

The Landfill Directive (99/31/EC) came into force in July 1999 and has now been transposed into UK law. One important aspect of the Directive is that it will drastically reduce the amount of municipal waste currently being landfilled:

a 65% reduction of 1995 levels by 2016. This will result in an increase in the amount of municipal waste that is incinerated. Whilst the Directive will deliver an important reduction in methane emissions (a significant contributor to global warming and climate change) from landfill sites, it will increase atmospheric emissions from incinerators (see Directives 89/369/EEC and 89/429/EEC relating to municipal waste incinerators).

8.12   ACID RAIN, OZONE, GLOBAL WARMING AND THE INTERNATIONAL DIMENSION

Air pollution is a global environmental issue and attracts international attention. The study of international environmental law falls outside the scope of this book, but the transboundary nature of atmospheric pollution and the global problem of greenhouse gas emissions and climate change make it necessary to include some commentary.

The UK (and the EC) has committed itself to a number of international conventions which require the government to take steps to reduce the emission of certain pollutants:

(a) *The 1979 Convention on Long Range Transboundary Air Pollution*

Agreed in Geneva in 1979, this convention, effective from 1983, was not ratified by the UK until 1980. The 30 current signatories have agreed to endeavour to limit and, as far as possible, reduce and prevent air pollution, especially pollutants associated with the production of acid rain (especially SO_2). The Convention has resulted in several international protocols including the reduction of sulphur dioxide (SO_2) emissions; emissions of oxides of nitrogen (NO_x); and emissions of volatile organic compounds (VOCs) and heavy metals.

(b) *The 1985 Vienna Convention and the 1987 Montreal Protocol relating to the Protection of the Ozone Layer*

Parties to the Vienna Convention, including the UK (and EC) which ratified it in 1987, have agreed the Montreal Protocol on Substances that Deplete the Ozone Layer. The Protocol requires the signatories to freeze, reduce and phase out the production of various CFCs, HCFCs, methyl bromide and halons. Trade restrictions apply to non-signatory States.

(c) *The 1992 UN Framework Convention on Climate Change*

This Convention was agreed by over 150 parties at the United Nations Earth Summit in Rio de Janeiro and is aimed at reducing emissions of greenhouse gases. The 1997 Kyoto Protocol to the Convention establishes targets for six greenhouse gases: carbon dioxide, oxides of nitrogen, methane, HFCs (hydrofluorocarbons), PFCs (perfluorocarbons) and sulphur hexafluoride (SF 6). The combined target for the six gases represents a very modest 5% reduction of 1990 emission levels for these gases. The targets are to be achieved by 2012. Developing countries, in contrast to developed countries, are not bound by the reduction targets.

The Rio Convention and Kyoto Protocol have generated some interesting debates with regard to the factors which may be taken into account when assessing whether a State has attained the Protocol targets. For example, to what extent should the presence of existing forests and the planting of new forests act as 'carbon sinks' locking up carbon dioxide generated by developed countries which are parties to the Convention and Protocol?

In order to meet the UK's targets for the reduction of the main greenhouse gases specified in the Kyoto Protocol (a reduction of 12.5% of 1990 levels of the six gases between 2008 and 2012), the government has, in the Finance Act 2000, introduced a new tax effective from April 2000 known as the 'climate change levy'. The tax is a levy on business energy usage and is intended to reduce energy consumption. By reducing energy consumption, the government intends to lower the production of greenhouse gases in the UK.

The levy is payable by energy suppliers of both primary fuels (such as coal and natural gas) and secondary fuels used for lighting, heating, powering appliances and machinery. Energy suppliers will recover the levy from their customers. There are some important exemptions, including: domestic use of fuel and power, vehicle fuel, fuel products which are not energy-related (for example, raw material usage and lubricants), renewable energy production and energy from combined heat and power plants. The levy is based on the energy content of the relevant fuel rather than its carbon content. There are reductions in the levy for energy intensive industries such as steel, glass, paper, aluminium, metal foundries, food and drink production, and cement (this is not an exhaustive list). In these sectors, the tax is to be reduced by up to 80%. Each of these sectors has entered into an agreement with DEFRA (or its predecessor, the DETR) which specifies the periodic targets which must be met for each industry sector to qualify for the relevant tax reductions.

8.13   FURTHER INFORMATION

Further reading

See Chapter 2 of *Sourcebook on Environmental Law*, 2nd edn, 2001, Cavendish Publishing, which contains the cases of *Budden v BP Oil, Halsey v Esso Petroleum*, important sections from the Clean Air Act 1993 and the Environment Act 1995, EC Directives (Ambient Air Quality, Large Combustion Plants, Industrial Air Pollution and Ozone Depletion) and international conventions (the Long Range Transboundary Air Pollution Convention, the UN Framework Convention on Climate Change and the Kyoto Protocol).

Bongaerts, J, 'Carbon dioxide emissions and cars: an environmental agreement at EU level' [1999] EELR 101.

Commission of the European Communities, Green Paper on Greenhouse Gas Emission, COM(2000)87.

DETR, *Air Quality and Traffic Management*, 1997.

DETR, *The UK National Air Quality Standards: Guidance for Local Authorities*, Circular 15/97, 1997.

Department of the Environment, *Ozone*, DoE Expert Panel on Air Quality Standards, 1994.

Department of the Environment, *Air Quality Strategy for England, Scotland, Wales and Northern Ireland*, Cm 4548, 2000, The Stationery Office.

Harvey, L, *Global Warming: The Hard Science*, 2000, Prentice Hall.

House of Commons Environment Committee (1999–2000 Session), *UK Climate Change Programme*, 5th Report, The Stationery Office.

Hughes, D, Parpworth, N and Upson, J, *Air Pollution Law and Regulation*, 1998, Jordans.

National Society for Clean Air, *Pollution Handbook* (updated annually).

Royal Commission on Environmental Pollution, *Air Pollution Control: An Integrated Approach*, 5th Report, Cmnd 6371, 1975.

Royal Commission on Environmental Pollution, *Transport and the Environment*, Cm 2674, 1994, The Stationery Office.

Royal Commission on Environmental Pollution, *Energy – The Changing Climate*, Cm 4749, 2000, The Stationery Office.

Stradling, D, 'The smoke of great cities: British and American efforts to control pollution 1860–1914' [1999] Environmental History 6.

United Nations, *Strategies and Policies for Air Pollution Abatement*, 1999, United Nations Economic Commission for Europe, ECE/E13.AIR/65.

CHAPTER 9

STATUTORY NUISANCE

9.1   INTRODUCTION

Chapter 11 considers the ways in which the common law can provide a means of protecting the environment and some of the inherent difficulties faced when bringing common law actions. Common law actions, especially tort actions, are now supplemented by the provisions of ss 79–82 of the Environmental Protection Act (EPA) 1990, which provides that certain matters may constitute 'statutory nuisances' and as such may, if not abated, result in the commission of criminal offences incorporated into the EPA 1990 (see s 80(4)). The control of statutory nuisances rests largely with the environmental health departments of the local authorities. However, it is also possible for a 'person aggrieved' by a statutory nuisance to commence proceedings in the magistrates' court in order to secure the abatement of the nuisance (effectively bypassing the local authority statutory provisions). The purpose of putting certain nuisances on a statutory footing was to provide a quicker, cheaper and more effective means of dealing with nuisances than by means of a common law action.

The current statutory nuisance provisions can be found in Pt III of the EPA 1990 (ss 79–82), as amended by the Noise and Statutory Nuisance Act (NSNA) 1993. However, the provisions are not new and, in fact, the EPA 1990 consolidates provisions from legislation dating back to the Public Health Act (PHA) 1875 and the PHA 1936, which first placed certain nuisances on a statutory footing in recognition of the growing health problems associated with industrial development and some of the limitations of the common law in addressing these problems. The PHA 1936 has now been repealed and re-enacted by the EPA 1990. One of the problems with this straightforward re-enactment is that there has been no redefinition of the statutory nuisances which were introduced by the PHA 1936 to protect public health, but are now intended to protect the environment. Although statutory nuisances were intended to control pollution, the main objective of the legislation was to protect public health rather than protect the environment. In addition to the original list of statutory nuisances, noise nuisances are drawn from the Control of Pollution Act (COPA) 1974 and also the NSNA 1993. Many of the cases cited in this chapter concern the PHA 1936, but are still relevant in the context of the EPA 1990. Section 79(1) of the EPA 1990 places a duty on local authorities to inspect their areas periodically for statutory nuisances; nevertheless, the regulation of statutory nuisances is a largely reactive regulatory tool.

Section 57 of the Environment Act (EA) 1995 has inserted a new Pt IIA into the EPA 1990 concerned specifically with contaminated land. The contaminated land provisions which are discussed at length in Chapter 7 are modelled on the statutory nuisance provisions in Pt III of the EPA 1990. As a consequence, s 79(1A) of the EPA 1990 states clearly that no matter shall constitute a statutory nuisance to the extent that it consists of, or is caused by, any land being in a contaminated state. This is clearly intended to avoid overlap of the provisions and where any land is deemed to be contaminated then it will not be dealt with under the statutory nuisance provisions discussed in this chapter.

9.2   WHAT ARE STATUTORY NUISANCES?

The matters or activities that constitute statutory nuisances are listed in s 79 as follows:

(a) any premises in such a state as to be prejudicial to health or a nuisance;

(b) smoke emitted from premises so as to be prejudicial to health or a nuisance;

(c) fumes or gases emitted from premises so as to be prejudicial to health or a nuisance;

(d) any, dust, steam, smell or other effluvia arising on industrial, trade or business premises and being prejudicial to health or a nuisance;

(e) any accumulation or deposit which is prejudicial to health or a nuisance;

(f) any animal kept in such a place or manner as to be prejudicial to health or a nuisance;

(g) noise emitted from premises so as to be prejudicial to health or a nuisance;

(ga) noise that is prejudicial to health or a nuisance and is emitted from or caused by a vehicle, machinery or equipment in a street;

(h) any other matter declared by any enactment to be a statutory nuisance.

It should be noted that point (ga) was added by the NSNA 1993. Noise nuisances are considered in greater detail in Chapter 10.

9.3   PREJUDICIAL TO HEALTH OR A NUISANCE

The list of matters that may potentially constitute statutory nuisances is wide and covers many different situations, ranging from noise as a result of a party to the accumulation of waste materials on land. In practice, many of the matters that are statutory nuisances are very localised incidents which may not generally be regarded as major or serious environmental problems. However, it is at the local level that most people are concerned about environmental problems. A vacant site used for dumping rubbish may not have serious or global environmental consequences but can cause considerable problems for people living and working near the site. It may attract vermin, it may give rise to noxious or offensive smells and it may result in a loss of local amenity. In that sense, the vacant site affects the environment of those affected by it and as such is no less of an environmental problem to the people concerned.

However, the matters listed in s 79 are not automatically statutory nuisances. They become so if they are either prejudicial to health or a nuisance. This phrase includes two separate and alternative limbs and it is not necessary to show that a matter is both a nuisance and prejudicial to health. This was affirmed in *Betts v Penge UDC* (1942).

9.3.1 Prejudicial to health

Section 79(7) defines 'prejudicial to health' as meaning 'injurious, or likely to cause injury'. This definition includes two limbs: 'injurious to health', that is, actual harm, and 'likely to cause injury', that is, anticipated harm. The definition is the same as that given in the PHA 1936. Its meaning was considered by the Divisional Court in the case of *Coventry City Council v Cartwright* (1975), which concerned a vacant site owned by the city council. The council took no steps to prevent people from depositing household refuse and building materials, such as brick, tarmacadam, earth, scrap iron and broken glass, on the site. A complaint was made by a local resident that the deposits constituted a statutory nuisance in that there was an accumulation or deposit which was prejudicial to health and a nuisance. The argument that it was a nuisance was based on the loss of amenity, an argument rejected by the court. However, the case is important because of its consideration of the meaning of the phrase 'prejudicial to health'. Initially, the magistrates found that the building materials on the site were prejudicial to health on the basis that anyone entering the site might injure themselves on the rubble and they consequently made an abatement order. However, on appeal, their decision was overturned by the Divisional Court. The Divisional Court concerned itself with the question of whether or not the inert materials on the site could be prejudicial to health and in doing so came to the conclusion that they could only be prejudicial to health if they were likely to cause a threat of disease or attract vermin. It was held that the definition of 'prejudicial to health' did not encompass inert materials which could cause physical injury to people who walk on them. In reaching this decision, the court considered that the statute (in the instant, the PHA 1936) defined 'prejudicial to health' as meaning 'injurious or likely to cause injury to health' and concluded that this did not extend to physical injury from cuts and the like. In his judgment, Widgery CJ stated that, in relation to the words prejudicial to health: '... the underlying conception of the section [s 92(1)(c) of the PHA 1936] is that that which is struck at is an accumulation of something which produces a threat to health in the sense of a threat of disease, vermin or the like.' This was confirmed in *R v Bristol City Council ex p Everett* (1999), where the Court of Appeal held that the risk of physical injury from a steep internal staircase did not fall within the definition of prejudicial to health. *Cunningham v Birmingham City Council* (1998) confirms that the test for whether something, such as the state of premises, is 'prejudicial to health' is an objective test (see also, *Southwark BC v Simpson* (1999) and *O'Toole v Knowsley Metropolitan BC* (1999)).

9.3.2 What is meant by nuisance?

The courts have equated nuisance in this context with common law nuisance, especially private nuisance involving interference with enjoyment of property. In *National Coal Board v Neath BC* (1976), it was held that the word 'nuisance' meant either a public or a private nuisance at common law. It therefore involved an act or omission materially affecting the comfort and quality of life of a class of the public or an interference for a substantial period with the use and enjoyment of neighbouring property. It should be noted that, like common law nuisance, the interference must emanate from a neighbouring property (*National Coal Board v Thorne* (1976)). This requirement was, however, relaxed in later cases, such as *Carr v*

Hackney London BC (1995), where the nuisance consisted of condensation, dampness and mould caused by the state of the premises as opposed to an interference from neighbouring property.

The problem with using the common law notion of private nuisance is that there is no clearly applicable standard and whether a nuisance exists will depend (subjectively) on the particular circumstances. As will be illustrated in Chapter 11, one of the features of the common law of nuisance is the achievement of a balance between competing rights, with each case turning on its facts. Where there is no actual physical damage to person or property, but only a reduction in the enjoyment of a property (for instance, as a consequence of loud noise or offensive smells), then the courts have also indicated that much will depend upon the location where the nuisance is complained of. In the often quoted case of *Sturges v Bridgman* (1879), Thesiger LJ stated that 'what would be a nuisance in Belgrave Square would not necessarily be so in Bermondsey'. This narrow approach is problematic in the context of environmental protection. Environmental problems often transcend spatially defined areas and should not be seen in such narrow terms. Moreover, it is precisely in the industrial and run-down areas where there are more likely to be statutory nuisances occurring, and there is no justifiable reason why in these more vulnerable areas the protection of the law should be less than in those areas where the chances of statutory nuisances occurring are more remote.

9.3.3   Interference with personal comfort

The courts require evidence that the nuisance interferes with a person's personal comfort, as opposed to land or physical possessions, largely because the concept of statutory nuisance was based on the need to protect public health. This was aptly demonstrated in *Wivenhoe Port v Colchester BC* (1985), where the court held that nuisance, in the context of statutory nuisance, did not have its wide common law meaning but should be confined to personal discomfort. In the judgment, Butler J made the following statement:

> To be within the spirit of the Act [PHA 1936] a nuisance, to be a statutory nuisance, had to be one interfering materially with the personal comfort of the residents, in the sense that it materially affected their well-being although it might not be prejudicial to their health. Thus, dust falling on motor cars might cause inconvenience to their owners; it might even diminish the value of their motor car; but this would not be a statutory nuisance. In the same way, dust falling on gardens or trees, or on stock held in a shop would not be a statutory nuisance. But dust in eyes or hair, even if not shown to be prejudicial to health, would be so as an interference with personal comfort.

Here, Butler J refers to the 'spirit of the Act', which was intended to protect public health. However, statutory nuisances are now contained in the EPA 1990 which has as its *raison d'être* the protection of the environment and thus quite different aims from public health legislation. The restrictive approach adopted by the courts would not serve such aims; indeed, dust falling on grass and trees is precisely the type of activity which causes environmental problems.

9.3.4 Criticisms of the present approach

The restrictive approach adopted by the courts has been criticised by the House of Commons Select Committee on the Environment which, in its report on *Contaminated Land* (1990), recommended that the concept of nuisance should be capable of being used to protect the natural environment as well as public health. Unfortunately, the government rejected this particular recommendation, claiming that it would result in local authorities being 'inundated with requests to take action from well-intentioned, but over-enthusiastic residents who had read a report in the *New Scientist* or had been influenced by a *Panorama* programme'. It therefore seems that the statutory nuisance provisions offer a means of protecting public health and interests in land but only a limited means of protecting the environment in its own right.

9.3.5 Identifying a statutory nuisance

In practice, the local authority environmental health officer will make an initial determination whether the matter complained of constitutes a statutory nuisance on the basis of it being prejudicial to health or a nuisance. The officer will therefore be required to take into account the nature of the neighbourhood and also whether the matter complained of amounts to a nuisance in common law or is just (as sometimes happens) a vexatious complaint. The environmental health officer (EHO) will pay particular attention to the following considerations: the nature of the activity alleged to constitute a nuisance; the locality; the relevant time; the duration of the alleged nuisance; and the utility of the activity creating the alleged nuisance. The EHO will only need to satisfy himself or herself on the balance of probabilities that a nuisance has occurred or is likely to occur before he or she is obliged to take abatement action. The local authority has no authority to act unless it is satisfied that a statutory nuisance exists or is likely to occur or recur (s 80(1) of the EPA 1990).

9.3.6 Burden of proof

The burden of proof which applies is the criminal one. In other words, it must be established beyond reasonable doubt that the matter complained of exists and that the defendant is responsible for it. This was clearly illustrated in the case of *London Borough of Lewisham v Fenner* (1995). Fenner commenced proceedings against the local authority under s 82 of the EPA 1990 (see below for a discussion of the way in which individuals can commence statutory nuisance proceedings under s 82). His complaint was against the noise from the dehumidifying equipment at a local swimming pool operated by the local authority. The principal issue in the case was the nature of statutory nuisance proceedings and the burden of proof. Fenner complained that the noise caused him to lose sleep. The Crown Court judge held that loss of sleep can be injurious to health. The Crown Court judge took the unusual step of visiting the pool during the day and the pool management agreed to shut down the dehumidifier voluntarily during the night. The noise itself was continuous and droning but fell below the recommended 30–40 decibels recommended in British Standard 8233. As a matter of fact, it was found that the noise had affected Fenner's health and had caused annoyance to another person but, on the basis that the noise fell within advisory standards, the court could not feel satisfied that the criminal burden of proof for a noise nuisance had been discharged.

9.4　EXEMPTIONS

Section 79(2)–(6) of the EPA 1990 provides a number of specific exemptions from the list of statutory nuisances. These are dealt with below under each category of nuisance:

(a) Section 79(1)(a) – 'Any premises in such a state as to be prejudicial to health or a nuisance'. Premises does not simply mean buildings, but is defined in s 79(7) as including land and any vessel other than one powered by steam reciprocating machinery. The definition clearly encompasses the garden of a dwelling house (see *Stevenage BC v Wilson* (1993)). This particular head of statutory nuisance has been used on occasion by council house tenants to force the local council to deal with defective council houses (for example, *Carr v Hackney London BC* (1995)). The premises may be in such a state as to be prejudicial to the health of the occupants, in which case a statutory nuisance may arise where there is no interference from a neighbouring property. Equally, the nuisance or prejudice to health need not arise on the premises, but may be caused by some external interference. Where the premises are in such a state that the occupants are disturbed from noise outside (for example, because of inadequate sound insulation), there may be a statutory nuisance (*Southwark London BC v Ince* (1989)). However, disturbance due to external, traffic-generated noise is excluded from the ambit of statutory nuisance (see *London Borough of Haringey v Jowett* (1999)). In *East Riding of Yorkshire Council v Yorkshire Water Services Ltd* (2000), it was held that sewers are not 'premises' within the meaning of the statutory nuisance regime contained in the EPA 1990. In addition, submissions based upon the potentially wider remit of statutory nuisance contained within an environmental statute (that is, the EPA 1990), as opposed to a public health statute, were rejected by the court.

(b) Section 79(1)(b) – 'Smoke emitted from premises so as to be prejudicial to health or a nuisance'. This particular statutory nuisance was not included in the Public Health Acts but replaces provisions from the Clean Air Act (CAA) 1956. Premises occupied by the armed forces are exempt from this section, as are certain activities listed in s 79(3) such as smoke emitted from a chimney of a private dwelling within a smoke control area and dark smoke emitted from a chimney of a building serving a boiler or furnace. These latter exempt activities will not constitute a statutory nuisance under Pt III of the EPA 1990 but are controlled under the provisions of the CAA 1993.

(c) Section 79(1)(c) – 'Fumes or gas emitted from premises so as to be prejudicial to health or a nuisance'. Section 79(1)(c) only applies to domestic premises. Fumes are defined as any airborne solid smaller than dust, and gas is defined as vapour and moisture precipitated from vapour.

(d) Section 79(1)(d) – 'Any dust, steam, smell or other effluvia arising on industrial, trade or business premises so as to be prejudicial to health or a nuisance'. Steam emitted from a railway locomotive engine is exempted. This is the only statutory nuisance which is limited to industrial, trade or business premises. The terms 'industrial, trade or business' have been given a wide interpretation and include activities such as manufacturing and service activities such as banking. The term 'effluvia' refers to the flow of harmful or unpleasant substances, such as vapours or gases, onto the complainant's property (see *Malton Board of Health v Malton Manure Co* (1879)).

(e) Section 79(1)(e) – 'Any accumulation or deposit which is prejudicial to health or a nuisance'. This has been held to mean 'an accumulation of something which produces a threat to health in the sense of a threat of disease, vermin or the like' (*Coventry City Council v Cartwright* (1975)). In this particular case, the accumulation of building materials, scrap iron and broken glass was not an accumulation that was prejudicial to health, so as to be within the intent (or purpose) of the legislation. The fact that the materials could cause injury when walked on was not relevant. In *R v Carrick DC ex p Shelley* (1996), it was held that pollution from sewage outfalls, such as sanitary towels and condoms washed up on a beach, constituted a statutory nuisance under s 79(1)(e). However, a mere accumulation that does not create any physical interference with the legitimate activities of anyone else is not likely to be a statutory nuisance. The relevant deposit need not result from human action (see *Margate Pier v Town Council of Margate* (1869), a case involving the natural accumulation of seaweed).

(f) Section 79(1)(f) – 'Any animal kept in such a place or such a manner as to be prejudicial to health or a nuisance'. Both smells and noise from animals may constitute statutory nuisances although, in *Morrisey v Galer* (1955), it was held that this particular statutory nuisance was intended to deal with nuisances arising from insanitary or defective premises where animals were kept and not noisy animals. Thus, in this case, the court placed a strict interpretation on the statutory provision. Nevertheless, noise from animals is covered under s 79(1)(g) below.

(g) Section 79(1)(g) – 'Noise emitted from premises so as to be prejudicial to health or a nuisance'. Noise nuisance was previously contained in ss 58 and 59 of the COPA 1974. 'Noise' is defined as including vibration. Aircraft noise (other than noise from a model aircraft) is exempt from this provision but controlled under other specific legislation. As in a smoke nuisance, premises occupied by the armed forces are exempt from this particular section.

(h) Section 79(1)(ga) – 'Noise that is prejudicial to health or a nuisance and is emitted from or caused by a vehicle, machinery or equipment in a street'. This statutory nuisance will be considered in full in Chapter 10.

(i) Section 79(1)(h) – 'Any other matter declared by any enactment to be a statutory nuisance'. This catch-all provision enables other statutory nuisances created by any other Act to be dealt with under the statutory nuisance procedures of the EPA 1990, for example, nuisances caused by mines and quarries (see the Mines and Quarries Act 1954).

9.5 RESPONSIBILITY OF THE LOCAL AUTHORITIES

Section 79(1) of the EPA 1990 places all district councils and London borough councils under a duty to inspect their area from time to time to detect any statutory nuisance actually occurring or likely to occur, which ought to be dealt with under ss 80 and 80A of the Act. They are also under a duty to take such steps as are reasonably practicable to investigate complaints made by people living in the area about statutory nuisances. The duty is therefore twofold. The local authority has to carry out its own checks and has to respond to complaints made. In practice, it is the environmental health departments and officers that are responsible for enforcing this legislation and they will carry out the inspections and deal with the complaints. In some areas, particularly the large cities, some local authorities have night patrols which are concerned primarily with noise control.

9.5.1 Duty to inspect

The duty to inspect and detect statutory nuisances is tempered by the requirement that these inspections only have to be carried out from time to time. One of the problems here is that the expression 'time to time' is not defined by the EPA 1990, thus making the obligation very imprecise.

9.5.2 Duty to respond to complaints

The duty to respond to complaints was established by the EPA 1990. Prior to its introduction, local authorities were not actually required to respond to complaints, although, in practice, complainants provided useful information about the occurrences of statutory nuisances within the local authority area. The duty to respond to complaints made by people living in the area is qualified by the fact that the authority only has to take such steps as are reasonably practicable to investigate the complaint. Again, this expression is not defined and could potentially cause problems.

However, if the complainant presents credible evidence of the existence of a nuisance to the local authority and the local authority declines to fulfil its statutory duty by inspecting the alleged nuisance, then the complainant could judicially review the local authority's adopted course of action.

In *R v Carrick DC ex p Shelley* (1996), the defendant local authority received a statutory nuisance complaint relating to the presence of sewage debris (from a sewage outfall pipe) washed up on a beach in its area. The authority refused to utilise its statutory nuisance powers pending the outcome of other proceedings which were not directly related to its statutory nuisance functions. The complainant successfully challenged, on a judicial review application, the authority's decision to do nothing. Once it was clear that a statutory nuisance existed, the authority was obliged by law to serve an Abatement Notice on the water and sewerage company responsible for the statutory nuisance. (See also *R v Falmouth and Truro Port Health Authority ex p South West Water Ltd* (2000).)

Local authorities are increasingly finding that they are facing severe financial problems. Whether the authority can take into account its own financial situation in determining what is reasonably practicable is not clear. However, if the Secretary of State finds that a local authority is in default of these duties, he can, by virtue of Sched 3 to the EPA 1990, transfer the function to himself.

9.5.3   Local authorities' investigative powers

In order to carry out their functions of inspection and investigation, local authority environmental health officers (EHOs) can enter any land with the people and equipment that they consider necessary. The officers can also carry out any inspections, measurements and tests and can also take away samples and articles. These powers are provided by Sched 3 to the EPA 1990. The purpose of the inspection and investigation is to establish whether or not there is a statutory nuisance (or whether one is likely to occur) and to gather any evidence which may be needed in subsequent court proceedings. The powers of entry are exercisable in respect of any premises. This means that the EHO can investigate not only the premises from which the alleged nuisance emanates, but also neighbouring premises in order to further the investigation. The EHO can exercise powers of entry at any reasonable time. However, where the premises are private dwellings, the EHO will need to obtain the occupiers' consent and also give 24 hours' notice. The EHO is not required to have a warrant, but one will be required where entry is refused or a refusal is apprehended, where the premises are permanently or temporarily unoccupied or where, in an emergency, the EHO believes there to be a danger to life or health. Where the EHO believes that a request for admission would defeat the purposes of entry (for example, where he or she anticipates that evidence may be concealed), then he or she should also secure a warrant. Sometimes, the EHO may be accompanied by a police officer. It is a criminal offence under Sched 3 to obstruct an EHO exercising his or her powers of entry.

9.6   ABATEMENT NOTICES

Section 80 of the EPA 1990 provides that an authority shall serve an Abatement Notice when it is satisfied that a statutory nuisance:

(a) exists;

(b) is likely to occur; or

(c) is likely to recur in its area.

Therefore, the authority can take preventive action in order to stop a statutory nuisance happening. The requirement to serve the Abatement Notice is mandatory. The authority has no discretion once it is satisfied the statutory nuisance exists. However, the section does not say anything about the need for the likely occurrence to be imminent. It is enough that it is likely to occur. Also, when one considers that the concept of 'prejudicial to health' also extends to 'likely to cause injury', the local authority must serve an Abatement Notice if it believes that circumstances exist which make injury likely.

9.6.1   The form of the Notice

Although there is no prescribed form for an Abatement Notice, it must nevertheless state the following in a manner which is clear and understandable to the recipient:

(a) the nature of the statutory nuisance and whether it exists or is likely to occur or recur;

(b) time limits for compliance;

(c) the rights of appeal to the magistrates' court.

The Abatement Notice must be dated and signed by an officer of the court.

Section 80 states that the Notice must state 'all or any' of the following requirements:

(a) the abatement of the nuisance or prohibiting or restricting its occurrence or recurrence;

(b) the execution of such works, and the taking of such other steps, as may be necessary for any of these purposes.

This specific section has given rise to a considerable and growing body of case law centring on whether local authorities should be required to specify the steps required to bring the nuisance to an end or whether they have discretion simply to require abatement of the nuisance. This question was considered by the Divisional Court in *Sterling Homes v Birmingham City Council* (1996), in which the court reviewed previous authorities and concluded that an Abatement Notice need not specify any works or other steps to be taken. In other words, the Abatement Notice could simply require abatement of the nuisance, leaving the recipient to work out how to do this. Alternatively, the local authority, exercising its discretion, could choose to include in its Notice a requirement for works or other steps to be carried out. However, in *Kirklees Metropolitan Council v Field and Others* (1998), a specially constituted three judge Court of Appeal held that in circumstances where the authority requires the recipient to take positive steps (as opposed to refraining from doing something), it 'could be necessary to specify those steps to avoid doubt'. In this case, the statutory nuisance constituted a rock face in serious danger of collapse. The Court of Appeal held that the Abatement Notice was invalid because it did not specify the works which were necessary to abate the nuisance. Rather confusingly though, the Court of Appeal approved the earlier decision in *Sterling Homes*, in that it approved the idea that a Notice may simply require the abatement of the nuisance. The decision in *Kirklees* was eventually overruled by the subsequent decision of the Court of Appeal in *R v Falmouth and Truro Port Health Authority ex p South West Water Ltd* (2000), on the basis that, in all cases, the authority could if it wished leave the choice of means of abatement to the perpetrator of the nuisance and should not be obliged to specify what works were necessary, since this could interfere with the ability of the recipient of the Notice to choose the works that would enable it to comply with the Abatement Notice.

However, if the local authority chooses to require works to be undertaken by the recipient of the Notice, then it must be clear to the recipient what is required. In *Network Housing Association Ltd v Westminster City Council* (1995), the city council served an Abatement Notice on the housing association requiring it to carry out alterations in order to reduce the noise between flats to a specific decibel level. Since the Abatement Notice was not sufficiently clear in defining what works were required, it was quashed. The degree of specification will no doubt vary on a case by case basis. Where the authority does prescribe steps to be taken, the recipient may choose to challenge these steps by way of appeal (see below). In view of this, it appears that the simplest option for a local authority is simply to require the abatement of the nuisance, thus passing the burden to the recipient to determine how best to do this and reducing the likelihood of appeal.

The Court of Appeal has also held in *R v Falmouth and Truro Port Health Authority ex p South West Water Ltd* (2000) that the local authority is not under a duty to consult the alleged perpetrator of a statutory nuisance before serving an Abatement Notice. Thus, for example, where a local authority elects to specify what steps are required to abate a nuisance, the authority is not required to conduct any prior consultation with the recipient of the Notice. Notwithstanding the fact that there is no duty to consult, the Court of Appeal did suggest that consultation may often be appropriate and that there may in some circumstances be a duty to consult where the recipient has a legitimate expectation of being consulted. On the facts in this case, the Court of Appeal held that the recipient did not have a legitimate expectation of being consulted, but also added that there was a strong case for consultation. In practice, many EHOs will actually embark on some form of dialogue with the parties involved before serving an Abatement Notice.

9.6.2 On whom must the Notice be served?

The provisions regarding the serving of Abatement Notices are contained in s 80 of the EPA 1990. Normally, the local authority is required to serve the Notice on the person responsible for the nuisance. Where the nuisance arises from any defect in the structural character of a building, then the Notice should be served on the owner of the premises. In circumstances where the person responsible for the nuisance cannot be found, or the nuisance has not yet occurred, then the Notice must be served on the owner or occupier of the premises. In relation to vehicles, machinery or equipment, the person responsible will be the driver or operator.

The person responsible for the nuisance is defined in s 79(7) as the person to whose:

(a) act;

(b) default; or

(c) sufferance,

the nuisance is attributable.

This is a wide definition and could include not only the person who created the nuisance, but also a third person/party who failed to take any appropriate preventive or corrective action where he or she had some legal requirement to do so. It can also include third persons who, on becoming aware of the problem, took no steps to remedy the situation. This was confirmed in *Clayton v Sale UDC* (1926), where an owner was held liable for a statutory nuisance on his land consequent upon the activities or defaults of another (see s 80(2)(c)). It would also appear that a local authority can serve a Notice on a previous owner of land, rather than the current owner, if it decides that the previous owner was the person who caused the nuisance rather than the present owner. The terms 'owner' and 'occupier' are not defined in the Act.

Where the statutory nuisance relates to a vehicle, the person responsible also includes the person in whose name the vehicle is registered and any other person who is the driver of the vehicle. Where the statutory nuisance relates to machinery or equipment, the person responsible can also include any person who is for the time being the operator of the machinery or equipment.

In *Carr v Hackney London BC* (1995), the Divisional Court held that where a tenant had refused to allow his landlord to enter in order to do works to abate the nuisance, the landlord could not be a person whose act or default or sufferance caused the nuisance to arise. See also *R v Metropolitan Stipendiary Magistrates ex p Mahmed Ali* (1997).

9.6.3 What if more than one person is involved?

Section 81(1) deals with the situation where more than one person is responsible for the statutory nuisance. In these circumstances, s 80 still applies to each of the persons, irrespective of whether or not that which any one of them is responsible for would, by itself, amount to a statutory nuisance. Therefore, if two persons are involved in an action which jointly amounts to a statutory nuisance, they will both be responsible for the statutory nuisance even if their individual actions do not by themselves amount to such a nuisance. Although the Abatement Notice should be served in the first instance on the person responsible for the nuisance, this should be read as meaning that the authority is obliged to serve separate notices on all the parties that may have contributed to the statutory nuisance.

9.7   APPEALS AGAINST AN ABATEMENT NOTICE

By virtue of s 80(3) of the EPA 1990, a person upon whom an Abatement Notice is served is entitled to appeal against it by making a complaint to the magistrates' court. He or she must be informed of this right in the Abatement Notice. Where a person decides to lodge an appeal, he or she must do so within 21 days from the day on which the Abatement Notice was served. The grounds of appeal are laid down in the Statutory Nuisance (Appeals) Regulations 1995 (SI 1995/2644). The grounds are as follows:

(a) the Abatement Notice is not justified by s 80 of the EPA 1990 – here the appellant would be arguing that the matter did not constitute a statutory nuisance;

(b) the Abatement Notice has some informality, or is defective or contains an error;

(c) the authority has refused unreasonably to accept compliance with alternative requirements, or the requirements laid down in the Abatement Notice are unreasonable or unnecessary;

(d) the period(s) for compliance in the Notice is (are) not reasonably sufficient for the purpose;

(e) there has been an error in the service of the Notice – for example, the Notice has been served on the wrong person. An appeal may also be made if the appellant argues that it is 'equitable' for the Notice to be served on some other person, either *instead of* the appellant or as well as him. Whether the wrong person has been served will be determined by reference to s 80(2);

(f) the best practicable means were used to prevent or counteract the effect of a nuisance from trade or business premises or, for a noise nuisance under s 79(1)(ga), that the best practicable means were used to prevent or counteract the noise from or caused by a vehicle, machinery or equipment being used for industrial or trade purposes;

(g) in relation to a nuisance under s 79(1)(g) or (ga), the requirements imposed by the Abatement Notice are more onerous than the requirements which may have been determined by means of other noise controls under the COPA 1974;

(h) in relation to a nuisance under s 89(1)(ga) (noise emitted from or caused by vehicles, machinery or equipment), the requirements imposed by the Abatement Notice are more onerous than the requirements of any condition of a consent given under the NSNA 1993 (provisions relating to loudspeakers in streets or on roads).

The magistrates' court has wide powers when dealing with appeals against Abatement Notices. It can:

(a) quash the Abatement Notice;

(b) vary the Abatement Notice in favour of the appellant;

(c) dismiss the appeal.

If a person has appealed on the grounds of some defect or error in the Abatement Notice, the court must dismiss the appeal if it is satisfied that the defect or error is not a material one. Therefore, there seems little value in appealing against 'minor' defects or informalities.

In addition to this, the court can also make an order as it thinks fit regarding:

(a) any works which need to be carried out and the contribution to be made by any person to the cost of the work; or

(b) the proportion of expenses that a local authority may recover from the appellant and from any other person.

9.7.1 Effect of an appeal upon an Abatement Notice

In general, and provided the Notice is appropriately worded by the relevant local authority, the lodging of an appeal will not suspend the Abatement Notice and the person served with the Notice will still be required to comply with the conditions of the Notice. This is particularly so where the nuisance to which the Abatement Notice relates is either injurious to health or likely to be of such a limited duration that suspension of the Notice would render it of no practical effect. However, the fact that the Notice will not be suspended pending the appeal should be clearly stated in the Notice. However, this general provision does not apply in the following alternative situations when the Abatement Notice will be suspended pending the appeal:

(a) where compliance with the Abatement Notice would involve any person in expenditure or the carrying out of works before the hearing of the appeal and the works or cost would be out of proportion in relation to the expected public benefit;

(b) in the case of a nuisance under s 79(1)(g) or (ga) of the EPA 1990, the noise to which the Abatement Notice relates is noise necessarily caused in the course of the performance of some duty imposed by law on the appellant.

These provisions are to be found in reg 3 of the Statutory Nuisance (Appeals) Regulations 1995 (SI 1995/2644).

9.7.2 Duration of an Abatement Notice

Unless it is otherwise stated, an Abatement Notice is of unlimited duration. In *Wellingborough DC v Gordon* (1991), the defendant, Mr Gordon, was served an

Abatement Notice in 1985 in respect of a noise nuisance. Three years later in 1988, the defendant held a birthday party at which the police intervened in the early hours of the morning requesting that the volume of the music be turned down. The district council prosecuted Mr Gordon for breach of the Abatement Notice served in 1985. The magistrates found the defendant not guilty but, on appeal, the High Court held that the Abatement Notice was still valid. Interestingly, in this case, there had been no complaints about the noise levels in 1988 and the High Court acknowledged that this was an isolated incident. In the court's view, however, these factors did not constitute a reasonable excuse for breaching the original notice.

9.8   NON-COMPLIANCE WITH AN ABATEMENT NOTICE

Section 80(4) of the EPA 1990 establishes that it is a criminal offence for a person served with an Abatement Notice either to contravene or fail to comply with any requirement or prohibition imposed by the Notice, without reasonable excuse. If an Abatement Notice is not complied with, the authority that has issued the Notice has three options:

(a) abate the nuisance and do whatever may be necessary in execution of the Notice;

(b) institute summary proceedings;

(c) take proceedings for an injunction in the High Court.

9.8.1   The authority can abate the nuisance

The authority can abate the nuisance and do whatever may be necessary in execution of the Notice (s 81(3)). A typical example of this is where audio equipment is removed to abate a noise nuisance (in *Liverpool City Council v Maudsley* (1992), a court order was made authorising the local authority to seize a radio). The authority can take this course of action irrespective of whether it takes proceedings for non-compliance. In the event that the authority does take action either to abate the nuisance or prevent it happening, then it can, by virtue of s 81(4), recover any expenses reasonably incurred. This would normally be from the person whose acts or omissions caused the nuisance. If that person is the owner of the premises, the expenses can be recovered from any person who is for the time being the owner of them. This would cover situations where, for instance, a previous owner caused a nuisance, but the present owner could be made responsible for the reasonable expenses incurred by the authority. Should the matter of cost recovery go before the court, the court has the power to apportion the expenses between persons whose acts (or omissions) caused the nuisance, in a manner that the court considers fair and reasonable.

The NSNA 1993 provides additional assistance to the local authorities in the form of a newly inserted s 81A of the EPA 1990, which enables the local authority serving a Notice to recover costs to make a charge on the premises owned by the person in default.

9.8.2   The authority can institute summary proceedings

If a person fails to comply with an Abatement Notice and commits an offence under s 80(4), the authority can only institute proceedings in the magistrates' court. The penalty for nuisance offences (see s 80(5) and (6)) depends on whether the nuisance has occurred on industrial, trade or business premises. For nuisances arising on non-industrial, trade or business premises, the maximum penalty is £5,000 plus a further £500 for each day that the offence continues after the conviction. However, where the nuisance occurs on industrial, trade or business premises, the maximum fine is £20,000 (but no additional daily fines can be made). The magistrates also have a discretion to make a compensation order of up to £5,000.

9.8.3 The authority can take proceedings in the High Court

The third option available to the authority against a person who fails to comply with or contravenes an Abatement Notice is to take proceedings in the High Court (s 81(5) of the EPA 1990). This option is available if the authority is of the view that proceedings in the magistrates' court (under s 80(4)) would afford an inadequate remedy. The aim would be to obtain an injunction to secure the abatement, prohibition or restriction of the statutory nuisance. The authority can take this course of action at any time after service of an Abatement Notice, even if summary proceedings have not been concluded (see *Hammersmith London BC v Magnum Automated Forecourts Ltd* (1978)). Failure to comply with an injunction may result in a prison sentence. In *Bristol City Council v Huggins* (1995), Mr Huggins was jailed for three months for breaching an injunction which was obtained by Bristol City Council after two prosecutions under the EPA 1990 failed. The circumstances surrounding the application for an injunction must be sufficiently serious otherwise there is little prospect of the High Court exercising its discretion to grant the remedy. See also *Lloyd v Symonds and Others* (1998).

9.9   DEFENCES AGAINST NON-COMPLIANCE WITH AN ABATEMENT NOTICE

Any person who contravenes or fails to comply with the terms of an Abatement Notice, without reasonable excuse, is guilty of an offence (s 80(4) of the EPA 1990). However, s 80(7) provides a defence of best practicable means. Subject to certain exceptions, it will be a defence to prove that the best practicable means were used to prevent or counteract the effects of the nuisance. Section 80(4) provides that it will only be an offence to contravene or to fail to comply with the requirements of an Abatement Notice provided the defendant does not have a reasonable excuse.

9.9.1 What is meant by 'reasonable excuse'?

The EPA 1990 does not define 'reasonable excuse'. The test laid down by the courts appears to be an objective one. That is whether a reasonable person would consider the excuse consistent with a reasonable standard of conduct. Therefore, what constitutes 'reasonable excuse' will be a matter of fact. In *Saddleworth Urban Development Corp v Aggregate and Sand* (1970), Aggregate and Sand argued that they had run out of funds to complete the work required by the Abatement Notice. The Divisional Court held that lack of finance could not constitute a reasonable excuse for non-compliance with the Notice.

Similarly, in *Wellingborough BC v Gordon* (1993), the court rejected a submission that there was a 'reasonable excuse' based on the length of time (three years) between service of the Abatement Notice and its breach. Neither is there a 'reasonable excuse' based on the argument that a common law action on identical facts would fail.

The alleged reasonable excuse must relate specifically to a problem encountered in attempting to comply with the Abatement Notice. The 'reasonable excuse' element of the offence under s 80(4) of the EPA 1990 cannot be used as the means to challenge the grounds upon which the Abatement Notice was served. Challenges to Abatement Notices are best addressed through the appeal process (see *AMEC Building Ltd v London Borough of Camden* (1997)).

If the defendant produces evidence to support its submission that the defendant had a reasonable excuse for carrying on the activity alleged to constitute a statutory nuisance, the local authority must prove, beyond reasonable doubt, that the activity was not reasonable (see *Polychronakis v Richards and Jerrom Ltd* (1998) and *Hope Butuyuyu v London Borough of Hammersmith & Fulham* (1997)).

9.9.2   The 'best practicable means' defence

Section 80(7) provides the defence that the best practicable means were used to prevent or counteract the nuisance. The defendant must be able to establish the defence on the balance of probabilities (that is, more likely than not) rather than beyond reasonable doubt. The definition provided in s 79(9) of the EPA 1990 states that best practicable means is to be interpreted by reference to the following provisions:

(a) 'practicable' means reasonably practicable having regard among other things to:

  (i)   local conditions and circumstances;

  (ii) the current state of technical knowledge; and

  (iii) the financial implications;

(b) the means to be employed include:

  (i)   the design, installation, maintenance and manner and periods of operation of plant and machinery; and

  (ii) the design, construction and maintenance of buildings and structures;

(c) the test is to apply only so far as compatible with any:

  (i)   duty imposed by law;

  (ii) safety and safe working conditions; and

  (iii) exigencies of any emergency or unforeseeable circumstances.

In circumstances where a code of practice under s 71 of the COPA 1974 (noise minimisation) is applicable, regard must be given to the guidance given in the code.

9.9.3   Limitations to the 'best practicable means' defence

The 'best practicable means' defence is, however, only available where the nuisance arises on industrial trade or business premises. Section 80(8) lists its availability as follows:

(a) in the case of nuisances (a), (d), (e), (f) or (g) of s 79(1), the defence is only available if the nuisance occurs on industrial, trade or business premises;

(b) if the nuisance falls under category (ga) of s 79(1), the defence is generally not available unless the noise is emitted from or caused by a vehicle, machinery or equipment being used for industrial, trade or business purposes;

(c) in the case of smoke emitted from premises (s 79(1)(b)), the defence of best practicable means is not available except where the smoke is emitted from a chimney;

(d) the defence of best practicable means is not available at all in relation to the nuisances under s 79(1)(c) and (h).

9.9.4 What is 'best practical means' in practice?

The onus is on the company or business seeking to rely on the defence to prove that the best practicable means were employed. The issue of the costs of employing best practical means and the effect on profitability was considered in *Wivenhoe Port v Colchester BC* (1985). The port authority argued that it had used the best practicable means but was not able to use certain dust arrestment equipment because of the cost and impact on profitability. The court accepted that the profitability of the defendant was a relevant factor to be taken into account, but went on to say that the company needed to show, on the balance of probabilities, that the operation would go from profit to loss, or become so uneconomical that the company could not profitably continue if the dust machinery was used. More recently, in *East Devon District Council v Farr* (2002), in the context of an appeal against an Abatement Notice, the Divisional Court upheld the magistrates' decision to quash an Abatement Notice where the recipient had done all that he could be expected to do in the circumstances to abate a noise nuisance. Following complaints about the noise from his small industrial unit, the Abatement Notice required that the doors on the industrial unit be kept closed when the machinery was in operation. Farr appealed the Abatement Notice on the grounds that, *inter alia*, he had investigated the possibility of installing air conditioning and dust extraction equipment so as to avoid having to open the doors, but had concluded that this would have been ineffective, noisier and expensive. Although Farr had not investigated all possible options, the magistrates were right to accept that he had taken all reasonable and practicable steps to reduce the noise.

In *Manley v New Forest DC* (1999), it was established that the defendant dog breeder was already using best practicable means to minimise noise at the time an Abatement Notice was served on him. The High Court reversed the decision of the Crown Court that best practicable means could be established by the defendant agreeing to relocate his business to a non-residential area. The court held that relocation in such circumstances was going beyond the purpose of the statutory nuisance controls contained in Pt III of the EPA 1990. See also *Chapman v Gosberton Farm Produce* (1993).

9.9.5 Special defences

Special defences exist regarding noise and other nuisances in relation to construction sites, and noise abatement zones (see Chapter 10).

9.10   ACTION BY CITIZENS

Section 82 of the EPA 1990 provides that any person aggrieved by a statutory nuisance has the right to complain to the magistrates' court in order to obtain a court order to bring the nuisance to an end. Failure to comply with a court order under the section is an offence. Section 82 enables any person to bypass the local authority statutory nuisance process.

The provision enables any person who is aggrieved by the nuisance to commence proceedings which are likely to be cheaper and quicker than a common law private nuisance action. There is no requirement that the complainant is an occupier of premises or a neighbour of adjoining premises.

The phrase 'person aggrieved' has appeared in various other statutes and has been widely interpreted by the courts. In *AG (Gambia) v N'Jie* (1961), Lord Denning asserted that the words 'person aggrieved' should not be subjected to a restrictive interpretation. However, he went on to say that the words:

> ... do not include, of course, a mere busybody who is interfering in things which do not concern him; but they do include a person who has a genuine grievance because an order has been made which prejudicially affects his interests.

It seems, therefore, that a person must at least be in some way prejudicially affected by the alleged nuisance. In *Sandwell Metropolitan BC v Bujok* (1990), a council tenant alleged that the defective state of her council house gave rise to a statutory nuisance under the PHA 1936. Mrs Bujok was entitled to bring proceedings against the council as a person whose health, and that of her family, was prejudicially affected by the premises. Section 82 is of particular value when the person concerned is complaining about a statutory nuisance created by a local authority and has been useful in enabling people to bring actions against the local authority in respect of council houses and premises which are prejudicial to health or a nuisance. The number of these cases has been increasing in recent years. The fact that the local authorities act as the statutory bodies responsible for controlling statutory nuisances does not provide them with any immunity against actions against them, as can be seen in the *Sandwell* case.

Aggrieved persons can only commence proceedings to secure the abatement of an existing nuisance or its recurrence. They cannot, under these provisions, bring an action to prevent a statutory nuisance, such as a potentially noisy party, since the magistrates' court, unlike the local authority, does not have anticipatory powers.

9.10.1 Section 82 proceedings

When a person complains to the magistrates' court, there is a requirement that the defendant is informed, in writing, of the matter complained of and that such action is going to be taken. For noise nuisances, the complainant must give three days' notice, but the period of notice is 21 days in respect of the other nuisances. Before taking action in proceedings brought under s 82, the magistrates must be satisfied of one of the following conditions:

(a) the alleged nuisance exists; or

(b) an abated nuisance is likely to recur on the same premises, or in the same street.

The court can make the following orders:

(a) requiring the defendant to abate the nuisance within a specified time and to carry out any works necessary for that purpose;

(b) prohibiting a recurrence of the nuisance and requiring the defendant to carry out any necessary works to prevent the recurrence. A time period for carrying out such works will be specified in the order;

(c) imposition of a fine of up to £5,000;

(d) requiring the relevant local authority to do anything which the convicted person was required to do by the court order, after it has given the authority the opportunity to be heard.

Where the nuisance is such as to render premises unfit for human habitation, the court can prohibit the use of the premises for human habitation until the court is satisfied that the premises have been made fit for such a purpose.

Failure to comply with a nuisance order from the magistrates is an offence and can result in a fine of up to £5,000 (plus £500 for each day that the offence continues).

9.11 ADVANTAGES OF THE STATUTORY NUISANCE PROVISIONS

From the point of view of a person subjected to a statutory nuisance, the provisions of Pt III of the EPA 1990 provide a relatively simple mechanism for addressing problems without recourse to expensive and lengthy litigation. In contrast to civil proceedings, which are expensive and usually very fraught, the statutory nuisance provisions enable the local authority to 'step in' to deal with problems before judicial action becomes necessary. The statistics produced annually by the Chartered Institute for Environmental Health Officers demonstrate that the vast majority of substantiated complaints that are dealt with can be resolved informally without legal action. The 'burden' of dealing with statutory nuisances rests with the local authority and the mechanisms, backed up by the possibility of criminal sanctions, can afford a very effective means of dealing with problems. Since proceedings under Pt III of the EPA 1990 are heard before the magistrates' court, the speed of dealing with cases is likely to be much faster than private actions before the county court and High Court. Moreover, from the point of view of the 'complainant', the legal costs are borne by the local authority.

9.12 CONTAMINATED LAND AND STATUTORY NUISANCES

As a consequence of Pt IIA of the EPA 1990, which establishes a statutory regime for dealing with contaminated land, s 79(1)(a) was inserted into Pt III of the EPA. This section states clearly that no matter shall constitute a statutory nuisance to the extent that it consists of, or is caused by, any land being in a contaminated state. Although the intention of the government was to avoid an overlap of the provisions, it has in fact created something of a lacuna in the law. The reason for this is that the definition of land that 'is in a contaminated state' provided by s 79(1)(b) includes any land on which contaminants are present and which may cause harm. Thus, land which falls within this definition cannot be dealt with under the statutory nuisance provisions. In contrast, the definition of 'contaminated land' under s 78A(2) of the EPA 1990 requires the presence of contaminating substances which cause significant harm or have a significant possibility of causing significant harm. Consequently, any land which is land which is in a contaminated state, but is not 'contaminated land' because the risks it poses are not significant, will effectively fall between the two regimes and a local authority will have no power to deal with it.

9.13   FURTHER INFORMATION

Further reading

Lewis, R, 'Dealing with nuisance: all about abatement' (2000) 3(6) Journal of Local Government Law 117.

This article considers whether Abatement Notices must spell out the necessary abatement requirements or whether the steps needed to abate the nuisance may be left to be determined by the perpetrator of the nuisance.

Lewis, R, 'Statutory nuisance Abatement Notices – a response' [2000] JPEL 1011.

This article examines a number of statutory nuisance cases and the possible implications of the implementation of the Human Rights Act 1998.

Loveland, I, 'And now wash your hands – statutory nuisance under the Environmental Protection Act 1990 section 79(1)' [2001] JPEL 1144.

This reviews the decision of the House of Lords in *Birmingham City Council v John Oakley* (2000) concerning statutory nuisance in a council house.

Malcolm, R, 'Statutory nuisance: the validity of Abatement Notices' [2000] JPEL 894.

McCracken, R, Jones, G and Pereira, J: a series of six articles on various aspects of the statutory nuisance regime published in the Solicitors Journal ((2001) 145(42) SJ 1028–29 to (2001) 145(47) SJ 1152–53).

The articles cover the following topics: scope of the regime, responsibilities of the local authorities, Abatement Notices, appeals and s 82 provisions.

Parpworth, N, 'Statutory nuisance Abatement Notices under s 80 of the Environmental Protection Act 1990' (2003) 167(12) Justice of the Peace and Local Government Law 204.

Websites

www.cieh.org

The official website of the Chartered Institute of Environmental Health. Documents available on the site include Policy Unit responses to Noise Act Review, annual statistics relating to noise complaints and statutory nuisance procedures.

www.defra.gov.uk/environment/noise/index.htm

The Department for Environment, Food and Rural Affairs website. See, in particular, updates on noise.

CHAPTER 10

NOISE POLLUTION

10.1 THE PROBLEM OF NOISE POLLUTION

Noise is a natural consequence of everything that we do. It forms part of our everyday background and for the most part we just accept it or at least tolerate it. Nevertheless, noise has the capacity to cause conflict between those who are generating it and those who hear it but do not wish to. Indeed, the Wilson Committee (Wilson, 1963) recognised the subjective and conflictual nature of the problem when it defined noise as 'sound which is undesired by the recipient'.

Noise regulation poses its own distinctive problems:

(a) noise is transient and mostly it is a source of temporary irritation;

(b) noise is not inherently dangerous. It does not accumulate in our bodies or the wider environment. It is not toxic to man and the environment as many chemical substances are;

(c) the impact of noise on humans is highly subjective. Although it is possible to measure the level at which noise begins to damage hearing, the impact of less damaging sound is problematic. The differential impact of noise upon humans varies with the time of day and the susceptibility of the individual. Unwanted noise at night which disturbs sleep is a serious issue;

(d) it may be difficult to disentangle offending 'noises' from background noises or the general noise level in the area;

(e) how should regulatory controls tackle the problem? Should controls 'bite' at (i) the immediate point of noise production (for example, motor vehicle exhaust systems and construction site noise), (ii) some point between the noise producer and the noise recipient (for example, construction of a noise barrier, either internally via sound insulation, or externally via a 'bund' to deflect noise away from the recipient), or (iii) the point at which the noise reaches the recipient's property (for example, installation of double glazing);

(f) what types of regulatory controls should be employed? The following list indicates some of the choices available: (i) product standards (noise emission limits applying to lawnmowers, car exhaust systems, etc), (ii) licence-based controls (for example, Integrated Pollution Prevention and Control (IPPC) installations and Health and Safety at Work controls in factories), (iii) reactive controls (for example, statutory nuisance), (iv) public order controls (Crime and Disorder Act 1998), and (v) separation controls (for example, planning controls providing geographical separation between incompatible land uses);

(g) noise is regulated by a patchwork of fragmented controls.

In most circumstances, unwanted noises will not cause people to complain, but there are clearly circumstances where either the volume, duration or repetition (or all three) will cause sufficient aggravation to cause the recipient of the unwanted noise intrusion to take legal action, or in some instances resort to more dramatic measures. Most people are familiar with complaints between neighbours concerning excessive noise from music systems, dogs barking or the constant drone of lawnmowers, but these complaints rarely lead to legal proceedings. However, people are increasingly more concerned about noise levels and neighbourhood noise in particular. They are also more aware of the effects that noise can have upon them and are consequently more likely to complain. This is clearly borne out by statistics, some of which are shown later.

Modern industrial society generates an enormous quantity of noise and it is bound to increase as more and more aeroplanes arrive and depart at airports and as more and more cars take to the roads. There are also more opportunities for creating noise in a society which relies heavily upon domestic appliances (the noisy washing machine and lawnmower). Stereo and audio equipment have become more sophisticated, more powerful, more affordable and more commonplace and people are able to play music at high volumes. The dawn of the ghettoblaster and the personal stereo means that loud music is something which frequently occurs in the street as well as in the home.

Although there is a general assumption that rural areas are quieter, they are not without their own noise problems. Heavy machinery used in farming can also be a source of aggravation to local residents (see *Chapman v Gosberton Farm Produce* (1993), below). Many people who move out of the inner cities and urban areas to the country are surprised at the lack of peace and quiet that they had envisaged.

10.2   THE LEGAL REGULATION OF NOISE

Whilst excessive or continued levels of noise may be unacceptable, certain levels of noise must be accepted in order that modern society can function. Construction sites, for instance, generate a significant amount of noise from mobile plant, pneumatic drills, etc and cause many local residents to complain. Yet we nevertheless expect and, in most instances, welcome new developments, which can create jobs and which can enhance towns and cities. All activities and processes generate noise and we all expect to be able to continue those activities without interference from others. This raises certain problems regarding the legal regulation of noise, in that there will necessarily be a need to achieve a balance between the rights of individuals, groups or companies to make noise and the rights of others not to suffer at their expense. This weighing of considerations is familiar in the common law of nuisance where the courts have to consider whether what is complained of is unreasonable.

The problem of aircraft noise raises numerous problems and litigation concerning aircraft noise is on the increase. The demand for more flights and the proposals to build new runways at various airports throughout the country has given rise to enormous controversy and raised issues of human rights and public interest. For an examination of these issues in the context of military aircraft, see *Dennis & Dennis v Ministry of Defence* (2003), in which the Divisional Court held that the noise from RAF Harrier Jets could not be classed as 'ordinary' and that, whilst a public interest argument might excuse what would otherwise be an actionable nuisance, the claimants in question should not bear the cost of that public benefit.

10.2.1 The subjectivity of noise problems

The other problematic feature of controlling noise is that it is a particularly subjective issue. What amounts to intolerable noise for one person may be disregarded or even considered desirable by others. Pop concerts, raves and parties are typical examples. Some people will be able to accept certain levels of noise, whereas others may suffer in terms of their mental or physical health as a consequence of that same noise. The sensitivity of hearing varies from person to person and other factors such as age can play a large part in determining responses. Noise may be problematic, not only in relation to its volume, but also with regard to its ability to irritate the recipient. Intermittent, disturbing and repetitive noises, whilst not inherently dangerous, may cause significant annoyance and emotional disturbance.

10.2.2 The nature of legal controls

Traditionally, noise problems have been addressed through the common law, principally by means of private nuisance actions. However, in more recent times, legislation has been introduced which attempts to control noise levels. There are various different ways in which legislation seeks to control the level of noise. In general, measures seek to control the level of noise emissions, either through product specifications or preventive action by means of prior consents. Alternatively, adverse levels of noise can be controlled through mechanisms which enable regulatory authorities to take measures to abate noise nuisances.

In the first instance, legislation exists to set precise noise emission levels for particular classes of machinery and vehicles and, in addition, there are a number of codes of practice which set out recommended noise levels for the likes of intruder alarms and ice cream van chimes. Predicted noise from construction works can be regulated in advance by means of a noise consent issued by a local authority (under the provisions of the Control of Pollution Act (COPA) 1974 (see below, on specific noise controls)).

The other mechanism for dealing with noise pollution is through a system of sanctions. In some instances, noise can be controlled where it constitutes a statutory nuisance. Local authorities have various powers which enable them to abate noise nuisances and bring criminal proceedings if the person responsible for the noise nuisance fails to comply with an Abatement Notice. The enactment of the Noise Act (NA) 1996 provides for immediate sanctions in the form of on the spot fines, designed to bring night-time noise nuisances to an immediate end. The provisions of the NA 1996 and the statutory nuisance provisions under the EPA 1990 are considered below.

In addition to these legal measures, the levels of noise can to some extent be controlled in the first instance through good planning which takes account of the potential noise generation of developments at the planning stage. Planning authorities are in fact required to consider the problems of noise when taking planning decisions in order to avoid noise nuisances occurring. Planning Policy Guidance Note 24 gives guidance to local authorities on the use of their planning powers to minimise the adverse impact of noise.

The following list provides a guide to the legislative controls in respect of various types of noise encountered:

Aircraft and airports	Civil Aviation Act 1982
Burglar alarms for cars and houses	Noise and Statutory Nuisance Act 1993
Construction sites	Control of Pollution Act 1974
Dogs and animals	Environmental Protection Act 1990
Domestic and neighbourhood noise	Environmental Protection Act 1990
Entertainment noise	Local Government (Miscellaneous Provisions) Act 1976
Loudspeakers	Control of Pollution Act 1974
Motor vehicles; cycles	Road Traffic Act 1988

The issue of noise has in recent years started to receive more attention from government and the European Community and, according to DEFRA (Noise Update 2002), 'noise policy in the UK and in Europe is undergoing a radical change'. The government has been aware of the difficulties faced in combating the problems of noise, and neighbourhood noise particularly. In 1994, the then Department of the Environment established a Working Group to review the effectiveness of the neighbour noise controls contained in Pt III of the EPA 1990 and the recommendations of that Working Group led to the enactment of the Noise Act (NA) 1996, which aimed at providing a quicker mechanism for dealing with domestic night-time noise. In 2000–01, DEFRA conducted a further review of the NA 1996. This review is considered fully below.

In 2001, the government embarked on a further consultation exercise to draw up a National Ambient Noise Strategy. The consultation proposed three distinct phases in the strategy covering the period 2002–07. It is envisaged that local authorities will continue to play a key role in the development and implementation of the strategy. It is anticipated that after the first phase of noise mapping and evaluation to assess the ambient noise climate in the country, new legislation will be necessary.

The European Community has also become considerably more active in the sphere of noise control in recent years. In 1996, the European Commission issued a Green Paper (COM(96)540) which set out various proposals and suggestions for further action to reduce noise pollution. The EC has enacted a number of directives on specific sources of noise (such as motor cycles and cars), but it appears that the Community is now moving towards a more comprehensive noise policy.

10.3   DAMAGE TO HEALTH

Although unwanted noise or excessively loud noise may be aggravating to those who do not wish to hear it, does it have any harmful effect? Unlike other types of pollution, noise is transient, it exists at the time that it is generated and cannot be said to have a permanent harmful effect on the environment in the same way that toxic wastes can contaminate land. Nevertheless, it can have a long term or even permanent detrimental effect on hearing, health or mental well being. CS Kerse in his book *The Law Relating to Noise* notes that exposure to excessive noise can result in a range of physiological effects. Quoting Dr Samuel Rosen he states that: 'At an unexpected or unwanted noise, the pupils dilate, skin pales, mucous membranes dry; there are intestinal spasms and the adrenals explode secretions. The biological organism, in a word, is disturbed.'

Noise can cause both temporary and permanent hearing loss. Temporary loss of hearing is typified by either sounds being perceived as muffled or a ringing in the ears. Once the exposure to the noise has ended, hearing should return to normal after about 45 minutes. Repeated exposure to noise might prevent the ear from recovering so readily and may cause permanent hearing loss.

Excessive levels of noise continued over a sustained period can cause serious damage to hearing and may, as stated above, even cause hearing loss (noise induced hearing loss). There are many occupations that expose workers to enough loud noise to cause this type of hearing loss. Equally, deafness may occur as a result of a very sudden and loud noise.

Loss of sleep and the associated health problems arising from loss of sleep is a more common complaint. Aeroplane noise in particular has a much more significant impact on sleep loss than do other noises. Residents living close to major airports, notably Heathrow, will testify to this particular problem. Loss of sleep can result in a person becoming irritable, he or she may find it difficult to concentrate and it may in turn result in a diminution of physical well being and health.

Unwanted noise is always likely to irritate after continued periods of time; however, it is also the case that it may cause actual physical discomfort. Apart from causing a headache, noise may result in feelings of severe discomfort such as nausea.

In *Dennis & Dennis v Ministry of Defence* (2003), the claimants described the noise caused by RAF Harrier Jets taking off from a nearby RAF air force base as not only deafening and highly intrusive but also 'frightening'. Similarly, in *Middlesbrough CC v Stevens* (1993), the constant and repetitive playing of Whitney Houston's song 'I Will Always Love You' was said to cause 'psychological torture' for a neighbour.

10.4   MEASURING NOISE

Despite the fact that responses to different noises vary widely, it is possible to measure sound objectively. Sound can be measured either in Hertz (Hz), which measures the frequency of sound (the number of pressure variations per second), or in decibels.

The decibel (dB(A)) measure is more widely used because it provides a better measure of the response of the human ear to loudness as the ear responds to changes in the noise level. The decibel is effectively a logarithmic scale with 0 dB corresponding to the quietest audible sound (the threshold of hearing) whilst 140 dB represents a sound at which pain would probably occur. As stated above, the usual form of measurement is dB(A) where the 'A' refers to the frequency weighting used in sound meters, enabling them effectively to mimic human hearing.

The Control of Noise (Measurements and Registers) Regulations 1976 (SI 1976/37) prescribe the decibel as the method for measuring noise in relation to the legal controls discussed in this chapter. In addition, they also provide some guidance on how noise levels can be calculated when it is not possible to make a precise measurement.

The courts are familiar with the use of decibels as measurements of noise although they will often seek a further description of the noise from the complainant. In *Halsey v Esso Petroleum Co Ltd* (1961), the use of decibels was affirmed by the court and an indication was given as to the effect of different levels of noise:

> Between 40 and 60 decibels the noise is moderate, and between 60 and 80 it is loud.
> Between 80 and 100 it is very loud and from 100 to 120 it is deafening.

10.5   NEIGHBOURHOOD NOISE

Neighbourhood noise, defined for the purposes of this text as the noise inside and outside homes, has been a growing area of concern for the last decade. The most reliable and up to date research into noise was carried out in 2000 on behalf of DEFRA. The National Noise Incidence Study concluded that some 55% of the population of England and Wales live in dwellings exposed to daytime noise levels above the World Health Organisation (WHO) recommended daytime level of 55 dB (decibels). In addition, the 2000 study found that 68% of the population of England and Wales live in dwellings exposed to night-time noise levels above the WHO recommended level of 45 decibels. Among the findings of the study research, which included a survey of more than 5,000 people, were the following:

- 21% of respondents reported that noise spoilt their home life to some extent, with 8% of respondents reporting that their home life was spoilt either 'quite a lot' or 'totally';

- 84% of respondents heard road traffic noise and 40% were bothered, annoyed or disturbed to some extent;

- 28% of respondents reported that road traffic noise at their homes had got worse in the last five years;

- 81% of respondents heard noise from neighbours and/or other people nearby and 37% were bothered, annoyed or disturbed to some extent;

- the proportion of respondents who reported being adversely affected by noise from neighbours has increased from 21% to 26% over the last 10 years whilst, for all other categories of environmental noise, the proportion adversely affected remained unchanged;

- only a small proportion of respondents who were bothered by noise from neighbours complained to the environmental health department of their local authority, which means that noise complaint statistics may greatly underestimate the extent of community dissatisfaction.

Although the statistics demonstrate that the overall outdoor noise levels have remained stable over the last decade, the fact remains that the number of complaints received by local authorities increased significantly. Local authorities in England and Wales received nearly five times as many complaints about noise in 2000/01 as in 1982/83.

The Chartered Institute of Environmental Health (CIEH) publishes annual statistics which provide a detailed breakdown of the number of complaints received by local authorities in England and Wales. In 2001/02, 308 local authorities (some 82%) received 228,704 complaints about domestic noise, representing the largest source of noise complaints by a significant margin (the next highest figure being 39,200 in respect of noise from commercial and leisure activities). Interestingly, of these 228,704 complaints received, only 36,236 were confirmed to be nuisances by the local authorities. The figures demonstrate that the public perception of noise as a problem is high, but that many complaints may be either too trivial or short-lived to constitute a confirmed nuisance.

The principal mechanism available for local authorities in dealing with domestic noise complaints is the statutory nuisance provisions contained in Pt III of the EPA 1990 (see Chapter 9 for a fuller discussion of these provisions). The 2001/02 CIEH statistics reveal that the vast majority of substantiated complaints were in fact resolved without any recourse to the formal proceedings under the Act:

2001/02 England and Wales

Complaints received re domestic noise	228,704
Complaints per million population	5,540
Sources complained of	193,301
Sources confirmed as a nuisance	36,236
Nuisances remedied without notices being served	26,781
Notices served	7,245
Number of seizures by local authorities	309
Prosecutions	565
Convictions	453

10.6 COMMON LAW

10.6.1 Nuisance

It is well established that adverse noise can constitute an actionable nuisance at common law. Noise may give rise to either a public nuisance or a private nuisance. In some circumstances it may be both.

In *Halsey v Esso Petroleum Co Ltd* (1961), it was held that a noise nuisance from tanker lorries at night on the public highway was both a public and a private nuisance. However, private nuisance actions are the most common because the impact of a public nuisance must be widely felt if it is to form the basis of a common law action.

10.6.2 Private nuisance

A private nuisance is one which unlawfully interferes with a person's use or enjoyment of land or some right connected with it. In terms of noise nuisances, the damage may be physical since vibrations may result in property damage or may damage hearing. However, it is more likely that a noise nuisance will interfere with a person's enjoyment of property through, for example, loss of sleep. There is no need to establish that the noise complained of is injurious to health to establish that it constitutes a nuisance (*Vanderpant v Mayfair Hotel Co Ltd* (1930)).

In a nuisance action, the courts are required to balance the rights of the owner of land to do what he or she wants against the rights of the owners of neighbouring land to be free from unreasonable interference. This necessarily involves the court dealing with each case on its merits taking into account all the relevant circumstances. The courts have developed a number of general principles and will take into account a number of factors.

10.6.3 Temporary interferences

The nature of the interference will be a significant factor in determining whether an action succeeds. A minor interference may still amount to a nuisance where there is physical damage, either to property or person, whereas in other cases the interference must be *substantial*. In *Walter v Selfe* (1851), the test was said to be whether there was 'an inconvenience materially interfering with the ordinary comfort physically of human existence, not merely according to plain and sober and simple notions amongst the English people'.

With regard to noise nuisances, it will clearly, like other nuisances, be a question of degree. It is here that noise can pose particular problems, because noise is often a temporary occurrence. As a general rule, the courts have found that a temporary interference is less likely to constitute a nuisance than one which is permanent or occurs regularly. A classic example of this reasoning can be found in the case of *Leeman v Montagu* (1936). Here it was held that the noise from cockerels sounding their dawn chorus was not an actionable nuisance whereas, if the noise from the cockerels had taken place in a residential area for weeks, damages and an injunction might have been granted. However, it is also clear that noise which results in loss of a single night's sleep can be a nuisance (*Andreae v Selfridge & Co Ltd* (1938)). In a more recent case brought under the statutory nuisance provisions of the EPA 1990, *East Northamptonshire DC v Fossett* (1994), the defendant F argued that 'nuisance' under the EPA 1990 has its common law meaning and therefore a single isolated instance of noise was not enough since there must be a 'course of action'. This argument was rejected by the Divisional Court, which stated that no case had held that excessive noise continuing all night could not amount to a nuisance to neighbouring residences.

The time of day, however, may be a factor for consideration. Noise disturbances during the night are more likely to constitute a nuisance than a noise made during the day.

10.6.4 Locality

It is well known that the courts will take into account the character of an area when determining whether an action is unreasonable and constitutes a nuisance (*Sturges and Bridgman* (1879)). The logical conclusion of this in relation to noise is that in peaceful suburban areas, the courts are more likely to regard noise as a nuisance than in built-up industrial areas. However, this does not exclude the possibility of bringing an action in private nuisance in industrial areas, nor does the fact that an area is already noisy remove the possibility of success. In *Roskell v Whitworth* (1871), a congregation at a Roman Catholic Church succeeded in obtaining an injunction to restrain the use of a steam hammer in an iron and steel works because it interfered with their prayers and the comfortable enjoyment of the rectory house (see also *Rushmer v Polsue and Alfieri Ltd* (1906)).

Since it is a well established principle in the law of nuisance that locality will have a bearing on whether a nuisance action will succeed, to what extent will the grant of planning permission alter the characteristics of a neighbourhood and provide a defence against a nuisance action? In *Gillingham BC v Medway (Chatham) Dock Co* (1992), planning permission had been granted to the Medway port authority for the construction of a port facility on the site of the former Chatham Royal Naval Dockyard. The Royal Naval Dockyard when it was operational had not generated much traffic, unlike the new port facility. Local residents complained to the local authority about the noise and other pollution from the round the clock heavy goods vehicle traffic to and from the port. In proceedings against the port authority, the council sought to restrain the passage of the heavy goods vehicles through the neighbourhood at night on the grounds that it constituted a public nuisance.

The court held that the grant of planning permission could alter the character of the area and may have the effect of rendering 'innocent activities which prior to the change would have been an actionable nuisance'. It was held accordingly that the noise from the traffic was not an actionable nuisance.

However, this ruling has since been considered by the Court of Appeal in *Wheeler v JJ Saunders Ltd* (1995). Here, planning permission was granted for two pig-weaning houses. An action in private nuisance was brought because of the smell generated by the pigs. The defendants in the action sought to rely on the *Gillingham* case by arguing that the grant of planning permission for the pig houses meant there could not be an actionable nuisance. This argument was rejected by the Court of Appeal, which held that the grant of planning permission was no defence to an action in nuisance. Staughton LJ was clear that:

> ... the court should be slow to acquiesce in the extinction of private rights without compensation as a result of administrative decisions which could not be appealed and were difficult to challenge.

10.6.5 Nature of the noise generating activity

The courts have also demonstrated some reluctance to interfere with noise arising from construction sites. This reflects the principle that the courts must have regard to the nature and desirability of the operation that is causing the alleged nuisance. In *Andreae v Selfridge & Co Ltd* (1938), the defendant company was developing a site close to the plaintiff's hotel. It was held that if operations of this particular nature are reasonably carried out, and all proper steps are taken to ensure that no undue inconvenience is caused to neighbours, then the neighbours must put up with the noise. However, in *De Keyser's Hotel Ltd v Spicer Bros Ltd* (1914), it was held that the defendant's building operations constituted a nuisance because they were not carried out in a reasonable and proper manner. The case was brought by the hotel on the grounds that the noise from the construction was so loud that the guests at the hotel and after-dinner speakers were unable to make themselves heard!

However, it appears that the courts have effectively recognised that building operations cannot happen without generating noise and that they are usually only short-lived operations where the benefits outweigh the temporary discomforts. Legislation now exists to control the noise from construction sites (ss 60 and 61 of the COPA 1974), although it is still possible to bring a private action in nuisance. See also *Dennis & Dennis v Ministry for Defence* (2003), in which the Divisional Court examined the public interest argument in the context of a claim against the Ministry of Defence in respect of the excessive noise caused by RAF Harrier jets.

10.6.6 Sensitivity of the claimant

It is well established that for an interference to be actionable, it must be one which affects an ordinary person and not one who is abnormally sensitive. In *Robinson v Kilvert* (1889), in which the plaintiff claimed that heat from the defendant's property which was situated in the basement was having an adverse effect on the brown paper stored in his premises, it was held that there was no actionable nuisance because:

> ... a man who carries on an exceptionally delicate trade cannot complain because it is injured by his neighbour doing something lawful on his property, if it is something which would not injure anything but an exceptionally delicate trade.

The rationale behind this principle is consistent with the law of nuisance. An example of abnormal sensitivity was given in *Heath v The Brighton Corp* (1908). In this case the vicar of a church sought an injunction to restrain the noise from the defendant's power station. The vicar failed because the noise was neither interrupting services nor had it affected attendance at church; it merely irritated the vicar. Therefore, it appears to follow that there can be no regard to a claimant who has an acute sense of hearing.

10.6.7 Intent of the parties

Finally, in relation to noise nuisances, the courts have been willing to take into account the malicious intent of the parties. In *Hollywood Silver Fox Farm Ltd v Emmett* (1936), the court granted an injunction to the plaintiff which restrained his neighbour from firing his guns during breeding time. The guns were fired by the defendant in spite, following an argument between the defendant and the plaintiff. Therefore, if the defendant's noise is made with the intention of causing annoyance to his neighbour, then he may be liable even if the interference would not amount to a nuisance if done in the ordinary and reasonable use of property. A good example of this occurred in *Christie v Davey* (1893). The defendant's intentional banging of trays on a party wall in retaliation for the noise caused by the neighbour's musical sessions was held to constitute a nuisance.

10.6.8 Remedies

The main remedies available in private nuisance actions are:

(a) abatement;

(b) injunction;

(c) damages.

The advantage of common law actions, despite the problems noted, is that they enable claimants to seek damages. If the intention of the claimant is to bring an end to the noise problem, a swifter and cheaper remedy is to ask a local authority to commence proceedings under the statutory nuisance provisions of the EPA 1990.

10.6.9 An interest in land

There are several problems in bringing an action in private nuisance and traditionally it has been necessary to demonstrate that the claimant has an interest in land. The House of Lords reaffirmed that a complainant must have an interest in land in *Hunter v Canary Wharf* (1997).

The creator of the relevant nuisance is the person who is liable and, unlike the claimant, does not need to have a proprietary interest in land where the nuisance arises. The occupier of the property from which the nuisance emanates will normally also be liable, although usually the creator of the nuisance and the occupier will be the same person (see *Sedleigh-Denfield v O'Callaghan* (1940)). A landlord will only be liable for any nuisance which emanates from premises where such a state of affairs is the ordinary and necessary consequences of granting the lease (see *Tetley v Chitty* (1986)).

10.6.10 Public nuisance

A public nuisance is defined as an unlawful act or omission which materially affects the reasonable comfort and convenience of a class of Her Majesty's subjects who come within the sphere or neighbourhood of its operation. Unlike private nuisance, there is no need to prove any interest in land.

In *AG v PYA Quarries Ltd* (1957), it was held that it is a question of fact whether a sufficiently large enough group of people have been affected for the nuisance to be called public.

A public nuisance is both a tort and a criminal offence and the case is brought by the Attorney General (or an individual with the consent of the Attorney General and in his name), who may seek an injunction to prevent a public nuisance.

For a private claimant to seek damages in a case of public nuisance, he or she must prove that he or she has suffered some special damage over and above that suffered by the general public. It is not necessary for the claimant to have an interest in land. Damages may be available to compensate for personal injury and for economic loss from the responsible party. As in private nuisance, an action may be brought against the creator of the nuisance, the occupier of premises and/or the landlord.

In relation to noise problems, public nuisance actions are rare.

10.6.11 The advantages and disadvantages of bringing an action in nuisance

Given the very nature of the law of nuisance and the weighing of considerations by the court, it will not always be easy to predict the likely outcome of a case. In addition, proceedings often take a very long time (which in noise disputes may often mean that the noise nuisance continues unabated) and are often very expensive.

Despite the disadvantages and problems of bringing a successful action in nuisance, there are a number of distinct advantages. On the one hand, the civil courts have the ability to award unlimited damages and the range of matters which can be complained of and which may constitute a nuisance is very wide.

10.7   CONTRACT AND LICENSING

An individual may also be able to secure a remedy through a contract. A good example would be a tenancy agreement whereby a claimant may bring an action based upon rights and covenants contained in a tenancy agreement. In any landlord and tenant relationship there is an implied (although it may also be expressly stated) covenant for the quiet enjoyment of the land, and this can be enforced by either of the parties to the agreement.

In addition, it will also be possible for a tenant, or the landlord at a tenant's request, to enforce a covenant, such as not to cause a nuisance, against another tenant.

10.7.1 Licensing

Licensing may in some circumstances provide a means of controlling noise. Under s 4 of the Licensing Act 1964, conditions aimed at reducing noise from licensed premises may be attached to the granting of an on-licence. The Local Government (Miscellaneous Provisions) Act 1982 (in London, the provisions are contained in the London Government Act 1963) provides for the licensing of music and dancing in public. Breach of a licence condition or failing to obtain a licence may result in a fine of up to £20,000 or six months' imprisonment on summary conviction. Outside London, the provisions only relate to indoor events. Whether an activity is public in this context depends upon whether any member of the public may participate, regardless of whether any payment is required.

The Private Places of Entertainment (Licensing) Act 1967 established similar controls in relation to private events promoted for private gain, but for the provisions of this Act to apply, they must be adopted by the relevant local authority.

10.8   STATUTORY CONTROLS

The main statutory provisions which relate to noise are as follows:

(a) the Land Compensation Act 1973;

(b) the Health and Safety at Work Act 1974;

(c) the COPA 1974;

(d) the Civil Aviation Act 1982;

(e) the EPA 1990;

(f) the Noise and Statutory Nuisance Act 1993;

(g) the Town and Country Planning Act 1990;

(h) the NA 1996.

The Health and Safety at Work Act 1974 deals with noise in the workplace, the Land Compensation Act 1973 deals with a local authority's duty to insulate buildings against noise created by public works such as road building, and the Civil Aviation Act 1982 deals with noise generated from civil aircraft. These are matters which fall outside the main environmental controls and are not considered in this book. (However, it should be noted that it is not possible to bring an action under the Civil Aviation Act 1982 in either trespass or nuisance in relation to noise generated from the flight of civil aircraft. Noise from civil aircraft is controlled by a separate regime under regulations.)

This chapter will concentrate on the provisions contained in the COPA 1974, the EPA 1990, the Noise and Statutory Nuisance Act (NSNA) 1993 and the NA 1996.

10.9   NOISE AS A STATUTORY NUISANCE

The provisions in the EPA 1990 relating to noise nuisances were amended by the NSNA 1993. The majority of the new provisions came into force in January 1994. In particular, the 1993 Act incorporated a new statutory nuisance into the EPA 1990 at s 79(1)(ga).

10.9.1 Section 79(1)(g) and (ga) of the EPA 1990

Section 79(1)(g) and (ga) of the EPA 1990 provide that noise can be a statutory nuisance in the following circumstances:

(a) *Section 79(1)(g)*: 'noise emitted from premises so as to be prejudicial to health or a nuisance'; and

(b) *Section 79(1)(ga)*: 'noise that is prejudicial to health or a nuisance and is emitted from or caused by a vehicle, machinery or equipment in a street'.

The EPA 1990 does not provide any particular definition of noise other than to say in s 79 that it includes 'vibration'.

10.9.2 Prejudicial to health or a nuisance?

Before considering the noise statutory nuisances in any detail, it is necessary to consider the general provisions relating to statutory nuisance. Although s 79 of the EPA 1990 lists certain states of affairs that may constitute statutory nuisances, they will only be statutory nuisances if they are either prejudicial to health or a nuisance. The definition includes two separate and alternative limbs and it is not necessary to show that a matter is both a nuisance and prejudicial to health. This was affirmed in *Betts v Penge UDC* (1942):

(a) *Prejudicial to health*

Section 79(7) of the EPA 1990 defines 'prejudicial to health' as meaning 'injurious, or likely to cause injury'. This definition includes two limbs, 'injurious to health', that is, actual harm, or 'likely to cause injury', that is, anticipated harm. The definition is the same as that given in the Public Health Act 1936. For a discussion of what is meant by the term 'prejudicial to health', see Chapter 9. However, in the context of noise nuisance it was held in *Southwark London BC v Ince* (1989) that a house which was inadequately insulated against noise, so that noise from a nearby railway adversely affected the occupants, was prejudicial to health.

(b) *What is meant by nuisance?*

The courts have equated nuisance in this context with common law nuisance, private or public, with the focus primarily on private nuisance, therefore involving interference with enjoyment of property. In *National Coal Board v Neath BC* (1976), it was held that the word 'nuisance' meant either a public or a private nuisance at common law. It should also be noted that, like the common law nuisance, the interference must be with *neighbouring* property (*National Coal Board v Thorne* (1976)).

In *Godfrey v Conwy County BC* (2000), in a case stated appeal, the Divisional Court held that noise can constitute a statutory nuisance even if it does not exceed background noise in the locality if it is of a character which makes it intrusive and irritating. It is not necessary for the noise to be prejudicial to health; it is sufficient that it merely interferes with another's quiet enjoyment of his or her property. In this case, G had converted a barn in a quiet rural area for use as a music studio where rock bands practiced. On investigation, the Environmental Health Officer was clearly able to hear the noise and accepted the complaints made, but she was unable to take a recording of the noise satisfactorily because of the interference of background noise caused by haymaking in the adjacent field. G argued that the noise from his recording studio was no higher than the background noise and that, in the absence of a decibel reading, the noise could not be prejudicial to health.

10.9.3 Noise from premises – s 79(1)(g)

Like all of the statutory nuisances in s 79 of the EPA 1990, noise from premises may only constitute a statutory nuisance if it is either:

(a) noise emitted from premises so as to be *prejudicial to health*; or

(b) noise emitted from premises so as to be a *nuisance*.

This particular statutory nuisance was not included in the Public Health Act 1936 but was drawn from ss 57–59 of the COPA 1974. The term 'premises' was not defined in the COPA 1974. In *Tower Hamlets LBC v Manzoni and Walder* (1984), the court held that the term premises did not include a street and therefore noise from a street could not be controlled under the statutory nuisance provisions of the COPA 1974. The EPA 1990, however, provided a definition of 'premises' as including land. It remains unclear whether this definition encompasses a street.

In the context of this particular head of statutory nuisance, the meaning of prejudicial to health was considered in *Southwark London BC v Ince* (1989). It was held that a house which was inadequately insulated against noise so that noise from a nearby railway adversely affected the occupants was a statutory nuisance because it was prejudicial to health.

Since noise is much more likely to interfere with enjoyment, rather than cause injury or be injurious to health, the nuisance limb needs some further definition. In general, the nuisance limb of statutory nuisance is based on the common law concept. This means that when the court is required to consider whether noise constitutes a nuisance, it will take into account various matters, including:

(a) the duration and time of the noise;

(b) the nature of the activity giving rise to the noise;

(c) the harm suffered by the person affected;

(d) the neighbourhood where the noise took place.

It also means that, in practice, the EHO who is usually responsible for exercising the local authority's statutory nuisance functions will need to make a similar determination.

10.9.4 Noise in a street which is emitted from a vehicle, machinery or equipment – s 79(1)(ga)

This particular statutory nuisance was incorporated into s 79 of the EPA 1990 by the NSNA 1993. The amendment was made largely because the EPA 1990 did not provide sufficient protection from noise in streets (see *Tower Hamlets LBC v Manzoni and Walder* (1984) above).

A street is defined as a 'highway and any other road, footway, square or court that is for the time being open to the public'. It is clear that a great deal of noise is generated in streets not only from vehicles but from ice cream vans, people playing loud music and of course the interminable sounds of car alarms going off. Not all street noises are covered. Certain exceptions are provided: it does not apply to noise created by traffic, the armed forces or by political demonstrations (or demonstrations supporting or opposing a campaign or cause). Traffic is understood to mean vehicles in motion.

Section 79(1)(ga) only refers to street noises emitted from vehicles, machinery or equipment. The question remains about the position of noise which emanates from the street but is not emitted from any of these particular sources.

In *Haringey LBC v Jowett* (2000), in a case concerning a complaint by a council house tenant about the noise from traffic caused by poor sound insulation of his property, the court found that although the lack of sound insulation meant that the premises were a potential source of injury to Jowett's health, the authority was not responsible for the statutory nuisance in respect of the traffic noises, the reasoning being that the restriction on traffic under s 79(1)(ga) was limited by s 79(6A) of the 1990 Act (as amended by s 2 of the NSNA 1993), thereby precluding traffic noise.

10.9.5 Responsibility of the local authorities

Section 79(1) of the EPA 1990 places all district councils and London borough councils under a duty to inspect their area from time to time to detect any statutory nuisance which ought to be dealt with under ss 80 and 80A of the EPA 1990. They are also under a duty to take such steps as are reasonably practicable to investigate complaints about statutory nuisances made by people living in the area. The duty is therefore twofold. The local authority has to carry out its own checks and has to respond to complaints. In practice, it is the environmental health departments and officers that are responsible for enforcing this legislation and they will carry out the inspections and deal with the complaints. In some areas, particularly the large cities, some local authorities have night patrols who are concerned primarily with noise control. According to the National Society for Clean Air, in *Controlling Neighbourhood Noise*, complaints about neighbours 'may be fully investigated, receive minimal attention or may not be investigated at all'.

In determining which complaints to investigate, many local authorities operate what is known as the 'three neighbour rule'. This effectively means that the local authority will not take action unless they have received complaints about noise from three separate sources. Some local authorities operate a policy of first sending a warning letter to the person they have received the complaint against:

(a) *Duty to inspect*

The duty to inspect and detect statutory nuisances is tempered by the requirement that these inspections only have to be carried out from time to time. One of the problems here is that the expression 'time to time' is not defined by the EPA 1990, thus making the obligation very imprecise.

(b) *Duty to respond to complaints*

This duty to respond to complaints was established by the EPA 1990. Prior to its introduction, local authorities were not actually required to respond to complaints made although, in practice, complainants provided useful information about the occurrences of statutory nuisances within the local authority area. The duty to respond to complaints made by people living in the area is qualified by the fact that the authority only has to take such steps as are reasonably practicable to investigate the complaint. Again, this expression is not defined and could potentially cause problems. Local authorities are increasingly finding that they are facing severe financial problems. Whether the authority can take into account its own financial situation in determining what is reasonably practicable is not clear. However, if the Secretary of State finds that a local authority is in default of these duties, he can, by virtue of Sched 3, transfer the function to himself.

(c) *Local authorities' investigative powers*

In order to carry out their functions of inspection and investigation, local authority environmental officers can enter any land with the people and equipment that they consider necessary. The officers can also carry out any inspections, measurements and tests and can also take away samples and articles. These powers are provided by Sched 3 to the EPA 1990. The purpose of the inspection and investigation is to establish whether or not there is a statutory nuisance (or whether one is likely to occur) and to gather any evidence which may be needed in subsequent court proceedings. Once a local authority environmental officer is satisfied that a statutory nuisance is occurring or is likely to occur, then an Abatement Notice must be served.

(d) *Determining whether a statutory nuisance exists*

In practice, the local authority environmental health officer will make an initial determination whether the matter complained of constitutes a statutory nuisance on the basis of it being prejudicial to health or a nuisance. He or she will therefore be required to take into account the nature of the neighbourhood and also whether the matter complained of amounts to a nuisance in common law or is just (as sometimes happens) a vexatious complaint. As with the common law, this makes it very difficult to predict whether or not a noise will amount to an actionable statutory nuisance. An EHO may have to make a number of visits to determine whether a nuisance exists, particularly in relation to noise nuisances which by their very nature are often sporadic. Complainants are well advised to keep a written record of the times and frequency that noise disturbances take place and also, where possible, to get third parties to witness the disturbances for evidential purposes.

In relation specifically to noise complaints, the environmental health officer may take noise measurements where this is possible.

Once an environmental health officer or local authority is satisfied that a statutory nuisance exists or is likely to occur, then an Abatement Notice must be served on the person responsible.

10.10 NOISE ABATEMENT NOTICES

As stated above, once it has been determined that a statutory nuisance exists or is likely to occur, then an Abatement Notice must be served on the person responsible.

Section 80 of the EPA 1990 provides that an authority must serve an Abatement Notice when it is satisfied that, in its area, a statutory nuisance:

(a) exists;

(b) is likely to occur; or

(c) is likely to recur.

Therefore, the authority can take preventive action in order to stop a statutory nuisance from happening. The requirement to serve the Abatement Notice is mandatory. However, s 80 does not say anything about the need for the likely occurrence to be imminent. It is enough that it is likely to occur. Also, when one considers that the concept of prejudicial to health also extends to 'likely to cause injury', the local authority must serve an Abatement Notice if it believes that circumstances exist which make injury likely.

10.10.1 The form of the Notice

Although there is no prescribed form for an Abatement Notice, it must nevertheless state the following in a manner which is clear and understandable to the recipient:

(a) the nature of the statutory nuisance;

(b) the action or works required to abate it;

(c) time limits for compliance;

(d) the rights of appeal to the magistrates' court.

The Abatement Notice can impose a variety of conditions, including:

(a) conditions requiring the abatement of the nuisance or prohibiting or restricting its occurrence or recurrence (s 80(1)(a));

(b) conditions requiring the execution of such works, and the taking of such other steps, as may be necessary for any of these purposes (s 80(1)(b)).

The provisions of s 80(1)(b) above were considered by the Divisional Court in *Lambie v Thanet District Council* (2001) in an appeal by way of case stated against an Abatement Notice served on Lambie. In this case, the Abatement Notice required L to abate the noise by allowing the authority to set up a sound restricting device on his premises. The Divisional Court held that the local authority's power under s 80(1)(b) was a wide one and could legitimately include a requirement to allow an officer to enter premises so as to install such a device.

There is no need to specify a time limit when prohibiting the recurrence of a nuisance. In *R v Birmingham City Justices ex p Guppy* (1988), the city council served an Abatement Notice on G who was having a noisy party. The Notice imposed the three following requirements:

(a) to prohibit the noise amounting to a nuisance;

(b) immediately to cease permitting the use of the sound equipment to produce a noise so as to be a nuisance; and

(c) to take all other steps as may be necessary for that purpose.

Two months later, the noise nuisance recurred on three successive nights and G was convicted of three offences of non-compliance with the Notice. G sought judicial review of the convictions specifically on the grounds that the prohibition of recurrence in the Notice was invalid since no time limit for compliance was specified. The High Court held that it is necessary for a Notice to include a time limit for compliance where it requires the abatement of a nuisance or the execution of works, but not where it prohibits the recurrence of a nuisance. The decision in *Guppy* was applied in *R v Tunbridge Wells Justices ex p Tunbridge Wells BC* (1996).

10.10.2 Should the Notice set a prescribed decibel level?

In *R v Fenny Stratford JJ ex p Watney Mann* (1976), three residents were disturbed by the noise from a jukebox in a local public house. Proceedings were brought under s 99 of the Public Health Act 1936 against the company that owned the pub and the local magistrates' court issued a nuisance order which stated that the 'nuisance should be abated' and 'the level of noise in the premises should not exceed 70 decibels'. Watney Mann applied for judicial review, arguing that the terms of the Notice were not clear. The High Court quashed the Notice on the grounds that it was void for reasons of uncertainty, in that:

(a) it did not state where the noise meter should be positioned; and

(b) the magistrates had failed to consider the likelihood and relevance of other sources of noise such as general conversation.

However, in two later cases, the courts appeared to take a more lenient attitude towards this issue. In *East Northamptonshire DC v Fossett* (1994), F was served with an Abatement Notice which required F to control all activities, including musical ones, so as not to cause a nuisance. The district council had served the Notice because it was aware that an all night rave was to take place at F's club. The rave took place and the noise could be heard within one mile of the club. F was prosecuted for breach of the Notice. The magistrates held that the noise levels amounted to a nuisance, but stated that the Abatement Notice was void on the grounds of imprecision and uncertainty. The district council appealed by way of case stated. In response F argued, following *Watney Mann* (see above), that a decibel level should have been set by the Notice. The Divisional Court distinguished that case as one on a recurrence of a nuisance. In *Fossett*, the Divisional Court held that since the Notice was served to prevent a likely nuisance, the district council would have had to speculate unnecessarily if they had tried to set a decibel level and, on the facts, the district council had been forced to act quickly. F further argued that the Notice was uncertain and he could not possibly know what an acceptable level of sound should be since the Notice had failed to set one down. The Divisional Court rejected these arguments.

In a further case, *Myatt v Teignbridge DC* (1994), M kept 17 dogs. The district council served an Abatement Notice on her which required her to 'cease the keeping of dogs'. A further Notice was served which stated that she had to 'reduce the number of dogs kept at the premises to no more than two and to take such steps as are necessary in the housing, welfare and management of the dogs to ensure they do not cause a nuisance'. M failed to comply with either Notice and was prosecuted by the district council. She appealed by way of case stated. The Divisional Court held that the issue was whether or not the recipient of the Notice knows what is wrong from the Notice. On the facts, the court held that M must have known what the cause of complaint was and, although the Notice could have been drawn up more carefully, it was sufficient to make it clear to the recipient what was wrong.

These two later cases suggest a more lenient attitude towards the drafting of Abatement Notices and suggest that it is not necessary to prescribe a decibel level. However, it is clear that the courts will not be too prescriptive and that they will take into account the facts of the case.

In *Lambie v Thanet DC* (2001), the Divisional Court held that a requirement in a Notice that 'amplified music and raised voices were not intrusive in nearby or adjoining properties' was too vague and too uncertain.

10.10.3 On whom must the Notice be served?

The provisions regarding the serving of Abatement Notices are contained in s 80 of the EPA 1990. Normally the local authority is required to serve the Notice on the person responsible for the nuisance. Where the nuisance arises from any defect in the structural character of a building, then the Notice should be served on the owner of the premises. In circumstances where the person responsible for the nuisance cannot be found, or the nuisance has not yet occurred, then the Notice must be served on the owner or occupier of the premises.

In relation to vehicles, machinery or equipment, the person responsible will be the driver or operator. In circumstances where the noise nuisance has not occurred or arises from an unattended vehicle, machinery or equipment, the Abatement Notice should be served on the person responsible for the vehicle. If that person cannot be found, the Abatement Notice can be affixed to the vehicle following a determination of the authority to that effect. This particular provision was introduced by the NSNA 1993 and is now contained in s 80(a) of the EPA 1990.

The Abatement Notice must specify the time for compliance. With noise nuisances, that may be immediately. Non-compliance with an Abatement Notice without reasonable excuse is a criminal offence.

10.10.4 The 'person responsible for the nuisance'

The person responsible for the nuisance is defined in s 79(7) of the EPA 1990 as the person to whose:

(a) act;

(b) default; or

(c) sufferance,

the nuisance is attributable. This is a wide definition and could include not only the person who created the noise nuisance, but also a third person/party who failed to take any appropriate preventive or corrective action where they had some legal requirement to do so. It can also include third persons who on becoming aware of the problem took no steps to remedy the situation. This was confirmed in the case of *Clayton v Sale UDC* (1926), where an owner was held liable for a statutory nuisance on his land consequent upon the activities or defaults of another.

In *Network Housing Association Ltd v Westminster CC* (1995), an Abatement Notice was served on a landlord in respect of noise under s 79(1)(e) of the EPA 1990 (noise emitted from premises) following a complaint from a tenant to the city council. The complainant claimed he was being disturbed by the ordinary residential use of the flat above. The Abatement Notice required the housing association to carry out alterations to the flat to reduce the noise levels to a prescribed decibel level. The court found that the noise in question was the noise of everyday living and it was the lack of sound insulation between his and a neighbour's flat that constituted it a nuisance. The housing association argued that there was no act on its part, nor indeed any default or sufferance, since it had no knowledge of the nuisance when it acquired the premises. However, the court rejected these arguments and held that the landlord was the person responsible. The housing association had allowed the nuisance to continue after it had come to its attention in 1991. However, on appeal to the Divisional Court, it was held that the Abatement Notice did not specify the type of works to be carried out and was void because of lack of certainty.

10.10.5 What if more than one person is involved?

Section 81(1) of the EPA 1990 deals with the situation where more than one person is responsible for the statutory nuisance. If two persons are involved in an action which jointly amounts to a statutory nuisance, they will both be responsible for the statutory nuisance even if their individual actions do not by themselves amount to such a nuisance. Although the Abatement Notice should be served in the first instance on the person responsible for the nuisance (s 80(2)), this should be read as meaning that the authority is obliged to serve separate notices on all the parties that may have contributed to the statutory nuisance.

10.11 APPEALS AGAINST AN ABATEMENT NOTICE

A person who is served an Abatement Notice is entitled to appeal against it by making a complaint to the magistrates' court (s 80(3) of the EPA 1990). He or she must be informed of this right in the Abatement Notice. Where a person decides to lodge an appeal they must do so within 21 days from the day when the Abatement Notice was served. The grounds for appeal are not laid down in the EPA 1990, but are provided in the Statutory Nuisance (Appeals) Regulations 1995.

The grounds are:

(a) the Abatement Notice is not justified by s 80 of the EPA 1990. In other words, the appellant argues that the matter did not constitute a statutory nuisance;

(b) the Abatement Notice contains some informality, is defective or contains an error;

(c) the authority has unreasonably refused to accept compliance with alternative requirements, or the requirements laid down in the Abatement Notice are unreasonable or unnecessary;

(d) the period for compliance in the Notice is not reasonably sufficient;

(e) there has been an error in the service of the Notice; for example the Notice has been served on the wrong person. An appeal may also be made if the appellant argues that it is 'equitable' for the Notice to be served on some other person either instead of the appellant or in addition to the appellant. Whether the wrong person has been served will be determined by reference to s 80(2). In relation to noise nuisances, an appeal may be brought on the grounds that the Notice should have been served on the person responsible for the vehicle, machinery or equipment instead of the appellant;

(f) the best practicable means (BPM) were used to counteract the effect of a nuisance from trade or business premises;

(g) in relation to a nuisance under s 79(1)(g) of the EPA 1990, the requirements imposed by the Abatement Notice are more onerous than the requirements which may have been determined by means of other noise controls under the COPA 1974 or the NSNA 1993 (such as consents relating to loudspeakers).

The magistrates' courts have wide powers when dealing with appeals against Abatement Notices. They can:

(a) correct any procedural defect in the Notice, quash the Notice or vary the Notice;

(b) dismiss the appeal;

(c) make such order as they think fit regarding:

    (i)   any works which need to be carried out and the contribution to be made by any person to the cost of the work; or

    (ii) the proportion of expenses that a local authority may recover from the appellant and from any other person.

10.11.1 Effect of an appeal upon an Abatement Notice

In general, the lodging of an appeal will not suspend the operation of an Abatement Notice and therefore the person served with a Notice will still be required to comply with the conditions of the Notice. However, this general provision does not apply in circumstances where:

(a) the Abatement Notice requires expenditure on works and the expenditure required would be out of proportion to the expected public benefit; or

(b) in the case of a nuisance under s 79(1)(g) or (ga), the noise to which the Abatement Notice relates is noise necessarily caused in the course of the performance of some duty imposed by law on the appellant.

These provisions are to be found in the Statutory Nuisance (Appeals) Regulations 1995 (SI 1995/2644).

10.12 NON-COMPLIANCE WITH AN ABATEMENT NOTICE

Section 80(4) of the EPA 1990 establishes that it is an offence for a person served with an Abatement Notice either to contravene or fail to comply with any requirement or prohibition imposed by the Notice, without reasonable excuse. If an Abatement Notice is not complied with, the authority that has issued the Notice has three options:

(a) *The authority can abate the nuisance and recover its cost*

The authority can abate the nuisance and do whatever may be necessary in execution of the Notice (s 81(3)). A typical example of this is where audio equipment is removed to abate a noise nuisance. Police support is often required when environmental health officers try to seize equipment. According to the Neighbour Noise Working Party, in its 1995 report, there had been some uncertainty about the use of s 81(3) to confiscate noise making equipment temporarily and, until amendments were introduced by the NA 1996, there was no specific provision for the return of seized equipment to owners. Local authorities often used s 43 of the Powers of Criminal Courts Act 1973 to obtain a court order to confiscate permanently equipment used to commit or facilitate the commission of an offence. The provisions relating to seizure of equipment were amended by the NA 1996 and are covered more fully at 10.14.6 below.

An authority can abate a nuisance irrespective of whether it takes proceedings for non-compliance. In the event that the authority does take action either to abate the nuisance or prevent it happening, then it can, by virtue of s 81(4) of the EPA 1990, recover *any* expenses reasonably incurred. This would normally be from the person whose acts or omissions caused the nuisance. If that person is the owner of the premises, the expenses can be recovered from any person who is for the time being the owner of them. This would cover situations where, for instance, a previous owner caused a nuisance, but the present owner could be made responsible for the reasonable expenses incurred by the authority. Should the matter of cost recovery go before the court, the court has the power to apportion the expenses between persons whose acts (or omissions) caused the nuisance, in a manner that the court considers fair and reasonable.

The NSNA 1993 provides additional assistance to the local authorities in the form of a newly inserted s 81A, which enables the local authority serving a notice to recover costs to make a charge on the premises owned by the person in default.

If the noise is from a car alarm, the officer has the power to open the vehicle, if necessary by force, and immobilise the alarm. The expenses incurred by a local authority in abating a nuisance can be recovered with interest (s 81A of the EPA 1990). The local authority can also place a charge (that is, a debt secured on property and recouped when the relevant property is sold) on the premises. This new provision was inserted into the EPA 1990 by s 10 of the NSNA 1993.

(b) *The authority can institute summary proceedings*

If a person commits an offence under s 80(4), the authority can institute proceedings in the magistrates' court. The penalty for nuisance offences depends on whether the nuisance has occurred on industrial, trade or business premises or not. For nuisances arising on non-industrial, trade or business premises, the maximum penalty is £5,000 plus a further £500 for each day that the offence continues after the conviction. However, where the nuisance occurs on industrial, trade or business premises, the maximum fine is £20,000 (but no additional daily fines can be made).

In *Lewisham LBC v Hall* (2003), the council appealed against a decision by the magistrates' court to acquit Hall on charges of contravening a noise Abatement Notice. Hall had failed to comply with the Notice and the council had commenced summary proceedings, but was unable to produce any acoustic measurement evidence, relying on the experience of the environmental health officer. The Divisional Court held that the production of acoustic measurement evidence (such as a decibel recording device used under the NA 1996) was not a precondition for conviction. It was open to magistrates to convict on the basis of the evidence of an environmental health officer or any other lay witness.

(c) *The authority can seek an injunction*

The third option available to the authority against a person who fails to comply with or contravenes an Abatement Notice is to take proceedings in the High Court (s 81(5) of the EPA 1990). This option is available if the authority is of the view that proceedings in the magistrates' court (under s 80(4)) would afford an inadequate remedy. The aim would be to secure an injunction to secure the abatement, prohibition or restriction. The authority can take this course of action even if summary proceedings have not been exhausted and equally there is no requirement that the authority has suffered damage from the nuisance. Failure to comply with an injunction may result in a prison sentence. In *Bristol CC v Huggins* (1994), Mr Huggins was jailed for three months for breaching an injunction which was obtained by Bristol City Council after two prosecutions under the EPA 1990 failed.

This enables the local authority to obtain an interlocutory injunction to stop a nuisance, despite the availability of appeal proceedings in the magistrates' court.

10.12.1 Defences

The following defences are available in relation to noise nuisances:

(a) *Reasonable excuse*

It will be a defence if the defendant can prove that there was a reasonable excuse for not complying with the Abatement Notice. Unfortunately, the EPA 1990 does not define 'reasonable excuse'. The test is whether it is an excuse that a reasonable man would consider consistent with a reasonable standard of conduct. What constitutes a reasonable excuse will therefore be a matter of fact. Reasonable excuses have included non-receipt of the Abatement Notice (*A Lambert Flat Management Ltd v Lomas* (1981)). A birthday celebration or party will not constitute a reasonable excuse.

(b) *The best practicable means (BPM) defence*

Where a noise nuisance has been alleged in relation to noise from a vehicle, machinery or equipment, then it is a defence to show that the best practicable means (BPM) were used to prevent or counteract the nuisance. The defence is only available where the vehicle, machinery or equipment is used for industrial, trade or business premises (s 80(8)(aa) of the EPA 1990). The defence was considered in *Chapman v Gosberton Farm Produce Co Ltd* (1993), where a company in Boston, Lincolnshire received prepared packed horticultural produce from heavy goods vehicles during the night. Complaints were made to the district council about the noise from the lorries and also about the noise from the refrigeration equipment. In proceedings before the magistrates' court, the company argued that the BPM had been used to counteract the effect of the noise. The company maintained that it had sought planning permission to erect a soil bank and screening (to provide a sound screen) as part of a wider application to extend its business and this fulfilled the BPM. The magistrates accepted this defence, but their decision was overruled by the Divisional Court. The upper court held that the burden of proof in establishing the BPM lies on the defendant (s 101 of the Magistrates' Court Act 1980) on a balance of probability, and it could not be said that a simple planning application was enough to discharge the burden of proof since the application for planning permission had not been determined.

Defendants have often found it relatively easy to take advantage of this defence on the basis that any work required would be too expensive in relation to their means (AJ Waite, 'Neighbourhood noise in the UK' (1994) 6(4) Environmental Law and Management 130–36).

In considering what constitutes BPM in this context, s 79 adds an additional factor not relevant in other statutory nuisances. In circumstances where a code of practice (issued under s 71 of the COPA 1974) is applicable, then regard must be had for the guidance given in the code.

(c) *Codes of practice*

Section 71 of the COPA 1974 enables the Secretary of State to prepare and approve codes of practice for the purpose of giving guidance on the appropriate methods of minimising noise in relation to specified types of plant and machinery. Codes of practice issued under s 71 include construction and open sites (SI 1984/1992, SI 1987/1730); audible intruder alarms (SI 1981/1829); ice cream van chimes (SI 1981/1828); and model aircraft (SI 1981/1830).

(d) *Additional defences*

In addition, s 80(9) of the EPA 1990 contains a defence specific to a failure to abate a noise nuisance or act in accordance with a prohibition or restriction in a noise Abatement Notice. The basis of this defence is essentially that the local authority has given its consent to a particular level of noise under the provisions of ss 60–67 of the COPA 1974 and that the Abatement Notice attempts to impose a higher standard. The provisions of ss 60–67 are described more fully below.

10.12.2 Burden of proof in statutory nuisance proceedings

Within the context of proceedings involving statutory nuisances, the burden of proof which applies is a criminal one. In other words, it must be established beyond reasonable doubt that the matter complained of exists and that the defendant is responsible for it.

10.13 AN AGGRIEVED CITIZEN'S ACTION – s 82 OF THE EPA 1990

The right exists in relation to all of the statutory nuisances contained in the EPA 1990 for an aggrieved person to make a complaint in the magistrates' court (s 82 of the EPA 1990). Before a person can do this, he or she must give notice. In relation to noise nuisances under s 79(1)(g) and (ga), three days' notice is required rather than the standard 21 days' notice.

One of the main limitations with the so called aggrieved citizen's action is that the magistrates' court cannot make an order unless a statutory nuisance has occurred. In other words, preventive action cannot be taken by an individual.

Before taking action in proceedings brought under s 82, the magistrates must be satisfied that one of the following conditions exists:

(a) the alleged nuisance exists;

(b) an abated nuisance is likely to recur on the same premises, or in the same street.

The court can make the following orders:

(a) requiring the defendant to abate the nuisance within a specified time and to carry out any works necessary for that purpose;

(b) prohibiting a recurrence of the nuisance and requiring the defendant to carry out any necessary works to prevent the recurrence. A time period for carrying out such works will be specified in the order;

(c) the imposition of a fine of up to £5,000, with a further fine of up to £500 for each day that the offence continues after conviction;

(d) order the relevant local authority to do anything which the convicted person was required to do by the court order, after it has given the authority the opportunity to be heard. This is only likely to happen where the court makes a second nuisance order because the first has not been complied with.

Where the nuisance is such as to render premises unfit for human habitation, the court can prohibit the use of the premises for human habitation until the court is satisfied that the premises have been made fit for such a purpose.

Failure to comply with a nuisance order from the magistrates is an offence and can result in a fine of up to £5,000 (plus £500 for each day that the offence continues).

10.13.1 Compensation

Since statutory nuisance proceedings are criminal proceedings, the magistrates' court can make a compensation order in favour of persons aggrieved by the nuisance under s 35 of the Powers of Criminal Courts Act 1973. This is limited to a sum of up to £5,000. No such limit exists if a compensation order is granted by the Crown Court.

10.14 THE NOISE ACT 1996

The NA 1996 received royal assent on 18 July 1996. The provisions of the Act do not create a new noise nuisance, but provide for a special summary procedure in relation to night-time noise.

The provisions of the Act are adoptive, that is to say local authorities are not obliged to comply with the provisions of the Act, and by s 1 must actually adopt a formal resolution to adopt its provisions. This adoptive element was criticised at the time with the suggestion that very few authorities would seek to adopt an Act which imposed significant resource implications. One of the requirements of the Act was that a review be conducted to evaluate the success and effectiveness of the Act. This review was undertaken by DEFRA in 2000 (see below). At the time that the review was published in December 2000, only 14 authorities had adopted the Act.

10.14.1 Complaints

The NA 1996 provides that in an area where the provisions have been adopted, the local authority is under a duty to respond to certain complaints. If a complaint is made by an individual present in a dwelling during night hours that excessive noise is being emitted from another dwelling, the local authority must ensure that an officer of the local authority takes reasonable steps to investigate the complaint. Night hours are defined as being between 11 pm–7 am.

10.14.2 Investigation and service of Warning Notice

If, after carrying out an investigation, the local authority officer (usually the EHO) is satisfied that:

(a) the noise is being emitted from a dwelling during night hours; and

(b) the noise, if it were measured from within the complainant's dwelling, would or might exceed the permitted level which is detailed in Circular 8/97 (the relevant noise levels are 35db (if the underlying noise level does not exceed 25db) or 10db above the relevant background noise (if the underlying noise level is 25db or more) – an increase of 10db over a background level of 25db will double the loudness of the noise),

the officer may serve a Warning Notice on any person at or near the offending dwelling who appears to be responsible for the noise. In the event that no such person can be found, the Notice can be left at the dwelling.

It is clear that it is the local authority officer who is responsible for making the decision as to whether the noise does or is likely to exceed the permitted level. He or she also needs to decide whether it is necessary to assess the noise levels either within or outside the complainant's dwelling. It is also a matter of discretion whether or not the noise level needs to be measured using any noise measuring device.

In deciding whether a nuisance exists, the local authority will primarily rely upon the results of its noise measuring instruments. Consequently, there is no need to take into account factors, such as locality, which are material to the exercise of the local authority's functions.

10.14.3 Person responsible for the noise

A person is responsible for the noise emitting from a dwelling if he or she is the person to whose:

(a) act;

(b) default; or

(c) sufferance,

the emission of the noise is wholly or partly attributable. This test is the same as that used under the statutory nuisance provisions discussed earlier.

10.14.4 The Warning Notice

The environmental health officer has discretion in relation to whether or not to serve a Warning Notice. The Warning Notice may start as little as 10 minutes after the service of the Notice and must end at 7 am. The Notice will state that the person responsible for any noise which exceeds the permitted levels has committed a criminal offence liable on summary conviction to a fine not exceeding level 3 on the standard scale.

10.14.5 Defences

The NA 1996 provides the defence that there was reasonable excuse for the act, default or sufferance.

Section 7 of the NA 1996 lays down the evidence that may be admitted to a court in summary proceedings for an offence under s 4. It includes:

(a) documentary evidence of an offence without the attendance in court of the local authority officer (unless by virtue of s 7(6) attendance is required by the defendant); and

(b) evidence from noise measuring devices.

10.14.6 Powers of entry and seizure and disposal of equipment

Section 10 of the NA 1996 provides a power of entry by force under a magistrate's warrant. The NA 1996 makes specific provision for the seizure and disposal of equipment, such as audio and stereo equipment. The relevant provisions are s 10 of and Sched 1 to the Act. The provisions of the NA 1996 in this regard also extend to the statutory nuisance provisions under the EPA 1990 and make it clear that the power of a local authority to abate a nuisance under s 81(3) of the EPA 1990 includes the power to seize and remove equipment which it appears to the local authority is being or has been used in the emission of a noise nuisance under s 79(1)(g) of the Act.

10.14.7 Fixed penalty notices

The NA 1996 was introduced to provide a speedy resolution of noise problems. In addition to a maximum penalty of £1,000, the 1996 Act introduced a fixed penalty procedure.

Where a local authority officer has reason to believe that a person:

(a) is committing an offence; or

(b) has just committed an offence under the Act,

the officer *may* issue a fixed penalty notice. This essentially gives the person in receipt of the penalty notice the opportunity of discharging any liability under the Act upon payment of a fixed penalty. The fixed penalty is currently set at £100.

10.14.8 Review of the Noise Act 1996

In 2000, DEFRA embarked on a consultation exercise to evaluate the effectiveness of the Noise Act (NA) 1996. In total, DEFRA received some 213 responses, representing a response rate of just under 50%. Of these, the vast majority (193) were from local authorities. The consultation document suggested three possible options for consideration, one of which was that the provisions of the Act be made mandatory for all local authorities. There was a clear rejection of this proposal, given the resource implications of the Act, with most authorities citing resources as the reason for non-adoption.

One of the significant criticisms of the Act is that it only really offered one advantage over the provisions of the EPA 1990, namely the possibility of serving a fixed penalty notice without having to go through the protracted procedures of serving an Abatement Notice. On the other hand, the legislation is perceived as being more limited than the EPA 1990, in that it only confers powers between certain hours and in relation to domestic noise only. The requirement that noise exceed a fixed threshold has also been criticised because of the need to invest in specific recording devices, and the difficulties in taking recordings (for a fuller examination of these criticisms, see the Chartered Institute of Environmental Health Policy Unit Consultation Response to the Review of the Noise Act 1996, available online via the CIEH website).

Although very few authorities have adopted the NA 1996, the conclusion of the consultation exercise was that the Act has acted as a form of catalyst in encouraging local authorities to operate some form of out of hours complaints service. In 1994, only 52% of authorities (responding to the consultation exercise) operated some form of out of hours service, whereas the percentage had significantly increased to 90% in 2000. More particularly, the review indicated that one of the key successes of the NA 1996 was the clarification of the powers of seizure and the clear incorporation of these powers into the EPA 1990.

Following the review of the Act, the government announced that it would seek to make amendments to the Act in order to make the night noise offence more accessible to local councils by allowing authorities to use the Act without having to adopt it formally.

10.15 BYLAWS

The first legislation in the UK expressly dealing with noise was in the form of bylaws. Section 235(1) of the Local Government Act 1972 allows district councils to make bylaws for the 'good rule and government of the whole or any part of the district or borough, as the case may be, and for the prevention and suppression of nuisances therein'. The Home Office has issued a number of model bylaws, including those on:

(a) noisy animals;

(b) noisy conduct at night;

(c) the playing of organs, wirelesses and gramophones;

(d) music near houses, churches and hospitals.

The breach of a bylaw is a criminal offence.

10.16 SPECIFIC SOURCE NOISE CONTROLS

10.16.1 Construction sites

In addition to the controls contained in the EPA 1990, the other main statutory provisions controlling noise can be found in Pt III of the COPA 1974, which replaced the Noise Abatement Act 1960.

The COPA 1974 includes a number of measures which enable local authorities to control various aspects of noise. In particular, ss 59A, 60 and 61 introduced the first legislative controls over noise from construction sites.

The COPA 1974 provides the means by which local authorities can control the level of noise in their areas arising from construction works. The definition of 'construction' extends to the erection, construction, alteration, repair or maintenance of buildings, structures or roads. It also includes demolition and dredging works. Where it appears to a local authority that any of these activities are being, or are going to be, carried out on premises, then the authority can serve a notice imposing requirements as to the way in which the work is to be carried out (s 60(2) of the COPA 1974). It is not necessary that a nuisance exists or could occur for the authority to resort to these powers. Sometimes, local authorities will publish details of the notice in the local press.

The notice can specify the following:

(a) plant and machinery which must or must not be used;

(b) permitted hours of operation;

(c) noise levels by reference to the time of the day or to a part of the site;

(d) the time within which the notice is to be complied with;

(e) the execution of works necessary for the purpose of the notice.

When the local authority issues its powers under s 60, it must take into account the matters specified in s 60(4) which are:

(a) relevant codes of practice issued under s 71 of the COPA 1974;

(b) the need to ensure that the best practicable means (BPM) are employed to minimise noise;

(c) the need to protect people in the locality from the effects of noise.

It should be noted that the definition of BPM under s 72 of the COPA 1974 is very similar to the definition provided under the EPA 1990 (s 79(9)). The local authority is required to serve the s 60 notice on the person who appears (to the local authority) to be either carrying out or going to carry out the works. In addition, a notice can also be served on the person(s) who is (are) responsible for or controlling the carrying out of the works. In *City of London Corp v Bovis Construction Ltd* (1989), it was held that it was sufficient that the notice was served upon the person having control of the site even if the contractor actually doing the work is not served.

It is an offence not to comply with a s 60 notice without reasonable excuse. The magistrates can fine up to £5,000 with a daily fine of £50 for continuing offences. However, it is possible to raise the defence of reasonable excuse. The phrase reasonable excuse is not defined in the Act, but was considered in the case of *City of London Corp v Bovis*, where Lord Bingham stated that:

> Nothing much short of an emergency, unless an event beyond a party's control, could in my view provide a reasonable excuse for contravention in a case such as this.

Where a party fails to comply with the s 60 notice, the local authority also has the option to apply for an injunction. The court may grant an injunction where it appears that the criminal proceedings will not provide an adequate remedy to ensure compliance with the notice and to protect the inhabitants from noise.

A right of appeal exists against a s 60 notice providing the appeal is made within 21 days of service. The grounds for appeal are set out in the Control of Noise (Appeals) Regulations 1975 (SI 1975/2116, as amended by SI 1990/2276). An appeal can suspend the notice unless the notice expressly states otherwise.

Given that local authorities have powers to restrict construction noise under s 60 of the COPA 1974, contractors have the right to reach some agreement with the local authority, in advance of the works taking place, about the levels and timing of noise that will take place. Section 61(3) provides that contractors can apply for consent prior to the construction work taking place. To do so, the applicant must provide details of the work that is to be carried out and also the method by which it is to be carried out. In addition, details must be given regarding the measures that will be taken to minimise the noise resulting from the works. If the authority considers that the application contains sufficient information that no s 60 notice would be served if the steps proposed are observed, then it must grant a consent. The authority, however, has the right to attach conditions to the consent. In setting the conditions, it must take into account the relevant codes of practice, BPM and the need to protect persons in the locality from noise.

The authority must respond to the application for prior consent within 28 days of receipt of the application. The authority can either refuse or approve the application, or alternatively it may approve the application subject to conditions. An applicant can appeal if the authority refuses to give its consent, fails to deal with the application within the 28 days, or attaches conditions to which the applicant objects. An appeal is made to the magistrates' court and must be lodged within 21 days after the expiry of the 28 days.

It is an offence to carry on the works other than in compliance with the terms of the consent. Obtaining the prior consent from the local authority can prove to be valuable since the existence of a consent can protect the contractor from any statutory nuisance proceedings brought by a local authority. However, the consent does not provide the same protection in relation to actions brought by private individuals (under s 82 of the EPA 1990). The existence and compliance with a prior consent will not provide a defence in such actions. A citizen can also seek an injunction in respect of a noise nuisance irrespective of whether there is a s 60 of the COPA 1974 prior consent. Although prior consent would appear to be a sensible step for any contractor, in practice relatively few have applied under these provisions. One of the suggested reasons for this is the view that contractors have thought that the local authorities would be too restrictive in setting conditions. Contractors have preferred to run the risk of proceedings under s 60.

10.16.2 Noise from loudspeakers

The noise from loudspeakers is controlled by s 62 of the COPA 1974, which provides that loudspeakers are not to be operated in streets at all for advertising any entertainment, trade or business. There is a blanket ban as far as advertising is concerned. Loudspeakers may be used for other non-advertising purposes, but they may not be operated in any event between 11 pm and 8 am the following morning. The Secretary of State can reduce these times, but has no power to extend the period (s 7 of the NSNA 1993).

Section 62(2) of the COPA 1974 provides exceptions for the use of loudspeakers:

(a) at any time in the street for, *inter alia*, various public service reasons, such as the police, the ambulance or fire service or the Environment Agency;

(b) in an emergency;

(c) inside vehicles for the entertainment of passengers;

(d) by ice cream vans (or vans selling perishable foods). They can play their music between noon and 7 pm;

(e) at pleasure fairs.

In relation to the last three of these exceptions, there is a caveat that the noise must not give reasonable cause for annoyance to persons in the vicinity.

Section 8 of and Sched 2 to the NSNA 1993 amended s 62 of the COPA 1974 in order to allow local authorities to permit the use of loudspeakers in certain circumstances where it would otherwise be a breach of s 62.

The maximum penalty for the illegal use of a loudspeaker in a street is £5,000.

10.16.3 Noise from burglar alarms

There cannot be many people who have not been annoyed by the sound of burglar alarms going off for what sometimes seems like forever in the middle of the night. Burglar alarms are designed to be noisy and to arouse attention, that is their very purpose. But all too often they go off for no other reason than the operator has misused the system or a 'door has blown open'.

Section 9 of the NSNA 1993 enables local authorities to adopt a regime to deal with the problem of burglar alarms. Local authorities may impose obligations on installers of audible intruder alarms and occupiers (or any person entitled to occupy if the premises are unoccupied) to ensure that where alarms are fitted, they comply with requirements to be set out in regulations by the Secretary of State. When a burglar alarm is installed, the police must be notified of details of current key holders and the local authority must be informed of the police station where that information has been recorded. Where an alarm sounds for more than one hour and is giving persons living or working in the vicinity reasonable cause for annoyance, the local authority officer has the power to enter the premises and turn it off. The officer cannot use force to do this. However, the EHO, accompanied by a police officer, can enter forcibly if a warrant has been obtained.

The alarm must comply with the prescribed requirements and, in particular, there must be a 20 minute cut-out device. Powers of entry are provided.

10.16.4 Emission standards and codes of practice

One way of reducing noise generated by certain types of transport, machines or activities is to set source emission standards. This is the approach that has been taken in a number of EC directives.

EC legislation controls noise for a variety of types of machinery including:

(a) lawnmowers;

(b) motorcycles;

(c) aircraft. Aircraft noise emission regulation is licence-based. No aircraft may take off or land at a UK airport unless it has a noise certificate issued by the Civil Aviation Authority (or an equivalent licence issued by a national licensing authority) complying with the Air Navigation (Noise Certification) Order 1990 (SI 1990/1514). The 1990 Order implements EC Directives 80/51/EEC, 83/206/EEC and 89/269/EEC which, in turn, give effect to the provisions of the 1944 Chicago Convention on Civil Aviation. Although aircraft noise controls have been 'ratcheted up' by EC Directives 92/14/EC and 98/20/EC (implemented in the UK by the Aeroplane Noise Regulations 1999 (SI 1999/1452)), the noise reductions achieved have been counterbalanced by an increase in air traffic. In consequence, the adverse impact of noise at some UK airports has significantly increased.

Aircraft noise is regulated by the Secretary of State under the Civil Aviation Act (CAA) 1982. Section 78 of the Act enables the Secretary of State to list specific airports (currently Heathrow, Gatwick, Stansted and Manchester) which require regulation in respect of the volume of air traffic and hours of operation. Under s 79, statutory noise insulation schemes may be set up which provide grant assistance for noise insulation works.

Noise and other environmental impacts are, by virtue of s 68(1) and (3), taken into account when operating licences are granted to airlines.

Tortious actions, such as trespass and nuisance, regarding noise disturbance caused by aircraft and airports will, in most cases, fail because of the exclusions of liability provided by ss 76 and 77, except to the extent that the airline or airport operator is acting unreasonably. In 1990, the validity of these exclusions was unsuccessfully challenged in a human rights action based on Arts 6, 8 and 13 of the European Convention on Human Rights (see *Powell and Rayner v UK* (1990));

(d) cars, buses and goods vehicles. Traffic-related noise nuisance arises from a combination of engine noise, road noise (caused by the composition of the road surface – tarmac or concrete) and the volume of traffic using a particular stretch of road. The EC has been influential in developing product-based controls, such as exhaust silencers and tyre standards, which help to combat these problems (see EC Directives 70/157/EEC, 77/212/EEC, 81/334/EEC, 84/372/EEC, 84/424/EEC and 92/97/EC). The main secondary legislation transposing these provisions into UK law are the Road Vehicles (Construction and Use) Regulations 1986 (SI 1986/1078), the Motor Vehicles (Type Approval) (Great Britain) Regulations 1984 and 1994 (SI 1984/81 and SI 1994/981) and the Motor Vehicles (EC Type Approval) Regulations 1998 (SI 1998/2051);

(e) tractors;

(f) construction plant and machinery.

The Secretary of State has the power under s 68 of the COPA 1974 to make regulations which reduce or limit the noise caused by plant or machinery both inside and outside factories and construction sites. As yet, this power has not been exercised and the Secretary of State has preferred the use of codes of practice rather than legally binding standards.

Section 71 of the COPA 1974 enables the Secretary of State to prepare and approve codes of practice for the purpose of giving guidance on the appropriate methods of minimising noise in relation to specified types of plant and machinery.

Codes of practice issued under s 71 include construction and open sites (SI 1984/1992, SI 1987/1730); audible intruder alarms (SI 1981/1829); ice cream van chimes (SI 1981/1828); and model aircraft (SI 1981/1830).

Although codes of practice are not legally binding, they may be taken into account in legal proceedings, for example, in determining whether BPM have been employed. The code of practice dealing with audible intruder alarms has now been incorporated into the NSNA 1993.

10.16.5 Anti-social behaviour orders

Anti-social, threatening and disruptive behaviour which causes, or is likely to cause, alarm, harassment and distress may be dealt with by means of an anti-social behaviour order under s 51 of the Crime and Disorder Act 1998. The Act is designed to provide the police and local authorities with power to address street disturbances, as opposed to neighbour disputes. Either the local authority or the police, after consulting one another, may apply to a magistrate for an order. Breach of an order is a crime punishable by a maximum penalty of an unlimited fine or a gaol sentence of up to five years.

10.16.6 'Rave' parties

The Criminal Justice and Public Order Act 1994 is relevant to the control of 'rave' parties. A 'rave' is defined as 'a gathering of one hundred or more people on land in the open air that includes the playing of amplified music'. Section 63 empowers the police to stop a rave in circumstances where the music is likely to cause serious distress to local residents.

10.17 PREVENTING NEIGHBOURHOOD NOISE

Environmental law is said to be based upon a number of principles, some of which are enshrined in the EC Treaty. One fundamental principle is the preventive principle – prevention being better than cure. In relation to noise, both EC and UK legislation exists which seeks to prevent noise nuisances occurring. The consequence of successful preventive action is the reduction in noise problems.

The noise controls that have been considered so far have largely been concerned with controlling existing noise problems and resolving noise disputes, although of course the statutory nuisance provisions can be used to prevent nuisances from arising.

The remaining part of this chapter is concerned with those measures which are intended to prevent noise problems from reaching unacceptable levels in the first place.

10.17.1 Noise abatement zones

In addition to the specific powers in ss 60–61 of the COPA 1974 (described above), local authorities can also take preventive action to control noise by designating noise abatement zones. The provisions relating to noise abatement zones are found in ss 63–67 of the COPA 1974. Section 63 of the COPA 1974 makes provision for local authorities to designate all or any part of their area as a noise abatement zone. The purpose of noise abatement zones is, according to DoE Circular 2/76, to 'prevent deterioration in environmental noise levels and achieve reductions in noise levels wherever practicable'.

If a local authority wishes to create a noise abatement zone, it must issue a 'noise abatement order' specifying the types or classes of premises to which the order applies (Sched 1 to the COPA 1974 defines the procedures for establishing noise abatement zones). Originally, such an order had to be confirmed by the Secretary of State, but this requirement was removed by the Local Government and Planning Act 1980.

Where a local authority designates an area as a noise abatement zone, it must measure the level of noise emanating from those classes of premises specified by the order. It is also under a duty to maintain a noise level register of all measurements taken. In a noise abatement zone, it is an offence to exceed the level of noise recorded in the noise level register without the written consent of the local authority. The local authority can consent to a noise level being exceeded by virtue of s 65 and any consent may be subject to conditions. Where such consent is denied by a local authority, an applicant can appeal to the Secretary of State. Where the local authority consents to the registered level being exceeded, then this is also recorded in the register.

If the local authority records a measurement in the register, then it is obliged to serve a copy of that record on the owner or occupier of the premises from which the measurement was taken. Any person who is served with a copy of a record has the right to appeal against the record to the Secretary of State within 28 days by virtue of s 64. The Control of Noise (Appeals) Regulations 1975 (SI 1975/2116) provide for the appeals procedure. The precise methods of measurement are determined by the Control of Noise (Measurement and Registers) Regulations 1976 (SI 1976/37).

In addition, the local authority can require the reduction of noise emanating from premises covered by the noise abatement order. The local authority will issue a noise reduction notice which will state:

(a) that the level of noise must be reduced to the stated levels;

(b) the noise level allowable at different times of the day and on different days;

(c) what steps are to be taken to achieve the noise reduction; and

(d) the deadline for achieving the noise reduction.

The noise reduction stated in the notice must be practicable and achievable at a reasonable cost. It must also generate some public benefit. Parties served with a noise reduction notice have the right to appeal to the magistrates' court against the notice (the appeal must be made within three months of service of the notice). Failure to comply with the terms of a notice without reasonable excuse constitutes an offence. By virtue of s 74 of the COPA 1974, the fines may not exceed level 5 on the standard scale (£5,000) and there is provision for a daily penalty of £50. As in statutory nuisance, the local authority may execute works itself and recover reasonable costs (s 69 of the COPA 1974).

Noise abatement zones have not found widespread support. This is probably because of the length of the procedures used and the resources that are needed to implement the provisions. Local authorities have largely relied on their powers under the statutory nuisance provisions in the EPA 1990 to control noise.

10.17.2 Planning and noise control

The town and country planning regime can play a large part in either causing or reducing noise problems. Bad planning can result in noisy developments being built alongside more noise sensitive operations. For this reason, planning authorities are required to consider the potential for noise problems in the exercise of their planning functions. In 1994, a new Planning Policy Guidance Note (PPG 24) was introduced on planning and noise. The PPG replaces advice previously given in DoE Circular 10/73. It also takes into account the recommendations of the Noise Review Working Party, which reported in October 1990.

PPG 24 provides advice to local authorities on how to use their planning powers to minimise the adverse impact of noise. In particular, it outlines the considerations that should be taken into account when the authority is considering planning applications for activities which will generate noise and also for proposals in noise sensitive areas. The PPG highlights the measures that may be taken to control noise. These include:

(a) ensuring that there is adequate distance between the source of noise and noise sensitive areas;

(b) engineering solutions to reduce noise at the point of generation;

(c) controlling the times when noise generating activities can take place.

10.17.3 Noise exposure categories

In addition, PPG 24 introduces the concept of 'noise exposure' categories (NECs) for residential developments. When determining an application for a residential development near a source of noise, such as a motorway, planning authorities must first determine into which of the four noise exposure categories the proposed site falls, taking account of noise levels during the day and night. The four NECs are rated A to D. An A category means that noise need not be considered as a determining factor in granting planning permission, whereas a D category means that planning permission should normally be refused. Annexe 2 of the PPG sets out detailed 'noise exposure' categories:

    A – noise need not be considered as a determining factor in granting planning permission.

    B – noise should be taken into account.

    C – planning permission should normally be granted, but where it is granted appropriate conditions should be applied.

    D – planning permission should normally be refused.

10.17.4 Planning conditions

Local planning authorities can grant planning permission for development subject to conditions which are aimed at minimising noise levels. PPG 24 is useful once again in that it describes the sorts of conditions that might be used to achieve this objective. For example, the planning authority can lay down conditions which determine that construction work cannot begin until a scheme for protecting a noise sensitive development has been approved by the authority. Other relevant conditions include:

(a) layout conditions;

(b) engineering conditions;

(c) administration conditions (such as operating times).

In *Penwith DC v Secretary of State for the Environment* (1977), the local planning authority, in relation to an application for the extension to a factory, granted permission subject to a condition that no machinery be operated in the extension or the existing factory between the hours of 6 pm and 6 am on weekdays or between

1 pm on Saturday and 8 am on Monday, or on statutory holidays. The court held that the planning authority could lawfully impose such conditions.

10.17.5 The Building Regulations

There can be no doubt that poor sound insulation, particularly in flats, is a contributing factor to neighbour noise problems. However, new buildings must comply with the Building Regulations which can to some extent prevent noise problems occurring. The Building Regulations are enacted under the Building Act 1984 and prescribe various technical requirements relating to building structures including noise insulation. It is a criminal offence to carry out building works in contravention of the Building Regulations. In late 2002, the government announced changes to the Building Regulations in relation to sound insulation standards for new and converted homes.

10.18 THE EC DIMENSION

Although the impact of the EC upon noise regulation in the UK is not as marked as in other contexts, nevertheless, the EC has had some effect on noise controls in a national context. So far the thrust of EC noise regulation has been product-based, especially with regard to motor vehicles (EC Directive 70/157/EEC as amended with regard to engine and exhaust system noise), aircraft (EC Directive 80/51/EEC regarding noise from sub-sonic aircraft), household appliances (EC Directive 86/594/EEC with regard to product information on noise levels), and construction equipment.

In 2000, the EC adopted a further Directive on noise emissions by equipment for use outdoors in order to harmonise national laws regarding noise emission limits and the labelling requirements of such equipment at the manufacturing stage. The Directive applies to equipment such as lawnmowers and construction machinery. The Directive has been implemented into UK law by the Noise Emission in the Environment by Equipment for Use Outdoors Regulations 2001 (SI 2001/1710).

During the mid-1990s, the EC issued a Green Paper on *Future Noise Policy* (COM(96)540) which highlighted the need for action with regard to railways, construction plant and other areas. Although the document makes some reference to environmental quality limit values, the general thrust of EC noise policy remains focused on product-based noise limits and the provision of information to consumers on product noise levels. Nevertheless, the Green Paper marks something of a new approach by the EC to the problems of noise and is seen by the EC as the first step in the development of a coherent noise policy with the aim that no person should be exposed to noise levels which endanger health and the quality of life. Following on from the Green Paper, the Commission has issued a Directive for the harmonisation of the assessment of noise exposure (Directive 2002/49/EC).

10.19 ALTERNATIVE DISPUTE RESOLUTION

Noise disputes are often part of a much wider neighbour dispute. Unwelcome noise is often a symptom of the disagreement between neighbours, rather than the original cause. In which case, the noise laws discussed above may be of limited use in controlling the noise and other alternative methods of resolution may be required, either in other branches of law or possibly through mediation. Equally, genuine noise disputes may be dealt with outside the framework of legal control discussed so far. The following section is intended to consider the possibilities of alternative forms of dispute resolution which may lend themselves to the resolution of noise disputes.

It will often be the case that a dispute between neighbours over noise can be resolved informally. Often an environmental health officer can facilitate this informal resolution by helping the neighbours to reach some sort of compromise solution.

The DoE (now DEFRA) has shown itself keen to encourage informal resolution of problems (*Bothered by Noise?*, 1994). However, it is recognised that not all problems can be dealt with so easily. Nevertheless, the DoE (now DEFRA) has also sought to promote the use of more formal means of alternative dispute resolution and has issued a guidance note on the mechanics and benefits of alternative dispute resolution, in particular, the use of mediation.

10.19.1 Mediation

Mediation is one form of alternative dispute resolution where an impartial third party seeks to help those in dispute reach a mutually acceptable agreement outside the framework of the courts. The DoE (now DEFRA) recognises that mediation will not always be the appropriate form of dispute resolution, but suggests that it is more likely to work.

The advantages of mediation are clear. Mediation is normally quicker and almost certainly less expensive than legal action because its use only requires one mediator. The costs of mediation are split between the parties involved.

Mediation is also claimed to be very successful. Mediation UK, a mediation service, claims that it has an 85% success rate of reaching lasting agreements (this claim relates to all types of disputes, not just noise disputes).

Mediation was argued for most strenuously during the passage of the Noise Bill before Parliament. According to the MP for Lewisham and Deptford, Joan Ruddock, 'about 60% of all mediated neighbour disputes involve noise, and estimates of their success range from 40% to 77%. Mediation is cost-effective and usually costs between £200 and £300 per hour' (*Hansard*, 16 February 1996 – during the Second Reading of the Noise Bill).

10.20 FURTHER INFORMATION

Further reading

Adams, M and McManus, F, *Noise and Noise Law*, 1994, Wiley Chancery.

McManus, F, 'Noise law in the United Kingdom – a very British solution?' (2000) 20(2) LS 264.

Dymond, A, 'Noise and the Limits of the Law' (2000) 3(1) Journal of Local Government Law 11.

Websites

www.environment-agency.gov.uk
Search for 'noise' on the website.

www.cieh.org
The official website of the Chartered Institute of Environmental Health. Documents available include Policy Unit Response to the Review of the Noise Act and annual statistics relating to noise complaints and statutory nuisance procedures.

www.defra.gov.uk/environment/noise/index.htm
The Department for Environment, Food and Rural Affairs. See, in particular, noise updates.

http://europa.eu.int/comm/environment/noise/home.htm
Information on developments in the European Community.

CHAPTER 11

THE PRIVATE REGULATION
OF ENVIRONMENTAL POLLUTION:
THE COMMON LAW

11.1   INTRODUCTION

Most of this book is devoted to a study of the public regulation of private pollution. Command and Control regulatory regimes are employed by the government to regulate the polluting emissions of private industry. Such legislative controls task public bodies, such as the Environment Agency and the local authorities, with regulating polluting emissions from a wide range of industries.

Command and Control legislation such as the Environmental Protection Act (EPA) 1990 and the Water Resources Act (WRA) 1991 are examples of public laws. These laws differ from criminal laws or civil laws in that each piece of legislation comprises an administrative framework designed to regulate a particular type of polluting activity, often through the use of licence-based controls.

In contrast to the regulation of pollution by public regulators 'policing' compliance with the law as detailed in legislation and licences, this chapter considers the role of the common law as a component of the patchwork of controls which currently comprise the environmental law of England and Wales. The common law, in contrast to the law in legislation, comprises various legal principles which have been developed by the judiciary in decided cases over many years. This is 'judge made' law rather than statute law (Acts of Parliament). Common law actions consist of 'one on one' disputes involving an action commenced by an injured claimant in the civil courts against the person (defendant) who allegedly caused the injury. Thus, the common law is a mechanism to regulate the legal relations between private persons, whether individuals or companies. In the context of this book, the relevant legal relations upon which we shall focus concern the resolution of disputes relating to pollution damage to property, property-related interests, or personal injury. Most of these disputes require the courts to resolve competing land uses.

The most important set of common laws which have application to environmental problems in general, and pollution in particular, is the law of torts (wrongs). The primary function of the law of torts is to provide a range of remedies for any person who suffers a wrong consisting of damage to property or person (personal injury) caused by the activities of another person.

11.2   COMMON LAW ACTIONS

Where a legal person, such as an individual or a company, has suffered environmental harm which takes the form of damage to person or property, an action in tort is usually the most appropriate response. The common law of torts is used to provide redress, usually in the form of compensation, for a victim of pollution-related damage.

Although common law actions have been criticised for 'being too expensive, too long winded and too uncertain' (Bell, 1997), nevertheless, they have, in recent years, proved to be a fertile ground for environmental litigation, although the judiciary have demonstrated a rather lukewarm response to attempts to use torts as a mechanism to control the adverse impacts of pollution on people, property and the wider environment. The courts have shown a preference for specific pollution legislation, such as the EPA 1990, and have shown minimal support for attempts to develop the common law as a means of resolving modern day environmental problems.

Before we consider each environmental tort in detail, a few general points will be made:

(a) common law actions are largely concerned with the protection of *private rights*. These rights, such as property rights, are 'private' in the sense that they relate to legal persons (individual humans and companies). Currently, no corresponding legal rights exist to bring an action on behalf of the environment or flora and fauna (Stone, 1972 and 1985). It is humans (and also companies) who resort to the common law to engage in civil litigation in order to protect their own interests from actual or threatened damage arising out of the use of a neighbouring landowner's property;

(b) in contrast to the Command and Control regulatory frameworks in the EPA 1990 and the WRA 1991, with their licence-based pollution controls linked to precise and monitorable licence conditions, the common law has traditionally been associated with imprecise standards. The common law attempts to balance competing private interests and looks to the reasonableness of the activities of competing landowners. It does not lay down strict numerical limits for substances contained in emissions from one person's property discharged into the environment and affecting a neighbouring property;

(c) proving that the defendant's activities caused the damage sustained (the process of causation) may be a difficult and expensive task, bearing in mind the degree of scientific uncertainty which may exist (see *Graham and Graham v ReChem International* (1996)). Damage caused by airborne pollutants may pose a significant evidential problem for the claimant, especially if the claimant's and defendant's properties are some distance from one another and there are other properties in the area which are generating identical or similar polluting emissions;

(d) the right to take action in most cases is strictly limited to those persons whose property or property-related interests have been harmed (see *Hunter v Canary Wharf Ltd* (1997) and *Blackburn v ARC Ltd* (1998));

(e) in a common law action, the court makes a largely subjective decision as to whether the defendant's activities are unreasonable, taking into account the degree of tolerance which would be expected of a reasonable neighbour;

(f) the grant of, and compliance with, a pollution discharge licence issued by a regulator under Command and Control legislation, such as the WRA 1991, does not prevent the defendant being liable in an action based on tort (except negligence);

(g) the common law is mainly a reactive and compensatory mechanism. Only rarely will the courts, in such an action, grant an injunction to prevent anticipated, future damage or interference;

(h) the usual remedy, in the event that an action is successful, is an award of damages to the claimant to put him or her back in the same position that he or she would have been in had the tort not been committed. Except in the case of negligence actions, the claimant may seek an injunction to restrain the defendant's behaviour which is causing injury to the claimant's interests. The award of an injunction will almost certainly be more important to both parties than damages. Injunctions are generally only awarded to stop or restrict continuing activities;

(i) a successful claimant is not obliged to spend any damages received on restoring the environment, even if this was the basis of the complaint;

(j) injury or damage relating to some aspect of the environment valued by the public or harm to man is often a powerful factor which motivates the claimant to pursue a case in order to make a defendant accountable for the alleged wrong (Pugh and Day, 1995);

(k) the legal standard of proof in civil cases requires the claimant to prove his or her case 'on the balance of probabilities'. In other words, it is more likely than not that the defendant's actions caused the relevant injury to the claimant or his or her interests.

11.3 REMEDIES

The common law offers various remedies which will be sought by the claimant depending upon the particular circumstances of each case. Each remedy is discussed below.

11.3.1 Damages

The object of damages in the law of torts is to put the claimant into the position he or she would have been in had the harm or damage not occurred. This is particularly difficult to calculate in relation to environmental damage, because it is often the case that the cost of environmental damage can never be calculated for many years, as clean-up may take several years, or the damage can never be fully rectified.

The most common form of damages to be awarded by the courts are compensatory damages, where the claimant is compensated for any loss that has been suffered.

There are several other forms of damages which may be awarded, for example:

(a) *aggravated damages* – awarded where the court wishes to express disapproval of the defendant's conduct and compensate the claimant who has suffered more than would normally be expected;

(b) *punitive/exemplary damages* – awarded where it is the court's intention to punish the tortfeasor (defendant) by adding an additional award onto the compensatory damages awarded, which may also have the effect of deterring others from acting in a similar fashion. The award of exemplary damages is largely governed by the rules established in *Rookes v Barnard* (1964), in which it was stated that damages of this type could be awarded in three classes of cases:

(i) where servants of the government act in an oppressive, arbitrary or unconstitutional way. In *Gibbons v South West Water Services Ltd* (1992), a claim in private nuisance, it was held that this could not apply to private individuals or corporations;

(ii) where the defendant's conduct was calculated to profit from the tort. This is particularly appropriate in environmental cases, because industrial operators may feel that it would be more profitable to continue with the polluting activity and to face the consequences when paying damages, rather than to cease production or to operate with less polluting techniques;

(iii) where the statute expressly permits the payment of exemplary damages.

11.3.2 Injunction

In addition, or as an alternative to damages, the claimant may seek an injunction.

Injunctions essentially allow the courts to require that the defendant discontinues the offending operation and/or takes action to prevent or remedy the damage or pollution that has been caused.

Injunctions can be classified as:

(a) mandatory injunctions, in which case the court will order the defendant to undo or remedy the damage, or prevent further damage from occurring;

(b) prohibitory injunctions, which order the defendant not to continue with the wrongful act. The duration of a prohibitory injunction is determined by the court with regard to the offending activity and the nature of its effects.

Injunctions provide the potential for a powerful common law weapon against polluters and their activities because they allow the courts to tailor the exact remedy to the nature of the damage being caused. For example, it may be possible for the court to order a mandatory clean-up of a gradual chemical spillage, or prohibit the operation of a polluting activity.

The effect of injunctions can be particularly damaging for those upon whom they are imposed; for example, in the Irish case of *Bellew v Cement Ltd* (1948), an injunction closed the defendant's cement factory for three months. The financial and commercial implications of injunctions are potentially very damaging, but common law injunctions are awarded in few cases.

Interlocutory injunctions allow the courts to compel the defendant to take action to cease operating or remedy the damage being caused pending the arrangement of a full hearing.

Injunctions are restricted in that they may only be granted by the court when the activity complained of is substantial, and when it would be reasonable. In order to determine this, it is necessary to balance the interests of the polluting activity and the significance of its impact on the environment.

11.3.3 Abatement

The remedy of abatement dates back many years, although it is rarely used today and its use is not encouraged by the courts. It is an important remedy in statutory nuisance actions. Under the common law, abatement is known as the 'self-help' remedy because an occupier of land affected may take action to abate the damage.

The definition of abatement was given in *Blackstone's Commentaries on the Laws of England Book III*:

> And the reason why the law allows this private and summary method of doing one's self justice, is because injuries of this kind, which obstruct or annoy or such things as are of daily convenience and use, require an immediate remedy; and cannot wait for the slow progress of the ordinary forms of law.

This point was discussed in *Burton v Winters* (1993), in which it was stated that abatement was a summary remedy which was only justified in clear and simple cases where the nuisance or trespass would not justify the expense of legal proceedings, or in an emergency where an urgent remedy is required.

A simple example of abatement was given in *Smith v Giddy* (1904), in which it was held that the plaintiff was entitled to cut back the overhanging branches of his neighbour's ash and elm trees which were damaging the growth of his fruit trees.

11.4 GENERAL DEFENCES TO INTENTIONAL TORTS

An action in tort may fail if the defendant can rely on one of the general defences discussed below. There are also defences which are specific to particular torts, which will be discussed in relation to each tort.

11.4.1 Statutory authority

If the tort has been authorised by a statute, then this will provide a complete defence, and will not allow the injured party to recover damages. The exact application of the defence of statutory authority will depend on the statute in question.

The defendant must prove that the conduct complained of has arisen as an inevitable result of the activity authorised by the statute and that the defendant has exercised reasonable care in carrying out that activity.

The authority to carry out the activity must be expressly or impliedly authorised by the statute.

An example of implied authority was given in *Allen v Gulf Oil Refining Ltd* (1979). The Gulf Oil Refining Act 1965 authorised the compulsory purchase of land, by the defendants, for the construction of a refinery. It did not explicitly authorise the operation of the refinery. The plaintiff claimed that the operation of the refinery caused a nuisance. The House of Lords held that the defence must apply because the operation of the refinery was implied by the statute and was therefore authorised.

However, this defence may not succeed where the Act specifically envisages that an action in nuisance may be brought (see *Lloyds Bank v Guardian Assurance, Trollope and Colls Ltd* (1986)).

In the case of *Budden v BP Oil Ltd and Shell Oil Ltd* (1980), the Court of Appeal accepted an argument put forward by the defendants that they had complied with the relevant statutory provision, s 75(1) of the Control of Pollution Act (COPA) 1974, and accepted that the statutory standard establishes the common law standard. However, the question of whether an authorisation or consent from the Environment Agency constitutes statutory authority remains unclear.

11.4.2 *Volenti non fit injuria* (consent)

Meaning literally 'no injury is done to a person who consents', the defence of *volenti non fit injuria* can be pleaded by the defendant. In order for this defence to succeed, the claimant must voluntarily assume the risk. In order to do this, the claimant must be in position to make a choice as to whether or not to assume the risk and he or she must also know of the nature and extent of the risk.

11.4.3 Necessity

The defence of necessity is used where the defendant must choose between causing damage to the claimant's property and preventing some greater damage to the public or to a third party. This defence is effective in limited circumstances. Where the defence is raised, it can only succeed if the necessity did not arise from the defendant's negligence. It must also be proved that the defendant has acted in the public benefit, or for the protection of his own property. When determining the applicability of the defence, it is necessary for the courts to judge which of the possible outcomes would be preferred. The limitation attached to the defence of necessity is that the defendant must have acted as a reasonable man in order to avoid a greater danger.

11.4.4 Contributory negligence

Section 1 of the Law Reform (Contributory Negligence) Act 1945 provides:

> Where any person suffers damage as the result partly of his own fault and partly of the fault of any other person or persons, a claim in respect of that damage shall not be defeated by reason of the fault of the person suffering the damage, but the damages recoverable in respect thereof shall be reduced to such extent as the court thinks just and equitable having regard to the claimant's share in the responsibility for the damage.

The burden of proof is placed on the defendant to establish that the claimant contributed to the damage resulting in his injuries.

This allows the amount of damages to be reduced in line with the claimant's contribution to his or her own loss or injury. Damages are often reduced by anything from 10% to 75%.

11.5   TORTS

The common law actions which are of most relevance to the private regulation of environmental pollution are the torts of nuisance, trespass, negligence and the rule in *Rylands v Fletcher*. Of all the four torts, it is nuisance which appears to be the most popular ground of action. We consider below the elements of each tort, relevant defences and available remedies.

11.6   NUISANCE

Actions in nuisance may be divided into private nuisance, public nuisance and also statutory nuisance as contained in ss 79–82 of the EPA 1990, and supplemented by the Noise and Statutory Nuisance Act 1993. Statutory nuisance was dealt with in Chapter 9. A distinction must be made between the three types of nuisance because they are each significantly different from the others. The tort of private nuisance attempts to reconcile the competing interests of landowners; public nuisance is a crime which protects public rights, although an individual may bring an action where he or she has suffered damage over and above that suffered by the public generally; a statutory nuisance is one which is largely controlled by local authorities exercising their statutory powers.

Today, the tort of nuisance is recognised as the area of common law which has contributed most significantly to environmental protection.

11.7   PRIVATE NUISANCE

Private nuisance attempts to achieve a balance of competing rights of neighbours to use their property as they wish. It must be stressed that not every interference with another's use or enjoyment of land can constitute a private nuisance. In order to be actionable, the conduct complained of must constitute an unreasonable interference with an occupier's interest in the beneficial use of his or her land. Most nuisance actions relate to continuing unreasonable land uses.

11.7.1 Definition

Private nuisance was defined in *Read v Lyons & Co Ltd* (1947) as the 'unlawful interference with a person's use or enjoyment of land or some right over, or in connection with it'.

11.7.2 The two categories of private nuisance

Traditionally, private nuisance has been sub-divided into two categories:

(a) actions involving physical damage to the claimant's land; and

(b) actions involving interference with the claimant's use or enjoyment of land (often referred to as the 'sensibility' cases).

Typically, private nuisance actions, in an environmental context, relate to physical damage to property and chattels caused by the defendant's polluting emissions which come into contact with and damage the claimant's property. For example, pollutants may be blown by the wind onto the claimant's land. This is the most common type of nuisance action and it is generally the easiest to prove. Successful actions in private nuisance have been taken against defendants engaged in running various types of activities, reported in the law reports, including: an oil depot, a metal foundry, a brickworks, a cokeworks, a landfill site and a coal distribution depot. The phrase 'physical damage' includes damage to premises, land, vegetation, chattels and livestock.

Private nuisance actions also relate to cases in which there is no physical damage to property, but injury is caused to the claimant's use or enjoyment of his or her land, for example, cases concerning interference with property stemming from unreasonable amounts of noise, unpleasant smells, dust, vibration and infestations emanating from the defendant's land. In order to succeed, the claimant must prove that he or she has suffered 'inconvenience materially interfering with the ordinary physical comfort of human existence, not merely according to elegant or dainty modes and habits of living, but according to plain and sober and simple notions and habits obtaining among the English People' (see *Walter v Selfe* (1854)). The focus in these cases is on what the ordinary claimant would find intolerable and not what an especially sensitive (that is, hypersensitive) person would find unreasonable and/or intolerable.

11.7.3 The characteristic features of private nuisance

The tort of nuisance is characterised by the following features:

(a) the nuisance must arise from a continuous state of affairs and not a one-off, isolated event; however, a sufficiently continuous state of affairs arose out of a single firework display in *Crown River Cruises Ltd v Kimbolton Fireworks Ltd* (1996);

(b) the defendant's actions do not have to have been the original cause of the problem. An action may be brought even though the nuisance arises as a result of pre-existing conditions on the defendant's land, for example, historic contamination. The nuisance must emanate from the defendant's land;

(c) the nuisance must affect land belonging to the claimant or in which the claimant has a proprietary interest. In *Hunter and Others v Canary Wharf Ltd* (1997), the House of Lords rejected the proposition that occupiers of property, other than owners and tenants, could sue in private nuisance. This decision has been followed in *Blackburn v ARC Ltd* (1998), in which the plaintiff's common law wife, who had no proprietary interest in the plaintiff's house, had her claim in nuisance rejected;

(d) the claimant must prove that the damage sustained, whether in the form of physical damage to person, premises, or chattels or personal discomfort, has been caused by the alleged nuisance. In many environmental pollution cases, it may be difficult to prove a causal link between the nuisance and the damage sustained by the claimant;

(e) the type of damage sustained by the claimant must have been reasonably foreseeable at the time when the actions which caused the damage occurred (see *Cambridge Water Co Ltd v Eastern Counties Leather plc* (1994)). The plaintiff water company in the *Cambridge Water* case failed in its nuisance action because, at the time polluting chemicals escaped from the defendant's tannery, it was not reasonably foreseeable that solvents could migrate through sub-strata over several years and travel significant distances before contaminating the aquifer from which the water company abstracted drinking water;

(f) where the nuisance causes personal discomfort, as opposed to physical damage, the characteristics of the neighbourhood where the alleged nuisance occurs is taken into account (*St Helens Smelting v Tipping* (1865)). Residents living in an established industrial area will be expected to be more tolerant than people living in a purely residential area;

(g) nuisance does not enable a hypersensitive claimant to obtain redress in circumstances in which the ordinary reasonable person would not find the defendant's activities to be a nuisance;

(h) the grant of planning permission will not confer immunity upon the defendant for liability in nuisance (*Allen v Gulf Oil Refining* (1981)) except to the extent that planning permission for a major development, when implemented, changes the character of the area (*Gillingham BC v Medway (Chatham) Dock Co Ltd* (1993) and *Wheeler v JJ Saunders Ltd* (1996)). Similarly the grant of, and compliance with, a licence to pollute issued by the Environment Agency will not provide the defendant with immunity from a common law action in nuisance;

(i) where a nuisance is found to exist, the claimant will generally be awarded damages to place him or her in the position he or she would have been in had the nuisance not occurred. However, where the defendant is liable for a nuisance which he or she did not originally cause, he or she will only be expected to have taken reasonable steps to remedy the situation in the light of his or her means. No remedy is available in nuisance for personal injury.

11.7.4 Reasonableness

The key issue in an action based on nuisance is that the court must judge whether the defendant is using his or her property reasonably. In *Saunders-Clark v Grosvenor Mansions and D'Allesandri* (1900), Buckley J stated the importance of this requirement of the tort of nuisance:

> ... the court must consider whether the defendant is using his property reasonably or not. If he is using it reasonably, there is nothing which at law can be considered a nuisance: but if he is not using it reasonably ... then the plaintiff is entitled to relief.

Whilst giving consideration to the question of whether the defendant is using his or her property reasonably, the court attempts to balance the competing interests of the claimant and the defendant. On the one hand, the defendant has a right to conduct activities on his or her land as he or she pleases, and on the other hand the claimant has a right to use and enjoy his or her property without an unreasonable amount of interference. The court must therefore determine whether, on the facts, the defendant is using his or her property unreasonably. In balancing the competing interests of the claimant and the defendant, the courts pay particular attention to the following factors:

(a) locality;

(b) duration;

(c) sensitivity of the claimant;

(d) intention of the defendant;

(e) the defendant's use of best practicable means (BPM) to minimise the nuisance;

(f) the foreseeability of the type of harm or damage complained of;

(g) the utility of the defendant's conduct.

Each of these is discussed below.

11.7.4.1 Locality

The character of the local environment is a key factor which the courts have regard to in the 'sensibility' nuisance cases (otherwise referred to as amenity damage, intangible damage or personal discomfort). These are nuisance actions which do not involve physical damage but the claimant claims that the defendant's actions have caused injury to the use or enjoyment of the claimant's property. As a general rule, a claimant who lives in a highly industrialised or urbanised neighbourhood must accept higher levels of noise and air pollution than might exist in a rural area. The classic statement of the 'locality doctrine' appears in the case of *Sturges v Bridgman* (1879): 'What would be a nuisance in Belgrave Square would not necessarily be so in Bermondsey.'

The locality doctrine does have limits. For example, in *Rushmer v Polsue and Alfieri Ltd* (1906), the House of Lords upheld the grant of an injunction to the plaintiff to stop the operation of the defendant's printing press during the night. The injunction was granted despite the existence of many other printing presses in the area also operating at night. The court expressed the limits of the locality doctrine as follows:

> It does not follow that because I live, say, in the manufacturing part of Sheffield I cannot complain if a steam-hammer is introduced next door, and so worked as to render sleep at night almost impossible, although previously to its introduction my house was a reasonably comfortable abode, having regard to the local standard; and it would be no answer to say that the steam-hammer is of the most modern approved pattern and is reasonably worked. In short, if a substantial addition is found as fact in any particular case, it is no answer to say that the neighbourhood is noisy, and that the defendant's machinery is of first class character.

Also of relevance to the locality doctrine is the decision in *Gillingham BC v Medway (Chatham) Dock Co Ltd* (1993). This case concerned the grant of planning permission to transform a former naval dockyard into a commercial port. The development generated high levels of heavy goods vehicle traffic throughout day and night which disturbed residents living adjacent to the roads giving access to the port. The local residents persuaded their local authority to take an action in public nuisance. The court held that the grant of planning permission had changed the character of the neighbourhood and therefore any allegation of nuisance was to be judged by reference to what was acceptable in a commercial, rather than a residential, area. The decision in the *Gillingham* case was subsequently clarified, by the Court of Appeal, in *Wheeler v JJ Saunders Ltd* (1996). Planning permission had been granted for development consisting of pig rearing units. A nuisance action was commenced with regard to smells emanating from the pig unit. The court rejected the proposition that the grant of planning permission automatically operates to create a defence to a nuisance action based on the grant of planning permission changing the character of the area. The plaintiff was awarded an injunction. The court sought to limit the application of the *Gillingham* case to developments which concerned 'strategic' planning developments (major developments). In the context of a planning decision relating to a commercial port, interference with private rights had been weighed against the public interest, and the level of interference was found to be acceptable. The decision clarified that it is the implementation of planning permission, rather than the grant of permission, which changes the character of the area.

11.7.4.2   Sensitivity of the claimant

Where the claimant is deemed to be abnormally sensitive to the defendant's activities, there can be no actionable nuisance. In *Robinson v Kilvert* (1889), the plaintiff claimed that heat from the defendant's property, which was situated below the plaintiff's premises in the basement, was having an adverse effect on the brown paper stored in the plaintiff's premises. It was held that there was no actionable nuisance because:

> ... a man who carries on an exceptionally delicate trade cannot complain because it is injured by his neighbour doing something lawful on his property, if it is something which would not injure anything but an exceptionally delicate trade.

The rationale behind this principle is consistent with the law of nuisance, namely that each owner of property should have a right reasonably to use and enjoy his land.

A further example of abnormal sensitivity was given in the case of *Heath v Brighton* (1908). In this case, the vicar of a church sought an injunction to restrain the noise from the defendant's power station. The vicar failed because the noise had neither interrupted services nor had it affected attendance at church; it merely irritated the vicar.

11.7.4.3   Duration of the nuisance

The ability to obtain redress in a nuisance action depends, in part, upon the claimant being able to prove that the activity alleged to constitute a nuisance is a continuing problem. In *Bolton v Stone* (1951), the Court of Appeal rejected a nuisance action relating to the activities of the defendant cricket club because the plaintiff could only establish that cricket balls had been hit out of the ground six times in 30 years.

There are exceptions where the application of this rule could be deemed unreasonable. An example of such unreasonableness was given in *De Keyser's Royal Hotel Ltd v Spicer Bros Ltd* (1914). The case was brought on the grounds that the defendant's building operations were so loud that guests at the hotel were unable to sleep and after-dinner speakers were unable to make themselves heard. It was held that the defendants were not carrying out the operations in a reasonable and proper manner.

Single incidents may give rise to a nuisance action. In *British Celanese v AH Hunt (Capacitors) Ltd* (1969), the defendant stored metal foil on its property. Foil was blown onto neighbouring property causing damage to an electricity sub-station. The court held that an isolated incident could create an actionable nuisance (see also *Crown River Cruises Ltd v Kimbolton Fireworks Ltd* (1996)).

11.7.4.4   Intention of the defendant

The defendant's motives may also be a factor in determining the reasonable use of property. In *Hollywood Silver Fox Farm v Emmett* (1936), the defendant's malicious intent to disrupt the plaintiff's fox farm by discharging a shotgun during the mating season was held to be an actionable nuisance. Environmental malice includes the deliberate making of noise to antagonise neighbours in neighbour disputes.

11.7.4.5 Utility of the defendant's conduct

If the defendant is carrying out operations which provide a general benefit to the whole community, then the nuisance will be more reasonable or justifiable than if his or her motive is purely selfish or malicious. There is clearly a link between the defendant's motives and the utility of his or her conduct. Whilst the courts do take account of the social utility of the defendant's activities, it appears that this factor is not a key consideration (*Kennaway v Thompson* (1981) and *Blackburn v ARC Ltd* (1998)).

11.7.4.6 The defendant's use of best practicable means to minimise the nuisance

The defendant's use of best available abatement technology to minimise the impact of the alleged nuisance upon the claimant will be taken into account by the court and will be given appropriate weight. Utilisation of the best practicable means (including 'best available techniques not entailing excessive costs' and 'best available techniques') by the defendant does not provide an automatic defence. The courts will have regard to the severity of the impact of the defendant's activities upon the claimant and whether any further preventive action could have been taken by the defendant. Thus, a defendant who is complying with the terms of a licence to pollute may not necessarily be able to defeat a nuisance action. In *Read v J Lyons and Co Ltd* (1947), the House of Lords, in a nuisance action in respect of an explosion at a munitions factory, held that if a man commits a nuisance, it is no answer to his neighbour's complaint that he took the utmost care not to commit the nuisance. Even if a factory has been operated with reasonable care, it is still open to the court to find that the defendant's activities constitute a nuisance.

11.7.4.7 The foreseeability of the type of harm or damage complained of

It is necessary for the claimant to prove that the type of damage caused to his or her use or enjoyment of land was *foreseeable at the time the relevant damage occurred*. The leading case on this issue is *Cambridge Water Co Ltd v Eastern Counties Leather plc* (1994). The House of Lords, in rejecting the plaintiff's private nuisance action, held that liability depended upon the foreseeability of the relevant type of damage occurring. The damage in this particular case consisted of the presence of polluting solvents in an aquifer from which the plaintiff abstracted drinking water. Although it was proved that the solvents had emanated from the defendant's property, the court held that at the time the spillages of solvents had occurred, it was not foreseeable that the escape of those solvents would result in damage to the aquifer.

11.7.4.8 Human rights

In *Marcic v Thames Water Utilities Ltd* (2002), the claimant brought a successful private nuisance action against his sewerage services provider based on a breach of

Art 8 of the European Convention on Human Rights (right to respect for a person's home and private life).

11.7.4.9 Public interest

The tort of nuisance continues to be a fertile basis of civil actions. In *Dennis v Ministry of Defence* (2003), the claimants owned an historic mansion located close to an RAF base at Wittering. The base was used for jump jet pilot training and the noise of aircraft was very loud (an average of 77–113 db(A)). The claimants sued the MOD in nuisance and Buckley J found that the operation of the jets constituted a very serious interference with the enjoyment of the claimant's property. The MOD put forward the following arguments (unsuccessfully) to justify its activities: (a) training pilots for the defence of the realm was one of the ordinary usages of mankind – the court held that the generation of such extreme noise was not an ordinary use of land; (b) defence of the realm was a public interest of a different and greater order than commercial interests (that is, the public interest 'trumped' the private commercial interests of the claimants). Buckley J declined to attempt a general answer to the question of the effect of public interest in a nuisance action; however, if the public interest were automatically to prevail (when balancing the competing interests of the parties) over private interests, then the claimants would have no remedy at all and would suffer unjust damage for the benefit of all. Buckley J was clearly of the opinion that public interest considerations were relevant to the question of the appropriate remedy (rather than whether the activities complained of constituted a nuisance). Thus, whilst the public interest might dictate that jump jet training continue, it was just that the claimants receive compensation; (c) the MOD submitted that the character of the neighbourhood was to be assessed in the context of the airbase as an established feature of the locality. This was rejected by the court as otherwise the defendant could change the character of the neighbourhood over time and create a nuisance with impunity; and (d) the MOD's argument that it had acquired a prescriptive right was also rejected because such a right was too uncertain.

The court also upheld the claimant's claim based on breach of their human rights (Art 8 – right to home and family life, and Art 1, Protocol 1 – peaceful enjoyment of possessions). The court awarded £950,000 damages based on property 'blight', loss of potential revenue from the commercial exploitation of the property, and loss of amenity.

11.7.5 Who can bring an action in private nuisance?

It is a long established principle that, in order to sue in nuisance, the claimant must have an interest in the land affected (see *Hunter and Others v Canary Wharf Ltd* (1997)). This will include the occupier of the land, a tenant in possession, and it can extend to those with a variety of other legal interests in land (such as a squatter with possessory title).

11.7.6 Against whom can a nuisance action be brought?

Action can be brought against a variety of parties, not only the 'polluter', but also those who allowed or authorised the pollution or environmental damage.

A nuisance action can be brought against the following:

(a) the creator of the nuisance: the party who creates the nuisance may always be sued. This is the case whether or not the creator of the nuisance is the occupier of the land at the time (see *Thompson v Gibson* (1841));

(b) the occupier of premises: the occupier will be liable in two situations:

  (i) if he or she creates the nuisance; or

  (ii) if the nuisance is caused by his or her servant or agent.

  In *Leakey v National Trust* (1980), it was stated that if the nuisance was not created by the occupier, he or she is only expected to do what is reasonable in the circumstances to prevent or minimise a known risk to his or her neighbour;

(c) the landlord: there is a generally recognised rule that a landlord will generally not be liable because he or she is not in occupation of the property and has no knowledge of the nuisance, unless he or she has authorised the nuisance, as in *Tetley v Chitty* (1986). In that case, the local authority, as landlord, was held liable for the noise caused by go-karting activities because the authority knew, or should have known, of the nuisance before the property was let.

11.7.7 Defences

11.7.7.1 *Statutory authority*

This defence is only available to bodies exercising statutory powers whose activities are alleged to be causing a nuisance. To be able to take advantage of this defence, the defendant must be able to show that it did not cause any unnecessary inconvenience in the way in which it carried out the activities authorised by the legislation. The court will take into account the methods and equipment used by the defendant to complete the works. It will also have regard to the scale of the development, its social utility and the timescale within which it took the defendant to complete the development. In *Allen v Gulf Oil Refining Ltd* (1981), a private Act of Parliament provided the defendant oil company with statutory authority to acquire land in Milford Haven for the purpose of building an oil refinery. Once the refinery was operational, local residents brought a nuisance action in regard to the smells, noise and vibration generated by the defendant's activities. The plaintiffs argued that the defence of statutory authority did not apply in this case because the relevant Act did not specifically refer to, and therefore authorise, the operation of the plant in a manner which created a nuisance. The House of Lords rejected this submission and held that the Act conferred an immunity for all acts inevitably flowing from the authority to build the refinery. The plaintiffs could only succeed if they could establish that the nuisance complained of was much greater than was necessary or where the defendant had carried out its activities negligently. In short, redress is only possible if it can be proved that the defendant failed to exercise reasonable care to minimise the nuisance. An example of a case in which the defendant failed to exercise reasonable care is *Tate & Lyle Industries Ltd v GLC* (1983). The defendant local authority constructed a ferry terminal with the benefit of statutory authority, but the development caused the silting up of the River Thames around the plaintiff sugar refiners' river jetties. The plaintiff sued in nuisance to recover the £50,000 it had incurred in dredging the river in order to maintain access to its jetties. The court found in favour of the plaintiff but awarded only 75% of its claim on the ground that even if the defendant had exercised reasonable care in the construction of the terminal, some dredging would still have been necessary.

Whilst it is clear that special Acts of Parliament will entitle a defendant to claim the defence of statutory authority, it seems that other legislative provisions, such as the grant of a pollution licence by the Environment Agency under the EPA 1990, will not, in most cases, entitle the defendant to the defence of statutory authority. In *Wheeler v JJ Saunders Ltd* (1996), Gibson LJ stated that 'the court should be slow to acquiesce in the extinction of private rights without compensation as a result of administrative decisions which could not be appealed and were difficult to challenge'. Gibson LJ went on to concede, however, that there might be instances where a regulatory body may legitimately override private rights.

One recent case to consider private nuisance in an environmental context is *Blackburn v ARC Ltd* (1998). The case concerned a landfill site which was alleged to be causing a nuisance due to (a) litter escaping from the site, (b) odour problems relating to the failure of the defendant properly to cover over the waste and also from landfill gases, and (c) noise from lorry traffic, site machinery and gas flare.

The High Court held that the defence of statutory authority only applied if the statutory authority changed the character of the area or there was direct statutory authorisation for the development. In this case, there was no change in character because the relevant planning permission and waste management licence were of a temporary nature. The plaintiff's claim would fail if the nuisance would have inevitably resulted from the authorised activities. However, in this case, the nuisance was not inevitable and could have been avoided if the defendant had operated its site properly. The court went on to hold that where the defendant's activities did inevitably lead to the release of odours and gas in circumstances where the release could not have been avoided, in order to establish nuisance, the plaintiff must prove that the defendant's use of land was not a reasonable use. It was clear that the use of land as a waste tip which generated odours and gases was not a reasonable use of land. If the odours and gas were more than must be tolerated in modern living conditions, the defendant would be liable. Additionally, the court held that the principle of 'give and take', applying to the activities of neighbouring landowners (and referred to by Lord Goff in *Cambridge Water*), depended upon the defendant's use of land being a reasonable use, but, in this case, the defendant's activities 'fell well outside any latitude which the law may have allowed'.

11.7.7.2 The defendant takes reasonable precautions to minimise the nuisance

The courts make a distinction between those cases in which the defendant is the original cause of the nuisance and those cases in which the defendant acquires land and continues a pre-existing nuisance. In the former case, the fact that the defendant took all reasonable care to minimise the nuisance will not provide a defence because liability is strict. In *Read v Lyons* (1947), Lord Symons stated: 'If a man commits a legal nuisance, it is no answer to his injured neighbour that he took the utmost care not to commit it. There the liability is strict.' In the latter case, in which the defendant subsequently becomes aware that a nuisance is being caused and takes all reasonable precautions to minimise the nuisance, then the defendant will have a defence.

11.7.7.3 The claimant came to the nuisance

It is not a defence for a defendant to argue that the claimant exposed himself to a nuisance by moving to it. This is relevant to the owners of factories which, at some point after construction, are surrounded by residential development. The law does not prevent residential property owners from taking action with regard to nuisance caused by the operation of factories. The leading case on this issue is *Bliss v Hall* (1838), in which the defendant established and operated a business as a tallow chandler. Three years later, the plaintiff moved into the neighbouring property and commenced a nuisance action against the defendant with regard to the fumes produced by the tallow works. Tindall CJ stated: 'The plaintiff came to the house he occupies with all the rights which the common law affords, and one of them is the right to wholesome air. Unless the defendant shows a prescriptive right to carry on his business in the particular the plaintiff is entitled to judgment.' Awareness of the possibility that conflicts might arise between competing property owners will not be allowed to interfere with the operation of the town and country planning system. The High Court held in *R v Exeter County Council ex p JL Thomas and Co Ltd* (1991) that a planning authority may grant planning permission for development which may give rise to complaints and legal action against the owners of existing development by owners of new developments.

11.7.7.4 One of many polluters

It is no defence to a nuisance action for the defendant to argue that the defendant's contribution to the nuisance suffered by the claimant is so insignificant that it is not actionable. The authority for this principle is *Blair v Deakin* (1887), a case in which effluent from several upstream defendants created a nuisance for a downstream factory owner. This principle should be viewed with some caution since the means to detect, measure, and identify pollutants is now very much more advanced than when this case was decided.

11.7.7.5 Prescription

The likelihood of this defence succeeding in most circumstances is remote. Whilst, in theory, it is possible to acquire an easement to pollute, in practice this defence is very difficult to establish. To succeed, the right to pollute which is claimed must be lawful (that is, not a discharge in breach of the conditions of a pollution licence), which is openly exercised, which continues for a period of at least 20 years, and which is exercised without the permission of the person against whom the right is being acquired. In *Sturges v Bridgman* (1879), the defendant had operated noisy machinery on his land for over 20 years. An adjoining landowner, a doctor, extended his premises by constructing a consulting room close to the boundary with the defendant's property. The doctor then commenced, and succeeded in, an action in nuisance against the defendant due to the unreasonable level of noise generated by the defendant's machines. The court rejected the defendant's argument that he had acquired an easement authorising the nuisance. The time from which the prescriptive right in this case was calculated was the time, or point, at which the nuisance began, and the time ran from the date of construction of the consulting rooms.

11.7.8 Remedies

11.7.8.1 Injunctions

To succeed in obtaining an injunction, the claimant must have a strong case. The courts are reluctant to grant injunctions unless there is good evidence that the defendant's activities are having a significant and adverse impact upon the claimant which justifies restricting, totally or partially, the defendant's activities which are causing the nuisance. The following cases illustrate the circumstances in which a claim for an injunction may succeed or fail. In *Halsey v Esso Petroleum Co Ltd* (1961), the plaintiff successfully obtained an injunction relating to the noise from the defendant's boilers and vehicle movements to and from the plant. In *Allison v Merton, Sutton and Wandsworth AHA* (1975), the plaintiff was granted an injunction to restrain the noise from the defendant's hospital boilers which interfered with the plaintiff's sleep and caused feelings of depression falling short of a clinical depressive illness. In *AG v Gastonia Coaches Ltd* (1977), the plaintiff successfully obtained an injunction against the defendant coach company to restrain a nuisance consisting of diesel odours and noise disturbance caused by the defendant 'revving' coach engines in a residential street. In *Blackburn v ARC Ltd* (1998), the plaintiff applied for an injunction to close down the defendant's landfill site which was alleged to be causing a nuisance due to litter, odour and vehicle movements. The landfill site only had a further three years of 'life' left and the court declined to grant an injunction closing the site down. Whilst the court accepted that the primary remedy for continuing nuisances was an injunction, it was a discretionary remedy and in the circumstances of this case damages provided adequate compensation for the diminution in value of the plaintiff's property. The court stated that it would be open to the plaintiff to seek a further injunction at any time in the future if a repetition of the serious failures of the past were to recur.

11.7.8.2 Compensation

Compensation may be awarded to the claimant with regard to damage to property and chattels. The position regarding the recovery of compensation for personal injury caused by nuisance is unclear and therefore the claimant ought to include a negligence claim to cover any personal injury.

11.7.8.3 Sensibility claims

An award of damages is the norm in such cases and the sum awarded will reflect the severity and persistence of the nuisance (see *Blackburn v ARC Ltd* (1998)).

11.7.8.4 Loss of profits

In contrast to negligence actions, in which pure economic loss is not recoverable, once damage has been proved in a nuisance action, liability is strict. In appropriate cases, loss of profits are recoverable. In *Blackburn v ARC Ltd* (1998), the plaintiff included a claim for loss of profits relating to renovation works carried out at the plaintiff's home. The court rejected the claim on the basis that such losses were not a foreseeable consequence of the particular nuisance. Although the loss of profits claim failed, the plaintiff did recover £25,000 in respect of the diminution of the value of his home.

11.7.8.5 Exemplary damages

The circumstances in which exemplary damages may be claimed are very limited. The claimant will succeed if the defendant has deliberately interfered with the claimant's property rights and has cynically calculated that his or her interference will produce a financial gain greater than the cost of the damage to the claimant (see *AB v South West Water Services Ltd* (1993)).

11.8   PUBLIC NUISANCE

The tort of public nuisance shares many of the elements of private nuisance, although there are several distinguishing factors. It is also possible for the nuisance to be actionable as both a public and private nuisance.

11.8.1 Definition

Public nuisance was defined in the case of *AG v PYA Quarries* (1957):

> A public nuisance is one which materially affects the reasonable comfort and convenience of life of a class of Her Majesty's subjects who come within the sphere or neighbourhood of its operation; the question whether the number of persons affected is sufficient to constitute a class is one of fact in every case and it is sufficient to show that a representative cross-section of that class has been so affected for an injunction to issue.

11.8.2 The characteristic features of public nuisance

Actions in public nuisance have the advantage that no interest in land is required by a claimant in order to commence an action. The House of Lords decision in *Hunter and Others v Canary Wharf Ltd* (1997), with its rejection of private nuisance actions by occupiers of property who have no legal rights as owners or tenants of property, is likely to increase interest in the use of public nuisance by licensees who cannot otherwise sue in nuisance.

Public nuisance must affect a wide class of the public. In contrast to private nuisance, public nuisance is a crime and this enables the Attorney General or a local authority to prosecute the defendant. An action in public nuisance may be brought by an individual or a group of citizens provided that he, she or they can establish that he, she or they have suffered special damage (damage over and above that which is suffered by the general public). Typically, public nuisance actions might relate to:

(a) repeated exposure to offensive smells generated by landfill sites or incinerators;

(b) intolerable noise created by a factory which is operating 24 hours a day and disturbs many people; or

(c) widespread contamination of water supplies posing a threat to the health of a large number of people.

Public nuisance is founded on the commission of an actionable wrong which has a material effect on a large number of people. Some guidance on the numbers of people who must be affected to justify an action in public nuisance is provided by the Docklands case (*Hunter v Canary Wharf* (1997)). In that action, approximately 600 people constituted a sufficiently wide class to mount an action relating to disturbance caused by construction dust and interference with TV reception. In contrast, in *R v Johnson* (1996), the Court of Appeal held that 13 women who had received harassing telephone calls were a 'class' upon which a nuisance action could be founded.

The case of *R v South West Water Authority* (1991) was brought following the water pollution incident at Camelford, Cornwall, which attracted a considerable amount of press coverage at the time.

In July 1988, 20 tonnes of aluminium sulphate was pumped into the wrong tank at a water treatment works. Although the alarm was raised almost immediately, remedial action was not taken for several hours, during which time there were reports that the water smelt and tasted foul, that it was black, it burnt mouths and hair and stuck fingers together. It was later reported that the water had caused considerable personal injury in the form of hair loss, nail deformities, rheumatism, diarrhoea and memory loss.

The action was brought as criminal proceedings against South West Water Authority. The authority was found guilty of committing a public nuisance by supplying water contaminated with aluminium sulphate which endangered the health or comfort of the public. The authority was fined £10,000 and ordered to pay costs of £25,000.

11.8.3 Who can bring an action in public nuisance?

Public nuisance actions may be commenced by members of the public, a local authority, or the Attorney General. Public nuisance actions will, as a general rule, only be commenced where the relevant local authority is unwilling to take action (using its statutory nuisance powers). If a member of the public commences an action, he or she must have suffered substantial damage (that is greater than that suffered by the public in general). The damage must also be of a type which was reasonably foreseeable. In *Halsey v Esso Petroleum Co Ltd* (1961), a public nuisance action was possible because oily smuts had damaged vehicles parked in the public highway, as opposed to being parked on private property. In addition, the noise of heavy vehicles travelling to and from the refinery on the public highway also justified an action in public nuisance. The special damage sustained by Halsey was damage to the paintwork of his motor car.

A public nuisance action may be commenced by a claimant where interference with a public right also violates the claimant's private rights. In *Tate & Lyle Industries Ltd v GLC* (1983), an action in public nuisance was possible because not only did the defendant's construction work interfere with public navigation rights, but it also interfered with the plaintiff's right of access to its river jetties.

Section 222 of the Local Government Act 1972 provides local authorities with a discretionary power to commence public nuisance actions. This power is used infrequently due to the preference of local authorities for using their statutory nuisance powers (see Chapter 9). In contrast to private nuisance, the use of best practicable means to abate a public nuisance is a complete defence to a statutory nuisance action. This may be a factor in the decision by the public to commence a public nuisance action rather than relying upon the local authority. Also, if a local authority does commence a public nuisance action, aggrieved citizens will not be able to claim compensation for the damage they have suffered. Worse still, if a local authority fails to establish that a public nuisance exists, it will not be able to claim injunctive relief and aggrieved citizens may be left without a remedy.

The Attorney General is entitled to take action to redress public wrongs. In the event that an individual who wishes to commence an action in public nuisance cannot prove that he or she has suffered special damage, he or she may request either the Attorney General or the local authority to take action.

11.8.4 Against whom can the action in public nuisance be brought?

As in private nuisance, an action may be brought against the following:

(a) the creator of the nuisance;

(b) the occupier of the premises;

(c) the landlord.

11.9 DEFENCES IN PUBLIC NUISANCE AND PRIVATE NUISANCE ACTIONS

The following are defences in public and private nuisance actions:

(a) statutory authority;

(b) contributory negligence;

(c) prescription (only available in private nuisance) – the law will not allow an action in nuisance to succeed if the state of affairs which constitutes the actionable nuisance has continued for more than 20 years. For this defence to succeed, the claimant must know that the actionable nuisance has run from the beginning of this 20 year period (*Sturges v Bridgman* (1879));

(d) consent of the claimant – in circumstances in which the claimant has consented, either expressly or impliedly, to the nuisance, the defendant cannot be liable, unless there is some negligence on his or her part (*Kiddle v City Business Properties Ltd* (1942));

(e) ignorance – ignorance of the nuisance can only be classed as a defence if it is not a result of the defendant's failure to act with reasonable skill and care in order to discover the nuisance;

(f) other defences – many other defences have been raised, although few have been successful; for example, it would be no defence for the defendant to argue that the claimant had 'come to the nuisance', nor could the defendant argue that the activity is of some use to the public in general, although it may be an issue which is considered in determining whether the defendant's use of the land is reasonable.

11.10 REMEDIES IN NUISANCE ACTIONS

Remedies in nuisance actions are:

(a) abatement;

(b) injunction;

(c) damages.

Damages are certainly available for physical damage to the claimant's property, although it is doubtful if damages can be awarded for personal injury. Some commentators feel that an action in negligence may be the only way to claim damages for personal injury. It is also possible that damages for economic loss may be available, although there is no clear judicial guidance on this point.

11.11 NEGLIGENCE

The largest volume of civil compensation claims are based upon the tort of negligence, but this tort has limited utility in an environmental context.

Negligence actions have advantages and disadvantages. The claimant does not require an interest in land in order to sue and damages are available to compensate personal injuries. Conversely, injunctions are not available, pure economic loss and exemplary damages are not recoverable, the negligent actions of the defendant's independent contractors may shield the defendant from liability, and in contrast to other torts, fault must be proved. A negligence claim may be the only option for some claimants who suffer damage but have no interest in the property which would enable them to commence actions in nuisance, trespass or the rule in *Rylands v Fletcher* (for example, a guest in a hotel who is poisoned by fumes emanating from a factory located adjacent to the hotel).

11.11.1 Definition

> Negligence is the omission to do something which a reasonable man, guided upon those considerations which ordinarily regulate the conduct of human affairs, would do, or doing something which a prudent and reasonable man would not do [*Blythe v Birmingham Waterworks Co* (1856) 11 Exch 781].

In order to establish negligence, the claimant must prove the following:

(a) the defendant owes the claimant a duty of care;

(b) the defendant breaches that duty; and

(c) the breach causes damage to the claimant.

11.11.2 Duty of care

The general duty of care in negligence was established in *Donoghue v Stevenson* (1932). The general principle behind the duty of care is the 'neighbour principle' –

meaning that 'you must take reasonable care to avoid acts or omissions which you can reasonably foresee would be likely to injure your neighbour'. Neighbours are defined as 'persons who are so closely and directly affected by my act that I ought reasonably to have them in contemplation as being so affected when I am directing my mind to the acts or omissions which are being called into question'.

The neighbour principle has, in recent times, been given a restrictive judicial interpretation. The judiciary generally favour an incremental approach (that is, they look to previous cases to ascertain whether a duty of care already exists) to the development of the law of negligence. In novel factual situations, the courts apply the approach set out in the case of *Caparo Industries v Dickman* (1990) in order to determine whether a duty of care is owed by the defendant to the claimant.

Three criteria must be established:

(a) the harm must be reasonably foreseeable (that is, an objective test of what the reasonable man would foresee and not what the defendant might foresee);

(b) the claimant and defendant must have a sufficiently proximate relationship; and

(c) it must be just, fair and reasonable to impose a duty of care.

The courts currently appear to be reluctant to take a principled, as opposed to an incremental, approach to the development of the law by upholding claims which support the imposition of a duty of care in novel environmental contexts. This is especially true where a claimant seeks to make a regulatory agency liable for loss caused by a failure (omission) to warn the claimant of danger (see *Dear v Thames Water Ltd* (1992), but contrast the decisions in *Barnes v Irwell Valley Water Board* (1939) and *Scott-Whitehead v NCB* (1987)).

11.11.3 Breach of duty of care

Once a duty of care has been established, it is necessary to go on to establish that the defendant was in breach of this duty of care and, further, that his or her breach resulted in damage to the claimant. In order to determine whether there has been a breach of the duty of care, it is necessary to look at the conduct of the defendant and ask whether he or she has achieved the standard of care that is necessary if he or she is not to be liable. The standard used is that of the 'reasonable man'. This is an objective standard and as such no concessions are made for individual weaknesses. The courts will look at the following factors to determine whether the defendant has acted as a reasonable man:

(a) the likelihood of harm;

(b) the seriousness of the risk;

(c) the end to be achieved;

(d) the cost and practicability of avoiding the risk.

Where the duty of care relates to a specialised area, then the duty of care expected is one which would be expected from someone with those skills in the same profession, as was decided in *Bolam v Friern Hospital Management Committee* (1957). Where industrial practices are concerned, one must look to standards which are deemed reasonable by the industry concerned.

11.11.4 Foreseeable damage arising from the breach of the duty of care

An action in negligence can only be brought where the negligence has caused, or contributed to, personal injury or damage to property. The courts usually use the 'but for' test to determine whether the defendant's breach of duty was the cause of the damage (that is, would the claimant's loss or injury have occurred in any event and irrespective of the defendant's negligence?). The classic illustration of the 'but for' test is *Barnett v Chelsea and Kensington Hospital Management Committee* (1969), in which a person, suffering from arsenic poisoning, attended hospital but would have died even if the hospital had not been negligent in its diagnosis. The 'but for' test and its limitations are examined below (see also the tort texts listed in the further reading section at the end of the chapter).

Damage must also be reasonably foreseeable, as the defendant will not be liable for the unforeseen consequences of his or her negligent act. (See, further, *Overseas Tankship (UK) Ltd v Morts Dock & Engineering Co Ltd (The Wagon Mound)* (1961).)

Following the House of Lords decision in *Cambridge Water Co Ltd v Eastern Counties Leather plc* (1994), foreseeability of the relevant *type of harm* or damage is a necessary prerequisite of liability in negligence, nuisance and the rule in *Rylands v Fletcher*. The test of foreseeability in the *Cambridge Water* case was based on what the reasonable supervisor, who was overseeing the operation of the defendant's tannery, would have foreseen as the consequence of repeated spillages of solvents over a prolonged period of time. The court held that, at the material time, the supervisor might reasonably have foreseen that repeated spillages of solvents, in relatively small quantities, might result in solvent fumes affecting the breathing of the defendant's employees, but not contamination of groundwaters. Little was known about the migration of chemicals in sub-surface strata at the relevant time the spillages were occurring and the supervisor could not reasonably have foreseen the relevant type of harm which actually occurred.

It should be noted that in recent years, greater emphasis has been placed on the prudence of businesses employing risk assessments to identify pollution risks associated with their activities. The harmful practices which formed the basis of the *Cambridge Water* litigation occurred in the late 1970s at a time when industrial practice regarding the identification of pollution risks tended to be reactive. It was not uncommon to find that industry would do little to address pollution risks until the regulator produced guidance on specific environmental risks which it had identified. This is no longer an acceptable practice (see *Thompson v Smiths Shiprepairers (North Shields) Ltd* (1984)) as employers and others have an obligation to keep up to date with best practice.

11.11.5 What counts as 'damage'

Environmental compensation claims often stem from actions based on the tort of nuisance; however, one significant property-related negligence action arose in *Blue Circle Industries plc v Ministry of Defence* (1998). This case concerned a claim for compensation arising out of a delayed sale of the claimant's property (the original purchaser dropped out when it realised that the property was contaminated) caused by flood waters emanating from MOD property carrying with them radioactive substances. Those substances became mixed with (and therefore formed part of) the defendant's soil (see the judgment of Aldous LJ).

Although the level of radioactive contamination posed no threat to human health, the level present in the defendant's land exceeded the level permitted by the Nuclear Installations Act (NIA) 1965. This aspect of the case is similar to that of *Cambridge Water v Eastern Counties Leather*, in which the House of Lords accepted that the presence of solvents in controlled waters in concentrations exceeding those permitted by the EC Drinking Water Directive could constitute actionable damage (see Carnwath LJ's judgment in *Blue Circle*).

In allowing the claimant's action for damages under the NIA 1965, the court drew attention to the physical damage to Blue Circle's land which constituted an adverse change in the property's usefulness and value (see the article by Maria Lee referred to at the end of this chapter).

In the comparable case of *Merlin v British Nuclear Fuels plc* (1990), the claimant was a homeowner living close to the Sellafield civil nuclear power plant in Cumbria. The claim for damages related to the presence of radioactive dust in the property which the claimant alleged had adversely affected (blighted) the value of his home. In rejecting the claim, the High Court held that the radioactive dust from Sellafield which was present in Merlin's home had not caused any damage to the property (that is, the presence of the dust did not constitute damage to property). Only the airspace within Merlin's home had changed and since the airspace was not capable of being owned by Merlin, there could be no damage to his property, in spite of the fact that the presence of dust adversely affected the market value of the property.

The *Merlin* case may be contrasted with *Hunter and Others v Canary Wharf Ltd* (1997), a nuisance case in which the presence of excessive levels of dust in Hunter's property was accepted (see the judgment of Pill LJ) as constituting property damage, provided cleaning costs (for example, in regard to internal fabrics) were reasonably incurred.

11.11.6 Damage is a prerequisite of liability

A claimant will fail in a negligence action unless damage is proved. Damage may comprise personal injury (including psychiatric injury), property damage, consequential losses, but not pure economic loss. Damage to the unowned environment is not a recoverable head of damages in England and Wales, although the EC Commission favours recognising 'impairment of the environment' as a form of recoverable damage (see the EC White Paper on *Environmental Impairment Liability*). In some circumstances, there might be difficulty in determining the precise date when the relevant damage occurred. For example, in the *Cambridge Water* case, the damage to the plaintiff's proprietary right to abstract wholesome water from its borehole only occurred when the water in the borehole became unwholesome and unsaleable. This occurred when a European Community (EC) Water Quality Directive (80/778/EC) was implemented in UK law which set maximum permissible levels for certain chemicals, including solvents. When tested, it was found that the presence of solvents in the water exceeded the limits contained in the Directive and the water could no longer be supplied for human consumption.

In the absence of statutory standards, the damage occasioned to the claimant must be 'substantial' if the negligence action is to be actionable. The courts employ a 'fact and degree' test to determine when damage is substantial. In the Docklands case (*Hunter v Canary Wharf Ltd* (1997)), the court referred to substantial damage as 'injury impairing value or usefulness'. In determining whether damage has occurred, the courts do not take into account the impact of continuing damage. This may cause problems for the claimant in deciding when to commence an action. If the action is commenced too early, there may be difficulties in establishing that damage has actually occurred, but if the claimant leaves it too long to commence an action, he or she may have his or her claim statute barred. The court has the power to strike out an action if it is of the opinion that the damage occurred at a much earlier time than the date on which the claimant commenced the claim (s 14 of the Limitation Act 1980).

11.11.7 Proof

The doctrine of *res ipsa loquitur* (the thing speaks for itself) (see *Scott v London & St Katherine's Docks Co* (1865)) may be invoked by a claimant to reduce the burden of proof in those cases where the claimant is alleging that the injury or damage was caused by negligence, such as the poor design or faulty operation of industrial plant. Any conviction which the defendant has and which is material to the claimant's claim, for example, a public nuisance conviction, may be used in evidence to support the claimant's claim. Depending upon the degree of relevance to the claim, this may be conclusive in establishing the culpability of the defendant.

11.11.8 Causation

The general rule is that the claimant must prove his or her case on the balance of probabilities (that is, it is more likely than not that the defendant's breach of duty caused the claimant's loss). Where there are conflicting explanations of the loss or injury sustained by the claimant, it is not the defendant's job to prove which of the competing explanations is the correct one.

Causation problems may arise in circumstances in which the defendant's conduct or actions, as a cause of the claimant's loss (or injury), competes with an 'innocent' (that is, non-negligent) cause of the loss. The problem often relates to the fact that medical science cannot prove (with the necessary degree of certainty) that the defendant's acts caused the claimant's loss because the relevant biological processes are not fully understood (see *Risk* by John Adams (1995, UCL Press) for an accessible account of scientific experimentation in proving that exposure to chemicals causes disease in humans). This problem is illustrated by the case of *McGhee v National Coal Board* (1973), in which the claimant, an employee of the defendant, contracted dermatitis due to exposure to brick dust whilst working in a brick kiln. Exposure to some brick dust during the working day was inevitable and lawful. The claimant's allegation of negligence related to the fact that the defendant had not provided shower facilities at work and the extra time the claimant was exposed to the dust, before he could shower at home, was the cause of the disease. The defendant admitted that it had been negligent in not providing showers, but argued that its negligence was not the cause of the disease. Whilst the medical evidence confirmed that exposure to brick dust caused dermatitis, nevertheless, medical experts could not agree that, on the balance of probabilities, the *additional* exposure to dust had caused the disease. The disease might have been caused by the 'innocent' lawful dust to which the claimant was exposed during working hours.

The House of Lords held the defendant liable because its failure to provide showers had *materially increased the risk* that the claimant would contract dermatitis. In circumstances in which the defendant may escape liability due to evidential difficulties, the courts may relax the 'but for' test in the interests of justice. Not to relax the burden of proof would be unfair to the claimant, since the claimant had sustained exactly the sort of damage which the defendant had a duty to protect the claimant against.

The decision in *McGhee* should be compared with *Hotson v East Berkshire AHA* (1987) (a 'lost chance' case) in which the delay in the treatment of the plaintiff's hip injury resulted in the plaintiff losing a 25% chance of making a full recovery from the injury. The House of Lords rejected the claim because the plaintiff had failed to prove his case on the balance of probabilities. There was a 75% chance that the disabling condition stemming from the injury would have occurred irrespective of the defendant's negligence. In *Hotson*, the court could, on the evidence before it, draw an inference that the plaintiff's injury had not been caused by the defendant's negligence, whereas in *McGhee*, the court based its decision on the evidence that the plaintiff's negligent additional exposure to brick dust was an operative cause of the plaintiff's disease materially contributing to its onset. Thus, the exposure to the 'guilty' dust need not be the main cause of the plaintiff's disease. A majority of the House of Lords treated a material increase in risk as equivalent to a material contribution to the disease. *McGhee* and similar cases are important to environmental litigants because negligence actions are a common basis of action in claims for personal injury concerning exposure to polluting substances (for example, dioxins from waste incinerator chimneys). Occasionally, litigation may be prompted by so called 'cancer cluster' cases in which emissions from a plant are alleged to have caused illness in the population living in the vicinity of the plant. Whilst expert evidence may be able to demonstrate that statistically there will be a 25% increase in cancer-related mortality in the area surrounding the plant in the next five years, it will be rare for the courts to allow claimants to succeed in such circumstances unless there are good reasons for relaxing the burden of proof.

In *Wilsher v Essex AHA* (1986), the House of Lords stated that *McGhee* supported the basic rule that the claimant must prove that the defendant caused the claimant's loss but, although the burden of proof remains with the claimant, the claimant may establish that the defendant's breach of duty was a material contributory cause of the loss. This interpretation of *McGhee* has not found support in the recent House of Lords decision in *Fairchild and Others v Glenhaven Funeral Services Ltd* (2002). In this case, negligent exposure of employees to asbestos fibres resulted in the claimant contracting mesothelioma, an invariably fatal type of cancer with a long latency period. Unfortunately, medical science does not fully understand the disease and this resulted in further causation problems. The claimant had worked for a number of employers who had all negligently exposed him to asbestos fibres. Mesothelioma is not, unlike pneumoconiosis, a cumulative illness (that is, the greater the exposure, the worse the disease). There is a minimum exposure (dose) level which has no adverse impact upon humans but, once that level is exceeded, it takes only one fibre to trigger the disease. Whilst the risk of contracting the disease increases with greater exposure to asbestos fibres, once the disease has been triggered, the severity of the disease does not increase with further exposure.

The claimant could not prove which of his former employers had exposed him to the 'fatal fibre' which had triggered the disease and, on the basis of the normal causation rules, his action was bound to fail. The House of Lords held that in the special circumstances of this type of case (fatal disease and breach of duty to protect the claimant from exposure to asbestos), the 'but for' test ought to be relaxed. Lord Bingham expressed the court's reasoning in the following terms:

> ... there is a strong policy argument in favour of compensating those who have suffered grave harm, at the expense of their employers who owed them a duty to protect them against that very harm and failed to do so, when the harm can only have been caused by the breach of that duty and science does not permit the victim accurately to attribute, as between several employers, the precise responsibility for the harm he has suffered.

Proving, to the satisfaction of the court, that the defendant's activities caused injury to the claimant is commonly an area where many negligence claims founder. For example, in *Graham and Graham v Rechem International Ltd* (1996), the court rejected an allegation of damage caused to the claimant's cattle due to dioxin poisoning from the defendant's chemical waste incinerator. In this action, the defendant supported his case by referring to the absence of regulatory enforcement action to indicate that its emission of dioxins was not causing harm.

11.11.9 Who can bring an action in negligence?

There is no need to prove an interest in the land which is affected, as there is in an action based on private nuisance. It is not necessary to demonstrate loss by other members of the public, which is necessary in cases brought on the grounds of public nuisance.

11.11.10 Against whom can an action in negligence be brought?

An action can be brought against any party where it can be proved that he or she owes a duty of care to the claimant, that there was a breach of this duty and that this resulted in foreseeable damage or injury to the claimant. There are, however, policy factors which will limit actions against certain defendants, for example, regulatory agencies.

11.11.11 Defences

11.11.11.1 Compliance with regulations

It has been suggested that the possession of a licence (for example, a planning permission or operating licence granted by the Environment Agency) may act as a defence to a negligence action. There is, however, no applicable blanket defence which applies automatically in such circumstances. In the *Budden* case, it was alleged that the defendant petrol companies had been negligent in not eliminating or reducing the lead content of their petrols by July 1978 and that this had caused personal injury to the plaintiffs. The defendants applied to have the action struck out on the basis that compliance with the relevant regulations made under s 75(1) of the COPA 1974 provided them with either a complete statutory defence or a complete answer to the allegation that the defendants had been at fault. The court accepted the second submission but not the first.

In *Blackburn v ARC Ltd* (1998), a case involving a claim (in nuisance) for an injunction and/or damages relating to odour and litter emanating from a poorly run landfill, the defendant argued unsuccessfully that possession of planning permission and a waste management licence provided it with a defence to the action. The court held that those licences would only provide the defendant with a defence if the relevant licence conditions were being observed so that any resulting nuisance would be an inevitable consequence of the defendant's licensed operations. This approach seems to accord with earlier authority regarding the application of the defence of statutory authority (see *Allen v Gulf Oil Refining Co Ltd* (1981)).

11.11.11.2 Fault

In order to avoid liability in negligence, industrial defendants must be able to establish that they were, at the material time, operating in accordance with the objectively determined standards of knowledge and best practice applicable in the relevant industry. In assessing whether the defendant has attained the standard required by the duty of care, the court will take a number of factors into account, including:

(a) the object to be attained;

(b) the practicability of taking precautions;

(c) the existence of approved or general practice;

(d) the defendant's compliance with approved or general practice; and

(e) the risks created by the defendant's activities.

In assessing whether the defendant kept reasonably abreast of emerging risks in the relevant industry, the court is likely to apply *Stokes v GKN* (1968), a case concerning awareness of developing knowledge of occupational health risks.

11.11.12 Remedies

11.11.12.1 Damages

It is a general principle of the tort of negligence that it is possible to claim damages for physical damage, to the person or to property, and for loss consequential to this damage. It is not possible to claim for pure economic loss (see, further, *Murphy v Brentwood DC* (1990)). Following this, it would be possible to claim damages for injuries caused by a chemical spillage which caused damage to people and property; it would be possible to claim for the clean-up costs, but it would not be possible to claim money for lost profits for the time the site was shut.

11.11.12.2 *Injunction*

In *Miller v Jackson* (1977), it was held that an injunction is not an available remedy in an action based in negligence.

11.12 TRESPASS

The tort of trespass to *land* has many functions. Its application for environmental purposes is a more recent development, although its use for such purposes appears to be limited as there are few reported cases.

There is some overlap between trespass to land and private nuisance, although it may be easier to bring an action on the basis of trespass because there is no requirement to prove actual damage as there is with nuisance. This is an obvious advantage and it may make an action in trespass in respect of fly-tipped waste, for example, more likely to succeed than an action in private nuisance.

11.12.1 Definition

Trespass to land is the unjustifiable physical interference with land, arising from intentional or negligent entry onto the land. A continuing trespass may be caused by continuing entry onto the land or by allowing physical matter to remain on the land.

In addition to trespass to land, an action may be brought with regard to trespass to the person. Whilst it is possible to envisage a situation in which pollution generated by the defendant's activities might give rise to a claim for trespass to the person, in practice the requirement that the interference to the claimant's property or person must be direct has restricted the development of this tort.

The defendant's activities in *McDonald v Associated Fuels Ltd* (1954) illustrate the significance of the intentional nature of the defendant's activities which it is necessary to prove if the claimant is to succeed. The defendant delivered sawdust to the plaintiff's home by blowing it from the defendant's lorry into a storage bin at the plaintiff's home. Exhaust gases from the defendant's lorry were blown into the plaintiff's home along with the sawdust. In consequence, the plaintiff was overcome by fumes, collapsed and suffered injury. The plaintiff's claim based on the negligent actions of the defendant was successful and the court went on to confirm that an action in trespass would also have been successful on the facts. Whilst the defendant did not intend to blow exhaust fumes into the plaintiff's home, it intended to do the act which directly caused the injury.

11.12.2 The characteristics of trespass

The following factors which must be present in order for an action for trespass to land or the person to be brought are:

(a) that the trespass was direct;

(b) that the act was intentional or negligent;

(c) a causal link must be proved between the directness of the act and the inevitability of its consequences.

11.12.3 Direct

The interference must be direct rather than consequential. For example, fly-tipping tyres onto someone's property would constitute trespass, whereas migration of methane from a landfill would not. The dumping of rubbish on land is a common form of trespass, even if it causes very little damage, as in *Gregory v Piper* (1820), in which the defendant disposed of his rubbish in such a way as to block a right of way. Some of the rubbish rolled against the plaintiff's wall and it was held that the defendant was liable in trespass. In this case, it was stated that, in order to be direct, the injury must result from an act of the defendant. An example of this may be found in *Jones v Llanrwst UDC* (1911), in which it was held that sewage, which had been released into a river and which had passed downstream and settled on the plaintiff's land, was direct and amounted to trespass.

If the trespass is indirect (see *Esso Petroleum Co Ltd v Southport Corp* (1956)), then any action should be brought in the law of nuisance.

11.12.4 Intentional or negligent

In order for a trespass to be actionable, it is necessary to prove that the defendant acted intentionally or negligently. The intent requirement essentially means that the defendant, or someone under his or her control, must voluntarily enter the claimant's land. Involuntary entry onto, or into, the claimant's land is not sufficient to constitute trespass.

11.12.5 Causal link between the directness of the act and its effects

It is also imperative to establish a causal link between the directness of the act and the inevitability of its consequences. If the effects of the act are indirect, there can be no trespass; however, there may be a remedy in nuisance or negligence. Establishing a causal link between the defendant's act and both the directness and inevitability of the resultant damage are important restrictions on trespass actions. In *Jones v Llanrwst UDC* (1911), sewage flowing from the defendant's drains polluted a section of riverbank belonging to the plaintiff. Whilst the defendant local authority had not intended to deposit sewage onto the plaintiff's land, the court held the defendant liable because it had intended the sewage to pass from its drains into the river. The court held that the trespass was sufficiently direct despite the plaintiff's property being some way downstream of the defendant's drain. By contrast, in *Esso Petroleum Co Ltd v Southport Corp* (1956), the defendant's tanker ran aground in the Ribble Estuary. To refloat the tanker, oil was emptied into the estuary where it was carried by the wind and the tide onto the plaintiff's beach. The House of Lords distinguished this case from *Jones v Llanrwst* on the ground that, unlike the inevitability of a river flowing downstream, it was not inevitable that the oil would wash up on Southport beach. The outcome of this case means that it is virtually impossible to bring a trespass action with regard to an air pollution incident due to the unpredictability of air currents which negates the necessary degree of directness. In contrast, rivers flow in defined channels.

11.12.6 Who can bring an action in trespass?

Any person who is in exclusive possession of the land can bring an action in trespass. Exclusive possession refers to the occupation or physical control of the land.

As trespass is actionable *per se*; the party bringing the action does not have to prove that the trespass has caused actual damage.

11.12.7 Against whom can a trespass action be brought?

The action can be brought against the wrongdoer who has interfered with the possession of the land. An example of this would be where someone has exceeded permission to remain on the land.

11.12.8 Defences

Defences are:

(a) necessity;

(b) licence. A licence gives the express or implied authority which will prevent the trespass from being actionable.

11.12.9 Remedies

Remedies are:

(a) *damages* – the amount of damages awarded in actions of trespass will usually depend upon the act complained of, particularly as trespass is actionable without any evidence of damage being caused. If the trespass is deemed to be trivial, then the damages awarded will usually be nominal. Substantial damage will, however, result in an appropriate award of compensation. Yet, where the trespass has physically damaged the land, the level of damages awarded will reflect the reduction in the value of the land rather than the costs of remediation (*Lodge Holes Colliery Co Ltd v Wednesbury Corp* (1908));

(b) *injunction* – it will generally be easier to obtain an injunction in an action for trespass than under any other tort because there is no need to prove any damage.

The claimant may require an injunction to prevent a continuing trespass, for example, to prevent the recurrence of tipping.

11.13 THE RULE IN *RYLANDS v FLETCHER*

11.13.1 Definition

The classic definition of this tort is found in the judgment of Blackburn J in *Rylands v Fletcher* (1868), that is, 'the person who for his own purposes brings on his land and collects and keeps there anything likely to do mischief if it escapes, must keep it in at his peril, and, if he does not do so, is *prima facie* answerable for all the damage which is the natural consequence of its escape'.

The case involved the construction of a reservoir on the defendant's land by independent contractors. The contractors failed to block off a number of mine shafts under the defendant's land which connected to the plaintiff's mine. When the reservoir was filled, the plaintiff's mine became flooded. The defendant, although personally not at fault, was held strictly liable for the damage. He had brought onto his land and collected there something which was likely to do damage if it escaped. The defendant failed in his duty to prevent the escape and was therefore liable for all the damage which was the natural consequence of the escape.

The *Rylands v Fletcher* principle imposes strict, but not absolute, liability for damage caused by the escape of dangerous things. The principle has been applied to a wide range of escapes of substances or objects including: water, fire, gases and fumes, electricity, oil, chemicals, colliery waste, poisonous vegetation, acid smuts, explosives, vibrations, trees and animals. Because the rule imposes strict liability, the claimant does not need to prove that the defendant was negligent. The claimant will succeed if he or she establishes a causal connection between the escape and the damage sustained.

An extra facet to the rule was added by Lord Cairns when the case reached the House of Lords. The rule was restricted to circumstances where the defendant had made a 'non-natural' use of his land. The rule applies to things not naturally (ordinarily) present on the defendant's land. The defendant incurs liability by bringing these things onto his or her land which subsequently escape and cause damage. This has, until the decision in *Cambridge Water*, played an important part in restricting the application of the rule. This restriction came to be associated with the idea that, to fall within the rule, the defendant's use of his land had to pose an increased risk of injury to others. This idea of 'non-natural' use was referred to in *Rickards v Lothian* (1913) as 'some special use bringing with it increased danger to others and must not merely be the ordinary use of the land or such a use as is proper for the general benefit of the community'. To be able to commence an action, the claimant was required to establish that the defendant's use of his or her land was an abnormal use involving an especially hazardous activity. This requirement is no longer good law.

11.13.2 Which factors must be established for the rule to apply?

In *Read v Lyons* (1947), the key criteria to establish liability under the rule in *Rylands v Fletcher* were stated to be:

(a) dangerous thing likely to do mischief;

(b) brought on to land;

(c) escape;

(d) non-natural user of the land.

(Note that the additional criterion that the type of damage sustained must be foreseeable was added by the decision in *Cambridge Water Ltd. v Eastern Counties Leather plc* (1994).)

11.13.3 Dangerous thing likely to do mischief

The first essential factor in the application of the rule in *Rylands v Fletcher* is that it applies to 'anything likely to do mischief if it escapes'. There are numerous examples of 'dangerous things', including oil (*Smith v Great Western Railway* (1926)); noxious fumes (*West v Bristol Tramways Co* (1908)); and explosions (*Miles v Forest Rock and Granite Co (Leicestershire) Ltd* (1918)).

In determining the presence of a 'dangerous thing', the courts will use a factual test 'whether the thing is likely to do mischief if it escapes'. Following the decision in *Cambridge Water v Eastern Counties Leather plc* (1994), it would appear that there is a requirement that the type of damage is foreseen as a result of the escape, and possibly that the escape itself is foreseeable (see 11.13.5 below). A seemingly innocuous substance, such as water, may be a 'thing likely to do mischief if it escapes' (note the circumstances of *Rylands v Fletcher* (1868)).

11.13.4 Brought on to land

It is not enough for the dangerous thing to be naturally present on the land; it must have been brought onto the land. In *Giles v Walker* (1890), there was no liability for self-sown thistledown which blew from the defendant's land onto the plaintiff's land. There may, however, be liability in nuisance or negligence in such circumstances (see 11.11 above).

11.13.5 Escape

There must also be an escape of the 'dangerous thing' from land before there can be any liability under the rule in *Rylands v Fletcher*. It is not sufficient that there was merely the potential for escape. This is clear from the case of *Read v Lyons*, in which it was held that escape meant an escape from a place where the defendant has occupation or control over land to a place which is outside his or her occupation or control.

11.13.6 Non-natural user of the land

It is a fundamental principle of the rule that the defendant should have brought onto his or her land something which was not naturally there. The term 'natural' was interpreted in *Rylands v Fletcher* to mean 'that which exists in or by nature and is not artificial', although more recent cases have centred around the wider definition which covers the concept that a non-natural use is one that brings with it 'increased danger to others and must not merely be the ordinary use of land or such a use as is proper for the general benefit of the community' (*Rickards v Lothian* (1913)). The *Rickards v Lothian* decision was followed in *Read v Lyons* by what was essentially a policy decision, that uses which provide some public benefit would be classed as 'natural'. This point was illustrated in *British Celanese Ltd v AH Hunt (Capacitors) Ltd* (1969):

> The manufacturing of electrical and electronic components ... cannot be adjudged to be a special use ... The metal foil was there for use in the manufacture of goods of a

common type which at all material times were needed for the general benefit of the community.

The decision of the House of Lords in *Cambridge Water Co v Eastern Counties Leather plc* (1994) has altered the 'non-natural user' requirement. In determining what was a non-natural use, the House of Lords took a fairly broad approach, in line with the original concept of non-natural use, and held that there should be a distinction between something naturally occurring, for example a flood, and an artificial creation such as a reservoir (see 11.14.6 below).

There is clearly less need to rely on the non-natural user restriction because the House of Lords has limited future claims by holding that foreseeability is now an essential requirement of the tort.

11.13.7 Foreseeability of the type of damage (remoteness)

In *Cambridge Water Co v Eastern Counties Leather plc* (1994), the House of Lords stated that the rule in *Rylands v Fletcher* should be considered as an extension of the law of nuisance relating to isolated incidents rather than continuing problems:

> ... it would moreover lead to a more coherent body of common law principles if the rule was to be regarded as essentially an extension of the law of nuisance to isolated escapes from land.

As a result of making this connection, it was stated that the damage must be foreseeable:

> The historical connection with the law of nuisance must now be regarded as pointing towards the conclusion that foreseeability of damage is a prerequisite of the recovery of damages under the rule.

11.13.8 Who can bring an action under *Rylands v Fletcher*?

It is not clear whether it is necessary for a claimant to have an interest in land in order to bring an action under the rule in *Rylands v Fletcher* (there are several cases where the claimant has not had an interest, although it was suggested in *Read v Lyons* that some interest in land will be necessary).

The House of Lords decision in *Cambridge Water Co v Eastern Counties Leather plc* suggests that the rule in *Rylands v Fletcher* is merely an extension of the law of nuisance and, if this is so, the ordinary principles of nuisance will apply, namely that the claimant must have an interest in land.

11.13.9 Against whom can an action in *Rylands v Fletcher* be brought?

It would appear that the defendant does not need to have any proprietary interest in the land; it is enough that he merely controls the 'dangerous thing', as was stated in *Rainham Chemical Works v Belvedere Fish Guano* (1921). This suggestion is consistent with the law of nuisance and reflects the close link between nuisance and *Rylands v Fletcher*.

11.13.10 Defences

Although it is widely acknowledged that the rule in *Rylands v Fletcher* created a regime of strict liability, liability is not absolute and the courts have developed a number of defences:

(a) statutory authority;

(b) necessity;

(c) act of God. The act of God defence is very limited and applies to 'forces of nature which no human foresight can provide against, and of which human prudence is not bound to recognise the possibility' (*Tennent v Earl of Glasgow* (1864));

(d) common benefit. Where the 'dangerous thing' is for the benefit of both the defendant and the claimant, the defendant will not be liable for its escape. This defence is very close to the defence of consent;

(e) independent act of a third party. The unforeseeable act of an independent third party is a defence where the defendant has no control over the actions of the third party. The burden of proving this defence lies with the defendant. Where the third party's act could have been foreseen or action could have been taken to prevent the consequences then the defendant will still be liable (*Northwestern Utilities v London Guarantee and Accident Co Ltd* (1936));

(f) default on the part of the claimant. Where the claimant suffers as a result of his or her own act or default, the defendant cannot be liable. Where there is contributory negligence on the part of the claimant, the provisions of the Law Reform (Contributory Negligence) Act 1945 apply.

11.13.11 Remedies

Because the rule in *Rylands v Fletcher* has its origins in nuisance, the remedies available appear to be the same as nuisance, namely:

(a) damages – although in *Read v Lyons* it was decided that damages would not be available for personal injury;

(b) injunction – although there is little judicial guidance on this point.

11.14 *CAMBRIDGE WATER CO v EASTERN COUNTIES LEATHER PLC*

The House of Lords decision in the case of *Cambridge Water Co v Eastern Counties Leather plc* (1994) has made a considerable impact on the interpretation and application of the common law to environmental problems.

11.14.1 The facts of the case

In September 1976, the Cambridge Water Company bought a piece of land which was formerly used as a paper mill at Sawston, Cambridgeshire, attached to which was a licence to abstract water from a borehole (linked to an underground aquifer) on the site. Cambridge Water Company began to abstract water from the aquifer for public consumption in June 1979. Unknown to the water company, the water was contaminated by solvents which had leached into the aquifer from a nearby tannery operated by Eastern Counties Leather. The spillages of the relevant solvent occurred regularly between 1950 and 1976, after which the tannery began to operate more efficiently. This contamination was not considered an issue (it did not make the water unwholesome and unusable) until, in 1976, the EC issued Directive 80/778/EC. This Directive set standards for drinking water used for human consumption and contained a limit relating to the maximum level of perchloroethylene solvent which could be present in the water. The water abstracted from the borehole was found to exceed these limits and use of the borehole was discontinued.

It was originally thought that the action would be brought under the WRA 1991; however, this proved to be impossible as the pollution pre-dated its enactment (the solvent took several years to migrate to and pollute the aquifer). Cambridge Water Company began civil proceedings against Eastern Counties Leather on the grounds of nuisance, negligence and the rule in *Rylands v Fletcher*.

11.14.2 The High Court decision

The action was dismissed in nuisance and negligence because it was held that the defendants, Eastern Counties Leather, could not at the relevant time that spillages of solvent were occurring have foreseen the damage caused to the aquifer.

Kennedy J also considered the application of the rule in *Rylands v Fletcher* and decided that the defendant's activities on its site, including the use of solvents, was a 'natural use' of land.

11.14.3 The Court of Appeal decision

The High Court decision was reversed by the Court of Appeal and Cambridge Water Company was awarded £1 million in damages plus costs.

The decision of the Court of Appeal was based on the tort of nuisance and the case of *Ballard v Tomlinson* (1885). The Court of Appeal held that the pollution of the aquifer by Eastern Counties Leather plc constituted an interference with Cambridge Water Company's 'natural rights' to abstract naturally occurring water which arrived beneath Cambridge Water's land by percolation through undefined underground channels. It was held that interference with this natural right to abstract uncontaminated groundwater constituted an actionable nuisance. The Court of Appeal did not comment on the rule in *Rylands v Fletcher*.

The Court of Appeal's reversal of the High Court's decision alarmed industry which feared that it could be liable for so called 'historic contamination'.

Appeal to the House of Lords was inevitable.

11.14.4 The House of Lords decision

The decision of the House of Lords was awaited with a great deal of interest as it was widely anticipated that the outcome would considerably affect the future application and development of the common law and that it would clarify the principles of the common law relating to environmental damage.

The judgment contained important pronouncements on the relationship between nuisance and the rule in *Rylands v Fletcher*.

11.14.5 Foreseeability

The House of Lords considered the issue of foreseeability in great detail. The following passage indicates the tone of the judgment:

> ... it by no means follows that the defendant should be held liable for damage of a type which he could not reasonably foresee; and the development of the law of negligence in the past 60 years points strongly towards a requirement that such foreseeability should be a prerequisite of liability in damages for nuisance, as it is of liability in negligence.

Lord Goff went on to state that foreseeability of harm 'is a prerequisite of recovery of damages in private nuisance, as in the case of public nuisance'. Therefore, there could only be liability where the interference was of a type which could be reasonably foreseen by a person in the defendant's position at the relevant time the solvents escaped from the defendant's control. The House of Lords therefore held that the damage caused to the aquifer by the solvents was not reasonably foreseeable at the time the pollution occurred.

11.14.6 Non-natural user

The House of Lords observed that 'the storage of substantial quantities of chemicals on industrial premises should be regarded as an almost classic case of non-natural use' and in so doing freed up this restriction on liability under the *Rylands v Fletcher* tort.

11.14.7 The courts and environmental protection

Also contained in the judgment was a statement referring to the development of the common law as a means of environmental protection. It was implied that it was the function of Parliament, rather than the courts, to create a statutory regime of liability for environmental damage:

> But it does not follow from these developments that a common law principle, such as the rule in *Rylands v Fletcher*, should be developed or rendered more strict to provide for liability in respect of such pollution. On the contrary, given that so much well informed and carefully structured legislation is now being put in place for this purpose, there is less need for the courts to develop a common law principle to achieve the same end, and indeed it may well be undesirable that they should do so.

11.14.8 The implications of the judgment

The judgment has been viewed by many environmentalists as being restrictive because of the introduction of the requirement of foreseeability of the type of damage as a component of the rule in *Rylands v Fletcher*. Critics of the judgment say that only very rarely will it impose liability for pollution cases such as this one.

However, many commentators feel that the judgment was the only reasonable and practicable step to be taken in the circumstances, because it is unfair to penalise anyone and impose retrospective liability for operations which were considered perfectly normal and effective at the relevant time. Neither is the judgment as restrictive as some originally interpreted, as it can provide the basis for liability where industry's poor environmental practices, after 1994, result in the escape of substances which contaminate neighbouring property. (We refer the reader, at the end of the chapter, to several articles which analyse the implications of the *Cambridge Water* case.)

11.15 AN EVALUATION OF THE COMMON LAW AS A MEANS OF ENVIRONMENTAL PROTECTION

Whilst it is clear that the common law torts do have a valid role to play in the protection of the environment, they do have a number of both limitations and advantages.

11.15.1 Disadvantages

The first fundamental problem associated with the use of the common law to secure environmental protection is that it cannot prevent damage (it is reactive) to the environment (although the use of an injunction can halt threatened damage or continuing damage); its purpose instead is to compensate the owner of the land affected. The availability of compensation to remediate environmental damage may not necessarily be used by the claimant for that purpose.

Because the development of common law controls has taken place over many years and at a time when the environment was not considered important, it does not meet the specific needs of environmental protection for a number of reasons:

(a) it operates on the basis of reactive 'cure' rather than prevention;

(b) the common law creates an uncertain level of liability (it does not set clear licence-based conditions which determine an acceptable level of pollution);

(c) it permits individuals to be guardians of the environment only on an *ad hoc* basis, given the uncertainty of establishing that the behaviour complained of was unreasonable and the evidential difficulties associated with this.

Modern (Command and Control) environmental laws which have been developed in response to specific environmental problems are better placed to address the needs of environmental protection because they contain express standards and provisions which relate directly to many industrial operations (they have industry-wide application).

Current environmental regulation is also better suited to the needs of industry as it provides clear standards of acceptable environmental behaviour via licence-based regulatory controls. Through these legislative frameworks, industry can also seek advice and guidance as to acceptable levels and types of pollution from the Environmental Agency.

In the late 19th century, it was established that the courts could not assume the place of the legislature in such cases. This was affirmed in *Cambridge Water Co v*

Eastern Counties Leather plc, in which the House of Lords confirmed that it would not be appropriate for the courts to develop the common law principles further.

11.15.1.1 Evidence

It may often be difficult to (a) prove the source of the pollution causing damage, and (b) establish a causal link between the pollution and the damage caused.

Experts may need to be employed to help prove the claimant's case and this often causes considerable delay and expense when bringing an action under the common law.

11.15.1.2 Costs

The cost of financing a common law action is often extremely prohibitive, especially as the availability of legal aid in such cases is very restricted. An example of a legally aided action is the Docklands litigation (*Hunter v Canary Wharf* (1997)).

Where legal aid is not available, it is usually only the wealthy who can take action, an example of this being the rock star Roger Daltry, who brought an action in respect of agricultural pollution which damaged his fish farm in *Beju-Bop Ltd v Home Farm (Iwerne Minster) Ltd* (1990).

The financial problems are exacerbated by the fact that an unsuccessful claimant may have to bear the defendant's legal costs as well as his or her own.

An action in the law of torts brought following environmental damage is often one that is hard fought by the defendant, who may be a large multinational company anxious to avoid defeat because this may damage the image of the company, with the potential to affect trade adversely. In order to avoid defeat, the defendant will spend a considerable amount of money on legal advice, representation and presentation of alternative scientific evidence (often far more than the claimant can afford to pay his or her own legal and scientific experts).

An example of such a case is that of *Hanrahan v Merck, Sharp and Dohme* (1988), an Irish case which, had it not been for the sheer determination of the plaintiff, and the hardship suffered by him and his family to raise the finances necessary to appeal, would not have reached the Supreme Court, where the earlier decision in favour of Merck, Sharp and Dohme was reversed.

The introduction of contingency fees by the Law Society is set to have a considerable impact on environmental litigation. The proliferation of claims handling companies and 'no win, no fee' deals are likely to stimulate an increase in environment-related claims.

11.15.1.3 Remoteness

The House of Lords decision in *Cambridge Water Co v Eastern Counties Leather plc* introduced the element of foreseeability as a prerequisite to the rule in *Rylands v Fletcher*.

The introduction of the foreseeability element will have the effect of limiting claims for historic pollution. However, as foreseeability is to be determined from the state of knowledge at the time the pollution takes place, it is unlikely that a great deal of the pollution which is currently taking place will be unforeseeable.

11.15.1.4 The Limitation Act 1980

A further limitation as to the effectiveness of the common law in the protection of the environment is that the Limitation Act 1980 applies. Section 2 of the Limitation Act 1980 provides:

(a) an action founded on tort shall not be brought after the expiration of six years from the date on which the cause of action actually accrued;

(b) where the action is brought in respect of personal injury, the basic limitation period is reduced to three years under s 11(4) of the Act, although the court has discretion to override this limitation period if it would be equitable to do so;

(c) the limitation period is calculated 'from the date on which the cause of action occurred'. The reason for the existence of the limitation period is that it would be unfair on the defendant if an action could be brought against him or her for an indefinite period of time.

11.15.2 Advantages

The strengthening of the statutory framework for the control of environmental pollution and environmental damage may lessen the significance of the common law. However, it still remains an important basis of action in several circumstances:

(a) for environmental pressure groups (for example, anglers' associations);

(b) for individuals who are affected by environmental damage and for whom there is no relief under statutory provisions;

(c) for enforcement agencies, such as the Environment Agency, where a prosecution under a statutory provision is not possible;

(d) where the pollution has taken place before the relevant legislation providing a remedy has come into force. This was the case in *Cambridge Water Co v Eastern Counties Leather plc*, where the pollution pre-dated the WRA 1991.

11.15.2.1 Supplementary to statutory provisions

An action under the common law may also supplement statutory provisions. For example, in the case of *National Rivers Authority (NRA) and Anglers Co-operative Association v Clarke* (1994), the NRA attempted to prosecute a pig farmer, Mr Clarke, who was responsible for the release of three million gallons of slurry into the river Sapiston in Suffolk, affecting a 75 km stretch of the river Sapiston and the Little Ouse and destroying a fishery. The action against Mr Clarke was brought under ss 31(1)(a) and 32(1)(a) of the COPA 1974 and s 4(1) of the Salmon and Freshwater Fisheries Act 1975. The Court of Appeal decided that the pig farmer could not be liable because his knowledge of the discharge could not be proven. (Had the NRA based the action on 'causing' pollution, it might have succeeded.)

Following the failure of the action under the statute, the NRA, along with the Anglers Co-operative Association who were representing the interests of the local angling club, then proceeded with a civil action against Mr Clarke. This time the action succeeded and the NRA was awarded £90,000 to cover its legal costs, to investigate the extent of the damage to the fishery and to pay for restocking.

The Anglers Co-operative Association was awarded £8,400 for legal expenses, and the local angling club was awarded £8,450 in damages.

11.15.2.2 Remedies

The chief remedy available in successful common law actions relating to environmental damage is damages. A significant advantage of an action under common law over statutory provisions is that the claimant may (depending upon the tort) recover damage for loss or personal injury. This is only rarely possible under statute. One example, however, is s 73(6) of the EPA 1990.

The remedies available in cases based on the common law are not specifically intended to meet modern environmental challenges; rather, their aim is to address affected property rights.

Injunctions can be granted in a variety of situations. They may be prohibitive, in which case they will simply require that the defendant should cease operations to prevent further damage from occurring; they may be mandatory, in which case the defendant will be required to take some positive action, such as the clean-up of a contaminated site. Both types of injunction may be granted on a *quia timet* basis, which would prevent damage being done where there was a threat of it occurring.

11.15.2.3 Actions need not be restrictive

A major advantage associated with a tort action is that it need not be brought on one ground alone and it is not uncommon for the torts of nuisance, negligence, trespass and the rule in *Rylands v Fletcher* to be tested in one case.

11.16 CIVIL ACTIONS UNDER STATUTE

11.16.1 Introduction

In addition to the civil law torts, legislation can also provide a means by which individuals can pursue civil claims for breach of environmental law.

Civil liability actions arising from statutes are available as follows:

(a) express statutory rights to be compensated for certain types of damage;

(b) breach of statutory duty;

(c) certain statutory provisions which extend, or sometimes restrict, rights under the common law.

Each of these will be considered in turn.

It may also be possible for an individual privately to prosecute a polluter for an offence under the statute, providing such action is not prohibited by the statute.

11.16.2 Express statutory rights to damages

An example of such an express provision is s 73(6) of the EPA 1990, which provides that where damage is caused by waste deposited in or on land, the person who deposited it, or knowingly caused or knowingly permitted it to be deposited, commits an offence under ss 33(1) or 63(2) and is liable in damages for the cost of remediation.

Section 73(6) provides that where the damage was wholly the fault of the person who suffered it, or the person who suffered voluntarily accepted the risk of the damage, the defences of contributory negligence and *volenti non fit injuria* are applicable.

It is not necessary for a prosecution to be brought in order to commence a statutory civil action; it is enough that the offence has been committed.

A further example is s 60 of the WRA 1991, which provides for damages where the Environmental Agency, under s 39 of the WRA 1991, has granted water abstraction rights which impair the existing rights of third parties.

11.16.3 Breach of statutory duty

The general rule defining breach of statutory duty was established in *Bishop of Rochester v Bridges* (1831):

> ... where an Act creates an obligation and enforces performance in a specified manner ... that performance cannot be enforced in any other manner.

A breach of statutory duty is only actionable where it can be shown that Parliament intends that the statute should grant a civil remedy. Many environmental statutes which prohibit an activity or make it a criminal offence also provide for some degree of civil liability.

The question of civil liability for breach of statutory duty is addressed in both the EPA 1990 and the WRA 1991.

In order to bring an action for breach of statutory duty, the claimant must prove the following:

(a) that the statute creates an obligation;

(b) that the statute intends to allow a civil action;

(c) that the harm suffered by the claimant is within the general class of risks at which the statute is directed;

(d) that the claimant is a member of the class of persons protected by the statute;

(e) that the defendant has breached the statute; and

(f) that this breach has caused the damage complained of.

11.16.3.1 Defences

There are two defences available for breach of statutory duty:

(a) *Volenti non fit injuria* – the defence of *volenti non fit injuria* (that is, voluntary assumption of risk) applies to cases of breach of statutory duty.

In *ICI v Shatwell* (1965), the House of Lords held that the defence applied in cases of breach of statutory duty except where there is a statutory provision to the contrary. This defence is not available where a worker sues his or her employer for breach of the employer's statutory duty.

(b) Contributory negligence.

11.16.3.2 *Example of actions in breach of statutory duty*

Gibbons and Others v South West Water Services (1992) was an action brought on behalf of 80 plaintiffs in respect of damage suffered by them when their drinking water supplies were contaminated with aluminium sulphate. The plaintiffs claimed damages on the grounds of breach of statutory duty, public nuisance and breach of contract. The defendants, South West Water Services, admitted liability for breach of statutory duty and the plaintiffs were awarded compensatory damages. The plaintiffs appealed because they also claimed exemplary and/or aggravated damages; however, the original decision was upheld.

11.17 STATUTORY PROVISIONS WHICH ALTER RIGHTS UNDER COMMON LAW

Statutory nuisance provisions in the EPA 1990 allow an individual to bring action in a magistrates' court against a person who has created the nuisance (s 82). This section is used where the local authority has not acted to prevent or abate the statutory nuisance (see Chapter 9).

An individual aggrieved by statutory nuisance may bring an action under s 82 of the EPA 1990 (which re-enacts s 99 of the Public Health Act 1936). These proceedings will be brought against the person responsible for the nuisance. If the responsible party cannot be found, the owner of the premises may be liable or, where more than one person is responsible for the nuisance, each party may be liable under s 82 'whether or not what any one of them is responsible for would by itself amount to a nuisance'.

This action can only be brought in a magistrates' court and there is no power enabling an individual to serve an Abatement Notice. Notice of the individual's intention to bring proceedings must be given to the responsible parties. In the case of a noise nuisance, three days' notice must be given and, in all other cases, 21 days' notice must be given.

11.18 THE EC AND CIVIL LIABILITY

Work is continuing within the European Commission on the preparation of a Draft Directive on Civil Liability for Damage to the Environment Caused by Waste. The purpose of the proposed Directive is to harmonise the systems of civil liability which are in place in Member States across the EC. The concept of civil liability in relation to environmental damage is already established in some Member States: it exists in Germany, Belgium, France and Italy, and has been introduced in the waste management sector in Spain.

The different systems in place in the Member States may lead to unequal conditions for competition, thereby creating artificial currents of investment and wastes from those countries where less stringent standards apply for the operators.

The proposed Directive encourages the polluter to take action to minimise the risks at the earliest possible stage. Its objectives are:

(a) to apply the 'polluter pays' principle on terms conducive to completing the goal of the single market;

(b) to establish a uniform system of liability;

(c) to ensure that industry's waste-related costs are reflected in the price of the product or service giving rise to the waste.

The draft Directive proposes to place primary liability on the producer of the waste; this could include any person who imports waste into the EC and persons responsible for waste installations.

It is not yet clear whether this draft Directive in its current form will be adopted. The issue is currently being considered in a wider dialogue on environmental liability within the Commission.

The EC Commission submitted proposals to the European Parliament and Council in early 2002 for a Directive on Preventing and Restoring Environmental Damage (see COM(2002)17 Provisional). Environmental damage is defined by reference to the protection of biodiversity at EC and Member State levels, waters regulated by the Water Framework Directive, and threats to human health caused by land contamination. Member States decide when action is required to be taken by licensed operators, competent authorities or third parties. If possible, in line with the 'polluter pays' principle, the operator responsible for the environmental damage (or imminent threat of damage) will bear the cost of the measures taken to prevent and/or restore the damage (that is, the cost of preventive action or to fund the cost of reparation, if damage has already occurred, via insurance). The Directive aims to make public authorities (local authorities) primarily responsible for taking action against polluters.

Personal injury and damage to goods are not covered and are to be regulated by the legal systems of Member States. Damage caused by diffuse sources of pollution is not covered and the Directive will have no retrospective effect. Where damage has been caused by activities which pose a potential or actual threat to humans or the environment, the operator responsible is strictly liable subject to limited defences (damage caused by events beyond the operator's control, damage caused by licensed (lawful) emissions and damage caused by emissions or activities which were not considered to be harmful at the relevant time but are later revealed to be so).

Non-governmental organisations and public interest groups have a role to play as 'qualified entities' (plus individuals with standing) to request competent authorities to take action (and challenge actions taken or omitted to be taken). The draft Directive also includes provisions relating to transboundary damage and financial security requirements.

DEFRA consulted on the proposals in early 2002 and a summary of the responses to the consultation can be found on DEFRA's website (see www.defra.gov.uk/environment/consult/liability2).

11.19 FURTHER INFORMATION

Further reading

Bell, S, *Environmental Law: The Law and Policy Relating to the Protection of the Environment*, 4th edn, 1997, Blackstone.

Bowman, M, 'Nuisance, strict liability and environmental hazards' (1995) Env Liability 105.

Brenner, 'Nuisance law and the Industrial Revolution' (1974) J Legal Studies 403.

Buckley, R, *The Law of Nuisance*, 1981, Butterworths.

Campbell, D, 'Of Coase and corn: a (sort of) defence of private nuisance' (2000) MLR 197.

Cane, P, 'Are environmental harms special?' [2001] JEL 3.

Conaghan, J and Mansell, W, *The Wrongs of Tort*, 2nd edn, 1998, Pluto.

Cross, D, 'Does the careless polluter pay?' (1995) 111 LQR 445.

Gearty, C, 'The place of nuisance in the modern law of torts' (1989) CLJ 214.

Greve, M, 'The private enforcement of environmental law' (1999) 65 Tulane L Rev 339.

Hilson, C, '*Cambridge Water* revisited' [1996] WLAW 126.

Holder, J, 'The Sellafield litigation and questions of causation in environmental law' (1994) CLP 287.

Jones, M, *Textbook on Torts*, 8th edn, 2002, OUP.

Lee, M, 'Civil liability in the nuclear industry' [2000] JEL 317.

Lowry, J and Edmunds, R (eds), *Environmental Protection and the Common Law*, 2000, Hart.

McLaren, J, 'Nuisance law and the Industrial Revolution: some lessons from social history' (1983) OJLS 155.

Newark, F, 'Non-natural user and *Rylands v Fletcher*' (1961) MLR 557.

O'Neill, O, *Justice, Property and the Environment*, 1997, Ashgate.

O'Sullivan, J, 'Nuisance, local authorities and neighbours from hell' (2000) CLJ 11.

Ogus, A and Richardson, G, 'Economics and the environment: a study of private nuisance' (1977) CLJ 284.

Penner, J, 'Nuisance and the character of the neighbourhood' [1993] JEL 1.

Pontin, B, 'Tort interacting with regulatory law' (2001) NILQ 597.

Pugh, C and Day, M, *Pollution and Personal Injury: Toxic Torts II*, 1995, Cameron May.

Rabin, R, 'Environmental liability and the tort system' [1987] Houston Law Review 27.

Rogers, WVH, *Winfield and Jolowicz on Tort*, 16th edn, 2002, Sweet & Maxwell.

Spencer, J, 'Public nuisance: a critical examination' (1989) CLJ 55.

Steele, J, 'Private Law and the environment: nuisance in context' (1995) 15 LS 236.

Steele, J, 'Remedies and remediation: foundational issues in environmental liability' (1995) MLR 615.

Steele, J and Jewell, T, 'Nuisance and planning' (1993) MLR 568.

Steele, J and Wikeley, N, 'Dust on the streets and liability for environmental concerns' (1997) MLR 265.

Stone, C, 'Should trees have standing?: towards legal rights for natural objects' (1972) Southern California L Rev 450.

Stone, C, 'Should trees have standing revisited. How far will law and morals reach – a pluralist perspective' (1985) 59(1) Southern California L Rev 1.

Tromans, S, 'Nuisance – prevention or payment?' (1982) CLJ 87.

Wetterstein, P, *Harm to the Environment: the Right to Compensation and the Assessment of Damages*, 1997, Clarendon.

Wightman, J, 'Nuisance – the environmental tort?: *Hunter v Canary Wharf* in the House of Lords' (1998) MLR 870.

Wilde, M, 'The EC Commission's White Paper on environmental liability: issues and implications' [2001] JEL 21.

See also the articles relating to the *Cambridge Water Co* case in Chapter 4.

CHAPTER 12

THE PRIVATE REGULATION OF ENVIRONMENTAL POLLUTION: PUBLIC CONCERN, PRIVATE PROSECUTION, JUDICIAL REVIEW, ACCESS TO INFORMATION AND HUMAN RIGHTS

12.1   INTRODUCTION

In Chapter 11, we noted that legal persons, such as individuals and companies, are able to use the law of torts to obtain redress for damage to property and person caused by the polluting activities of other persons. The role of private individuals, companies and other organisations or groups is not, however, confined to litigation in the civil courts. Legal persons also have an important role to play in ensuring that the Command and Control regimes we encountered in Chapters 4–10 are properly regulated and the relevant regulators are made accountable for their decisions. Private persons have two courses of action open to them if they are unhappy with any regulatory action (or inaction) or decision. First, in the event that a regulator exercises its discretion not to prosecute a person who has breached environmental law, any person who disagrees with this decision may exercise the right (provided the right is not excluded by the relevant statute) to mount a private prosecution to bring the alleged offender to account before the criminal courts. Secondly, any person may challenge a wide range of regulatory decisions by means of an application to the courts to have the relevant decision judicially reviewed. These two mechanisms enable the private person to 'police' the activities of public regulators. In order for private persons effectively to police the decisions of the regulators, it is essential that such persons have access to regulatory records, especially those relating to breaches of environmental law and pollution licences (that is, applications for licences, the conditions attached to licences, the monitoring of polluting emissions to confirm that licences are complied with, etc). The importance of the participation of private citizens in the protection of the environment is widely recognised, especially by the European Community (EC) and the international community. The EC in particular has played an important part in ensuring that Member States make environmental information available to the public. More recently, the Human Rights Act 1998 has provided the basis for a number of interesting environmental claims.

12.2   PUBLIC CONCERN

12.2.1 What is public concern and why is it important?

Public concern, in an environmental pollution context, is the fear of actual or threatened adverse impacts of emissions from industrial, commercial and agricultural activity upon an individual's core interests. Therefore, anything which threatens the security of an individual, especially with regard to health, family, property, money or employment will trigger a strong defensive reaction. Quite simply, the public will vehemently oppose those pollution-related risks which it considers to be unacceptable. Furedi (1997) captures the essence of such concerns when he observes:

Safety has become the fundamental value of the 1990s. Passions that were once
devoted to a struggle to save the world (or keep it the same) are now invested in
trying to ensure that we are safe.

In order to appreciate fully the significance of public concern and its potential
impact on government, regulatory agencies, and regulated businesses, we must take
note of the role of the media. The media reports on what it believes to be the chief
concerns of its principal client, the public. The media, through their editorial control
of the items they deem newsworthy, sensitise the public to selected risks. Currently,
pollution-related concerns are high on the media's agenda and, over time, pollution-
related issues have become a pressing concern for most people. This shift in the
public perception is borne out by one leading law firm specialising in pollution-
related claims which has noted the 'enormous increase in public concern regarding
environmental pollution' (Pugh and Day, 1995).

The public is assailed on all sides by both local and global threats including
climate change, acid rain, destruction of habitat, resource depletion, industrial
pollution and nuclear waste disposal. At the same time, public confidence in science
and scientific experts has been severely dented by a string of environmental
controversies which have been linked with adverse health impacts: BSE, foot and
mouth disease, genetically modified crops, ozone depletion and traffic-related
asthma.

What the public values and what the public fears are two related issues which are
capable of forming important inputs into environmental policy and environmental
decision making. The public values a healthy environment and any development,
such as the construction of a waste incinerator, which appears to threaten such
deeply held values, beliefs or convictions is likely to generate controversy. Currently,
the planning system seems to be the main forum in which development decisions,
relating to permission to build 'risky' developments, come head to head with public
concerns relating to health, safety and environmental issues. Almost without
exception, any development proposal which is believed to impact adversely upon
humans will stimulate vociferous opposition. Controversies over the siting of waste
incinerators, landfill sites, electricity power lines, low level nuclear waste storage
facilities and similar unwanted developments are reported daily in the media.

The issues which concern the public undoubtedly have an influence upon what
the media deem newsworthy. The more the media report on an issue of public
concern, such as environmental pollution, the more the public are sensitised to that
issue and its attendant risks. In turn, public concern impacts upon government pre-
occupations and may generate policy proposals, at both central and local levels. In
some instances, public concern may force the government to propose new
legislation, as in the case of dangerous dogs or firearms (following the Dunblane
massacre). Public concerns permeate society and impact upon the activities of the
regulators (as can be seen in the Environment Agency's enforcement and
prosecution policy, and in its agreement to trial an extended public consultation
process with regard to licensing applications which generate high levels of public
concern) and the regulated (as is evident in the decision of Shell to reverse its plan to
decommission the Brent Spar oil rig at sea).

Public concern is not only instrumental in influencing government policy and
proposals for new legislation but it can also have a powerful, localised, impact on

regulators and regulated businesses. Media coverage of pollution incidents may alert the public to the pollution risks associated with the operation of specific company plants. In turn, this may result in public pressure on the regulator to prosecute the offending polluter. Regulators such as the Environment Agency operate in a political environment and are acutely aware that they need to be seen to be doing their job as this is understood by the public. In such circumstances, the regulator may exercise its discretion to prosecute to placate the public rather than employing its administrative enforcement powers. Regulated businesses are also increasingly aware of the power of public concern and opposition. Unpopular development proposals, such as the proposed construction of a new factory or extension to an existing facility, may be blocked by widespread opposition to the relevant proposal. Usually, public concern is expressed at the planning stage, but increasingly the public will seek participation in the decision making of environmental regulators, especially with regard to the issue and variation of licences.

12.2.2 Public concern and the legitimacy of environmental decision making

Tapping into public concerns and values is problematic for both central and local government. It is not easy to discern, or measure, the extent of public concern with regard to a specific risk. The public is not an homogeneous group whose opinions are easily sounded out. Experience at local government level in the drafting and consultation upon development plans (which comprise a collection of policies guiding development control decisions in the planning process) is illustrative of the problem. Only major landholders and businesses tend to make inputs into the development plan process. They do so primarily to protect their own interests. In contrast, few individuals bother to master the background detail to the consultation process (which requires a major investment of time and effort) prior to making any input into the process. In an effort to address this problem, both central and local government have experimented with focus groups, citizen juries and citizen advisory forums, in an effort to ascertain reliable indications of public values and concerns. These initiatives recognise, to a greater or lesser extent, the need to bring the public 'up to speed' before reliable information on public concerns and values may be elicited. Obtaining accurate information is vital because only then will the government be reasonably certain that its policies will be perceived as legitimate by the public. Values and concerns thus form an essential element of policy making. Policies which do not reflect the true concerns and values of the public will be unreliable guides for decision makers. Failing to consult properly can wrongfoot the government and lead to a public outcry which may force the government to rethink its proposals. An example of the consequences of failing to obtain reliable information on public concerns can be seen in the public outcry and subsequent rejection, by Hampshire county council, of a proposal to build a large waste incinerator on the outskirts of Portsmouth (Stanley, 2000).

Until the late 1990s, the principal Command and Control decision making process in which the public vented its concerns about the tolerability of risks created by development proposals was the town and country planning system. There are signs that the demand for public participation in the licensing decisions of the Environment Agency and the local authorities is growing. The Environment Agency has been trialing a system of improved and extended consultation with the public with regard to a selected number of sites which raise matters of significant public concern. The Environment Agency has announced that its objective in engaging in extended consultation is to 'provide an opportunity for fully informing the public and engaging them in debate during the decision making process. In this way, decisions will be better informed, and because they have greater public involvement, more widely accepted'. So far, the extended consultation process has been piloted at several facilities, including a power station, a waste treatment plant, a cement works, and a nuclear plant. The Environment Agency anticipates that 20–50 licence applications each year will utilise the extended consultation process.

In the past, the government has responded to important shifts in public concern by adopting reactive, legislative 'fixes', as demonstrated by the passage of the Deposit of Poisonous Wastes Act 1972 and the Clean Air Acts of the 1950s. These laws were passed in response to environmental problems (fly-tipping dangerous waste and the health effects of smogs) which captured the attention of the public and media and led to demands for decisive action. Legislation which goes with the grain of society's perceptions of acceptable environmental behaviour will have widespread support because it is perceived as necessary. The government must learn the lesson that it cannot afford to wait until a situation becomes intolerable before it acts. There are encouraging signs that the government is beginning to adopt a less reactive approach to environmental pollution problems as demonstrated by its proactive policy development of the national air, waste and water strategies (although it could be argued that the government is only responding to EC pressure for change).

12.2.3 The causes of high levels of public concern

Since public concern often arises from actual or threatened exposure to levels of pollution which the public perceives as too risky and therefore unacceptable, we need to consider the following linked issues: what is risk, and what factors help to generate public perception of unacceptable risk exposure?

12.2.3.1 What is risk?

Every one of us, of necessity, is a risk taker. In the act of a crossing a public highway, overtaking another vehicle in our own motor car, or smoking cigarettes, we are all involved in a continual process of risk taking. Our own experiences of risk taking, be they rewards or losses, influence our own risk taking behaviour and the opinion each of us holds of what constitutes a 'risky' activity. Why then are some risks surrounded by controversy and considered to be less acceptable than other activities which involve the taking of risks? Why is environmental pollution, such as the airborne emissions from waste incinerators, associated with unacceptable risk taking and the creation of high levels of public concern?

These questions can only be effectively answered if we develop a better understanding of the concept of risk (Royal Society, 1992). John Adams, a leading author on risk, has divided risk into three categories in an effort to explain why the public is more fearful of some risks rather than others (Adams, 1995). Risks may be directly perceptible to each of us through our own, unaided senses; risks may be perceptible with the aid of science and technology; or risks may be 'virtual risks'. In crossing a busy road, we are using our own unaided senses to perceive the direct risk that oncoming vehicles may injure us. We do not need to carry out a formal risk assessment to convince us that we should exercise a high degree of care in such circumstances. Similarly, the risks and rewards of driving fast are directly apparent to us. Each individual has an 'in-built' risk thermostat which guides his or her risk taking behaviour. Some people are risk seeking whilst others are risk averse and the setting of each individual's risk thermostat will vary with that person's life experiences. Occasionally, an individual's risk thermostat will conflict with attempts by regulators and safety experts to manage risks for him or her. We may choose to ignore speed limit warning signs in the pursuit of speed. Despite the efforts of government, many of us will continue to insist on taking more risks than the safety authorities believe we should take.

Risks perceived through science require us to use scientific apparatus to perceive the relevant risk. We cannot see a virus with the naked eye but we can observe it under the microscope. However, without training, we cannot understand what we are seeing or form any impression with regard to the risk of infection. Science helps us to assess risk in those cases in which the mechanism between exposure to infection and the onset of the disease is well known. It also helps us assess the relevant risk and its acceptability or tolerability. In those cases where the science is uncertain, we may resort to the use of objective risk assessments to provide us with statistical information to guide our risk taking behaviour. In the world of risk assessments, activities which have less than a 'one in a million' risk of resulting in death are generally considered to be safe. Risk assessments are frequently used in assessing the risk of workplace accidents and they have also been used to demonstrate the relatively remote risk of chemical spillages occurring at a waste transfer station (see *Envirocor Waste Holdings Ltd v Secretary of State for the Environment* (1996)). Whilst these assessments are helpful aids in environmental decision making, they nevertheless represent an expert's best 'guestimate' of the likelihood of an adverse outcome actually materialising. Whilst risk experts may be familiar with the statistical risk ratings of various activities, the ordinary individual may have rather more difficulty in coming to a satisfactory conclusion on whether a one in a million risk of dying of cancer caused by polluting emissions from a new factory is an acceptable risk.

Virtual risks are those risks, such as the risk to health associated with the consumption of meat potentially infected with BSE, which are surrounded by great uncertainty and with regard to which scientists themselves cannot agree whether the relevant activity is safe. An environmental pollution example is the public concern, generated by the emission of carcinogenic dioxins from waste incinerators. When faced with scientists who profoundly disagree with one another, the public is forced to impose meaning on uncertainty. In such circumstances, the public makes an assessment of the relevant risk based upon the subjective criteria discussed below.

Public concern is increasingly relevant to environmental decision making. Public concern is now a consideration which, when relevant, must be taken into account by local planning authorities when determining the outcome of planning applications. The pollution risks associated with the granting of licences to industry to discharge substances into the environment may generate public concern. Increasingly, affected members of the public wish to participate in regulatory decisions which affect their well being. Public concern is also instrumental in the commencement of some common law actions in which residents living in the vicinity of polluting industry choose to take on big business in the courts because of the fear of the ill effects of pollution in their neighbourhood.

12.2.3.2 *The factors generating public perception of unacceptable risk exposure*

Research has demonstrated that the public uses 'rules of thumb' to reduce the burden involved in processing the mass of information available to it with regard to the assessment of risks. The public largely relies upon what it is able to recall about a particular risk when calculating the likelihood of an event occurring or recurring. This may lead to significant differences of opinion between what activities the risk experts tell us is safe and what the public perceives as safe. For example, the public tends to overestimate the risk of death and injury from infrequent causes, such as hurricanes, but underestimate the loss of life from asthma.

The nature and extent of media coverage of a risk is a key factor influencing public perception and public concern. A specialist law firm, which has considerable experience of environmental pollution claims, believes that media interest in environmental pollution will ensure that health problems associated with these activities are well reported. The same firm reported that it had received a total of 1,500 telephone calls from potential plaintiffs, concerned about the risks of breast implants, following two television appearances by a representative of the firm on the ITN news (Pugh and Day, 1995).

The types of events which the media deem newsworthy, the graphic imagery employed and the timescale within which an issue remains newsworthy all influence public recollection. The media report on what they believe to be of most concern to most of the public for most of the time. Reporting is biased in favour of stories relating to health, money, crime, education and the environment. Media reporting of industrial accidents causing death, injury and environmental damage create a climate in which the public will voice its objections to both existing and proposed developments which threaten the fundamental concerns of the public: the ability to live in a healthy, pollution-free and safe local environment. It is not surprising to discover that the public is concerned with threats to its health. Where industrial activities threaten these fundamental concerns, the following expressions of concern are to be expected: is this waste incinerator poisoning the neighbourhood with toxic atmospheric emissions?; will the construction of this chemical plant close to residential properties blight property values? These are typical and rational reactions to what the public perceives as threats to its core concerns.

The degree of public trust in the organisation which will be managing a risk influences the opinion of the public as to the acceptability of the activity creating the risk. If the organisation which will be managing the risk has a poor track record in risk management, it can expect public opposition. For example, would the public in the immediate years after the Bhopal disaster have been behaving irrationally if it steadfastly resisted a proposal by Union Carbide to build a chemical plant in the heart of the British countryside, even though the chemical company could demonstrate, using objectively calculated risk assessments, that the proposed plant would be safe?

If a hazard is perceived by the public as being imposed on it, the risks created by the relevant activity will be less acceptable than if the risks were assumed voluntarily. *R v Secretary of State for Trade and Industry ex p Duddridge* (1996) illustrates the heightened public opposition to risky development which the public perceives as being unjustly imposed upon it against its will. If the public believes that it has no personal control over a risk, then the level of public concern experienced will be higher than in those circumstances in which the public retains some degree of control over risk exposure. For example, public concern relating to polluting emissions from a new factory may be defused if the site operator provides equipment and training to enable the public to monitor plant emissions independently of data collected by the factory itself.

The number of people potentially at risk from, for example, the risk of explosion at a petro-chemical plant is a further factor which the public takes into account when assessing the tolerability of a hazard. Also of significance is the way in which the hazard manifests itself. Contrast the graphic media depiction of how the victims of the Piper Alpha oil rig inferno met their deaths and the minimal media interest in the plight of shipworkers whose hearing has been severely damaged by constant exposure to loud noises. In the former incident, the injuries caused were immediate, graphic and horrific, whilst in the case of widespread deafness in shipyards, the injuries were neither observable nor immediately apparent.

New risks are problematic because the public is unfamiliar with the extent and nature of the risks generated by the relevant activity. Genetic engineering, biotechnology and the risks of exposure to electro-magnetic field radiation are three examples of the uncertainty created by newly emergent risks which are not yet fully understood by experts and the public. Any accident involving new technologies, such as biotechnology, may be perceived by the public as confirmation that the activity is inherently dangerous and therefore any risks associated with such risky technology are not acceptable.

Man-made risks, such as those associated with the nuclear power industry, cause the public to fear far more than hazards which are 'natural', such as the risk of property damage caused by living on a flood plain.

The perception that risks are inequitably distributed in society also affects their acceptability. The waste industry is currently grappling with this issue with regard to finding sites to 'host' new landfills or waste incinerators. The perception of the local community that it is to be the dumping ground for waste generated by the entire county often galvanises affected members of the public to take action to resist the proposal.

Research has demonstrated that a combination of the factors outlined above may combine to evoke a powerful negative public reaction. Hazards may cause 'dread' or 'unknown' risk reactions amongst the public. Dread risks are those which are characterised by a lack of personal control, the inequitable distribution of risks and benefits, the existence of a threat to future generations, the fact that the risk increases over time, and the fact that the risk has catastrophic potential to injure people or the environment. The issues raised by objectors to the construction of a waste incinerator in Gateshead illustrate the dread risk caused by public concern over exposure to dioxins emitted from the incinerator. 'Unknown' reactions relate to hazards which are unobservable, which are not fully understood by science, and whose impacts on people and the environment are difficult to assess. Hazards generated by nuclear power plants may prompt this type of extreme reaction. Occasionally, the combination of public concern criteria produces a public outcry compelling the government and the regulators to take swift and decisive action to address such concerns. The post-Dunblane disaster 'Snowdrop' campaign subjected the then government to intense and sustained pressure to ban certain types of firearms.

One final, yet significant issue is the failure of stakeholders in risk decision processes to hear and understand one another's points of view. The supporters of an objective perspective on risk and hazards favour the use of statistics to calculate the probability and severity of a range of adverse incidents. They may fail to appreciate the wide range of factors which the public employs to 'calculate' risk and its tolerability. This problem is neatly encapsulated in Sandman's equation 'Risk = Hazard + Outrage' where hazard is 'objective' risk and outrage is public, 'subjective' risk.

Public concern continues to raise its head in planning disputes. In *Trevett v Secretary of State for Transport, Local Government and the Regions and Others* (2002), the applicant challenged the grant, on appeal, of planning permission for the erection of three police radio masts on the ground that the inspector, who heard the planning appeal, had regarded the public perception of health risks as irrelevant. The High Court rejected this submission and held that the inspector had considered the perceived health risks from the radio masts, but had concluded, on the facts, that the perceived risks did not justify refusing planning permission (see the article by Ray Kemp [2003] JPL 13 with regard to public concern and telecommunication masts).

12.3 PRIVATE PROSECUTIONS

The enforcement of environmental law is not the monopoly of the pollution control authorities. Neither the Environment Agency nor the local authorities exercising their respective pollution control functions have the financial resources or personnel to ensure full enforcement of the environmental controls laid down in statute or in the permissive authorisations (licences) granted. It is for these reasons that the individuals and pressure groups can play a role in the enforcement of environmental law by bringing private criminal prosecutions. The environmental legislation considered in this book contains a number of provisions which enable citizens to bring their own prosecutions against those who commit offences under specific pollution control legislation. The Environmental Protection Act (EPA) 1990, for example, provides considerable scope for citizens to bring private prosecutions (except in the case of Pt IV, s 118(10), which deals with genetically modified organisms). Other examples of the restricted right to bring a private prosecution include s 211 of the WIA 1991, s 7(4) of the WIA 1991 and s 38 of the Radioactive Substances Act 1993. However, it appears that these rights have not been widely recognised or taken up. There are several reasons why this might be the case and these are considered below.

12.3.1 The right to bring a private prosecution

At common law, it is a well established rule that a citizen has the right to bring a private prosecution under an Act of Parliament. In *R v Stewart* (1896), the High Court allowed a private prosecution to be brought by the Royal Society for the Prevention of Cruelty to Animals under the Diseases of Animals Act 1894. The court held that a citizen has a right to prosecute under any statute unless an Act specifically precludes that right in clear words. Various statutes do contain provisions which explicitly give individuals the right to enforce the statutory provisions by means of private prosecutions and clearly these rights are of particular importance in the context of pressure groups and the environment. But even in the absence of a specific statutory provision, an individual or pressure group can still bring a private prosecution under an Act of Parliament, providing that the Act does not expressly and clearly preclude such a right and providing the prosecution is not vexatious.

In the context of environmental protection where most businesses have statutory authority to pollute (in accordance with the conditions imposed in authorisations), it is necessary to establish whether an offence has been committed. Access to information about polluting activities is essential and the public registers described below may provide the information necessary in order to assist people in identifying the firms or businesses that are committing offences. From the information on the registers, it should be possible, for example, to ascertain who is responsible for a particular discharge into a river, what the discharge consent conditions are, whether any monitoring data has been collected revealing breach of licence conditions, any notices served, or previous offences recorded. Where a person or group of persons believes that an offence has been committed, is being committed or is likely to be committed, the easiest and cheapest course of action will be to complain to the regulatory authority and ask it to take enforcement action. It has already been stated that the pollution control authorities do not have the resources to monitor every discharge or emission all of the time and they therefore rely on reports and complaints brought by people in this respect. For instance, the anglers' associations were often the first to draw the NRA's attention to pollution incidents and fish kills. In fact, the NRA established a 24 hour hotline telephone number enabling the public to report incidents to it and this has been continued with the transfer of functions to the Environment Agency.

However, the alternative course of action is for an individual or pressure group to bring a private prosecution (often using the information obtained from the public registers). An example of a statutory right to bring a private prosecution is s 82 of the EPA 1990 where the aggrieved citizen is given the right to prosecute statutory nuisances. This is one of the more well known 'rights' and is covered in Chapter 9. Well-heeled defendants in civil and criminal litigation may be tempted to use their financial muscle to restrict and stifle tactically civil claims and private prosecutions by increasing the length, complexity and costs of the litigation with the intention of exhausting the claimant's limited financial resources. In addition, a defendant could resort to a 'SLAPP' (strategic lawsuit against public participation) to head off unwelcome interest in its activities by environmental groups and others.

12.3.2 Problems for private prosecutors

Although private prosecutions are arguably more commonplace, nevertheless, there are a number of problems associated with starting such litigation. It may not always be necessary to commence a legal action; it is possible that the threat of litigation will produce the desired results. The financial cost of commencing a criminal prosecution must be taken into account. Although the criminal courts do have a discretion to award prosecution costs to private prosecutors (*Practice Direction (Crime: Costs)* (1991)), the discretion is generally exercised irrespective of whether the private prosecution is successful or not, provided there was a good reason for bringing the case. Very often, prosecutors will need to employ costly scientific evidence to 'prove beyond reasonable doubt' that the defendant was responsible for the offence. The legal costs of litigation will also be considerable.

Problems also arise in relation to admissible evidence. Private prosecutors are not entitled, like the pollution control authorities, to enter premises and take samples, records, etc. They therefore have to rely on other evidence, such as samples taken by themselves without trespassing on the defendants' property and information entered on the public registers.

Evidential problems could conceivably arise in a private prosecution involving the use of self-monitoring data entered on the public register. A defendant's privilege against self-incrimination enables a criminal court to decline to hear such evidence (s 78 of PACE 1984 and *R v Director of Serious Fraud Office ex p Smith* (1993)). The privilege against self-incrimination and the use of a challenge under Art 6 of the European Convention on Human Rights in an environmental context has been restricted following the decision in *R v Hertfordshire County Council ex p Green Environmental Industries Ltd and Another* (2001).

12.4 JUDICIAL REVIEW IN ENGLISH LAW

Judicial review is available with regard to actions of State or public authorities exercising the powers granted by statute. On a successful judicial review challenge, the court has a discretion to make orders of certiorari, mandamus or prohibition. The effect of these orders is discussed at 2.7.5.9 above.

12.4.1 Judicial review: individuals

The Command and Control regulatory regimes examined in this text contain provisions enabling an applicant to appeal to the Secretary of State against a number of regulatory decisions including: (a) the refusal to grant a licence; (b) the grant of a licence but subject to conditions which the applicant finds unacceptable; (c) Enforcement Notices; (d) Works Notices; (e) Prohibition Notices; and (f) Revocation Notices. Whilst an aggrieved applicant has a statutory right to challenge the regulator's decision, there is no equivalent right for concerned citizens ('third parties'). In order that a concerned citizen may have a role to play in regulatory decision making and policy making, he or she must have a sufficient interest in the legal proceedings which he or she wishes to challenge. The courts refer to this requirement as 'standing' (s 31(3) of the Supreme Court Act 1981 and Pt 54 of the Civil Procedure Rules).

As a general rule, individuals who are geographically proximate to the subject matter of the relevant proceedings, or who are personally affected by them, will have a sufficient interest providing them with standing. Any challenge by a citizen with standing will proceed by way of a judicial review application. The following Command and Control regimes make specific provision for judicial review if aggrieved citizens have standing: the TCPA 1990, the EPA 1990, the WRA 1991, the

WIA 1991 and the PPCA 1999. Judicial review applications must be made within the strict time limits specified in the relevant legislation. Recent decisions on standing in an environmental context give rather mixed messages on the degree of interest which will suffice (see *R v North Somerset District Council ex p Garnett* (1998) and *R v Somerset District Council ex p Dixon* (1998)). The more liberal approach to standing evident in the *ex p Dixon* decision is to be preferred, since the question of standing should operate as a filter to eliminate vexatious or unmeritorious claims. In contrast, the *ex p Garnett* decision supports the view that the question of standing can only be determined by analysing the relevant statutory regime to assess whether the legislation expressly or impliedly provides the applicant with standing. The later case of *North West Leicestershire ex p Moses* (2000) supports this restrictive approach.

12.4.2 Judicial review: environmental pressure groups (NGOs)

The ability of an environmental group (NGO) to seek judicial review in circumstances in which either no individual member of the NGO is affected or there is no individual willing to take action is the subject matter of a long-running debate.

The concept of a group action is one which presumes that citizens generally should be able to bring judicial review actions in the public interest without having to show any individual harm over and above that suffered by the general community. Although no such right of action exists in English public law, it has received some judicial support. In particular, Lord Diplock in *R v Inland Revenue Comrs ex p National Federation of the Self-Employed and Small Businesses Ltd* (1982) asserted that:

> It would, in my view, be a grave lacuna in our system of public law if a pressure group, like the federation, or even a single public-spirited taxpayer, were prevented by outdated technical rules of *locus standi* from bringing the matter to the attention of the court to vindicate the rule of law and get the unlawful matter stopped.

In order to challenge administrative decisions, it is necessary for the person, persons or group seeking judicial review to demonstrate the requisite *locus standi*. The test for standing is contained in s 31(3) of the Supreme Court Act (SCA) 1981. The SCA 1981 requires a person or group to have 'sufficient interest' in the matter to which his or her application for judicial review relates. The courts have developed rules on what amounts to sufficient interest. Initially, the courts placed a restrictive interpretation on NGO 'standing' and have in a number of instances ruled that environmental pressure groups could not satisfy the test. More recent decisions suggest that the courts are more willing to accept that pressure groups do have sufficient interest.

12.4.2.1 NGOs: the restrictive approach

The case of *R v Secretary of State for the Environment ex p Rose Theatre Trust* (1990) illustrates the restrictive approach to judicial review actions adopted by the courts in the case of NGOs. Developers had been granted planning permission to build an office block on the site of an Elizabethan theatre (the Rose Theatre) in London. A trust company was set up by numerous campaigners to preserve the remains of the theatre, which was of particular historical importance because it claimed to be the venue of two first performances of Shakespeare's plays. The Rose Theatre Trust sought to persuade the Secretary of State to designate the site as one of national importance and include it in the list of monuments under the Ancient Monuments and Archaeological Areas Act 1979. If the Secretary of State had so listed the site, it would have meant that no work could begin on the site without his consent. The Secretary of State agreed that the site was of national importance, but decided that it did not fall within the relevant legislation. The Theatre Trust brought the action for judicial review, alleging that the Secretary of State's decision was unlawful. The question was whether or not the Trust had 'sufficient interest' to bring such an action. Members of the Trust argued that since they had entered into correspondence with the Secretary of State, they had the necessary interest. However, the court found that the Trust did not have *locus standi.*

Schiemann J stated that it was necessary to consider the statute to determine whether it afforded standing to these individuals in this instance. On the facts of the case, the court held that no individual could point to anything in the statute that would serve to give him or her a greater right or interest than any other person that the decision would be taken lawfully. The case resulted in a great deal of criticism and was a blow to the notion of public interest litigation. Among other things, it appeared that the court was not concerned that no one could sue in such a situation, leaving the decision of the Secretary of State beyond challenge.

12.4.2.2 NGOs: the liberal approach

In *R v Her Majesty's Inspectorate of Pollution ex p Greenpeace (No 2)* (1994), Greenpeace applied for a judicial review of the decision by HMIP to allow testing at British Nuclear Fuels Thermal Oxide Reprocessing Plant (THORP) at Sellafield. British Nuclear Fuels Ltd (BNFL) argued that Greenpeace had failed to establish a sufficient interest and that its application should be set aside. However, this argument was rejected by the court. Otton J held that Greenpeace was an eminently respectable and responsible organisation and that its genuine interest in the matter was sufficient for it to be granted *locus standi.* In reaching this welcome decision, the court took into account the following factors:

(a) Greenpeace's genuine concern relating to the health of the 2,500 Greenpeace supporters in the Cumbria region;

(b) the nature of Greenpeace ('guardians of the environment') as a campaigning group whose prime objective was the protection of the environment;

(c) the fact that Greenpeace as a responsible and respected environmental organisation had been accredited by the United Nations (UN) and several other international bodies.

Otton J stated that a denial of standing would mean that the people represented by Greenpeace would not have 'an effective way to bring the issues before the court'. Otton J declined to follow the decision in *Rose Theatre Trust* and stated that a denial of standing to Greenpeace would have meant that an application for judicial review would have had to have been brought either by an individual employee of BNFL or a near neighbour. Neither would have had the resources or the expertise to bring such an action and this would have resulted in a less well informed challenge which would have stretched the court's resources.

The decision in this case is greatly welcomed. With a less restrictive view of standing, environmental pressure groups such as Greenpeace, which represent people who are directly affected by the challenged decision or action, are more likely to succeed in achieving *locus standi*. However, a note of caution: in the judgment, the court referred to the advantages of an application from Greenpeace which, with its particular experience in environmental matters and its access to experts in the realms of science, technology and law, could bring a focused, relevant and well argued challenge. It seems, therefore, that the larger national or international NGOs are more likely to satisfy the test than small *ad hoc* or localised groups without the benefit of a 'deep pocket' and expert back-up.

The trend towards recognising the standing of pressure groups was given further support in *R v Secretary of State for Foreign Affairs ex p World Development Movement Ltd* (1995). The World Development Movement (WDM) was an NGO whose main objective was to bring about improvements in the provision of overseas aid and WDM applied for a judicial review of the Foreign Secretary's decision to provide aid to construct the Pergau Dam against the advice of the Overseas Development Administration. Rose LJ held that the WDM had sufficient interest to challenge the government's decision to provide aid for the Pergau Dam scheme, on the basis: (a) that there were few other parties that could challenge the decision; and (b) of the prominence of the WDM in the protection of aid to under-developed countries. The WDM was granted standing even though its members had no direct personal interest in the issue before the court. The Court of Appeal's decision in this case is important not least because it drew attention to the growing willingness of the courts to grant 'surrogate' standing to interest groups. Rose LJ observed that the real question 'is whether the applicant can show some substantial default or abuse, and not whether his personal rights or interests are involved'. In contrast to the *Rose Theatre Trust* decision, the court made it clear that if standing were not granted, then a clear illegality would not be subject to challenge.

In *R v Secretary of State for the Environment ex p Friends of the Earth and Andrew Lees* (1994), Friends of the Earth (FOE) and Andrew Lees (who was FOE's campaign director before his tragic death) challenged the decision of the Secretary of State to accept undertakings from water companies which were in breach of the EC Drinking Water Directive (80/778/EEC) rather than take enforcement action. In this case, Andrew Lees was a resident in the area supplied by one of the water companies, Thames Water, and clearly had a direct health interest in the decision. Like the *Greenpeace* case, the fact that local people who had a local interest (in both cases the interest was in health rather than the protection of the environment *per se*) in the issue and were joined in the action with a pressure group appears to have been relevant. When the *Friends of the Earth* case was considered by the Court of Appeal, it was merely noted that the High Court had granted standing and there was no further discussion of the point.

Standing will normally be granted in cases where a pressure group or individual expects to be consulted in relation to a decision and is not. For example, in *R v Poole BC ex p Beebee and Others* (1991), the applicants represented the Worldwide Fund for Nature and the British Herpetological Society (BHS). They sought to challenge the refusal of the Secretary of State for the Environment to 'call in' a decision of Poole Borough Council to grant planning permission for a new housing development on land which was part of a Site for Special Scientific Interest (SSSI). The applicants had no legal interest in the land in question, but the High Court decided that they did have sufficient interest because one of the conditions of planning permission was that the developers would inform the BHS in advance of any development in order that the BHS could take steps to protect and relocate any protected species. The fact that the applicants had been given the right to be informed in these circumstances was enough to give them the necessary *locus standi*. Similarly, in *R v Swale BC and Medway Ports Authority ex p the Royal Society for the Protection of Birds (RSPB)* (1991), the RSPB was granted standing in a judicial review action. The RSPB sought to challenge a decision by Swale Borough Council to grant planning permission to the Medway Ports Authority to reclaim and develop 125 acres of mud flats known as the Lappel Bank. The RSPB was granted standing on the basis that it had a legitimate expectation, based on correspondence from the Borough Council, that it would be consulted as an interested party before planning permission was granted and that the Borough Council had failed to consult it.

In order to qualify for standing in human rights-based judicial review proceedings, NGOs must qualify as 'victims' (see s 7(3) of the Human Rights Act 1998 and *Greenpeace Schweiz v Switzerland* (1997)).

There are many examples in planning law of individuals seeking judicial review of planning decisions which may adversely affect them. Examples in the field of environmental law include *R v Secretary of State for Trade and Industry ex p Duddridge and Others* (1994). This case concerned parental fears relating to the risk of their children contracting leukaemia due to exposure to the electromagnetic field radiation (EMFs) from high voltage electricity cables. The Secretary of State took a decision not to limit the level of EMFs, although he had the power to do so under the provisions of the Electricity Act 1989. Standing was granted to the parents who sought to force the Secretary of State to exercise his powers to reduce EMF levels. Interestingly, in this case, the applicants argued that the Secretary of State's action was in breach of the precautionary principle laid down in Art 174 (formerly Art 130r) of the EC Treaty. In rejecting the parents' claim, the Court of Appeal held that Art 174 was intended to lay down principles upon which future EC environmental policy might be based. It was not a principle that could bind the Secretary of State.

12.5 ACCESS TO INFORMATION

One of the most important, if not *the* most important, requisites for individuals and pressure groups to take action is that they are equipped with the necessary information (a) enabling them to understand the relevant issues, and (b) providing them with evidence of unlawful activity. Public access to information on the environment may lend itself to improved environmental protection. Since most environmental offences involve the carrying out of unauthorised activities, the public must have access to information to ascertain whether an activity is authorised (licensed) or not and, if it *is* authorised, whether all of the conditions attached to the authorisation are being complied with. Environmental information may also be used for less litigious purposes, for instance, by consumers and customers to identify the environmental track record of companies and factor such information into their respective decision making processes.

Businesses have traditionally favoured less disclosure of information and have perceived public registers as a threat.

Public *information* needs are twofold: access and comprehensibility. Once the information has been gathered, read and understood, the public may then have *access to justice* needs: (a) access to and participation in policy making and decision making processes; (b) the ability to challenge (by way of judicial review and statutory appeals) regulatory policies and decisions perceived as unfair and unjust; and (c) the ability to take civil actions for injunctive relief and compensation arising out of damage caused by the unlawful actions of polluters. The public is especially interested in access to environmental information with regard to: (a) the polluting activities of industry (as revealed in the data recorded in pollution registers); and (b) the activities of the pollution regulators, especially with regard to securing the accountability of the regulator for its decisions. Public trust in the ability of the regulator to protect the public from the effects of unlawful pollution may be damaged by paying too little attention to the information needs and the justice needs of the public (see 12.2 above).

Historically, the UK has been characterised by limited public access to environmental information. The dearth of information available has, arguably, increased the public's concerns regarding the adverse health impacts of exposure to polluting emissions and undermined the public's trust of regulators and government.

Access to information is achieved in a variety of ways including: (a) the series of public registers corresponding to the Command and Control environmental regimes (the WRA 1991, the WIA 1991, the EPA 1990 and the PPCA 1999); (b) the Environmental Information Regulations 1992; (c) the general legislative provision of information – the Local Government Act 1972 and the Freedom of Information Act 2000; (d) the important influence of international law on the future shape of EC law and that of Member States (the Aarhus Convention); and (e) access to a wide range of publicly-available information, including the publications of the Environment Agency and other regulators, the reports of the House of Commons and House of Lords Select Committees, reports published by the RCEP, reports published by NGOs such as Friends of the Earth, and the wealth of information published on the Internet.

12.5.1 Current restrictions on effective public access to environmental information

The following restrictions limit effective public access to environmental information:

(a) Statutory registers maintained by the Environment Agency may only be accessed in Environment Agency premises save that there has been some discussion of allowing Internet access to the relevant registers.

(b) The statutory registers contain bare data. There is no interpretative guidance which would assist the public in assessing whether the breach of licence conditions from a nearby industrial facility poses any threat to health.

(c) A fee is payable for copying data.

(d) Regulatory systems are unable to engage the public meaningfully in environmental policy making and decision making processes. Generally, the public will only consider accessing information in response to a perceived threat.

12.5.2 Who uses registers and for what purpose?

NGOs (for example, Friends of the Earth and Greenpeace) will access information with a view to lobbying the regulator and government departments with regard to policy changes and licensing/siting decisions; individual victims of pollution may use the register data as evidence of breach of the law in civil compensation claims; individuals and NGOs may use the data on the registers as the basis of a private prosecution; NGOs and individuals may use the register data with regard to judicial review challenges of policy, licensing decisions and the use of the regulator's discretion not to prosecute; environmental consultants use registers to target customers regarding sales of pollution abatement technology and environmental services; industry and commerce may attempt to use register data to gain insight into a competitor's process and products (so called 'reverse technology'); and the finance sector (banks) may use registers in order to assess the level of their clients' environmental risk exposure (for example, contaminated land) with regard to current landholdings and proposed acquisitions.

12.5.3 Content of the statutory registers

The information available includes details of applications for licences, licences granted (with conditions), administrative notices served by the Environment Agency (for example, Enforcement Notices), appeals, applications to remove information from the register (national security or commercial confidentiality reasons), monitoring data (including sampling data), details of breaches of licence conditions (for example, the number of breaches) and enforcement action (including the outcome of prosecutions).

The registers do not contain information relating to breaches of the law by non-licence holders.

12.5.4 The Royal Commission on Environmental Pollution

The Royal Commission on Environmental Pollution can take much of the credit for ensuring the introduction of the statutory provisions which established publicly accessible pollution control registers. In its 2nd Report, the RCEP suggested that the arguments in favour of restricting the accessibility of commercial environmental information were not well founded:

> We doubt some of the reasons for this confidentiality and our doubts are shared by many of the witnesses from industry with whom we have spoken. It is a practice which on occasion hinders the flow of information and it leads to risks of misunderstanding on the part of the public which may be harmful to industry and government alike.

In its 10th Report, the Royal Commission recommended that the public should be entitled to the fullest possible information with regard to all forms of environmental pollution and that the onus should be placed on the polluter to substantiate a claim for exceptional treatment (that is, exclusion of information). It accordingly recommended that a guiding principle behind all legislative and administrative controls relating to environmental pollution information should be a presumption in favour of unrestricted access for the public to information which the pollution control authorities receive by virtue of their statutory powers, with protection for secrecy only in those circumstances where a genuine case can be substantiated. It was also suggested that cases where genuine secrets are involved are, in fact, comparatively rare.

The basic premise of the Royal Commission's arguments is that the public has a right to know, that there is a need to restore public confidence in the enforcement system and, importantly, that the public has a beneficial interest in the environment.

The EPA 1990 introduced important new provisions requiring that information held by the regulatory bodies empowered by the Act be available for inspection by the public. The stated aim was that:

> Information must be freely available. Unnecessary secrecy undermines public confidence that pollution has been properly controlled. The new system of public registers which the Act introduces will increase confidence in pollution control. Furthermore it will facilitate public participation in helping to protect the environment. It will mean that every individual can become an environmental watchdog in his or her own right.

The EPA 1990, the WIA 1991 and the WRA 1991, as amended by the EA 1995 and the PPCA 1999, provide for the creation of public registers, maintained by the regulatory authorities. The registers are required to be available for inspection at all reasonable times and copies of entries can be obtained at a reasonable charge. The specific statutory provisions are further supplemented by the Environmental Information Regulations 1992 (SI 1992/3240). In relation to all of these provisions, information may be excluded from the registers on the grounds that its disclosure would be a threat to national security or breach commercial confidentiality. The relevant registers are referred to in Chapters 4–10.

12.5.5 Other sources of environmental information

In addition to the registers of information maintained by regulators such as the Environment Agency, the local authorities and the privatised water companies, pressure groups and individuals can obtain additional information from other sources, including environmental information held by local authorities. This should be available to the general public under the Local Government (Access to Information) Act 1985. In addition, the Clean Air Act (CAA) 1993 provides that local authorities have powers to arrange for research and publicity with regard to air pollution. However, under s 34(2) of the CAA 1993, it is a criminal offence to disclose any information obtained under the CAA 1993 provisions which is a trade secret. Details of hazardous substances consents can be found in registers maintained by the Hazardous Substances Authorities who are under a duty to maintain the registers by virtue of s 28 of the Planning (Hazardous) Substances Act 1990. A number of large companies voluntarily publish information on their environmental performance, usually as an adjunct to their annual reports. In 2001, the European Commission produced non-binding guidelines on how EU businesses should treat environmental issues in annual reports and financial accounts.

12.5.6 Environmental Information Regulations 1992

The Environmental Information Regulations 1992 (SI 1992/3240) make provision for freedom of access to information on the environment held by public bodies. The requirements of the Regulations are more extensive than the system of public registers, but they have a number of weaknesses. In particular, they include a long list of exceptions and provide no statutory right of appeal against a refusal to provide information.

The Regulations give effect to Directive 90/313/EEC on Freedom of Access to Information on the Environment. They place a duty on 'every relevant person' who holds any information to which the Regulations apply to make the information available to every person who requests it, subject to the exceptions. The person supplying the information can make a charge for the supply of the information.

12.5.6.1 Environmental information

By reg 2(1), the Regulations apply to any information which relates to the environment. Information relates to the environment if, and only if, it relates to any of the following:

(a) the state of any water or air, the state of flora or fauna, the state of any soil or the state of any natural site or other land;

(b) any activities or measures giving rise to noise or any other nuisance which adversely affect anything mentioned in sub-para (a) above or are likely adversely to affect anything so mentioned;

(c) any activities or administrative or other measures (including any environmental management programmes) which are designed to protect anything so mentioned.

12.5.6.2 Information

'Information' includes anything contained in records; it therefore includes information held in registers, reports and returns, as well as computer records or other records kept otherwise than in a document.

12.5.6.3 Relevant persons

The duty to furnish information is placed on 'relevant persons'. They are defined in the regulations as Ministers of the Crown, government departments, local authorities and other persons carrying out functions of public administration at a national, regional or local level and which have responsibilities in relation to the environment (for example, the Director General of OFWAT). The definition has a second limb and a person or organisation may be a relevant person if he, she or it has public responsibilities for the environment which do not fall within the above description but are under the control of a person falling within that description. This second limb is capable of including the privatised water companies and sewerage undertakers which have environmental responsibilities and are in the control of Ministers of the Crown and the Environment Agency. In *Griffin v South West Water* (1995), it was held that South West Water was an emanation of the State for the purposes of an EC directive concerned with employment rights. It therefore follows that the water companies may also be subject to the Regulations. However, this particular point has not yet been considered by the courts.

It is clear that the definition includes information held by DEFRA and the local authorities in their various capacities as well as the Environment Agency.

12.5.6.4 The duty to make information available

The duty to make information available is owed to the person requesting the information. The persons or organisations subject to the duty to make information available must ensure that:

(a) every request made for information is responded to as soon as possible;

(b) no such request is responded to more than two months after it is made;

(c) where the response to such a request contains a refusal to make information available, the refusal is in writing and specifies the reasons for the refusal.

The Regulations make provision for the 'relevant person' to:

(a) refuse a request for information in cases where a request is manifestly unreasonable or is formulated in too general a manner;

(b) impose a charge in respect of the costs reasonably attributable to the supply of the information;

(c) make the supply of any information conditional on the payment of such a charge;

(d) make the information available in such a form, and at such times and places, as may be reasonable.

12.5.6.5 Exceptions to disclosure

The Regulations allow for certain categories of information to be excluded from the duty of disclosure. A distinction is drawn between information which must be excluded and other information which may be excluded depending upon the exercise of discretion by the relevant person holding the information.

Certain information must be regarded as confidential and therefore cannot be disclosed. It will be treated as such if:

(a) the information is treated as confidential and its disclosure in response to a request for information would contravene any statutory provision or a rule of law or would involve a breach of any agreement;

(b) the information is personal information contained in records held in relation to an individual who has not given his or her consent to disclosure;

(c) the information is held by the relevant person in consequence of having been supplied by a person who was not under, and could not have been put under, any legal obligation to supply it to the relevant person and has not consented to its disclosure;

(d) the disclosure of the information in response to that request would, in the circumstances, increase the likelihood of damage to the environment affecting anything to which the information relates.

In addition, information may be treated as confidential in the following circumstances:

(a) information relating to matters affecting international relations, national defence or public security;

(b) information relating to anything which is or has been the subject of, any legal or other proceedings (whether actual or prospective);

(c) information relating to the confidential deliberations of any relevant person or to the contents of any internal communications of a body corporate or other undertaking or organisation;

(d) information contained in a document or other record which is still in the course of completion;

(e) information affecting matters to which any commercial or industrial confidentiality attaches or any intellectual property.

12.5.6.6 *Right of appeal*

The Regulations do not provide any specific right of appeal against a refusal to supply information. However, it is possible that a person could seek judicial review of a decision to refuse to supply information since the person from whom the information is requested is under a duty to provide it. Judicial review relates only to the legality of the decision process. It is not a re-hearing of the original decision.

12.6 RECOGNITION OF THE NEED FOR PUBLIC PARTICIPATION

12.6.1 International recognition

At the UN conference on environment and development held in Rio de Janeiro in 1992, over 150 States and the EC agreed to Principle 10 of the Rio Declaration that 'environmental issues are best handled with participation of all concerned citizens, at the relevant level'. Non-governmental organisations (NGOs) have traditionally played an important role in the development of international law and this was particularly the case at the Rio 'Earth Summit'. Not only were many NGOs accredited at the UN conference, many of them played a significant part in the parallel negotiations leading up to the Bio-Diversity Convention (1992) and the Convention on Climate Change (1992). The role played by NGOs was well recognised and in fact a whole Chapter of Agenda 21 was devoted to their activities.

In 1998, further progress was made internationally with regard to access to environmental information with the adoption of the Aarhus Convention on Access to Information, Public Participation in Decision Making and Access to Justice in Environmental Matters. This Convention mirrors the EC Directive on Access to Environmental Information (90/313/EEC), save that its remit is wider, both in regard to the number of State signatories and the types of information which are to be made available (for example, the Aarhus Convention covers access to health and safety information).

12.6.2 EC recognition of the role of the public

The EC's Fifth Environmental Action Programme also envisaged an important role for the citizens of Europe in ensuring that environmental legislation is enforced:

Individuals and public interest groups should have practicable access to the courts in order to ensure that their legitimate interests are protected and that prescribed environmental measures are effectively enforced and illegal practices stopped.

Environmental pressure groups have been particularly active at the European level in two principal ways. First, by participating in the development of environmental law and policy and, secondly, by monitoring compliance with EC environmental law and complaining to the European Commission with regard to cases where EC law has been breached or inadequately enforced. The Fourth Environmental Action Programme (1987–92) stated that one of the aims of the EC's environmental policy was to ensure that directives are not only legally implemented, but are also practically enforced. This monitoring of compliance does not rest entirely with the European Commission or the national regulatory authorities but is supported by individuals and pressure groups.

12.6.3 National recognition

The Department of the Environment produced a publication, *Green Rights and Responsibilities: A Citizen's Guide to the Environment*, which set out the government's thinking on public participation in environmental protection.

In the Secretary of State's Foreword to the *Guide*, the following statement is made:

Government provides the law and institutions within which we exercise our environmental rights and discharge our responsibilities. But unless each one of us plays our own part, no amount of law-making will make any difference to the quality of the environment.

These environmental rights are described as:

(a) the right of access to environmental information which is held by public bodies;

(b) the right to participate in the decision making process on environmental issues; and

(c) the right to seek appropriate remedies in the event of a breach of environmental laws or failure to provide environmental services.

12.7   ENVIRONMENTAL PRESSURE GROUPS

There is a long history of environmental pressure group activity in the UK and such groups are expert in mobilising public opinion. There are now numerous environmental pressure groups (note: they are often referred to as NGOs), some of which have very large memberships and are interested in global environmental and conservation issues. Greenpeace, Friends of the Earth (FOE) and the World Wide Fund for Nature are the obvious ones. In addition, there are many groups which are formed around specific issues, such as the protection of birds or particular species of animal. The RSPB enjoys a particularly large membership, is well resourced and has demonstrated its willingness to take legal action to protect specific bird habitats.

Today, the large pressure groups such as Greenpeace and FOE boast large membership numbers throughout the world, in countries as diverse as Guatemala, Russia and Tunisia. These groups have developed into large organisations with significant financial and technical resources and also highly trained staff (and often volunteers) ranging from scientists to lawyers. The larger pressure groups have become skilled in organising professionally-run campaigns, mobilising public support and media interest.

12.7.1 Using EC environmental law to protect the environment

Environmental pressure groups have been able to exert an influence on both the introduction and enforcement of EC environmental law and have been able to use EC environmental law rights to bring legal actions within the national courts of Member States.

12.7.2 Lobbying at the European level

Given that so much of our current environmental legislation emanates from the EC and that the UK is obliged under Art 5 of the EC Treaty to implement and enforce such legislation, pressure groups have realised the importance of influencing the content of legislation at the European level. Indeed, the same can be said for almost all areas of EC law and Brussels now is a major centre for professional lobbyists. Environmental pressure groups representing a wide range of general and specific interests have been particularly active in bringing pressure on the EC institutions to influence the content of legislation. This has involved lobbying the European Parliament and the Commission, suggesting amendments, providing technical advice and participating in the drafting of directives. There are numerous examples of successful lobbying at EC level.

12.7.3 Environmental pressure groups and the enforcement of EC environmental law

Although it is generally only the larger and well resourced pressure groups that can exert influence on the law making process and the content of environmental legislation, almost all environmental pressure groups can play a role in the enforcement of environmental law. However, this is subject to at least two limitations: first, not all groups will have the financial and technical resources to bring costly legal actions, particularly where they run the risk of having to bear the other side's costs. Secondly, not all pressure groups will be able to challenge decisions made by planning authorities, the pollution regulatory authorities or the Secretary of State by means of judicial review actions because of the difficulties in proving that they have *locus standi*. However, most groups can play a role in terms of monitoring compliance with EC law and they all have the right to complain directly to the European Commission when they believe that EC law is being breached.

12.7.4 Article 226 (formerly Art 169) direct actions

The European Commission receives thousands of complaints each year from pressure groups, their members and aggrieved citizens concerning breaches of environmental law. The legal action brought by the Commission (under Art 226 (formerly 169) of the EC Treaty) against the UK in *Commission v UK* (1993) concerning breaches of the Bathing Water Directive reputedly arose from a complaint received by the Commission in a postcard from an aggrieved holidaymaker at Blackpool. However, the Commission is not under a duty to follow up every complaint it receives and it exercises its discretion as to whether to take action against the Member State involved. Therefore, although the Art 226 procedure offers aggrieved citizens and pressure groups an inexpensive means of attempting to secure compliance, it does not guarantee that the Commission will take any action.

12.7.5 Challenging EC environmental law before the ECJ

In addition to the possibility of complaining to the Commission, environmental pressure groups may also, where relevant, seek judicial review of EC actions under Art 230 (formerly Art 173) and Art 232 (formerly Art 175) of the EC Treaty. Article 230 involves the review of actions, whereas Art 232 is concerned with omissions or the failure of the EC institutions to act. According to the EC Treaty, natural and legal persons (as opposed to the institutions and the Member States) can only seek judicial review against a decision addressed to that person or against a decision which, although in the form of a regulation or a decision addressed to another person, is of direct and individual concern to the complainant. Unlike Member States and the Community institutions, individuals and pressure groups have limited access to the European Court of Justice (ECJ) in judicial review actions. Not all 'acts' are reviewable, only decisions or regulations which are decisions in substance. The test for *locus standi* is that a person is directly and individually concerned. In a number of cases largely concerned with market regulations, the ECJ has placed a very restrictive interpretation on what is meant by the phrase 'direct and individual concern', effectively barring many applicants from bringing such actions. The test which was laid down in the leading case of *Plaumann* (1963) is that a person other than one to whom a decision is addressed will only be individually concerned:

> ... if that decision affects them by reason of certain attributes which are peculiar to them, or by reason of circumstances in which they are differentiated from all other persons, and by virtue of these factors distinguishes them individually just as in the case of the person addressed.

In terms of environmental law, two problems become immediately apparent. First, most environmental measures are in the form of directives and are therefore *prima facie* not reviewable via judicial review actions brought by individuals. It is rare for the Commission to take a formal decision concerned with environmental protection but, as the case below illustrates, it can take decisions which have a bearing on the enforcement of environmental laws, albeit indirectly. Secondly, the *locus standi* test itself is very difficult for environmental pressure groups to satisfy, notwithstanding that the Court of First Instance, which has first instance jurisdiction in judicial review actions brought by natural and legal persons, has, like the English courts, been forced to consider the position of environmental pressure groups.

12.7.6 NGO standing in an EC context: *Stichting Greenpeace Council and Others v EC Commission* (1993)

This case illustrates the importance of judicial review as a means of ensuring that environmental policy and law are enforced and complied with, not only by the pollution control authorities but also by the authors of environmental policy and law, in this instance the European Commission. The Commission, which is responsible for initiating legislation and ensuring compliance, was, in this case, challenged by a number of applicants because of its decision to award financial assistance through the structural funds (regional funds to support infrastructure projects in certain regions throughout the Community) for a project which had not been made subject to the Environmental Assessment Directive (85/337/EEC).

The project in question involved the construction of two power plants in the Canary Islands. The applicants included local farmers and residents, two Canary Island environmental groups and Greenpeace. They sought annulment of the Commission's decision to award a 12 million ECU grant to the projects on the ground that the grant was made for a project for which an environmental assessment should have been carried out in accordance with EC Directive 85/337/EC, and this amounted to a violation of EC law. In order for an individual or association to bring a judicial review action under Art 173 (now Art 230) of the EC Treaty, the complainants had to show that the decision being challenged was either addressed to them or, if addressed to another person, was of 'direct and individual concern to them'. Thus, Greenpeace had to satisfy the ECJ that it was directly and individually concerned with the Commission decision. The ECJ, following a string of previous decisions including *Plaumann*, held that there was no evidence to show that the applicants were affected by virtue of features peculiar to them or that their circumstances differentiated them from all others; therefore, the applicants could not prove that they were individually concerned. It is clear from the case law on Art 173 (now Art 230) that the ECJ has placed a very narrow interpretation upon the phrase 'directly and individually concerned' and even in circumstances such as the case in point, it will be very difficult for pressure groups to satisfy the necessary *locus standi* in such judicial review actions.

12.8   HUMAN RIGHTS

Human rights represents an emerging area in which individuals and environmental groups may use rights-based arguments to challenge the decisions of public authorities. The courts, as well as regulatory agencies, are public bodies for the purposes of the Human Rights Act (HRA) 1998 and are therefore constrained to act in a way which is compatible with the rights enshrined in the European Convention on Human Rights (ECHR). The HRA 1998 requires the courts to take into account, in their decisions, not only the rights granted to citizens by the Convention, but also the judgments and opinions of the European Court of Human Rights and the Commission. National legislation must, as far as possible, be read so as to give effect to the Convention rights, even if this means that the court will depart from a previous decision which would otherwise have been binding on it. It will be unlawful for the courts, and other public bodies, to act in ways which are incompatible with Convention rights (unless the public authority could not have acted differently because of the existence of incompatible legislation).

National courts are empowered to grant such remedies which they consider 'just and appropriate'. This power will enable the courts both to award damages for breach of human rights and, in appropriate cases, quash incompatible subordinate legislation.

Debate as to the potential impact of the ECHR and HRA 1998 currently centres upon two issues: (a) to what extent the ECHR and the HRA 1998 guarantee substantive environmental human rights; and (b) to what extent the ECHR and the HRA 1998 guarantee procedural environmental human rights.

12.8.1 Substantive environmental human rights

The Convention does not directly address the question of whether an individual has a right to a healthy environment. Early ECHR environmental litigation supported the view that the Convention did not provide a right to environmental protection or standards of environmental quality. Nevertheless, the ECHR has been used by litigants as the basis of a number of claims the objective of which was to secure an acceptable level of environmental quality.

12.8.1.1 *The right to life*

Article 2 of the ECHR provides that 'Everyone's right to life shall be protected by law'. At first sight, it seems unlikely that such a right could serve the interests of environmental protection, but it would appear that breaches of Art 2 are not restricted to the protection of physical life. Both significant interference with the quality of life and a threat to life caused by the activities of a public authority could form the basis of an Art 2 action. For example, in *Guerra v Italy* (1998), two members of the European Court of Human Rights were of the opinion that a government which withheld information about circumstances which created a foreseeable and substantial risk of damage to physical health and physical integrity could amount to a breach of Art 2. In the *Guerra* case, the applicants lived only 1 km from a chemical plant which was discharging large quantities of inflammable gases into the environment. It was argued that the gases could cause chemical reactions leading to the release of highly toxic substances. The chemical plant had a 'checkered' operational history. Various accidents had occurred, including an incident in 1976 when 150 people had been hospitalised with serious arsenic poisoning. The applicants complained that the 'Seveso' Directive on the Control of Major Accident Hazards had not been complied with. The Directive required local authorities to advise the local population with regard to the relevant hazards from the plant and the procedures and plans in place to safeguard the local population, but this had not been done. Although the court ruled that the claim under Art 2 was inadmissible, since it had already decided the case on the basis of Art 8, the comments of the two concurring members of the court are significant because they indicate that in certain circumstances, public authorities have a positive obligation to safeguard a citizen's right to life.

Guerra is also significant in that Jamboek J called for the development of implied human rights such as the right to an environment free from health-threatening pollution. The question of liability for failing to warn the public also arose in *LCB v UK* (1998). This case concerned the UK's alleged failure: (a) to warn LCB's parents that LCB might develop leukaemia due to her father's exposure to radiation whilst serving on Christmas Island during nuclear weapon testing; and (b) to monitor LCB's health. Whilst LCB's action failed, the case confirmed that a State is under a duty to take positive action to safeguard the lives of people within its territory, although what action, if any, a State is obliged to take will vary with the circumstances.

The action which a State takes in response to hazards has been the subject of further judicial consideration in *McGinley and Egan v UK* (1998). In this case, it was the government itself which undertook hazardous activities, rather than a private company, as in *Guerra*. Where such activities could pose hidden health risks for workers or others (that is, pollution victims), then the duty to provide information to the potential victims includes both the provision of documents and effective procedures to access that information.

Whilst decision makers in public authorities must be mindful of the need to protect the health and well being of the authority's citizens, Art 2 does not oblige a public authority to provide a healthy environment for its population. Article 2 actions are therefore only likely to stand a reasonable prospect of success where the relevant claim relates to allegations of unreasonable exposure to pollution risks. Even then the court will be wary of imposing unreasonable burdens upon public authorities. Thus, in *Osman v UK* (1998), an Art 2 claim based on negligent policing, the court stated that the right to life 'must be interpreted in a way that does not impose an impossible or disproportionate burden on the authorities. Accordingly, not every risk to life can entail for the authorities a Convention requirement to take operational measures to prevent the risk from arising'. In view of this decision, it remains to be seen whether the suggested link between traffic pollution and asthma could form the basis of a successful Art 2 action. Nevertheless, it is conceivable, following *Osman v UK*, that any public authority (for example, the Environment Agency, local authority, etc) which in full knowledge of the existence of a serious risk to public health (or in circumstances in which it ought to have known of the risk) fails to take reasonable preventive measures (such as closing down a risky activity or at least warning the public of the relevant risks) which results in injury to an identifiable member or section of the public will be liable for breach of Art 2.

12.8.1.2 The right to privacy and family life

Article 8 provides that:

(1) Everyone has the right to respect for his private and family life, his home and his correspondence.

(2) There shall be no interference by a public authority with the exercise of this right except such as is in accordance with the law and is necessary in a democratic society in the interests of national security, public safety or the economic well-being of the country, for the prevention of disorder or crime, for the protection of health or morals, or for the protection of the rights and freedoms of others.

Article 8 imposes a positive obligation on States to take reasonable and appropriate measures to secure the rights of applicants and a negative obligation not to interfere with Art 8 rights unless these are justified by Art 8(2). In *Powell and Rayner v UK* (1990), the applicants who lived close to Heathrow airport based their action on Art 8. The applicants alleged that the noise from the airport adversely affected the quality of their private lives and the scope for enjoying the amenities of their homes and so breached their Art 8 rights. The applicants, along with approximately 6,500 other residents, lived in an area considered to be one of high noise annoyance. The court rejected the applicants' action because of the qualification, in Art 8(2), to strike a balance between the competing interests of the applicants and the wider community. In balancing the relevant interests, the court had regard to (a) the fact that residents had received compensation for noise disturbance, (b) the noise abatement measures which had been taken by the airport, (c) the economic importance of Heathrow airport to the country (for example, in 1998, Heathrow handled cargo to the value of £26.3 billion, contributed £16 million in local rents and rates, generated £200 million to the UK's balance of payments, and provided over 48,000 jobs), and (d) the use, by the UK government, of a regulatory regime to control noise pollution rather than favouring the use of civil actions to resolve noise disputes. Whilst the court found that aircraft noise was interfering with the applicants' use of their homes, the interference was justified in the particular circumstances. The measures taken by the UK government to address the problem were held to be within the UK's margin of appreciation.

In the later case of *Hatton v UK* (2001) concerning sleep disturbance due to night flights at Heathrow Airport, the European Court of Human Rights came to a contrary decision to *Powell and Rayner v UK* (1990) and held that a fair balance had not been struck between the national interest and Hatton's Art 8 right to respect for a private life, family life and the home. In 1993, a noise quota system was introduced for each airline operator at Heathrow Airport permitting a greater number of take-offs and landings of quieter aircraft or a smaller number of noisier aeroplanes. The applicant, Hatton, challenged the quota system, alleging that it constituted a breach of his Art 8 rights. At the hearing, it was accepted that noise levels had increased following the introduction of the quota system. The European Court of Human Rights held that States have a duty to take reasonable and appropriate measures, by fixing a fair balance between individual rights and those of the wider community, to protect Art 8 rights. Interference with these rights could not be justified on purely economic grounds. The State (or a public authority) should minimise the adverse environmental impacts of such schemes on the Art 8 rights of identifiable victims by undertaking a detailed study of the economic benefits of the scheme and its environmental impacts on identifiable victims.

In *Lopez Ostra v Spain* (1995), waste treatment plants were constructed on municipal land just 12 metres from the applicant's home. The operators omitted to acquire a licence authorising their 'nuisance causing' activities. The applicant alleged that odour and noise emissions from the waste treatment plants were causing health problems and were disrupting home life. The court found that as the emissions exceeded permitted limits, they could endanger the health of citizens living nearby. The court stated that 'severe environmental pollution may affect individuals' well being and prevent them from enjoying their private and family life adversely, without however, seriously endangering their health'. The court found in favour of the applicant and awarded 4 million pesetas compensation. There had been an interference with the applicant's Art 8 rights and the interference was not justified by the Art 8(2) qualification. The court noted that whilst the key objective of Art 8 was to protect citizens against arbitrary interference by public authorities, a public body's duty under Art 8 included a positive obligation to ensure effective respect for private and family life. The court concluded that the economic benefit of the treatment plants to the local community did not outweigh the applicant's right to respect for her home and home life. Article 8 could therefore be a fertile source of human rights litigation in circumstances where inaction by a public body exposes citizens to the adverse impacts of environmental pollution. For example, a judicial review action against a regulator is possible in circumstances where the regulator refuses to take enforcement action against a person, such as an IPPC licensed facility, whose emissions are interfering with the Art 8 rights of citizens living close to the polluter.

There is an interesting contrast between the decisions in *Lopez Ostra* and *Powell and Rayner*. In the successful *Lopez Ostra* case, the economic interests were relatively narrow economic interests comprising the private tanneries who used the waste treatment plants. In *Powell and Rayner*, the relevant economic interests at Heathrow airport were of a different order of magnitude altogether and were not confined to a narrow range of private interests.

In *Khatun and Others v UK* (1998), a complaint was made to the European Court of Human Rights arising out of the disturbance caused by the Canary Wharf development. Residents living close to the development were affected by construction dust, could not use their gardens and were forced to close their windows in the height of summer, resulting in excessive heat levels in their homes. The court rejected the claims and accepted the developer's submissions relating to the public benefit arising from the regeneration of Docklands. The court recognised the 'pressing social need' of the project and concluded that a fair balance had been struck between the interference with the applicants' home and private life and the wider public benefit. The *Khatun* case provides an example of the private interests of a developer winning out, as a result of a public decision, over the adverse impacts of the development on the applicants. In this case, the court was able to identify a public economic benefit which justified the interference complained of.

The significance of the HRA 1998 in the context of Art 8 rights is illustrated by the planning case involving the Kings Hill Collective (a group of people who believe in pursuing a sustainable lifestyle). The Collective constructed a number of low impact dwellings known as 'benders' (wooden and canvas shelters) on land near Shepton Mallet without the benefit of planning permission. A planning Enforcement Notice was served on the Collective requiring the removal of the benders. The Collective appealed unsuccessfully to the Secretary of State for the Environment against the Enforcement Notice. Subsequently, the Collective made an application to the High Court to have the Secretary of State's decision judicially reviewed. On appeal, the Court of Appeal confirmed the decision of the High Court that the Secretary of State had erred in not considering whether or not a decision adverse to the Collective would breach Art 8. The decision was remitted to the Secretary of State for reconsideration and the original decision was reversed. Although the erection of the benders was a development which was contrary to the planning policies in the relevant development plan (and therefore the presumption was that the outcome of the appeal would be in accordance with the development plan – see s 54(A) of the Town and Country Planning Act 1990), the appellants' human rights were material considerations of significant weight. Upholding the Enforcement Notice was a serious interference with the appellants' Art 8 rights. Breach of the right to a private and home life had to be balanced against the wider public interest issues comprising the effect of the benders on the surrounding landscape, traffic generation and the potential precedent effect of the bender development. The

Secretary of State concluded that the development would not have a significant adverse impact on the public interest and, after taking Art 8 into account, he concluded that these factors outweighed the planning presumption in favour of development which accords with the development plan. Accordingly, the Enforcement Notice appeal was upheld and retrospective planning permission was granted. The *Kings Hill Collective* case runs somewhat contrary to the general run of similar UK planning cases in which human rights issues have arisen. For example, in *Buckley v UK* (1996), the applicant, a gypsy who purchased land on which she parked her caravans, did not obtain planning approval for the use of her land which resulted in the local planning authority taking enforcement action for breach of planning control. Mrs Buckley argued that the enforcement proceedings prevented her from living a gypsy lifestyle contrary to Art 8. Whilst the court held that Art 8 could apply in such cases, it concluded that the interference with the applicant's Art 8 rights was justified on road safety and public health grounds (see also *Brazil v Secretary of State for Transport, Local Government and the Regions* (2001), *Chapman v UK* (2001), *Clarke v Secretary of State for Transport, Local Government and the Regions* (2001) and *Porter v South Buckinghamshire District Council* (2001)).

In addition to planning cases, Art 8 may be used in the early stages of judicial review proceedings, private nuisance and statutory appeals.

In *Marcic v Thames Water Utilities Ltd* (2002), the claimant sued his sewerage services provider in (a) nuisance, (b) breach of statutory duty, and (c) breach of Art 8 and Protocol 1, Art 1. The case arose out of the continued overflow of the sewage treatment system flooding the claimant's property. Although the defendant was aware of the problem, it gave it a low priority in the selection of projects it was able to undertake each year. The Court of Appeal held (a) that the inadequacy of the sewage treatment system constituted a nuisance, and (b) that the defendant had infringed the claimant's human rights.

In *McKenna and Others v British Aluminium Ltd* (2002), the Birmingham District Registry of the High Court heard an application to strike out a claim by claimants (miners) relating to alleged mental distress and physical harm caused by the operation (environmental emissions, noise and invasion of privacy) of the defendant's factory in the context of the claimants' occupation and/or enjoyment of their homes. The defendant sought to strike out the relevant claims in nuisance and *Rylands v Fletcher* on the basis that the claimants had no proprietary interest in their homes (see *Hunter v Canary Wharf Ltd* (1997) and *Cambridge Water Co v Eastern Counties Leather plc* (1994)) and therefore had no reasonable prospect of winning their case. The claimants argued that their claim should not be struck out on human rights grounds because of: (a) the existence of their Art 8 right to respect for private and family life; and (b) s 6 of the Human Rights Act 1998, which required public authorities (including courts) not to act incompatibly with their ECHR rights. The claimants also relied on *Douglas v Hello! Ltd* (2001) as authority requiring the courts to develop the common law so that it accorded with their ECHR rights.

The court refused to strike out the claim. Although the court thought that an interest in land was probably necessary to found a claim in *Rylands v Fletcher* (on the basis of the reasoning in *Cambridge Water* that the *Rylands v Fletcher* principle was an extension of the law of nuisance), the case ought to proceed to trial as the court should develop the common law so as to be compliant with the ECHR. There was a powerful argument that the claimant's Art 8 rights would not have been properly given effect to if the claimant (with no proprietary interest in his or her home) could not bring an action himself or herself and was therefore at the mercy of the owner of his or her home as the only person allowed to bring proceedings.

12.8.1.3 The right to property

Article 1 of Protocol 1 states that:

> Every natural or legal person is entitled to the peaceful enjoyment of his possessions. No one shall be deprived of his possessions except in the general public interest and subject to the conditions provided for by law and by the general principles of international law.

> The preceding provisions shall not, however, in any way impair the right of a state to enforce such laws as it deems necessary to control the use of property in accordance with the general interest or to secure the payment of other taxes or contributions or penalties.

In *Powell and Rayner v UK*, it was stated that Art 1 of Protocol 1 does not, in principle, guarantee a right to the peaceful enjoyment of possessions in a pleasant environment. It is unlikely that the Article will be capable of forming the basis of an action relating to loss of amenity, such as a pleasant view. Any person (including a company) may be able to rely on the Art 1 right to challenge the decisions of public bodies which, although taken with the object of protecting the natural environment for the general benefit of society (the general public interest), interfere with his or her right to peaceful enjoyment of his or her possessions. In *Fredin v Sweden* (1991), the applicant's licence to extract gravel from his land was revoked (by a public body) following changes in Swedish nature conservation law. In rejecting the applicant's claim, the European Court of Human Rights took note of the following factors: (a) the revocation decision was a property-related control; (b) the Swedish authorities had a legitimate objective in revoking the permission – environmental protection; and (c) the applicant had no legitimate expectation that the permission would not be revoked. It seems that interference with the right to property will be justified where the interference is in conformity with planning laws and is designed to protect the environment (see *Pine Valley Developments v Ireland* (1991)).

The European Court of Human Rights has so far adopted a liberal interpretation of the term 'possessions' in Art 1 of Protocol 1. Licences authorising the development of land (*Pine Valley Developments Ltd v Ireland* (1991)), mineral extraction (*Fredin v Sweden* (1991)), waste management (*R v Leicestershire County Council ex p Blackfordby and Boothorpe Action Group Ltd* (2001)) and public entertainment (*Catscratch Ltd and Lettuce Holdings Ltd v Glasgow Licensing Board* (2001)) are all possessions with significant economic values. Article 1 has also been used as the basis of an action to recover the cost of salmon destroyed without payment of compensation under a Fish Health Regulation Order (*Booker Aquaculture Ltd v Secretary of State for Scotland* (1998)).

Similarly, any State or public authority decision to deprive (or refuse to license) an individual of a possession (for example, planning permission) can be challenged on the basis that the State or public authority has failed to strike a fair balance between the individual's Convention rights and the rights of the wider community. The aims of the State or public authorities must be legitimate and actions in furtherance of the relevant aims must be necessary, proportionate and fair. Human rights-based challenges may not only arise in relation to refusal of planning permission and enforcement of planning control, but also in regard to restrictive policies included in Development Plans which are alleged to breach Art 1 of Protocol 1 (*Katte Klitsche de la Grange v Italy* (1994)).

12.8.2 Procedural rights

12.8.2.1 The right to a fair trial

Article 6(1) states:

> In the determination of his civil rights and obligations or of any criminal charge against him everyone is entitled to a fair and public hearing within a reasonable time by an independent and impartial tribunal established by law.

The European Court of Human Rights has liberally construed the reference in Art 6 to a person's 'civil rights and obligations'. These include a range of property-related rights benefiting both the private and commercial sectors (for example, planning permission, revocation of permission and compulsory purchase). If a person's property is affected by a State or public authority decision and that person has no effective means of challenge, then it is probable that the person's right to a fair hearing by an independent and impartial tribunal will have been breached (Art 6).

Article 6 may be subdivided into the following rights: access to a tribunal, (impartial, independent and lawfully constituted), a fair hearing, a prompt hearing, a public hearing and a public judgment.

In *Benthem v Netherlands* (1985), the applicant was granted a licence to operate a liquid petroleum gas plant by a local authority, but this was later revoked by a central government decree. The European Court of Human Rights held that the applicant's Art 6 rights had been breached because the rights had not been subjected to an adjudication by an independent tribunal. In *Ortenberg v Austria* (1994), the applicant's property adjoined a new housing development and she feared that her right to the enjoyment of the amenities of her property would be infringed by the construction works. She also feared that the value of her property would be adversely affected by the adjoining development. She unsuccessfully attempted to challenge the grant of planning permission in the Austrian Administrative Court. Ultimately, the matter came before the European Court of Human Rights, at which juncture it was held that Art 6 did apply to the circumstances of the applicant's case and although the applicant was attempting to protect her own private pecuniary interests, nevertheless, her Art 6 rights should have been considered by an appropriate tribunal.

Only 'victims' may rely upon Art 6: those persons whose civil rights and obligations are in issue. NGOs such as Greenpeace will generally not have sufficient standing to mount Art 6 challenges (see *R (on the Application of Vetterlein) v Hampshire County Council* (2001)).

Article 6 challenges may be based not only on allegations concerning failures in access to, impartiality and independence of tribunals, but also with regard to procedural failures such as timely access to information, the giving of adequate reasons for a decision, the imposition of inadequate time limits or the lack of proper notice that a tribunal's decision was pending.

The *Alconbury* case (2001) concerned a planning application to develop a redundant Ministry of Defence airfield (government property) as a distribution centre. Planning permission had been refused by the planning committee of the local planning authority and an appeal against the refusal followed. The Secretary of State used his 'call in' power (s 77 of the TCPA 1990) to recover jurisdiction in the case at the appeal stage. This was a case in which the government stood to gain from a decision to allow the development to proceed. A legal challenge was launched against the Secretary of State's action based on Art 6 (the right to a hearing before an 'independent and impartial tribunal').

The High Court ruled in favour of the applicants and held that the Secretary of State's role as both policy maker and decision maker on the 'called in' planning application was incompatible with Art 6 of the ECHR. In effect, the Secretary of State was judge in his own cause. The court went on to state that, in its opinion, the inquiry system provided an adequate safeguard for the public where a planning inspector took a decision with regard to a planning appeal, but not where the Secretary of State took the decision. An appeal to the House of Lords followed swiftly. The House of Lords reversed the High Court's ruling and held that the Secretary of State's powers are not incompatible with the Human Rights Act 1998. The court held that whilst the Secretary of State's consideration of the case, using his 'call in' power, was not an impartial hearing, nevertheless, this was not the decisive factor. It was enough that the Secretary of State's decision was subject to a judicial body which did provide the Art 6 guarantees. (In such cases, a right exists enabling the applicant to apply to the higher courts against the decision of the Secretary of State on a point of law.) Importantly, the judicial control over the Secretary of State's hearing of the matter did not require a rehearing of the merits of the case in order for the current process to amount to a sufficient review of the legality of the decision and the procedures which were followed in reaching that decision. The courts' judicial review powers and the accountability of the Secretary of State to Parliament were adequate safeguards under the Human Rights Act 1998.

The right to a fair hearing may also be the subject of legal challenge relating to the use of this administrative powers of regulatory bodies. Regulators such as the Environment Agency often have legal powers which may be used to elicit information which causes defendants to incriminate themselves. In *Hertfordshire County Council ex p Green Environmental Industries Ltd and John Moynihan* (2000), the county council in its capacity as WRA conducted an investigation into allegations of illegal fly-tipping of waste by Mr Moynihan contrary to s 33(1) of the EPA 1990. The council used its powers (under s 71(2) of the EPA 1990) to require Mr Moynihan to assist the council with its inquiries into alleged waste offences. Mr Moynihan challenged the use of the council's powers on the grounds that their use infringed the rule against self-incrimination and the right to remain silent which is implied in the Art 6(1) right to a fair trial/hearing. Both the Court of Appeal and House of Lords rejected these arguments and dismissed the case. The House of Lords approached this issue by reference to EC law (the Waste Framework Directive (91/156/EEC)), UK law (Pt II of the EPA 1990 and the Waste Management Regulations 1994), and the principles and case law of the European Court of Human Rights, which form part of EC jurisprudence. The court relied on the cases of

Saunders v UK (1996), in which the European Court held that the privilege against self-incrimination did not apply to extra-judicial inquiries, and Case 374/87, *Orkem v Commission* (1989), in which the applicant received a questionnaire from a regulator containing a request for information which, when completed, would amount to an admission of guilt. The questionnaire was held by the European Court to breach the Art 6 privilege against self-incrimination. The House of Lords in *Saunders* held that as the s 71(2) of the EPA 1990 notice was a request for purely factual information, the notice did not breach Art 6 even though the answers provided might be incriminating. Thus, compulsory questioning does not automatically result in a breach of Art 6. Even if a subsequent case were to hold that such a practice breached the information provider's Art 6 rights, there appears to be no bar to a regulator (public authority) issuing multiple requests for information to several individuals on a site where illegal activity is suspected. The information provided by one individual might incriminate another person and vice versa. In these circumstances, there seems to be no breach of Art 6.

In considering the evidence in a criminal prosecution (for example, s 33 of the EPA 1990), a judge is entitled to exclude evidence obtained, via the exercise of a s 71 of the EPA 1990 notice if: (a) the questions are designed to extract an admission of guilt; or (b) the information was unfairly obtained, or was obtained without proper regard to due process. Section 71 of the EPA 1990 or similar information gathering interview powers are not subject to the same strict requirements as interviews conducted by the police under the Police and Criminal Evidence Act 1984.

What happens if information provided via a s 71 or similar information gathering power is subsequently relied upon as evidence in a later criminal trial? Does a breach of Art 6 occur? This issue was considered in *Stott (Procurator Fiscal Dunfermline) v Brown* (2001), not in an environmental context, but with regard to the s 172 of the Road Traffic Act 1972 power to obtain information. In reaching the conclusion that the use of the s 172 power was not a breach of Art 6, the court drew attention to the following factors: (a) the ECHR did not expressly guarantee that a defendant had a right not to incriminate himself or herself; (b) the scope of the privilege against self-incrimination is not set out in detail; and (c) none of the Art 6 rights, express or implied, was absolute. The court went on to hold that a State may limit Art 6 rights, provided (a) in restricting Art 6, the State's objectives were clear and proper; and (b) the limitation of Art 6 was the minimum necessary to enable the State to achieve its objectives. In view of the widespread problem of motor accidents and consequent injuries and deaths, some form of regulation was necessary. Section 172 required the provision of information only with regard to the identity of the driver of a motor vehicle and that information of itself did not incriminate anyone. The penalty for refusing to respond to s 172 was a moderate fine (with no custodial option) and there was no suggestion that the defendant had been coerced into responding to the s 172 request. As s 172 applied equally to all motorists, the restriction on Art 6 was not disproportionate to the objective of the legislation – to improve road safety through identifying and punishing motorists who broke the relevant law.

Compulsory questioning does not breach Art 6 provided: (a) there is a good reason for restricting Art 6; (b) questions are clear and are not designed to extract an admission of guilt; and (c) the information provider is not coerced to supply the information. Any threat relating to the penalties for failure to supply information is likely to amount to coercion and breach of the article (*Heaney and McGuinness v Ireland* (2001)).

12.8.2.2 *The right to freedom of expression*

Article 10 provides:

1   Everyone has the right to freedom of expression. This right shall include freedom to hold opinions and to receive and impart information and ideas without interference by public authority and regardless of frontiers ...

2   The exercise of these freedoms, since it carries with it duties and responsibilities, may be subject to such formalities, conditions, restrictions, or penalties as are prescribed by law and are necessary in a democratic society ...

In *Guerra v Italy* (see 12.8.1.1 above), the application of Art 10 to the facts of the case was considered. Both the Commission and the European Court had interesting remarks to make concerning the relevance of Art 10 rights in circumstances in which State inaction exposes citizens to environmental risks. The failure of the Italian authorities to inform the applicant about the pollution risks generated by the waste treatment plants and the failure to provide information, as required by the Control of Major Accident Hazards Directive, infringed Art 10. The Commission was of the opinion that the provision of information to the public was an essential means to protect the health and well being of the population. Article 10 conferred on the local population who had been affected, or who might be affected, by the activity representing a threat to the environment, a right to receive such information. The court agreed with the Commission but found, in the particular circumstances, that there was no positive obligation on the State to collect and disseminate such information.

12.9   FURTHER INFORMATION

Further reading

See Chapter 7 of *Sourcebook on Environmental Law*, 2nd edn, 2001, Cavendish Publishing, which contains *Guerra v Italy, Booker Aquaculture Ltd v Secretary of State for the Environment, Powell and Rayner v UK* and extracts from the ECHR.

Adams, J, *Risk*, 1995, UCL Press.

Alston, P (ed), *The EU and Human Rights*, 1999, Clarendon.

Beck, U, *Risk Society*, 1992, Sage.

Birtles, W, 'A right to know: the Environmental Information Regulations 1992' [1993] JPL 615.

Boyle, A and Anderson, M (eds), *Human Rights Approaches to Environmental Protection*, 1996, Clarendon.

Brinkman, R, Jasonoff, S and Ilgen, T, *Controlling Chemicals*, 1985, Cornell UP.

Cane, P, 'Standing up for the public' [1995] PL 276.

De Merieux, M, 'Deriving environmental rights from the ECHR' (2001) OJLS 521.

English, R and Havers, P (eds), *An Introduction to Human Rights and the Common Law*, 2000, Hart.

Feldman, D, 'Public interest litigation and constitutional theory in comparative perspective' [1992] MLR 44.

Furedi, F, *Culture of Fear*, 1997, Cassell.

Grant, W, *Pressure Groups, Politics and Democracy in Great Britain*, 2nd edn, 1995, Harvester Wheatsheaf.

Hadfield, B, *Judicial Review: A Thematic Approach*, 1995, Macmillan.

Hallo, R, *Access to Environmental Information in Europe: The Implementation and Implications of Directive 90/313/EEC*, 1996, Kluwer.

Hart, D, 'The impact of the European Convention on planning and environmental law' [2000] JPL 117.

Hilson, C and Cram, I, 'Judicial review and environmental law: is there a coherent view of standing?' (1996) Legal Studies 1.

Jendroska, J and Stec, S, 'The Aarhus Convention: towards a new era in environmental democracy' (2001) Env Liability 140.

Jewell, T and Steele, J (eds), *Law in Environmental Decision-Making*, 1998, Clarendon.

Miller, C, *Environmental Rights: Critical Perspectives*, 1998, Routledge.

Mowbray, A, '*Guerra v Italy*: the right to environmental information under the ECHR' (1998) Env Liability 81.

Pugh, C and Day, M, *Pollution and Personal Injury: Toxic Torts II*, 1995, Cameron and May.

Ridley, F and Jordan, G, *Protest Politics: Cause Groups and Campaigns*, 1998, OUP.

Robinson, D and Dunkley, J (eds), *Public Interest Perspectives in Environmental Law*, 1995, Wiley.

Rowan-Robinson, J, 'Public access to environmental information: a means to what end?' [1996] JEL 19.

Rowell, A, *Green Backlash: Global Subversion of the Environmental Movement*, 1996, Routledge.

Royal Commission on Environmental Pollution, *Tackling Pollution: Experience and Prospects*, 10th Report, Cmnd 9149, 1984, HMSO.

The Royal Society, *Risk: Analysis, Perception, and Management*, 1992.

Sandman, P, *Responding to Community Outrage: Strategies for Effective Risk Communication*, 1993, American Industrial Hygiene Association.

Schiemann, K, *'Locus standi'* (1990) PL 342.

Simpson, D, *Pressure Groups*, 1999, Hodder & Stoughton.

Stanley, N, 'Public concern: the decision-maker's dilemma' [1998] JPL 919.

Stanley, N, 'Contentious planning disputes: an insoluble problem?' [2000] JPL 1226.

Steele, J, 'Participation and deliberation in environmental law: exploring a problem-solving approach' (2001) OJLS 415.

Symonides, J (ed), *Human Rights – New Dimensions and Challenges*, 1998, Ashgate.

Thornton, J and Tromans, S, 'Human rights and environmental wrongs incorporating the ECHR; some thoughts on the consequences for UK environmental law' [1999] JEL 35.

Vick, D and Campbell, K, 'Public protests, private lawsuits and the market: the investor response to the McLibel case' (2001) Journal of Law and Society 204.

Vogler, J, *The Global Commons: A Regime Analysis*, 1995, Wiley.

Wilson, D, *The Secrets File*, 1984, Heinnemann.

APPENDIX

LEGAL RESOURCES: A BASIC GUIDE
FOR NON-LAWYERS

Non-law students embarking upon the study of environmental law for the first time may be intimidated at first by the materials which are the stock in trade of the lawyer: textbooks packed full of information, reports of court cases contained in a variety of law reports, legislation (both primary legislation – Acts of Parliament – and secondary legislation – regulations) and academic/professional journal articles. However, based on our own experience of teaching a variety of environmental courses to both law and non-law students, we can state with confidence that non-lawyers find, after an initial period of familiarisation, that they can perform just as well as law students.

This chapter introduces non-law students to the most important sources of information on environmental law.

CASES

You will find reports of legal cases/decisions in law reports which are to be found in most university libraries (provided the relevant university has a law department).

There are a whole range of reports, for example, the All England Reports, and these are arranged alphabetically and by year. Your course textbooks and case reports will cite (refer to) previously decided cases as authority for the statements made in the chapters of each text. The relevant case may look something like this: *Alphacell Ltd v Woodward* [1972] 2 WLR 1320. This means that this case is reported in the Weekly Law Reports, for the year 1972, in the second volume for that year, commencing on page 1320. Often, a case is reported in more than one report and you will therefore have a choice of which set of reports to refer to. The abbreviations used to describe the relevant set of reports are often explained in a pamphlet which your university library will make available. Alternatively, there should be a notice or board in the law library which explains which reports are stocked and where they are to be found. Law libraries should stock the British Libraries Legal Index. This is a publication which records academic journal articles published on a year-by-year basis. At the front of each part of the Index, you will find an explanation of the abbreviations (for example, JEL – Journal of Environmental Law) used in the Index.

When you have successfully located the case which you have been looking for, you will usually find the case report divided up into (a) a summary of the main facts of the case, (b) a note of what the case actually decided (look for the heading 'Held'), (c) the cases and legislation which were referred to by the advocates in the case, and (d) the individual judgments of the judges making up the court. Cases decided in the Court of Appeal and the House of Lords will each contain a series of judgments, whereas cases decided in the High Court will usually be decided by a single judge.

Currently, there is only one series of reports which focuses on reporting environmental cases decided in the UK or decisions of the ECJ which will have a bearing on future cases in the UK (the Environmental Law Reports – cited as Env LR and published by Sweet & Maxwell). Other law reports which often report environmental decisions are listed at the end of Chapter 1.

TEXTBOOKS

There are several good books which cover environmental law in England and Wales (see the texts and other materials listed at the end of Chapter 1, which also refer to texts covering environmental law in Scotland and Northern Ireland). Non-lawyers will quickly come to realise that the information in legal textbooks cannot be absorbed by a cursory browse through the chapters which correspond to the topics on your module. The contents of textbooks have to be read and re-read until the reader understands the points which are being made. Your course/module handouts will almost certainly not provide you with all the information you must know and be able to apply to enable you to answer examination questions and assessed essays. Your course handouts provide you with a framework for your studies. That framework must be supplemented by studying your textbook(s), case reports, relevant extracts from legislation and journal articles. If you are prepared to devote an appropriate amount of time to your studies, you should do well. If for any reason you encounter problems understanding the course material, the onus is on you to discuss the matter with your environmental law tutor. At the end of Chapter 1, we have also referred you to environmental casebooks which contain key extracts of legislation and case reports. At the end of most of the chapters in this text, we have made a reference to the corresponding chapter in the *Sourcebook on Environmental Law*, written by Sunkin, Ong and Wight.

JOURNALS

The main environmental law journals are referred to in the materials at the end of Chapter 1.

LEGAL DICTIONARIES

The law section of your library should contain a number of copies of legal dictionaries. Non-law students often find legal terminology a little alien at first, but being aware of where to find a legal dictionary ought to soothe any concerns you may have that you will not understand 'legal language'.

THE LIBRARY CATALOGUE

It is highly likely that your university will have a catalogue of contents which can be searched electronically. Provided you have a password, you may even be able to search the catalogue from your own PC rather than attending the library in person. The most common searches are: author searches, title searches and key word searches. Students (whose university has a law department) will probably be able to access WESTLAW, Lexis/Nexis, Lawtel and other databases of legal information online through their university library home page. These databases contain reported cases (UK and other jurisdictions), legislation, and journal articles (refer to your library for full details of the extent of these resources).

WEBSITES

At the end of Chapter 1, we have included a number of website addresses which will enable you to access a wide range of materials relating to environmental law and policy.

INTER-LIBRARY LOAN SYSTEM

Your university will be able to obtain for you via this system a book, article, report, etc, which is not held in your own library collection (a modest fee is payable for this service).

PUBLIC LIBRARIES

Public libraries in major cities in the UK will often have a legal section both in the reference section and the lending library. As might be expected, the range of materials is limited when compared with university collections. Public libraries operate a similar system of inter-library loans to that used by university libraries (a fee is payable).

THE COURT SYSTEMS

Non-lawyers should note the basic division of our legal system into criminal law and civil law. We set out below a simple diagram overleaf distinguishing between the criminal and civil court systems.

HOUSE OF LORDS

(Hears appeals from the Court of Appeal (criminal and civil appeals) and the High Court (civil appeals))

COURT OF APPEAL

CIVIL DIVISION

(Hears appeals from the High Court, county courts and tribunals)

CRIMINAL DIVISION

(Hears appeals from the Crown Court)

HIGH COURT

CHANCERY DIVISION

(Hears equity, trusts, probate, tax and bankruptcy cases)

FAMILY DIVISION

(Hears matrimonial cases and cases concerning children)

QUEEN'S BENCH DIVISION

(Hears contract and tort cases)

DIVISIONAL COURT

(Hears county court appeals regarding bankruptcy and land registration cases)

DIVISIONAL COURT

(Hears appeals from county courts and magistrates' courts relating to the family)

DIVISIONAL COURT

(Hears appeals from the Crown Court and magistrates' courts and judicial review cases)

CROWN COURT

(Hears trials of indictable offences and appeals from the magistrates' courts)

COUNTY COURTS

(Hears most civil cases)

MAGISTRATES' COURTS

(Hears summary cases)

INDEX

Aarhus Convention. 295, 471, 476

Abandoned mines. 122

Abatement Notices 357–65
  appeals. 360–62, 391–92
  best practicable
    means. 363, 364–65, 394
  case stated 388, 389
  citizens, action by. 366–67
  codes of practice. 364, 394
  consultation. 359
  criminal offences 362–67, 393
  defences against
    non-compliance with. 363–67
  duration of. 361–62
  environmental health
    officers 359
  expenses, recovery of
    local authority. 392
  fines 363
  form of 357–59,
    387–88
  High Court proceedings 363
  injunctions. 363, 393
  Integrated Pollution
    Control 290
  landlords 359–60
  local authorities. 357–59, 362–63,
    366, 389–92,
    394–95
  more than one person,
    involvement of 360
  motor vehicles. 359
  noise 358, 361–62, 373,
    387–95, 398
  non-compliance with. 362–63, 392–95
  reasonable excuse. 363–64, 393–94
  service of 387, 391–92
    more than one
      person, on 360
    persons who
      should receive. 359–60, 389–90
  time for compliance 388, 390
  works
    execution of. 358
    specification of 358

Abatement, remedy of 414–15

Absolute discharge 63

Access to information. . . . .
  Aarhus Convention 471
  appeals. 474, 476
  atmospheric pollution 473
  Command and
    Control regulation 471
  comprehensibility
    of information. 471
  confidentiality. 473, 475–76
  contaminated land 314
  criminal offences 473

  duty to make
    information available. 475
  EC law 110, 471, 474
  Environment Agency. 159–60, 471
  environmental information,
    definition of. 474
  exceptions to disclosure 465–76
  hazardous substances 473
  information, definition of 474
  interest groups 472
  local authorities 473
  private prosecutions 465
  private regulation
    of pollution 470–76
  public bodies. 473–74
  public concern. 459
  public registers 470–74
  regulators, trust of 471
  relevant persons 474–75
  restrictions on 471–72
  sewerage undertakers 474
  trade secrets 473
  water 159–60, 171, 474

Accumulators. 239

Acid rain 346–47

Acts of God. 444

Administration 29–68
  Command and
    Control regime 6, 29
  courts 59–55
  discharge consent
    licences 129
  Environment Agency. 48
  Integrated Pollution
    Prevention and
    Control 299
  licences. 9
  local authorities 30
  notices,
    non-compliance with. 46
  planning. 30
  reasons for changes in 35–37
  regulation 9
  waste management
    licensing. 215–18

Advisory Committee on
Business and the
Environment. 59

Advocates General 80

Agenda 21 14

Aggravated damages 413

Aggregates Levy 18

Agriculture . . . .
  common agricultural policy 109
  criminal offences 149
  due diligence. 149
  EC law 109, 153

Nitrate Sensitive Areas,
    agreement on...................... 155
Nitrate Vulnerable Zones 156
sewage sludge....................... 109
silage, slurry and fuel oil............ 153
water.................... 122, 149, 151,
                             153, 155–56
Air pollution
    See Atmospheric pollution
Air Quality Management
    Areas 329–31, 333
Air Quality Plans................... 331–32
Aircraft noise................ 372, 375, 380,
                          383, 402–03, 423
Alarms, noise
    from burglar...................... 402
Alkali works................... 30, 260, 328
Alternative dispute
    resolution 408
Amenity groups
    See Interest groups
Amenity, loss of.................. 351, 486
Animals............................ 355
Anti-Pollution
    Works Notice 52, 157–59
Anti-social
    behaviour orders............... 403–04
Appeals
    Abatement Notices........ 360–62, 391–92
    access to information........... 474, 476
    carriers, registration of 251
    charging orders notices.............. 322
    Command and
        Control regulation 10
    contaminated land............... 322–23
    damages........................ 217, 220
    discharge consent licences 132–33
    Enforcement Notices 301
    Environment Agency............. 219–20
    expenses........................... 323
    inspectors 220
    Integrated Pollution
        Control................... 283, 288–89
    Integrated Pollution
        Prevention and Control............. 301
    licences........................ 283, 288
    noise 391–92,
                             400, 405
    public registers 220
    regulation......................... 5–11
    Remediation Notices 322–23
    Secretary of State 219–20, 288–89
    sentencing 61
    smoke............................ 341
    Suspension Notices 217, 220, 301
    trade effluent consents 164
    Variation Notices 301

waste management 222–23, 251
    licensing.................. 217, 219–20
    Works Notices..................... 159
Asbestos **308**
Atmospheric pollution............. **327–48**
    See also Local Authority
        Air Pollution Control
        (LAAPC); Smoke
    access to information................ 473
    acid rain........................ 346–47
    Air Quality
        Management Areas 329–31, 333
    Air Quality Plans 331–32
    alkali works....................... 328
    BATNEEC 344
    benzene emissions 342
    BPEO 278
    carbon monoxide 342–43
    charging schemes.................. 332
    chlorofluorocarbons................ 345
    Climate Change
        Convention 346
    climate change levy 347
    climatic disruption,
        threat of severe 327–28
    codes of practice................ 402–03
    contingency plans 331
    criminal offences 327
    crop residue burning 334
    EC law 327, 330, 344–46
        chlorofluorocarbons................ 345
        framework directive on............. 115
        hydrofluorocarbons 345
        industrial plant,
            emissions from large 344
        Integrated Pollution
            Prevention
            and Control 344
        motor vehicle
            emissions 115, 343, 345
        ozone layer 345
        power stations..................... 344
        quality standards 115, 345
        waste............................ 238
    ecosystems, threats to 327
    effects-based approach 329
    emergencies.................... 331, 343
    energy suppliers,
        climate change levy and 347
    Environment Agency................ 39
    fuel, composition of 343
    global warming 328, 346–47
    Geneva Convention on
        Long Range
        Transboundary
        Air Pollution 346
    government policy.............. 328–29
    guidance 329

Her Majesty's Inspectorate
    of Pollution 333
highways, lighting fires on 334
historic controls 328
human health, threats to 327
hydrocarbons 343
hydrofluorocarbons 345
incinerators 187, 243, 333, 346
industrial plant,
    emissions from large 344
industrial processes,
    licensing for 332
Integrated Pollution
    Control 327, 333
Integrated Pollution
    Prevention and Control 327, 344
international law 346–47
Kyoto Protocol 346–47
Large Combustion
    Plant Directive 344
licensing 332
local air quality management 329
Local Air Quality
    Management Areas 330–31
local authorities 329–33, 343–44
motor vehicle emissions 327, 329,
                                        342–44
    EC law 343, 345
    fuel, composition of 343
    local authorities 343–44
    quality standards 115, 345
National Air Quality
    Strategy 327, 330, 333
nuisance 333, 342
ozone layer 345–46
planning 333–34
power stations 344
problems caused by 327–28
product quality
    standards 345
quality standards 115, 329, 331,
                                        344, 345
Rio Convention 346–47
Secretary of State,
    role of 330, 332
separated and
    integrated control of 6
smog 328
traffic re-routing 343
traffic restrictions 329, 344
waste 187, 236, 345–46
Authorisations
See Licences

BAT
See Best available
    techniques (BAT)
Bathing waters **135, 175**

BATNEEC
See Best available technology
    not entailing
    excessive cost (BATNEEC)
Batteries **239**
Benzene emissions **342**
**Best available techniques
    (BAT)** **291–92, 296–99**
    available, meaning of 297
    BAT reference 297
    best, meaning of 297
    best available
        technology not
        entailing excessive
        cost (BATNEEC) 292
    call in power 298
    clean-up 298
    costs and benefits 297
    definition 297–98
    EC law 297
    Environment Agency 298
    IPPC Information
        Exchange Forum 297
    permits 298–99
    proportionality 297
    Secretary of State 298
    techniques, meaning of 298
    waste management
        licences 298
**Best available technology
    not entailing excessive
    cost (BATNEEC)**
    atmospheric pollution 344
    best available techniques 292
    BPEO 277–78
    conditions 276–78
    criminal offences 277
    definition 276
    Environment Agency 275–78
    guidance notes 277
    implied conditions 276–77
    Integrated Pollution Control 274–78
    licences 275–77
    local authorities 275–77
    Local Authority Air
        Pollution Control 277, 334
**Best practicable
    environmental option
    (BPEO)** **259, 261–62**
    atmospheric emissions 278
    BATNEEC 277–78
    definition 262, 278
    Environment Agency 262, 278
    Integrated Pollution
        Prevention and Control 259, 292
    Local Authority Air
        Pollution Control 334
    Royal Commission on
        Environmental Pollution 261, 278

seriously polluting
  processes 262
Best practicable means
  Abatement Notices 363, 364–65, 394
  noise 394, 400–01
  nuisance 422, 430
**Best practicable
  techniques** 317
Biodiversity 111, 114, 476
Birds 98
Bowsers 168
BPEO
  See Best practicable
  environmental
  option (BPEO)
Breach of statutory duty
  civil proceedings 352–53
  contributory negligence 453
  criminal offences 46
  damages 453
  defences 452–53
  volenti non fit injuria 452–53
Brokers 205, 247–48
Bruntland Report 14, 40, 109
Building regulations 407
**Burglar alarms,
  noise from** 402
Burning 334, 338–39
Bylaws 399
Byproducts 195

Cambridge Water **case** 445–48
  common law 445–46, 448–49
  EC law 448
  foreseeability 433, 447
  non-natural users 447
  nuisance 446–47
  private regulation
  of pollution 445–46
  Rylands v Fletcher 446, 447
  water pollution 445–48
**CAP (common
  agricultural policy)** 109
Caravan sites 485
Carbon monoxide 342
Carriers
  See Transport
Cases, legal resources and 493–94
Catalogues 494–95
Cement kilns 197–98
Certiorari 66
Change of use 242–43
Charging order notices 322
Charging schemes
  atmospheric pollution 332

Command and Control
  regulatory schemes 19
  discharge consent licences 130
Environment Agency
  risk assessment 19
  Her Majesty's Inspectorate
  of Pollution 32
  licence fees 19
  operation pollution
  risk appraisal 19
  regulation 19
  risk assessment 19
Chemicals 2–3, 308
Chimneys 340–41
Chlorofluorocarbons 345
Civil proceedings
  breach of statutory duty 452–53
  common law 451–53
  courts 495–96
  damages, express statutory
  rights to 452
  EC law 453–54
  enforcement 20
  private regulation
  of pollution 451–53
  statute, under 451–53
  waste management 223–24, 247, 255
Clean-up
  See also 'Polluter pays' principle
  allocating the costs of 319–21
  appropriate person 317–19
  best available techniques 298
  Class A persons 318–21
  Class B persons 318–21
  contaminated land 290, 303, 310
  definition 316
  EC law 454
  expenses of 222–23, 317–21
  Integrated Pollution
  Control 290
  Integrated Pollution
  Prevention and Control 298
  neighbouring land 217
  Remediation Notice 290, 314–17,
                                               321–24
  standard of 310, 316–17
  suitable for use concept 310
  Superfund 310
  Remediation Notices 322–23
  waste management 217, 218,
                                               222–24, 324
  water 122, 151, 157–59,
                                               172, 324
Climate change
  atmospheric pollution 346–47
  energy suppliers and 347
  global warming 328, 346–47
  greenhouse gases 18–19

levy 347
  precautionary principle 16
  public participation 476
Coastal waters **127**
Combustion processes **269**
Command and
  Control regulation. **5, 29**
  access to information 471
  administration 6, 29
  alternatives to 16–20
  appeals. 10
  charging schemes. 19
  common law 411–12
  continuous. 10
  courts 59
  criminal offences 8, 46, 53, 224
  enforcement. 47
  Environment Agency. 6
  Integrated Pollution
    Control 259
  Integrated Pollution
    Prevention and
    Control 259
  investigations 8
  judicial review 466
  legislation 6
  licences. 6–8
  main regimes. 10–11
  private regulation
    of pollution 411
  public registers 10
  waste management 185, 190
  waste offences. 224
  water 121
Committee on Environment,
  Public Health and
  Consumer Protection **80**
Committee on Sustainable
  Development **59**
Common agricultural policy **109**
Common law **411–54**
  abatement, remedy of 414–15
  advantages 450–51
  Cambridge Water case 445–46, 448–49
  civil actions 451–53
  Command and
    Control regulation 411–12
  common law 411–53
  contingency fees. 449
  contributory negligence 416
  costs 449
  damages. 413–14
  defences. 415–16
  disadvantages. 448–50
  EC law, civil
    liability and 453–54
  evidence. 449
  foreseeability. 449–50

injunctions. 412, 414–15, 451
limitation periods. 450
necessity. 416
negligence 431–39
noise. 377–82, 384–85
nuisance 351–52, 377–78,
                                384, 417–31
private regulation
  of pollution 411–53
private rights,
  protection of 412
remedies 413–15, 451
remoteness. 449–50
Rylands v Fletcher 441–45
statutory authority. 415–16
torts. 411–12, 415–16
trespass 439–41
volenti non fit injuria 416
Companies
  contaminated land 321
  criminal offences 47, 60, 61, 63,
                     148, 229–31, 255
  directors, liability of 47, 146,
                         229–30, 255
  Environment Agency,
    information from 153
  fines 63
  health and safety 229–30
  Integrated Pollution Control 287
  Integrated Pollution
    Prevention and Control. 302
  liability of 47, 50, 287,
                           302, 321
  managers, liability of 229–30, 255
  officers, personal liability
    of senior 47, 50
  prosecutions 50
  regulation. 11–13
  sentencing 60, 61, 63
  small. 51, 153
  waste offences. 229–31, 255
  water pollution. 146, 148
Compensation
  See Damages
Compensation orders **396**
Compulsory questioning. **489–90**
Conditional discharge **63**
Confidentiality
  access to information 473, 475–76
  criminal offences 473
  Integrated Pollution
    Control 279–80, 288
  Integrated Pollution
    Prevention and Control. 301
  public registers 220, 279–80,
                          301, 473
  trade secrets 473
  waste management
    licensing 220

Consignment
note system **253–54**
Construction sites **399–401**
Containerisation **250**
Contaminated land **307–26**
abandonment of 309
access to information 314
activities typically
associated with 307
allocating the costs of. 319–21
appeals
charging order notices 322
Remediation Notices 322–23
appropriate person. 317–19, 321
asbestos 308
best practicable
techniques 317
causing or knowingly
permitting contamination. 318–19
charging order notices. 322
chemicals. 308
clean-up 290, 303, 323–24
allocating the costs of. 319–21
appropriate person. 317–19
Class A persons. 318–21
Class B persons. 318–21
definition 316
expenses of 317–21
Remediation Notice 290, 314–17,
321–23
standard of 310, 316–17
suitable for use concept. 310
combined impact of
more than one
parcel of land. 313
companies, liability of 321
consultation. 315–16
criminal offences 314, 322
definition of. 311, 368
enforcement. 313
English Nature 315
Environment Agency 39, 290,
314–15, 324
exclusions 320–21
expenses of . . . .
appeals. 323
charging order notices. 322
clean-up 317–21
fines 322
government objectives. 310
groundwater 308
guidance 311
identify, duty to 314–15
interface with
other controls 323–25
inspection 314
Integrated Pollution
Control. 290, 303, 324

Integrated Pollution and
Prevention Control. 303, 324
investigations 314–15
licences. 323
linkage 312–13
local authorities 54, 309, 312,
314–15
nature conservation 315
notify, duty to 315–16
nuisance, statutory 313–14, 317,
324–25, 349–50,
367–68
owners and occupiers,
liability of. 318–19
planning. 316, 322, 325
polluter pays. 318
potentially 315
pre-existing
contamination. 303
property blight
and stigma 308
public registers 309, 314,
316, 323
abandonment of,
reasons for 309
Remediation Notices 322
receptors, definition of 312–13
recognition of the
problem of 308–09
Remediation Notice 290, 314–17,
321–24
risk assessment 311, 313
risks associated with 308
sale of land 320
significant harm 311–13
solvents 308
special sites 290, 313–15
specific incidents 307
statutory framework 313–17
strict liability. 318
subsidiary role of
contaminated land
controls 323–24
Superfund 310
tax incentives 323
waste management 219, 245
water 172, 315, 308, 324
Contingency fees. 449
Contracts **20, 203–04,
249, 382**
Contributory negligence **416, 452, 453**
Costs
common law 449
private prosecutions 48, 465–66
sentencing 63–64
Costs/benefits
best available techniques 297
Environment Agency. 43–44

precautionary principle 15
Scottish Environmental
    Protection Agency 43
Council of the European Union 76–77
Countryside Council for Wales 58, 210
Courts
adjudication function 59–60
administration, role in 59–66
Command and
    Control regulation 59
Court of First Instance 80–81
criminal and civil law
    systems of 495–96
criminal offences 59–60
Department for
    Environment, Food and
    Rural Affairs 66
enforcement, role in 59–66
European Court of Justice 71, 80–81,
    100–02
Grant Report 66
interpretative role 64
judicial review 64–66
role of 59–66
sentencing 60–64
specialist court, need for 66
statutory interpretation 64
supervisory body 64–66
Covenants 20
Criminal offences
See also Private prosecutions;
    Prosecutions; Sentencing;
    Waste offences;
    Water offences
Abatement Notices 362–67, 393
access to information 473
administrative notices,
    non-compliance with 46
atmospheric pollution 327
BATNEEC 277
breach of statutory duty 46
causing or knowingly
    permitting pollution 46
choice of offences 53
Command and Control
    regulation 8, 46, 53
compensation orders 396
contaminated land 314, 322
courts 59–60, 495–96
directors 47
discharge consent
    licences 129, 131
drinking water 169
EC law 241
enforcement 50
Environment Agency 46–47, 149
fitness for human
    consumption 169

health and safety 229–30
inspections 46
Integrated Pollution
    Control 262, 268–69, 284,
        286–90, 292, 300–03
licences 3, 8, 46
Local Authority
    Air Pollution Control 286
marine pollution 180
noise 373, 381, 382,
        393, 395–400, 405
nuisance 367, 429
officers, personal
    liability of
        senior company 47
oil pollution 180
packaging 241
regulation 8
Remediation Notices 322
sewage 163–64
smoke 327, 336–40
strict liability 47
trade secrets 473
waste
    EC law 241
    management
        licensing 206, 209, 211,
            218, 222–23, 248
    packaging 241
water 169
Crop residue burning 334
**Curtilage, waste
    within the 208**
Custodial sentences
Integrated Pollution
    Control 288
Integrated Pollution
    Prevention and Control 302
waste management
    licensing 218, 222
waste offences 228–29, 231, 255
water pollution 150

Damages
aggravated 413
breach of
    statutory duty 453
civil litigation 12, 452
common law 413–14
contributory negligence 416, 452
directives, failure
    to implement 94–96
discharge consent
    licences 133
exemplary 413–14, 428
Human Rights Act 1998 480
judicial review 66
loss of profits 427–28

Member State liability 94–96
negligence 434, 438
noise 381–82
nuisance 381–82, 419,
                      427–28, 430–31
punitive 413–14
riparian waters 160
Rylands v Fletcher 445
statutory right to,
    express 452
trespass 441
volenti non fit injuria 452
waste management 223, 247, 255
    licensing 214–15, 217, 220
water 160, 168
Works Notices 159
Dams **146**
Dangerous substances
See also Hazardous substances
discharge consent licences 135
EC law 97, 114–15
licensing 174
packaging and labelling 97
waste management
    licensing 213
water 174, 213
Databases **485**
Decisions,
    EC legislation and **75**
Definition of environment **3**
Definition of
    environmental law **1, 4**
Definition of pollution **2, 292**
Demolition sites **336–37**
Department for
    Environment, Food
    and Rural Affairs. **55–56**
Deposit and refunds schemes. **20**
Detergents. **176**
Development of
    environmental law **5**
Dictionaries **494**
Dioxins **239**
Direct effect **88, 90–93**
Directives
    See also Waste
       Framework Directive
atmospheric pollution 115
bathing water 175
damages 92–96
dangerous substances 174
detergents 176
direct effect 91–93
Directive on Civil Liability
    for Damage to the Environment
    Caused by Waste (Draft) 453–54
drinking water 175, 176

emanations of the State 92–93
Environmental Impact
    Assessment Directive. 304
failure to implement 74–75, 92–96
fisheries 176
framework 115
horizontal direct effect. 92–93
landfill 236–38
Member State liability 94–96, 116
oil pollution. 180
packaging 240–41
Seveso Directive on
    Control of Major
    Accident Hazards. 481, 490
shellfish 176
standards 7
sulphur dioxide 341
surface water. 175
titanium dioxide. 176–77
transposition of 13, 69, 74, 83, 91,
                      94–96, 116–17
Urban Waste
    Water Directive 177
waste management
    licensing 205, 207, 214
Director of Public
    Prosecutions **161**
Directors, liability of **47, 229–30, 255**
Discharge consent
    licences **121, 129–37**
administration 129
advertising 130
Anti-Pollution Works Notice 157–58
appeals. 132–33
applying for. 129–30
bathing waters 135
charging schemes 130
compensation for variation
    or revocation of 133
compliance with 123–24
conditions 130–34
consultation. 129–30
criminal law offences 129, 131, 137–39,
                           145–48
dangerous
    substances 135
diffuse sources
    of pollution 133
EC law 135
Environment Agency. 129–36, 159–60
fees 130
fisheries 135–36
improvements in
    water quality 136
inspection powers 136–37, 159–60
judicial review 131
National Rivers
    Authority 130, 137

National Water
  Council 134
  prohibition notices 134
  public registers 159–60
  publicity requirements 129–30
  quality of works 130–31
  review of 133
  revocation of 133
  sampling 137
  sewerage 57, 132, 162–63
  surface water 135–36
  variation
    of conditions 133
  water 134–39, 145–48
  weaknesses in the
    system of 133
Drains 148, 151
Drinking water
  criminal offences 169
  EC law 92, 168–69, 176
  fines 169
  fitness for human
    consumption 169
  maximum admissible
    concentrations 92
  private supplies of 169
  quality standards 92, 168–71, 176
Drought permits 168
Due diligence 147, 149, 154–55, 228
Dumping
  criminal offences 224, 226
  fly-tipping 224, 226, 441
  sea, waste at 181
  toxic waste 188
  trespass 441
  waste 181, 188
Duty of care 246–55, 431–32

EC law 5, 69–119
  See also Directives
  access to information 110, 471, 474
  agriculture 153
  aims of the EC 71
  air quality, framework
    directive on 115
  annulment 71, 73, 85
  atmospheric pollution 327, 330,
                                        344–46
    chlorofluorocarbons 345
    hydrofluorocarbons 345
    industrial plant,
      emissions from large 344
    Integrated Pollution
      Prevention and Control 344
    motor vehicle emissions 343, 345
    ozone layer 345
    power stations 344
    quality standards 345
  best available techniques 297

biodiversity 111, 114
Bruntland Report 109
Cambridge Water case 448
case law 75
chlorofluorocarbons 345
civil liability 453–54
clean-up 454
co-decision procedure 79, 82, 99
common agricultural
  policy 109
common law 453–54
competences 71–73, 89, 96,
                                        100, 103
competition,
  distortion of 97, 99
competitiveness
  of the EU 72–73
consultation procedure 82
co-operation procedure 82, 100
Council of the
  European Union 76–77
  composition of 76
  European Parliament 80
  functions of 76–77
  legislation 82
  meetings 76
  qualified majority voting 77
  unanimous voting 77–78
Court of First Instance 80–81
criminal offences 231
damages 94–96
dangerous substances 97, 114–15
decisions 75
deposit and
  refund schemes 20
development of the EU 69–70
direct actions against
  Member States 84
direct and individual
  concern 86
direct applicability 74, 91
direct effect 88, 90–93
  conditions for 91
  directives 91–93
  drinking water 92
  emanations of
    the State 92–93
  environmental
    assessments 92
  horizontal 92–93
  interest groups 93
discharge consent
  licences 135
discrimination 107
drinking water 92, 168–69
economic, fiscal and
  legal instruments 111
education 110–11
emanations of the State 92–93

enforcement of EC law 83–86
    interest groups 478
    legislation...................... 115–17
    national courts,
       indirect through 87–88
enlargement 69–70
environmental action
    programmes............. 98–99, 109–15,
                           476–77
environmental
    assessments 92, 304
environmental policy............. 96–117
European Commission 78
    composition....................... 78
    Directorates General 78
    dismissal of 79–80
    enforcement 78
    functions of 78–79
    guardian of the treaties 78, 116
    independence of 78
    legislation................... 78–79, 82
    services.......................... 78
European Court of Justice 71, 80–81,
                           100–02
    Advocates General.................. 80
    case law of 75
    judicial notice of
       decisions of 75
    jurisdiction....................... 80
    opinions, reasoned 84
    preliminary rulings 87–88
    role of 80
European Economic
    Community to
    European Community............. 70–71
European Environment
    Agency 117
European Information
    and Observation Network 117
European Parliament 79–80
    balance of powers
       between Member States 81
    co-decision procedure 79
    Committee on Environment,
       Public Health and
       Consumer Protection.............. 80
    composition....................... 79
    Council of the
       European Union.................. 80
    European Commission,
       votes of censure and 79
    functions of 79–80
    interest groups,
       petitions to...................... 80
    legislation...................... 79–80
    maladministration 80
Fifth Environmental
    Action Programme....... 109–11, 476–77
financial instruments 111
fines 85

First Action Programme 109–10, 112
Fourth Environmental
    Action Programme................. 477
framework directives............... 115
free movement of goods 100–11
hazardous waste.................... 231
hydrofluorocarbons................. 345
indirect effect 94
industrial plant,
    emissions from large 344
information 110–11
institutions 69, 70
    competences of 71–73
    framework of.................... 76–81
Integrated Pollution
    Control 259, 274
Integrated Pollution
    Prevention and Control 259, 290–91,
                 295, 304, 344
integration principle 100, 113
interest groups 110, 478–80
    petitions to....................... 80, 84
    standing 86, 93
international
    co-operation 111, 114
interpretation 87, 93–94
judicial notice 75
judicial review 71, 85–86, 470
    grounds for 86
    standing 85–86
    time limits 86
Kyoto Protocol 111
legislation.................... 13, 74–79,
                       114–17
    co-decision procedure 82
    consultation procedure 82
    co-operation procedure............. 82
    Council of the
       European Union.................. 82
    enforcement of 115–17
    European Commission,
       initiation of 82
    initiation of 82–83
    objective of....................... 82
    procedure.................... 76, 81–83
    reviewable acts 85–86
maladministration 80
measures having
    equivalent effect........... 101, 104–05
Member States' liability 83–85,
                 94–96, 116
motor vehicle emissions 343, 345
national courts, indirect
    enforcement through............. 87–88
National Rivers Authority 33
nationality discrimination 83
natural and legal persons,
    status of 86
new legal order, as 88–89
noise................... 374, 403–04, 407

ombudsman for
  maladministration,
  appointment of 80
opinions 75
ozone layer 345
polluter pays 454
power stations 344
precautionary principle 16, 113, 470
preliminary rulings 87–88, 100
private regulation
  of pollution 453–54
privileged
  applicant status 86
product quality
  standards 115
proportionality 102, 105–06
public awareness 110–11
public participation 476–77
qualified majority
  voting 77
quality standards 114, 345
quantitative
  restrictions 101, 104–06
recommendations 75
regional diversity 113
regulations 73–74
Rio Summit 110
Royal Commission on
  Environmental
  Pollution 69
rule of reason 101–02, 105–07
secondary legislation 73, 81, 85
shared responsibility 110
Single European Act 70, 71, 96, 99,
                                             102–03
Sixth Environmental
  Action Programme 74–75, 111, 114
sources of
  environmental law 13, 73–75
standards 7, 97, 108,
                                           115, 117
standing 85–86, 93
Stockholm Conference 98
subsidiarity 89
supremacy of EC law 89–90
sustainable development 100, 109–10
Treaty of Amsterdam 70, 71, 100
Treaty of Nice 70, 71, 100
Treaty of Rome 70, 71, 96–98
Treaty on
  European Union 70, 71,
                                        99–100, 110
UK law and 89
unanimous voting 77–78
vehicle emission
  standards 115
voting 77–78, 99
waste management
  licensing 205, 207–08, 214

waste offences 231
water 168–70, 173–78
  abstraction 170
  drinking 92
  framework
    directive on 115
  quality 173
wild birds 98
EC law, waste and 185, 193–99
See also Waste Framework
  Directive
accumulators 239
agriculture 239
atmospheric pollution 238
batteries 239
controlled waste,
  definition of 234
criminal offences 241
decision making 235
definition of waste 191
dioxins 239
directive waste 191–93
duty of care 255
Environment Agency 240–41
groundwater 238
hazardous waste 199, 237–38
incineration 187, 237–39
Integrated Pollution
  Prevention and Control 237, 245
Landfill Directive 236–38
  acceptance procedures 237
  groundwater 238
  Integrated Pollution
    Prevention and
    Control 237
  licensing 237
  liquid waste 237–38
  planning 236
  site conditioning plans 237
  targets in 236
  transposition of 236
  water 237–38
licensing 237
oils 239
packaging 240–41
planning 236, 242
policy, significance
  of EC waste 234–36
polychlorinated
  biphenyls (PCBs) 240
polychlorinated
  terphenyls (PCTs) 240
prior notification
  of movement 238
producer responsibility 240–41
recycling 234, 240–41
sewerage sludge 239
Sixth Environmental
  Action Programme 234

special waste 238
titanium oxide. 239
transport 238
water 237–38
Ecosystems, threats to. 327
Eco-taxes
    See Tax
Education 110–11
Either way offences. 62
Emergencies
atmospheric pollution 331, 343
contingency plans 331
criminal offences 147–48
drought orders 168
traffic re-routing 343
waste management 223, 232
waste offences. 228
water 147–48, 152
Emissions trading 18–19
Agreement
    Participants 19
credits. 18
Direct Entry
    Participants 19
Environment Agency. 18
greenhouse gases 18–19
Kyoto Protocol 18–19
regulation 18–19
review of 18
voluntary scheme. 18
Energy
discharge of. 2–3
waste management 197
Enforcement. 29–68
Anti-Pollution
    Works Notice. 52
civil proceedings 20
circumstances surrounding
    the breach. 51
Command and
    Control regulation 47
compliance
    history of polluter. 51
    policy 48–49
    pyramid 49
contaminated land 313
courts 59–66
criminal offences,
    range of. 50
EC law. 83–88,
                            115–17, 478
Environment Agency. 19, 47–53, 149
    name and shame. 19
    waste management 190, 214–18
    water. 149–51
European Commission 79–80
Her Majesty's
    Inspectorate of Pollution. 31–32

incentives. 19–20
interest groups 478
Integrated Pollution
    Control 281–87
Integrated Pollution
    Prevention and
    Control 299–303, 478
key considerations 51–52
licences. 19, 170
Local Authority Air
    Pollution Control 287
notices 282–84, 299–302
nuisance, statutory. 304
objectives of. 49
penal policy of 49, 52
principles of 50
prosecutions 19, 49
publicity. 19
reasons for change 35–37
regulation 19–20, 47
resources, limits on 52
sanctioning style of 49, 52
smoke. 335
strict liability offences 51
styles. 48–49
tools 50, 52
waste management 190, 215–18
water 149–51, 170
English Nature. 58, 315
Entertainment licences. 382
Entry, rights of 44–45, 221–22,
                              285, 341, 357,
                              397–98
Environment Agency 37–54
access to information 159–60, 471
accountability of. 38
administrative powers. 48
advice and information. 151–52
aims of 40
air quality 39
annual reports. 160
appeals. 219–20
BATNEEC 275–78
best available techniques 298
BPEO 262, 278
charging schemes. 19
codes of practice. 44
Command and
    Control regulation 6
composition. 38
conservation 42, 128
contaminated land 39, 290,
                            314–15, 324
costs and benefits. 43–44
creation 36–38
criminal offences
    and proceedings 46–47, 138–41,
                       145–51, 225–27, 248

criticisms of 53–54
discharge consent
   licences 129–36, 159–60
duties of 41–44
EC law 240–41
education 50
emissions trading 18
enforcement . . . .
   name and shame 19
   penal style of 53
   policy 47–53
   powers 149
   waste management 190, 214–18
   water 149–51
expenses 40, 44
fines, instances of 48
fragmentary system of
   control before creation of 29–30
guidance 40
Her Majesty's
   Inspectorate of Pollution 39
incidents, number of 48
independence of 38
inspectors, powers of 44–46,
                           284–85
Integrated Pollution
   Control 32, 172, 262–63,
                        269–73, 279–90
Integrated Pollution
   Prevention and
   Control 32, 291–95, 303
Local Authority Air
   Pollution Control 334
local fisheries
   advisory committees 39
motor vehicles,
   seizure of 222
National Rivers
   Authority 39
NETREGS 19
Nitrate Sensitive Areas 155
non-pollution control duties 42
pollution control 41–42
pollution, definition of 41
private regulation of pollution 411
prosecution 47–53
public concern 459–60
regional environmental
   protection advisory
   committees 38–39
regional structure 38–39
regulation 47
risk assessment 19
role of 29, 41, 128
sentencing 63–64
sewage 165
sites of special interest 43
small and medium-sized
   companies 153
smoke 342
structure of 38
sustainable development 14, 40
transfer of functions 39
transport of waste 205, 250–51
umbrella organisation, as 37
waste
   EC law 240–41
   management 185, 190,
                     199–203, 205–22,
                   233, 250–51, 253
   offences 225–27, 248
   regulation
      authorities 39
water 41–42, 121–22, 127
                     149–60, 165–68,
                   172, 303, 324
   criminal offences 138–41, 145–51
   resource management 128
website 19, 24, 49–50
Welsh Advisory
   Committee 38
Environmental
health officers **353, 357, 359**
Environmental
remediation
See Clean-up
Equipment,
noise from **385, 397–98, 405**
Ethics **15**
European Commission **78–80, 82, 116**
European Convention
on Human Rights
amenity, loss of 486
compulsory questioning,
   evidence obtained
   as a result of 489–90
fair trials 487–90
family life, right to 423, 482–87
freedom of expression 490
gypsy caravan sites,
   planning for 485
home, right to
   respect for 423, 483–84
Human Rights
   Act 1998 . . . . 480–81, 488
independent and
   impartial tribunals 487–88
life, right to 481–82
night flights 482–83
noise 403
nuisance 422–23
peaceful enjoyment
   of possessions 486–87
planning 484–88
privacy, right to 423, 482–86
procedural rights 487–90
public bodies 481–89

Rylands v Fletcher 485–86
self-incrimination,
    privilege against 488–89
Seveso Directive on
    Control of Major
    Accident Hazards. 481, 490
sewerage 485
substantive
    environmental rights 481–87
victims 487
warn, failure to 481
European Court of Justice. 71, 80–81,
                                                                    100–02
European
    Environmental Agency. 58, 117
European Environment
    Information and
    Observation Network. 58, 117
European Parliament 79–80
European Union
    See EC law, waste and
Evidence, admissibility of. 466
Exclusive possession 441
Exemplary damages. 413–14,
                                                                    426, 428
Expenses
    See also 'Polluter pays' principle
    Abatement Notices. 392
    appeals. 323
    charging order
        notices. 322
    clean-up 222–23, 317–21
    contaminated land 317–23
    Environment Agency. 40, 44
    investigations 157
    waste management 222–23
    water 157
Explosives. 201

Fair trials. 487–90
Family life, right to 423, 482–87
Fifth Environmental
    Action Programme 109–11, 476–77
Financial instruments. 111
Fines. 60–63
    Abatement Notices. 363
    companies, size of 63
    contaminated land 322
    drinking water 169
    EC law 85
    Environment Agency. 48
    Integrated Pollution
        Control 287–88
    Integrated Pollution
        Prevention and Control. 302
    low level of 63
    noise. 395
    prosecutions 52

regulation 36
smoke. 336
waste management
    licensing. 218, 222
waste offences. 228–29, 231, 255
water 122, 157–58
Works Notices. 157–58
Fires, lighting. 334, 338–39
First Environmental
    Action Programme
Fisheries
    criminal offences 172
    directive on 176
    discharge consent
        licences 135–36
    Environment Agency. 39
    interference with rights 160
    Integrated Pollution
        Control 273
    local fisheries
        advisory committees 39
    nuisance. 160
    quality 176
    shellfish 175
Fit and proper purpose. 211–12, 255
Fitness for human
    consumption. 169
Fitness for human
    habitation 395
Fixed penalty notices 398
Fly-tipping 224, 226, 439–41
Foreseeability 422, 433, 442,
                                                                    444, 447
Fourth Environmental
    Action Programme 477
Free movement of goods 100–11
Freedom of expression 490
Fuel. 153, 343, 341
Fumes. 354
Function of
    environmental law 4–5
Furnaces 339–40

Gas 354
General Permitted
    Development Orders 243
Global warming 328, 346–47
Grants 20
Greenhouse gases 18–19
Grit, dust and fumes. 339–40
Groundwater
    definition. 126, 175
    EC law 175, 238
    landfill 238
    waste management
        licensing. 172, 210

Guilty pleas 61
Gypsy caravan sites,
 planning and 485

Harbours 180, 273
Hazardous substances
 See also Dangerous substances
 access to information 473
 criminal offences 231
 EC law 199, 231, 237–38
 Hazardous Waste
  Inspectorate 30
 local authorities 54
 marine pollution 178
 planning 246
 waste 199, 237–38
Health and safety 60–62, 229–30
Health and Safety
 Executive 57, 61, 210, 273
Hearing loss 375
Her Majesty's
 Inspectorate
 of Pollution (HMIP) 30–32, 37
 atmospheric
  pollution 333
 authorisations 31–32
 charging scheme 32
 composition 30–31
 enforcement 31–32
 Environment Agency 39
 financing 32
 Integrated Pollution
  Control 31, 32, 35, 261,
        269, 271, 288–89
 licences 31
 monitoring 31–32
 National Rivers
  Authority 35, 127
 predecessors to 30
 prosecutions 31–32
 regulation 30–32
 responsibilities of 31, 35
 sentences 32
 water 127
Highways 148, 334
Historic built environment 11
HMIP
 See Her Majesty's
 Inspectorate of Pollution
Home, right to
 respect for the 423, 483–84
House of Commons
 Select Committee on
 Environment, Food
 and Rural Affairs 58
Hosepipe bans 171
Human Rights Act 1998
 damages 480

European Convention
 on Human Rights 480–81, 488
 national courts 480
 private regulation
  of pollution 480–90
 public bodies 480
 remedies 480
 standing 470
 victims 470
Hydrocarbons 343
Hydrofluorocarbons 345

Illegality 64
Incineration
 atmospheric pollution 187, 239,
         333, 346
 dioxins 239
 EC law 187, 199, 237–39
 oils 239
 planning 243
 waste 186–88, 199,
         237–39, 243
Independent and
 impartial tribunals 487–88
Industrial plant
 atmospheric pollution 344
 EC law 344
 grants 20
 Integrated Pollution
  Prevention and Control 292–93,
         296, 302
 large, emissions
  from 344
 mobile 207, 218, 292–93,
         296, 302
 noise 394, 403
 waste management 207, 218
Information
 See Access to information
Injunctions
 Abatement Notices 363, 393
 common law 412, 414–15, 451
 Integrated Pollution
  Prevention
  and Control 302
 mandatory 414
 negligence 439
 noise 378–79, 393, 400
 nuisance 420–21, 427
 prohibitory 414
 Rylands v Fletcher 445
 trespass 441
 waste management
  licensing 218
 water 159, 160
 Works Notices 159
Inland waters 126, 138, 166
Insolvency 219

Inspections
appeals. 220
contaminated land 314
criminal offences 46
discharge consent
  licences. 136–37, 159–60
entry, powers of 44–45
Environment Agency. 44–46, 284–85
Integrated Pollution
  Control 284–85
licences. 44
Local Authority Air
  Pollution Control 44–45
National Rivers Authority 34
nuisance, statutory. 356, 357
public registers 159–60, 473
waste management
  licensing. 218, 220–22
water 121–22

**Integrated Pollution
Control (IPC) 259–92**
See also Best practicable
  environmental
  option (BPEO)
Abatement Notices. 290
activities, definition of. 262–63
advertising 273
air, substances
  released into the 266, 268, 288
Alkali Inspectorate. 260
appeals. 283, 288–89
applications. 269–73
atmospheric pollution 327, 333
BATNEEC 274–78
burden of proof. 268
carrying on a
  prescribed process,
  definition of. 264
charges. 271–72
clean-up. 290
combustion processes 269
Command and
  Control regulation 259
companies, liability of 287
components. 272
confidentiality. 279–80, 288
consents 263
consultation. 273
contaminated land 290, 303, 324
criminal offences 146, 262, 268–69,
                                    284, 286–90
custodial sentences. 288
district councils. 273
EC law 259, 274
enforcement. 281–86
entry, powers of 285
Environment Agency 32, 172, 262–63,
                                269–73, 279–90
exemptions 267–68

fees 271–72
fines 287–88
fisheries committee,
  local. 273
harbour authorities 273
harm
  definition of. 264
  remedy, powers to 286
Health and Safety
  Executive 273
Her Majesty's Inspectorate
  of Pollution. 31, 32, 35, 261,
                                269, 271, 288–89
industrial sectors 265–66
information
  applications, for 271
  inspectors, powers of. 285–86
inspectors, powers of
  Environment Agency. 284–85
interface between IPC
  and other pollution
  controls. 289–92
Integrated Pollution
  Prevention and Control. 270, 290–92
land, substances
  released onto 267–68
licences 3, 262–64, 266,
                                        268–72
  appeals 288
  conditions 272, 273–75
  monitoring. 280–81
  review of 281
  revocation of 283
  sewers, discharge into 290
  templates 272
  transfer of. 280
  variation of 281–83
  waste management 289
local authorities 263, 273,
                                        284, 290
Local Authority Air
  Pollution Control (LAAPC). 262–66,
                                    271–72, 284
Ministry of Agriculture,
  Fisheries and Food 273
monitoring. 280–81, 286
more than one process,
  plants operating 266
National Rivers
  Authority 289
national security. 279
Nature Conservancy
  Council. 273
new processes. 269–70
nuisance, statutory. 289–90
one stop shop, as 259
overlapping regulation 260
overview of 262–63
Part A processes 262–66

Part B processes 262–66, 268, 287
penalties........................ 287–88
phasing in 269
planning............. 269–70, 274–75, 304
polluter pays....................... 271
pollution of
    the environment.................. 264
prescribed processes 262–71
prescribed substances 262–71
process, definition of 263–64
Prohibition Notices 284, 287
prosecutions 281, 284
public registers.............. 279–80, 288
publicity requirements,
    exemption from 279
quality standards 260, 274–75, 281
quotas............................. 275
Remediation Notices 324
Revocation Notices 283
Royal Commission
    on Environmental
    Pollution...................... 260–61
Secretary of State,
    role of 274, 284, 288–89
sentencing 287–88
sewage 273, 290
substantial change
    definition of...................... 270
    processes
        undergoing 270, 282–83
transferability
    of pollution 261
variation of conditions 282–83
waste management 244, 289
Waste Regulation
    Authorities...................... 289
water.................... 121, 146, 172,
                          261, 266–68

**Integrated Pollution
Prevention and Control
(IPPC)........................ 259–60**
See also Best available
    techniques (BAT)
administrative powers............... 299
advertising applications 294–95
appeals........................... 301
atmospheric pollution 327, 344
best practicable
    environmental option 259, 292
clean-up.......................... 298
Command and
    Control regulation 259
companies, liability of 302
confidentiality...................... 301
consultation....................... 295
contaminated land 303, 324
coverage......................... 291–92
criminal offences 147, 292, 300–03
custodial sentences................. 302

definition
    of pollution 292
EC law 259, 290–91, 295
    waste and..................... 237, 245
Enforcement Notices 299–302
enforcement powers 299–303
Environment Agency...... 32, 291–95, 303
Environmental Impact
    Assessment Directive.............. 304
exemptions 293–94
externalities....................... 292
fines 302
industry groupings 293
Information Exchange
    Forum.......................... 297
information, powers
    to acquire 300–01
injunctions........................ 302
installations.................. 291–93, 302
Integrated Pollution
    Control 270, 290–92
interface with other
    regulatory controls of 303–04
landfill 237, 244–45, 303
listed activities 293
listed substances................... 293
local authorities 291–92, 295
Local Authority Air
    Pollution Control 334–35
management, liability of 302
mobile plant................... 292–93,
                          296, 302
nuisance, statutory.................. 304
one stop shop, as 259
Part A processes 299
Part B processes 291–92
permits....................... 3, 291–99
    advertising..................... 294–95
    applications for................. 294–95
    conditions 291, 293, 296,
                          299–300, 303
    consultation.................... 295
    exemptions 293–94
    injunctions 302
    material
        considerations................ 295–96
    review.......................... 300
    transfer and
        surrender of................. 298–99
planning................. 294, 296, 304
prescribed activities 293
proportionality 292
public participation 295
public registers.................... 301
quality standards 260
regulation 291–92
remedial powers................. 302–03
Remediation
    Notice 324

Revocation Notice 300
Royal Commission
    on Environmental Pollution 260
sentencing 302
sewer discharges 304
Suspension Notice 300–02
Variation Notice 300–01
waste
    EC law 237, 245, 296
    framework
        directive on 296
    management 244–45, 296,
                                            298, 303
    water pollution 121, 147, 172, 303–04
Interest groups
    access to information 472
    challenging EC
        environmental law 479
    direct actions 478–79
    EC law 80, 83–84, 93,
                                            478–80
    enforcement 478
    European Parliament 80
    influence of 477–78
    judicial review 467–70, 479, 480
    lobbying at the
        European level 478
    members, number of 477–78
    private prosecutions 4, 123,
                                            161–62, 465
    private regulation
        of pollution 477–80
    public participation 476, 477
    public registers 472
    regulation 11–12
    standards 65
    standing 4, 86, 93,
                                            467–71, 479
    structural funds 480
    water pollution 123
Inter-library
    loan systems **495**
Intra-generational
    equity **14**
Investigations
    Command and
        Control regulation 8
    contaminated land 314–15
    expenses of 157
    local authorities 357
    noise 386, 396–97
    nuisance, statutory 357
    regulation 8
    water 157
Irrationality **65**

Judicial review
    certiorari 66

Command and
    Control regulation 466
courts 64–66
damages 66
delegation of powers,
    improper 65
discharge consent licences 131
discretion 10
EC law 85–86, 470
    grounds for 86
    illegality 64
    individual applicants 466–67
    Integrated Pollution
        Prevention and Control 479, 480
    interest groups 467–70
    irrationality 65
    legitimate expectations 65
    mandamus 66
    precautionary principle 470
    private regulation
        of pollution 457, 466–70
    procedural flaw 64
    procedural unfairness 65
    prohibition 66
    public bodies 64–65
    regulation 10, 12
    relevant and
        irrelevant
            considerations 64
    standing 10, 12, 65, 466–67
        EC law 85–86
        interest groups 467–70
    third parties 466
    time limits 66, 86, 467
    waste management
        licensing 219

Kyoto Protocol **18–19, 111, 346–47**

Labelling **97**
Landfill
    acceptance procedures 237
    contaminated
        land exemption 17
    credit scheme 241–42
    criminal offences 225–26
    directive, on 236–38
    exemptions 17
    groundwater 238
    Integrated Pollution
        Prevention
        and Control 237, 244–45, 303
    licensing 237
    liquid waste 237–38
    local authorities 232
    operation of 17–18
    planning 236, 243
    risk assessment 219
    site conditioning plans 237

tax 17–18, 234,
241–42
waste management 186, 219, 232,
234, 236, 243–45, 303
waste offences. 225–26
water 186, 237–38
Landlords
Abatement Notices. 359–60
noise. 382
nuisance. 424
tenancy agreements,
covenants in. 382
Law of the Sea Convention 15, 178–79
Law reports. 493–94
Legal resources 493–94
Legitimate expectations 65
Licences. 3
See also Discharge consent
licences; Waste
management licensing
administrative powers. 9
advertising 294–95
anticipatory. 6–7
appeals. 283, 288
atmospheric pollution 332
BATNEEC 275–77
categories of 6–7
charging schemes. 19
Command and
Control regulation 6–8
compliance 8
conditions. 6–7, 9, 272–75,
291, 293, 296,
299–300, 303
breach of. 3
prosecutions 51
regulation. 7–8
water. 167–68
consultation. 295
contaminated land 323
criminal offences 3, 8, 46
dangerous substances 174
discharge, authorising. 6–7
discretion. 10
EC law 237
enforcement. 19, 170
entertainment 382
fees 19
Her Majesty's
Inspectorate of Pollution. 31
industrial processes 332
injunctions. 302
inspections. 44
Integrated Pollution
Control 3, 283, 262–64,
266, 268–75,
280–83, 289–90

Integrated Pollution
Prevention
and Control 3, 291–300, 302–03
landfill 237
Local Authority Air
Pollution Control 334
material
considerations. 295–96
monitoring. 280–81
negligence 437–38
noise. 382
operational 6–7
prosecutions 51
public register 170
regulation 7–8
review of 281, 300
revocation of 283
sewers 165, 290
standards. 7–8
surrender of. 298–99
templates 272
transfer of 280, 298–99
variation of 281–83
waste management 289
water 3, 165–68, 170
Life, right to 481–82
Listed buildings. 11
Loan systems,
inter-library 495
Local air quality
management. 329
Local Air Quality
Management Areas. 330–31
Local authorities
See also Local Authority
Air Pollution
Control (LAAPC)
Abatement Notices 357–59, 362–63,
366, 389–92, 394–95
access to
information 473
administration 30
atmospheric
pollution 329–33, 343–44
BATNEEC 275–77
burglar alarms,
noise from 402
construction sites 400–01
contaminated land 54, 315
emissions. 54
environmental
health officers 353, 357, 359
hazardous substances 54
Integrated Pollution
Control. 263, 273, 274, 290
Integrated Pollution
Prevention
and Control 291–92, 295

investigations 357
landfill 232
licensing 189
loudspeakers,
    noise from 401–02
motor vehicle
    emissions 343–44
noise 373, 376–77, 381,
                                    383, 385–87,
                                    394–400, 404–05
nuisance 430
planning 35–36, 54, 242–43
research and
    data collection
    responsibilities 341–42
smoke 341–42
statutory nuisance 54, 304, 349, 353,
                                    355–57, 367
transfer of
    responsibilities 54
waste management 188–89, 202, 232,
                                    234, 242–43
waste regulation
    authorities 34–35, 54
water 171–72, 303–04
Local Authority Air
Pollution Control
(LAAPC) **36, 334–35**
BATNEEC 277, 334
BPEO 334
criminal offences 286
enforcement 287
Environment Agency 334
fees and charges 272
inspections 44–45
Integrated Pollution
    Control 262–66,
                                    271–72, 284
Integrated Pollution
    Prevention and Control 334–35
licences 334
phasing out 334–35
prescribed industrial
    processes 334
public registers 279
Locus standi
    See Standing
Loudspeakers, noise from **401–02**
Loss of profits,
    damages for **427–28**

Machinery, noise from **385, 394, 403**
Managers, liability of **229–30, 255, 302**
Mandamus **66**
Marine pollution **178–81**
criminal offences 148, 180
dumping of waste at sea 181
EC law 180

harbours, reporting
    oil spills in 180
hazardous substances 178
Law of the
    Sea Convention 15, 178–79
MARPOL 179
offshore installations,
    disposal of 181
oil pollution 179–80
OSPAR Convention 181
pipelines 180
ports, refusal
    of entry to 180
preventive principle 15
reception facilities 180
salvage 180
ships
    detention of 180
    surveys of 179
waste 178, 181
MARPOL **179**
Media
    See Publicity
Mediation **408**
Medicinal products **198, 201**
Mineral
    extraction waste **194–95, 243**
Mines **122, 148**
Ministry of Agriculture,
    Foods and Fisheries **273**
Mortgagees **222**
Motor vehicles
    Abatement Notices 359
    atmospheric pollution 115, 327, 329,
                                    342–45
    criminal offences 226–27
    EC law 115, 343, 345
    Environment Agency 222
    fuel, composition of 343
    local authorities 343–44
    noise 385, 389, 393
    quality standards 115, 345
    seizure 222
    stop and search 251
    traffic
        re-routing 329, 343–44
        restrictions 329, 344
    waste offences 226–27
Mobile plant **207, 218, 292–93,**
                                    296, 302

Name and
    shame policy **19**
National Air
    Quality Strategy **327, 330, 333**
National Ambient
    Noise Strategy **374**

National Rivers
  Authority **33–34, 37, 124,**
                                    127–28
  advice and information 151–52
  Code of Practice on
    Conservation, Access
    and Recreation 128
  consents 36
  conservation 127–28
  discharge consent
    licences 130, 137
  EC law 33
  Environment Agency 39
  Her Majesty's Inspectorate
    of Pollution 35, 127
  inspectors 34
  Integrated Pollution Control 289
  prosecutions 34
  regional advisory
    committees 33
  regulation 24, 33–34
  river police 34
  role 33–34, 35, 127
  structure of 33
  Water Pollution
    Inspectorate 30–31
National security
  Integrated Pollution
    Control 279–80
  public registers 279–80, 473
  waste management 220
National Water Council **134**
Nationality discrimination **83**
Nature Conservancy
  Council **210, 273**
Negligence . . . .
  breach of duty of care 432
  breach of statutory duty 453
  causation 435–37
  common law 431–39
  contributory 416, 452, 453
  criminal offences 171
  damage,
    what amounts to 433–36
  damages 416, 452,
                                    434, 438
  defences 437–38
  definition 431
  duty of care 431–32
  fault 438
  foreseeability 433
  injunctions 439
  licences 437–38
  material contribution
    to harm 435–37
  neighbour principle 431–32
  private regulation
    of pollution 431–39
  proof 435

remedies 438–39
res ipsa loquitur 435
standard of care 432
standing 437
trespass 440
water 161, 171
Neighbour principle **431–32**
Neighbouring land
  clean-up 217
  noise and 378
  nuisance, statutory 357
  waste management
    licensing 217
NETREGS **19**
Night flights **482–83**
Nitrate Sensitive Areas,
  agreement on **155**
Nitrate Vulnerable Zones **156**
Noise **371–409**
  Abatement Notices 358, 361–62, 373,
                                    387–95, 398
  abatement zones 404–05

  aggrieved citizens'
    action 395–96
  aircraft 372, 375, 380, 383,
                                402–03, 423, 482–83
  alternative
    dispute resolution 408
  anti-social
    behaviour orders 403–04
  appeals 391–92, 400, 405
  best practicable
    means 394, 400–01
  building regulations 407
  burden of proof 395
  burglar alarms,
    noise from 402
  bylaws 399
  codes of practice 373, 394, 402–03
  common law 377–82, 384–85
  compensation orders 396
  complaints on 377, 386, 396
  construction sites 399–400
  consultation 398–99
  contract 382
  criminal offences 373, 381, 382,
                                393, 395–400, 405
  damages 381–82
  defences 393–95
  EC law 374, 403–04, 407
  emission standards 402–03
  enjoyment of property,
    interference with 378, 384
  entertainment licences 382
  entry, powers of 397–98
  equipment
    disposal of 397–98
    noise from 385, 407

European Convention
  on Human Rights 403, 482–83
exposure categories 406
fines 395
fitness for human
  habitation 395
fixed penalty notices 398
health, damage to 374–75, 383–84
hearing loss 375
injunctions 378–79, 393, 400
inspections 386
intent of the parties 380
interests in land 381
investigations 386, 396–97
landlords 382
licensing 382
local authorities 373, 376–77, 381,
                            383, 385–87,
                  394–400, 404–05
locality 378–79
loudspeakers,
  noise from 401–02
machinery,
  noise from 385, 394, 403
measurement of 375–76, 387, 393,
                              397, 405
mediation 408
motor vehicles,
  noise from 385, 389, 393
National Ambient
  Noise Strategy 374
nature of 373–74
neighbourhood noise 371–72, 374,
                   376–79, 386, 394
  mediation 408
  prevention of 404–07
neighbouring land 378
night time 373–74,
                       396, 482–83
noise generating
  activity 379–80
nuisance 355, 377–87,
                    399–401, 423
persons responsible for 397
planning 373, 379, 394,
                            405–07
plant, noise from 394, 403
premises, from 384–85
prescribed decibel
  levels in Abatement
  Notices 388–89
psychological effects 375
public interest 372, 380
rave parties 404
reasonable excuse 393–94
regulation 371–74
remedies 380–81
rural areas 372
sanctions 373

Secretary of State 403
seizure 397–98
sensitivity of
  the claimant 380
sources of, specific 399–404
statutory controls 382–83
statutory nuisance 355, 383–87, 396
street, noise from the 385
subjectivity of
  problems concerning 373
temporary interferences 378
tenancy agreements,
  covenants in 382
traffic 403
trespass 403
types of 374
Warning Notices, service of 396–97
Wilson Committee 371
**Non-governmental
organisations**
See Interest groups
Notices
See also Abatement Notices
administration,
  non-compliance with 46
Anti-Pollution
  Works Notices 52, 157–59
charging order 322
Command and
  Control regulation 7
criminal offences 46, 157–58
Enforcement Notices 287, 299–302
fixed penalty 398
private supply 172
prohibition 134, 284, 287
public registers 322
regulation 7
Remediation Notices 290, 314–17,
                        321–24
Revocation Notices 216–17, 283, 300
service of 396–97
Suspension Notices 217–18,
                     220, 300–02
trade effluent 163–64
Variation Notices 215, 282, 300–01
Warning Notices 396–97
Waste Removal
  Notices 222–23
water 172
Works Notices 157–59
Nuisance
See also Statutory nuisance
abatement 414–15
aircraft noise 423
atmospheric pollution 333, 342
best practicable means 422, 430
Cambridge Water case 446–47
characteristic
  features of 418–19, 428–29

coming to the nuisance,
    claimant 426, 430–31
common law. 351–52, 377–78,
                                            384, 417–31
criminal offences 429
damages 381–82, 419,
                                            427–28, 430–31
defences 424–26
definition 417, 428
duration of
    the nuisance. 421
enjoyment of land,
    interference with 417, 419–20
European Convention
    on Human Rights. 422–23
exemplary damages. 428
fishing rights,
    interference with. 160
foreseeability. 422, 447
home, family and
    private life, right to
    respect for 423
hypersensitivity 419
ignorance of
    the nuisance. 430
injunctions. 420–21, 427
intention of
    the defendant 421–22
landlords 424
local authorities 430
locality 420
loss of profits,
    damages for. 427–28
more than
    one polluter 426
noise 377–78,
                                            399–401, 423
occupiers 424
physical damage. 417–18, 420
planning. 419–20, 425, 426
precautions 425
prescription. 426, 430
private. 160, 342, 377–78,
                                            417–28, 439–40
private regulation
    of pollution 417–31
public 161, 342, 381,
                                            428–31
public interest 423
reasonableness 419–23
remedies 427–28, 431
riparian rights. 159, 160
Rylands v Fletcher 444
self-help 415
sensibility claims 427
sensitivity of
    the claimant. 421
sewerage 160
standing. 423, 429–30

statutory authority,
    defence of. 424–25
trespass 439–40
utility of the claimant 422
water 159–61

Office of Water Services,
    role of. 57
Officers, personal liability
    of senior 47, 50
Offshore installations,
    disposal of 181
Oil pollution 179–80
Oils. 153–54, 239
Ombudsman. 80
Onerous property,
    disclaimer of. 219
Operator and Pollution
    Risk Appraisal. 215
Operator Performance
    Appraisal. 215
OSPAR Convention 181
Ozone layer 345–46

Packaging 97, 240–41, 249
Parliamentary
    select committees 58
PCBs
    (polychlorinated
    biphenyls). 240
PCTs
    (polychlorinated
    terphenyls) 240
Peaceful enjoyment
    of possessions 486–87
Pipelines,
    oil pollution from 180
Planning
    administration 30
    atmospheric pollution 333–34
    authorisations. 35–36
    change of use 242–43
    conditions 243
    contaminated land 325
    Department of Transport,
        Local Government and the
        Regions. 56
    EC law 236, 242
    Environment Statement. 304
    Environmental Impact
        Assessment Directive. 304
    European Convention on
        Human Rights. 484–88
    General Permitted
        Development Orders. 243
    gypsy caravan sites 485

hazardous substances 246
incineration 243
Integrated Pollution
    Control 304
Integrated Pollution
    Prevention
    and Control 294, 296, 304
land use 304
landfill 236, 242–43
local planning
    authorities 35–36, 54, 242–43
material
    considerations 325, 333
mining 243
noise 373, 379, 394, 405–07
nuisance 419–20, 425, 426
permission 35–36, 244
public concern 458–60, 464
regulation 11
standing 469–70
Waste Framework
    Directive 242
waste management 188, 209, 213,
                               232, 236, 242–44,
                               246, 304

Plant
    See Industrial plant
'Polluter pays' principle
    clean-up 16
    contaminated land 318
    EC law 454
    Integrated Pollution
        Control 271
    waste management licensing 210
**Polychlorinated
    biphenyls (PCBs)** **240**
**Polychlorinated
    terphenyls (PCTs)** **240**
Ports, refusal of entry to **180**
Precautionary principle **15–16**
    Climate Change
        Convention 16
    cost/benefit test 15
    EC law 16, 113, 470
    judicial review 470
    Paris Convention 16
    Rio Declaration 15–16
Precedents **12**
Preliminary rulings **87–88, 100**
Prescription **426, 430**
Pressure groups
    See Interest groups
Preventive principle **15**
**Principles of
    environmental law** **13**
Privacy, right to **423, 482–86**

Private nuisance **161, 377–78,
                                        417–28, 439–40**
Private prosecutions **12, 47**
    access to information 465
    Attorney General 161
    consent to 48, 161
    costs 465–66
    Director of
        Public Prosecutors 161
    evidence,
        admissibility of 466
    Integrated Pollution
        Prevention
        and Control 4
    interest groups 123, 161–62, 465
    private regulation
        of pollution 457, 464–66
    public registers 465, 466, 472
    right to bring 464–65
    self-incrimination,
        privilege against 466
    water pollution 123, 161–62
**Private regulation
    of pollution** **457–92**
    access to information 470–76
    Cambridge Water case 445–46
    civil actions 451–53
    Command and
        Control regulation 411
    common law 411–53
    defences 415–16
    EC law, civil
        liability and 453–54
    Environment Agency 411
    Human Rights
        Act 1998 480–90
    interest groups 477–80
    judicial review 457, 466–70
    negligence 431–39
    nuisance 417–31
    private prosecutions 457, 464–66
    public concern 457–64
    public participation 476–77
    remedies 413–15
    Rylands v Fletcher 441–45
    trespass 439–41
    water 160–62
Procedural unfairness **65**
Prohibition **66**
Prohibition notices **134, 284, 287**
**Property blight
    and stigma** **308**
Proportionality
    best available
        techniques 297
    EC law 102, 105–06
    Integrated Pollution
        Prevention and Control 292

Prosecutions
See also Private prosecutions
aggravating and
  mitigating circumstances 50
companies 50
consequences of 52
constraints of...................... 48
discretion.......................... 50
enforcement...................... 19, 49
Environment Agency.............. 47–53
evidence............................ 50
fines, level of 52
Her Majesty's
  Inspectorate
  of Pollution 31–32
insolvency 219
licences, compliance
  with conditions of................. 51
National Rivers Authority 34
presumption of 50–51
public interest...................... 50
regulation 39
senior company officers, of.......... 50
small companies,
  bias towards prosecuting 51
tests of 50
water pollution.................. 149–50

Public bodies
See also Local authorities;
  Particular bodies
  (eg, Environment Agency)
access to information............. 473–74
European Convention
  on Human Rights............... 481–89
Human Rights Act 1998.............. 480
judicial review 64–65

Public concern
access to information............... 459
causes of high levels of 460–64
consultation...................... 459–60
decision making 458–61
definition....................... 457–58
EC law 110–11
Environment Agency............. 459–60
exposure, public
  perception of
  unacceptable risk 462–63
government policy............... 458–59
media 458–59, 462–63
planning.................... 458–60, 464
private regulation
  of pollution 457–64
public participation 459–60
risk, meaning of 460–61
Public nuisance **160, 381, 428–31**
Public participation
Aarhus Convention 295, 476
Biodiversity Convention............. 476

Climate Change
  Convention 476
EC law 476–77
Fifth Environmental
  Action Programme.............. 476–77
Fourth Environmental
  Action Programme................ 477
Integrated Pollution
  Prevention and Control............ 295
interest groups 476, 477
international recognition
  of need for 476
national recognition
  of need for 477
private regulation
  of pollution 476–77
public concern................... 459–60
recognition of need for 476–77
Rio Summit 476
waste management
  licensing 210
Public registers
access to information............. 470–74
appeals........................... 220
Command and
  Control regulation 10
confidentiality 220, 279–80, 288,
                                301, 473
contaminated land 309, 314, 316,
                                322–23
contents of 472
copies of entries 159–60, 473
discharge consent
  licences....................... 159–60
exemptions 279
inspection 159–60, 473
Integrated Pollution
  Control 279–80, 288
Integrated Pollution
  Prevention and Control............ 301
interest groups 472
licences........................... 170
Local Authority Air
  Pollution Control 279
national security............. 279–80, 473
private prosecutions 465, 466, 472
purpose of 472
regulation 10
Remediation Notices 322
Royal Commission
  on Environmental
  Pollution..................... 472–73
use of 472
waste management
  licensing........................ 220
water abstraction 170
**Public regulation of
private pollution**
See Regulation

Publicity
criminal offences 229
discharge consent licences 129–30
enforcement. 19
Integrated Pollution
 Control 279
public concern. 458–59, 462–63
sentencing 63
waste offences. 229
Punitive damages **413–14**

Quality
Air Quality
 Management Areas 329–31, 333
Air Quality Plans 331–32
atmospheric pollution 329–31, 331–33,
 344–45
bathing water 175
discharge consent
 licences 130–31
drinking water 92, 168–71, 176
EC law 114–15, 344–45
fisheries 176
Integrated Pollution
 Control 260, 274–75, 281
Integrated Pollution
 Prevention
 and Control 260
local air quality
 management 329
Local Air Quality
 Management Areas 330–31
motor vehicle
 emissions 345
product standards 115, 345
shellfish waters. 176
surface water. 175
water 165, 168–69, 173,
 175–76
Quarries. **148, 195**

Radioactive waste 202
Radiochemical
 Inspectorate 30
Rave parties 404
RCEP
See Royal Commission on
 Environmental Pollution
Reception facilities 180
Recycling
EC law 234, 240–41
waste management 193–94, 204, 234,
 242, 244
Recommendations. 75
Regional advisory
 committees 33, 38–39
Regional Water
 Authorities 125

Registers
See Public registers
Regulation **5–11, 35–36**
See also Command and
 Control regulation;
 Private regulation of pollution
administrative
 functions of 6
administrative powers. 9
appeals. 10
charging schemes. 19
Command and Control 5–11
companies,
 role of private 11–13
continuous control 10
criminal offences 8, 127
definition of key
 legislative terms 9
deposit and
 refund schemes. 20
developers. 35–36
discretion. 8, 10
eco-taxes 17–18
emerging mechanisms. 16–17
emissions trading. 18–19
enforcement 19–20, 47
Environment Agency. 47
environmental covenants 20
fines 36
function of
 environmental law 4–5
grants 20
guidance 9
Her Majesty's
 Inspectorate of
 Pollution. 30–32
historic build
 environment 11
Integrated Pollution
 Prevention and Control. 291–92
interest groups 11–12
investigations, regulator's
 powers of 8
judicial review 10, 12
licences 6–9, 11
market mechanisms. 17
National Rivers Authority 24, 33–34
noise. 371–74
nature conservation 11
notice-based regimes 7
nuisance, statutory. 349
official guidance. 9
planning control 11
policing functions of 6
pollution control. 11
primary legislation. 6
private persons 11–12
prosecutions 39
public registers 10
reasons for change 35–37

secondary legislation 9
self-regulation 247
separate and
    integrated regulation 6
subsidies 20
waste management 202–05, 244–46
waste regulation
    authorities 34–35
water 122–23, 127–32,
                                              137, 173–78
Regulations **73–74**
Regulatory offences **161**
**Rehabilitation
    of offenders** **212**
Remediation
    See Clean-up
Remediation Notices **290, 314–17,
                                              321–24**
Remedies
    See Damages; Injunctions
Res ipsa loquitur **435**
Revocation Notices **216–17, 283, 300**
Ringlemann Chart **337, 339**
Rio Summit **14–16, 110,
                                              346–47, 476**
Riparian rights **160–61, 165–66**
Risk assessment **19, 219, 311, 313**
Rivers
    See National Rivers Authority
**Royal Commission on
    Environmental Pollution** **2**
    BPEO 262
    EC law 69
    Integrated Pollution Control 260–61
    Integrated Pollution
        Prevention and Control 260
    legislation 57
    public registers 472–73
    reports 57
    role 57
Rule of reason **101–02, 105–07**
Rural areas, noise in **372**
Rylands v Fletcher **441–45**
    acts of God 445
    Cambridge Water case 444, 446, 447
    common benefit 445
    common law 441–45
    damages 445
    dangerous things
        likely to do mischief 443, 444
    default of the claimant 445
    defences 445
    definition 441–42
    escapes 442
    European Convention
        on Human Rights 485–86

factors to be established 442
foreseeability 442, 444
injunctions 445
non-natural user 442–43
nuisance 444
private regulation
    of pollution 441–45
standing 444
strict liability 442
third parties, acts of 445

Salvage **180**
**Scottish Environmental
    Protection Agency** **38, 43**
Secretary of State
    appeals 219–20, 288–89
    atmospheric pollution 330, 332
    best available
        techniques 298
    Department for
        Environment, Food
        and Rural Affairs 56
    Integrated Pollution
        Control 274, 284, 288–89
    noise 403
    role of 56
    smoke 342
    waste management
        licensing 219–20
Seizure **222, 397–98**
Self-help **415**
**Self-incrimination,
    privilege against** **222, 466, 488–89**
Self-regulation **247**
Sentencing
    See also Custodial sentences; Fines
    absolute discharge 63
    aggravating features 61, 63
    appeals 61
    companies 61
    conditional discharge 63
    conduct 61–62
    costs 63–64
    courts 60–64
    Crown Court,
        committal to the 62
    either way offences 62
    Environment Agency 63–64
    guilty pleas 61
    health and safety 60–62
    Health and Safety
        Executive 61
    Her Majesty's
        Inspectorate of Pollution 32
    individuals 61
    Integrated Pollution Control 287–88
    Integrated Pollution
        Prevention and Control 302

judicial guidance 60–62
magistrates' courts 62–64
mitigating features 61, 63
publicity, bad. 63
Sentencing Advisory
    Panel guidance 61–62
seriousness of offences 63
small companies 62, 63
types of 62, 63
warnings, failure
    to heed 60, 63
waste management
    licensing 219, 222
waste offences. 228–29, 231, 255
water unfit for
    human consumption,
    supplying 61
Seveso Directive on Control
    of Major Accident Hazards 481, 490
Sewers and sewerage 162–65
access to information 474
agriculture 239
consents 57
controlled waters,
    discharges into 162–63
criminal offences 148, 163–64
discharge consent
    licences 57, 132, 162–63
EC law 239
Environment Agency 165
European Convention
    on Human Rights 485
Integrated Pollution
    Control 273, 290
Integrated Pollution
    Prevention and Control 304
licences 290, 304
nuisance 160, 356
sludge 239
special category effluents 165
third parties, discharges
    caused by 162
trade effluent consents 163–65
trade effluent notices 163–64
undertakers 57, 162,
                                          273, 474
Urban Waste
    Water Directive 177
waste management 239
water 122, 125–26, 145,
                          148, 160, 162–65, 177
Shellfish 176
Ship surveys 179
Ships,
    detention of 180
Silage 153
Sixth Environmental
    Action Programme 74–75, 111,
                                  114, 234

Sludge 239
Sluices 146
Slurry 153
Smells 246
Smog 328
Smoke 328, 335–42
appeals 341
burden of proof 337–38
burning 338–39
chimneys
    definition of 335
    height, control over 340–41
criminal offences 327, 336–39
    dark smoke 336–39
    defences 338–39
    exemptions 338, 340
    grit, dust and fumes 339–40
    notification of 337
dark smoke 336–39
definition of 335
demolition sites 336–37
enforcement 335
entry, powers of 341
Environment Agency 342
fines 336
fuel, definition
    of authorised 341
furnaces
    cold, lighting from 339
    installation of non-domestic,
        control over 339–40
grit, dust and fumes 339–40
installation of
    non-domestic furnaces,
    control over 339–40
local authorities 339–41
    research and data
    collection,
    responsibilities of 341–42
monitoring 340, 342
notification of offences 337
nuisance, statutory 342, 354
research and data
    collection responsibilities 341–42
Ringlemann Chart 337, 339
Secretary of State, powers of 342
smog 328
Smoke Control Areas 341
strict liability 336–38
Sulphur Dioxide
    Directive 341
Solvents 308
Sources of
    environmental law 12–13
    EC law 13, 73–75
    international sources 13
    legislation,
        evolution of 12
    national sources 12–13

Stand pipes........................ **168**
Standard of care..................... **432**
Standards
  atmospheric pollution....... 115, 329, 331,
                                        344–45
    directives, as 7
    drinking water 92
    EC law...................... 7, 97, 108,
                                    114–15, 117
  Integrated Pollution
    Control 260, 274–75, 281
  Integrated Pollution
    Prevention
    and Control 260
  interest groups 65
  licences.......................... 7–8
  motor vehicle
    emissions 115, 345
  noise......................... 402–03
  product....................... 115, 345
  source-based 7–8
Standing
  definition........................ 10
  direct and individual
    concern...................... 479–80
  EC law 83, 85–86, 93
  Human Rights
    Act 1998 470
  Integrated Pollution
    Prevention
    and Control 4, 479
  interest groups 86, 93, 467–71
  judicial review 86, 467–70
  negligence 437
  nuisance.................. 423, 429–30
  planning....................... 469–70
  Rylands v Fletcher 444
  sufficient interest 467–70
  trespass 441
  victims,
    Human Rights
    Act 1998 and 470
Statutory nuisance **349–69**
  See also Abatement Notices
  accumulations
    or deposits...................... 355
  amenity, loss of.................... 351
  animals.......................... 355
  atmospheric pollution........... 333, 342
  burden of proof................. 353–54
  comfort,
    interference
    with personal 352
  complaints,
    duty to respond to 356
  contaminated land 313–14, 317,
                                324–25, 349–50,
                                        367–68

criminal offences 367
definition of nuisance 351–52
dust, steam, smell or
  other effluvia.................. 354–55
enforcement....................... 304
entry, powers of 357
environmental
  health officers 353, 357
exemptions 354–55
fumes........................... 354
gas............................. 354
identifying....................... 353
inspections................... 356, 357
Integrated Pollution
  Control 289–90
Integrated Pollution
  Prevention
  and Control 304
investigatory powers
  of local authorities 357
list of........................... 350
local authorities 54, 188, 304, 349,
                            353, 355–57, 367
neighbouring
  premises....................... 357
noise................... 355, 383–87, 396
prejudicial to health,
  definition of..................... 351
regulation 349
sewage.......................... 356
smells........................... 246
smoke......................... 342, 354
waste
  management 188, 219, 245–46
Stop and search **251**
Street, noise from the **385**
Strict liability
  criminal offences 47, 138, 143,
                                    145, 148
  enforcement....................... 51
  Remediation Notices 318
  Rylands v Fletcher 442
  smoke......................... 336–38
  waste management 223
  water pollution........ 138, 143, 145, 148
Structural funds.................... **480**
**Study of environmental
  law, scope of**....................... **4**
Subsidiarity **89**
Subsidies........................... **20**
Sulphur dioxide..................... **341**
Superfund.......................... **310**
Surface water **135–36, 175**
Suspension Notices **217–18, 220, 300–02**
Sustainable development **14–15**
  Agenda 21 14
  Bruntland Report 14, 40, 109

Committee on
  Sustainable
  Development.......................59
definition..........................40
EC law 100, 109–10
education...........................40
Environment Agency..............14. 40
ethics 15
guidance 40
integration.........................15
inter-generational
  equity 14–15
international
  environmental law.................14
intra-generational
  equity 15
policy documents....................14
Rio Summit.........................14
sustainable use 15

Tax
  Aggregates Levy.....................18
  climate change levy 347
  contaminated land..................323
  landfill 17–18, 234, 241–42
  regulation 16–17
  waste management 234
Tenancy agreements,
  covenants in 382
Textbooks 494
Titanium oxide................176–77, 239
Toolbox,
  environmental law as a 4
Trade effluent consents 163–64
Trade secrets........................473
Tradeable pollution
  permits
  See Emissions trading
Traffic 329, 343–44, 403
Transport
  See also Motor vehicles
  consignment note
    system.........................253–54
  criminal offences 249–50
  EC law 238
  Environment Agency.........205, 250–51
  registration 205, 250–51
  special waste......................199
  stop and search....................251
  waste   198–99, 204–05,
                              238, 249–54
Treaties and
  conventions 13
Trespass...........................439–41
  causal link 440
  characteristics of...................439
  common law 439–41

continuing........................439
criminal offences 140–41
damages...........................441
defences..........................441
definition.........................439
direct interference 440
exclusive possession 441
fly-tipping......................439–41
injunctions........................441
intention..........................440
negligence 440
noise.............................403
nuisance, private and..............439–40
person, to.........................439
private regulation
  of pollution 439–41
riparian eights......................161
standing..........................441
water pollution.................140–41

Variation Notices..........215, 282, 300–01
Vehicles
  See Motor vehicles
Victims, status of.................470, 487
Volenti non fit injuria 416, 452–53

Wales........................38, 58, 210
Warn, failure to 481
Warnings Notices 396–97
Waste Framework
  Directive 189, 190–95
  controlled waste,
    definition of.....................234
  criminal offences 224
  direct effect 235
  Integrated Pollution
    Prevention
    and Control 296
  national waste policy.............232–33
  objectives of....................234–36
  planning 242
  sustainable
    water policy.....................115
  transposition of...................235
  waste carriers 204–05
  waste offences....................224
  water 177–78
Waste management...............185–257
  See also EC law, waste and;
    Waste Framework Directive;
    Waste management
    licensing; Waste offences
  appeals....................222–23, 251
  atmospheric pollution 187, 345–46
  breach of the
    duty of care 255
  brokers...................205, 247–48

byproducts 195
carriers 198, 204–05,
                                        238, 250
    authorised 250, 252
    consignment note
        system for
            special waste 253–54
    Environment Agency 205, 250–51
    prior notification 238
    registration 205, 250–51
    special waste 199
    stop and search
        of vehicles 251
cement kilns 197–98
change of use 242–43
civil liability for
    deposit of waste,
        statutory 223–24, 247, 255
clean-up 222–24, 324
code of practice 247, 248, 254–55
Command and
    Control regulation 185, 190
commercial waste 191–92, 204
consignment note system
    for special waste 253–54
consignment waste 199
containerisation 250
contaminated land 245
contracts 203–04, 249
controlled waste 191–92, 234, 237
damages 223, 247, 255
definition of
    special waste 198–99
definition of waste 185, 190–202
development control 242–44
development of
    waste controls 188–89
dioxins 239
directive waste 190, 191–93, 222
discarded,
    meaning of 196
disposal 232
    co-disposal 186
    contractors 203–04
    licensing 189
    methods of 186–89
    operations, what
        constitutes disposal 196–98
    plans 242
    waste brokers 205
    water pollution 245
dumping
    sea, at 180
    toxic waste 188
duty of care 246–55
eco-taxes 234
emergencies 223, 232
energy, generation of 197
enforcement 190
Environment Agency 39, 185, 203

carriers 251
consignment
    note system 253
    creation of 202–03
    enforcement 190
    special waste,
        transport of 199
    strategy for England
        and Wales 233
    transport 205, 250–51
environmental
    assessments 188
escape of waste from
    holders' control 249–50
exemptions 251
expenses, recovery
    of clean-up 222–23
explosives 201
General Permitted
    Development Orders 243
groundwater pollution 245
guidance on
    special waste 199–200
hazardous waste 199–201
household waste 191, 203, 204
incineration 186, 187–88
    advantages and
        disadvantages of 187
    atmospheric
        pollution 187, 239
    dioxins 239
    planning 243
industrial waste 191, 204
Integrated Pollution
    Control 244, 289
Integrated Pollution
    Prevention
        and Control 244–45, 296,
                                        298, 303
landfill 186–87
    disadvantages 186
    Integrated Pollution
        Prevention
            and Control 244–45
    local authorities 232
    planning 243
    water pollution,
        from 186
landfill tax 234, 241–42
local authorities 34–35, 54, 202, 234
    landfill 232
    licensing 189
    planning 242–43
    statutory
        nuisance 188
local plans 242–44
marine pollution 178, 181
medicinal products 198, 201
mineral extraction
    waste 194–95, 243

mortgagees,
  repossession and 222
national waste policy 232–42
nuisance, statutory 188, 245–46
oils 239
packaging 249
planning 188, 232, 236,
                                     242–44, 304
  change of use 242–43
  conditions 243
  General Permitted
    Development Orders 243
  hazardous substances 246
  incineration 243
  landfill 243
  local authorities 242–43
  mining 243
  permission,
    withdrawal of 244
problem of waste 185–88
public health
  protection 188
quarries 195
radioactive waste 202
records of
  special waste 199
recovery operations 193–98
recycling 193–94, 204,
                                     234, 242, 244
registration of
  waste carriers 250–51
regulation 202–05
  interface with
    other pollution
      regimes 244–46
reorganisation of 190
self-regulation 247
sewerage sludge 239
shipment of waste 198
special waste 198–202, 238,
                                     253–54
specialist recovery
  operations 197
stop and search 251
strategy for England
  and Wales 232–42
strict liability 223
toxic waste,
  dumping of 188
transfer of waste 249–52
  authorised
    persons, to 250
  notes 252
  written descriptions 252–53
waste brokers 205, 247–48
Waste Collection
  Authorities 202, 204, 244
Waste Disposal
  Authorities 189, 202–04

Waste Regulation
  Authorities 34–35, 39, 54,
                                     202, 203, 289
Waste Removal
  Notices 222–23
water pollution 186, 237–38, 245
Waste management
  licensing 185, 190, 202,
                                     205–24
  administration 215–18
  appeals 217, 219–20
  applications procedure 209–13
  best available
    techniques 298
  biodegradable waste 208–09
  carriers, renewal and
    surrender of licences for 251
  certificates of completion 218
  charges 210
  civil liability 223
  clean-up 217, 218
  compensation 214–15, 217, 220
  conditions 207, 210–14, 220
  confidentiality,
    registers and 220
  consultation 210–11
  contaminated land 219
  Countryside Council
    for Wales 210
  criminal offences 206, 209, 211,
                                     218, 223–29
    duty of care 248
    information,
      requests for 222
  curtilage, within the 208
  custodial sentences 218, 222
  dangerous substances 213
  death of licence
    holders 219
  definition of waste
    management licence 207
  directive waste 205, 208
  disposal 189, 208
  duty of care 248, 255
  EC law 205, 207–08, 214, 237
  enforcement 215–18
  entry, powers of 221–22
  Environment Agency 206–19
    appeals 219–20
    enforcement 214–18
    officials, powers of 220–22
    seizure of vehicles 222
    supervision
      and monitoring 220–22
  Environment Appraisal 215
  exemptions and exclusions 207–09
  false statements 209
  financial resources 212
  fines 218, 222

fit and proper person 211–12, 255
groundwater 172, 210
Health and
    Safety Executive 210
information,
    request for 222
injunctions. 218
insolvency 219
inspections. 218, 220–22
Integrated Pollution
    Control 289
Integrated Pollution
    Prevention
    and Control 245
judicial review 219
knowingly causing
    or permitting disposal
    of controlled waste 209
landfill
    completion. 219
    directive on 236
    Integrated Pollution
        Prevention
        and Control 245, 303
    risk assessment 219
local authorities 189
mobile plant 207, 218
monitoring. 220–22
national security. 220
national waste strategy 233–34
Nature Conservancy
    Council for England. 210
neighbouring land,
    clean-up on 217
nuisance, statutory. 219
occupation. 207
onerous property 219
Operator and Pollution
    Risk Appraisal (OPRA) 215
Operator Performance
    Appraisal 215
planning 209, 213, 243–45
polluter pays. 210
public participation 210
public register. 220
publicising
    the application. 210–11
records 218–19
rehabilitation
    of offenders 212
rejection
    necessary to
        prevent pollution 212–13
    notices of 209
renewal 251
Revocation Notices 216–17
Secretary of State 219–20
seizure of vehicles 222
self-incrimination,
    privilege against 222

sentencing 218, 222
sites 189, 207,
                                                     213–14, 218
smells, statutory
    nuisance and 246
special waste. 216–17
strategy for England
    and Wales. 233–34
supervision 220–22
surrender. 218–19, 251
Suspension Notices 217–18, 220
technical competence. 211–12
third parties,
    compensation to 214–15
variation. 211, 215–16
Variation Notices 215
waste brokers 205
Waste Management
    Directive. 205, 207, 214
water 172, 210, 245
    dangerous substances,
        escape of. 213
    works, carrying out 210–11, 214
    compensation 214
    injunctions 218
    neighbouring land,
        clean-up on 217
    notices. 210
    Suspension Notices 217–18
Waste offences 224–31
carriers 249–50
Command and
    Control regulation 224
companies 229–31, 255
consent. 230
custodial sentences 228–29,
                                                     231, 255
defences. 228
deposit 224–25
    meaning of. 225–26
    special waste 230
directive waste 224, 226
directors, liability of 229–30, 255
due diligence. 228
duty of care 247, 249–50, 255
EC law, hazardous
    waste and. 231
emergencies. 228
Environment Agency. 225–27, 248
fines. 228–29,
                                                     231, 255
fly-tippers 224, 226
harm to human health. 225
household
    waste exemption 227
knowingly causing. 224–26
knowingly permitting 224–26
landfill 225–26
licences. 224–29
managers, liability of 229, 255

motor vehicles,
deposited from 226–27
penalties. 228–29, 231
precautions,
taking all reasonable 228
personal liability. 229–30
publicity 229
records 230
sentencing 228–29, 231, 255
special waste and 199, 229–31
hazardous waste,
replacement
with term 231
proposed changes
to control of 231
transfers of. 249, 250
Waste Framework Directive 224
Waste Removal Notices,
non-compliance with. 223
Water **41–42**
See also National Rivers
Authority; Water offences;
Water pollution
abstraction. 165–68
compensation 168
conditions 167–68
EC law 170
enforcement licences 170
licensing. 165–68, 170
register of licences 170
riparian owners 165–66
statutory controls 166
succession to licences. 167
surface waters,
quality of 175
Water Bill 170
access to information. 171, 474
bathing. 135
compensation 168
criminal offences 169
discharge consent
licences 135–36
draft flow statements. 166
drinking water 168–71
criminal offences. 169
EC law and 92, 168–69
fines. 169
fitness for human
consumption. 169
maximum admissible
concentrations. 92
private supplies of 169
quality 92, 168–71
drought permits 168
drought-related powers 168
EC law 92, 168–70
emanations of
the State 93
framework directive. 115

waste. 237–38
water quality 173
emergency
drought orders 168
enforcement licences 170
Environment Agency. 128, 165–68
fitness for human
consumption 61, 169
groundwater 210, 238
hosepipe bans 171
inland waters,
acceptable flows of. 166
Integrated Pollution
Control 261, 266–68
landfill 237–38
licensing. 165–68, 170
local authorities 171–72
National Water
Council. 134
Office of Water
Services. 57
private supplies of 169, 171–72
private supply notices 172
privatised companies. 93, 474
public register of
abstraction licences 170
quality 165, 168–69, 173
classification
systems for. 134
discharge consent
licences. 134–36
drinking 92, 168–71
statutory standards 135–36
surface 175
resources 42, 128, 165
riparian owners 165–66
sentencing 61
stand pipes
and bowsers. 168
succession to
abstraction licences 168
surface waters. 135–36, 175
variation of
abstraction licences 168
waste 213, 237–38
Water Bill. 170–71
wells. 169
Water offences **122–24, 137–51**
agriculture. 149
aggravating factors 149
authorised
discharges 146–49
'causing'. 138–43
controlled matters,
definition of. 144–45
Crown Court. 151
custodial sentences. 150
dams, weirs and sluices,
removal of 146

defences 146–49
directors, liability of 146
discharge consent
    licences 137–39, 145–48
discharge,
    definition of 143–44
disrepair 171
drains open,
    entitlement to keep 148
due diligence defence 147, 149
effluent, definition of 145
emergencies 147–48
entry 143
Environment Agency 138–41, 145–51
fact and degree test 141
fines 150–51,
                                                     157–58
fisheries 172
fittings, disrepair of 171
Highway Authority 148
information,
    provision of 160
inland fresh water 138
interest groups,
    private prosecutions by 123
Integrated Pollution
    Control authorisations 146
Integrated Pollution
    Prevention
    and Control 147
'knowingly permitting' 138, 143
landfill 186
latent defects 141–42
magistrates' courts 150–51
major incidents 149
mines or quarries,
    depositing refuse from 148
mitigating factors 149
neglect, acts of 171
omissions 140
penalties 150–51
poisonous, noxious or
    polluting matter 137–38, 144
private prosecutions 123, 161–62
privatised
    water companies 148
proof of
    water pollution 149
prosecutions 149–50
regulation 137
regulatory offences 161
sewage 138, 145, 148
significant incidents 149–50
strict liability 138, 143, 145, 148
substance, definition of 145
third parties 141, 146
trade effluent,
    definition of 145
trespassers, actions of 140–41

vessels, causing or
    permitting
    discharge from 148
Water Protection Zones **154**
Water pollution **121–84**
See also Discharge consent
    licences
abandoned mines 122
access to information 159–60
advice 151–53
agriculture 122, 151, 153,
                                                     155–56
annual reports 160
Anti-Pollution
    Works Notice 157–59
aquatic environment 122
Bathing Water Directive 175
Cambridge Water case 445–48
clean-up 122, 151, 157–59,
                                                     172, 324
coastal waters 126–27
Command and
    Control regulation 121
contaminated land 172, 308, 315
control over 121–22
controlled waters 126–27
damages 160
dangerous substances 213
Dangerous Substances
    Directive 174
deliveries 151
Detergents Directive 176
Director General of
    Water Services 126
drains 151
Drinking Water
    Directive 176
due diligence
    defence 154–55
EC law 156, 173–78, 448
emergency
    planning 152
enforcement 149–51
Environment Agency 121–22,
                                                     127, 128
    access to information 159–60
    advice and information 151–52
    annual reports 160
    contaminated land and 324
    enforcement 149–51
    Integrated Pollution
        Control 172
    Integrated Pollution
        Prevention and Control 303
    nitrate sensitive areas 155
    Pollution Prevention
        Guidance notes 152
    remedial work 157
    prevention 151–52, 157

small and medium-sized
    enterprises,
    information for 153
fines 122
fisheries 160, 176
foreseeability................... 433, 447
Freshwater Fish
    Water Directive 176
fuel oil 153
groundwater 126, 172,
                                175, 308
Her Majesty's Inspectorate
    of Pollution 127
historical development
    of the public regulation of........ 124–25
industry and commerce 122
information 151–53
injunctions...................... 159, 160
inland fresh waters................. 126
inspectors 121–22
Integrated Pollution
    Control 121, 172
Integrated Pollution
    Prevention and Control 121, 172,
                                303–04
investigations,
    expenses of....................... 157
licences....................... 3, 172, 175
local authorities 303–04
main water polluters 122
marine pollution................. 178–81
National Rivers
    Authority 124, 127–28,
                                151–52
negligence 161
Nitrate Sensitive Zones 155
Nitrate Vulnerable Zones 156
non-natural users................... 447
nuisance................. 159–61, 446–47
oil storage 153–54
poisonous, noxious or
    polluting matter 153, 157
polluting activities 122–24
polluting substances 122–24
Pollution Prevention
    Guidance notes................... 152
preventive powers 122, 151–58
pricing policies 178
private regulation of 160–62
privatisation 124, 125
public nuisance..................... 161
quality 175–76
Regional Water
    Authorities....................... 125

regulation 173–78
regulatory agencies 122–23, 127–32
reorganisation of
    the industry...................... 125
riparian rights................... 160–61
river basin
    management 177–78
River Boards 125
run-off 122
Rylands v Fletcher 446, 447
security 152
separated and
    integrated control of................. 6
sewage 122, 125–26,
                                160, 162–65, 177
Shellfish Waters
    Directive......................... 176
silage 153
site drains 151
slurry 153
small and medium-sized
    enterprises,
    information for 153
storage 152, 153–54
Surface Water
    Directive......................... 175
territorial waters................... 126
Titanium Dioxide
    Directive....................... 176–77
training 152
trespass 161
Urban Waste Water
    Treatment Directive 177
waste management............. 172, 186,
                                237–38, 245
Water Framework
    Directive....................... 177–78
Water Protection
    Zones 154–55
watercourses,
    definition of...................... 126
Works Notice.................... 157–59
**Water Pollution
    Inspectorate** **30–31**
Websites **495**
Weirs **147**
Wells **169**
Wild birds.......................... **98**
Works, execution of................. **358**
Works Notice **157–59**